POLYHISTOR

STUDIES IN THE HISTORY AND HISTORIOGRAPHY
OF ANCIENT PHILOSOPHY

PHILOSOPHIA ANTIQUA

A SERIES OF STUDIES ON ANCIENT PHILOSOPHY

FOUNDED BY J.H. WASZINK AND W.J. VERDENIUS

EDITED BY

J. MANSFELD, D.T. RUNIA
J.C.M. VAN WINDEN

VOLUME LXXII

K.A. ALGRA, P.W. VAN DER HORST, D.T. RUNIA (EDS.)

POLYHISTOR

STUDIES IN THE HISTORY AND HISTORIOGRAPHY OF ANCIENT PHILOSOPHY

POLYHISTOR

STUDIES IN THE HISTORY AND HISTORIOGRAPHY OF ANCIENT PHILOSOPHY

Presented to Jaap Mansfeld on his Sixtieth Birthday

EDITED BY

KEIMPE A. ALGRA
PIETER W. VAN DER HORST
DAVID T. RUNIA

E.J. BRILL
LEIDEN · NEW YORK · KÖLN
1996

The paper in this book meets the guidelines for permanence and durability of the Committee on Production Guidelines for Book Longevity of the Council on Library Resources.

ISSN 0079-1687
ISBN 90 04 10417 8

PRINTED IN THE NETHERLANDS

CONTENTS

Part Five: Imperial Philosophy

Part Six: Dialectic and Doxography

Part Seven: History of Scholarship

Bibliography

Indices

INTRODUCTION

χρὴ γὰρ εὖ μάλα πολλῶν ἵστορας φιλοσόφους ἄνδρας εἶναι...
Naar wijsheid strevende mannen dienen heel veel zaken onderzocht en in hun mars te hebben....
Nach Weisheit strebende Männer müssen sehr viele Dinge erforschen...[1]

Of Immanuel Kant it has often been observed that he spent his entire life in the territory of Königsberg, but that this did not prevent his fame from spreading throughout the whole of Europe and beyond. In a somewhat similar way Jaap Mansfeld has never lived anywhere else than Utrecht and its vicinity, and has never been associated with any other institution than its University, but this has not stopped him from becoming a dominant force in the study of ancient philosophy in the final quarter of the 20th century.

Jaap was born in Utrecht and gained his first knowledge of Greek and Latin at its Stedelijk Gymnasium, where he was taught by Peter Breemer, later a life-long friend. In 1954 he enrolled at Utrecht University, began to study Classics and Philosophy, and completed his Bachelors and Masters degree in rapid time. After a brief period in Bern, where he studied under Willy Theiler, he obtained his doctorate in 1964 with an innovative study on the poem of Parmenides. Supervisor of his research was his teacher Cornelia de Vogel. About this time lecturers began to be appointed at Dutch Universities, and Jaap soon obtained a position in the newly established Philosophical Institute. He did not have much to do, for Professor De Vogel was not about to allow a young whippersnapper to take on the heavy responsibility of giving lectures in her department. For a time Jaap was enthusiastic about the new wave of democracy that spread through the Dutch universities in the early 70's, and served as chairman of the elected University council. But in 1973 De Vogel retired and he was swiftly appointed as her successor. Since then he has held the chair of Ancient and

[1] Clement of Alexandria, *Stromateis* 5.141, = Heraclitus fr. B33 Diels-Kranz. Translations by Jaap Mansfeld in *Heraclitus Fragmenten* (Amsterdam 1979) 26, *Die Vorsokratiker* (Stuttgart 1983–86) 1.249.

Patristic (later Medieval) philosophy. On various occasions he has been Dean of the Faculty—continuously since 1990—, building it up into a flourishing institution within the larger University context.

Such are the bare bones of a successful Academic career. We briefly mention the details, first because not everyone knows them, but more importantly because they form the backdrop to what has above all motivated the contributors to this book, his enormous contribution to the study of ancient philosophy. All those who know Jaap personally are well aware of his dislike of any form of pomp and circumstance. It was with some trepidation, therefore, that we decided we did not want his 60th birthday to go entirely unnoticed. When we approached Jaap's many friends and colleagues in the field, we discovered that they were of the same mind. In many cases they were already heavily committed, and the last thing they wanted was yet another request to contribute to a Festschrift. But when they heard that it was for Jaap, they quickly gave in. The result is this collection of papers, which all of us—publisher, editors and contributors—offer to him with feelings of respect, gratitude and friendship.

When we first wrote to the contributors, we asked them to submit articles with the following double focus: (a) on historical aspects of the study of ancient philosophy; (b) where possible on subjects that have been dealt with by Jaap in his many writings or that will be of particular interest to him. The result of our request can be seen in the twenty-four papers contained in this volume. They cover virtually the entire length and breadth of the field of ancient philosophy. Since in most of them reference is made to contributions made by Jaap himself, they are in themselves an impressive testimony to the staggering range of Jaap's interest and participation in the research on the history of ancient philosophy. All will agree that he himself has put into practice, in a manner befitting the end of the twentieth century of course, the Heraclitean injunction which we have exploited for the title of this Festschrift.

The papers in this collection have been organized largely in chronological order. As things turned out, there are few papers on the Presocratics, despite Jaap's major contributions to this area. This is perhaps an indication of a decline of activity in the field. In contrast the many papers on Hellenistic and Imperial philosophy correspond not only to Jaap's own interests and research, but also to a major concentration of effort by other scholars at the present time. A special section is reserved for papers in the area of doxography, in which—as various scholars point out—Jaap's influence is perhaps more dominant than in any other. At the end of the volume we include a complete bibliography of Jaap's scholarly writings up to the end of 1995. Here too we felt a Heraclitean title was appropriate, for, given the large number of contributions awaiting publication and other works in progress, we cheerfully predict that this bibliography will one day *deis volentibus* appear to be very incomplete.

For the editors it has been particularly gratifying that there turned out to be a common thread through most of the papers submitted, i.e. the indissoluble link between the ideas and themes of ancient philosophers and the writings in which those ideas and themes have been presented, whether directly or through the intermediation of the tradition. This has been the chief insight which Jaap has developed in a myriad of ways during the past thirty years. Its continued exploration has given the collection of essays a modicum of unity and an additional sense of purpose.

The chief purpose of the volume, however, is to honour Jaap. We hope that this gift will inspire and challenge him in the continuation of his scholarly activities. May he long remain faithful to the saying of Heraclitus that forms the *Leitmotiv* for this collection.

On a more practical note we would like to offer our warm thanks to the publishing firm of E. J. Brill in Leiden and especially its editors Julian Deahl and Albert Hoffstaedt. They responded with enthusiasm to our initial suggestion and so made the publication of this book possible. We also thank Mrs Gonni Runia-Deenick for efficiently coping with all our demands in the area of type-setting. The most difficult task we confronted was to impose a measure of standardization on the diversity of conventions used by the various contributors (e.g. Diogenes Laertius abbreviated as DL, D.L. or Diog. Laert. etc.). We are the first to admit that we have not been entirely successful in this area and have no choice but to beg the reader's clemency. Because of this problem we tried to limit the number of abbreviations used throughout the book. For those that remain the reader is advised to consult *L'année philologique* in the case of Journals and the well-known Lexica of Oxford University Press (Liddell, Scott and Jones, Glare, Lampe) in the case of ancient authors and standard reference works.

The editors
Utrecht & Leiden, May 1996

PART ONE

THE PRESOCRATIC TRADITION

ANAXAGORAS' OTHER WORLD REVISITED

Malcolm Schofield

Very short papers are not what his readers most immediately associate with the name of Jaap Mansfeld. But his piece entitled 'Anaxagoras' Other World' runs to less than three full pages of text, and the notes cover only half a page more.[1] Perhaps its brevity is one of the reasons for its neglect. Schofield in his light revision of Raven's chapter on Anaxagoras in *The Presocratic Philosophers* does not refer to it.[2] Nor do more recent articles such as Inwood's or Furth's.[3] The neglect is unfortunate. Of the difficult text Mansfeld takes as his topic, 'Anaxagoras' Other World' seems to me much the most persuasive account available in the scholarly literature. In what follows I shall advance further considerations in favour of its interpretation of the mysterious 'other world', and against some of the alternatives favoured in other quarters.

The text in question is as usual preserved by Simplicius, and since its analysis by Hermann Fränkel known to afficionados as Fragment 4a.[4] Here is the text, followed by a translation. Anaxagoras' prose as often contains ambiguities. For example, in the first sentence there is a present infinitive in *oratio obliqua*, which I have taken as probably representing a present indicative, although I once thought it reflected an imperfect. My version borrows from Furley's and Raven's[5] (in KRS):[6]

> τούτων δὲ οὕτως ἐχόντων χρὴ δοκεῖν ἐνεῖναι πολλά τε καὶ παντοῖα ἐν πᾶσι τοῖς συγκρινομένοις καὶ σπέρματα πάντων χρημάτων καὶ ἰδέας παντοίας ἔχοντα καὶ χροιὰς καὶ ἡδονάς. καὶ ἀνθρώπους τε συμπαγῆναι καὶ τὰ ἄλλα ζῷα ὅσα ψυχὴν ἔχει. καὶ

---

1 Mansfeld (1980) 1–4.

2 Kirk, Raven and Schofield (1983) 352–89.

3 Inwood (1986) 17–33; Furth (1991) 95–129.

4 Fränkel (1955) 287 and n. 1. For information about Simplicius' citations see Diels–Kranz (1952) 59 B4: the relevant passages are in his commentaries on *De Caelo* 609.3–11 and *Physics* 34.28–35.9 and 156.2–4, 157.9–16.

5 Furley (1989) 56; Raven in Kirk, Raven and Schofield (1983) 369 and 379.

6 Text as in KRS nos. 483 and 498, except as indicated in n. 7.

τοῖς γε ἀνθρώποισιν εἶναι καὶ πόλεις συνημμένας καὶ ἔργα κατεσκευασμένα, ὥσπερ παρ' ἡμῖν, καὶ ἠέλιόν τε αὐτοῖσιν εἶναι καὶ σελήνην καὶ τὰ ἄλλα, ὥσπερ παρ' ἡμῖν, καὶ τὴν γῆν αὐτοῖσι φύειν πολλά τε καὶ παντοῖα, ὧν ἐκεῖνοι τὰ ὀνήϊστα συνενεγκάμενοι εἰς τὴν οἴκησιν χρῶνται. ταῦτα μὲν οὖν μοι λέλεκται περὶ τῆς ἀποκρίσιος, ὅτι οὐκ ἂν παρ' ἡμῖν μόνον ἀποκριθείη, ἀλλὰ καὶ ἄλλῃ.

These things being so, it is right to think that there are, in all the aggregates, many things, of all kinds, and seeds of all things—[seeds] having forms and colours and savours of every kind; and that human beings were formed and the other living creatures that have soul; and that among the humans there are cities that have been constructed and buildings that have been manufactured, as is the case with us;[7] and that they have sun and moon and the rest, as is the case with us; and that the earth grows for them many things, of all kinds, of which they collect together the best into their dwelling and make use of them. This, then, is my story about the separation: that separation would have taken place not only with us, but elsewhere too.

1. *Simplicius' interpretation*

Simplicius was puzzled by the passage. The first time he presents it in the *Physics* commentary, in his discussion of *Physics* I 2, he treats it as good evidence for his Platonist interpretation of Anaxagoras. This makes Anaxagoras explain the generation of our perceptible *kosmos* as a replication of a purely intelligible *kosmos*—the 'other world' specified in Fr. 4a. That *kosmos* is generated timelessly in its turn from an original intelligible unity, which is how Simplicius reads Fr. 1. On his account, Fr. 1 presents the original unity of things not as *temporally* prior to the present *kosmos* we inhabit, but as *ontologically* more primitive. What Fr. 4a then does is describe the generation of the intelligible *kosmos* from that *ur*-condition, adding as it goes along comparison with the way things are with us, in our derivative perceptible *kosmos*.[8]

---

[7] Sense and at one point textual reading in this clause are disputed. I follow Sider (1981) 69–70, and in particular his decision to read συνημμένας, not συνῳκημένας.

[8] Simplicius *in Physica* 34.18–35.21.

Everybody nowadays dismisses Simplicius' interpretation as hopelessly ahistorical. It is one thing to see in Anaxagoras anticipations e.g. of Plato's idea of participation in Forms, as some recent writers have suggested;[9] it is another actually to make him a Platonist, or rather a Neoplatonist. Of more importance for our present inquiry is that Simplicius himself evidently had doubts about his account: not a global doubt about Anaxagoras' Neoplatonism, but a local doubt over whether Fr. 4a really was good evidence of his conceiving of an intelligible *kosmos*. Already in the discussion of *Physics* I 2 he concedes that some might think Anaxagoras was talking there not of an intelligible *kosmos* but of other parts of the earth we inhabit.[10] By the time he reaches Aristotle's sustained treatment of Anaxagoras in *Physics* I 4 Fr. 4a is no longer Simplicius' prime evidence for ascribing to him the idea of an intelligible *kosmos*, as it was earlier: now he puts greater weight on Fr. 12 and Fr. 14. He would clearly like to enlist Fr. 4a too, but spends most of his space on it attacking first the possibility that Anaxagoras is describing an earlier phase of our present perceptible *kosmos*, and secondly once again the suggestion that other parts of the earth are in question. At the end of the discussion he concludes aporetically with the remark: 'Yet it would be worth inquiring further as to whether this or some other stance on these issues is correct.'[11]

One curious feature of Simplicius' treatment of Fr. 4a is the feebleness of the alternatives that he considers to his own preferred interpretation, and their power nonetheless to unsettle him. The idea that Anaxagoras might be talking about an earlier phase of the perceptible *kosmos* is decisively refuted by Simplicius' own observation[12] that he uses the present indicative to describe the behaviour of the humans described in the text (although most of the verbs are infinitives or participles, 'make use of' near the end of the passage is not). His reasons for discounting other parts of the earth are admittedly less compelling. He argues that if that is what Anaxagoras had had in mind, he would have said not 'they have sun and moon' but they have '*the* sun and *the* moon'.[13] Not necessarily, we might reply, noting that Anaxagoras anyway

[9] E.g. Denyer (1983) 315–27; Furley (1989) 62–4.
[10] *In Physica* 35.9–13.
[11] *In Physica* 157.5–24.
[12] *In Physica* 157.18–20.
[13] *In Physica* 157.20–4.

talks of '*the* earth' in this context. In the commentary on *Physics* I 2 Simplicius also takes the reference to 'seeds' as showing that an 'intelligible prototype' of our world (to use Mansfeld's nice formulation) is meant.[14] But he does not repeat the argument when he comments on I 4, and it will certainly not sway the modern reader. Some scholars of our era, notably Cornford[15] and Guthrie,[16] have actually supposed that the 'other parts of the earth' reading of Fr. 4a is correct. This must be wrong, for a reason pointed out by Vlastos.[17] Talk of *the* separation is for Anaxagoras in this kind of context talk about *cosmogony*. Reference to its happening 'elsewhere' cannot therefore relate to the possibility or necessity of civilization in other places on earth, but has to concern the creation of one or more other worlds, which are envisaged as containing civilizations like our own. Given that Fr. 4a comes from an early part of Anaxagoras' book (as Simplicius says it does),[18] in which the main theses of his system were evidently enunciated and (some of them) argued, it is hard anyway to see what the point would be of discussing the existence of civilization elsewhere on earth. It is quite unclear what light it could throw on the general themes of the mixture of all things and their separation out which Anaxagoras was developing here.

If Simplicius felt as he plainly did that even so some uncertainty hung over Anaxagoras' meaning in Fr. 4a,[19] it seems fairly safe to infer that that must be at least in part because he could find nothing in the surrounding context or indeed elsewhere which helped to clarify the issue. This conclusion is in fact the most interesting and important thing to emerge from consideration of Simplicius' evidence. Its significance is muted if Simplicius had access only to a selection of Anaxagorean texts from what he refers to as 'Book I of

---

14 *In Physica* 35.13.

15 Cornford (1934) 7–8.

16 Guthrie (1965) 314–15.

17 Vlastos (1975) 354–5.

18 *In Physica* 34.28–9, 156.1–2.

19 Raven (in Kirk, Raven and Schofield (1983) 380) is certainly correct in concluding that this is Simplicius' 'considered view'. Vlastos (1975) 358 tries to downplay the importance and reduce the scope of Simplicius' doubts, referring *inter alia* to their absence in the *De Caelo* commentary (608.31–609.12). But that commentary probably antedates the *Physics* commentary: so Hadot (1990) 289–90. Vlastos is right however that Simplicius betrays no sign of being tempted by a plurality of worlds interpretation.

On Nature'.[20] Most scholars, however, think that the range of material he can cite from the early parts of Anaxagoras' work, and his quite numerous indications of the order within it of texts he cites, suggest that he had access to a complete copy of Anaxagoras, or at least 'Book I' of Anaxagoras, himself. If they are right, it is plausible to infer the further conclusion (drawn e.g. by Fränkel[21] and Vlastos)[22] that Fr. 4a was the *only* passage in which Anaxagoras spoke of another 'separation'.

2. *A plurality of universes?*

In his discussions of Fr. 4a Simplicius nowhere entertains the possibility that Anaxagoras was arguing for the existence of other physical and in principle perceptible worlds like our own, such as are very clearly attested for the atomists Leucippus and Democritus,[23] and more controversially for e.g. Anaximander.[24] This is surprising, since *prima facie* it is an obvious way to read the passage. But Anaxagoras does not appear on standard ancient lists of proponents of a plurality of worlds, nor does Aristotle ever number him in that company (although he does not explicitly attribute to him the belief that there is only one world, as Simplicius and Aëtius do).[25] It is true that Simplicius once cites a passage of Theophrastus which in a comparison between Anaximander's infinite and Anaxagoras' mixture credits Anaxagoras with the generation of 'the worlds' as a result of the activity of mind. But he does not exploit this claim of Theophrastus; and we can probably not determine whether it was Theophrastus' considered view of

---

20 As argued by Schofield (1975) 11.

21 Fränkel (1955) 288 n. 1.

22 Vlastos (1975) 357.

23 E.g. Diog. Laert. IX.31 (= DK 67 A1), Hippol. *Ref.* I.13.2–4 (= DK 68 A40).

24 E.g. Stob. *Ecl.* I.22.3 (= DK 12 A 17), Simp. *Phys.* 1121.5–9. For a case against the correctness of this attribution see e.g. Kirk in Kirk, Raven and Schofield (1983) 122–6. I believe the attribution to be sound: see Schofield (1997) for a brief statement for the defence, Burnet (1930) 58–61 for a fuller argument, and Conche (1991) ch. 5 for a thorough refutation of scepticism on the issue.

25 For the standard lists see the texts cited in n. 24; for Anaxagoras as proponent of a single world see Stob. *Ecl.* I.22.2 (= DK 59 A63), Simp. *Phys.* 178.23–6. The grounds on which Anaxagoras was regarded as a one world theorist may well have been dubious: very likely the mention of 'the one *kosmos*' in Fr. 8, which however is probably primarily a reference to its internal unity.

Anaxagoras, or a careless intrusion in his account of a position of Anaximander's which was *not* replicated by Anaxagoras.[26]

So ancient testimony gives strangely little support to those modern scholars such as Burnet and Barnes[27] who take Fr. 4a as asserting or implying belief in a plurality of worlds. Or perhaps not so strangely. In atomism it makes perfect sense that the random movements of atoms should over infinite time result in the chance formation of an infinite variety of *different* universes.[28] In Anaxagoras' theory creation of a universe requires the activity of mind. Why should his divine mind *want* to create several contemporaneous universes that are all the *same*? For that separation produces the same results elsewhere as it does with us is what Fr. 4a insists. Given a divine mind at work, one would expect either one world only, the best of all possible worlds, or different worlds, achieving the goal of optimal variety. A mind which has no wish or no option but to replicate the same product simultaneously over and over again forfeits its claim to *be* a mind.[29]

There is also a textual problem. If Fr.4a is to be construed as making claims about a plurality of worlds, where does Anaxagoras announce that he is introducing a reference to plural worlds? It can only be either in a passage lost to us but closely preceding the fragment, or in its first sentence, presumably in the phrase 'in all the aggregates'. These two options probably collapse into a single hypothesis, viz. that 'aggregates' (the word συγκρινόμενα occurs only here in the fragments) must here be understood as 'worlds';[30] and that shortly before Fr. 4a he has affirmed the production of a

---

26 See Simp. *Phys.* 27.15–17 (= Theophr. *Phys. Op.* Fr. 4, in *Dox.* 479.7–9). On the other hand it might be that Theophrastus' mention of 'worlds' in the plural is explained by his allegiance to the Mansfeld interpretation of Fr. 4a.

27 Burnet (1930) 269–70; Barnes (1979) 2.294 (n. 17).

28 See e.g. Hippol. *Ref.* I.13.2–4 (= DK 68A40). Barnes (1979) 2.294 (n. 17) points out that when, as this text reports, Democritus denied that all worlds have a sun and a moon, he very likely intended to be denying something he took Anaxagoras to have been asserting. (The text also uses the 'in our case' locution found in Fr.4a of Anaxagoras.) But this does not (*pace* Barnes) help us much with the interpretation of Fr.4a. Democritus' remark would be pointful on any of the readings of Anaxagoras' position examined in this paper (leaving aside Simplicius' Neoplatonist version).

29 The Stoic divine providence (memorably discussed by Mansfeld (1979) 129–88) is not a counter-example to this thesis. It aims to produce the best possible world, but the only way it can make this achievement permanent, given the refractoriness of matter, is to replicate the world it creates in successive incarnations by a process of conflagration (ἐκπύρωσις) and renewal.

30 For this suggestion see Lanza (1966) 202.

plurality of aggregates as the principal outcome of the process of separation, in such a way as to make it tolerably clear that he is talking about worlds. The rest of Fr. 4a will then have to be interpreted as effectively governed by 'in all the aggregates', i.e. as spelling out the developments which must be supposed to occur within them all.

None of this is impossible. But positing a lost part of Anaxagoras' book to do the key work in the hypothesis, with precious little encouragement from the reactions of its ancient readers, is precarious speculation. And as I argued before, it yields a philosophically unappetizing theory.

3. *A* Gedankenexperiment?

A novel attempt at interpretation, taking a quite different approach, was offered by Fränkel in the 1950s.[31] His proposal found some weighty supporters in the shape of Gregory Vlastos and David Furley.[32] In essence Fränkel's Anaxagoras says not that there *is* a world besides our own (as in Simplicius) or a plurality of such worlds (as on the view examined in Section 2), but that given the initial conditions of an original mixture operated on by the separating activity of mind, any other world it created *would* be just like ours. I.e if mind decided to intervene at some other point of the original mixture, exactly the same process of separation would occur there as resulted in *our* universe. On this reading of Anaxagoras the point of Fr. 4a could be expressed in terms of contemporary possible worlds metaphysics as follows: what is true in our world is true in every possible world—which is a way of arguing that things in our world are *necessarily* the way they are.

Fränkel's interpretation puts a lot of emphasis on two features of the Greek. First, it stresses that Fr. 4a begins with a thesis not about reality, but about the correct theory of reality. Starting from the assumption that 'these things are so', it states what we must then *suppose* (δοκεῖν) to be the case.[33] In effect this is already a claim not that things happened in a certain way, but that given the conditions specified in the theory elaborated so far, no other outcome is

[31] Fränkel (1955) 284–93.
[32] Vlastos (1975) 354–60; Furley (1989) 56. I accepted the Fränkel interpretation myself in Schofield (1980) 102–3.
[33] Fränkel (1955) 290; cf. Vlastos (1975) 357.

possible. Second, Fränkel argues that in the crucial assertion at the end of the passage Anaxagoras uses the construction of optative with ἄν in a manner familiar in early Greek, not as a muted, polite form of assertion, but as a true potential, designed once again to insist on the inevitability of what is being envisaged. To say that 'the separation would have taken place not only with us, but elsewhere too' is a bit like saying: 'I had to do it—anyone else would have done the same'.[34]

Fränkel's story about Frag. 4a has some undeniable attractions. It is consistent with the ancient testimony that makes Anaxagoras one of the physicists who talks of a single *kosmos* only. It is alert to some conceivably crucial details of the text. And its account of Anaxagoras' train of thought gives the fragment a good point in the context. In Mansfeld's pithy formulation, 'things in our world are as they have to be'.[35]

In his critique of Fränkel's interpretation Mansfeld concentrated on the linguistic arguments. I think his objection to what it claims about the use of the optative with ἄν misfires. He points out that elsewhere in Anaxagoras (Fr. 6) the construction is twice employed, not to conduct a *Gedankenexperiment*, but to express 'a *necessary inference*'.[36] But on Fränkel's account the final sentence of Fr. 4a where the construction occurs is not part of the *Gedanken-experiment*. Rather, it tells us what we may conclude from the *Gedankenexperiment*. As Mansfeld's own account of the account already brings out, a necessary inference is precisely what on that view Anaxagoras *should* at this point be trying to draw from the argument he has been developing in the rest of the passage. So Mansfeld's counter-evidence from Fr. 6 actually turns out to give welcome support to Fränkel.

On δοκεῖν, 'suppose', Mansfeld makes the telling point that on Fränkel's view this word really does two quite different jobs in Anaxagoras' argument.[37] On the one hand, taken as governing the account of sun and moon, agriculture and urban life, it introduces what Fränkel calls the *Gedankenexperiment*. Here it has to mean something like 'counterfactually suppose' what he construes as the imaginary scenario of a duplicate civilization. But in the first

---

34 Fränkel (1955) 288–9; cf. Vlastos (1975) 355–6.
35 Mansfeld (1980) 1.
36 Mansfeld (1980) 1.
37 Mansfeld (1980) 1.

clause of the fragment it must function quite differently, for as Mansfeld says (and Fränkel concedes)[38] 'the fact that seeds etc. of all things are contained in all compounds...is a main feature of Anaxagoras' theory, not a "*Gedankenexperiment* "'. This time δοκεῖν must be equivalent to 'hold' in an assertoric mood. Although Mansfeld does not elaborate on its significance, his diagnosis of ambiguity is quite devastating for the Fränkel interpretation. For how are readers meant to *know* as they progress through the passage that when they reach 'and that human beings were formed', they are to take the implicit δοκεῖν governing the clause as switching without warning to a counterfactual mood? The indicative at the end of the supposedly counterfactual section ('make use of') gives an opposite signal.[39] Nor is ἄν attached to any of the infinitives in the sequence. Fränkel argues that archaic Greek does not use ἄν with the infinitive even when it carries counterfactual force. This enables him to claim that the absence of the ἄν marker is no evidence against his hypothesis that Anaxagoras' infinitives are potential.[40] But equally it can provide no evidence *for* the hypothesis either, which has to rest solely on an unmarked shift in the sense of an unexpressed δοκεῖν.

4. *Furley's variation*

The only way out for adherents of the Fränkel interpretation is to abandon the whole idea of a shift in the sense of δοκεῖν, and with it the notion that Anaxagoras conducts a Gedankenexperiment about an imagined duplicate world. This is the route taken by David Furley in his acute discussion of Fr. 4a.[41] Furley takes δοκεῖν to have more of the flavour of '(reasonably) expect'. On his version of Fränkel's reading, Anaxagoras is doing the same thing throughout the passage: viz. spelling out the thesis that, given the initial conditions, it is 'only reasonable to expect' that the world has turned out exactly as it has and as we know it—with just the variety in the aggregates (seeds of all sorts, humans, animals, civilization, heavenly bodies) that we are familiar with. That is to say, Anaxagoras is not describing another world which he compares with ours, but asserting that there had to be a world just like ours. Thus

38 Fränkel (1955) 290.
39 As was pointed out by Strang (1975) 379.
40 Fränkel (1955) 290 and n. 2; cf. Vlastos (1975) 357.
41 Furley (1989) 56 and n. 37.

when he reiterates 'as is the case with us', this is the 'as' not of comparison but of exemplification or illustration.[42]

This highly ingenious reinterpretation of Fr. 4a, mostly tucked away in a footnote, is of course rather startling. Everybody—Simplicius and modern readers alike—has supposed that the fragment is talking about *another* world or another civilization. The disagreement has been over the identity and status of that world or civilization. On Furley's view everybody (including Fränkel) has got the passage wrong. It is not about *another* world at all.

The part of Fr. 4a which is hardest to accommodate within Furley's exegesis is the concluding sentence:

> This, then, is my story about the separation: that separation would have taken place not only with us, but elsewhere too.

The contrast 'not only with us, but elsewhere too' seems designed to round off an account of another world that has been compared with our own: first Anaxagoras tells us about another world just like ours that is also produced by the separation, then like the preacher he tells us that he has told us. Furley has to give a more convoluted explanation of the role of the sentence.[43] He must say that the *point* of the main part of the fragment is to argue that the initial conditions must produce a world such as ours is. We can then infer that if those conditions were to obtain at some other place or time, the same *would* happen or have happened there. Anaxagoras has not spelled out that inference in the main passage: it is *not* 'the story about separation' he has *actually* told. But if we assume it was in his sights all along, Furley might suggest, it is not too hard to understand why he should have claimed that he has. As I say, this is pretty convoluted.

There is also a whole cluster of difficulties with the suggestion that by 'it is right to think (δοκεῖν)' Anaxagoras means 'it is only (i.e. uniquely) reasonable to expect', i.e. something amounting to a claim that what follows is the necessary consequence of the conditions just referred to ('these things being so'). The expression *could* in appropriate circumstances mean something as strong as that, but it cannot be said to be obvious that it does here. It is also rather puzzling that Anaxagoras should *wish* to make such a strong claim

[42] My gloss on Furley: not his own formulation.

[43] Again, this account of Furley's position is partly extrapolation from his very brief discussion of the text.

about the outcome of the initial conditions he has evidently been articulating. For the most part he is content in the surviving fragments either simply to assert that things *are or were* so (as e.g. in Fr. 1 on the original state of things or in Fr. 12 on mind's cosmogonic activity) or to argue that they are so, not that they could not conceivably be otherwise (as e.g. in the proof that everything has a portion of everything in Fr. 6). It is hard to see why he would be motivated to be so insistent on necessity in this instance, yet paradoxically without ever explicitly and decisively employing any of the rich vocabulary of necessity now available in Greek philosophy. Puzzlement mounts when we recall that among the initial conditions being referred to at the beginning of Fr. 4a is presumably the separating activity of *mind.* It would seem odd of Anaxagoras to be making the implicit assertion that mind would or *could* have produced no other world than our own. Why ever not? It is not as though he went out of his way to portray the *kosmos* as the best possible ordering of things: Plato and Aristotle notoriously complained precisely that he did no such thing.[44] Perhaps they went too far in suggesting that there was no teleology in Anaxagoras' system at all. Fränkel was right to draw attention to the thoroughgoing anthropocentric focus of our text, with 'sun, moon, stars and earth...mentioned only as existing for men, i.e. for human uses', and the reference to earth's bounty particularly striking.[45] It seems likely that Anaxagoras conceives of these features of the *kosmos* as providentially designed by mind. But mind could surely have devised a *kosmos* which was *not* providentially constructed, or providentially constructed but in some other way.

We may conclude that Furley makes Fr. 4a say something which comports rather strangely with Anaxagoras' general style and philosophical outlook; and which, had he wanted to say it, he would have said differently.

5. *Microscopic worlds*

'I believe', said Mansfeld, 'that the inquiry should start elsewhere'.[46] The Anaxagorean idea he proposed as the key to Fr. 4a is what he identified as a theory about the infinity, or more specifically the

---

44 Plato *Phaedo* 97B–99D; cf. Arist. *Metaph.* 985a18–21.
45 Fränkel (1955) 285–6, 292–3.
46 Mansfeld (1980) 2.

infinitely small, but which I should prefer to call the thesis that complexity is no function of size.[47] It is the idea not merely that there is no lower limit on how small a thing can be ('there is no least', Fr. 3 and 6), but that the small is just as complex as the large (Fr. 6). The crucial text is Fr. 6.

> And since, too, there are portions equal in number belonging to both the large and the small, in this way too all things will be in everything. Since the least cannot be, none of them could be separated, nor come to be on its own; but as in the beginning, so too now all things must be together. And in all things there are many even of the things that are separating off, equal in number in both the larger and the smaller.

Like most of Anaxagoras' prose, this is not without its ambiguities and densities, some of which have inevitably been ironed out in translation. There remain irreconcilable differences over its analysis.[48] Nonetheless most interpreters would agree that the main proposition advanced here is Anaxagoras' central doctrine that in everything there is something of everything, and that the passage focuses on a particular way of enunciating that doctrine. For Fr. 6 is chiefly concerned with the way the world is now, when there has been and continues to be separation from the original mixture. And it formulates the doctrine as something true both of larger things and smaller things in this differentiated world. So formulated it states that anything, whether larger or smaller, contains as many ingredients (even ingredients which are being 'separated out') as anything else.

What Mansfeld proposes is that it is this thesis about the larger and the smaller which underlies Fr. 4a. Assume that 'the larger', taken collectively, is the world of macroscopic objects all around us and including us, and that 'the smaller', taken generically, is the way things are or might be at the microscopic level.[49] Then in

---

[47] See Schofield (1980) 79–94.

[48] For a very different reading of Fr. 6 from mine see e.g. Inwood (1986) 17–33 (especially 31–32), broadly endorsed by Furth (1991) 95–129 (especially 111–19).

[49] Mansfeld (1980) 2–3 consistently speaks only of the *possibility* of worlds 'far below the level of sense-perception'. This is perhaps because of the empiricism he detects in Anaxagoras' allegiance to the principle that the phenomena are our window on the unapparent (Fr. 21). But Fr. 4a is not couched in terms of 'might'; and it seems to me that if its argument depends on Fr. 6 Anaxagoras must be arguing for the *existence* of micro-worlds. I shall assume this version of the interpretation in what follows.

Fr. 4a Anaxagoras is best understood as encouraging us to believe that at that microscopic level there is or might be a duplicate of the world-system we are familiar with at the macroscopic level—i.e. the system consisting of earth and heavenly bodies sustaining humans and other animals, and in particular human civilization. Separation—his point would be—occurs not just at the macro-level. If you could penetrate below the level of the perceptible, you would find that separation has operated and is operating there too, in just the same way and to just the same effect as 'with us'. Suggesting that our entire differentiated world-system is replicated at the micro-level is a dramatic and unexpected way of making that point, designed to get the reader to sit up and take notice.

Mansfeld's proposal[50] coheres well with various features of the fragments. In the first place, preoccupation with the infinite, the small, and the infinitely small, and with the need to think of larger and smaller in the same way, surfaces one way or another in many of them (notably in Fr. 1, 2, 3, 6, 12; 5 and 7 pursue related concerns, albeit no longer altogether intelligibly). Indeed the very first sentence of the work signals Anaxagoras' decision to place such concerns at the heart of his enterprise:

> All things were together, unlimited both in quantity and in smallness—for the small was indeed unlimited.

Secondly, it is not unlikely that Anaxagoras had articulated his specific thesis about the equal complexity of the smaller and the larger before he reached the passage which survives as Frag. 4a. We are told by Simplicius that Fr. 4a came 'shortly after the beginning of Book I of *On Nature*', and again that it came shortly after Fr. 2, placed by him in its turn shortly after Fr. 1.[51] But these are relatively vague indications, and need not preclude the possibility that Anaxagoras made some other substantive points before Fr. 4a. Presumably there was rather more about cosmogonic separation than the brief statement about air and αἰθήρ contained in Fr. 2. And the first sentence of Fr. 4a seems to presuppose that the important doctrine of a portion of everything in everything has already been enunciated:

---

[50] Mansfeld (1980) 3 points out that the main idea of the proposal (viz. that Anaxagoras is talking in Fr. 4a about micro-worlds) was anticipated in 'an apparently forgotten paper', viz. Leon (1927) 133–41. It is also advocated by Strang (1975) 379 n. 28.

[51] Simp. *Phys.* 34.28–9, 156.1–2.

> These things being so, it is right to think that there are, in all the aggregates, many things, of all kinds, and seeds of all things.

Given that the aggregates are things in a world or worlds where separation has taken place and is still occurring, it is hard to see how Anaxagoras could justify the claim he makes here unless 'these things being so' includes a reference to the contention that in everything there still is something of everything, even though the original mixture is no more. But so paradoxical is that contention that he must have mentioned some arguments in its favour when introducing it. The reference to seeds at the beginning of Fr. 4a makes it likely that among them was a proof of the sort reflected in the scholium which gives us Fr. 10: 'How could hair come to be out of not hair, and flesh out of not flesh?', and which specifically talks about seeds containing such bodily parts.[52] Our evidence, however, suggests that when Anaxagoras argued for the doctrine of everything in everything he presented a *set* of proofs,[53] so the one recorded in Fr. 6 (which announces itself as one of a series: 'And since, too,...in this way too') was probably one of those accompanying the proof from seeds. The reference to separation in Fr. 6 is also consistent with its having occurred in the same part of Anaxagoras' book as Fr. 2 and Fr. 4a. It is perhaps significant that Fr. 4a begins in argumentative fashion. This too is a feature it shares with the material in the fragments and testimonia on the everything in everything doctrine, in contrast with the explanatory narrative style used to propound the major claims about the original mixture and about the cosmogonic activity of mind.[54]

Mansfeld's proposal that Fr. 4a is in effect an elaboration of Anaxagoras' conception of 'smaller' things equal in complexity to 'larger' things suggests an explanation of some opaque locutions in Fr. 12. Anaxagoras speaks there of mind's control of 'all the things that have soul, both the larger and the smaller', and again of how all mind is the same, 'both the larger and the smaller'. It sounds as though he has something specific in view when he employs these

---

52 Fr. 10 is contained in a scholium on Gregory of Nazianzus (see *PG* XXXVI 911; cf. 521). I discuss it in Schofield (1975) 14–24 and Schofield (1980) 133–43. My use of Fr. 10 here is, I think, in line with the valuable observations in Mansfeld (1982) 361–3.

53 Cf. e.g. Arist. *Phys.* 187a26–b7.

54 Anaxagoras' expository and argumentative styles are one of the major themes of Schofield (1980).

expressions. If Mansfeld is right, and in Fr. 4a Anaxagoras has already given an account of the microscopic world contained in the 'smaller' things, we can identify what specific reference he is intending. The larger things that have soul will be humans and other animals in our macroscopic world, the smaller things that have soul the corresponding humans and other animals in the microscopic world of Fr. 4a; and so *mutatis mutandis* for the larger and the smaller mind.

One difficulty with the other interpretations of Fr. 4a we have examined was that none offered an account of it which cohered at all well with the other evidence we have of the content, structure and intellectual style of Anaxagoras's book. Mansfeld's interpretation integrates the fragment and its 'other world' with many of the other fragments, and gives it a thoroughly intelligible point at just the juncture in Anaxagoras' book that it occupies. In the context of his story about cosmogonic separation, Mansfeld's Anaxagoras develops the line of thought of Fr. 4a in order to give explicit and striking expression to the idea that 'the smaller' is just as complex as the 'larger': separation is not, as one might say, skin-deep.[55]

So the microscopic world's reading of Fr. 4a scores heavily on its strategic advantages. And it does not contradict the impression most ancient readers seem to have gained that Anaxagoras did not believe in the kind of plurality of worlds to which Anaximander and the atomists were committed: 'micro-worlds' within a single macrocosm don't make him a recruit to their party. Nor is there the problem faced by other modern interpretations that mind is so constrained as to be able or willing to undertake only *one kind* of cosmic programme. Mansfeld's Anaxagoras takes no stance on that issue. All he is insisting on in Fr. 4a is that however the cosmogonic separation initiated by mind works out at the macro-level, we have to suppose it works out in just the same way at the micro-level.

[55] Mansfeld's account of Fr. 4a thus presents a strong challenge to the contention of Inwood (1986) 17–33 (especially 22) that the small is by definition mixed and as such not 'separated out', or of Furth (1991) 95–129 (especially 111–112) that (i) the latent is 'small' (ii) that is latent of which there are 'few' or 'less' (iii) latent things are 'together' and 'commingled', not 'separated out' or 'distinguished'. On the other hand Mansfeld's interpretation is consistent with the suggestion in Sorabji (1988) 61–66 that for Anaxagoras, 'the small' is like an infinitesimal powder.

The interpretation needs to be able to show that it makes satisfactory sense of the detail of the passage as well as its strategic purpose. Here the only hard question it faces is where or whether the text itself indicates that it is talking about a micro-world. The key phrases are once again those of the opening clause:

> These things being so, it is right to think that there are, in all the aggregates, many things, of all kinds.

The most obvious way of taking 'aggregates' is as perceptible compounds in the separated world with which we are familiar. Then Anaxagoras is to be construed as claiming that within any such aggregate or compound is a micro-world consisting *inter alia* of all the things mentioned in the rest of the fragment—humans, animals, heavenly bodies, urban civilization, agriculture. The space within a perceptible object is 'the smaller'; and by relying on the principle of equal complexity in the larger and the smaller he will have believed himself entitled to argue that that internal space is as heavily populated as the external space in the world about us.

The crucial moves in this reading of Fr. 4a are (a) the decision to take 'in all the aggregates' as governing the whole sequence of clauses that follow, and (b) the inference that the inventory of things contained within an aggregate is designed to illustrate the complexity of 'the smaller'. The decision is not something the text forces upon us, but equally it doesn't go against the grain of the prose, and justifies itself by its results—it enables us to see *how* the passage introduces the other world which the concluding sentence clearly takes it to have been talking about. The inference is not explicitly legitimated by anything said *in* Fr. 4a. It depends on the supposition that Anaxagoras has been talking about the complexity of 'the smaller' shortly before, and on the reader's making a connection between that idea and the introduction of a world within an aggregate. But I hope I have shown reason to think both the supposition and the connection are attractive.

Neither (a) nor (b) is entirely obvious, however. This is just as well, since otherwise there would be the difficulty of having to explain why Simplicius and subsequent commentators failed to hit upon either (a) or (b). Until Mansfeld,[56] of course.

---

[56] And Leon (1927) 133–41 and Strang (1975) 379 n. 28.

Vlastos wrote:[57]

> Had Anaxagoras travelled further along the road of infinity, he might have glimpsed the enchanting prospect of a world in every seed, and so worlds within worlds *ad infinitum*, matching or bettering Leibniz's doctrine that 'each portion of matter may be conceived as like a garden full of plants and like a pond full of fishes; but each branch of every plant, each member of every animal, each drop of its liquid parts is also some such garden or pond' (*Monadology* 67). Anaxagoras' imagination took him far, but not so far.

If Mansfeld is right—and I have tried to show why and that he is—in Fr. 4a we see Anaxagoras' imagination taking him exactly where Vlastos thinks it did not reach.[58]

St John's College, Cambridge

[57] Vlastos (1975) 359.

[58] This paper is a development of material presented in a lecture in the University of Fribourg in October 1995 to celebrate the publication of the French translation of Kirk, Raven and Schofield (1983). I am grateful to Dominic O'Meara and Hélène-Alix de Weck for their kindnesses on that occasion. It is a great pleasure to be able to offer these thoughts to Jaap Mansfeld, from whom like so many colleagues I have learned an enormous amount not only about ancient philosophy but about how to work on it.

BIBLIOGRAPHY

Barnes, J. (1979) *The Presocratic Philosophers*, Vol. 2 (London).

Burnet, J. (1930) *Early Greek Philosophy*, 4th edn. (London).

Conche, M. (1991) *Anaximandre: Fragments et Témoinages* (Paris).

Cornford, F.M. (1934) "Innumerable Worlds in Presocratic Cosmogony", *Classical Quarterly* 28:1–14.

Denyer, N.C. (1983) "Plato's Theory of Stuffs", *Philosophy* 58: 315–27.

Diels, H. and Kranz, W. (1951–2) *Die Fragmente der Vorsokratiker*, 6th edn., 2 vols. (Berlin).

Fränkel, H. (1955) *Wege und Formen frühgriechischen Denkens* (Munich).

Furley, D.J. (1989) *Cosmic Problems* (Cambridge).

Furth, M. (1991) "A 'Philosophical Hero'? Anaxagoras and the Eleatics", *Oxford Studies in Ancient Philosophy* 9: 95–129.

Guthrie, W.K.C. (1965) *A History of Greek Philosophy*, Vol. 2 (Cambridge).

Hadot, I. (1990) "The Life and Work of Simplicius in Greek and Arabic Sources", in *Aristotle Transformed*, ed. R. Sorabji (London) 275–303.

Inwood, B. (1986) "Anaxagoras and Infinite Divisibility", *Illinois Classical Studies* 11: 17–33.

Kirk, G.S., Raven, J.E. and Schofield, M. (1983) *The Presocratic Philosophers*, 2nd edn. (Cambridge).

Lanza, D. (1966) *Anassagora* (Florence).

Leon, P. (1927) "The Homoeomeries of Anaxagoras", *Classical Quarterly* 21: 133–41.

Mansfeld, J. (1979) "Providence and the Destruction of the Universe in early Stoic Thought", in *Studies in Hellenistic Religions*, ed. M.J. Vermaseren (Leiden). Reprinted in his *Studies in Later Greek Philosophy and Gnosticism* (London 1989).

—— (1980) "Anaxagoras' Other World", *Phronesis* 25: 1–4.

—— (1982) Review of Schofield (1980), *Mnemosyne* 35: 360–366.

Schofield, M. (1975) "Doxographica Anaxagorea", *Hermes* 103: 1–24.

—— (1980) *An Essay on Anaxagoras* (Cambridge).

—— (1997) "The Ionians", in *The Routledge History of Philosophy*, Vol. 1, ed. C.C.W. Taylor (London).

Sider, D. (1981) *The Fragments of Anaxagoras* (Meisenheim am Glan).

Sorabji, R. (1988) *Matter, Space and Motion* (London).

Strang, C. (1975) "The Physical Theory of Anaxagoras", in *Studies in Presocratic Philosophy*, Vol. 2, ed. R.E. Allen and D.J. Furley (London) 361–80.

Vlastos, G. (1975) "One World or Many in Anaxagoras?", in *Studies in Presocratic Philosophy*, Vol. 2, ed. R.E. Allen and D.J. Furley (London) 354–60.

LE FRAGMENT DK 70 B 1 DE MÉTRODORE DE CHIO[1]

JACQUES BRUNSCHWIG

La pièce la plus célèbre du dossier de Métrodore, le représentant le plus important du "scepticisme atomistique" post-démocritéen, est certainement la formule qu'on pouvait lire, selon Cicéron[2] et Eusèbe de Césarée,[3] au commencement de son traité *De la Nature.* Cette formule, selon Eusèbe, "donna de fâcheuses impulsions à Pyrrhon, lequel vint par la suite"; le scepticisme paraissait s'y radicaliser en se prenant dans son propre champ. Son aspect provocant et sa situation en tête de livre lui ont valu une grande célébrité,[4] à en

---

1 Jaap Mansfeld est l'un des éditeurs de la *Cambridge History of Hellenistic Philosophy*, actuellement en préparation à la Cambridge University Press. Les collaborateurs de ce volume se sont réunis à Utrecht en août 1991, ce qui m'a donné l'occasion de visiter cette ville pour la première fois. J'étais chargé de rédiger un chapitre sur les débuts du scepticisme hellénistique. A cette occasion, j'avais présenté une étude assez longue sur l'ensemble du dossier de Métrodore, étude dans laquelle j'examinais les questions qu'il pose traditionnellement: la théorie de la connaissance de Métrodore, apparemment partagée entre "scepticisme" et "rationalisme", la compatibilité entre son "scepticisme" et son adhésion à l'atomisme de Démocrite, le sens de son intérêt pour les problèmes météorologiques. De tout cela, il ne restera guère que deux ou trois pages dans la *Cambridge History*. Pour exprimer à Jaap Mansfeld mon admiration et mon amitié, j'ai repris, bien plus à fond que je ne l'avais fait en 1991, l'examen d'un point limité du dossier de Métrodore, le fragment DK 70 B 1. On raille souvent les auteurs qui, pour contribuer à un volume de Mélanges, envoient ce que l'on appelle un "fond de tiroir". J'espère que Jaap Mansfeld voudra bien s'apercevoir que l'étude qu'on va lire est, pour le moins, un fond de tiroir longuement revisité et entièrement retravaillé.—J'exprime ici mes remerciements à Tiziano Dorandi et à Carlos Lévy, qui m'ont aidé à compléter ma documentation et à clarifier mes idées sur les témoignages de Philodème et de Cicéron, ainsi qu'à Jean-Pierre Lefebvre, qui m'a révélé le sens d'une abréviation dans le commentaire de Langerbeck (1935) 122, et à Richard Goulet pour son secours informatique.

2 *Acad. pr.* II 73 = DK 70 B 1.

3 *Praep. ev.* XIV 19 9 = DK 70 B 1. La source de ce passage n'est pas Aristoclès de Messine, à la différence des larges extraits du Περὶ φιλοσοφίας de cet auteur qui figurent dans le contexte. Cette source est de bonne qualité, comme le montre Mansfeld (1992) 33 n. 24 en comparant la version donnée ici du début du traité *Des dieux* de Protagoras (XIV 19 10) et celle, moins complète, qu'Eusèbe donne ailleurs de ce même début (XIV 3 7).

4 Le rapprochement qu'Eusèbe effectue entre la formule de Métrodore et le début, non moins célèbre et provocant, du traité *Des dieux* de Protagoras repose aussi sur le sensualisme qu'il prête aux deux philosophes (XIV 9 8), et peut-

juger par les nombreuses références et allusions qui lui sont faites dans la doxographie.

La rançon de cette célébrité est que la parole de Métrodore nous est transmise sous des formes très diverses, plus diverses qu'on ne le dit parfois.[5] La tâche que je me fixe, et qui ne semble pas avoir été faite jusqu'ici de façon systématique,[6] est d'étudier les témoignages qui la concernent, de les comparer, et d'essayer de voir si l'on peut identifier la version qui a les meilleures chances d'être authentique. Je présente d'abord ces témoignages, dans un ordre qui n'est pas chronologique (ni à l'endroit ni même à l'envers), mais qui est plutôt celui de leur longueur et de leur complexité croissantes.[7]

A = μηδένα μηδὲν ἐπίστασθαι (Epiphane, *Adv. haer.* III 2,9 = DK 70 A 23, DDG 590,35).

B = μὴ [εἰδέ]ναι μηδ' αὐτὸ τοῦ[το (Philodème, *Rhet.* fr. inc., *Pap. Herc.* 224, II 169 Sudhaus = DK 70 A 25).

C = ἔλεγε μηδ' αὐτὸ τοῦτ' εἰδέναι, ὅτι οὐδὲν οἶδε (Diogène Laërce, IX 58 = DK 69 A 2, 72 A 1).[8]

être sur la tradition selon laquelle Métrodore et Protagoras auraient été tous deux les disciples de Démocrite (Clem. Alex., *Strom.* I 64 = DK 70 A 1).

5 Pour présenter la parole de Métrodore, beaucoup de commentateurs se contentent de citer l'un des témoignages disponibles. D'autres traitent assez cavalièrement la question de savoir comment les harmoniser. Ainsi Zeller-Mondolfo (1969) 314 n. 69 cite Eusèbe et ajoute que l'on trouve "la même chose" chez Sextus, Diogène Laërce, Epiphane et Cicéron; cf. aussi, entre autres, Ernout et Robin (1926) 2.227. Le plus influent de cet écrasement des différences a certainement été le collage opéré par DK 70 B 1 entre le texte d'Eusèbe et une rétroversion partielle du texte de Cicéron. J'y reviendrai naturellement. Je signale en passant que Shorey (1919) 393-394 porte, malgré son titre aujourd'hui trompeur, sur ce qui est maintenant DK 70 B 2.

6 Ce qui s'en approche le plus est Langerbeck (1935) 121-123.

7 Je ne compte pas ici parmi les témoignages sur la parole de Métrodore la célèbre réfutation du scepticisme chez Lucrèce (IV 469-477), bien qu'un nombre considérable de commentateurs aient considéré que la version du scepticisme visée par Lucrèce (et déjà par Epicure) était celle de Métrodore (voir entre autres Ernout et Robin (1926) 2.226-227, Bailey (1947) 3.1238, DeLacy (1971) 605 n. 30, Burnyeat (1978) 204, Isnardi-Parente (1984) 106-121, Gigante (1990) 79). Je me rangerai plutôt parmi les rares qui en doutent (Vander Waerdt (1989) 242 n. 48). En effet, Lucrèce *objecte* à son adversaire sceptique qu'il "ne peut pas savoir qu'on ne peut rien savoir, puisqu'il professe ne rien savoir"; puis il lui *concède* tactiquement (473) qu'il possède un tel savoir au second degré. Cet adversaire, contrairement à Métrodore, prétend donc savoir qu'on ne peut rien savoir. Métrodore paraît avoir voulu précisément désarmer, par anticipation, ce genre d'objection (cf. Straume-Zimmermann *et al.* (1990) 414).

8 Curieusement, **C** n'est pas repris dans DK 70, le chapitre consacré à Métrodore.

D = οὐδὲν ἴσμεν, οὐδ' αὐτὸ τοῦτο ἴσμεν ὅτι οὐδὲν ἴσμεν (Sextus Empiricus, *Adv. Math.* VII 88 = DK 70 A 25).

E = οὐδεὶς ἡμῶν οὐδὲν οἶδεν, οὐδ' αὐτὸ τοῦτο, πότερον οἴδαμεν ἢ οὐκ οἴδαμεν (Eusèbe, *Praep.Ev.* XIV 19 9 = DK 70 B 1).

F = *(i) nego scire nos sciamusne aliquid an nihil sciamus, (ii) ne id ipsum quidem nescire aut scire <scire> nos, (iii) nec omnino sitne aliquid an nihil sit* (Cicéron, *Acad. pr.* II 73 = DK 70 B 1).[9]

Reprenons maintenant l'examen de ces témoignages.[10]

A

La version d'Epiphane, saint homme généralement renommé pour la faible valeur de ses informations, est la plus courte de celles qui subsistent de l'énoncé de Métrodore. La doxographie contenue dans son ouvrage *Contre les hérétiques* contient des notices sur les opinions physiques, cosmologiques, éthiques, épistémologiques des philosophes; mais celle concernant Métrodore ne retient que ses conceptions épistémologiques. En voici l'intégralité: "*Métrodore de Chio a dit (i) que personne ne sait rien, mais (ii) que nous ne savons pas avec exactitude les choses que nous croyons connaître, et (iii) qu'il ne faut pas attacher de valeur aux sensations; (iv) car toutes choses relèvent de la croyance*".[11] L'originalité de ce témoignage tient à ce que la portée de l'énoncé d'apparence brutalement sceptique **Ai** est immédiatement précisée par le complément que lui apporte **Aii**: si pour Métrodore il existe des choses (au pluriel: ταῦτα) que nous croyons connaître (γινώσκειν), et que pourtant nous ne savons pas avec exactitude ou avec certitude (ἀκριβῶς οὐκ ἐπιστάμεθα), la position qui lui est attribuée est probablement que ce qui nous est refusé est un savoir au sens fort (ἐπίστασθαι), équivalent à la certitude que notre opinion sur telle ou telle question particulière est justifiée de

---

[9] La troisième occurrence de *scire* est donnée de seconde main par les mss AB (voir l'apparat critique de Plasberg (1922) 62). La plupart des éditeurs (sauf Plasberg lui-même) introduisent ce mot dans leur texte, avec des crochets obliques (ainsi Straume-Zimmermann *et al.* (1990) 188) ou même sans (ainsi DK 70 B 1, Reid (1885) 262, Rackham (1933) 560).

[10] J'espère que l'ordre dans lequel je les étudie n'a pas induit d'effets artificiels dans l'interprétation que j'en donne. Je puis en tout cas assurer le lecteur que j'ai abordé cette étude sans avoir la moindre idée du résultat auquel elle aboutirait.

[11] M. ὁ Χῖος ἔφη μηδένα μηδὲν ἐπίστασθαι, ἀλλὰ ταῦτα, ἃ δοκοῦμεν γινώσκειν, ἀκριβῶς οὐκ ἐπιστάμεθα οὐδὲ ταῖς αἰσθήσεσι δεῖ προσέχειν· δοκήσει γάρ ἐστι τὰ πάντα .

façon appropriée par les faits. Il se peut que cette opinion soit "objectivement" justifiée;[12] mais nous ne pouvons en être certains. Vraisemblablement, la raison pour laquelle nous ne pouvons en être certains est que, de cela même, nous ne pouvons avoir qu'une croyance ou une opinion; mais cette subsomption d'une opinion sous une opinion portant sur cette opinion même n'est présente, au mieux, qu'en filigrane dans l'ensemble de **A**.

Si cette interprétation est correcte, **Aiv**, qui explique ce qui précède (γάρ) par la domination universelle de la δόκησις, se relierait fort bien à **Ai** et **Aii**.[13] En revanche, l'attaque contre les sensations (**Aiii**) fait figure d'élément perturbateur. En effet, **Ai** et **Aii** ne se rapportent pas particulièrement à telle ou telle source prétendue de connaissance, et l'on ne voit pas bien en quoi l'explication fournie par **Aiv** serait spécifiquement pertinente à l'égard des sensations.[14] Comme l'hostilité de Métrodore envers les sensations est attestée dans d'autres témoignages doxographiques, mais sans être rapportée à sa proclamation sceptique,[15] on peut faire l'hypothèse d'un collage maladroit opéré par Epiphane, ou par sa source, entre plusieurs renseignements d'origine diverse.

Dans leur apparat critique, Diels et Kranz invitent le lecteur à comparer **A** avec le vers 4 du célèbre fragment 21 B 34 de Xénophane. Ils y sont évidemment conduits par l'écho assez direct que l'on peut entendre entre la formule du Colophonien, δόκος δ' ἐπὶ

---

[12] Cette possibilité caractérise ce que certains philosophes anglo-saxons actuels appellent une épistémologie "externaliste": cf. Hankinson (1995) 19 et 118-119, qui se réfère à Bonjour (1980) 53-73; le terme et le concept ont été introduits par Armstrong (1973). Une telle épistémologie admet que les conditions qui font d'une croyance un savoir peuvent être satisfaites en fait, indépendamment de la conscience qu'en a le sujet connaissant, et donc sans qu'il sache ou même qu'il puisse savoir si elles le sont. On peut donc, selon cette épistémologie, savoir des choses sans savoir qu'on les sait.

[13] L'écho δοκοῦμεν-δοκήσει rattache lui aussi **Aiv** à **Aii**.

[14] Langerbeck (1935) 122, sans doute le commentateur le plus indulgent à l'égard d'Epiphane, rapproche **Aiv** de **Aii**, sans préciser ce qu'il entend faire de **Aiii**: "Der Ton liegt ganz auf dem οὐκ ἀκριβῶς unseres Wissens, bzw. dem δοκήσει εἶναι der Dinge".

[15] Aëtius IV 9 1 (cité incomplètement par DK 70 A 22, complètement par DDG 396, 12-16): "les sensations sont fausses, selon Pythagore, Empédocle, Xénophane, Parménide, Zénon, Mélissos, Anaxagore, Démocrite, Métrodore, Protagoras, Platon". Cette notice, pour ce qui concerne Métrodore, prend sans doute appui sur son adhésion à l'atomisme démocritéen; elle est en contradiction au moins apparente avec Eusèbe, *Praep. Ev.* XIV 2 4 (absent de DK) et 19 8 (DK 70 B 1), d'après lequel, selon Métrodore et Protagoras, "il ne faut se fier qu'aux sensations du corps".

πᾶσι τέτυκται, et celle qui est ici prêtée à Métrodore, δοκήσει γάρ ἐστι τὰ πάντα.[16] Mais on peut certainement aller plus loin que ce rapprochement ponctuel:[17] la position résumée ci-dessus peut en effet constituer une interprétation tout à fait décente du fragment de Xénophane.[18] Ce ne serait pas le seul exemple d'un rapprochement ancien entre Métrodore et Xénophane: Mansfeld[19] a brillamment montré que plusieurs anomalies de la doxographie d'Hippolyte[20] (Xénophane y vient après Démocrite, et son explication de la salinité de la mer est mise en contraste, en plein milieu du chapitre qui lui est consacré, avec celle de Métrodore) viennent de ce que, dans l'esprit d'Hippolyte, les deux penseurs devaient être associés pour une raison plus importante que leur divergence d'avis à propos de la salinité de la mer: à savoir, leur commune inclination au scepticisme. Mansfeld ne cite pas **A** dans ce contexte; mais on peut assez aisément voir en **A** le résultat d'une sorte de contamination doxographique, explicitant le sens du scepticisme affiché en **Ai** par des considérations (**Aii** et **Aiv**) d'inspiration plus ou moins directement xénophanienne.

B

La version de l'énoncé de Métrodore conservée dans un fragment de la *Rhétorique* de Philodème[21] est à peine plus longue que **A**. Dans le cours d'une énumération qui paraît avoir pour fonction de dénoncer quelques célèbres paradoxes philosophiques, que l'Epicurien exprime de façon très condensée, et qu'il tient manifestement pour insoutenables,[22] Philodème glisse celui-ci, rapporté à Métrodore de

---

16 Si cette hypothèse d'un écho est correcte, **A** témoignerait que ἐπὶ πᾶσι, chez Xénophane, a été interprété par certains, dès l'Antiquité, comme un neutre (alors que la plupart des modernes y voient un masculin).

17 Il y en a d'ailleurs peut-être un autre: cf. ἀκριβῶς dans **Aii** et σαφές chez Xénophane.

18 Voir par exemple Lesher (1978) 1-21, Hussey (1990) 18-22, Lesher (1992) 155-169 et 182-186. Hankinson (1995) 53 considère que l'une des interprétations possibles de l'énoncé sceptique de Métrodore (qu'il reproduit cependant, à cet endroit, d'après la version de Sextus Empiricus) lui attribue "une position cohérente avec celle de Xénophane, peut-être même une version de cette dernière".

19 Mansfeld (1992) 32-36.

20 *Ref.* I 14 = DK 21 A 33, DDG 565, 20 – 566, 10.

21 Pap. Herc. 224, II 169 Sudhaus = DK 70 A 25. Le contexte est cité par Crönert (1906) 192 et Gigante (1990) 79.

22 "Tout est dans tout" (Anaxagore), "le tout est un" (Parménide, Mélissos), "parce que les sensations sont fausses" (le texte s'interrompt ici). Bizarre-

Chio:[23] "*personne ne donnerait son accord à la formule «ne pas même savoir cela même»*".[24]

Dans cette formulation, intéressante bien qu'elliptique, ou mieux, parce qu'elliptique, s'introduit une expression caractéristique de toutes les versions qu'il nous reste à examiner: μηδ' αὐτὸ τοῦτο. Cette expression a pour fonction, selon toute apparence, de faire d'un non-savoir ou d'une ignorance de premier degré ("ne pas savoir$_1$", disons une "ignorance$_1$") l'objet d'un non-savoir ou d'une ignorance de second degré, d'une méta-ignorance ("ne pas même savoir$_2$ ne pas savoir$_1$", disons une "ignorance$_2$"). Mais ce qui est tout à fait remarquable, en comparaison surtout de quelques-unes des versions que nous examinerons par la suite, c'est que l'ignorance$_1$ ne fait pas l'objet d'une assertion explicite indépendante. Tout se passe comme si l'ignorance$_2$ était prise tellement au sérieux qu'il n'est même pas possible de désigner son objet comme étant précisément une ignorance$_1$. C'est d'ailleurs logique: si nous parlons d'un objet que nous ne connaissons pas, il n'y a pas de bonne raison de le désigner comme ceci (par exemple comme une ignorance), plutôt que comme cela.

J'introduirai ici une réflexion que je dois à l'étude de Myles Burnyeat sur la réfutation du scepticisme chez Lucrèce.[25] Supposons qu'un sceptique (peu importe ici qu'on l'identifie ou non à Métrodore) admette les deux propositions suivantes:

(1) "Il n'y a aucune proposition qui soit connue comme vraie".

Donc (2) "La proposition (1) n'est pas une proposition qui soit connue comme vraie".

---

ment, Gigante (1981) 64 subordonne à la proposition de Métrodore toutes les autres propositions de ce passage, dont il donne la paraphrase suivante: "in Filodemo possiamo solo ricordare che nella *Retorica* viene rispinta la nota proposizione di Metrodoro di Chio che nulla sappiamo né se tutto è in tutto (con Anassagora) né se uno è il tutto (con Parmenide e Melisso) perché le sensazioni sono false". Cette construction paraît exclue par la syntaxe du passage et par l'ordre dans lequel sont présentés les divers énoncés paradoxaux (Anaxagore, Métrodore, Parménide et Mélissos).

[23] Le papyrus contient ici une lacune: κατὰ τὸ[ν] Χεῖον Μήτ[... . La place disponible étant petite, Wilamowitz (1899) 636 a suggéré de lire Μητ[ρᾶν], sobriquet dont était affublé Métrodore dans une comédie d'Antiphane (DK 70 A 1a). Crönert (1906) 192 propose de lire Μήτ[ρωνα], autre sobriquet ironique, qui remplirait mieux la lacune. De toute façon, l'identification avec notre philosophe est assurée par le toponyme.

[24] οὐδ' ἂν] κατὰ τὸ[ν] Χεῖον Μήτ[ρωνα] ὁμολογῴη τῶι μὴ [εἰδέ]ναι μηδ' αὐτὸ τοῦ[το.

[25] Burnyeat (1978) 197-206, en particulier 204-206.

De (1) et de (2), on ne peut certainement *pas* déduire logiquement: (3) "La proposition (1) est fausse".

En effet, la proposition (1) pourrait être vraie sans être connue comme telle. Cependant, Burnyeat suggère de façon très éclairante qu'il faut replacer ce genre de discussion dans un contexte dialectique. Dans un tel contexte, la position du sceptique qui admet (1) et (2) devient fragile, parce que "*no sense is left to his furnishing reason, evidence or proof for (1)*". Tel est le sens qui donne sa plus grande plausibilité à l'argumentation anti-sceptique de Lucrèce: en un sens large du terme, la position de *ce sceptique* tombe sous le coup d'une περιτροπή; dialectiquement, sinon logiquement, elle "se réfute elle-même".

Mais, s'il en est ainsi, la conséquence à tirer de l'analyse de Burnyeat est que le principe de charité invite à privilégier, s'il s'en trouve, les témoignages qui n'attribuent *pas* à Métrodore l'assertion de (1). **B** est l'un de ces témoignages, et nous verrons qu'il y en a d'autres.

Remarquons encore que **B** ne donne pas de sujet à l'infinitif μὴ εἰδέναι. Qui ne sait pas ? On n'en sait rien.

C

Diogène Laërce ne consacre aucune notice à Métrodore, et c'est dommage. Il est impossible de savoir pourquoi il ne l'a pas fait, puisque le philosophe de Chio ne lui est pas inconnu. Il le mentionne au début de sa notice sur Anaxarque (IX 58), à l'intérieur d'une "succession" démocritéenne qui fait de lui, d'une part le maître de Diogène de Smyrne, lui-même maître d'Anaxarque, d'autre part l'élève de Nessas de Chio, ou selon certains, de Démocrite lui-même.[26] A cette occasion, Diogène Laërce mentionne l'opinion sans doute la plus frappante de Métrodore: "*il disait ne même pas savoir cela même, qu'il ne savait rien*".[27]

26 Sur les variantes de cette succession, cf. Eus. *Praep. Ev.* XIV 17 10 = DK 69 A 1 (Métrodore élève de Nessas, lui-même élève de Démocrite), *id. ibid.* XIV 17 8 = DK 70 B 1 (Métrodore élève de Démocrite), Clem. Alex., *Strom.* I 64 = DK 70 A 1 (Métrodore élève de Démocrite). Ces variantes sont sans doute liées à des incertitudes sur la chronologie exacte de Métrodore. Je ne puis m'attarder ici sur ce problème (voir aussi DK 70 A 2 et Alfieri (1953) 28); une datation relativement haute (fixant la naissance de Métrodore vers la fin des années ~420) semble être la seule compatible avec la mention faite de lui par Antiphane (cf. n. 23), dans une comédie que les spécialistes datent de ~388.

27 Μητροδώρου τοῦ Χίου, ὅς ἔλεγε μηδ' αὐτὸ τοῦτ' εἰδέναι, ὅτι οὐδὲν οἶδε.

Par rapport à **A**, **C** introduit d'abord une variante qui ne se retrouvera nulle part ailleurs, et qui est en elle-même assez suspecte: elle fait parler Métrodore de sa propre ignorance, non de celle des hommes en général. Faut-il supposer qu'à tel ou tel moment de la transmission a circulé une version de l'énoncé de Métrodore qui, comme **B**, ne contenait aucune précision à ce propos, et que la version de Diogène Laërce résulte d'une conjecture destinée à combler cette lacune ? On peut au moins se poser la question.

On observe aussi et surtout, en **C**, un embryon d'expression autonome de l'ignorance$_1$ ("cela même, *qu'il ne savait rien*"). Cette expression met dans une lumière plus vive la difficulté déjà évoquée: si je ne sais$_2$ même pas que je ne sais$_1$ rien, pourquoi désigner par "je ne sais$_1$ rien" l'objet sur lequel porte mon ignorance$_2$, plutôt que, par exemple, par "je sais$_1$ quelque chose" ? Une position cohérente, semble-t-il, serait plutôt de dire: "je ne sais$_2$ pas *si* je sais$_1$ quelque chose *ou si* je ne sais$_1$ rien".

D

Un pas décisif dans l'évolution vers une assertion autonome de l'ignorance$_1$ est franchi par la formule que Sextus Empiricus attribue à Métrodore. Ce dernier figure au nombre de ceux qui, selon le Sceptique, ont "aboli le critère";[28] du moins, précise-t-il au moment de s'en expliquer plus en détail, un nombre non négligeable de gens ont dit qu'il l'avait fait.[29] Leurs raisons tiennent tout entières dans l'énoncé qu'ils lui prêtent, et qui se présente ici sous la forme suivante: *"(i) Nous ne savons rien, (ii) nous ne savons même pas cela, que nous ne savons rien"*.[30]

Cette formulation est probablement la plus claire et la plus transparente de toutes celles qui nous sont transmises (ce qui ne signifie pas nécessairement qu'elle soit la plus digne de confiance

---

[28] Xénophane, Xéniade, Anacharsis, Protagoras, Dionysodore, Gorgias, Métrodore, Anaxarque, Monime (*Adv. Math.* VII 48).

[29] Cette précision est donnée en *Adv. Math.* VII 87, à propos des trois derniers philosophes de la liste reproduite dans la note précédente. Elle peut s'expliquer, soit par le fait que Sextus estime ne pas disposer d'une documentation suffisante en ce qui les concerne (les paragraphes VII 49-87 contiennent en effet, par contraste, des textes et des commentaires assez développés concernant Xénophane, Xéniade, Anacharsis, Protagoras et surtout Gorgias), soit parce qu'il n'est pas sûr de l'interprétation qu'il convient de donner aux brefs énoncés qu'il est en mesure d'attribuer à Métrodore, Anaxarque et Monime.

[30] Οὐδὲν ἴσμεν, οὐδ' αὐτὸ τοῦτο ἴσμεν ὅτι οὐδὲν ἴσμεν.

sur le plan historique—peut-être même au contraire, bien entendu). On y voit notamment que l'incertitude qui affecte le sujet de l'énoncé en **B**, et qui était levée au profit de la première personne du singulier en **C**, se trouve maintenant levée au profit (assurément plus plausible) de la première personne du pluriel: c'est nous, les hommes en général, qui sommes les victimes d'une ignorance redoublée.

Mais surtout, **D** contient (pour la première fois dans l'ordre de notre examen) une expression explicite et parfaitement assertorique de notre ignorance$_1$ universelle (**D**i), ainsi qu'une expression claire de la subsomption de cette ignorance$_1$ par une ignorance$_2$ (**D**ii).

Il importerait beaucoup, pour notre enquête, de savoir quelle a été la genèse de cette formulation. En suivant la suggestion de Burnyeat, je tenterai de replacer le problème dans un contexte dialectique. On peut au moins imaginer, entre Métrodore et un interlocuteur que je nommerai Antidore, deux enchaînements de dialogue qui auraient pu aboutir au même résultat, par des voies très différentes.

Le premier enchaînement serait le suivant:

Métrodore: "Nous ne savons$_1$ rien" (= **D**i).

Antidore: "Si tu l'affirmes, c'est que nous savons$_2$ au moins ceci, que nous ne savons$_1$ rien (ton scepticisme est inévitablement ce qu'on appellera un jour un métadogmatisme négatif)".[31]

Métrodore: "Non, nous ne savons$_2$ même pas cela, que nous ne savons$_1$ rien" (= **D**ii).[32]

---

[31] Barnes (1992) 4252 n. 54 et 4254 n. 72 a très utilement distingué le "dogmatisme négatif", qui consiste à soutenir des doctrines, mais seulement des doctrines de forme négative, et le "métadogmatisme", qui consiste à soutenir des doctrines, positives ou négatives, sur le statut cognitif de certaines propositions. Bien entendu, comme le souligne Barnes, on peut être métadogmatique négatif, si l'on soutient des doctrines négatives sur le statut cognitif de certaines propositions. Si l'on ne distingue pas les niveaux de savoir ou d'ignorance, l'objection d'Antidore tend à montrer que la position initiale de Métrodore se réfute elle-même.

[32] **D** a été souvent rapproché de l'attitude d'Arcésilas par rapport à l'ignorance socratique (*Arcesilas negabat esse quidquam quod sciri posset, ne illud quidem ipsum, quod Socrates sibi reliquisset*, Cicéron, *Acad.* I 45). Mais cela ne signifie pas nécessairement que Métrodore ait influencé Arcésilas: Langerbeck (1935) 121-122 estime à juste titre que les versions **D** et **C** peuvent résulter de l'insertion de la position de Métrodore dans un environnement platonico-socratique qui l'éloigne irrémédiablement de son environnement démocritéen originaire. Selon Straume-Zimmermann *et al.* (1990) 414, l'agnosticisme de Métrodore s'exprime de façon à désarmer l'objection de la περιτροπή, mais sa formulation paraît aussi "in irgendeiner Beziehung zur Aporetik des plato-

Antidore pourrait alors objecter, comme on l'a indiqué, que si nous ne savons$_2$ pas que nous ne savons$_1$ rien, il n'y a aucune raison déterminante de dire que nous ne savons$_1$ rien; or, c'est ce que Métrodore avait commencé par dire. En admettant qu'il ait ajouté **D**ii à **D**i pour éviter de tomber sous le coup d'une περιτροπή, sa position, telle qu'elle est exprimée par la conjonction de **D**i et de **D**ii, pourrait donc tomber sous le coup d'une περιτροπή de second degré.

On peut cependant tenter d'éviter cette conséquence en imaginant un autre enchaînement dialogué:

Métrodore: "Nous ne savons$_2$ même pas cela même" (cf. **B**).

Antidore: "Que signifie cette énigme ? Qu'est-ce que ce «cela même» que nous ne savons$_2$ même pas ? Est-ce «nous ne savons$_1$ rien» ? Dans ce cas, ta formule reviendrait à dire «nous ne savons$_2$ rien, même pas cela, que nous ne savons$_1$ rien» (= **D**). Es-tu d'accord sur ce point ?".

Métrodore: "Non. Ce «cela même», dont je dis que nous ne le savons$_2$ même pas, ce n'est pas *que* nous ne savons$_1$ rien (ma position serait alors fragile); c'est *si* nous savons$_1$ quelque chose *ou si* nous ne savons$_1$ rien. Ne confondons pas une complétive avec une interrogative indirecte. Je me résume: nous ne savons$_2$ même pas si nous savons$_1$ quelque chose ou si nous ne savons$_1$ rien".

Antidore pourrait sans doute montrer que cette formulation, si elle évite la contradiction, risque d'entraîner une régression à l'infini. Mais le schéma que nous venons d'imaginer aurait au moins l'intérêt de montrer: (i) que **D** pourrait être, non l'expression directe de la pensée de Métrodore, mais une reconstruction conjecturale de cette pensée; (ii) que cette reconstruction pourrait être concurrencée, non sans avantage, par une autre dans laquelle l'objet de l'ignorance$_2$ serait exprimé par une interrogative indirecte double, et non par une complétive.

E

L'interrogative indirecte double que nous avons vu poindre en filigrane, dans notre discussion de **D**, apparaît en toutes lettres dans **E**, la version donnée par Eusèbe. Après avoir donné un rapide

---

nischen Sokrates zu stehen". Cette expression prudente est cependant quelque peu démentie par la suite de leur commentaire, où ils affirment avec assurance qu'Arcésilas "hat den Satz Metrodors geradezu im Hinblick auf Sokrates interpretiert und übernommen".

aperçu des principes démocritéens adoptés par Métrodore, Eusèbe dit que ce dernier a commencé son traité *De la nature* par une entrée en matière du genre que voici (εἰσβολῇ τοιαύτῃ):[33] "*(i) Aucun d'entre nous ne sait rien, (ii) même pas cela même, si nous savons ou ne savons pas*".[34]

E présente un certain nombre de caractères communs avec **D**: l'assertion explicite de l'ignorance$_1$ (**E**i), la détermination du sujet de cette ignorance$_1$ (non pas simplement "nous", comme en **D**, mais "aucun d'entre nous"), et bien sûr la formule caractéristique οὐδ' αὐτὸ τοῦτο. La différence à ne pas négliger est l'absence de la complétive ὅτι οὐδὲν ἴσμεν et la présence de l'interrogative indirecte double πότερον οἴδαμεν ἢ οὐκ οἴδαμεν.

Avant de voir quel parti l'on peut tirer de cette différence, il importe de résoudre l'ambiguïté syntaxique de **E**ii. Il est possible que l'interrogative indirecte serve à expliciter le contenu de οὐδ' αὐτὸ τοῦτο. La formule signifierait alors: nous ne savons$_2$ même pas cela même, i.e. si nous savons$_1$ ou ne savons$_1$ pas. Dans cette hypothèse, les verbes οἴδαμεν et οὐκ οἴδαμεν n'auraient pas de complément, et signifieraient, pris en un sens absolu, "nous avons un savoir" ou "nous n'avons pas de savoir". Cette construction a été presque unanimement adoptée.[35] Pourtant, l'emploi absolu de εἰδέναι ne paraît pas attesté.[36] De plus et surtout, la comparaison avec **D** invite à penser que οὐδ' αὐτὸ τοῦτο a pour fonction de reprendre ce qui précède, plutôt que d'annoncer ce qui suit (quitte à répéter explicitement ce qui précède dans ce qui suit, comme c'est le cas en **D**). Sur ce modèle, on serait conduit à construire οὐδ' αὐτὸ τοῦτο comme se référant à ce qui précède, c'est-à-dire à l'expression de l'ignorance$_1$, et comme étant grammaticalement le complément, lancé en prolepse, des verbes οἴδαμεν ἢ οὐκ οἴδαμεν. L'interprétation

---

33 Eusèbe signale peut-être ainsi que sa citation n'est pas textuelle.

34 Οὐδεὶς ἡμῶν οὐδὲν οἶδεν, οὐδ' αὐτὸ τοῦτο, πότερον οἴδαμεν ἢ οὐκ οἴδαμεν.

35 Voir par exemple la traduction de DK (1952) 2.234 ("Niemand unter uns weiß irgend etwas, nicht einmal eben das, ob wir wissen oder nicht wissen"). Traductions similaires chez Bailey (1947) 3.1238, Cappelletti (1979) 109, Barnes (1982) 559, Des Places (1987) 169, Dumont (1988) 946, Vander Waerdt (1989) 239 n. 39. Quelques traducteurs paraissent avoir senti la difficulté de cet emploi absolu des verbes οἴδαμεν et οὐκ οἴδαμεν, auxquels ils fournissent des compléments dans leurs traductions: ainsi Brochard (1923^2) 47-48 ("Nous ne pouvons rien savoir, pas même si nous savons quelque chose ou rien"). De même Zeller-Mondolfo (1969) 313-314, Sedley (1983) 14.

36 Sauf au participe (οἱ εἰδότες: ceux qui sont au courant, les gens bien informés).

à laquelle on aboutit pour **E** devient la suivante: "*(i) Nous ne savons rien, (ii) nous ne savons même pas si nous savons ou ne savons pas cela même (i.e. que nous ne savons rien)*".

L'intérêt de cette construction est qu'elle introduit un *troisième niveau* dans l'étagement des degrés d'ignorance. En effet, si l'on veut préciser les choses, on aboutit au résultat suivant: nous ne savons$_3$ même pas si nous savons$_2$ ou ne savons$_2$ pas que nous ne savons$_1$ rien. L'enchaînement dialectique qui pourrait faire comprendre la genèse de cette formulation serait le suivant:

Métrodore: "Nous ne savons$_1$ rien" (= **E**i).

Antidore: "Mais au moins nous savons$_2$ que nous ne savons$_1$ rien".

Métrodore: "Non, nous ne savons$_3$ même pas si nous savons$_2$ ou si nous ne savons$_2$ pas que nous ne savons$_1$ rien" (= **E**ii).

Antidore pourrait une fois de plus objecter: "mais alors, quelle bonne raison as-tu de dire que nous ne savons$_1$ rien (= **E**i) ?". La vulnérabilité à cette objection est décidément le prix à payer, semble-t-il, si l'on tient à détacher de façon autonome, en tête de formule, l'expression assertorique d'une ignorance$_1$, comme c'est le cas avec **D**i et **E**i.

F

Il est temps d'aborder le témoignage de Cicéron, le plus long, le plus complexe, et aussi le moins éloigné de Métrodore dans le temps. Il figure dans une longue énumération des diverses autorités qui peuvent appuyer, à des titres divers, la position de l'Académie philonienne. Après avoir parlé de Démocrite, Cicéron passe à Métrodore, "celui qui a le plus admiré" ce dernier.[37] Confirmant l'indication d'Eusèbe, il dit qu'au début de son livre *Sur la nature*, Métrodore avait écrit ce que Cicéron traduit en latin de la façon suivante: *(i) nego scire nos sciamusne aliquid an nihil sciamus, (ii) ne id ipsum quidem nescire aut scire <scire> nos, (iii) nec omnino sitne aliquid an nihil sit.*[38]

---

37 *Is qui hunc maxime est admiratus.* Malgré Mansfeld (1992) 33 n. 25 ("«Greatest» pertains to the importance of Metrodorus"), il ne semble pas que l'on puisse comprendre ici que Métrodore a été le plus important des admirateurs de Démocrite.

38 Sur la troisième occurrence de *scire*, voir ci-dessus, n. 9.

Ce passage pose des problèmes d'établissement du texte, de construction syntaxique et d'interprétation. Comme ceux-ci sont concentrés dans la section **Fii**, on peut déblayer le terrain en traduisant les sections **Fi** et **Fiii**, qui ne soulèvent pas de problèmes philologiques particuliers:

(**Fi**) "Je dis que nous ne savons$_2$ pas si nous savons$_1$ quelque chose ou si nous ne savons$_1$ rien". Il est capital que l'assertion initiale d'ignorance posée par **Fi** soit ici posée d'emblée au niveau de l'ignorance$_2$ (par contraste avec **Di** et **Ei**), et que l'objet de cette ignorance$_2$ soit exprimé par une interrogative indirecte double (comme dans **Eii**) et non par une complétive (comme dans **Dii**).

(**Fiii**) "<Je dis aussi que nous ne savons> pas non plus le moins du monde[39] s'il existe quelque chose ou s'il n'existe rien". Cette ignorance "ontologique" est entièrement nouvelle, par rapport à toutes les versions examinées jusqu'à présent; il faudra y revenir.

Mais d'abord, examinons de façon plus précise la section **Fii**. Quel que soit le texte adopté, il faut bien reconnaître avec Langerbeck que **Fii** est "stilistisch unschön und gedanklich unklar".[40] Je dresserai d'abord une petite typologie (non exhaustive[41]) de quelques-unes des traductions données de **Fii**, afin de faire apercevoir l'embarras des traducteurs et la variété parfois déconcertante de leurs tentatives.

A tout seigneur tout honneur: il convient de citer tout de suite l'influente retraduction en grec d'un morceau de **F** (à savoir **Fii** et **Fiii**) que DK ne craignent pas d'ajouter à leur citation de **E**:[42] οὐδ' αὐτὸ τὸ μὴ εἰδέναι καὶ[43] τὸ εἰδέναι οἴδαμεν[44] (ὅτι ἔστιν).[45] On

39 Ou peut-être: "nous ne savons pas non plus s'il existe absolument quelque chose ou rien".

40 Langerbeck (1935) 122.

41 Je ne mentionne que pour mémoire la traduction aberrante de Cappelletti (1979) 108: "Niego ... hasta que sepamos esto mismo: si en absoluto existe algo o nada".

42 L'apparat critique (2.234) indique que cette reconstitution est due à "Diels + Friedländer". Je n'ai pas trouvé dans quel livre, article ou compte-rendu se trouve la contribution de Friedländer, et je ne sais donc pas quelles sont les parts exactes de chacun des deux érudits dans le résultat final (le nom de Métrodore ne figure pas dans l'index de Friedländer (1969)). Cependant, on peut déduire des indications d'Alfieri (1936) 335 que l'idée d'ajouter la rétroversion de **Fiii** à **E** revient à Diels; par élimination, on peut inférer que c'est Friedländer qui a eu l'idée d'en faire autant pour **Fii**.

43 *Sic* (le latin porte ici *aut*).

44 J'ai déjà signalé (n. 9) que DK, dans leur citation de Cicéron, acceptent l'occurrence de *scire* ajoutée par A^2B^2.

45 L'addition de **Fii** et de **Fiii** à **E** aboutit ainsi à une cascade assez suspecte

remarquera que DK n'écrivent pas οὐδ' αὐτὸ τοῦτο, ce qui leur permet d'accrocher directement οὐδ' αὐτό aux infinitifs substantivés qui traduisent *nescire* et *scire*. Cette décision a pour conséquence que, dans le texte composite obtenu par le collage **Ei** + **Eii** + **Fii** + **Fiii**, la liaison par οὐδ' αὐτό n'a plus pour fonction de subsumer une ignorance$_n$ sous une ignorance$_{n+1}$. Autre conséquence: les infinitifs substantivés τὸ μὴ εἰδέναι καὶ τὸ εἰδέναι n'ont pas de complément.[46] Ces deux conséquences, on l'a remarqué plus haut, ne vont pas sans difficultés. De plus, l'expression τὸ μὴ εἰδέναι καὶ τὸ εἰδέναι οἴδαμεν n'est guère satisfaisante, ni sur le plan syntaxique ni sur le plan sémantique; c'est ce qui a conduit DK à ajouter la parenthèse (ὅτι ἔστιν). On ne sait d'ailleurs pas exactement quel sens ils veulent donner aux parenthèses qui entourent ὅτι ἔστιν: s'agit-il d'une glose ou d'une conjecture à introduire dans le texte ? La deuxième hypothèse est probablement la bonne, si l'on en juge par la traduction allemande qui est donnée de ce texte à la même page ("noch eben vom Nichtwissen und Wissen wissen wir, daß es ist").

Beaucoup de traducteurs et de commentateurs de **Fii** ont été plus ou moins influencés, sur ce point, par DK. Les uns acceptent exactement l'interprétation suggérée par la rétroversion de DK et l'adjonction de ὅτι ἔστιν.[47] D'autres préfèrent implicitement remplacer l'adjonction de DK, ὅτι ἔστιν, soit par εἰ ἐστιν,[48] soit par τί ἐστιν.[49] Quelques traducteurs s'écartent pourtant du schéma de DK: au lieu de construire *nescire aut scire* en un sens absolu, ils lui donnent pour complément l'affirmation exprimée par **Fi**, attribuant ainsi à la clause *ne id ipsum quidem*[50] la fonction rétroactive qui est celle de οὐδ' αὐτὸ τοῦτο dans les textes grecs.[51]

---

de clauses introduites par "même pas", celle de **Eii** (οὐδ' αὐτὸ τοῦτο), celle que l'on tire de **Fii** (*ne id ipsum quidem*) et celle de de **Fiii**.

46 C'était déjà le cas pour οἴδαμεν et οὐκ οἴδαμεν dans la traduction DK de **Eii** (cf. ci-dessus, n. 35).

47 Ainsi Mansfeld (1992) 33, qui semble bien ne pas accepter l'insertion du *scire* supplémentaire ("[I deny] ... even the mere fact that we do not know or do know"). Traduction similaire chez Rackham (1933) 561.

48 Ainsi Dumont (1988) 945 ("Nous ne savons même pas s'il existe un ignorer et un connaître"). Cf. déjà Goedeckemeyer (1905) 3.

49 Ainsi Bailey (1947) 3.1238 ("[I deny] ... even that we know what is ignorance or knowledge"); de même Appuhn (s.d.) 429-431, Barnes (1982) 559, Conche (1984) 1821.

50 Correctement à mon sens, puisque *id* doit être la traduction cicéronienne de τοῦτο.

51 Cf. Alfieri (1936) 334 et Dal Pra (1975^2) 1.52, dont la traduction suppose

Devant un texte aussi difficile, on peut s'étonner que les tentatives de correction conjecturale aient été relativement rares.[52] La plus intéressante me paraît être celle de Langerbeck, qui, après avoir critiqué le montage opéré par Diels, remarque que l'insertion de <*scire*> n'arrange rien, et note très cursivement: "Offenbar ist das *nescire* von Cicero der stilistischen blendenden Antithese zuliebe eingefügt".[53] Dans sa hâte, il a oublié de dire que si l'on supprime *nescire*, il faut aussi supprimer *aut*. Mais il me semble que si l'on suit jusqu'au bout la piste ouverte par Langerbeck, on aboutit à un texte et à un sens tout à fait satisfaisants. Le texte de **Fii** devient: "(*nego*) ... *ne id ipsum quidem scire nos*". Le sens qu'on peut donner à ce texte (Langerbeck lui-même ne l'explicite pas) est le suivant:[54] "(je nie) ... que nous sachions$_3$ cela même (i.e. **Fi**, i.e. que nous ne savons$_2$ pas si nous savons$_1$ quelque chose ou rien)".

Les avantages de cette hypothèse sont multiples. Tout d'abord, on peut imaginer sans peine une genèse dialectique de l'ensemble **Fi** + **Fii**, à partir de l'enchaînement suivant:

Métrodore: "Nous ne savons$_2$ pas si nous savons$_1$ quelque chose ou rien" (= **Fi**).

Antidore: "Mais cela, nous le savons$_3$ (i.e. que nous ne savons$_2$ pas si nous savons$_1$ quelque chose ou rien) ?"

Métrodore: "Non, nous ne savons$_3$ même pas cela même (i.e. que nous ne savons$_2$ pas si nous savons$_1$ quelque chose ou rien) (= **Fii**).

Deuxième avantage: si l'on suppose (plus ou moins littéralement) authentique l'original grec de *nego scire nos sciamusne aliquid an nihil sciamus, ne id ipsum quidem scire nos*, on voit assez bien comment le texte de Cicéron a pu se corrompre en se compliquant: dans un premier temps, l'alternative *nescire aut scire* se substitue au simple *scire*, soit pour bâtir une antithèse séduisante (comme le

---

que l'on conserve <*scire*>("[Io affirmo] ... che non sappiamo neppure se sappiamo o non sappiamo questa cosa stessa"); de même, mais sans <*scire*>, Barigazzi (1969) 291 et Straume-Zimmermann *et al.* (1990) 189.

52 Une autre hypothèse, suggérée par Carlos Lévy (*per litteram*), serait que **Fi** soit la traduction du texte de Métrodore par Cicéron, et **Fii** une traduction alternative de ce même texte, effectuée soit par Cicéron lui-même, soit par un correcteur postérieur. Il n'y aurait donc pas lieu de chercher une différence de sens entre **Fi** et **Fii**. La difficulté est alors que *ne id ipsum quidem* perd sa valeur de surenchère par rapport à ce qui précède.

53 Langerbeck (1935) 122.

54 Rappelons qu'en syntaxe latine, quand la locution *ne ... quidem* suit une négation, elle ne l'annule pas.

pense Langerbeck), soit plutôt, peut-être, par contamination avec **E**ii; dans un second temps, l'adjonction d'un *scire* supplémentaire paraît nécessaire à la construction syntaxique de la phrase.

Troisième avantage: toujours dans la même hypothèse, l'apparition des variantes présentées par les différents témoignages s'explique assez bien. La version de **F** à laquelle nous arrivons contient à la fois une interrogative indirecte double dans la section (**F**i) (*sciamusne aliquid an nihil sciamus*) et une complétive simple dans la section (**F**ii) (*scire nos*). Ces deux éléments se séparent et se présentent isolément, l'interrogation double dans **E**, la complétive dans **D**. En outre, **F** ne contient pas d'assertion indépendante d'ignorance$_1$ universelle, mais seulement une assertion d'ignorance$_2$, ce qui est aussi le cas pour **B**. L'assertion d'ignorance$_1$ commence à se détacher dans **C**, qui permet de voir comment l'on aura éprouvé le besoin d'extraire une telle assertion de l'assertion métrodorienne de l'ignorance$_2$. Une fois ce mouvement parvenu à son terme, l'assertion d'ignorance$_1$ s'énonce expressément (avec tous les dangers dialectiques que cela comporte pour la position de Métrodore) dans **D** et dans **E**. Dans **A**, enfin, il ne reste plus qu'elle; pour cacher sa maigreur, on l'accompagne d'un commentaire inspiré de Xénophane.

Il reste à dire un mot de **F**iii, présent dans **F**, absent de tout le reste de la documentation. Peut-on attribuer à Métrodore le scepticisme ontologique de **F**iii ? Oui, répondent implicitement Diels-Friedländer, par le seul fait d'intégrer la rétroversion de **F**iii dans DK 70 B 1. Ils ont été suivis, ou même précédés, par un nombre considérable d'érudits.[55] Une voix dissonante[56] suggère qu'"il est fort possible que cette idée [i.e. celle de **F**iii] soit une addition personnelle" de Cicéron. Je suis assez enclin à adopter pareille

---

[55] Cf. Goedeckemeyer (1905) 3, Dumont (1988) 946, Dal Pra (1975^2) 1.52, Barnes (1982) 559. Mansfeld (1992) 33 déclare expressément que l'énoncé sceptique de Métrodore est "partly preserved in Greek and complete in Cicero's Latin" (y compris **F**iii). Langerbeck lui-même, qui n'est pourtant pas indulgent pour la rétroversion de Diels, et qui admet que Cicéron a pu rassembler plusieurs énoncés à partir de sa source pour obtenir de belles antithèses, estime que **F**iii est "gedeckt durch die Intention der ganzen Stelle". En effet, juste avant d'aborder le cas de Métrodore, Cicéron (*Acad. pr.* 73) avait présenté Démocrite comme le tenant d'un scepticisme radical (*verum esse plane negat*). Puisque Démocrite avait dénié "l'être du vrai", ajoute Langerbeck (1935) 123, "il n'est que trop vraisemblable que Métrodore aussi avait affirmé un tel non-savoir à propos de l'être".

[56] Ernout et Robin (1926) 2.227.

hypothèse: en effet, l'ignorance exprimée par **Fiii** redevient une ignorance$_1$, alors que nous avons trouvé dans **Fi** et dans **Fii** des raisons de penser que Métrodore n'avait décrit que des ignorances de degré supérieur; de plus, il serait assez étrange qu'une déclaration aussi fracassante que **Fiii** n'ait laissé aucune autre trace dans la tradition[57].

Concluons en laissant ouverte la question posée par **Fiii**. Il semble en tout cas que **Fi** + **Fii**, historiquement et philosophiquement, constituent la version la plus plausible de la parole de Métrodore.

Université de Paris I

RÉFÉRENCES BIBLIOGRAPHIQUES

Alfieri, V.E. (1936) *Gli Atomisti. Frammenti e Testimonianze* (Bari).
—— (1953) *Atomos Idea* (Firenze).
Appuhn, Ch. (s.d.) *Cicéron: De la Divination – Du Destin – Académiques* (Paris).
Armstrong, D.M. (1973) *Belief, Truth and Knowledge* (London).
Bailey, C. (1947) *Titi Lucreti Cari De Rerum Natura Libri Sex* (Oxford).
Barigazzi, A. (1969) "Epicure et le scepticisme", in *Actes du VIIIe Congrès de l'Association Guillaume Budé*: 286-93.
Barnes, J. (1982²) *The Presocratic Philosophers* (London).
—— (1992) "Diogenes Laertius IX 61-116: The Philosophy of Pyrrhonism", in *Aufstieg und Niedergang der römischen Welt*, ed. W. Haase (Berlin) II.36.6, 4241-4301.
Bonjour, L. (1980) "Externalist theories of empirical knowledge", *Midwest Studies in Philosophy* 5: 53-73.
Brochard, V. (1923²) *Les sceptiques grecs* (Paris).
Burnyeat, M. F. (1978) "The Upside-Down Back-to-Front Sceptic of Lucretius IV 472", *Philologus* 122: 197-206.
Cappelletti, A.J. (1979). *Ensayos sobre los Atomistas Griegos* (Caracas).
Conche, M. (1984) "Métrodore de Chio", in *Dictionnaire des Philosophes*, ed. D. Huisman (Paris) 2.1821.
Crönert, W. (1906) *Kolotes und Menedemos* (Leipzig).
Dal Pra, M. (1975²) *Lo scetticismo greco* (Roma–Bari).

[57] Pour défendre l'authenticité métrodorienne de **Fiii** contre les doutes d'Ernout et Robin, Conche (1984) 1821 écrit: "Métrodore a pu s'apercevoir de la contradiction qu'il y avait, chez Démocrite, à poser des atomes réels pour expliquer un sensible sans vraie réalité, et être ainsi conduit du scepticisme à l'égard des sens au nihilisme ontologique". Mais Métrodore, autant que nous sachions, n'a pas répudié l'ontologie atomistique; de plus, le "nihilisme ontologique" n'est que l'une des branches de l'alternative dans laquelle **Fiii** nous laisse en suspens.

DeLacy, Ph. (1971) "Οὐ μᾶλλον and the Antecedents of Ancient Scepticism", in *Essays in Ancient Greek Philosophy*, ed. J.P. Anton and G.L. Kustas (Albany) 593-606.

Des Places, E. (1987) *Eusèbe de Césarée: La Préparation évangélique*, Livres XIV-XV (Paris).

DDG = Diels, H. (1879) *Doxographi graeci* (Berlin).

DK = Diels, H. und Kranz, W. (1956^8) *Die Fragmente der Vorsokratiker* (Berlin).

Dumont, J.P. (1988) *Les Présocratiques* (Paris).

Ernout, A. et Robin, L. (1962^2) *Lucrèce: De Rerum Natura. Commentaire exégétique et critique* (Paris).

Friedländer, P. (1969) *Studien zur antiken Literatur und Kunst* (Berlin).

Gigante, M. (1981) *Scetticismo e Epicureismo* (Naples).

—— (1990) "Quelques précisions sur le scepticisme et l'épicurisme", in *Le scepticisme antique – Perspectives historiques et systématiques*, ed. A.J. Voelke (Genève–Lausanne–Neuchâtel) 69-83.

Goedeckemeyer, A. (1905) *Die Geschichte der Griechischen Skeptizismus* (Leipzig).

Hankinson, R.J. (1995) *The Sceptics* (London).

Hussey, E. (1990) "The beginnings of epistemology: from Homer to Philolaus", in *Epistemology*, ed. S. Everson, Companions to Ancient Thought: 1 (Cambridge) 11-38.

Isnardi-Parente, M. (1984) "I democritei e l'antiscetticismo di Epicuro (*Ratae Sententiae XXIII-XXIV*)", in *La storia della filosofia come sapere critico – Studi in onore di Mario Dal Pra* , ed. F. Angeli (Milano): 106-121.

Langerbeck, H. (1935) *ΔΟΞΙΣ ΕΠΙΡΡΥΣΜΙΗ : Studien zu Demokrits Ethik und Erkenntnislehre* (Berlin).

Lesher, J.H. (1978) "Xenophanes' Scepticism", *Phronesis* 23: 1-21.

—— (1992) *Xenophanes of Colophon: Fragments* (Toronto).

Mansfeld, J. (1992) *Heresiography in Context: Hippolytus'* Elenchos *as a Source for Greek Philosophy* (Leiden).

Plasberg, O. (1922) *Academicorum reliquiae cum Lucullo* (Leipzig).

Rackham, H. (1933) *Cicero: De Natura Deorum – Academica* (Cambridge Mass.–London).

Reid, J.S. (1885) *M. Tulli Ciceronis Academica* (London).

Schäublin, C. und Graeser, A. (1995) *Cicero: Academica* (Leipzig) (*non vidi*).

Sedley, D. (1983) "The Motivation of Greek Skepticism", in *The Skeptical Tradition* , ed. M. Burnyeat (Berkeley–Los Angeles–London) 9-29.

Shorey, P. (1919) "Note on Metrodorus, fragm. 1", *Classical Philology* 14: 393-4.

Straume-Zimmermann L., Broemser F., Gigon O. (1990) *Hortensius – Lucullus – Academici libri* (München–Zürich).

Vander Waerdt, P. A. (1989). "Colotes and the Epicurean Refutation of Scepticism", *Greek, Roman and Byzantine Studies* 30: 225-267.

Wilamowitz-Möllendorf, U. v. (1899) "Lesefrüchte", *Hermes* 34: 601-639.

Zeller, E., Mondolfo, R. (1969) *La filosofia dei Greci nel suo sviluppo storico. Parte I, volume V: Empedocle, Atomisti, Anassagora a cura di A. Capizzi* (Firenze).

PART TWO

PLATO

OBSERVATIONS ON PLATO'S THRASYMACHUS: THE CASE FOR *PLEONEXIA*

Keimpe Algra

1. The second half of the first book of Plato's *Republic*, which contains a discussion between Socrates and Thrasymachus on justice, is undoubtedly among the most widely studied parts of the work. This popularity is not surprising, for the episode not only makes for pleasant reading, but also constitutes an intriguing piece of philosophical dialogue. It is intriguing because it sets an important philosophical challenge which the rest of the *Republic* tries to answer, whereas the dramatic presentation is apparently such as to have given rise to quite divergent interpretations of what exactly Thrasymachus is made to say.[1] The present paper does not pretend to offer an entirely novel interpretation of the Thrasymachus episode. It rather contains some observations which support and elaborate existing scholarly interpretations, most notably those of Kerferd on Thrasymachus' definitions, Kahn on the way *Rep.* I fits into the rest of the work, and Rutherford on the literary and dramatic elements.[2] By bringing these various approaches together, I hope to be able to contribute to an account of Thrasymachus' position which is both coherent and securely based on Plato's text.

I have had to be selective in my references to the extensive scholarly literature on the Thrasymachus episode. Only those studies are mentioned which I took to be directly relevant to the points I wish to make. I have also had to refrain from adding detailed discussions of (1) the question of the genesis of the *Republic* and of the ancestry of book I, (2) the question of whether Plato's Thrasymachus represents the sophist Thrasymachus of Chalcedon, and (3) the relative merits and demerits of the various approaches to Plato (more purely 'analytic', or more literary and 'Wilamowitzean'). A few dogmatic statements to mark off my

[1] For a convenient overview of the various ways in which the position defended by Thrasymachus, and in particular his definitions of justice, have been interpreted and labelled see Cross/Woozley (1964) 29-41 and Kerferd (1947) 545-548.

[2] Cf. Kerferd (1945) and (1981), Kahn (1993), and Rutherford (1995).

position on these matters must here suffice. As to (1), although the view that *Rep.* I is to be traced back to an originally separate 'Socratic' dialogue, which some have even christened *Thrasymachus*, still does find some support,[3] it is now generally assumed to rest on poor evidence. For our present purpose, many of the items which are at stake in the context of this discussion may be ignored, except for the following points. First, book I is definitely less 'Socratic' than it may at first blush appear to be. Although it formally ends in *aporia*, it has Socrates defend what is, albeit *in nuce*, a dogmatic position.[4] Secondly, as was already pointed out by Wilamowitz, we shall have to assume that, even if Plato originally wrote a *Thrasymachus* as a separate piece, he must have redesigned it subsequently to fulfill a meaningful role in the *Republic* as a whole.[5] He explicitly refers to it as a *prooimion* to the rest of the work (357a2), and he refers back to Thrasymachus' position on various occasions in the later books of the *Republic*.[6] Moreover, as has now been forcefully argued by Charles Kahn, the first book contains so many detailed anticipations of themes that are further worked out in the course of the *Republic* that even the hypothesis of a secondary reworking becomes rather implausible, because in that case we would have to assume that Plato re-wrote more than half of the whole piece.[7] As to question (2), I shall be assuming that even if the character of Thrasymachus in *Rep.* I could be proved to be identical with the historical Thrasymachus of Chalcedon—which it clearly

[3] A sustained, though not very strong, defense of the hypothesis of a separate *Thrasymachus* was provided by Von Arnim (1914) 71-109, and (1927). A qualified and more sensible version of the hypothesis was defended by Wilamowitz (1920) 2. 182-184, and Friedländer (1964) 2. 45-60. It is still defended by Vlastos (1991) 250, and in a slightly modified form, by Gigon (1976) 82, who thinks that *Rep.* I in its present state represents an abbreviated version of an earlier work, with a number of additions designed to make it fit into the whole of the *Republic*. For a more extensive survey of the history of the 'Thrasymachus' hypothesis and connected issues, see Zeller (1922) 2. 1. 488 n. 1 and 555-556; Guthrie (1975) 437, and Kahn (1993) 131-133.

[4] This point has been well brought out by Gigon (1976) 81-82.

[5] Wilamowitz (1920) 2. 182-185. According to Wilamowitz Plato did not publish the original dialogue, because he had in the meantime written the *Gorgias* which more or less covered the same material in a better way, and later re-worked it for the *Republic*.

[6] The position defended by Thrasymachus in book I is referred to in *Rep.* II, 358a-c; 367a5; 367c2; 368b5; VIII 545a8; IX, 590d3

[7] Cf. Kahn (1993) 136 and 139. The fact that much of book I actually foreshadows what is to follow later on in the *Republic* has of course been noted by others as well, most notably by White (1979). That there were any such prefigurations in book I was flatly denied by Von Arnim (1914) 72.

cannot—historical accuracy was obviously not Plato's primary aim. He rather appears to have presented Thrasymachus as the fountainhead of a dialectical position to be refuted.[8] This means that we should first and foremost study Thrasymachus as a *persona* in Plato's dialogue (as the title of this paper indicates), and that we should realize that the discussion between Socrates and Thrasymachus is basically Plato's own creation. That should alert us to the fact that the way Socrates and Thrasymachus interact may be determined by Plato's overall aims rather than by the actual contents of what the two characters are made to say. In other words, the dialogue should be compared to a (skilfully staged) piece of work of a dramatist, rather than to the report of a game of chess.[9]

Finally, as to question (3), we may note that in 1975 Guthrie could still write that 'in discussing the views attributed to Thrasymachus the most recent practice had been to consider all possible alternatives as they appear to a philosopher today, and by exhaustive examination of the dialogue endeavour to decide which of them is being maintained by Thrasymachus'. He added that 'such clarification can be most valuable, yet may err by neglecting (as it is never wise to do with Plato) the dramatic situation and emotional tension between the speakers'.[10] Since Guthrie wrote these line there has been a growing tendency to complement the predominantly analytical approach of Plato's philosophical arguments—an approach which in the case of the Thrasymachus episode came down to focusing primarily on the definitions of justice and their alleged philosophical import—with an approach which takes account of the larger context, philosophical as well as dramatic.[11] It

---

[8] It is therefore methodologically preferable to refrain from using what little is known of the philosophical ideas of Thrasymachus of Chalcedon to interpret the text of *Rep.* I, as has been done by Guthrie (1971) 3. 92-97, and esp. 297, who tries to square the picture of Thrasymachus which arises from *Rep.* I with the evidence of Thrasymachus of Chalcedon fr. 1 Diels-Kranz (a speech to the Athenian assembly in which Thrasymachus appears to speak in praise of justice and which would thus seem to be at odds with *Rep* I.) by interpreting the Thrasymachus of the *Rep.* as a desillusioned and bitter man, a claim for which there does not appear to be any clear evidence in the text.

[9] Cf. the pertinent remarks in Reeve (1988) 276, note 5, and Annas (1981) 56. The recognition that neither Socrates nor Thrasymachus are writing their own lines should make us skeptical about the possibility of separating an allegedly 'original' position of Thrasymachus from additions which are supposedly due to Plato; an example of such an approach is Maguire (1971), on which see below, n. 39.

[10] Guthrie (1971), vol. 3, 91 .

[11] An extremely useful example of this approach is Rutherford (1995); but

will be clear from what follows that I happily endorse the latter approach.

The present paper is structured as follows. Section 2 contains a summary which will serve as a basis for the analysis which is to follow. Section 3 discusses the way the Thrasymachus episode connects with the rest of the *Republic.* Section 4 will deal with Plato's literary and dramatic presentation. Section 5, finally, contains some observations on how Thrasymachus definitions of justice interrelate and how they are to be interpreted.

2. After the vivid introduction of Thrasymachus as a *persona* (336b-337a, on which see section (4) and after some initial quarrelings between Thrasymachus and Socrates about method (337a-338c), the discussion gets started with Thrasymachus' claim (put forward with characteristic self-consciousness: ἀλλὰ τί οὐκ ἐπαινεῖς) that justice is 'the advantage of the stronger' (τὸ τοῦ κρείττονος [...] συμφέρον, 338c). Of course put like this the claim lacks philosophical precision. Hence the Socratic method is applied in order to get things straight. It turns out that Thrasymachus is not speaking of corporeal strength, and that by 'the stronger' he means the person or persons in power (τὸ τῆς καθεστηκυίας ἀρχῆς συμφέρον, 339a1).[12] In others words, in the context in which he launches this first definition he is primarily thinking of justice in the *political* sphere, of justice in the state.

---

see also Stokes (1986), where, however, the *Rep.* is not discussed; Müller (1981) represents a similar approach, but pays little attention to the Thrasymachus episode.

[12] Note, first, that the phrase τὸ τῆς καθεστηκυίας ἀρχῆς συμφέρον clearly figures as a further specification of the first definition ('the advantage of the stronger'), as may be inferred from what immediately follows: αὕτη δέ που κρατεῖ, ὥστε συμβαίνει τῷ ὀρθῶς λογιζομένῳ πανταχοῦ εἶναι τὸ αὐτὸ δίκαιον, τὸ τοῦ κρείττονος συμφέρον, 339a2-4). It does not involve any shift of position on Thrasymachus' part. Secondly Thrasymachus makes it quite clear that he regards it as an empirical fact that rulers legislate in their own interest (338e1-2: τίθεται δέ γε τοὺς νόμους ἑκάστη ἡ ἀρχὴ πρὸς τὸ αὑτῇ συμφέρον). It follows that, when at 339b7 he assents to Socrates' suggestion that justice is 'obeying the rulers' (πείθεσθαι [...] τοῖς ἄρχουσιν) he takes it to be implied all the way along that these rulers as a matter of course serve their own interest. Accordingly, *pace* Maguire (1971) 143, we cannot read 339b7 as containing a new and independent definition of justice. Thirdly, the notion of τὸ συμφέρον is prominent right from the beginning of Thrasymachus' account; this means that the label 'conventionalism' is not very suitable to describe this position, *pace* Annas (1981) 40. What may count as justice is never a matter of *mere* convention.

Socrates now points to the possibility of the rulers being mistaken as to their own interests. Thrasymachus rejects the suggestion of Cleitophon that he can dodge this objection by specifying that justice consists in whatever the rulers (rightly or wrongly) *think* to be in their own interest. Instead he boldly claims that the rulers *qua* rulers—i.e. *qua* possessing their specific skill (τέχνη)—are never mistaken. Interestingly, Socrates does not challenge this claim as such. He rather takes advantage of the fact that Thrasymachus is willing to speak of the ruler's job as a τέχνη, and of a ruler 'in the strict sense', and of the fact that he is prepared to compare the ruler's art to the art of, say, a doctor. Socrates does so, however, by shifting the ground. He retorts that anyone exercising a τέχνη *in the strict sense* is not acting in his own interest. By way of an elenctic procedure which Thrasymachus is unable to withstand, he concludes (342e6-11) that the ruler, *qua* ruler, will always be guided by the interests of his subjects. This conclusion is presented as a reversal of Thrasymachus' own account (ὁ τοῦ δικαίου λόγος εἰς τοὐναντίον περιειστήκει, 343a2), which it obviously is to the extent that the rulers are now said to decree whatever they decree in the interest not of themselves but of others, viz. their subjects.

However, instead of going along with this conclusion Thrasymachus accuses Socrates of naïveté (he doesn't 'know about sheep and shepherd', 343a8). It is now his turn to shift the focus from the political level to the level of individual human beings who, he suggests, are not as Socrates pictures them. And he vigorously restates his own position in what I shall henceforth refer to as his 'speech' (343b1-344d1). As his primary definition he now proposes that justice is 'what is good for someone else' (ἀλλότριον ἀγαθόν, 343c2) in the sense that it is contrary to the subjects' own interests. He contrasts a number of examples of just and unjust behaviour to show that the unjust, if successful, always gain the advantage, and repeats that justice is the advantage of the stronger, whereas injustice is 'one's own profit and advantage' (344c8).

Socrates replies with a series of questions (345b7-347e1) designed to show that the example on which Thrasymachus has based his case—a shepherd tending his flock in his own interest—was wrong, because the shepherd (*qua* shepherd) turns out to act in the interest of his flock. In general, he argues, this goes for every τέχνη, including governing according to the rules (καλῶς τῇ τέχνῃ, 347a1), which is why *good* rulers are so difficult to get. In fact they are only willing to govern if they get a proper compensation, or rather in order to evade the punishment of being ruled by others who are less competent. In a city where this risk would have been eliminated—i.e. in a city consisting of good people only—everybody would prefer the status of being a subject to that of being a ruler (347d1-8). For the time being Socrates continues to disagree with Thrasymachus' contention that justice concerns the advantage of the ruler, but he announces that this subject is to be further treated later on (347e2: ἀλλὰ τοῦτο μὲν δὴ καὶ εἰς αὖθις σκεψόμεθα).

He now turns instead to what he takes to be the more important issue, viz. Thrasymachus' claim that the life of the unjust is better and happier than the life of the just. This will be the subject of the rest of the discussion (347e7-354a11). A brief survey may here suffice. Socrates comes up with three arguments which are rather different in kind. First of all, he tries to establish that Thrasymachus' claim that injustice is a kind of ἀρετή gets him into trouble, for this would involve that justice is a κακία, a view so counter-intuitive that not even Thrasymachus is willing to endorse it (348b8-349a8).[13] Furthermore, the injust cannot be superior in φρόνησις either, since φρόνησις, which is the possession of a particular skill, entails that one only wants to outdo those who are inferior insofar as they do not have that skill. This criterion applies to the just, not to the unjust who want to outdo *everybody* (the words used are πλέον ἔχειν and πλεονεκτεῖν, both connected to the noun πλεονεξία), i.e. both the just and the unjust (349b1-350d10). Secondly (350d-352b), Socrates challenges Thrasymachus' contention that injustice is a source of strength. It appears that injustice, on the contrary, involves faction, hatred and disunity, on the level of states as well as between individuals, and even within a single individual. Thirdly, each thing has its proper function (ἔργον); exercising this function well is what virtue (ἀρετή) amounts to; living is the function of the soul; since justice is the the particular virtue of the soul (this is an element which in the present context is question-begging, and which Thrasymachus need not accept), living well amounts to living a life of justice. The final section of the book shows us a Thrasymachus who is more or less silenced, but who remains unconvinced, and a Socrates who admits that he has not as yet done his job properly: he has been hopping from

[13] See on this Annas (1981) 47-49.

subject to subject without clearly realizing that the main question, the definition of justice, needs to be answered first. This, of course, is what will be his task in the rest of the work.

3. The passages we have just summarized contain various elements which foreshadow the more elaborate discussions which are to follow in the rest of the *Republic*:

(1) Socrates' claim that true and competent rulers do not rule in their own interest but in the interest of their subjects anticipates the discussion in books III and IV of the characteristics of the rulers in the ideal state (starting with the claim at 412c13-4 that the rulers will have to be κηδεμόνας τῆς πόλεως), and in book VII, 540b (ἄρχοντας [...] τῆς πόλεως ἕνεκα).

(2) Related to (1) is Socrates' insistence (345b7-346e1) on the fact that a good ruler's ruling will never be entirely voluntary, which foreshadows his claim later on (519d-521b) that the rulers in the ideal state will take on their job only unwillingly. Indeed, as we already noted, he even explicitly states that this is a subject which will be postponed until later.

(3) Socrates's claim (352d-254a) that justice is a virtue of the soul in the sense that it constitutes its health and its proper functioning, is not justified in the context of *Rep.* I and indeed only becomes intelligible against the background of the moral psychology worked out in book IV, in particular 444a-e.

(4) The idea that unjustice is a source of strife (στάσις) at the level of states or smaller social groups (350d-352b) might in principle be justified, independently of the philosophical commitments of Socrates or Plato, by an appeal to common sense—for this reason it is within the limited context of *Rep.* I certainly the most powerful argument raised against Thrasymachus—but the idea that this same analysis applies to the injust *individual* is neither an element of common sense, nor a claim to which Thrasymachus needs to be committed.[14] In fact it anticipates the thesis of the parallelism between (the parts of the) *polis* and (the parts of the) individual which is developed later on in book IV (368d-e and 435e-436a); the conception of *stasis* within an individual soul is of course further developed in the context of the theory of individual justice being a healthy harmony between the three parts of the soul (441c-442d), and in book VIII-IX, in the extensive account of the decline of the ideal state and in the subsequent analysis of happiness in relation to psychic constitution (576b-592b, esp. 588e-589a).

(5) The general theme of the unresolved controversy between Thrasymachus and Socrates in the final part of *Rep.* I (viz. whether justice or injustice is more beneficial to its possessor) is taken up again at the end of book IX, in 588b ff., where the question is answered on the basis of the findings of the *Rep.* as a whole (591a-592b; see also X, 612b).

---

[14] See also Annas (1981) 53, who does not consider the possibility of an 'anticipatory' function of this passage.

(6) The idea of injustice as *pleonexia* (which occurs in Thrasymachus' speech in 341b-344d, and in 349a-350c) and the idea that people are naturally inclined to *pleonexia* and will accordingly only behave justly if they *have to* (an idea which runs through the whole of Thrasymachus' account; on which see my remarks in the next sections) recur at the beginning of book II, in 358a-362c, where Glaucon slightly reformulates Thrasymachus' position by way of a challenge to Socrates; the concept of *pleonexia* itself reappears in the discussion of the tyrant in book IX (574a8; 586b1).

(7) Thrasymachus' reference to tyranny as the ultimate form of injustice (τελεωτάτη ἀδικία, 344a) has its more elaborate counterpart in book VIII-IX, where Plato presents his account of the decline of the ideal state as a means to make clear how perfect justice stands to perfect injustice (tyranny). His aim is to get us in a position to decide whether Thrasymachus or Socrates was right (545a: ἵνα τὸν ἀδικώτατον ἰδόντες ἀντιθῶμεν τῷ δικαιοτάτῳ καὶ ἡμῖν τελέα ἡ σκέψις ᾖ, πῶς ποτε ἡ ἄκρατος δικαιοσύνη πρὸς ἀδικίαν τὴν ἄκρατον ἔχει εὐδαιμονίας τε πέρι τοῦ ἔχοντος καὶ ἀθλιότητος, ἵνα ἢ Θρασυμάχῳ πειθόμενοι διώκωμεν ἀδικίαν ἢ τῷ νῦν προφαινομένῳ λόγῳ δικαιοσύνην).

On the basis of this list—which, I believe, covers the main issues, but which may not be exhaustive[15]—I would like to make the following observations.

First, I take it to be obvious that we are here dealing with a number of instances of what Charles Kahn has labelled 'proleptic composition'. In introducing this label Kahn took his cue from a 1971 study on Aeschylus and his imagery by Anne Lebeck. In Aeschylus, according to Lebeck, we witness that 'the significance of a recurrent image unfolds in successive stages' and 'in its early occurrences the image is elliptical and enigmatic'.[16]

In the present case, however, we need not resort to such remote parallels in Aeschylean drama, interesting though they may be in themselves. As we noted, right at the beginning of the second book Socrates remarks that at this point he thought the discussion was completed, but that it turned out that the whole thing had really been nothing but a *prooimion* (ἐγὼ μὲν οὖν ταῦτα εἰπὼν ᾤμην λόγου ἀπηλλάχθαι· τὸ δ'ἦν ἄρα, ὡς ἔοικε, προοίμιον, 357a1). Now we

---

[15] Kahn (1993) 136-140 provides a somewhat differently structured list, which at any rate does not include my items (5) and (6). On the other hand he provides two extra examples which I have here left out, because I found them not quite as obvious and convincing as the other ones: (1) the perfect knowledge which Thrasymachus' rulers are supposed to possess serves to introduce, according to Kahn, the general theme of the perfect ruler (*op. cit.* 138), and (2) the claim that different *technai* have different capacities serves to prepare the distinction between knowledge and opinion in book V (esp. 477d1).

[16] Lebeck (1971) 1.

know from ancient rhetorical treatises that a proem was supposed to attract the attention of the readers or the public and to announce the theme(s) of the main body of the work. As Aristotle puts it (with special regard to drama and epic poetry), 'in prologues and epic poetry a foretaste of the theme is given, intended to inform the readers of it in advance instead of keeping their minds in suspense'.[17] But we can also turn to Plato's own words. In the fourth book of the *Laws* the Athenian tells his two companions that ideal laws need to have preambles (*prooimia*) and that their own conversation from early morning onwards, while walking through the Cretan mountains, has in fact been such a *prooimion*. He then adds: 'What do I mean? I want to say this: in all kinds of speeches and other vocal performances there are proems and, so to speak, preliminary exercises (προοίμιά τε ἐστιν καὶ σχεδὸν οἷόν τινες ἀνακινήσεις) containing a skilled first approach which is useful with regard to what is going to be accomplished (ἔχουσαί τινα ἔντεχνον ἐπιχείρησιν χρήσιμον πρὸς τὸ μέλλον περαίνεσθαι).[18]

The two main elements of this description—viz. (1) a proem is a kind of preliminary exercise and (2) it must be useful with regard to what follows—both neatly apply to the discussion of book I. It is clearly a *preliminary* exercise in so far as it broaches the subject of justice and shows some of the main items with which a full discussion should deal. It is also *useful* with regard to the rest of the work, in so far as Plato's own view as well as the view diametrically opposed to it (Thrasymachus') are both introduced in such a way as to attract the attention of the reader.

Like the 'proleptic' passages in Aeschylus discussed by Lebeck and referred to by Kahn, a proem will often contain elements which are more or less enigmatic in so far as they merely summarize or announce subjects which will be worked out more fully later on in the work. In this respect Aristotle's claim, quoted

---

[17] *Rhet.* 1415a13-14. See also *Rhet. Alex.* 29.1.

[18] *Leg.* 722d2-6. Note that the attached example of a musical *prooimion* - i.e. a prelude, which precedes the melody proper (νόμος: of course the choice of this homonym of νόμος in the sense of 'law' is deliberate) - is also used by Plato in *Rep.* 532d7 ('let us now move to the melody proper and perform it just as we have performed the prelude') and in *Tim.* 29d5 ('we liked your prelude, now proceed with the melody'). For examples of Plato's use of προοίμιον (and προοιμιάζεσθαι) in the general sense of 'introductory conversation', see *Phdr.* 266d7; *Lach.* 179a1; *Rep.* 432e8; for the use of *prooimion* in the sense of a 'preamble' to a law, see the whole context of *Leg.* 722-725. On the *prooimion* of the *Tim.* see now Runia (1996).

above, that proems are meant to clarify matters and to *minimize* suspense, should be qualified. Jaap Mansfeld, to whom this article is dedicated, has convincingly argued that in the case of some Presocratic proems we encounter a form of *intentional* unclarity, designed precisely to strengthen the element of suspense.[19] In the case of *Rep.* I we are arguably dealing with a weaker, but comparable, form of intentional unclarity: the diametrically opposed positions of Socrates and Thrasymachus are clear in themselves, but the arguments needed to clinch the issue will only be provided later on. And here also this procedure arguably creates a kind of suspense. Like Glaucon, at the beginning of the second book, the average reader will probably sympathize with Socrates's position rather than with that of Thrasymachus. And like Glaucon, he will ask for more: he will not be satisfied with the avowed inadequacy of Socrates' critique nor with the formal *aporia* which concludes the book.[20]

If, then, the arguments in book I sometimes appear to be truncated and if the discussion as a whole often strikes us as incomplete, we should realize that we are only dealing with an ἀνακινήσις, a first sounding of the important *Leitmotive* of the rest of the work. There is accordingly no need to to go along with Gigon's hypothesis that what we have before us is an abridged version of a more elaborate original and separate dialogue.[21] Indeed, the recognition that *Rep.* I has a prefatory character may help us to understand why the piece is not all that aporetic, despite its 'Socratic style' and despite Socrates' final admission that he still 'knows nothing' (354b59-c1). Thrasymachus is introduced in order to set out a position which is the exact counterpart of the position Socrates is going to work out later on in the *Republic*, and this means that Plato could not use a neutral, non-knowing Socrates in book I, but opted instead for a Socrates who opposes Thrasymachus with conviction and vigour on all accounts (on whether the rulers' ruling is in their own interest, on whether injustice is profitable). In addition the prefatory character of the Thrasymachus episode arguably offers an explanation of why Thrasymachus is made to

---

19 Mansfeld (1996).

20 Cf. Glaucon's words at 357a5: πότερον ἡμᾶς βούλει δοκεῖν πεπεικέναι ἢ ὡς ἀληθῶς πεῖσαι ὅτι παντὶ τρόπῳ ἄμεινόν ἐστι δίκαιον εἶναι ἢ ἄδικον. And 358b2-6: Θρασύμαχος γάρ μοι φαίνεται πρῳαίτερον τοῦ δέοντος ὑπὸ σοῦ ὥσπερ ὄφις κηληθῆναι, ἐμοὶ δὲ οὔπω κατὰ νοῦν ἡ ἀπόδειξις γέγονεν περὶ ἑκατέρου.

21 Gigon (1976) 82-83.

come up with two different—although, as I shall try to show coherent—definitions of justice ('the advantage of the stronger' in 338c, and 'what is good for someone else' in 343c). It is usually assumed either that this reflects the fact that Thrasymachus is simply a confused thinker, or that he merely states his position in an obscure way in 338c but is forced by Socrates' criticisms to come up with a better version in 343c.[22] As I noted in the introductory section, however, neither Thrasymachus nor Socrates are writing their own lines. We should therefore perhaps first ask whether Plato had a reason for this 'double' presentation. If we realise that the discussion is supposed to be a kind of proem, we are presented with such a good reason. As is well known, there are two main strands in Plato's discussion of justice in the rest of the *Republic.* The investigation is carried out at two different levels: justice in the state (with the concomitant issues of who should rule and why) and justice in the individual (with the concomitant issue of what constitutes the happy life). Of course the two strands are connected in various ways, most noticeably by Plato's anthropology (i.e. his tripartite psychology). My suggestion is that Plato wanted his *prooimion* to contain an exposition of the position diametrically opposed to his own *on both accounts,* i.e. he wanted Thrasymachus to define justice both at the political level ('the advantage of the stronger') and at the level of the individual ('what is good for someone else').

4. On the basis of the evidence discussed in the previous sections it may reasonably be suggested that Thrasymachus' position is to be characterized as being essentially a defense of *pleonexia.* The term πλεονεξία as well as the connected verbs πλέον ἔχειν and πλεονεκτεῖν all occur prominently, and *exclusively,* in those passages in the *Rep.* which refer to Thrasymachus' position, i.e. his own speech, the rephrasing of his position by Glaucon and Adeimantus in book II, and the description of (Thrasymachean) tyranny in book VIII-IX.[23] We appear to be dealing with key-words. The typically Thrasymachean motif of unlimited self-assertion appears to have

[22] See below, nn. 39 and 40.

[23] In the Thrasymachus episode in book I we find πλεονεξία at 359c5, πλέον ἔχειν at 343d5; 349b3-e12 (4 times) and πλεονεκτεῖν at 344a1; 349 b8-350c1 (10 times). In the 'paraphrase' in book II we find πλεονεκτεῖν at 362b7 (2 times) and 365d6. In the context of the discussion of tyranny in book VIII-IX we find πλεονεξία at 586b1, and πλέον ἔχειν at 574a8. This is the extent of the use of these terms in the *Republic.*

been deliberately opposed to Socrates' (and Plato's) own stress on order and limitation. And just as Plato's own two accounts of justice (political and individual) are linked by what we might call his anthropology of restraint and self-control (characterised by such words as κόσμος, κόσμιος and ἥμερος),[24] so also Thrasymachus' two definitions may be seen as linked by what we might call an implicit anthropology which is governed by the notion of *pleonexia*: people are naturally inclined not to respect other people and their possessions, to intrude into the areas of others and to set the rules for them, and to disregard any limits that might check such behaviour. I want to suggest that this general picture of Thrasymachus defending *pleonexia* is skilfully supported by the way Plato has fleshed out the *persona* of Thrasymachus dramatically.

In general, it is worth noting that Plato's characterisations of Socrates' interlocutors are usually more than simply the icing of the cake. Their character and behaviour are often made to contrast strongly with Socrates, thus underlining the fact that they are committed to an entirely different philosophical outlook or way of life. One of the most striking examples is Alcibiades in the *Symposium*. Others are Polus and Callicles in the *Gorgias*. But also in a more general way—i.e. apart from any intended dramatic contrast with the *persona* of Socrates—Plato's *personae* are often adapted to the ideas they are made to express. Here again the *Symposium* offers a most vivid example in the persons of the tragic poet Agathon and his foil Aristophanes. But one may of course add Euthyphro in the dialogue bearing his name, (exemplifying piety), Laches and Nicias in the *Laches* (exemplifying various conceptions of courage), the youthful quartet of Hippothales, Lysis, Ctesippus and Menexenus in the *Lysis* (exemplifying erotic *philia*), and Charmides in the *Charmides* (exemplifying *sôphrosunê*).[25]

---

[24] Most notably in 410e1-3, where the philosopher is said to have a nature which is ἥμερος and which, if properly trained, will turn out to be ἥμερος τε καὶ κόσμιος. For κόσμος and κόσμιος see further 329d4; 331b1; 339e11 (κοσμίου τε καὶ ἀνδρείου); 403a7 (κοσμίου τε καὶ καλοῦ); 408a8 (ὑγιεινούς τε καὶ κοσμίους); 430e6 (σωφροσύνη as κόσμος and ἐγκράτεια); 443d4; 486b6 (κόσμιος opposed to ἄδικος); 503c4; 539d4 (κοσμίους [...] καὶ στασίμους); 587b3 (κόσμιαι ἐπιθυμίαι opposed to τυραννικαὶ ἐπιθυμίαι). For ἥμερος see e.g. 416c2 (rulers educated so as to be ἥμεροι towards their subjects); 486b11 (ψυχὴ δικαία τε καὶ ἥμερος opposed to δυσκοινώνητος καὶ ἀγρία); 571c4 (λογιστικὸν καὶ ἥμερον καὶ ἄρχον); 588c-591b.

[25] Some of the dramatic and literary aspects of the *Laches*, *Protagoras* and *Symposium* are discussed in Stokes (1986). On the *Lysias* see Hoerber (1945). Woodruff (1982) contains a useful analysis of the literary aspects of the *Hippias*

If we now return to *Rep.* I, we may note that in a number of respects the dramatic picture which Plato draws of Thrasymachus is reminiscent of other scenes in Platonic dialogues which feature sophists. This goes for Thrasymachus' criticisms of and impatience with Socrates' dialectical procedure,[26] for the way in which Socrates' rational elenchus is opposed to the much more self-assertive form of reasoning which is typical of the rhetorical practice of the sophists, i.e. the set speech,[27] for Thrasymachus' scoffing approach, especially the way he laughs at Socrates,[28] and for his sullen and insincere resignation at the end of the conversation of *Rep* I.[29] But there is more to it than just the familiar opposition between Socratic philosophy and sophistical rhetoric. Plato's portrayal of Thrasymachus contains a number of interesting traits which, I believe, are meant to present this *persona* as in some respects being himself an *exemplum* of the philosophical position he is made to defend.

At 336b-338b Plato starts out with a vivid sketch of Thrasymachus' behaviour during the conversation between Socrates and Polemarchus, and of the way he interrupts the conversation. He is pictured as a man who is conspicuously lacking in self-restraint: he is only prevented from intruding into the conversation between Socrates and Polemarchus by the others (ὑπο τῶν παρακαθημένων διεκωλύετο) and as soon as he gets the chance he leaps in like a wild animal, ready to tear his opponents apart (ὥσπερ θηρίον ... ὡς διαρπασόμενος, 336b2-3). Socrates indirectly compares him to a wolf in 336 d6-7 ('if I had not seen him before he saw me, I really believe I should have been struck dumb'),[30] and to a lion in 341c1

Maior (suggesting, among other things, that Hippias exemplifies a certain outlook on the theme of the *kalon*); for a different literary analysis of the same work, see Ludlam (1991). A most valuable guide in these matters is now Rutherford (1995).

26 Cf. Critias in the *Charmides*, esp. 165e, and the indignant outbursts of Polus and Callicles in the *Gorgias*: 467b10; 473a1, 480e (Polus); and 490d1; 491a1; 494 e7; 497b6 (Callicles).

27 Cf. *Gorg.* 449b-c; see also *Prt.* 334c-335a. See also Nicholson (1974) 230. Thrasymachus himself delivers a kind of set speach of considerable length, pooring out a flood of words over his company (344d: ὥσπερ βαλανεὺς ἡμῶν καταντλήσας κατὰ τῶν ὤτων ἀθρόον καὶ πολὺν τὸν λόγον), after which he has to be prevented by the others from leaving the stage right away.

28 Cf. Polus in the *Gorgias*. On this 'rhetorical' use of laughter, see Rutherford (1995) 155; De Vries (1985) 378-381.

29 Cf. the way Callicles is made to behave at the end of his exchange with Socrates in the *Gorgias* (esp. 510a1; 513e1; 516b).

30 On this reference to an element of popular superstition, see Adam (1969) 1. 24.

('do you think me foolish enough to beard a lion and to try to outwit Thrasymachus?'). I believe these descriptions and comparisons are there on purpose. Later on in the *Republic* the tyrant, after all Thrasymachus' ideal example of unbridled *pleonexia*, is compared to a wolf (565d-566a), and in general Plato is wont to use the irrational ferocity of animals as a metaphor for the irrational parts of the soul (the appetitive element drags us ὥσπερ θηρίον (439b4),[31] the tripartite soul is depicted as a triad of man, lion and many-headed beast (588b-591a).[32] And like Thrasymachus, the raging bestial tendencies of the lower part of the soul also have to be kept in check from outside (i.e. by the rational part).[33] Thrasymachus, in other words is depicted as himself being in some ways the embodiment of the unlimited *pleonexia* (as against rational moderation) which he is made to defend.

This general characterization is further supported by what Thrasymachus is actually made to say. He attacks Socrates for merely asking questions in his customary way instead of coming up himself with anything like a detailed account of justice—i.e. for being not as self-assertive as Thrasymachus himself is—and makes clear that he regards Socrates and Polemarchus as a couple of wets who are only too ready to give way to each other (336c: τί εὐηθίζεσθε πρὸς ἀλλήλους ὑποκατακλινόμενοι ὑμῖν αὐτοῖς;).[34] He proceeds to set the rules for the conversation which is to follow: Socrates should know that a number of potential definitions of justice are not allowed (336c6: καὶ ὅπως μοι μὴ ἐρεῖς ὅτι τὸ δέον ἐστὶν μηδ' ὅτι τὸ ὠφέλιμον μηδ' ὅτι τὸ λυσιτελοῦν μηδ' ὅτι τὸ κερδαλέον μηδ' ὅτι τὸ συμφέρον). Socrates' reaction in its turn reinforces the reader's impression of Thrasymachus as an aggressive character (336b6: ἐγώ τε καὶ ὁ Πολέμαρχος δείσαντες διεπτοήθημεν, 336d5: ἐγὼ ἀκούσας ἐξεπλάγην καὶ προσβλέπων αὐτὸν ἐφοβούμην, and 336e2, with what may be a pun on Thrasymachus' name: Ὦ Θρασύμαχε,

---

[31] See also 430b8, 535e4, 571c5. At 411e1 people whose mind has not been properly cultivated by education are also said to be ὥσπερ θηρίον.

[32] One may also compare the description of the common people, the *demos* with their irrational desires, as 'the great beast' (*Rep.* 493b-c), and the lion-like strong men of which Callicles speaks in *Gorg.* 483e. See on this Rutherford (1995) 161, who provides an excellent discussion of the animal metaphors.

[33] For the use of κωλύειν in this connection, see 439c6-9; and 589b3 (τὰ δὲ ἄγρια ἀποκωλύων φύεσθαι).

[34] For the meaning of εὐηθίζεσθε and ὑποκατακλινόμενοι see Adam (1969) 1. 23 and 24.

μὴ χαλεπὸς ἡμῖν ἴσθι).[35] According to Gigon this portrayal of Thrasymachus and of Socrates' reaction is 'beinahe peinlich': 'Der Dichter Platon hat hier, so möchten wir wohl meinen, des Guten ein wenig zuviel getan'.[36] This may be true if we judge the passage merely from the point of view of naturalistic aesthetics. But such a judgement should at least be qualified once we recognize that Plato's dramatic characterization of Thrasymachus serves a philosophical purpose and that Thrasymachus' behaviour, at least at the beginning of the discussion, parallels the philosophical position which he is made to defend.[37]

5. The picture which I have been drawing thus far will call for further clarification, precisely in so far as it presupposes that Plato presents Thrasymachus' position as a clearly recognizable and basically coherent (though of course ultimately untenable) counterposition to his own. After all it has often been assumed that Thrasymachus does *not* present a coherent position at all, or at least that his two definitions are strictly speaking incompatible. Such 'incompatibilist' interpretations usually focus exclusively on the definitions and on what may be inferred from them (i.e. they study the definitions in isolation from their context), and they claim that these definitions can be written out as two basically unconnected items, viz. :[38]

(a) justice is the advantage of the stronger/ruler;

and

(b) justice is another one's good.

---

35 We know from Aristotle (*Rhet.* 1400 b 20) that the Greeks were certainly sensitive to the connotations of this name; on the possibility that Plato is here making a word-play, see Adam (1969) 24.

36 Gigon (1976) 48.

37 We may note that later on his aggressive behaviour loses some of its edge as his self-confidence apparently diminishes (in 350d he is presented as sweating and blushing). Gigon (1976) 82 finds this strange ('Die Wandlung vom furchterregenden Wüterich zum herablassenden Weltmanne bleibt etwas befremdlich'), but Plato's point is presumably that Thrasymachus' blunt self-assertion is unable to stand up to the rationality of the Socratic elenchus. We may perhaps even go so far as to see the development of the *persona* of Thrasymachus from mere aggression, via sullen resignation (at the end of book I), to a kind of friendly cooperation (later on in the *Republic,* cf. 545a, 590d) as exemplifying the 'domestication' of the irrational faculties under the guidance of reason.

38 An extreme example of such a purely 'analytical' procedure is Reeve (1988) 16-19.

Thus presented, and taken at face value, the definitions would certainly appear to add up to an incoherent position. Take, for instance, the example of the typically Thrasymachean ruler who rules exclusively in his own interest. According to definition (a) he will be just (for he pursues his own interest). According to (b) he will be be unjust (for he ignores the good of others).[39]

An interpretation which tries to square the two definitions has been proposed by George Kerferd, and has been taken over by various other scholars. According to Kerferd (b) is entirely consistent with (a), provided one thing is accepted, namely that the statement that justice is to seek the interest of the ruler was made by looking at the matter from one viewpoint only, namely the viewpoint of the ruled.[40] I believe that this interpretation goes a long way into the right direction, but requires further qualification on some points.[41] In particular, like most other interpretations it still presupposes that we are indeed dealing with two fully *independent* definitions, given in entirely different contexts. This is why Kerferd can claim that definition (a) is in fact incomplete and occurs in a context which (unlike the context of (b)) discusses the matter at issue only from a partial perspective. Kerferd accordingly adds that 'once we ask what about justice from the viewpoint of the ruler, we can no longer say that justice consists in seeking the interest of the ruler, we must say that it consists in seeking the interest of the ruled'.[42]

However, if we really take the context into account and turn to the way Plato actually presents these definitions, we are in for a surprise. Plato has Thrasymachus actually *combine* the two defini-

---

[39] Incompatibilist interpretations along these lines have been provided by Guthrie (1971), vol. 3, 94; and Gigon (1976) 60. Other interpretations of Thrasymachus' position (as presented in his definitions) as basically incoherent and confused (Jowett, Sidgwick, Cross and Woozley) are summarized by Nicholson (1974) 213. According to Maguire (1971) the inconsistency is basically due to Plato, who distorts Thrasymachus' original position by adding (b); on which see above, n. 8.

[40] Cf. Kerferd (1947) 560-561; and (1981) 121-122. An interpretation rather similar to Kerferd's has been defended by Nicholson (1974). Annas (1981) 45-46 takes a middle position between 'incompatibilists' like Guthrie (see previous note) and the view defended by Kerferd by arguing *both* that the two definitions are *formally* in conflict, *and* that they reflect the same spirit. According to Annas, 46, Thrasymachus is being 'driven from a partial and muddled to a clear formulation'

[41] Apart from qualifying remarks which I have made in the text, I would like to note that I see no justification for the thesis of Kerferd (1947) 561 that Thrasymachus' injustice is a *moral* obligation.

[42] Kerferd (1981) 122.

tions in the course of his speech: according to Thrasymachus Socrates does not know that 'justice' is 'in truth another one's good, the advantage of the stronger and the ruler' (ἀλλότριον ἀγαθὸν τῷ ὄντι, τοῦ κρείττονός τε καὶ ἄρχοντος συμφέρον, 343c3-4). And when in the second book Adeimantus refers back to Thrasymachus' position he simply follows in Thrasymachus' footsteps and connects the two definitions: 'Or should we agree with Thrasymachus that justice is another one's good and the advantage of the stronger' (ἀλλότριον ἀγαθόν, συμφέρον τοῦ κρείττονος, 367c). Two things are worth noting. First, neither here nor in the first book is there any suggestion that the two definitions are incompatible and that Thrasymachus' position is internally incoherent, although it *is* of course suggested that this position is *wrong*.[43] Secondly, these passages show that the two definitions are *not* independent, as was implicitly supposed by Kerferd, but that they apparently belong together as two sides of the same coin, as two ways of saying the same thing: (a) is so to speak placed in apposition to (b) as an explanatory tag (ἀλλότριον ἀγαθόν, συμφέρον τοῦ κρείττονος, 367c). This does not suggest that (a) is written from a more limited perspective, or that the cases described by (a) are only a subclass of the cases described by (b).[44] Both definitions apply to *everybody*, and they are meant to describe reality *as it is*, *not* to cover every imaginable situation (including the situation where a ruler might be just). Now *as things are* the fact that justice (at the level of the

---

[43] It is true that in 345b7 ff. Socrates asks Thrasymachus to stand by his own words from now on, or at least, if he does change his position, to do so openly. This passage has been adduced by Annas (1981) 46-47, in support of her view that the two definitions are according to Socrates/Plato formally incompatible and that Thrasymachus is driven from the confused position expressed by the first definition to the clearer view expressed by the second. Yet, as becomes clear from Socrates' immediately following words, he is not referring to Thrasymachus' having presented different definitions but to the fact that after having introduced the notion of the physician 'in the strict sense' he has not in a like manner discussed the shepherd *in the strict sense* (345b9-c3: νῦν δὲ ὁρᾷς ... ὅτι τὸν ὡς ἀληθῶς ἰατρὸν τὸ πρῶτον ὁριζόμενος τὸν ὡς ἀληθῶς ποιμένα οὐκέτι ᾤου δεῖν ὕστερον ἀκριβῶς φυλάξαι). In other words, the instability which Socrates ascribes to Thrasymachus does not concern the latter's main position, as crystallized in the two definitions, but the arguments by which he has defended his main position. It will be clear from all this that I do not see any reason to go along with Maguire (1971) 155, who claims with regard to the two definitions that 'Plato is at pains to indicate the logical difficulties in holding both positions simultaneously'.

[44] For the contrary view, however, see Nicholson (1974) 224 and 227 and Annas (1981) 45-46.

individual) is someone else's good, *comes down* (at the political level) to justice being the advantage of the stronger/ruler. In other words, Thrasymachus consciously and *exclusively* links justice to the weak: what justice amounts to for the really strong is a question which is not even considered.[45] For them, in actual practice, there simply *is* no such thing as justice, because there is no need for them to consider the interest of others.

This picture appears to be confirmed if we turn from the definitions to the larger context of Thrasymachus' story and the way it is summarized at the beginning of book II. Immediately after the definition of justice in 343c, we are told that injustice is 'the opposite' (τοὐναντίον) and that it 'rules over those who are truly simpletons and just' (καὶ ἄρχει τῶν ὡς ἀληθῶς εὐηθικῶν τε καὶ δικαίων, 343c6-7).[46] The just are simply identified with the losers who have to obey the rules set by others.[47] In the paraphrase in book II they are referred to as those who are neither able to act injustly themselves nor to escape the injustice done to them by others (359a1).[48] Those, on the other hand, who end up on top in

---

[45] This claim is not invalidated by the fact that Thrasymachus at 343e1 refers to the example of just people taking *some* office (ἀρχήν τινα). The way they get themselves into trouble shows that they do not qualify for the position of 'real', i.e. strong, rulers (cf. 343b5: οἱ ὡς ἀληθῶς ἄρχουσιν).

[46] This phrase, and indeed the whole context of Thrasymachus' speech may be taken to invalidate the rather relativistic interpretation of Nettleship (1964) 32, which claims that 'if the doer of unjust things is strong enough, then what he does is called justice by weaker men'. A similar view has now been defended by Reeve (1988) 19: 'By breaking all the laws, the tyrant reveals himself as completely unjust. By simultaneously overthrowing them, and the power behind them, he destroys the standard by reference to which he is unjust. Justice is now his advantage'. On the basis of the observations which I have here made, we may object that although the ruler determines what may count as just, his own unjust deeds and commands are and remain unjust from each and every perspective. It is only the obeying of the ruled to his unjust commands - not those commands themselves - that is to be called just.

[47] See also 348c-d, where Thrasymachus refers to justice as γενναία εὐήθεια and where the *successfully* injust (οἵ γε τελέως [...] οἷοί τε ἀδικεῖν, πόλεις τε καὶ ἔθνη δυνάμενοι ἀνθρώπων ὑφ' ἑαυτοὺς ποιεῖσθαι) are called φρόνιμοι and ἀγαθοί.

[48] It is to be noted, however, that in Glaucon's paraphrase the perspective has changed slightly. *Pleonexia* is still described as the motive force behind human behaviour, and the best life is still described as a life of unbridled self-assertion, but it is now argued that justice is a kind of contract by which the weak secure, by way of a second-best solution, at least some protection against the *pleonexia* of the strong. Nothing of this sort was maintained by Thrasymachus, where it was argued that the contents of justice are completely determined by the self-interest of the rulers. There is no justification in the text of book I for the claim of Gigon (1976) 61 that 'der Starke wird mit ihm (scil. dem Begriff der Gerechtigkeit) seine Stärke aufs Spiel setzen, der

the struggle for power resulting from what we might call Thrasymachus' implicit anthropology of *pleonexia*,[49] can do what they want. This is why Thrasymachus ends his speech by claiming that injustice is not only stronger and more powerful than justice, but also more indicative of freedom (ἐλευθεριώτερον). Justice, apparently, is a matter of compulsory self-restriction, a matter of limits and bonds. The really strong and powerful, with the tyrant as the most shining example, are free of such bonds. For them justice does not exist.[50]

6. We may summarize our findings as follows. The general picture which emerges from our analysis is that of Thrasymachus putting forward, apparently on empirical grounds, the case for *pleonexia*. This position foreshadows Plato's vivid sketch of the quasi-freedom of the tyrant, whose passions rule in complete lawlessness (ἐν πάσῃ ἀναρχίᾳ καὶ ἀνομίᾳ, 575a1). It thus serves as a counterpoint to Plato's own insistence in his moral psychology on limit and moderation, elements which in the last analysis, and in ways which need not concern us here, appear to be connected to his metaphysical conception of the Good.[51] The overall dramatic characterization of Thrasymachus as a *persona* confirms this picture by presenting him as animal-like, aggressive and incontinent, in short as in some respects an embodiment of the position he is made to defend. It appears that Thrasymachus' two definitions of justice belong together and are both connected with his general anthropology: justice sets limits to one's tendency towards *pleonexia*, and one only lets this happen if one *has to*. Consequently for the really strong justice does not exist.[52]

Utrecht

Schwache dagegen hat die Aussicht, den Starken bei ihm behaften zu können'.

[49] This anthropology is made explicit, however, in Glaucon's paraphrase in book II, 359c4: διὰ τὴν πλεονεξίαν, ὃ πᾶσα φύσις διώκειν πέφυκεν ὡς ἀγαθόν.

[50] We may recall that according to Thrasymachus the ruler 'in the strict sense' makes no mistakes, i.e. he is always successful in ruthlessly pursuing his own interests. Note the way this feature is underlined by Plato's use of the vocabulary of power and success (τὸν <u>μεγάλα δυνάμενον</u> πλεονεκτεῖν, 344a1; ἀδικία <u>ἱκανῶς γιγνομένη</u>, 344c5-6; δυνάσθω δὲ ἀδικεῖν ἢ τῷ λανθάνειν ἢ τῷ <u>διαμάχεσθαι</u>, 345a5; οἵ γε <u>τελέως</u> [...] <u>οἷοί τε</u> ἀδικεῖν, 348d5).

[51] On which see especially *Rep*. 500c.

[52] I would like to thank David Runia and Teun Tieleman for their comments on an earlier draft of this article.

References:

Adam, J. (1969) *The Republic of Plato*: edited with Critical Notes, Commentary and Appendices by James Adam; second edition with an Introduction by D. A. Rees, 2 vols. (Cambridge).

Adkins, A. W. H. (1972) *Moral Values and Political Behaviour in Ancient Greece* (London).

Annas, J. (1981) *An Introduction to Plato's Republic* (Oxford).

Arnim, J. von (1914) *Platons Jugenddialoge und die Entstehungszeit des 'Phaidros'* (Leipzig).

——(1927) Platons Dialog 'Thrasymachos', *Mededeelingen der Koninklijke Akademie van Wetenschappen*, afdeeling letterkunde deel 63 (Amsterdam), 201-232.

Classen, C. J. (ed.) (1976) *Sophistik* (Darmstadt).

Cross, R. C. / Woozley, A. D. (1964) *Plato's Republic*; A Philosophical Commentary (London).

Friedländer (1964) *Platon*, 2 vols., 3. Auflage (Berlin).

Gigon, O. (1976) *Gegenwärtigkeit und Utopie*; eine Interpretation von Platons 'Staat'; Erster Band: Buch I-IV (Zürich/München).

Guthrie, W. K. C. (1975) *A History of Greek Philosophy*, 6 vols. (Cambridge).

Hoerber, R. G. (1945) 'Character Portrayal in Plato's *Lysis*', *The Classical Journal* 41, 271-273.

Kahn, C. H. (1983) 'Drama and Dialectic in Plato's *Gorgias*', *Oxford Studies in Ancient Philosophy*, 1: 75-121.

——(1993) 'Proleptic Composition in the *Republic*, or Why Book 1 was never a separate dialogue', *The Classical Quarterly* 43: 131-142.

Kerferd , G. B. (1981) *The Sophistic Movement* (Cambridge).

——(1947) 'The Doctrine of Thrasymachus in Plato's *Republic*', *Durham University Journal* 40; repr. in Classen (1976) 545-563.

Lebeck, A. (1971) *The* Oresteia: *a Study in Language and Structure* (Washington DC).

Ludlam, I. (1991) *Hippias Major:* an Interpretation (Stuttgart).

Maguire, J. P. (1971) 'Thrasymachus ... or Plato', *Phronesis* 16: 142-163.

Mansfeld, J. (1996) 'Insight by Hindsight: Intentional Unclarity in Presocratic Proems', *BICS*, 42: 225-232 .

Müller, G. (1981) *Platons Dialog vom Staat: Kunstform und Lehrgehalt*, Wiesbaden.

Nettleship, R. L. (1964) *Lectures on the Republic of Plato*, (London); reprint of the second edition of 1901.

Nicholson, P. P. (1974) 'Unravelling Thrasymachus' Arguments in 'The Republic'', *Phronesis* 19: 210-232.

Reeve, C. D. C. (1988) *Philosopher-Kings*; The Argument of Plato's Republic (Princeton).

Runia, D. T., (1996) 'The literary and Philosophical Status of Timaeus' *Prooemium*', forthcoming in the Proceedings of the International Plato Society conference, Granada 1995.

Rutherford, R. B. (1995) *The Art of Plato: Ten Essays in Platonic Interpretation* (London)

Stokes, M. C. (1986) *Plato's Socratic Conversations* (London).

Vries, G. J. de (1985) 'Laughter in Plato's Writings', *Mnemosyne* 38: 378-381.

White, N. P. (1979) *A Companion to Plato's Republic* (Indianapolis).

Wilamowitz-Moellendorff, U. von (1920) *Platon*, 2 vols. (Berlin).

Woodruff, P (1982) *Plato: Hippias Major* (Indianapolis).

Zeller, E. (1922) *Die Philosophie der Griechen in ihrer geschichtlichen Entwicklung*, 5. Auflage, Band II, 1 (Leipzig).

KOMPSOI ASKLEPIADES: LA CRITICA DI PLATONE ALLA MEDICINA NEL III LIBRO DELLA *REPUBBLICA*

Mario Vegetti

Jaap Mansfeld ha sostenuto a più riprese (cfr. nota 17) che il metodo di Ippocrate cui Platone si riferisce nel celebre passo di *Phaedr.* 270c–d trova in *Arie acque luoghi* il suo testo principale di riferimento. Un'analisi della violenta critica che Platone rivolge nel libro III della *Repubblica* alla medicina dietetica contemporanea non può portare conferme o smentite dirette a questa tesi, e quindi contribuire alla soluzione della *vexatissima* 'questione ippocratica'. La polemica platonica costituisce tuttavia un documento significativo degli sviluppi della medicina nel IV secolo, e della loro valutazione nell'ambito della discussione etica e politica. Da questo punto di vista, qualche indicazione sia pure indiretta su quella questione può venir ricavata dalla *Repubblica*: si tratta, da un lato, del rilevante impiego platonico del linguaggio diagnostico e psico-etnologico di *Arie acque luoghi*, dall'altro del principale bersaglio della polemica del libro III, che, attraverso Erodico, sembra colpire soprattutto il *Regime*. Di questi dati andrà forse tenuto conto nell'interpretazione della 'testimonianza' del *Fedro*, e sembra plausibile pensare che essi possano almeno marginalmente confortare la lettura propostane da Mansfeld.

1. Il passaggio dalla prima città (definita «sana», ὑγιής, 372e7), alla seconda, che «vive nel lusso», le ragioni e le forme della patologia che affligge quest'ultima, infine le vie possibili per il suo risanamento, vengono discussi facendo largamente ricorso alle categorie diagnostiche e terapeutiche proprie della medicina dietetica del V e IV secolo.

La *polis* lussuosa soffre di gonfiore da infiammazione (φλεγμαίνουσα, 372e8). Non si tratta soltanto dell'impiego metaforico di termini medici in ambito morale, che è consueto in Platone. L'eziologia di questa malattia endemica è indicata da Platone nella cattiva dieta e nella corrispondente mancanza di esercizi (ἀργία καὶ δίαιτα, 405d); quanto al primo aspetto, si tratta soprattutto della dieta carnea, introdotta nella πόλις τρυφῶσα[1] (373b–c). Ora, questo nesso diagnostico ed eziologico è diffuso nella medicina dietetica, a partire dai più antichi *Luoghi nell'uomo (L.H.)* e *Arie acque luoghi (A.A.L.)* fino al più recente *Regime* e allo stesso Erodico, principale bersaglio della critica platonica. Il termine φλεγμαίνειν ricorre con grande frequenza in *L.H.*; per il gonfiore da infiammazione si vedano soprattutto 13.1 e 29.1. Il *Regime nelle malattie acute* (37) menziona l'alimentazione carnea (κρεηφαγίη)[2] tra le cause di flatulenze (φῦσαι: come si vedrà più avanti, questo termine gioca un ruolo centrale nella polemica platonica).

L'eccessivo riempimento di cibo (πλησμονή), non compensato da adeguati esercizi (πόνοι) produce, secondo il *Regime*, tanto κατάρροι (3.70.1: anche questo termine è impiegato polemicamente da Platone), quanto φῦσαι (3.74.1). Era questa, a quanto attesta l'Anonimo Londinense, anche la dottrina di Erodico: le malattie nascono dall'eccesso di alimentazione non compensato da πόνοι sufficienti (9.20 sgg.).

La medicina dietetica offre dunque a Platone gli strumenti per la diagnosi di una malattia sociale che è al tempo stesso morale, per la dedizione intemperante ai piaceri del lusso, ed organica, per i danni che questi piaceri producono alla salute pubblica.

Ma essa offre anche le indicazioni necessarie alla sua terapia. Platone insiste sulla necessità di «purificare» la *polis* (καθαίρειν, διακαθαίρειν, 399e): egli gioca indubbiamente anche sulla valenza religiosa del termine (c'è un *miasma* collettivo da scongiurare), ma è chiaro che in questo contesto dietetico il riferimento principale è quello alle purghe dimagranti dei medici. In questo senso il termine è frequentissimo in *L.H.* (cfr. soprattutto 13.4, 28.1), e ampiamente usato nel *Regime* (2.40–85). La «purga» morale e intellettuale che Platone somministra alla *polis tryphosa* mira a mettere sotto controllo l'abuso dei piaceri del lusso. Ad essa fa seguito la costruzione di un ambiente in cui sia possibile il risanamento e la

---

[1] Questo termine non appartiene al linguaggio della medicina. Il participio con valore aggettivale si trova, in questo stesso senso, in Aristoph. *Nub.* v. 48. In Xen. *Mem.* 1.6.10 Socrate accusava Antifonte di identificare la felicità con la τρυφή. Lo stesso Antifonte sembra aver elaborato una teoria fisiopatologica della φλεγμονή (DK B29a).

[2] Né qui né altrove nei testi medici c'è tuttavia una condanna dietetica dell'alimentazione carnea (anche la focaccia d'orzo, per es., può causare *physai*). Le proprietà alimentari dei diversi tipi di carni sono ampiamente discusse nel *Regime*, 2.46–49.

formazione armoniosa del ceto politico-militare cui verrà affidata la guida della nuova città. Questi giovani dovranno crescere, dice Platone, «in un luogo salubre» (ἐν ὑγιεινῷ τόπῳ), in senso morale, intellettuale e anche estetico, da cui siano positivamente influenzati come da «un'aura che reca salute, proveniendo da luoghi benefici» (αὔρα φέρουσα ἀπὸ χρηστῶν τόπων ὑγίειαν, 401c).

Anche a questo proposito, non è difficile individuare i riferimenti medici della terapia platonica. Il termine αὔρα, raro in prosa, compare in *A.A.L.* 6. Ed è ben noto come questa stessa opera dedichi una grande attenzione all'influenza dei venti sulla salute psicofisica delle popolazioni (cfr. soprattutto cap. 5). Più in generale, è altrettanto noto che l'autore 'ippocratico' ritiene essenziale il ruolo che i *nomoi*, cioè un buon assetto costituzionale, possono giocare, in aggiunta ai fattori ambientali, riguardo ai costumi (ἤθη) e alla εὐψυχία di individui e popoli (capp. 16, 23).

Già da quest'ultimo punto di vista, il rapporto fra la terapia platonica della *polis* e il pensiero medico-politico di *Arie acque luoghi* esce da un contesto solo metaforico, com'era quello fra l'aura educativa e i venti salubri del trattato medico. Ci sono tuttavia altri riscontri, più marginali ma proprio per questo forse più significativi. I suoi «atleti della guerra», scrive Platone, saranno esposti durante le loro campagne a frequenti «mutamenti» (μεταβολαί) nella dieta, nel clima e nelle stagioni, e al tempo stesso dovranno risultare «insonni» (ἄγρυπνοι), acuti nella vista e nell'udito e di salute costante (404a–b). Platone aggiunge altrove che il carattere psicologico dominante di questi guerrieri sarà l'impulsività animosa, lo spirito θυμοειδές, che a seconda dell'educazione può volgere verso la selvatichezza (τὸ ἄγριον) collerica o verso una benevola mitezza (ἡμερότης) (410d–e).

Questo intero complesso concettuale e linguistico relativo ai rapporti fra condizioni ambientali e caratteri psicologici ha il suo unico e puntuale precedente proprio nelle analisi di *Arie acque luoghi*. Qui è sistematicamente discussa l'influenza delle *metabolai* stagionali, e delle ἐκπλέξεις psico-somatiche che ne conseguono, sulla condizione morale e psicologica dei diversi popoli. Gli Asiatici, il cui clima è esente da bruschi mutamenti, mancano perciò di coraggio, di capacità di sopportare gli sforzi, di *thymoeides* (il termine non è altrove attestato prima di Platone) (12: τὸ δὲ ἀνδρεῖον καὶ τὸ ταλαίπωρον καὶ τὸ ἔμπονον καὶ τὸ θυμοειδὲς οὐκ ἂν δύναιτο ἐν τοιαύτῃ φύσει ἐγγίνεσθαι).

Essi sono inoltre più miti (ἡμερώτεροι) degli Europei, perché non esposti alle *metabolai* e alle conseguenti *ekplexeis* che inselvatichiscono il carattere, eccitano lo *thymoeides*, tengono desta la mente come accade appunto per i popoli d'Europa (16: τὴν ὀργὴν ἀγριοῦσθαί τε καὶ τοῦ ἀγνώμονος καὶ θυμοειδέος μετέχειν [...] αἱ γὰρ μεταβολαί εἰσι τῶν πάντων αἱ ἐπεγείρουσαι τὴν γνώμην). La frequenza e la violenza dei mutamenti rende al contrario questi uomini selvatici, impulsivi, coraggiosi, disposti agli sforzi (23: τό τε ἄγριον καὶ τὸ ἄμεικτον καὶ τὸ θυμοειδὲς ἐν τοιαύτῃ φύσει ἐγγίνεται [...] ἀπὸ τῆς ταλαιπωρίης καὶ τῶν πόνων αἱ ἀνδρεῖαι), duri, tonici, insonni, indipendenti di giudizio, acuti nell'esercizio delle tecniche, migliori combattenti (24: σκληρούς τε καὶ ἰσχνούς [...] καὶ ἐντόνους [...]. τό τε ἐργατικὸν ἐνεὸν ἐν τῇ φύσει τῇ τοιαύτῃ καὶ τὸ ἄγρυπνον [...] καὶ ἰδιογνώμονας, τοῦ τε ἀγρίου μᾶλλον μετέχοντας ἢ τοῦ ἡμέρου, ἔς τε τὰς τέχνας ὀξυτέρους τε καὶ συνετωτέρους καὶ τὰ πολέμια ἀμείνους εὑρήσεις).

Esattamente il quadro dei caratteri, dunque, che Platone richiede ai suoi «atleti della guerra», preoccupandosi per altro di temperarne l'asprezza «europea» con il ricorso all'addolcimento che può venire da una buona educazione musicale.

La diagnosi della patologia sociale tracciata nei libri II e III della *Repubblica*, la sua eziologia, la sua terapia, sembrano così largamente ispirate ai testi della medicina dietetica; in particolare, il rapporto fra il linguaggio psicologico di Platone con quello di *Arie acque luoghi* è così stretto da rendere improbabile l'ipotesi di una coincidenza casuale.[3] Abbiamo qui, come altrove, un Platone attento lettore dei testi di medicina, e pronto a fruire della loro concettualizzazione metodica tanto come riferimento metaforico quanto come strumento analitico.

2. Tanto più sorprendente risulta il violento attacco alla medicina contemporanea a base dietetica che Platone lancia a partire da 405a.

Il punto di partenza è il nesso che viene stabilito fra patologia sociale e sviluppo della medicina[4] (parallelo a quello, in ambito

---

[3] Si può inoltre rilevare un'eco della critica ai sacrifici di *A.A.L.* 22 nel discorso di Adimanto (II 365e sgg.).

[4] Può essere interessante notare che la denuncia di Platone non è soltanto basata su di un'indignazione moralistica. C'è stato in effetti nel IV secolo un peggioramento della salute pubblica in Grecia dovuto all'abbandono dell'agricoltura, con il conseguente mancato drenaggio delle paludi, e alla sovrappopolazione urbana. Ne conseguì un aumento delle malattie malariche, delle gastro-enteriti, del tifo e della tubercolosi. L'età media al momento della

morale, tra decadenza dei costumi ed espansione della pratica giuridica). L'abuso intemperante dei piaceri alimentari determina una rottura del quadro nosologico tradizionale, che includeva secondo Platone soltanto lesioni traumatiche (come le ferite sui campi di battaglia) e malattie a decorrenza stagionale (ἐπέτεια νοσήματα: qui è ancora chiara l'influenza di *Arie acque luoghi* 2 e di *Epidemie* I–III) (405c).

La diffusione di nuove malattie interne determina la proliferazione dei medici e dei loro ambulatori, che costituiscono dunque un effetto e un sintomo della malattia morale della società, ma che, come vedremo, finiscono per diventarne una delle cause. In queste circostanze, la medicina, come l'avvocatura, viene ad assumere un'indebita 'aria di distinzione' (σεμνύνονται), motivata anche dal fatto che «molti uomini liberi» vi si dedichino con impegno professionale, cosa che Platone sembra trovare sorprendente (405a).

Questa sorpresa va interpretata come un segnale del crescente umore polemico di Platone; mai altrove, nei numerosissimi riferimenti alla medicina presenti nelle sue opere (e del resto anche nel I libro della *Repubblica*) egli ha messo in dubbio che la *techne* medica sia degna di uomini liberi. E c'è soprattutto il celebre passo delle *Leggi* in cui la medicina praticata dai liberi viene contrapposta a quella degli schiavi come modello per l'azione del buon legislatore nella sua opposizione rispetto al tiranno (IV 720a–e).

Il nuovo quadro patologico, causato dalla dieta malsana e dalla inattività fisica proprie della *polis* lussuosa, comprende ῥεύματα e πνεύματα, «flussi» e «arie» che ribollono nei corpi come in paludi limacciose (405d). Si tratta di termini medici diffusissimi, che indicano processi morbosi relativi (in linguaggio moderno) all'apparato respiratorio e soprattutto a quello digestivo. Di fronte a queste novità nella patologia, «i raffinati Asclepiadi» (κομψοὶ 'Ασκληπιάδες, 405d) sono chiamati a un lavoro di precisazione linguistica e concettuale del loro lessico fisio-patologico, vista l'inadeguatezza di quello tradizionale. Due osservazioni sono qui necessarie. Κομψοί ha certamente una sfumatura polemica, indicando un eccesso di

---

morte per gli uomini passò dai 45 anni in epoca classica ai 42,4 nel IV e III secolo. Si vedano i dati raccolti in M. Grmek, *Les maladies à l'aube de la civilisation occidentale* (Paris 1983) 32, 141–42, 157–58. È dunque vero che lo sviluppo della medicina scientifica coincide in Grecia con il declino delle condizioni generali di salute.

raffinatezza che diventa 'sofisticazione'[5] (e infatti il principale bersaglio dell'attacco, Erodico, è definito «sofista a nessuno inferiore» insieme con un altro dietetico, Icco di Taranto, in *Prot.* 316e).

In secondo luogo: quando Platone parla di Asclepiadi, non intende sottolineare la discendenza della professione medica dal dio guaritore (alla cui tradizione essa viene anzi poco dopo esplicitamente contrapposta), bensì designare la corporazione (κοινόν) dei medici, ben nota nella vita pubblica dell'Atene dei suoi tempi.[6] Si trattava di un gruppo numeroso di professionisti colti, socialmente prestigiosi e ben visibili, l'appartenenza al quale segnalava l'affermazione e la competenza del singolo medico. Quando Platone cita lo stesso Ippocrate egli non manca di qualificarlo come Asclepiade (*Prot.* 311b, *Phaedr.* 270c), per rafforzarne l'autorevolezza. C'è dunque un'intenzionale ironia polemica quando Glaucone, approvato da Socrate, definisce a loro volta πάνυ κομψοί, «davvero raffinati» (408b), i figli di Asclepio, la cui medicina tradizionale è stata contrapposta a quella moderna dei 'sofisticati' Asclepiadi.

Per tornare appunto alle loro innovazioni terminologiche, esse vengono esemplificate da Platone con le parole φῦσαι, che specializza πνεύματα, e κατάρροι, che tecnicizza ῥεύματα.[7] «Flatulenze» e «catarri»: termini che Glaucone qualifica prontamente come «nuovi e assurdi» (καινὰ καὶ ἄτοπα, 405d).[8]

Non tanto «nuovi», si può osservare, al tempo in cui Platone scriveva la *Repubblica* (ed è improbabile che egli pensasse qui alla

---

[5] Κομψότεροι sono per es. definiti in *Theaet.* 156a i seguaci di Protagora sostenitori di una gnoseologia empiristica. Cfr. anche *Phil.* 53c.

[6] Sul *koinon* dei medici ateniesi, cfr. S. Aleshire, *The Athenian Asklepieion* (Amsterdam 1989); V. Nutton, "The medical Meeting place", in *Ancient Medicine in its socio-cultural context*, eds. Ph.J. Van der Eijk *et al.* (Amsterdam 1995) 1.3–25 (4). A Delfi era riconosciuto e privilegiato un *koinon* degli Asclepiadi di Cos e di Cnido: cfr. J. Bousquet, "Delphes et les Asclépiades", *Bulletin de Correspondance hellénique*, 80 (1956) 579–93.

[7] O. Gigon, *Gegenwärtigkeit und Utopie* (Zürich–München 1976) 309 sgg., nota che questi termini, che definiscono le «Zivilisations-krankheiten», compaiono per la prima volta in Platone al di fuori della letteratura medica (rivestendo così un netto valore citazionale).

[8] *Antica medicina* polemizza a sua volta contro gli inventori di una καινὴ ὑπόθεσις: il termine vale «di nuova invenzione», e anche «straniero» (cfr. Festugière *ad loc.*). Può quindi darsi che Platone rivolga deliberatamente contro i medici il loro stesso linguaggio polemico. Ma lo stesso Socrate (*Eutyphr.* 3b) definisce ἄτοπα le accuse che gli vengono rivolte di introdurre dèi 'nuovi' e 'stranieri' (καινούς).

sua 'data drammatica'). Essi compaiono infatti in testi che a Platone, come si è visto, dovevano essere ben noti e ormai vecchi di qualche decennio. Κατάρροος è usato in un gruppo di scritti piuttosto vicini tra loro, come *Luoghi nell'uomo* (29.2), che offre inoltre un'elaborata teoria dei ῥόοι, «flussi» (9–10), *Male sacro* (6, 7, 8—dove è identificato appunto a ῥεῦμα, 13—dove è discusso il rapporto fra πνεύματα, «venti», e κατάρροι che scendono dal cervello), e infine in *Arie acque luoghi* (3—dove si parla di φλέγμα ἐπικατάρρεον, 10).

Quanto a φῦσα, il termine compare in *Luoghi nell'uomo* (45.3), *Antica medicina* (10, 22—dove viene tracciata una sorta di anatomo-fisiologia delle *physai*), *Regime nelle malattie acute* (23, 37).

Del resto, secondo la pur discutibile testimonianza dell'aristotelico Menone riassunta nell'Anonimo Londinense, il concetto di φῦσα occupava un ruolo centrale nell'eziologia dello stesso Ippocrate (5.35 sgg.).[9]

Nulla di particolarmente 'nuovo', dunque, nell'uso di questi termini in quanto tali. Ma si possono forse indicare alcuni testi, questi sì nuovi al tempo in cui Platone scriveva la *Repubblica*, e forse anche dal suo punto di vista «assurdi», che documentano il lavoro linguistico degli Asclepiadi e le sue conseguenze in termini medici: essi costituiscono, con ragionevole margine di probabilità, il termine immediato di riferimento dell'aggressione polemica di questi passi della *Repubblica*. Dal primo punto di vista, sono senza dubbio significative le precisazioni del capitolo 3 dei *Venti*, un'opera appunto dedicata al ruolo eziologico delle *physai*, che tracciano nell'ambito dei *pneumata* una distinzione fra l'aria esterna, *aer*, e quelle interne, appunto le *physai*: πνεύματα τὰ μὲν ἐν τοῖσι σώμασι φῦσαι καλέονται, τὰ δὲ ἔξω τῶν σωμάτων ἀήρ.

Lo πνεῦμα esterno, secondo questo autore, entra nel corpo insieme con i cibi, e la relativa πλησμονή determina le flatulenze interne (7); le φῦσαι sono a loro volta causa dei ῥεύματα organici.

C'è dunque in questa recente opera della medicina dietetica una

---

9 A prima vista, questa testimonianza sembra riferirsi allo scritto sui *Venti*. Qui, tuttavia, le *physai* sono legate all'immissione di aria esterna, mentre Menone, aristotelicamente, le mette in rapporto con i residui (περισσώματα) dei cibi ingeriti: cfr. G.E.R. Lloyd, *La questione ippocratica*, in Id., *Metodi e problemi della scienza greca* (trad. it. Roma–Bari 1993) 348–50. Per quanto la testimonianza sia inattendibile, e l'Anonimo sembri aver riassunto in modo impreciso il testo di Menone, essa documenta comunque l'esistenza di un'autorevole dottrina eziologica delle *physai* tra la fine del V e l'inizio del IV secolo.

precisa traccia del lavoro di sistemazione linguistica alla quale si riferisce polemicamente Platone.

Il nodo concettuale e terminologico che egli ha di mira nel nostro passo della *Repubblica* non è tuttavia reperibile tanto nei *Venti*, quanto nel *Regime*, dove credo esso possa venir rintracciato nella sua completezza.

Anche quest'opera distingue tra πνεῦμα, respiro dell'aria esterna, e φῦσα, flatulenza interna, che si connettono nel processo digestivo (2.40.2). Ma è soprattutto importante la sequenza che viene istituita fra prevalenza dei cibi sui πόνοι, e conseguente πλησμονή, e formazione di κατάρροι (3.70.1), da un lato, dall'altro di φῦσαι, sempre dovute alla πλησμονή (3.4.1). Qui sembra pienamente articolato quel rapporto fra eccesso dietetico, mancanza di esercizio fisico, e formazione di φῦσαι e κατάρροι, nell'ambito dei πνεύματα e dei ῥεύματα, che Platone individuava nei recenti e discutibili sviluppi della medicina dietetica.

E che il *Regime* possa venir considerato il più diretto bersaglio della polemica platonica[10] sembra confermato da altre considerazioni, relative alla collocazione sociale della medicina. Platone, come vedremo, vorrebbe che la terapia dei ricchi venisse assimilata a quella dei poveri e degli artigiani,[11] con il comune obbiettivo di ripristinarne il più rapidamente possibile la capacità di erogare prestazioni socialmente utili, lavorative nel caso dei secondi, politiche in quello dei primi (406d–407a).

L'autore del *Regime*, al contrario, sostiene che la sua δίαιτα (invero μακρὰ δίαιτα, per dirla con Platone in 406d3–4), non è fruibile dalla massa (πλῆθος) dei poveri, che devono per forza guadagnarsi la vita (ἐξ ἀνάγκης διατελεῖν τὸν βίον, e cfr. in Platone 406c: ἔργον ὃ

---

[10] Diventa da questo punto di vista rilevante il problema della collocazione cronologica di *Regime*. R. Joly, *Recherches sur le traité pseudo-hippocratique du Régime* (Paris 1960) 203 sgg., lo data intorno al 400 (cfr. anche la sua introduzione all'ediz. Budé, 1967). J. Mansfeld, *The Pseudo-Hippocratic Tract peri hebdomadon ch. 1–11 and Greek Philosophy* (Assen 1971) 25 n. 116, 105 n. 195, considera il trattato precedente il *Timeo*, ma lo colloca dopo il 370 in base al calendario implicato in 3.68. Neppure questa datazione più bassa escluderebbe la possibilità che Platone abbia conosciuto il *Regime* durante la stesura della *Repubblica*. Si tratta in ogni caso di argomenti altamente congetturali, date le modalità 'fluide' di pubblicazione e di circolazione di questi testi di scuola.

[11] G. Cambiano, *Platone e le tecniche* (Roma–Bari 1991^2) 149 sgg., mette in luce come la polemica di Platone colpisca anche il carattere 'classista' della medicina dietetica, fruibile, per ragioni di tempo e di costo, solo da parte dei ricchi.

ἀναγκαῖον ἐργάζεσθαι). Il nuovo regime è invece messo a disposizione dei ricchi, i quali sono più attenti alla salute (3.69): esattamente, dunque, quello stravolgimento di interesse, dal bene pubblico alla salute privata, che Platone condanna nella medicina dietetica. È proprio in questo modo che essa si trasforma, da sintomo ed effetto, in concausa della malattia sociale.

3. L'eroe negativo di questa metamorfosi della nuova medicina, appropriata alla *polis tryphosa*, è individuato da Platone nella figura di Erodico di Selimbria.[12] Erodico era stato accusato nel *Protagora*, come si è visto, di essere un sofista «travestito» e potente; nel *Fedro* (227d), Platone ironizzava sulle lunghe e faticose passeggiate cui Erodico sottoponeva se stesso e presumibilmente i suoi pazienti (un eccesso di esercizi per cui evidentemente era famoso e anche aspramente criticato da altri medici).[13] Tutto ciò dipendeva probabilmente dalla sua teoria secondo la quale era necessario riportare il rapporto fra alimentazione ed esercizi al suo equilibrio naturale (*Anon. Lond.* 9.20 sgg.).

Nella *Repubblica*, Erodico viene accusato di aver fatto deviare la medicina dalla sua efficace tradizione terapeutica trasformandola in un controllo minuzioso e ossessivo del regime di vita dei malati. Fattosi medico dopo esser stato maestro di ginnastica (παιδοτρίβης), egli ha «mescolato» e confuso la ginnastica con la medicina (406a–b): si allude evidentemente alla cura degli esercizi fisici raccomandata da Erodico. Ha praticato con rigore ossessivo il rispetto della dieta consueta e prescritta (406b), di lunghissima durata (406d). In questo modo, ha trasformato la medicina da terapia in «pedagogia delle malattie» (406a),[14] in una νοσοτροφία

---

[12] Le testimonianze su Erodico sono raccolte in H. Grensemann, *Knidische Medizin. Teil I* (Berlin–New York 1975) 15 sgg. Cfr. ora A. Jori, "Platone e la svolta dietetica della medicina greca. Erodico di Selimbria e le insidie della techne", *Studi italiani di filologia classica* 11 (1993) 157–95, che propone una cronologia di Erodico fra il 460–50 e il 380.

[13] Cfr. *Epidemie* 6.3.18. Probabilmente a causa della polemica di Platone, Erodico era già diventato proverbiale al tempo della *Retorica* di Aristotele (1.5 1361b 4–6: «molti sono sani nel senso in cui si dice sano Erodico; nessuno invidierebbe la loro salute, perché devono astenersi da tutte le soddisfazioni umane o dalla maggior parte di esse»).

[14] Nel *Timeo*, al contrario, Platone avrebbe raccomandato di παιδαγώγειν διαίταις le malattie croniche, invece di irritarle con farmaci, nei limiti di tutta la σχολή disponibile (89c–d): un ritorno 'erodiceo', dunque, da annoverarsi fra le molte tensioni nel pensiero platonico determinate dalla polemica di *Repubblica*.

(407b), che prolungano un'esistenza malaticcia distogliendo l'attenzione e le energie dei cittadini dalla vita sociale per concentrarle in modo morboso—noi diremmo ipocondriaco—sulle condizioni di salute e le loro minime variazioni quotidiane.

Va detto che molte delle accuse platoniche colpiscono l'intera medicina dietetica, compresa quella di ispirazione 'ippocratica', e non soltanto la figura di Erodico. La continuità fra ginnastica e medicina era per esempio stata fortemente sottolineata in *Antica medicina* (3, 4, 7), e del resto condivisa da Platone (*Crito* 47b; *Gorg.* 464b; una contrapposizione tra le due arti, forse proprio in polemica contro Erodico, era stata però stabilita in *L.H.* 35). I pericoli derivanti da un mutamento della dieta consueta erano stati enfatizzati nella stessa opera (10–11), e confermati in *Regime delle malattie acute* (26).

Perché dunque Platone ha deciso di fare di Erodico il suo principale bersaglio polemico, il capofila emblematico della generazione degli Asclepiadi che li rende complici dei vizi della città del lusso?

Una risposta può forse venire proprio dagli altri due dialoghi in cui il medico di Selimbria è citato esplicitamente.

Nel *Protagora,* all'attacco contro Erodico «sofista» corrisponde la menzione di Ippocrate di Cos come maestro per antonomasia di medicina, al pari di Policleto e Fidia per la scultura (311b–c). Il *Fedro,* che si apre con l'ironia su Erodico, culmina nel celebre elogio del metodo di Ippocrate, cui si deve ispirare la riforma dialettica della retorica (270b–c).

Erodico sembra dunque configurarsi come l'anti-Ippocrate: concentrare sul suo nome l'aggressione polemica poteva significare per Platone mettere al riparo da essa la medicina ippocratica, che, nonostante le sue ovvie tendenze dietetiche, manteneva ai suoi occhi un rilevante valore metodologico (e anche, stando al primo libro della *Repubblica,* deontologico).

Del resto, più specificamente, se è vero—come qui si è cercato di dimostrare—che Platone individuava gli eccessi degenerativi e socialmente pericolosi della medicina dietetica in opere come il *Regime,* può darsi che egli fosse al corrente di quello stretto rapporto fra quest'opera e il pensiero di Erodico, che è stato a più riprese ipotizzato dai moderni.[15]

---

15 Un rapporto fra Erodico e il *Regime* era stato sostenuto già da C. Fredrich, "Hippokratische Untersuchungen", *Philol. Untersuchungen* 15 (Berlin 1899) e in seguito riproposto da K. Deichgräber, "Die Epidemien und das

Questo può comportare una conseguenza di rilievo per la stessa 'questione ippocratica'. Se esiste in Platone una contrapposizione fra Ippocrate ed Erodico, e se quest'ultimo può essere avvicinato alla dietetica del *Regime* (al quale è se non altro accomunato dalla stessa polemica platonica), è allora da escludere che l'opera attribuibile a Ippocrate secondo il «metodo» descritto nel *Fedro* sia proprio il *Regime*, secondo la tesi sostenuta da W.D. Smith.[16] Per contro, l'ampio uso che Platone fa di *Arie acque luoghi* nella diagnostica sociale e nella psicologia collettiva del libro III può confermare che questo testo sia fra quelli riferibili a Ippocrate alla luce della testimonianza del *Fedro*.[17]

4. Torniamo ora alla discussione del libro III. Come si è visto, la medicina dietetica era servita a Platone come strumento diagnostico per la malattia della *polis tryphosa*; sul piano sociale, il suo sviluppo era stato considerato come un effetto della degenerazione morale di questa città, con i suoi abusi alimentari e la sua 'pigrizia', e infine anche, negli eccessi erodicei, a sua volta come una causa capace di confermare quella degenerazione.

Una riforma della medicina è dunque indispensabile, parallelamente alla «purificazione» della città. Essa sarà mirata ad un corretto uso politico delle procedure terapeutiche, destinate soltanto ad un sollecito ripristino delle prestazioni lavorative e pubbliche dei cittadini, ricchi o poveri che siano.

Da questo punto di vista, Platone ritiene necessario un ritorno alla medicina tradizionale, che si ispira a quella praticata sui campi di battaglia dai «figli di Asclepio», contrapposti così alla corpora-

---

Corpus Hippocraticum", *Abhandl. d. Preuss. Akad. d. Wissensch.*, Phil.-Hist. Klasse, 3 (Berlin 1933) 58–64. R. Joly, introd. a *Du régime* (Paris 1967) nega che Erodico possa venir considerato l'autore dell'opera, in base alla critica ai ginnasti di 1.24, ma ammette che le sue dottrine sono riprese e sviluppate nel *Regime* (p. 13).

16 Cfr. W.D. Smith, *The Hippocratic Tradition* (Ithaca–London 1979) 44 sgg. Smith condivide la datazione del *Regime* proposta da Joly (p. 60).

17 Per questa tesi, dopo Deichgräber, *op. cit.* (n. 15), cfr. soprattutto J. Mansfeld, "Plato and the Method of Hippocrates", *Greek Roman and Byzantine Studies*, 21, 1980, 341–62, e Id., "The historical Hippocrates and the origins of scientific medicine", in *Nature Animated*, ed. M. Ruse (Dordrecht 1983) 49–76. Per una posizione simile, ma con argomenti diversi e meno convincenti, cfr. R. Joly, "La question hippocratique et le témoignage du Phèdre", *Revue des Etudes grecques*, 74, 1961, 69–92, e Id., "Platon, Phèdre et Hippocrate: vingt ans après", in *Formes de pensée dans la Collection hippocratique*, eds. F. Lasserre–P. Mudry (Genève 1983) 407–22. La testimonianza del *Fedro* è discussa in M. Vegetti, *La medicina in Platone* (1969, Venezia 1995) cap. IV.

zione professionale dei moderni Asclepiadi. Se essi non si dedicavano alle raffinatezze dietetiche proprie di questi ultimi, era perché avevano ben chiari i compiti sociali e collettivi della loro arte, non certo per «l'ignoranza e l'inesperienza» che i sofisticati medici moderni attribuiscono ai loro predecessori tradizionali (406c: è forse possibile scorgere in queste parole una confutazione polemica di *Male sacro* 1–2, che appunto attribuiva ἀπειρία e ignoranza ai guaritori ciarlatani legati alla superstizione religiosa).

Ma il richiamo ad Asclepio e ai suoi figli è evidentemente solo polemico ed ironico. Lo sottolineano due pungenti battute di Glaucone: «davvero raffinati (κομψοί) li descrivi, i figli di Asclepio» (408b); e «un politico (πολιτικόν) ne fai di Asclepio» (407e).

Al contrario, Platone appare molto serio, e perfettamente informato, quando prescrive i requisiti per la medicina adatta alla città purificata.

(a) Essa deve trattare solo malattie ben circoscritte (νόσημα ἀποκεκριμένον, 407d). Qui Platone si oppone alla tendenza della medicina moderna, inclusa quella ippocratica, a farsi carico dell'intero organismo malato, e, al limite, dell'intera esistenza del paziente, a scopo sia terapeutico sia profilattico. Una tendenza, del resto, che egli aveva condiviso e approvato. Secondo il *Carmide* (156b–c), i «buoni medici» (ἀγαθοὶ ἰατροί, qui sicuramente gli 'ippocratici'), se si rivolge loro uno che ha una malattia agli occhi, «gli dicono che non si può cominciare a curare solo gli occhi, ma che bisognerebbe curare anche la testa se si vuole guarire gli occhi; e dicono ancora che è un'assurdità pensare di curare la testa per se stessa senza tenere conto dell'intero corpo. Così [...] cercano di curare e guarire la parte applicando un regime all'intero corpo» (διαίται ἐπὶ πᾶν τὸ σῶμα). Ma i buoni (e ippocratici) medici del *Carmide*, benché esemplari metodicamente, non sono socialmente utili nella «città sana» della *Repubblica*.

(b) Il trattamento di queste malattie locali deve essere rapido e immediatamente efficace: esso non impiegherà dunque diete ma solo farmaci catartici, cauterizzazioni e incisioni chirurgiche (406d). Questa triade è naturalmente canonica, ma anche qui Platone corregge gli ippocratici e se stesso. *Arie acque luoghi*, per esempio, aveva sottolineato la necessità di astenersi dal somministrare φάρμακον, τάμνειν e καίειν durante i mutamenti di stagione (11). E anche Platone nel *Protagora* (354a) aveva indicato come rimedi *standard* della medicina φάρμακον, καῦσις e τομή, aggiungendovi tuttavia anche le restrizioni dietetiche (λιμοκτονία), che qui vengono omesse in polemica contro la medicina dietetica e probabilmente come inutili in una *polis* dove il regime alimentare è già politicamente controllato.

(c) La medicina inoltre dovrà rifiutarsi di trattare quanti siano di costituzione malferma e incapaci perciò di rendersi socialmente utili, «lasciandoli morire», proprio come i giudici dovranno mandare a morte coloro che siano incurabili nell'anima (410a).

Il punto di vista di Platone è qui perfettamente chiaro. L'esistenza individuale non ha alcun valore se non in funzione della sua utilità sociale; sopravvivere senza essere in grado di contribuire al benessere comune non ha alcun senso né personale né pubblico. Questo punto di vista non ha naturalmente paralleli nella deontologia medica, anche se vi compare a volte (cfr. per es. *p. technes* 3) il rifiuto di affrontare la terapia degli incurabili, dovuto soprattutto alla preoccupazione che la loro morte possa venir addebitata al medico invece che alla malattia. È qui il caso di accennare che il parallelo platonico fra medicina e giustizia,[18] con l'obbligo per la seconda di mandare a morte chi sia moralmente irricuperabile, e per la prima di lasciar morire gli invalidi permanenti, era destinato ad inaugurare una lunga tradizione di pensiero tanto etico quanto medico. Essa sarebbe culminata, con Galeno (*Quod animi* 11, K. 4.815–6), in un singolare rovesciamento.[19] Poiché le devianze morali sono secondo Galeno determinate da malformazioni organiche, spetta al medico—che si appropria così anche della funzione del giudice platonico—di diagnosticare chi sia incurabile nel corpo e (dunque) anche nell'anima e di decretare la condanna a morte di coloro che risultano tanto «irrimediabilmente malvagi» da «non poter essere rieducati dalle Muse stesse né migliorati da Socrate o da Pitagora» (e neppure, s'intende, curati dallo stesso Galeno). In Platone, c'è ancora parallelismo, e non convergenza, fra sentenza di giustizia e diagnosi medica, anche se, come si è visto, la patologia morale influenza quella organica e viceversa. La nuova medicina, frutto di una purificazione della città, contribuirà comunque a sua volta a

---

[18] Il parallelo fra medicina e giustizia, ma senza riferimento ai rimedi estremi del nostro passo, era stato elaborato in *Gorg.* 478a sgg.

[19] Per questa vicenda, anche in rapporto al riferimento aristotelico alla «punizione medica o politica» (*Eth. eud.* 1.3), cfr. M. Vegetti, "Cura dei tribunali, punizioni della medicina", in *Immaginario e follia*, ed. F. Rosa (Trento 1991) 29–36.

depurarla dagli individui inutili, al contrario di quella dietetica che l'aveva invece intossicata prolungando, alla maniera di Erodico, la loro malsana esistenza.

5. L'atteggiamento platonico verso la medicina nei libri II e III della *Repubblica* risulta dunque piuttosto articolato e complesso. Da un lato, Platone non dimentica la fruibilità metodica del modello medico: essa sarà certo enfatizzata soprattutto nel *Fedro*, e nella *Repubblica* viene messa in secondo piano per il privilegio che i suoi libri centrali riconoscono alle matematiche, ma anche qui, come si è visto, la medicina offre utili strumenti diagnostici e modelli terapeutici per la patologia sociale della *polis tryphosa*. Anche sul piano etico, il rapporto medico-paziente, che dal *Gorgia* alle *Leggi* costituisce un possibile paradigma del potere giusto, non manca di venir richiamato, nello stesso senso, nel I libro del nostro dialogo.

Dall'altra parte, però, Platone attacca violentemente il ruolo sociale della medicina dietetica in quanto solidale alla patologia morale della *polis tryphosa*. In un 'regime di salute pubblica', quale è quello necessario alla purificazione della città, questa medicina non può a sua volta che essere destinata all'evacuazione purgativa, diventando così vittima dei suoi stessi canoni terapeutici. Il necessario ridimensionamento della funzione pubblica della medicina è al tempo stesso una premessa e una conseguenza del risanamento della città: nella *polis* sana, moderata e temperante, serviranno certamente meno medici, meno *iatreia*, meno diete (come anche meno tribunali e avvocati). E intanto, le energie sociali necessarie a questo risanamento andranno ricuperate distogliendo l'attenzione dalla vicenda privata e individuale delle terapie dietetiche per reinvestirla nella sua prioritaria destinazione pubblica.

Ma in questa drastica svolta, Platone cerca comunque di salvare il salvabile, e ne è un segno il fatto che la sua polemica risparmi qui il nome di Ippocrate. Serviranno ancora buoni medici (408c–d), presumibilmente di ispirazione 'ippocratica' nel metodo e nell'*ethos* (gli *agathoi iatroi* menzionati nel *Carmide*). Essi dovranno però essere 'politicizzati', al pari dell'Asclepio rivisitato da Platone, e di tutti gli altri cittadini-pazienti. Che la «buona medicina» descritta nel *Carmide* e nelle *Leggi* sia suscettibile di questa politicizzazione, secondo il modello della sbrigativa «terapia dell'artigiano» a base di farmaci, incisioni e cauterizzazioni approvata nel libro III, è un serio problema concettuale, che Platone non affronta in questa sede, sotto l'urgenza del progetto di riforma etico-politica e anche sanitaria della *polis*. In seguito, il ridimensionamento di questo progetto consentirà alla medicina di riassumere, in forme variabili, la sua funzione di paradigma metodico e di modello etico, senza l'asprezza delle tensioni prodottesi nella *Repubblica*.[20]

Pavia

[20] Una versione leggermente modificata di questo testo compare anche, in forma di *pre-print*, nel II fascicolo di *Platone. Repubblica*, traduzione e commento a cura di M. Vegetti (Dipartimento di filosofia, Pavia 1996).

Γέγονεν (PLATON, TIM. 28 B 7)
IST DIE WELT REAL ENTSTANDEN ODER NICHT?

MATTHIAS BALTES

Von allen Fragen, die der Platonische "Timaios" aufwirft, ist über keine so viel diskutiert und gestritten worden wie über die hier gestellte. Das gilt für die lateinische und griechische Antike, aus der uns zu diesem Problem mehr Äußerungen erhalten sind als zu allen anderen[1]. Das gilt in ähnlicher Weise für das lateinische, griechische und arabische Mittelalter[2], die beginnende Neuzeit und die neueste Zeit. Wie schon in der Antike, so zeichnet sich auch unter den heutigen Interpreten kein Konsens ab: Die einen sind nach wie vor der Meinung, Platon lehre im "Timaios", die Welt sei zeitlich oder, wenn schon nicht zeitlich, so doch wenigstens in einem einmaligen Schöpfungsakt entstanden, während die Gegenseite ebenso beharrlich die Auffassung vertritt, der Schöpfungsakt, von dem der "Timaios" spricht, sei nur ein bildlicher Ausdruck für ein immerwährendes Schöpfungs-Geschehen, für eine *creatio continua* oder *perpetua*: die Darstellung entfalte das, was sich im Kosmos immerfort gleichzeitig abspiele, in einem zeitlichen Nacheinander, um auf diese Weise die innere Struktur des Kosmos und der Vorgänge in ihm einsichtig zu machen[3]. Beide Seiten können sich dabei nicht nur auf Passagen

[1] Vgl. M. Baltes, *Die Weltentstehung des Platonischen Timaios nach den antiken Interpreten* I–II (Leiden 1976–78); H. Dörrie – M. Baltes, *Der Platonismus in der Antike* III (Stuttgart-Bad Cannstadt 1993) 296 ff.

[2] C. Baeumker, "Die Ewigkeit der Welt bei Plato", *Philosophische Monatshefte* 23 (1887) 514 ff; M.-D. Chenu, "Die Platonismen des XII. Jahrhunderts", in *Platonismus in der Philosophie des Mittelalters*, hgg. von W. Beierwaltes (Darmstadt 1969) 274 ff. 287; M. Fakhry, "A Tenth-century Arabic Interpretation of Plato's Cosmology", *Journal of the History of Philosophy* 6 (1968) 15 ff = *Philosophy, Dogma and the Impact of Greek Thought in Islam* (Brookfield, Aldershot 1994) VI 15 ff; F. van Steenberghen, "La controverse sur l'éternité du monde au XIIIe siècle", *L'Academie Royale de Belgique. Bulletin de la Classe des Lettres et des Sciences Morales et Politiques*, 5e série, 58 (1972) 267 ff; H. Simon, "Weltschöpfung und Weltewigkeit in der jüdischen Tradition", *Kairos* 14 (1972) 31 ff; R. Sorabji, *Time, Creation and the Continuum* (London 1983) passim; ders., *Matter, Space and Motion* (London 1988) 259 ff; Dörrie-Baltes III 298 mit Anm.4.

[3] Die Hauptvertreter der beiden Richtungen werden vorgestellt bei W. Scheffel, *Aspekte der platonischen Kosmologie* (Leiden 1976) XI ff und R. Hackforth, "Plato's Cosmogony (*Timaeus* 27 D ff)", *Class. Quart.* N.S. 9 (1959) 17; die

des "Timaios" selbst berufen, sondern auch auf Stellen aus anderen Platonischen Dialogen; vor allem der "Staat", der "Politikos", der "Philebos", der "Kritias" und die "Nomoi" spielen in dieser Diskussion eine große Rolle[4]. Beide Seiten ziehen für ihre unterschiedlichen Ansichten zudem die unmittelbaren Platonschüler heran, Aristoteles einerseits und Speusipp, Xenokrates und Herakleides Pontikos andererseits[5]. Schon in der Schule Platons, der Akademie, war man sich also offenbar nicht einig darüber, wie der Schöpfungsbericht im "Timaios" zu verstehen sei. Wenn nun aber schon Platons direkte Schüler in dieser Frage uneins waren, wie sollen wir da in der Lage sein, die Sache zu entscheiden?! Die Situation scheint völlig verfahren, das Rätsel unlösbar zu sein.

Bei unserem Versuch, das Rätsel zu lösen, wollen wir uns ausschließlich auf den "Timaios" konzentrieren und zunächst seinen *Aufbau*, genauer den Aufbau der *Rede* des Timaios im "Timaios" betrachten. Unter dem Gesichtspunkt einer zeitlichen oder einmaligen Schöpfung ist dieser Aufbau geradezu chaotisch. Denn

---

älteren Vertreter werden genannt bei E. Zeller, *Die Philosophie der Griechen in ihrer geschichtlichen Entwicklung* II 1 (Leipzig 1922[5], Nachdr. Darmstadt 1963) 792, Anm.1; G. Vlastos, "The Disorderly Motion in the *Timaeus*" (1939), in *Studies in Plato's Metaphysics*, ed. R.E. Allen (London 1965) 379 und H. Cherniss, *Aristotle's Criticism of Plato and the Academy* (Baltimore 1944) 424, Anm.357. Über die dort Genannten hinaus treten heute ein

– für die nichtzeitliche Auffassung der Weltentstehung im "Timaios": M. Landmann, *Ursprungsbild und Schöpfertat* (München 1966) 162 ff; E. Ostenfeld, "Disorderly Motion in the Timaeus", *Classica et Mediaevalia* 29 (1968) 22 ff; L. Tarán, "The Creation Myth in Plato's *Timaeus*", in *Essays in Ancient Philosophy*, ed. J.P. Anton and G.L. Kustas (State University of New York Press, Albany 1972) 372 ff; L. Brisson, *Le même et l'autre dans la structure ontologique du Timée de Platon* (Paris 1974) 82 f; K. Alt, "Die Überredung der Ananke zur Erklärung der sichtbaren Welt in Platons Timaios", *Hermes* 106 (1978) 460 f;

– für die zeitliche Auffassung: F. Solmsen, *Aristotle's System of the Physical World* (Ithaca, New York 1962) 51; G. Vlastos, "Creation in the *Timaeus*: Is it a Fiction?" (1964), in *Studies in Plato's Metaphysics*, ed. R.E. Allen (London 1965) 401-419; J. Pépin, *Théologie cosmique et théologie chrétienne (Ambroise, Exam. I 1,1-4)* (Paris 1964) 85 f; H.J. Easterling, "Causation in the Timaeus and Laws X", *Eranos* 65 (1967) 25; T.M. Robinson, *Plato's Psychology* (Toronto 1995[2]) 64-104, bes. 68 f; ders., "The Argument of *Tim.* 27 d ff", *Phronesis* 24 (1979) 105 ff; W.K.C. Guthrie, *A History of Greek Philosophy* V (Cambridge 1978) 301 ff; Sorabji, Matter 248-259. 273-282; ders., Time 272 ff; J. Mansfeld, "Rez. Scheffel, Kosmologie", *Mnemosyne* 35 (1982) 168 ff; R.D. Mohr, *The Platonic Cosmology* (Leiden 1985) 64 ff; G. Naddaf, "The Atlantis Myth: An Introduction to Plato's Later Philosophy of History", *Phoenix* 48 (1994) 202; vgl. dens., *L'origine et l'évolution du concept grec de 'phusis'* (Lewiston 1992) 391 ff, bes. 413;

– für eine unzeitliche, aber reale Weltentstehung: Scheffel, *Kosmologie*.

[4] Vgl. Baltes, *Weltentstehung* I 210. 216 mit Verweisen (s. auch die Indices I 237 f) und II 166 f.

[5] Zu diesen vgl. Tarán, "Creation Myth" 389 f (zu Herakleides speziell 404, Anm.113); Baltes, *Weltentstehung* I 5 ff. 94 ff.

die Schritte, in denen sich der Schöpfungsakt im "Timaios" vollzieht, sind derart über die Rede des Timaios verstreut, daß man größte Mühe hat, sie zusammenzustellen. Es sind die folgenden:

1. Die Situation, bevor der Gott eingreift: in dieser existieren drei Dinge, das Seiende, der Raum und das Werden (ὄν, χώρα, γένεσις, 51 D 3). Die γένεσις bezeichnet den Zustand, in dem die Ideen (ὄν) auf den Raum (χώρα) wirken und in ihm Spuren (ἴχνη ἄττα, 53 B 2) von Elementen hervorrufen[6], die sich zwar noch in vollkommener Unordnung befinden (52 D 3 – 53 A 8), aber doch auch schon Andeutungen ihrer künftigen Eigenschaften besitzen (68 E 1 ff), beispielsweise Schwere, Dichte (53 A 1 f) und Sichtbarkeit (52 E 1). Da die ἀνωμαλία in diesem vorkosmischen Chaos zu einer Schüttelbewegung der Chora führt (52 E 1 ff; vgl. 57 D 7 ff), findet in diesem Stadium sogar schon eine Art Gruppierung der Spurenelemente statt (52 E 5 ff)[7]. Dies ist der Zustand πρὸ τῆς τοῦ οὐρανοῦ γενέσεως (48 B 3 ff; 52 D 4; 53 A 7), in dem die ἀνάγκη herrscht (47 E 4 f; 68 E 1. 6 f) und den der Gott vorfindet, bevor er einschreitet (30 A 2-4; 69 B 2 f. 5 ff).
2. Auf der zweiten Stufe tritt der Gott auf, der in dieses Chaos eingreift und es ordnet, indem er die Spuren der Elemente durch Gestalt und Zahl formt (διεσχηματίσατο εἴδεσί τε καὶ ἀριθμοῖς, 53 B 4 f). Nun erst gelangen Ordnung und Maß in das Chaos (53 B 1 – 7; 69 B 4 f); denn nun werden die einzelnen Elemente und auch der Kosmos als ganzer nach den fünf Platonischen Körpern gestaltet (53 B 7 – 56 C 7). Erst auf dieser Stufe herrschen die mathematischen Gesetze unter den Elementen (69 B 4 f), erst jetzt gibt es einen Kosmos[8], in dem die einzelnen Glieder durch Proportion gebunden sind und in Freundschaft miteinander leben (31 B 4 – 32 C 4). Dies ist der Zustand, in dem der νοῦς die Herrschaft übernimmt und die ἀνάγκη überredet, so daß diese zum Besseren des Ganzen nachgibt (47 E 5 – 49 A 5; 56 C 5 f). Von nun an herrschen im Kosmos νοῦς und φρόνησις (34 A 2; 39 C 2; 47 B 7; 90 C 7 ff).
3. Wo bleibt nun aber in dieser Abfolge die Weltseele? Nach dem, was der "Timaios" über die ersten beiden Stufen lehrt, ist die Weltseele

---

[6] Zu diesem Wirken der Ideen auf die χώρα vgl. Prokl. In Plat. Tim. I 387,8 ff; 388,16 ff. 28 ff Diehl; L. Robin, "Études sur la signification et la place de la physique dans la philosophie de Platon", in *La pensée hellénique des origines à Épicure*, publ. par P.M. Schuhl (Paris 1942, Nachdr.1967) 258; Baltes, *Weltentstehung* I 17, Anm.46 und 48; Scheffel, *Kosmologie* 103 ff. 142, dem ich jedoch nicht in allen Einzelheiten zustimmen kann.

[7] Daß nach dieser Gruppierung der Spurenelemente die ungeordnete Bewegung aufhören müßte, kann ich Tarán, "Creation Myth" 386 ff nicht zugeben; denn die Ideen wirken ja immerfort weiter auf die χώρα und rufen in ihr ständig neue Spurenelemente hervor, deren ἀνωμαλία die χώρα weiterhin in Bewegung setzt, so daß die Schüttelbewegung andauert. Ebenso kann ich ihm nicht zugeben, daß die Seele im "Timaios" Quelle *aller* Bewegungen ist (a.O. 384 u.ö.); sie ist nur Quelle aller *geordneten* Bewegungen.

[8] Auf den Gedanken, daß es "the world" schon vor dem Eingreifen des Demiurgen gibt, kann man nur kommen, wenn man die Leistung des Demiurgen unerlaubterweise so sehr minimalisiert, wie Mohr, *Platonic Cosmology* 66 f es tut.

später als die dort entstehenden Körper, einschließlich des Kosmoskörpers. Jedenfalls wird sie auf diesen Stufen nirgends erwähnt. Dagegen ist der Kosmoskörper nach 30 A 6 – C 1 *von Anfang an* beseelt, und nach 34 B 10 ff ist die Weltseele sogar früher als der Kosmoskörper; dieser wird ja in die schon erstellte Seele *hineingebaut* (36 D 9 f), und die Sterne werden erst *nach* ihrer Erstellung in die Umläufe der Seele hineingesetzt (38 C 7 f; 40 A 4 f). Also ist die Weltseele nach Platon wirklich früher als die Weltkörper. Aber wann ist sie dann entstanden? Auf der ersten Stufe oder erst auf einer Zwischenstufe nach der ersten und vor der zweiten Stufe? Tim. 34 B 10 ff scheint für die zweite Alternative zu sprechen[9].

Auch bei der Erschaffung der Zeit tun sich Schwierigkeiten auf; denn nach der Erzählung des Timaios schafft der Gott die Zeit *nach* der Weltseele und dem Weltkörper, aber *vor* den Gestirnen (37 C 6 ff); doch korrigiert Timaios sich sogleich, indem er sagt, die Zeit sei *zusammen mit* dem Himmel entstanden (38 B 6 ff). Obschon also die Darstellung des Timaios dies zunächst suggeriert, bildet die Erschaffung der Zeit dann doch keine eigene Stufe.

4. Auf der vierten Stufe erfolgt die Erschaffung der Gestirngötter und der δαίμονες (39 C 3 – 41 A 6).
5. Erst danach entsteht auf der fünften Stufe der unsterbliche Teil der Menschenseele, der aus den zweit- und drittrangigen Resten der Ingredienzien der Weltseele geschaffen wird (41 D 3 ff). Dieser Teil der Menschenseele entsteht *nach* den Götterseelen (vgl. 38 E 5 f; 40 B 5). Auch die Götterseelen müssen also aus Resten der Ingredienzien der Weltseele entstanden sein, doch wird man annehmen können, daß diese Reste nicht zweit- und drittrangig waren. Also ist vor der Entstehung des göttlichen Teils der Menschenseele und der Gestirnkörper zwischen der dritten und fünften Stufe die Entstehung der Götterseelen anzusetzen, die der "Timaios" nur voraussetzt, aber nicht behandelt.
6. Auf der sechsten Stufe zieht der Gott sich zurück, denn er hat seine Aufgabe erfüllt, und die Untergötter lösen ihn ab. Sie schaffen jetzt den menschlichen Körper, binden die göttliche Seele in diesen und fügen dann den sterblichen Teil der Menschenseele hinzu (42 E 5 ff; 69 C 5 ff). Dabei entsteht nur der Mann (41 E 3 ff; 90 E 6 ff). Wie die Stellung des Berichts im Ganzen nahelegt, werden auf derselben Stufe die Pflanzen erschaffen, die den entstandenen Menschen als Nahrung dienen sollen (76 E 7 – 77 C 5).
7. Auf der siebten Stufe entstehen die Frauen und mit ihnen auch die Fortpflanzungsorgane des Mannes (42 B 5 ff; 76 D 8; 90 E 6 ff).
8. Auf der achten Stufe entstehen die Tiere (42 A 1 – D 2; 76 D 8 ff; 91 D 6 ff).

---

[9] Trotzdem bleibt auch diese Lösung schwierig; denn wenn Tim. 48 A der νοῦς die ἀνάγκη zu *überreden* vermag, muß diese schon *von sich aus* Seele besitzen, wenn denn der Satz gelten soll, daß νοῦς ohne Seele niemandem zukommen kann (Tim. 30 B 3). Hat also das vorkosmische Chaos schon vor dem Eingreifen des Gottes Seele? Oder wird die Seele der ἀνάγκη in dem Augenblick mitgegeben, in dem der Gott sie anspricht? Eine unlösbare Schwierigkeit.

Diesen Aufbau der Handlung kann man unter dem Gesichtspunkt einer zeitlichen Schöpfung nur als katastrophal bezeichnen. Es *kann* nicht Platons Absicht gewesen sein, den wirklichen Verlauf der Schöpfung darzustellen, und es *war* auch nicht seine Absicht. Was Platon mit seiner Darstellung wirklich intendierte, war keine Entstehungs- und Entwicklungsgeschichte des Kosmos, sondern eine Analyse der Leistungen der einzelnen Faktoren, die bei der Schöpfung zusammenwirken. Daß dies so ist, hebt Timaios selbst im Verlauf seines Vortrags mehrfach hervor. So sagt er beispielsweise, daß der Abschnitt 27 D 5 – 29 D 3 als προοίμιον zu gelten hat, in dem die für die Darstellung notwendigen Vorfragen geklärt werden (29 D 4-6).

An das προοίμιον schließt sich 29 D 7 – 47 E 2 zunächst ein Abschnitt an, der die Entstehung des Kosmos unter dem Gesichtspunkt betrachtet, was in ihr die Vernunft leistet; es folgt der Abschnitt 47 E 5 – 68 D 7, der danach fragt, was die Notwendigkeit (ἀνάγκη) zur Kosmogenese beiträgt (47 E 3-5). Am Ende dieses Abschnitts stellt Timaios ausdrücklich fest, daß nunmehr die *Analyse* beendet sei und die *Synthese* der restlichen Darstellung beginnen könne: "Die Gattungen der Ursachen liegen *säuberlich getrennt* bereit, aus welchen es nun die restliche Darstellung *zusammenzuweben* gilt" (παράκειται τὰ τῶν αἰτίων γένη διυλισμένα, ἐξ ὧν τὸν ἐπίλοιπον λόγον δεῖ συνυφανθῆναι, 69 A 6 f).

Daß Timaios dieses Verfahren wählt, ist um so auffälliger, als er selbst zugeben muß, daß beide Abschnitte, der über die Leistung der Vernunft und der über das Wirken der Notwendigkeit, nicht ganz ohne das Wirken des jeweils anderen Prinzips auskommen (vgl. πλὴν βραχέων, 47 E 3). Daß Timaios dieses Vorgehen trotzdem vorzieht, hat seinen Grund in der 46 D 7 ff geäußerten Überzeugung, daß jeder vernünftige Mensch zuerst die vernunftbestimmten Ursachen erforschen müsse und dann erst die durch die Notwendigkeit vorgegebenen. Denn nur die Suche nach den ersteren führe zu einem glücklichen Leben (68 E 7 f)[10].

Die Darstellung ist also nicht durch die zeitliche oder sachliche Abfolge, sondern durch systematische und axiologische Überlegungen bestimmt. Timaios weist ja öfter selbst darauf hin, daß die Reihenfolge der Darstellung nicht der sachlichen Reihenfolge entspricht (34 B 10 ff; 48 A 7 ff; E 2 ff). Ja, gelegentlich hebt er

---

[10] Dazu Scheffel, *Kosmologie* 126 ff.

sogar hervor, daß er um der Darstellung willen Zusammengehöriges trennen muß (61 C 3 – D 5).

Timaios gibt auch klar und deutlich zu verstehen, warum er dieses Vorgehen wählt: Er ist überzeugt, daß seine Zuhörer auf diese Weise besser verstehen, was er sagen will (27 C 7 – D 4). Dies gilt vor allem für die Zweiteilung in die Abschnitte "Werke der Vernunft" und "Werke der Notwendigkeit"; denn erst nachdem Timaios seine Zuhörer mit den leichter verständlichen Werken der Vernunft vertraut gemacht hat, fügt er die "unerhörte und ungewöhnliche Darlegung" (ἄτοπος καὶ ἀήθης διήγησις, 48 D 5 f) über "die schwierige und dunkle Art" (χαλεπὸν καὶ ἀμυδρὸν εἶδος), die "Aufnehmerin allen Entstehens" (πάσης γενέσεως ὑποδοχή, 49 A 3-6) an, eine bis dahin vollkommen unbekannte Realität, über die noch nie jemand gesprochen habe (48 B 5 ff).

Die genannte Erklärung gilt in gleicher Weise für die Binnenstruktur der einzelnen Teile. So wird im Abschnitt über die Werke der Vernunft die einfachere Entstehung des Kosmoskörpers (29 D 7 – 34 A 7) *vor* der komplizierteren Entstehung der Weltseele (34 A 8 – 36 D 7) behandelt, obschon die Weltseele "früher" ist als der Weltkörper[11]. Ebenso wird die Entstehung der Zeit *nach* der Entstehung des Kosmos besprochen (37 C 6 ff), obschon sie doch *zusammen mit* dem Kosmos entstanden ist (38 B 6 ff). Aus denselben didaktischen Gründen wird die Entstehung der Gestirnkörper 38 C 3 ff vor ihrer Belebung behandelt, die erst in 38 E 3 ff erwähnt wird[12].

Mit anderen Worten, die Darstellung der Weltentstehung im "Timaios" ist durch *didaktische* Absichten bestimmt; so, wie sie ist, ist sie διδασκαλίας χάριν bzw. σαφηνείας ἕνεκα. Das haben schon Speusipp und Xenokrates gesehen. Doch sind diese noch einen Schritt weitergegangen. Sie haben behauptet, nicht nur die *Darstellung* der Weltentstehung, sondern auch der *dargestellte Akt* sei nichts weiter als ein Zugeständnis an die διδασκαλία. Wie in der Geometrie zum Zweck der Unterweisung und der Verdeutlichung ein Dreieck aus vorgegebenen Größen *konstruiert* werde, das doch *niemals* entstanden sei, so lasse Platon im "Timaios" den Kosmos nur zum Zweck der Unterweisung und um der größeren Deutlichkeit willen durch den Demiurgen *konstruiert werden.* In Wirklich-

---

11 Vgl. Robinson, *Plato's Psychology* 65. 68.

12 Ebenso wird im zweiten Teil des "Timaios" zunächst die weniger Vorwissen erfordernde χώρα behandelt (48 E 2 – 53 B 7), dann erst die "ungewöhnliche Darstellung" (ἀήθης λόγος) der Elementenlehre, die erhebliche mathematische Vorkenntnisse voraussetzt (53 B 7 ff).

keit sei der Kosmos ebensowenig entstanden wie die geometrische Figur[13].

Was ist von dieser Interpretation zu halten? In der Tat führt die Erzählung der Weltentstehung, wenn man sie als Schilderung eines sukzessiven Geschehens auffaßt, zu unüberwindlichen Schwierigkeiten, von denen ich nur einige aufzähle:

1. Woher kommt der Gott, der auf der zweiten Stufe so plötzlich auftaucht? Auf der ersten Stufe wurde er unter den Prinzipien ja nicht erwähnt. Wenn er aber, woran nicht zu zweifeln ist, Prinzip ist, dann muß er auch schon auf der ersten Stufe existiert haben; dann aber kann er nur mit dem auf der ersten Stufe genannten ὄν (52 D 3) identisch sein. Nun ist aber mit diesem ὄν nach 48 E 2 ff das ideale Vorbild gemeint. Also bleibt nur die Schlußfolgerung, daß der Gott und das ideale Vorbild identisch sind.
2. Bestätigt wird dies durch die Aussage, daß das νοητὸν ζῷον *alle* νοητὰ ζῷα in sich enthält (30 C 5 ff; 31 A 4 f). Wenn der Demiurg, was nicht bezweifelt werden kann, ein νοητὸν ζῷον ist, dann gibt es nur die Alternative, daß er entweder ein Teil oder das Ganze des νοητὸν ζῷον ist. Wäre er ein Teil, so wäre er unvollkommen (30 C 4 f)[14]. Da das undenkbar ist, kann er nur das Ganze des νοητὸν ζῷον sein; denn er ist ja "das beste der intelligiblen und immerseienden Dinge" (τῶν νοητῶν ἀεί τε ὄντων ... τὸ ἄριστον, 37 A 1).
   Daß der νοῦς, der die ἀνάγκη überredet, der νοῦς des Gottes ist, den Timaios 36 D 8 und 39 E 7 im Vorübergehen erwähnt, kann man vermuten, es wird aber nicht gesagt. Wie er zu deuten ist, werden wir später zu klären versuchen. So viel scheint jedoch klar, daß die vorher genannte zweite Stufe der Kosmogenese nicht einfach damit erklärt werden kann, daß plötzlich ein Demiurg auftritt, der vorher nicht da war.
3. Wohin zieht sich der Gott zurück, nachdem er sein Werk auf der fünften Stufe beendet hat? Ja, zieht er sich überhaupt zurück? Zwar scheint die Aufgabenverteilung zwischen Gott und Göttern vollkommen klar zu sein; der Gott will mit der Erschaffung des sterblichen Teils der Menschenseele und des menschlichen Körpers, aber auch mit der Erschaffung der Tiere nichts zu tun haben (41 B 7 – D 3; 42 D 2 – E 4). Gleichwohl wird die Trennung im Folgenden nicht aufrechterhalten; denn an die Stelle der Götter tritt häufig der Gott (46 C 7; E 8; 47 B 6; 71 A 7; E 2 f; 73 B 8; 74 C 6; D 6; 75 D 1; 76 C 6; 78 B 2; 80 E 1; 92 A 3). Ist der Gott also doch nicht abgetreten? Sind der Gott und die Untergötter etwa gar identisch? Sind der Demiurg und die Untergötter vielleicht nur Hypostasen für einzelne Stufen des Handelns des Gottes?

[13] Vgl. Speusipp, fg.54 Lang = fg.61 Tarán = fg.94 f Isnardi Parente; Xenokrates, fg.54. 68 Heinze = fg.153 ff. 188 Isnardi Parente; Baltes, Weltentstehung I 18 ff.

[14] Dieses Problem hat schon der Platoniker Attikos gesehen; vgl. fg.34 des Places.

4. Kann man wirklich annehmen, daß der Gott die Weltseele *vor* dem Weltleib erschafft, gleichsam eine Seele ohne Aufgabe? Denn diese Aufgabe erhält sie ja erst nachträglich dadurch, daß der Gott den Weltkörper in sie hineinbaut (36 D 9 f; 38 C 7 f; 40 A 4 f)[15].
5. Kann man wirklich annehmen, daß die Zeit erst *mit* dem Kosmoskörper entstanden ist?[16] Ist dem so, dann waren die vorkosmischen Bewegungen nicht "in der Zeit". Waren sie dann überhaupt noch Bewegungen? Welchen Sinn hat es dann noch, daß Timaios davon spricht, daß sie "vor der Entstehung des Himmels" waren (48 B 3 f; 52 D 3; vgl. 37 E 2) und daß der Urzustand und das Eingreifen des Gottes als zeitliches Nacheinander dargestellt werden (53 A 7 ff; 69 B 2 ff; 30 A 2 ff)[17]?
   Die Interpreten helfen sich hier mit der Annahme einer ungeordneten vorkosmischen Zeit (so schon der Platoniker Attikos)[18] bzw. mit einer unendlichen Dauer ("an ἄπειρον of duration"), die nicht periodische Zeit sei, weil sie sich nicht wie diese gemäß der Zahl bewegt (so Skemp und Hackforth)[19]. Aber kann es in dieser "Dauer" überhaupt ein Früher und Später geben, wenn es kein *Maß* gibt, woran beides gemessen wird?
   Vlastos nimmt analog zu den Spurenelementen "Spuren einer zeitlichen Ordnung" ("'traces' of temporal order") im vorkosmischen

---

[15] Dagegen schon Prokl. In Plat. Tim. I 287,11 ff; 104,4 ff; 115,2 f Diehl.

[16] Es ist falsch zu behaupten, daß, "when Plato says that the Demiurg makes time, he means that the Demiurge makes a clock, nothing more" (Mohr, *Platonic Cosmology* 54); denn die Zeit ist zwar ihrem Wesen nach ein bewegtes und der Zahl nach fortschreitendes Abbild der Ewigkeit (37 D 6 f; 38 A 7 f), aber sie ist keine Uhr; denn eine Uhr *ist* nicht Zeit, sie *mißt* die Zeit. Die Interpretation Mohrs ist nicht unvoreingenommen; denn sie geht davon aus, daß es auch vor dem Kosmos eine 'Zeit' gibt: Platon "means that time is a clock, a clock by which we measure time, where 'time' here is used in a colloquial sense, as that about motion and rest which is measurable" (ebd. 59). Platon kennt diese zweite Art von 'time' nicht, und es stimmt nicht, daß "the technical sense of time and this ordinary sense exist side by side through the text we are discussing (e.g., 38c2: ὁ δ'...χρόνον [?])" (a.O.). Grotesk wird es, wenn neben dieser ersten Art von 'time' eine zweite eingeführt wird, nämlich 'time' im Sinne von dem, "which is measurable *as actually having been measured*" [Hervorhebung von mir], und wenn gesagt wird, diese Bedeutung von 'time' "appears in the description of the planets as 'the instruments of time(s)' (42d5; 41e5)" (a.O. und 64).

Ganz unmöglich ist die Behauptung Mohrs ebd. 67 f, die vom Demiurgen geschaffene Zeit unterliege keinem Wandel und sei ewig. Platon sagt doch deutlich, sie sei eine εἰκὼν κινητός τις αἰῶνος (37 D 5) und ihre εἴδη Vergangenheit und Zukunft seien Bewegungen (38 A 2). Weder als bewegt noch als Abbild der Ewigkeit kann sie selbst wirklich ewig und unveränderlich sein. Die Zeit ist zwar nicht "in der Zeit", aber das heißt noch lange nicht, daß sie wirklich ewig (im Sinne des Vorbildes) ist. Siehe unten Anm.33.

[17] Vgl. zudem Tarán, "Creation Myth" 378 ff.

[18] Plutarch und Attikos bei Prokl. In Plat. Tim. I 276,32 ff; 286,26 ff; III 37,11 ff Diehl; dazu Sorabji, *Time* 273 f (dagegen Prokl. In Plat. Tim. I 286,29 ff Diehl; s. Baltes, *Weltentstehung* II 40 ff). Vgl. schon Epikureer bei Cicero, De nat. deor. 1,21 und dazu Baltes, *Weltentstehung* I 26.

[19] J. Skemp, *The Theory of Motion in Plato's Later Dialogues* (Amsterdam 1967²) 111; Hackforth, "Plato's Cosmology" 22; ähnlich Guthrie, *History* V 301 f und Mansfeld, "Rez. Scheffel, *Kosmologie*" 172.

Chaos an[20]. Doch von den letzteren sagt der Platontext nichts. An anderer Stelle[21] unterscheidet Vlastos die geschaffene Zeit als einen "einförmigen und meßbaren Zeitfluß" ("uniform and measurable time-flow") von einer vorkosmischen "unumkehrbaren zeitlichen Abfolge" ("irreversible temporal succession"), einer "quasi-time"[22]. In der letzteren gebe es zwar ein Früher und Später, aber die Intervalle zwischen beiden seien nicht meßbar: "If A, B, C, are successive instants we would have no means of telling if the interval, AB, is as long as the interval, BC, or longer, or shorter."[23] Ich möchte bestreiten, daß es überhaupt sinnvoll ist, in einem vorkosmischen *Chaos* von einem Früher und Später zu sprechen. Ein Früher-und-Später impliziert in jedem Fall eine zählbare Abfolge, also ein Voranschreiten der Zahl nach (κατ' ἀριθμὸν ἰέναι, 37 D 6)[24]; d.h. es impliziert eine Ordnung, die es im vorkosmischen Chaos nicht gibt. Wer immer also ein Früher oder Später im vorkosmischen Chaos konstatiert, kann selbst nicht zu diesem gehören, vielmehr betrachtet er das Chaos gleichsam von außen, von der Ordnung seines Erkenntnisorgans aus; er *überträgt* also etwas auf das Chaos, was nicht in ihm ist.

Auch darf man m.E. nicht hingehen und, wie Vlastos es tut, Vergangenheit, Gegenwart und Zukunft für die genannte zeitliche Abfolge ("temporal succession") in Anspruch nehmen[25]. Denn Platon bezeichnet diese doch ausdrücklich als χρόνου γεγονότα εἴδη, d.h. als Unterarten der *Zeit* (37 E 4)[26], die zusammen mit dieser *entstanden sind*: χρόνου ταῦτα αἰῶνα μιμουμένου καὶ κατ' ἀριθμὸν κυκλουμένου γέγονεν εἴδη (38 A 7 f).

Jedes Postulat einer wie auch immer gearteten Zeit ist für das vorkosmische Chaos abzulehnen; denn die einzige Zeit, von der Platon spricht, ist die Zeit, die "zusammen mit dem Himmel entstanden ist" und die zusammen mit dem Himmel vergehen kann (38 B 6 f); d.h. ebensowenig wie es nach einem Vergehen des Himmels Zeit geben würde, hat es vor dem Entstehen des Himmels Zeit gegeben. Die geordnete Bewegung des Himmels ist ja die Bedingung der

---

[20] Vlastos, "Disorderly Motion" 390. Mansfeld, "Rez. Scheffel, *Kosmologie*" 171/172 spricht in ähnlichem Sinne von "a faint sort ... of 'matter' of time" bzw. von "a sort of precosmic time–'matter'".

[21] Vlastos, "Creation" 409 ff

[22] Vlastos, "Creation" 414. Andere meinen, Platon nehme zwar keine vorkosmische Zeit, aber eine vorkosmische "durée" an; vgl. Naddaf, *L'origine* 437, Anm.1. Nichts im "Timaios" weist auf eine solche hin.

[23] Vlastos, "Creation" 411. Ähnlich urteilt Mohr, *Platonic Cosmology* 58 ff. 63. 64 ff.

[24] Das haben selbst Plutarch und Attikos zugegeben; vgl. Prokl. In Plat. Tim. I 277,6 f Diehl.

[25] Vlastos, "Creation" 411 ff

[26] Strenggenommen bezeichnet Platon nur "war" und "wird sein" als Arten der Zeit, aber das schließt nicht aus, daß auch das "ist" eine Art der Zeit ist; denn Platon sagt nicht, daß *nur die beiden* Arten der Zeit seien, vielmehr daß sie nur von der Zeit, nicht von der Ewigkeit ausgesagt werden dürfen, für die nur das "ist" zulässig ist (Tim. 37 E 4 ff). Daß dies richtig ist, zeigt Tim. 38 C 2 f: ὁ δ' αὖ διὰ τέλους τὸν ἅπαντα χρόνον γεγονώς τε καὶ ὢν καὶ ἐσόμενος. Vgl. C. Eggers Lan, *Las nociones de tiempo y eternidad de Homero a Platon* (México 1984) 177 f.

Möglichkeit für die Existenz von Zeit (38 C 3 ff; 38 E 4 f; 41 E 5; 42 D 5), und die kosmische Zeit ist "die ganze Zeit", wie Platon ausdrücklich betont (36 E 5; 38 C 2). Dementsprechend verwendet Platon den Begriff χρόνος nie, wo er vom vorkosmischen Zustand redet. Ist aber Zeit nur im kosmischen Zustand möglich, dann kann Platon keine Schöpfung im zeitlichen Sinne gemeint haben.
Ferner ist folgendes zu bedenken: Wenn die Zeit erst mit dem Kosmoskörper entstanden ist, dann ist die Weltseele, die ja vor ihm geschaffen wurde, weder *in* der Zeit noch *mit* der Zeit entstanden, noch erfolgen ihre Bewegungen "in der Zeit", obschon doch eben diese Bewegungen, wenn die Gestirne in sie hineingesetzt werden, die Zeit erzeugen und ihre Bewegungen dann πρὸς τὸν σύμπαντα χρόνον erfolgen (36 E 4 f). Sind aber nicht einmal die *Bewegungen* der Weltseele *unmittelbar nach* ihrer Erschaffung in der Zeit, dann ist erst recht ihre *Erschaffung* nicht in der Zeit erfolgt.

6. Kann man wirklich glauben, daß Platon einen Zustand angenommen hat, in dem es auf Erden nur Männer gab, keine Frauen und keine Tiere? Diese Frage stellt sich um so dringlicher, als die menschliche Natur (ἡ ἀνθρωπίνη φύσις) nach Platon zwiefältig ist (διπλῆ), d.h. aus Mann *und* Frau besteht (42 A 1 f). Die menschliche Natur wäre in ihrem ersten Stadium—ohne die Frau—also unvollständig. Erst durch die Verfehlung des Mannes würde sie vollständig (42 B 5 f). Zudem muß man fragen, wie denn diese ersten Männer entstanden sein sollen, wenn nicht aus einer Frau oder Frauen?[27] Aber Frauen gab es ja noch nicht[28].
7. Kann man wirklich annehmen, daß der Gott bei der Erschaffung der Weltseele "Reste" übrigläßt, aus welchen er anschließend die Seelen der Götter und Menschen schafft (41 D 4 ff)? Oder daß die Götter bei der Erschaffung des menschlichen Körpers erst einmal einen Vorrat an Knochenmark, Sehnen und Fleisch erschaffen, um diese erst danach zu verwenden (73 B 1 – 75 D 5)?
8. Darf man glauben, daß der Demiurg etwas Unvollkommenes schafft? Das tut er, indem er nur den Kosmos und die unsterblichen Wesen in ihm hervorbringt, die Erschaffung der sterblichen Wesen aber den Untergöttern überläßt. Sagt er doch selbst, daß der Kosmos ohne die sterblichen Wesen "unvollkommen" (ἀτελής) ist (41 B 8).

Diese und andere Schwierigkeiten machen die Annahme unmöglich, daß der Kosmos nach Platon *sukzessive* entstanden ist. Darf man also daraus schließen, daß er überhaupt nicht entstanden ist? Das zu behaupten wäre voreilig; denn es bleibt ja noch die Erklärung, er sei in einem realen Schöpfungsakt sozusagen auf

---

[27] Platons *erste* Menschen, die Männer-Generation, werden zwar von den Untergöttern erschaffen, also nicht geboren (42 E ff; 69 C ff), aber wie entsteht die zweite Generation? Oder präziser: Wie entsteht *die erste Frau* in der zweiten Generation?

[28] Vgl. Prokl. In Plat. Tim. III 282,27 ff; 293,32 ff Diehl; dazu Baltes, *Weltentstehung* II 199 ff. Zur Ambiguität der Äußerungen Platons über die Entstehung des Menschen vgl. Naddaf, *L'origine* 393 ff.

einen Schlag entstanden[29]. Aber auch diese Annahme bereitet unüberwindliche Schwierigkeiten, die sich zum Teil mit den schon genannten decken:

1. Platon deutet an keiner Stelle an, daß er eine solche Vorstellung im Sinn gehabt hat, weder im "Timaios" noch in seinen anderen Dialogen[30].
2. Timaios sagt 52 A 3: Das, was sich immer gleich verhält—gemeint sind die Ideen—das geht nirgendwohin (οὔτε εἰς ἄλλο ποι ἰόν). Wie ist es damit vereinbar, daß die ἀμέριστος οὐσία, das ἀμέριστον ταὐτόν und das ἀμέριστον θάτερον, d.h. Ideen, in die Weltseelenmischung eingehen (35 A)?[31]
3. Wenn es zum Wesen des νοητὸν ζῷον gehört, παράδειγμα zu sein, dann hat das νοητὸν ζῷον vor dem Kosmos sein Wesen verfehlt; denn dann war es Vorbild von nichts. Ist das aber undenkbar, dann muß es das Abbild dieses Vorbildes, den Kosmos, immer gegeben haben[32]. Daß Platon dies wirklich meint, zeigt ein unscheinbares Wörtchen in 37 D 7, wo er die Zeit eine αἰώνιος εἰκών, "ein ewiges Abbild" der Ewigkeit nennt[33]. Nun ist aber die Zeit ebenso existentiell mit dem

---

29 Vgl. Scheffel, *Kosmologie* 59. 73 f. 122 f. 130 f. 140 ff. Derselben Ansicht waren auch manche christlichen Schriftsteller hinsichtlich des Schöpfungsberichts der Genesis, beispielsweise Basileios, In Hexaem. 1,6 S.110-112 Giet; Ioh. Philoponos, De aet. mundi 1,3 S.6,2 ff; 11,13 S.367,19 ff u.ö. Rabe.

30 Bei einer schlagartigen Schöpfung würde der Demiurg des "Timaios" zudem in ein und demselben Augenblick auftreten und abtreten.

31 Selbst Hackforth, "Plato's Cosmology" 20, der doch der Ansicht ist, daß die Weltentstehung im "Timaios" im Sinne eines zeitlichen Aktes zu verstehen sei, hält es für "ridiculous" anzunehmen, auch die Mischung der Weltseele sei als ein einmaliges Geschehen in der Vergangenheit aufzufassen; diese Mischung sei vielmehr nichts weiter als "an analysis of the cosmic soul's faculties of cognition and motion".

32 Vgl. Prokl. bei Ioh. Philoponos, De aet. mundi II S.24,1 ff Rabe; Baltes, *Weltentstehung* I 214 mit Verweisen; II 136. Dieselbe Argumentation ließe sich übrigens auch auf den Demiurgen (vgl. Prokl. a.O. III S.42,1 ff Rabe; Baltes a.O. II 136 ff) oder die Zeit anwenden (Prokl. a.O. V S.103,20 ff Rabe; Baltes a.O. II 140).

33 Mit Recht schreibt Tarán, "Creation Myth" 397, Anm.60: "Since the word αἰώνιος is applied to the model and to the copy, it cannot mean in the case of the latter only imperishability: there must be something common to the model and the copy in order that both may be said to be αἰώνιος. And *Timaeus* 37 C 6 – 38 B 5 implies the answer: both model and copy are αἰώνιος, but whereas the former is eternal and atemporal, the latter possesses the eternity of infinite duration." Ähnlich urteilt Eggers Lan, *Eternidad* 175 ff.

Platon selbst ist noch expliziter: Es war nicht möglich, die αἰώνιος φύσις (d.h. den αἰών) *vollkommen* auf den Kosmos zu übertragen (παντελῶς προσάπτειν); d.h. der Kosmos konnte nicht *schlechthin* αἰώνιος werden; aber ein Kompromiß war möglich: Der Kosmos konnte die εἰκὼν αἰῶνος anfnehmen, die Zeit, die selbst wieder αἰώνιος ist: weil sie ja nicht "zeitlich" (ἔγχρονος) sein kann. Αἰώνιος muß auch im letzteren Fall so etwas wie "ewig" heißen, d.h. anfangs- und endlos, weil ja nur so das Ziel erreicht wird, daß die Zeit der Ewigkeit "*möglichst* ... ähnlich ist" (ἵν' ὡς ὁμοιότατος αὐτῷ κατὰ δύναμιν ᾖ, 38 B 8 f; vgl. 37 D 2).

Daß Platon wirklich annimmt, die Zeit sei anfangs- und endlos, zeigt die Parallelität des Satzbaus in Tim. 36 C 1-3:

Kosmos verbunden wie die Ewigkeit mit dem Vorbild. Wenn also die Zeit ein 'ewiges' Abbild der Ewigkeit ist, dann muß der Kosmos ein 'ewiges' Abbild des Vorbildes sein. Folglich ist er nicht entstanden.

4. Spricht schon die Bezeichnung der Zeit als αἰώνιος εἰκών gegen eine Entstehung derselben, so wird diese Ansicht durch folgende Überlegung untermauert: Vergangenheit und Zukunft sind Arten der Zeit (χρόνου ... εἴδη, 37 E 3 – 38 A 8); d.h. sie sind εἴδη des γένος Zeit. Wenn die Zeit nun gleichsam mit einem Schlag ins Sein gesetzt worden wäre, dann wäre sie unvollständig ins Sein gesetzt worden; denn in diesem ersten Augenblick hätte es noch keine Vergangenheit gegeben, sondern nur Gegenwart und Zukunft. Das aber ist unmöglich, denn
 a) der Gott hätte in diesem Fall etwas Unvollkommenes geschaffen[34], was undenkbar ist, und
 b) es ist unvorstellbar, daß das γένος Zeit einmal das εἶδος Vergangenheit nicht umfaßt.
 Also kann die Zeit nicht entstanden sein[35].
5. Wenn die Welt das schönste aller entstandenen Dinge und der Gott die beste aller Ursachen ist (29 A 5 f) und wenn der gute Gott keinen Neid kennt und alles möglichst gut machen (29 E 1 ff), ja, wenn er überhaupt in seinem Handeln immer das Schönste will (30 A 7 f), warum hat er dann die Welt nicht schon vorher erschaffen?[36] Dies gilt um so mehr, wenn es vor dem Anfang der Welt das vorkosmische Chaos der ersten Stufe gab. Wie konnte der Gott dieses überhaupt mit ansehen, ohne einzugreifen?[37] Man wende nicht ein, daß es nicht sinnvoll sei, vor der Entstehung der Zeit von einem *Vor* zu sprechen. Gewiß, es gab kein zeitliches Vor, aber doch ein sachliches: Unordnung vor Ordnung bzw. das Nichts vor dem Sein. Wie ist das bei einem guten Gott möglich?
6. Gott ist "immer seiend" (34 B 8), ja, er ist das Beste der intelligiblen Dinge (37 A 1), d.h. er ist keinem Wandel unterworfen (27 D 6 – 28 A 2). Wieso kann er sich dann überhaupt plötzlich zur Erschaffung der Welt entschließen? Ein solcher Entschluß würde doch notwendiger-

---

τὸ μὲν ... παράδειγμα *πάντα αἰῶνά* ἐστιν ὄν,
ὁ δ' αὖ ... *τὸν ἅπαντα χρόνον* γεγονώς τε καὶ ὢν καὶ ἐσόμενος.
Ewigkeit und Zeit existieren *parallel.*
Anzunehmen, die Zeit sei nur in einer Richtung ewig, würde 1. die Ewigkeit zeitweise ihrer Ursächlichkeit berauben und 2. sozusagen ein amputiertes Abbild erzeugen. Vgl. Proklos bei Ioh. Philoponos, De aet. mundi XVIII S.607,24 ff Rabe (Baltes, *Weltentstehung* II 162) und auch Cherniss, *Aristotle's Criticism* 419, Anm.350.

34 Später tadelte man dergleichen als ἡμιτελὴς δημιουργία; Ioh. Philoponos, De aet. mundi 9,10 S.344,15 f.

35 Vgl. in diesem Zusammenhang auch Cherniss, *Aristotle's Criticism* 419 f.

36 Vgl. Porphyrios bei Ioh. Philoponos, De aet. mundi 6,27 S.224,18 ff Rabe = fg.456a Smith; Porphyrios bei Prokl. In Plat. Tim. I 394,12 ff Diehl; Proklos selbst: In Plat. Tim. I 367,2 ff. 13 ff Diehl; dazu Baltes, *Weltentstehung* I 90. 92. 159. 160 f; II 74 ff; Proklos bei Baltes, a.O. II 134 ff.

37 Vgl. Tarán, "Creation Myth" 381; Baltes, *Weltentstehung* I 215 mit Verweisen.

weise einen Wandel implizieren[38]. Wie kann er sich nach der Erschaffung der unsterblichen Wesen und Dinge zurückziehen (42 E 5 f)? Eigentlich kann er sich doch nur immer gleich verhalten; denn er gehört ja zu den ἀεὶ κατὰ ταὐτὰ καὶ ὡσαύτως ἔχοντα (29 A 1; 35 A 2; 37 B 3; 38 A 3; vgl. 28 A 6 f; 52 A 1). Also kann er sich auch zur Schöpfung nur immer gleich verhalten.

7. Wenn der Gott "immer seiend" ist, dann gibt es für ihn keine Vergangenheit und keine Zukunft. Dann kann er auch nicht über "den Gott, der einmal sein wird", d.h. den Kosmos, nachdenken (34 A 8 f), zumal die Zeit noch gar nicht existiert. Ist aber dieser Akt unmöglich, dann ist auch die einmalige Schöpfung unmöglich[39].
8. Wo befindet sich der Gott vor der Weltentstehung? Wo nach seinem 'Abtritt' (42 E 5 f)? Wie verhält er sich in diesen beiden Stadien zum νοητὸν ζῷον? Blickt er auf es? Aber wozu? Blickt er nicht darauf? Wohin dann?

Wenn man beachtet, daß Platon sowohl im vorkosmischen (52 D 1 ff) als auch im kosmischen Zustand (50 C 7 ff; vgl. 51 E 6 ff) nur drei Wirklichkeiten anerkennt, das Seiende (τὸ ὄν, τὰ ὄντα, d.h. die Ideen), den Raum (τιθήνη, χώρα) und das Werden bzw. die werdenden Dinge (γένεσις, τὸ γιγνόμενον), wenn man ferner beachtet, daß im kosmischen Zustand das Seiende als Wirkursache *und* paradigmatische Ursache bezeichnet wird (τὸ ὅθεν ἀφομοιούμενον φύεται τὸ γιγνόμενον, 50 D 1 f)[40], dann drängt sich mit Notwendigkeit der Schluß auf, daß der Demiurg sowohl im kosmischen als auch im vorkosmischen Zustand mit dem idealen Vorbild identisch ist; d.h. er tritt nur im Zustand der Kosmogenese gleichsam als eigenes Wesen aus dem idealen Vorbild heraus und kehrt anschließend wieder in dieses zurück. Da aber ein Wandel, wie gesagt, im "immer Seienden" undenkbar ist, und da, wie Platon ausdrücklich sagt, das Seiende *nichts* in sich aufnimmt (52 A 2 f), ist es auch unmöglich, daß das Auftreten und Abtreten des Gottes real zu verstehen ist. Dann aber kann der Demiurg—*pace* T.M. Robinson[41]—nichts anderes sein als der schöpferisch-ordnende Aspekt des Seienden, so wie das Vorbild der paradigmatische ist. Dieser schöpferisch-ordnende Aspekt wirkt

---

[38] Vgl. Prokl. In Plat. Tim. I 288,14 ff Diehl; dens. bei Ioh. Philoponos, De aet. mundi XVIII S.604,14 ff Rabe; s. Baltes, *Weltentstehung* I 213 mit Verweisen; II 43 ff. 159 ff.

[39] Sucht man eine Erklärung, dann ist die des Proklos, In Plat. Tim. II 101,3 ff Diehl noch immer die vernünftigste: "Als 'Gott, der einmal sein wird', hat Platon den *in seiner Darstellung* (ἐν τῷ λόγῳ) Teil für Teil entstehenden Gott bezeichnet; denn der Gott läßt die Teile und das Ganze mit einem Mal (ἀθρόως) entstehen, die Darstellung (ὁ λόγος) hingegen zerlegt das, was zusammen entstand, läßt das entstehen, was unentstanden ist, und zerteilt das, was immerwährende Dauer besitzt, der Zeit nach. 'Der Gott, der einmal sein wird', ist also offensichtlich ein solcher *mit Rücksicht auf die Darstellung* (τῷ λόγῳ), die mit Analyse und Synthese arbeitet." Vgl. dazu Baltes, *Weltentstehung* II 100. 101 f.

[40] Vgl. καὶ δὴ καὶ προσεικάσαι πρέπει ... τὸ δ' ὅθεν πατρί, 50 D 1 f; das Seiende ist das Prägende: 50 C 5; D 4. 6.

[41] Robinson, *Plato's Psychology* 102. Wenn es den Gott zum Gott macht, bei den Ideen zu sein (Phaidr. 249 C 5 f), dann versteht man, daß der Demiurg der höchste Gott ist, weil er in gewisser Weise die Ideen *ist*.

aber auch im Kosmos. Denn Platon sagt ja ausdrücklich, daß dort, wo der Gott abwesend ist, Unordnung herrscht (53 B 3 f)[42]. Ist somit die Gegenwart des Gottes unabdingbare Voraussetzung für jede Ordnung, dann auch für den Kosmos. Der Gott *kann* also nicht abtreten, soll der Kosmos bestehen bleiben[43].

Bestätigt wird das durch eine wunderliche Aussage des Timaios, die den modernen Interpreten einiges Kopfzerbrechen bereitet hat. Timaios sagt 42 E 5 f: Nachdem der Gott den Untergöttern seine Aufträge für das weitere Schaffen erteilt hatte, "verharrte er in der seiner Art entsprechenden gewohnten Haltung/Seinsweise" (ἔμενεν ἐν τῷ ἑαυτοῦ κατὰ τρόπον ἤθει). Hier drängt sich doch geradezu die Frage auf, ob sich der Gott vorher—während seiner Schöpfertätigkeit—nicht "in der seiner eigenen Art entsprechenden gewohnten Haltung/Seinsweise" befunden hat. Da man diese Frage nicht bejahen kann, hat der Gott *immer* "in der seiner Art entsprechenden gewohnten Haltung/Seinsweise verharrt". Das Imperfekt ἔμενεν, das den Interpreten solche Schwierigkeiten bereitet hat, vermag diese Interpretation zu stützen.

Auch folgendes ist zu bedenken: Wie soll das "intelligible Lebewesen" wirklich *Lebewesen* sein, ohne zu wirken? Also darf es wohl als gesichert gelten, daß der Demiurg nichts anderes ist als der schöpferisch-ordnende Aspekt des Seienden, so wie das Vorbild sein paradigmatischer Aspekt ist[44]. Ist dies richtig, dann versteht man auch, warum Platon eigentlich nur *zwei* Ursachen gelten läßt (δύ' αἰτίας εἴδη), die notwendige und die göttliche (τὸ μὲν ἀναγκαῖον, τὸ δὲ θεῖον, 68 E 6 ff), den νοῦς und die ἀνάγκη (47 E 3 ff)[45].

Allerdings ist eine Einschränkung zu machen: Der Gott ist nicht das aktive Prinzip des Seienden schlechthin, sondern nur das aktiv *ordnende* Prinzip. Aktiv sind ja auch schon die Ideen, die auf die χώρα einwirken (50 C 4 f; 51 A 7 f; 52 D 4 ff)[46].

Ein vorletztes Argument kann das bisher Gesagte stützen: Das aktiv ordnende Prinzip des νοητὸν ζῷον nennt Platon auch einfach νοῦς. So sagt er 39 E 7 ff, daß es der νοῦς ist, der die vier Hauptideen der Lebewesen im νοητὸν ζῷον sieht und im Kosmos zu verwirklichen strebt, und 47 E 5 ff hebt er hervor, daß es der νοῦς ist, der die ἀνάγκη überredet. An beiden Stellen wird nicht erklärt, wem der νοῦς gehört.

---

42 Vgl. Plat. Polit. 272 D 6 – 273 E 1.

43 Vgl. Proklos bei Ioh. Philoponos, De aet. mundi XVIII S.606,9 ff; 608,11 ff Rabe; Baltes, *Weltentstehung* II 160 ff.

44 Daher kann man denn auch verstehen, daß Aristoteles dem Platonischen Demiurgen kaum Aufmerksamkeit schenkt (Cherniss, *Aristotle's Criticism* 609 f; Tarán, "Creation Myth" 382. 391), ja, daß er sogar sagen kann, Platon verwende nur *zwei* Ursachen, τῇ τε τοῦ τί ἐστιν καὶ τῇ κατὰ τὴν ὕλην, wobei er unter τῇ τοῦ τί ἐστιν die Ideen versteht; vgl. Arist. Met. A 6 988 a 7 ff.

45 Ebenso spricht er 48 E 3 ff bei der Rekapitulation von 27 D 5 – 47 E 2 nur von δύο εἴδη, dem παράδειγμα und dem μίμημα παραδείγματος, während er den Demiurgen völlig übergeht. Offenbar sind auch hier Demiurg und Paradigma identisch.

46 Es stimmt also nicht, daß "the Platonic Ideas are to be viewed as standards *and as nothing else*" (Mohr, *Platonic Cosmology* 55; Hervorhebung von mir).

Natürlich hat man, wie schon gesagt, an den νοῦς des Demiurgen gedacht, von dem einmal die Rede ist (36 D 8), aber das ist nicht mehr als eine Vermutung. Nach unserer Interpretation ist dieser νοῦς der demiurgisch schaffende und ordnende Aspekt des intelligiblen ζῷον, der mit dem Demiurgen identisch ist.
Als letztes Argument sei schließlich die Beobachtung von Theodor Ebert angeführt, daß im sog. προοίμιον (27 D 5 – 29 D 3), ja, im ganzen "Timaios" nie bewiesen wird, daß es einen *Baumeister* (δημιουργός) der Welt gibt, sondern nur, daß es eine *Ursache* (αἴτιον) für sie gibt[47]. Diese Ursache wird unmittelbar nach ihrer ersten Nennung 28 A 4-6 in die Aspekte Demiurg und Vorbild zerlegt (28 A 6 – B 2), ohne daß dafür eine Begründung gegeben wird. Dadurch entsteht sogar ein leichter Bruch im Gedankengang, der den Leser offenbar aufhorchen lassen und darauf hinweisen soll, daß die Ursache, von der Timaios spricht, mehrere Facetten hat: Sie ist absichtsvoll planende (δημιουργός) und nach einem rationalen Plan (παράδειγμα) verfahrende Ursache (αἴτιον).
Nach all diesen Überlegungen versteht man es besser, daß Platon gleich zu Anfang sagt, schon den Schöpfer und Vater des Alls *zu finden* sei schwierig, und es sei völlig unmöglich, ihn allen Menschen zu verkünden (τὸν μὲν οὖν ποιητὴν καὶ πατέρα τοῦδε τοῦ παντὸς εὑρεῖν τε ἔργον καὶ εὑρόντα εἰς πάντας ἀδύνατον λέγειν, 28 C 3 ff). Er ist in der Tat schwer zu finden, wenn er sich im Zustand der Kosmosordnung gleichsam im göttlichen Vorbild versteckt und erst durch das Hilfsmittel der Kosmogenese wirklich Konturen annimmt[48].

Dies also sind die Schwierigkeiten, die sich einstellen, wenn man annimmt, die Welt sei in einem einmaligen Schöpfungsakt entstanden. Sie alle sind nur dann zu lösen, wenn man zugibt, daß Platon auch den Schöpfungsakt selbst nicht als zeitlich oder einmalig aufgefaßt hat. Wie vor allem das Beispiel des Demiurgen zeigt, hat Platon in der Kosmogenese nur ein Hilfsmittel gesehen, um in dem immer gleichen und daher nur schwer durchschaubaren Geschehen im Kosmos sauber zu unterscheiden, was in dieser Ordnung auf die göttliche und was auf die notwendige Ursache zurückzuführen ist: Der göttlichen Ursache verdankt sie alles Gute (29 E 1 ff), der notwendigen Ursache die Einschränkungen, die der Verwirklichung dieses Guten auferlegt sind (48 A 3; 56 C 5 f; 75 A 7 ff; 77 A 1 f). In der göttlichen Ursache ist der Aspekt des παράδειγμα von dem des δημιουργός zu unterscheiden.

---

47 T. Ebert, "Von der Weltursache zum Weltbaumeister", *Antike und Abendland* 37 (1991) 51 f

48 Die Untergötter des "Timaios", die oft mit dem Demiurgen zusammenzufallen scheinen, können nach diesen Überlegungen nichts anderes sein als 'Ausläufer' des demiurgischen Aspekts des Seienden, die auf unterster Ebene wirken.

Der erstere begründet die Existenz der Dinge (52 D 2 ff), der letztere ihre Ordnung (διακόσμησις, τάξις, 53 A 7 ff; 69 B 2 ff).

Die Argumente, die ich bisher für die Auffassung vorgetragen habe, die Welt sei nach Platons "Timaios" nicht in einem einmaligen Akt entstanden, sind nur die stärksten, die der "Timaios" zu bieten hat, und sie sind m.E. unwiderlegbar. Ist somit eine einmalige Weltentstehung in grauer Vergangenheit undenkbar, so stellt sich nun mit noch größerer Dringlichkeit die Frage, wie der entscheidende Passus 28 B 6 – C 2 zu verstehen ist.

Nimmt man den *Beweisgang* für das Entstehen der Welt 27 D 5 – 28 C 2 ernst, dann wird in ihm nur nachgewiesen, daß die Welt ein γιγνόμενον ist[49]; denn alle *entscheidenden* Verbalausdrücke stehen in diesem Abschnitt im Präsens. Die einzige Ausnahme bildet γέγονεν (28 B 7).—Auf den Ausdruck ἀπ' ἀρχῆς τινος ἀρξάμενος komme ich später zurück.—Man beachte nun, wie die Begründung für dieses γέγονεν wieder auf das Präsens rekurriert: Die Welt ist entstanden, weil sie sichtbar, tastbar und mit einem Körper ausgestattet ist und sich alles dergleichen als γιγνόμενα καὶ γεννητά/γενητά gezeigt hatte.

Man wende nicht ein, wie man es zu tun pflegt, daß der Ausdruck γεννητά/γενητά die Vergangenheit impliziere. Täte er es, dann wäre der Beweisgang nicht einwandfrei. Aber er tut das ebensowenig wie bei den im gleichen Satz verwendeten Verbaladjektiven ὁρατὸς καὶ ἁπτός (28 B 7). Γεννητά/γενητά meint dem Zusammenhang nach nichts anderes, als daß die unter ihm subsumierten Gegenstände in der einen oder anderen Form die Fähigkeit zum γεννᾶσθαι oder γίγνεσθαι haben[50].

---

[49] Dies ist die Auffassung vieler antiker Interpreten; vgl. Baltes, *Weltentstehung* I 86 f. 108 mit Anm. 116; 121 f. 128 f.

[50] Vgl. R. Kühner – F. Blass, *Ausführliche Grammatik der griechischen Sprache. Erster Teil: Elementar- und Formenlehre*, II (Leipzig [1]1892, Hannover 1978) 288 f; E. Bickel, "Die φευκτά der Stoa bei Ausonius", *Rhein. Mus.* 86 (1937) 287 f; E. Schwyzer, *Griechische Grammatik* I (München 1939) 501.

Zu diesem Gebrauch des Verbaladjektivs vgl. περὶ θεῶν *ὁρατῶν καὶ γεννητῶν* (40 D 4); *γεννητόν, πεφορημένον ἀεί, γιγνόμενόν τε* ἔν τινι τόπῳ ... (52 A 5 f). In beiden Fällen ist nicht die Bedeutung "entstanden/geworden" intendiert. Auffällig ist der Gebrauch in 28 B 1 f: οὗ δ' ἂν εἰς γεγονός (sc. βλέπει ὁ δημιουργός), γεννητῷ παραδείγματι προσχρώμενος ... Wenn hier γεγονός und γεννητῷ dasselbe bedeuten, dann ist der Ausdruck tautologisch. Der Vergleich mit 28 A 6 f zeigt jedoch, daß γεννητῷ im Gegensatz zu τὸ κατὰ ταὐτὰ ἔχον zu verstehen ist; dann aber liegt die Bedeutung "dem Werden und Entstehen unterworfen" näher als die Bedeutung "entstanden/geworden". Ambivalent ist schließlich die Ausdrucksweise in 37 D 4, wo mit τῷ γεννητῷ entweder "das entstandene" oder "das dem Entstehen unterworfene (All)" gemeint

Wenn das richtig ist, dann ist auch γέγονεν (28 B 7) nicht im Sinne eines einmaligen Schöpfungsaktes zu verstehen—für diesen hätte man ja auch eher die Form ἐγένετο erwartet. Γέγονεν besagt vielmehr, daß das Werden und Entstehen im Zustand der Vollendung ist: Die Welt ist als eine entstandene, γεγονὼς ἔστιν, wie Platon vom Kosmos selbst sagt (31 B 3)[51].

Daß dies wirklich so zu verstehen ist, legt eine weitere Überlegung nahe: Wenn alles, was sichtbar, tastbar und körperlich ist, in einem einmaligen Akt entstanden ist, dann ist auch das vorkosmische Chaos in dieser Weise entstanden[52], das ebenfalls sichtbar (30 A 3; 52 E 1), tastbar und körperlich ist (vgl. 30 A 3 ff; 52 E 1 ff)[53]. Da das vorkosmische Chaos nach Platon aber offenbar nur γένεσις im Sinne des ständigen γίγνεσθαι ist (52 D 3), folgt daraus, daß auch die γένεσις des Kosmos nur im Sinne des ständigen γίγνεσθαι zu verstehen ist. Ist dem so, dann versteht man auch besser, warum 29 D 7 γένεσις und τὸ πᾶν gleichgesetzt werden (δι' ἥντινα αἰτίαν γένεσιν καὶ τόδε τὸ πᾶν ὁ συνιστὰς συνέστησεν; vgl. E 4): Der Kosmos *ist* γένεσις.

Man wende nicht ein, das vorkosmische Chaos werde zwar als γένεσις bezeichnet, nicht aber wie der Kosmos als γεγονός. Das ist nicht wahr; denn 28 C 5 ff wird die Möglichkeit erwogen, daß der Demiurg die Welt nach einem entstandenen Vorbild (γεγονὸς παράδειγμα) geschaffen hat. Dieses Vorbild kann nur das vorkosmische Chaos sein, in dem schon eine gewisse Ordnung der Spurenelemente herrschte (52 E 5 ff). Nur diese kann mit dem entstandenen Vorbild gemeint sein, denn sonst gab es ja nichts (52 D 2 ff)[54].

Nun könnte man darauf hinweisen, daß Platon ja nicht nur danach fragt, ob der Kosmos entstanden sei oder nicht, sondern danach, ob er immer *war* ohne jegliche ἀρχή oder ob er *geworden sei*, beginnend von einer gewissen ἀρχή. Hier scheint der Gegensatz klar und deutlich zeitlich zu sein. Darauf könnte vor allem das Imperfekt ἦν im Gegensatz zu dem Perfekt γέγονεν hindeuten. Aber

sein kann.

[51] Oder, wie Prokl. In Plat. Tim. I 290,23 ff Diehl es wortreich nachweist, der Kosmos ist ἀεὶ γιγνόμενος ἅμα καὶ γεγενημένος. Vgl. dazu Baltes, *Weltentstehung* II 52 ff.

[52] Vgl. Prokl. In Plat. Tim. I 283,31 ff Diehl und dazu Baltes, *Weltentstehung* II 30 ff; auch Zeller II 1, 793.

[53] Beides ist Voraussetzung für das 30 A 3 ff und 52 E 1 ff geschilderte vorkosmische Geschehen; vgl. Prokl. In Plat. Tim. I 387,10 ff Diehl.

[54] Vgl. Mansfeld, "Rez. Scheffel, *Kosmologie*" 171.

das Imperfekt ist überhaupt seltsam; denn nach dem Argumentationszusammenhang erwartet man ein ἔστιν: *Ist* der Kosmos immer oder ist er geworden? Also ist das Imperfekt nur kolloquial zu verstehen wie auch andere Imperfekte im "Timaios" (29 E 1; 37 D 3). Ist dies richtig, dann lautet der Gegensatz: Ist die Welt immer seiend oder das Ergebnis eines Entstehungsprozesses? Über den Beginn des Entstehungsprozesses ist damit noch nichts gesagt, und auch die zweifache Betonung der ἀρχή weist nicht unbedingt in diese Richtung. Denn schon in der Antike hat man auf den auffälligen Gegensatz ἀρχὴν ἔχων οὐδεμίαν—ἀπ' ἀρχῆς τινος ἀρξάμενος aufmerksam gemacht[55]. Es scheint, daß Platon mit diesen Formulierungen darauf hinweisen wollte, daß der Begriff ἀρχή zu den vieldeutigen Begriffen (πολλαχῶς λεγόμενα) gehört und er ἀρχή nur in einem ganz bestimmten Sinne verwendet. Da die Methode der begrifflichen Differenzierung in Platons Akademie gepflegt wurde[56], wußte jeder Platonschüler, daß auch der Begriff ἀρχή viele Bedeutungen hat und daß Platon hier nur auf eine bestimmte ἀρχή hinauswill (ἀρχή τις), ohne allerdings klar anzugeben, welche ἀρχή er wirklich im Sinne hat. Aber immerhin war der Schüler davor gewarnt, ἀρχή hier einfach in der Alltagsbedeutung zu nehmen.

Aber weist nun nicht gerade das ἀρξάμενος ganz entschieden in die Richtung der Alltagsbedeutung? Hier haben wir doch den erwarteten Aorist. Aber was für einen Aorist? Keinen Indikativ, der mit dem Augment als Vergangenheitszeichen *allein* mit Sicherheit das einmalige vergangene Ereignis hätte ausdrücken können. Hätte Platon geschrieben: ἤρξατο, so wäre klar gewesen, daß er den einmaligen Akt in der Vergangenheit gemeint hätte; ebenso wenn er formuliert hätte: ἐγένετο ἀπ' ἀρχῆς τινος ἀρξάμενος; dann nämlich hätte das voraufgehende Tempus auch auf das Partizip abgefärbt. Zusammen mit dem Perfekt γέγονεν besagt das Partizip ἀρξάμενος nicht mehr, als daß eine ἀρχή dem jetzigen Zustand voraufgeht, d.h. zugrunde liegt.

Auch der Hinweis auf 28 C 2 f: τῷ δ' αὖ γενομένῳ φαμὲν ὑπ' αἰτίου τινὸς ἀνάγκην εἶναι γενέσθαι hilft nicht wirklich weiter; denn auch hier liegen keine finiten Verbformen vor, und strenggenommen besagt dieser Satz nicht mehr als: "wenn er nun aber entsteht,

---

55 Prokl. In Plat. Tim. I 279,30 ff; 285,21 ff und Baltes, *Weltentstehung* I 143 ff

56 Vgl. Arist. Met. Δ 1/2; vgl. z.B. auch E. Heitsch, "Argumentation und Psychagogie", *Philologus* 138 (1994) 219 ff.

dann entsteht er, wie wir gesagt haben, notwendigerweise durch eine Ursache". Da der Ausdruck τῷ ... γενομένῳ das τὸ γιγνόμενον von 28 A 4 aufnimmt, weist die Aussage nicht auf einen einmaligen Akt, sondern auf den speziellen Fall hin[57].

Damit ist klar, daß der Ausdruck γέγονεν (28 B 7) nicht im Sinne eines zeitlichen oder einmaligen Aktes verstanden werden darf. Was also ist mit ihm gemeint? Er will besagen, daß die Welt Ergebnis eines Entstehungsprozesses ist, der von einer Ursache abhängt, die sich zerlegen läßt in einen aktiv schaffenden, einen ordnenden und einen paradigmatischen Aspekt. Diese Ursache ist die ἀρχή seines Entstehens. 'Αρχή bezeichnet also nicht den zeitlichen Beginn des Entstehungsprozesses—eine solche Annahme würde in ausweglose Schwierigkeiten führen, wie wir gesehen haben—vielmehr bezeichnet es das Woher des Entstehens im ursächlichen oder ontologischen Sinne.

Warum aber ist Platon im "Timaios" so änigmatisch? Warum sagt er nicht frei heraus, was er denkt? Möchte er seine Leser hinters Licht führen? Gewiß nicht. Bevor ich eine Antwort zu geben versuche, möchte ich auf folgende auffällige Erscheinungen hinweisen: Platon läßt seinen Hauptunterredner Timaios immer wieder darauf hinweisen,

1. daß die Darstellung des Gemeinten schwierig sei (27 D 3 f; 28 C 3 ff; 48 C 2 ff);
2. daß es von seiner Seite eine große Anstrengung erfordere, seine Gedanken adäquat zum Ausdruck zu bringen (27 D 3 f);
3. daß es unmöglich sei, die Darstellung vollkommen widerspruchsfrei zu halten (29 C 4 ff)[58], ja, daß sie nicht einmal frei von Zufällen sei (34 C 2 f);
4. daß die Mitunterredner des Timaios zwar hochgebildete Leute sind[59]

---

[57] Auffällig ist, daß im Folgenden (28 C 5 – 29 B 1) keine Aoriste vorkommen, sondern nur Imperfekte und Perfekte, die die Dauer und den Endzustand der Handlung festhalten und nicht auf die Einmaligkeit deuten. Aoriste begegnen erst wieder ab 29 D 7 ff, d.h. vom Beginn des *Schöpfungsmythos* an. Wie jede Erzählung muß auch dieser Mythos selbstverständlich auf weite Strecken im Aorist erzählt werden.

[58] Dazu gehört etwa, daß Timaios sich gelegentlich unscharfer kolloquialer Ausdrucksweise bedient, so beispielsweise, wenn er 28 B 6 statt πότερον ἔστιν ἀεί von πότερον ἦν ἀεί spricht; desgleichen ist das Imperfekt in 29 E 1 und 37 D 3 unscharf gebraucht (vgl. Prokl. In Plat. Tim. I 278,29 ff Diehl und Baltes, *Weltentstehung* I 133 f).

[59] Der "Timaios" ist der einzige Dialog Platons, in dem die Unterredner einigermaßen gleichrangig sind (vgl. Tim. 19 E 8 ff; T. Szlezàk, "Gespräche unter Ungleichen. Zur Struktur und Zielsetzung der platonischen Dialoge", *Antike und Abendland* 34 (1988) 99-116), und dennoch betont Timaios immer

und ein gehöriges Vorwissen besitzen (53 B 7 ff), Timaios aber trotzdem auf sie Rücksicht nehmen muß (27 D 2), ja, daß auch ihnen 'die letzten Dinge' in der gegenwärtigen Form nicht mitgeteilt werden können (48 C 2 ff); denn diese könnten nur Götterlieblinge erfahren, die die Zuhörer trotz ihrer Bildung offensichtlich nicht oder zumindest nicht alle sind (53 D 6 f).

Ja, nicht nur 'die letzten Dinge' können ihnen nicht mitgeteilt werden; wird doch an zahlreichen Stellen auf eine weitere Präzisierung auch auf niedrigerer Ebene ausdrücklich verzichtet (38 B 3 ff; D 6 ff; 40 C 2 ff; 59 C 5 ff; 86 B 8 f; 89 D 7 ff; vgl. 68 B 6 ff). Ferner wird immer wieder auf die Schwäche der menschlichen Erkenntnis hingewiesen, die eine exakte Darlegung unmöglich macht (29 C 8 f; 68 D 2 ff; 72 D 5 ff), und gelegentlich wird die Vorläufigkeit der getroffenen Entscheidung herausgestellt (54 A 7 ff; 55 D 4 ff).

So nachdrücklich wie in keinem anderen Dialog streicht also Platon immer wieder heraus, daß die Sachverhalte, die darzustellen er sich anschickt, nicht so einfach sind, wie sie erscheinen. Besonders auffällig ist sein Hinweis, daß der Demiurg schwer zu finden sei und daß es, wenn man ihn gefunden habe, unmöglich sei, ihn allen Menschen zu verkünden (28 C 3 f). Das ist vordergründig doch eine wirklich seltsame Aussage; denn verglichen mit anderen Gegenständen—dem idealen Vorbild, der Seele, der χώρα, der Zeit—gehört der Demiurg zu den Größen des "Timaios", die man am ehesten zu verstehen glaubt. Und doch sagt Platon, er sei schwer zu finden und schwer mitzuteilen. Ist das nicht ein deutlicher Hinweis darauf, daß Platon seine Darstellung nicht *prima facie* verstanden wissen will? Wie sich das Wesen des Demiurgen erst dem langen Nachdenken über die Aussagen des "Timaios" erschließt, ebenso steht es mit dem idealen Vorbild, ebenso mit der Zeit, ebenso mit dem vorkosmischen Chaos, ja, mit allem. Platon fordert offenbar den *mitdenkenden* Leser, der nicht beim vordergründigen Wortlaut hängenbleibt, sondern über diesen hinaus zu dem vordringt, was Timaios eigentlich meint (ᾗ διανοοῦμαι, 27 D 3).

Daß Platon so verfährt, hat einen besonderen Grund: Die Frage danach, ob die Welt entstanden sei oder nicht, war in seiner Schule, der Akademie, offenbar heftig umstritten. In der Topik nennt Aristoteles zweimal als Beispiel für ein φυσικὸν πρόβλημα

wieder die Schwierigkeiten, die sich einem angemessenen Verständnis des Gesagten entgegenstellen.

die Frage, πότερον ὁ κόσμος ἀίδιος ἢ οὔ (A 11 104 b 8; A 14 105 b 24 f). Diese Frage hatte in der Akademie offenbar dieselbe Aktualität wie die, πότερον ἡ ἡδονὴ αἱρετὸν ἢ οὔ, die Aristoteles im gleichen Zusammenhang anführt (A 11 104 b 7). In De caelo widmet Aristoteles dem Problem der Weltentstehung drei ganze Kapitel (I 10-12), in welchen er sich auch mit der Ansicht seiner Mitschüler auseinandersetzt, die Welt sei nach Platons Lehre nicht entstanden. Platon selbst kennt die Diskussion, wie einzelne Äußerungen in seinen Dialogen zeigen[60], und er nimmt selbst Stellung dazu, nicht nur im "Timaios", sondern auch im "Politikos", doch tut er es in *beiden* Dialogen änigmatisch. Warum?

Offenbar will er durch beide Dialoge zu dieser Frage Stellung beziehen, aber nicht in der Weise eines αὐτὸς ἔφα, das aufgrund des großen Ansehens, das Platon im Kreise seiner Schüler genoß[61], die Diskussion, wenn nicht beendet, so doch gefährdet hätte. Was Platon mit seinem "Timaios", seinem "Politikos", ja mit all seinen Dialogen wollte, war: Probleme zu benennen oder aufzugreifen[62], den Leser zum Mitdenken und Nachdenken anzuregen und Hinweise zu geben, wo nach seiner Meinung die Lösung zu suchen sei. Eben dies tut er im "Timaios".

Daß Aristoteles ihn anders verstanden hat als Speusipp, Xenokrates und Herakleides Pontikos, hat Platon nicht beunruhigt; auf diese Weise blieb die Frage als ein Problem im Raum, kam das Nachdenken darüber nicht vorzeitig zur Ruhe. Ja, nicht nur in der Alten Akademie kam diese Frage nicht mehr zur Ruhe, sondern die ganze Antike, das Mittelalter und die Neuzeit hindurch bis auf unsere Tage, wie wir anfangs gesagt haben. Ich glaube, daß eben dies Platons Anliegen war: das Problem zu formulieren, zum Nachdenken darüber anzuleiten und Wegweisungen für eine mögliche Lösung zu bieten. Jeder sollte seine *eigene* Lösung finden—ganz dem Wort Goethes entsprechend: "Was du ererbt von deinen Vätern hast, erwirb es, um es zu besitzen!"

Westfälische Wilhelms-Universität, Münster

---

60 Plat. Staat 546 A 2: γενομένῳ παντὶ φθορά ἐστιν (vgl. Tim. 41 A 8: τὸ μὲν οὖν δὴ δεθὲν πᾶν λυτόν); Phaidr. 245 D 3 f: ἐπειδὴ δὲ ἀγένητόν ἐστιν, καὶ ἀδιάφθορον αὐτὸ ἀνάγκη εἶναι; vgl. Nomoi 781 E f; Epin. 981 E f; Proklos bei Ioh. Philoponos, De aet. mundi XVII S.589,6 ff Rabe.

61 Zu Platons Ansehen in der Akademie vgl. M. Baltes, "Plato's School, the Academy", *Hermathena* 155 (1993) 8 f. 18.

62 Vgl. Philodemi Academicorum historia Y 2 ff S.126 Dorandi = S.152 Gaiser.

PART THREE

THE ACADEMY AND THE PERIPATOS

SPEUSIPPUS ON PLEASURE

John Dillon[1]

The task of rescuing from oblivion, and properly evaluating, the philosophical contributions of Plato's nephew and successor as head of the Academy, Speusippus, is one that is by no means over yet. Aristotle, whether through pique or genuine conviction, gives the distinct impression of not taking him seriously,[2] and modern scholars have in general been content to follow his lead.

I have already ventured to come to the defence of his metaphysics,[3] and I am glad to observe that other scholars are coming to share my view that he is a thinker to be taken seriously.[4] What I wish to come to the defence of on the present occasion is a basic principle of his ethics, intimated to us in a text of Clement of Alexandria,[5] namely the doctrine that happiness, or well-being (εὐδαιμονία), for man consists in 'freedom from disturbance' (ἀοχλησία),[6] and that pain and pleasure are evils in an equal

[1] This essay I offer, with some apprehension, to a great master in the art of interpreting doxographic materials. With Speusippus all, sadly, is dependent on doxographic reports (in the broader sense), many of them hostile.

[2] Good examples of this attitude would be *Metaph.* Z 2. 1028b21ff. (on his first principles); *PA* I 2, 642b5ff. (on his logic); and *EN* VII 14, 1153b1ff. (on his ethical theory).

[3] 'Speusippus in Iamblichus', *Phronesis* 29 (1984) 325-32. I was in fact only developing insights first contributed by Philip Merlan in his stimulating work *From Platonism to Neoplatonism* (The Hague 1954, 1960², 1968³), and criticizing what seemed to me the excessive scepticism of Leonardo Tarán in his otherwise very valuable edition of the fragments of Speusippus, *Speusippus of Athens* (Leiden 1983). An important recent contribution both to our understanding of Speusippus and of the ancient interpretation of Plato's *Parmenides* is contained in an article of Jens Halfwassen, 'Speusipp und die metaphysische Deutung von Platons *Parmenides*', in *Hen kai Plêthos*, Festschrift Karl Bormann, edd. L. Hagemann & R. Glei (Würzburg 1993).

[4] Notably Margherita Isnardi Parente and (despite what seems to me to be his perversity on various points) Leonardo Tarán in their respective collections of the fragments; and R.M. Dancy, particularly in 'Ancient Non-Beings: Speusippus and Others', *Ancient Philosophy* 9 (1989) 207-43, repr. in *Two Studies in the Early Academy* (Albany 1991).

[5] *Str.* 2.133.4 = Fr 77 Tarán.

[6] This term, if Clement can be trusted, would seem to have been invented by him. It is attested later for Epicurus and his followers, which is slightly bothersome, but it would be odd of Clement to employ this precise term in

degree, extending away from this 'mean' in an indefinite series of gradations in either direction, so to speak.

It will be no harm, perhaps, to quote Clement's testimony in full, since we have little enough apart from this to go on in reconstructing Speusippus' position.

> Σπεύσιππός τε ὁ Πλάτωνος ἀδελφιδοῦς τὴν εὐδαιμονίαν φησὶν ἕξιν εἶναι τελείαν ἐν τοῖς κατὰ φύσιν ἔχουσιν ἢ ἕξιν ἀγαθῶν, ἧς δὴ καταστάσεως ἅπαντας μὲν ἀνθρώπους ὄρεξιν ἔχειν, στοχάζεσθαι δὲ τοὺς ἀγαθοὺς τῆς ἀοχλησίας. εἶεν δ' αἱ ἀρεταὶ τῆς εὐδαιμονίας ἀπεργαστικαί.
>
> Speusippus, the nephew of Plato, declares that happiness is a perfect state in the area of what is natural,[7] or the state of (possession of)[8] goods, which is a state for which all men have a (natural) impulse, while the good aim at freedom from disturbance. It would be the virtues that are creative of happiness.

We see here a very summary (but, we hope, basically accurate) sketch of Speusippus' doctrine. He recognises that most men strive for happiness, but seems to introduce as a qualification of this that the good aim at ἀοχλησία. There must be some ellipse, though, here, I think, doubtless as the result of Clement's compression of his source. The state (κατάστασις) for which all men have ὄρεξις may be εὐδαιμονία, but Speusippus may well have gone on to say that most men believe, foolishly, that this lies in the acquisition and enjoyment of pleasure, while only the wise understand that it really resides in attaining freedom from disturbance. In that case, Speusippus would grant this much to the proponents of hedonism (such as Aristippus, founder of the Cyrenaic School, and his own colleague Eudoxus of Cnidos), that pleasure is indeed a natural object of striving for all living creatures, but he would deny that that proves what it is claimed to prove: that pleasure is the good for man. Instead, Speusippus wishes to maintain that for man, as a

---

characterizing Speusippus' doctrine, if it were known to be an Epicurean term, unless it was in fact Speusippus' coinage.

[7] In view of the problem arising below as to what sort of φύσις the δυσχερεῖς, or 'cranky ones', of *Phlb.* 44a were 'experts' (δεινοί) in, we may note the ambiguity of the word here. It could refer either to human nature or to the 'nature of things'.

[8] This represents a rather waffling attempt to render what seems to be a variation between the meanings of the two uses of ἕξις here. It seems almost incredible that Clement would use ἕξις in two different senses, 'state' and 'possession', in the space of one line, but the ambiguity may be more apparent in English than in Greek.

rational being, pleasure as an end must be transcended, as a consequence of dialectic, and supplanted by a rational striving for ἀοχλησία.

Speusippus appears to have used a number of arguments to support his position (which seems to have been developed in opposition to that of his colleague Eudoxus, who maintained that pleasure was the only good, as being the natural object of appetition),[9] one of which in particular comes in for trenchant criticism from Aristotle,[10] but this does not go to the core of his doctrine, which is not addressed by Aristotle—not unnaturally, since his purpose is primarily polemical. It is only, I would maintain, if one considers Speusippus' ethics against the background of his metaphysics, that its inner logic becomes apparent.[11]

---

9 It seems fairly clear to me that Philebus, in Plato's *Philebus,* is intended substantially to represent Eudoxus, and that Eudoxus is being gently teased throughout the dialogue (the reference at the end, 67B, to drawing deductions from the behaviour of animals, is particularly pointed). We do not, I think, have a title for any work he composed on this subject, and it is possible that he advanced his views merely orally, though we do not need to assume that. (By saying that Philebus is intended 'substantially' to represent Eudoxus, by the way, I do not wish to imply that Philebus is intended as a *portrait* of Eudoxus, nor that his position is a full or fair representation of that of Eudoxus. Philebus is rather crass person, as Eudoxus was not, and his hedonism is really a sort of 'lowest common denominator' of the overall hedonist position, which does not involve the use of certain arguments which we know to be distinctive of Eudoxus. All I wish to claim is that it is Eudoxus' revival of the hedonist position within the Academy—and Speusippus' attempts to counter him—that has provoked Plato to compose this dialogue.)

As for Speusippus, his doctrine was no doubt set out primarily in his treatise *On Pleasure,* perhaps in response to Eudoxus' exposition of his doctrine; but his dialogue *Aristippus* very probably also dealt with the same theme, this time featuring Aristippus, follower of Socrates and founder of the Cyrenaic school, and a notable propounder of hedonism, but no doubt also aimed primarily at Eudoxus. I see the *Philebus* as Plato's ironic commentary and judgement on this ongoing dispute between two of his most distinguished followers. There is no reason to assume, after all, that the views of either of these men were published only after Plato's death, or even later than the composition of the *Philebus*—a point which is of some importance to my argument. After all, by the generally agreed date of the *Philebus* (c. 355 BC), Speusippus was already in his fifties (he is generally agreed to have been born c. 410-8 BC), and Eudoxus (born c. 390) probably already dead, in his mid-thirties.

10 At *EN* VII 14, 1153b1-7 (= Fr. 80 Tarán), and X 2, 1173a5-28 (= Fr. 81 Tarán).

11 It is interesting, in this connection, that one of the few positive things reported by Diogenes Laertius (on the authority of an unknown Diodorus, in Book I of his *Memoirs*) in his very wretched 'life' of Speusippus (IV 2) is that he 'was the first to discern the common element in all subjects of study (ἐν τοῖς μαθήμασι ἐθεάσατο τὸ κοινόν), and tried to coordinate (συνῳκείωσε)

I hope that it may now be taken as reasonably certain that ch. 4 of Iamblichus' *De Communi Mathematica Scientia* preserves (by one means or another, at either first or second hand) a conspectus of Speusippus' metaphysical position.[12] There we find a metaphysical scheme involving a pair of principles, One, or Unity, and Multiplicity, very much on the lines of those attributed to Plato in his oral teaching[13] (and which are in effect present in the *Philebus* in the guise of Limit and the Unlimited). It is by the action of Unity on Multiplicity that every level of being in the universe is generated.

It is not, fortunately, necessary to our purpose on this occasion to go through all the details of this multi-level process (which is certainly complex, though not, I think, deserving of the satirical treatment which Aristotle gives it in *Metaph.* Λ 10). All I want to focus on is what seems to me to be Speusippus' basic intuition, reflected in the *Philebus,* that, on the human level, *aretê* consists in the imposition of *peras,* 'limitedness', on the indefiniteness of human emotions.

What I conceive to be his view is actually well expressed, much later and on the basis of a more elaborate theory of the virtues,[14] by Plotinus in *Ennead* I 2.2.15-18, as follows:[15]

> The virtues do genuinely set us in order and make us better by giving limit and measure to our desires, and putting measure into all our experience; and they abolish false opinions, by what is altogether better and by the fact of limitation, and by the exclusion of the unlimited and indefinite and the existence of the measured; and they are themselves limited and clearly defined' (trans. Armstrong).

---

them as far as possible with one another.' Diodorus is, as I say, otherwise unknown, but the fact that he is writing 'memoirs' (ἀπομνημονεύματα), in which Speusippus features in Book I, might indicate that he was a hanger-on of the Old Academy, and thus not a bad source.

[12] On this see my article 'Speusippus in Iamblichus' (above, n. 1) 325-32, in which I endeavour to defend Philip Merlan's hypothesis (in *From Platonism to Neoplatonism,* ch V) against the scepticism of Leonardo Tarán, *op. cit.* pp. 86-107.

[13] Cf. Ar. *Metaph.* A 6.

[14] Plotinus is speaking here of the 'civic' (πολιτικαί), as opposed to the 'cathartic' or 'purificatory' virtues, which is a distinction unknown to Speusippus. For our purposes, for 'civic' virtue one may understand virtue in general.

[15] Αἱ ... ἀρεταί... κατακοσμοῦσι μὲν ὄντως καὶ ἀμείνους ποιοῦσιν ὁρίζουσαι καὶ μετροῦσαι τὰς ἐπιθυμίας καὶ ὅλως τὰ πάθη μετροῦσαι καὶ ψευδεῖς δόξας ἀφαιροῦσαι τῷ ὅλως ἀμείνονι καὶ τῷ ὡρίσθαι καὶ τῶν ἀμέτρων καὶ ἀορίστων ἔξω εἶναι καὶ τὸ μεμετρημένον, καὶ αὐταὶ ὁρισθεῖσαι.

The repetition of various verbal and nominal forms of the concepts *horos* and *metron* in this passage is quite remarkable. One does not need to postulate any direct influence from Speusippus on Plotinus here, of course. He is merely reflecting a deeply-ingrained Platonist doctrine. I pick it out merely because I find it a particularly clear expression of what I conceive Speusippus' position to have been.

Speusippus, to reiterate, is criticized by Aristotle[16] for presenting pleasure as just as much of an evil as pain, in his argument that, because pleasure is the opposite of pain, it does not follow that if one of them—pain—is an evil, the other is a good, since both may be evils, opposed to some third thing, which is a good—even as the greater may be opposed both to the less and to equal. Aristotle does not object to this argument as such—he can hardly do that, since it is integral to his own argument in favour of virtue as a mean between extremes—but tries to pick holes in it on the specific ground that, if something is an evil, it is to be avoided (φευκτόν), and men do not in fact seek to avoid pleasure, while they do seek to avoid pain.

This is not, however, an argument which Speusippus needs to accept. His position could well be that pleasure is indeed a thing that is to be avoided, even though men do not in fact generally seek to avoid it. What men are seeking is in fact happiness (εὐδαιμονία)[17], and they wrongly imagine this to be attainable through pleasure, or even to consist in pleasure. What all too few of them realise, but which all *should* realise, is that the state which constitutes true happiness is that in which the soul has reached the perfect balance between pleasure and pain, which is attained by the scientific application of *peras* to the unlimited spectrum of more and less that runs from extreme pain to extreme pleasure, either condition constituting a grave disturbance of the organism, and of the soul which presides over it. It is this median state which Speusippus denominates 'freedom from disturbance' (ἀοχλησία), and which Epicurus later termed 'katastematic pleasure', and the Stoics χαρά, 'joy'.[18]

---

16 *EN* VII 13 1153b1-7 (= Fr. 80 Tarán); *EN* X 2 1173a5-28 (= Fr. 81 Tarán).

17 That Speusippus held this (fairly obvious) fact to be the case is attested by the doxographic report of Clement (Fr. 77 Tarán), where he declares that *eudaimonia* is a state for which all men strive (ἧς δὴ καταστάσεως ἅπαντας μὲν ἀνθρώπους ὄρεξιν ἔχειν).

18 For the Stoic conception of χαρά (as εὔλογος ἔπαρσις) see D.L. 7.116, =

To a certain cxtent, this whole argument may seem to turn on a semantic quibble as to what constitutes ἡδονή, but this may not after all be the case. Speusippus would not wish to deny, I think, that his state of ἀοχλησία is in some sense pleasant, but his objection to 'pleasure' in its usual connotation in Greek is that it is essentially a *process*, and an open-ended, disorderly one at that, while what he is aiming at, and recommending, is a *steady state*. The Stoics later developed a term for this to rival ἡδονή, to wit χαρά, but Speusippus did not have this at his disposal, or rather did not get round to inventing it.[19] Instead, he fastened on this rather negative-sounding term for his ideal state—without, however, I am sure, intending it to be taken as something merely negative.

And this brings me to the main topic of this discourse, the identity of 'the enemies of Philebus' in *Phlb.* 44A-D. A great many scholars before this, of course, have taken up positions on this question, many in favour of the identification with Speusippus, notably Döring,[20] Wilamowitz,[21] Philippson,[22] Burnet,[23] Taylor,[24] Friedländer,[25] Gauthier & Jolif,[26] Düring,[27] Krämer,[28] and most recently Malcolm Schofield.[29] That is a pretty impressive line-up, I think it would be generally agreed, but Leonardo Tarán, in his collection of the fragments of Speusippus (pp. 78-85), nothing daunted, proposes to dismiss the identification as based on misunderstandings and inadequate evidence. Tarán is not alone in his scepticism,[30] of course, but he is the most recent negative voice, and

---

SVF 3.431.

[19] But see below, n. 35, on the suspicious concentration of uses of χαίρειν in *Phlb.* 43-4.

[20] 'Eudoxos von Knidos, Speusippos, und der Dialog *Philebos', Vierteljahrschrift für wiss. Philos. und Soziol.* 27 (1903) 113-29 (esp. 125-7).

[21] *Platon* (Berlin, 1919) 2.272-3.

[22] 'Akademische Verhandlungen über die Lustlehre', *Hermes* 60 (1925) 444-81, esp. 452-3 & 470-4.

[23] *Greek Philosophy, I: Thales to Plato* (London 1914) 324f.

[24] *Plato, The Man and his Work* (London 1937⁴) 409-10, 423 with n. 1, 434-5; *A Commentary on Plato's Timaeus* (Oxford 1928) 455-6.

[25] *Plato* vol. 3: *The Dialogues, Second and Third Periods* (Princeton 1969) 339 & 540, n. 61.

[26] *L'Ethique à Nicomaque* (Louvain-Paris 1970²) 2.2.777, 788, 801.

[27] *Aristoteles. Darstellung und Interpretation seines Denkens* (Heidelberg 1966) 457, n. 157.

[28] *Platonismus und hellenistische Philosophie* (Berlin 1971) 205-9, with n. 88.

[29] 'Who were οἱ δυσχερεῖς in Plato, *Philebus* 44Aff.?', *Museum Helveticum* 28 (1971) 2-20 and 181.

[30] August Diès, in his Budé edition (pp. LVII-LXII) also rejects it, for one, but for reasons which Tarán rightly dismisses ('not consistent with what we

a powerful one, and it is he with whom I propose to deal here. He begins with what seems to me to be a misconception of his own:

> Because of his extreme anti-hedonism, several scholars have ascribed to Speusippus the doctrine espoused by Philebus' enemies in Plato's homonymous dialogue (44B-D), according to which pleasure is merely the cessation of pain. This conception of pleasure as *something purely negative* (my italics) can hardly have been part of Speusippus' doctrine, however, since for him the neutral state between pleasure and pain coincides with the good. This neutral state he must have identified with the freedom from disturbance (ἀοχλησία) which for him is the necessary condition of virtue and happiness. Hence, according to Speusippus the virtuous man must free himself from both pain and pleasure; and, if pleasure were nothing but the cessation of pain, he would not have considered it an evil, nor would he have thought that the virtuous man must avoid it as such.

It seems to me that Tarán's mistake here is to take Plato too literally, even as he frequently seems to me to take Aristotle too literally in his attacks on Speusippus[31]. There is certainly nothing *negative* about Speusippus' doctrine on pleasure, but that does not mean that his uncle's satirical presentation of it might not seek to present it as negative—even as he is doubtless distorting in various ways the hedonistic arguments of Eudoxus.

The dispute between Speusippus and Plato, after all, can be viewed as at least partly a semantic one. The mere cessation of

---

know of Speusippus' character from the sources'). Hackforth too (*Plato's Examination of Pleasure,* Cambridge 1945, pp. 87-8) finds it impossible to reconcile the position of the δυσχερεῖς with what he feels he knows of Speusippus' doctrine, and opts cautiously for Grote's suggestion that they were 'Pythagorizing friends' of Plato. But, as I shall argue, he is wrong to make an absolute contrast between the assertion of the δυσχερεῖς that pleasures are nothing but escapes from pain and the belief of Speusippus that pleasure is real, but an evil.

31 As a notable instance of this one might take his interpretation of Aristotle's criticism of Speusippus at *Metaph.* N 4, 1092a11-17 (= Fr. 43 Tarán), where Aristotle is drawing as a polemical conclusion of Speusippus' position that his first principle 'would not even be any sort of being (ὥστε μηδὲ ὄν τι εἶναι τὸ ἕν αὐτό)'. Even if, as Tarán asserts (and I do not agree), the ὥστε with infinitive construction implies that Speusippus himself did *not* draw this conclusion, that would not in itself guarantee that that was indeed the case. See my discussion in 'Speusippus in Iamblichus' (above, n. 3). Another example is his treatment of Theophrastus' polemical criticism of Speusippus (*Metaph.* 11a18-26 = Fr. 83 Tarán) for limiting the good in the universe to a little patch in the middle, with vast stretches of evil on either side of it, which is a malicious conflation of his doctrine that 'good' only arises at the level of soul, the One not properly being describable as 'good' (see below), with his ethical doctrine of the good lying between the twin evils of pain and pleasure. Tarán takes this far too seriously (*op. cit.* (n. 3) 444-9).

pain could, after all, be presented as a type of pleasure; but it need not be, and Speusippus chose not to present it as such. He wishes to reserve the term 'pleasure' to describe one of the equally reprehensible extremes which flank his ideal state, whereas Plato, it would seem, wishes to extend the notion of 'pleasure' to take in also the state which Speusippus sees as transcending both pleasure and pain, and even to give it the title of 'true' or 'pure' pleasure. This would not be the only area, we may note, in which Speusippus ventures to oppose what he feels to be a looseness in terminology on his uncle's part. On the important question of whether goodness can properly be predicated of the first principle, he is at odds with him (at least if we may take into evidence the survey of metaphysical doctrine preserved in Iamblichus' *De comm. math. sc.* ch. 4, as I contend we may). There (p. 16, 10-14 Festa) he declares: 'The One should not be called either fine or good, by virtue of the fact that it is superior to both fineness and goodness; for it is only as nature proceeds further from the first principles that, first, the fine makes its appearance, and secondly, and at a level of elements which are at a yet further remove, the good.'

Now Plato could argue that he is only calling the first principle the Good in the sense of being the ultimate object of all striving, but such terminology could nonetheless be criticized as involving misleading connotations—and in particular as tending to an improper characterization of the indefinite dyadic principle opposed to the One as 'evil'. Whether this somewhat impertinent correction of the Master was aired before or only after his death we have no means of knowing, but there is no reason to assume that Speusippus did not advance it while Plato was still alive. At any rate, this seems to be the line he is taking on the question of whether the perfectly balanced intermediate state which he postulates between pleasure and pain may itself properly be described as pleasure. He plainly feels that such a characterization would be seriously misleading, and prefers to reserve the term ἡδονή for those unlimited and mobile areas on the spectrum stretching out on the opposite side of his ideal state to painful ones.

On the other hand, he was left with certain terminological problems. It is unfortunate that Speusippus felt constrained to use a negative term to describe his ideal state, instead of, say, something like the later Stoic χαρά, but that does not mean that he intends anything negative by it. Indeed, he undoubtedly wished to claim that this state was productive of profound satisfaction, not to say joy. He may, however, for want of a better adjective, have been constrained to describe it as ἡδύ, 'pleasant', though denying that it involved any form of ἡδονή, and this could have given his uncle the chance to stick the knife in.[32]

Let us look now closely at the crucial passage of the *Philebus,* and see if we can divine just what sort of position is being criticized. We may begin at 43c. Socrates has just secured Protarchus' agreement that not all changes in our constitution produce pleasure or pain, but only fairly considerable ones. He continues (43c8–d10):[33]

> *Socr.:* In that case, the form of life I mentioned just now would become a possibility again.
> *Prot.:* What one is that?
> *Socr.:* The one we said would be without distress or enjoyment (ἀλυπός τε και ἄνευ χαρμονῶν).
> *Prot.:* Certainly it would.
> *Socr.:* To sum up, then, let us posit three forms of life, one of pleasure, one of distress, and one of neither. What would you say on the subject?
> *Prot.:* Just what you have said, that there are these three lives.
> *Socr.:* Now not being in distress would hardly be the same as enjoying oneself (χαίρειν), would it?
> *Prot.:* Of course not.
> *Socr.:* So when you hear people say that the pleasantest thing (ἥδιστον πάντων) is to live all one's life free from distress, what do you think they are saying?
> *Prot.:* They seem to be saying that not being in distress is pleasant (ἡδύ).

Let us pause here for a moment. Somebody, or some class of person, is being accused of claiming that the life without pain is the most pleasant (ἡδύ) of all.[34] If this is Speusippus, then one would

---

32 An interesting reflection of how difficult it is to avoid using parts of ἡδύς when one is in need of a positive value word may be seen at *Phlb.* 66a (where, indeed, Plato may be making some linguistic play with this fact, as is suggested by Diès, *op. cit.* Intro. p. LXXXIX).

33 I borrow here the translation of J.C.B. Gosling, *Plato, Philebus* (Oxford, 1975).

34 This, of course, is not the first time that this argument has come up. In Book IX of the *Republic* (583c-585a), Plato criticizes those who postulate that pleasure consists essentially in cessation of pain (παῦλα λύπης, λύπης ἀπαλλαγή), whereas that is like thinking you have reached the top of a mountain, say, when you have in fact only struggled up from the bottom as far as the mid-point. But the opponents here sound more like hedonists of some sort than anyone maintaining Speusippus' position, unless he is being seriously

like to think that he is being deliberately misrepresented; otherwise, he is being notably careless in his language. Speusippus does, admittedly, have a problem, as I have suggested above. He needs some positive value word to characterize his ideal psychic state, but he must be wary of employing words of the same root as ἡδονή for that purpose. The fact, however, that Plato also uses χαίρειν repeatedly[35] in this passage to describe this state might indicate that this was in fact the preferred term of the supporters of this position, and that the Stoics were actually anticipated in their technical use of this term. The difficulty here is, however, that there is no obvious adjective from χαρά available to characterize the preferred state,[36] and this might have led Speusippus to fall back incautiously on ἡδύ, which would allow Plato to win a terminological argument against him.

Let us continue, however (43e1–44b3):

> *Socr.:* Take any three things now, say one gold, one silver, one neither, just to have fine names.
> *Prot.:* All right.
> *Socr.:* Could the one that is neither possibly become either gold or silver?
> *Prot.:* How on earth could it?
> *Socr.:* Similarly, it would be a mistake for anyone to believe and therefore to say that the midway life was either pleasant (ἡδύς) or distressing; at least if we are to be strict.
> *Prot.:* How could it be?
> *Socr.:* Yet we find people who say and believe these things.
> *Prot.:* Certainly.
> *Socr.:* Do they then think they are enjoying themselves (χαίρειν) on the occasions when they are not in a distressed condition?
> *Prot.:* That's what they say, at any rate.
> *Socr.:* So they believe they are then enjoying themselves (χαίρειν), or they wouldn't say it.
> *Prot.:* Probably.
> *Socr.:* Yet they are making a false judgement about enjoyment if, that is, enjoyment and lack of distress are two quite different things.
> *Prot.:* But they turned out to be quite different things.

---

misrepresented.

35 Five times between 43d3 and 44a5, together with χαρμοναί once, at 43c7.

36 There is, of course, as the editors pointed out to me, χαρτός, which, though a rather poetical word, is actually presented as a synonym for ἡδύς (along with τερπνός) at *Prot.* 358a, but Speusippus would still have the problem of defining a special meaning for this term; otherwise he might as well use ἡδύς.

Socr.: We have a choice, then. We could hold as we did just now, that there are three alternatives, or that there are only two, first distress, which we would say was a human evil, and secondly release from distress, which, being itself good,[37] we should call pleasurable.

I think we can see various instances of unfair argumentation in this passage. First of all, to produce 'gold' and 'silver' as examples of two extremes between which there is to be a third thing which is neither of them is profoundly tendentious. First of all, they are not opposites; and secondly, they are selected in such a way that any other item in the same class (presumably of metals) is going to be worse than they are—unless, perhaps, it be the fabled orichalc!

Further, Socrates is attempting to convict the protagonists of this position of wishing both to condemn pleasure, and to commend their chosen intermediate state as pleasant, which it would certainly be inconsistent of them to do, without allowing that they may have wished to claim that their intermediate state was characterized by a condition of mind far superior to pleasure, precisely as being the result of the imposition of limit and order on the disorderly and unlimited spectrum of sensations of which pleasure is one 'wing', so to speak. They may have had difficulty in finding an adjective to describe this (and so may have incautiously fallen back on ἡδύ), but it rather looks as if their preferred verb/noun for it was χαίρειν/χαρά.

This, after all, would by no means be the only time that Socrates was less than fair to a position of which he disapproved. But let us press on. Socrates now gets round (44b4–c2) to identifying a group which he describes as 'the enemies of Philebus', who are characterized as being 'experts in natural science' (δεινοὶ τὰ περὶ φύσιν) and as being afflicted with a certain 'crankiness arising from a not ignoble nature' (τὶς δυσχέρεια φύσεως οὐκ ἀγέννους):[38]

---

[37] This may be a rather weak rendering of αὐτὸ τοῦτο ἀγαθὸν ὄν. Perhaps, 'being just what it is to be good'?

[38] I borrow the translation of Gosling here, with some amendments. The particular point of the repeated mention of δυσχερεῖς/δυσχέρεια has been well explored by Malcolm Schofield in his article, cited above (n. 29). His thesis is not strictly provable, I think, but I am attracted by the notion that δυσχερής was known to be Speusippus' favourite adjective for describing a difficulty, and that a gently teasing allusion is being made to that which we are meant to pick up on ('we', of course, being Academic auditors or readers of the dialogue). Certainly, Aristotle's four uses of δυσχερ- when discussing doctrines of Speusippus in the *Metaphysics* (1086a2-5; 1090a7-10; 1091a33-b1; 1091b22-5) would seem to back up this conjecture.

Prot.: Why are we raising this question at this stage, Socrates? I don't see what you are getting at.

Socr.: Don't you know the real enemies of Philebus here?

Prot.: Who are you referring to?

Socr.: People with a considerable reputation as experts in the science of nature,[39] who deny any real existence to pleasures.[40]

Prot.: How do they do that?

Socr.: According to them, what Philebus and his friends at present call pleasures are nothing but cases of release from distress (λύπων ἀποφυγαί).

The question to be faced here is whether the position stated here is in any way compatible with what appears from our other evidence to have been Speusippus' doctrine. On the face of it, one would be compelled to doubt it. After all, Speusippus is not attested to have denied the *existence* of pleasures; rather, he declared that they were just as much of an evil as pains, which would seem to recognise their existence at least to the same extent.

But then one asks oneself, could anyone in his right mind have denied the *existence* of pleasures? Surely what we have here from Plato is the conclusion, rather tendentiously put, of a polemical argument against pleasure. The argument, I submit, would go something like this (and a complementary argument could in theory be employed against the substantial existence of pain, except that there was no need to wean people from an irrational attachment to pain!). Any pleasure you care to name, if you analyse it, can be discerned as the result of freeing the organism from some form of distress or other, resulting from a disequilibrium in one

---

[39] The real meaning of the appellation δεινοὶ λεγόμενοι τὰ κατὰ φύσιν is a troublesome question. It does not necessarily refer, as it is often taken to do, to expertise in, or enthusiasm for, what we would call' natural science', though it may include that. It can just as well refer to what we would term 'the human sciences', including ethics. I take it, though, to be a good-naturedly teasing reference to Speusippus' well-known concern to give a comprehensive account of the relations of all branches of knowledge to one another, attested by Diogenes Laertius (IV 2; cf. above, n. 11)—with which may be linked his assertion, criticised by Aristotle at *A.Po.* B 13, 97a6ff. (= Fr. 63 Tarán), that knowledge of each thing requires knowledge of its differentiae in respect of everything else, which would lead to the sort of frenzied classificatory activities satirized by Epicrates in his famous fragment (Fr. 11 Kock), and exemplified in the many volumes of Speusippus's *Homoia*.

[40] There is some problem here as to what the Greek (τὸ παράπαν ἡδονὰς οὔ φασιν εἶναι) really means. Gosling wishes to translate 'who completely deny that *they* (sc. the pleasures arising from cessation of distress) are pleasures'. This would admittedly make better sense, but it is not the most natural meaning of the Greek, I think. I give a translation compatible, I hope, both with the Greek and what I take to be its real meaning.

direction. What is called 'pleasure' is simply the tilting of the disequilibrium in the other direction. So pleasures do not have a substantial existence, in that their manifestation is always a by-product of the removal of pain. You do not experience a sensation of pleasure except in the context of the relief of some painful organic imbalance or other.[41]

Now this is a pretty tendentious argument, certainly, but at least it is not manifestly insane, as an outright denial of the existence of pleasure would be; and I think that it is a position that Speusippus could have taken up, consistently with his known views.[42] The great problem that it leaves him with—and this is where his 'crankiness' (δυσχέρεια) comes in—is that he is forced to deny that what Plato would wish to term 'pure pleasures' (51aff.), such as those of smell or hearing, where there has been no previous unpleasantness, or indeed most pleasures of the mind, are to be described as pleasures at all.

But of course this is just what Speusippus wishes to deny, and it here that his semantic dispute with his uncle becomes acute. Plato, at 52c–d1, actually makes very much the distinction that Speusippus must have made, but he makes it between 'impure' and 'pure' pleasures, whereas Speusippus would have made it between 'pleasures', which he would regard as intrinsically unmeasured

---

41 We seem to get a reflection of this argument is the admittedly rather casual remark of Socrates at the beginning of the *Phaedo* (60b), as he sits up on his bed and rubs his legs after they have been released from the irons, that pain and pleasure seem in a way to be Siamese twins, springing from a common root.

42 The position of certain 'sophisticated persons' (κομψοί τινες) later, at 53d, that pleasure is always a state of *coming to be* (γένεσις), never of being (οὐσία), is an interesting problem. The original argument, that pleasure is 'a kind of smooth motion, issuing in sensation' is pretty certainly attributable to Aristippus (cf. D.L. 2.85), and is thus a hedonist argument (see Diès' excellent discussion *op. cit.* LXII-X), but it is less clear that Aristippus would have wished to characterize pleasure as a *genesis,* as it lays him open to the counter-argument presented here. The identification of *kinêsis* as a *genesis* sounds more like a hostile deduction. We must recall, in this connection, that Speusippus composed an *Aristippus* (though whether before or after the *Phlb.* is unfortunately uncertain). In such a work he must inevitably have sought to counter the main feature of Aristippus' position. My suggestion would be that Plato is here borrowing an argument from Speusippus (though he makes Socrates ironically thank the original proposers of the argument at 54d4-5, for providing material for their own refutation). Even if Speusippus' *Aristippus* is judged to be the later work, it seems to me that he must have used this argument, and that this is reflected later in Aristotle's reference to it at *EN* VII 12 1152b12ff.

and disorderly, and sensations arising out of his ideal state of equilibrium:

> So now we have an orderly sorting out of the purified pleasures from what should be called unpurified cases. As a further point we ought to attribute to violent pleasures disorderliness (ἀμετρία), and to those that are not, orderliness (ἐμμετρία). Those that admit of great degrees and intensity, whether becoming such commonly or only rarely, we should put in the category mentioned earlier of that which is indeterminate (τὸ ἄπειρον γένος) and more and less and in varying degrees permeates both body and soul. The others we should put in the category of ordered things.

Socrates goes on (52d5ff) to argue that the disorderly and indeterminate class of pleasures can properly be declared 'false', and only the ordered ones 'true', for very much the reasons that οἱ δυσχερεῖς back in 44b-c were criticised for denying the substantial reality of pleasure. Even there, we may note, the position of the δυσχερεῖς is not absolutely rejected; they are rather treated, ironically, as 'inspired prophets' (μάντεις, 44c5), who have grasped an intimation of the truth through a certain natural talent, but have not worked it out dialectically. This, it seems to me, is a very suitable form of put-down for Plato to use when dealing with a bumptious nephew. In fact, their two positions are not that far apart; it is just that Plato does not see the sense of denying the title of 'pleasure' to those states of the human organism which he has identified as 'pure' pleasures, whereas for Speusippus the essential distinction between these states and what he wants to designate 'pleasures' is precisely that they are *states,* and the others are *processes,* or motions, admitting of indefiniteness and 'more and less'.

Plato's contention is that the position of the δυσχερεῖς, while doing them credit, has not been properly thought out. It seems to me, on the other hand, that there is a certain amount to be said for it, even if it presents difficulties. After all, if we bear in mind Speusippus' Pythagoreanizing world-view (which is not, indeed, very different from that presented in the *Philebus*), it is important that, in the sphere of ethics, one postulates the existence of perfect states, representing the imposition of *peras* on the disorderly substratum of *apeiria,* and that it is such states that generate *eudaimonia.* The problem of how to describe the by-products of such states, which may include the enjoyment of the smell of roses, or the sounds of birdsong or Beethoven's string quartets, as well as of philosophizing, is something that he may not have quite mastered, though it seems possible, as we have seen, that he made use of the verb χαίρειν in this connection.

To complete our exegesis of the passage 44b-d, however: we may derive from it (or rather from its continuation, 44e-45d) a further polemical argument against pleasure which may well have been advanced by Speusippus. Socrates, at any rate, with his usual irony, thanks the δυσχερεῖς warmly for supplying him with it.

The argument goes as follows. If we want to get a clear view of the nature of a given thing, we should look at it in its most extreme or unadulterated form. In the case of hardness, for example, we should examine the hardest things that we can find, if we wish to acquire an accurate idea of what hardness is. In the case of pleasure, then, we look for the most extreme forms of pleasure, if we wish properly to comprehend the nature of pleasure. But then we are led to admit that people suffering from illness, either physical or mental—the argument glosses over the question whether *all* illnesses qualify in this regard, or only certain ones—experience more pleasure in more extreme forms (as a relief from their various pains or distresses) than healthy people. Thus it is argued that it is the most unbalanced natures that experience the most extreme pleasures. And so it is indicated (I hesitate to say *proved*) that pleasure is essentially connected with imbalance in the organism, and is thus the antithesis of a desirable state.

I see no reason not to accept that Plato is in fact borrowing this argument from Speusippus, and using it for his own purposes. He makes Socrates thank the δυσχερεῖς for it, as I say. If anything, it brings home to us how close their positions really were. This does not, however, mean that Plato was any the less displeased with Speusippus for taking up such a position. Plato would not appreciate his nephew taking up a position on his 'right', so to speak, on such a sensitive question as the status of pleasure. Mainly, though, he seems to have regarded this super-austerity of Speusippus as deficient in dialectical rigour. The sensations of the virtuous and self-controlled have enough in common with those of the dissolute and intemperate to merit being given the same generic name. A more correct way of evaluating them is to make the distinction that he works out in the latter part of the dialogue between 'adulterated' and 'pure', 'false' and 'true' pleasures, rather than being left with a class of sensations for which no proper name at all had been developed. This is, after all, just the role that the 'heavenly tradition' set out in 16-19 in meant to fulfil, making the correct distinctions within the previously vague and amorphous concept denominated 'pleasure'.

It may after all turn out, though, that Speusippus has the best of this argument. The Stoics were deficient to none in logical rigour, and they, it seems to me, sided, in retrospect, with Speusippus. The Stoic theory of εὐπάθειαι, or 'equable states', after all, is precisely developed to provide a set of sensations, including pleasurable ones, which are appropriate to a wise man who is quite free from πάθος, and that is the sort of Pythagorean sage that Speusippus seems to be envisaging. For them, the experiences of the sage are not to be confused with those of the vulgar, despite superficial resemblances between them, and that is surely very much the position of Speusippus before them.[43]

Trinity College, Dublin

[43] By way of an irreverent concluding footnote, one may record the (doubtless malicious, but possibly accurate) report of Diogenes Laertius in his *Life of Speusippus* (4.1) that the philosopher was 'prone to anger and vulnerable to pleasures' (ὀργίλος καὶ ἡδονῶν ἥττων ἦν). If so, he would not be the first or last philosopher whose personal life did not quite come up to his principles—though it must be said that the instances given by Diogenes to back up this assertion are puerile and incoherent in the extreme.

ON ARISTOTLE'S SEMANTICS IN *DE INTERPRETATIONE* 1–4

L.M. De Rijk

1. *Introduction**

By and large, in *De interpretatione* Aristotle is concerned with our capability to speak about all that presents itself to our mind. From chapter 4 onwards, he deals with the statement-making expressions (affirmation and negation), which are the main tools for conveying our thoughts about things. This discussion is prepared (chapters 1-3) by some important observations concerning the basic elements of such expressions, *viz.* ὄνομα and ῥῆμα. The present contribution contains some comments on Aristotle's view of the proper nature of statement-making as put forward in *De interpretatione.*[1] First, I would like to highlight Aristotle's, what Sir David Ross has called[2] 'frankly 'representative' view of knowledge' by discussing the terms ὁμοίωμα and πρᾶγμα. Next, I will discuss what is meant by a term's 'time-connotation', and finally I will examine the semantics of ὄνομα, ῥῆμα and λόγος.

2.1. *Meaning and Representation: What does ὁμοίωμα refer to?*

In the opening chapter, Aristotle's attention is focussed on the representative character of expressions and thoughts, respectively: 'Spoken utterances are symbols of 'affections in the soul' (*i.e.* thoughts), and written marks symbols of spoken utterances' (16a3-4), [...] what these (*sc.* expressions) are in the first place signs of—affections of the soul—are the same for all people; and what these affections are 'likenesses' of—things—are surely the same' (16a6-

---

* Twenty years ago Jaap Mansfeld and I worked together on the Festschrift for our common teacher and his predecessor in the chair of Ancient and Patristic philosophy at Utrecht. It now gives me great pleasure to be able to contribute this little offering to his Festschrift, on the occasion of his 60th birthday.

[1] The present author has greatly profited from the rich literature on the subject, especially the pioneering work by John Ackrill (1963), E. Montanari's (1988) extensive commentary on *De int.*, chs 1-4, and the exemplary work by Hermann Weidemann (1994).

[2] Ross (1949) 25.

8). The author is not interested in the psychological aspects of making utterances, which aspects he regards (16a8-9) as 'not belonging to the present subject', but to 'the work on the soul' (i.e. *De anima* III 3-8).

The pivotal notion of ὁμοίωμα ('likeness') has already drawn the attention of the Ancient Greek commentators of *De interpretatione.*[3] The English word 'likeness', however, does not cover the entire semantic area of Greek ὁμοίωμα. In addition to the basic sense of 'likeness', 'image', 'replica', the Greek word as used by e.g. Plato and Aristotle connotes the idea of 'being substitutable for' or 'representative of' the object the thing called ὁμοίωμα is said to be the likeness of, to the effect that an object's nature may be designated and clarified by its ὁμοίωμα. In order to illustrate this wider meaning I shall give some significant passages from Aristotle.

In *Nicomachean Ethics* VIII 10, 1160b21ff. Aristotle claims that there are resemblances between different types of political constitutions and the relationships between the members of a household; e.g. the relation between a father and his sons corresponds with a monarchy, whereas that between man and wife may stand for the aristocratic constitution, and so on for timocracy and democracy. The general idea is that the different types of household may elucidate the different natures of their respective counterparts in politics. This discussion is introduced as follows: 'One may find resemblances (ὁμοιώματα) to the constitutions, and, as it were, patterns (παραδείγματα) of them even in households (1160b21-2).'

In *Politics* VIII 5, in which the nature of musical expression is discussed, it is argued (1340a16-8) that 'there is clearly nothing which we are so much concerned to acquire and to cultivate as the power of forming right judgements, and of taking delight in good dispositions and noble actions.'[4] With regard to the role of musical expression, Aristotle points out that *qua* representations (ὁμοιώματα) of anger, gentleness, courage and all other kinds of qualities of character, rhythm and melody are practically equivalent in their effects on our souls to the affections they represent. We know from our own experience, he argues (a23-5), that the propensity of

---

[3] See Weidemann (1994) 134-51, and also Ackrill's (1963) 113 criticism of 'grave weaknesses in Aristotle's theory of meaning'.

[4] Oxford Translation (B. Jowett, revised by W.D. Ross). Most of the translations have been taken from the Oxford Translation.

feeling pleasure or pain at mere representations is not far removed from our experience of the same feelings when brought about by reality (τὴν ἀλήθειαν). So ὁμοίωμα, which is juxtaposed to μίμησις (a12) and μίμημα (a39)[5] as their equivalent, stands for some entity that is regarded as representative of something else, with which it has its effectiveness in common.

In *Metaphysics* A 5 Aristotle discusses the importance attached to mathematics by the Pythagoreans, 'who were the first to take up mathematics (and) not only advanced this study, but also having been brought up in it thought its principles were the principles of all things (985b24-6).' In numbers the Pythagoreans seemed to see, Aristotle argues (985b27-32), as many 'ὁμοιώματα to the things that exist and come into being, more than in the traditional basic ontological elements, fire, earth and water, such and such a modification of numbers being justice, another being soul and reason, another being opportunity, and similarly almost all other things being numerically expressible.' 'Since, again', he continues (985b32-986a2), 'they saw that the modifications and the ratios of the musical scales were expressible in numbers; since, then, all other things seemed in their whole nature to be modelled (ἀφωμοιῶσθαι) on numbers, and numbers seemed to be the first things in the whole of nature, they supposed the elements of numbers to be the elements of all things.' In the Pythagoreans' view, the various entities could adequately be represented by the corresponding numerical ratios. In this context, the notion of ὁμοίωμα goes beyond just likeness; rather, it expressly connotes the idea that different numerical ratios are representative of, and may stand for, different entities and that, accordingly, the nature of these entities can be represented by the corresponding number.

To my mind, it is this pregnant notion of ὁμοίωμα that is found in the opening lines of *De interpretatione,* in which expressions are said to primarily refer to thoughts ('affections of the soul'), which, in their turn, refer to πράγματα. In order to determine more precisely Aristotle's view of 'representative thought' the next subject that presents itself for examination is the proper meaning of πρᾶγμα.

---

[5] The genuine meaning of μίμησις and its cognates ('representation') is thoroughly discussed in Kardaun (1993), who has convincingly shown that the common rendering 'imitation' is incorrect.

2.2. *Meaning and Representation: What does πρᾶγμα properly stand for?*

Serious doubts may be raised against the rendering 'actual thing' for πρᾶγμα.[6] According to Boethius, Alexander of Aphrodisias already put forward the question of why—given the claim in *De interpretatione*, ch. 1 that expressions act as names referring to things—, Aristotle says that utterances are *primarily* (16a6 πρώτων) signs of thoughts rather than of actual things.[7] Alexander thinks that Aristotle possibly means to say that, although expressions are names of things, we do not use them in order to signify things, but rather to signify the thoughts ('affections of the soul') we have of things in our mind. Aristotle justly claimed, he says, that utterances are primarily signs of thoughts, because they are properly used to signify the *thoughts* we have of the things involved.[8] Some lines further on, our spokesman Boethius rightly comments that in calling the ὁμοιώματα 'affections of the soul' Aristotle means to say that to think is precisely 'to receive an object's proper image in the soul's reflections'.[9]

Alexander—speaking for Aristotle—appears to reject the opposition between thinking and reality that is implied in the question 'do the utterances refer to *either* thoughts *or* (actual) things?' Not the objects as such are the proper objects of signifying but the thoughts that are formed of the (actual) things; in Boethius words 'quae ex rebus nobis innatae sunt animae passiones'. In other words,

---

[6] E.g. Ackrill's rendering of πράγματα at 16a7 and 17a38 (as in *Cat.* 5, 4a36ff; 12, 14b19ff.); cf. Boethius II 22.2-6. It is righty rejected by others, e.g. Weidemann (1994) 138-9.

[7] Boethius II, 40.30-41.7: [...] quaerit Alexander: si rerum nomina sunt, quid causae est ut primorum intellectuum notas esse voces diceret Aristoteles? Rei enim ponitur nomen, ut cum dicimus 'homo', significamus quidem intellectum, rei tamen nomen est, idest animalis rationalis mortalis. Cur ergo non primarum magis rerum notae sunt voces quibus ponuntur potius quam intellectuum?

[8] *Ibid.*, 41.7-13: 'Sed fortasse quidem ob hoc dictum est, inquit, quod, licet voces rerum nomina sint, tamen non idcirco utimur vocibus ut res significemus, sed ut eas quae ex rebus nobis innatae sunt animae passiones. Quocirca propter quorum significantiam voces ipsae proferuntur, recte eorum primorum esse dixit esse notas.' The flavour of innatism ('innatae sunt passiones animae') in Alexander's exposition would surely not have amused Aristotle.

[9] *Ibid.*, 43.12-16: 'Similitudinem vero passionem animae vocavit, quod secundum Aristotelem nihil aliud est [omitted by Meiser; see however the older editions, e.g. Migne, *PL* 64, 414 B13] intellegere nisi cuiuslibet subiectae rei proprietatem atque imaginationem in animae ipsius reputatione suscipere.'

neither actual things (or states of affairs) by themselves nor our intellections as such are under consideration, but 'things' (whether or not actually existent) *in as far as they are conceived of and referred to by expressions.* [10] Admittedly, the Ancient thinkers, realists as they were, believed that there is a real world existing independent of human thinking, and that man is capable of grasping it by thinking, but this does not alter the fact that, when actually thinking, a realist's thinking, too, does not go beyond things *as conceived of*; to conceive of a thing as it is independent of conceiving is flatly contradictory.

The notion of πρᾶγμα ('thing or state of affairs as conceived of') deserves our special attention. W. Wieland already claimed that, generally speaking, to Aristotle πρᾶγμα has its *locus naturalis* only *within* what he calls 'the linguistic horizon' and merely is that which one has in mind in each case when using a word or a phrase.[11] I could not agree more. This 'horizon' of 'things (states of affairs) taken as being conceived of, and as such obtaining or not-obtaining' is frequently found in Aristotle.[12] Wieland (*loc. cit.*) rightly adduces *De interpretatione* 7, 17a38ff. to corroborate his view. In this passage, Aristotle distinguishes between universal and particular πράγματα, and claims that the universal one is 'that which is by its nature said of a plurality of things and the particular that which is not'. Now, it is not actual things that are said of something else, but their concepts; moreover, unlike Plato, Aristotle rejects the actual existence of universal things, because to him, whatever exists is particular.[13] Therefore, πρᾶγμα must stand, not for 'actual thing', but for the content of an expression, i.e. a thing (rather a state of affairs) *as conceived of*, irrespective of its actuality.

---

[10] For that matter, also Weidemann's (1994, 148-9) diagram of two dovetailed semiotic triangles is based, it seems, upon a mistaken opposition of 'thing' and thought, and thus seems to obscure the crucial point.

[11] Wieland (1970) 170-1 (dealing with Aristotle's *Physics*): '[...] das pragma seinen Ort nur *innerhalb* des sprachlichen Horizontes hat'; '[...] es ist nur das, was man mit dem Wort oder mit der Rede jeweils meint'. See also Weidemann (1994) 139.

[12] For a more detailed survey of its occurrence in Aristotle see De Rijk (1987) 36-39.

[13] See our note 21 below. In *Cat.* 10, 12b5-16 and in *Metaph.* Δ 29, 1024b19ff. even nonexistent (false) states of affairs are called πρᾶγμα . See De Rijk (1987) 38-9; Weidemann (1994) 138.

3. *On time-connotation and timelessness*

In the remaining part of the opening chapter (16a3-9), Aristotle goes on to clarify the distinction between statement-making expressions on the one hand and their constituents, ὄνομα and ῥῆμα on the other. The decisive difference between them is that statements are susceptible of truth-values, whereas ὀνόματα and ῥήματα are not. In order to have a truth-value, a thought, and its linguistic expression, require the addition of 'is' or 'is not', because ὀνόματα and ῥήματα by themselves, like thoughts when taken by themselves, are neither true nor false (16a9-15).

A serious difficulty arises at 16a18, where this addition of 'is' or 'is not' (εἶναι and μὴ εἶναι, respectively) is qualified by the phrase ἢ ἁπλῶς ἢ κατὰ χρόνον ('either simply or with reference to time'). Ackrill prefers the common explanation of this phrase in terms of the opposition 'present time versus past and future times' to taking ἁπλῶς to allude to the timeless or to the omnitemporal present tense. Yet he feels that the distinction between present time and past and future times 'would not be very happily expressed by the disjunction 'either simply or with reference to time'.'[14] The same phrase is also used at *A.Pr.* I 15, 34b7-8 and, somewhat modified, at *Topica* I 5, 102a22-30 and *De anima* III 10, 433b5-10. To my mind, these parallel passages provide clues that point to the alternative interpretation of this phrase, *viz.* as referring to the opposition between time-connotation and timelessness.[15]

Some preliminary remarks should be made on Aristotle's use of the word ἁπλῶς (*simpliciter*). Aristotle defines it on two occasions. At *Topica* II 11, 115b29-35 it is described by the claim (b29-30) that 'what is honourable *simpliciter* is that which without any addition you are prepared to say is honourable.' The honourable *simpliciter*, e.g. to honour the gods, is opposed to what is honourable to some people, such as to sacrifice one's own father, which is only honourable *secundum quid.* A similar opposition between *simpliciter* and *secundum quid* is also found elsewhere.[16] Another definition of the word occurs at *GC* I 3, 317b5-7: 'The word 'simpliciter' either

---

[14] Ackrill (1963) 115.

[15] Weidemann (1994) 157 adduces only *A.Pr.* I 15, 34b7-8, but does not regard it as a parallel, and joins Ackrell's interpretation.

[16] E.g. *SE* 5, 166b22-167a20; 6, 168b11-16; 25, 180a23-31; *Phys.* I 1, 184a18; I 7, 190b 2 ('substances, *i.e.* anything that can be said *to be* without qualification'); *GC* I 3, 317b2-5; b11-13; *Metaph.* Δ 11, 1018b11; Z 3, 1029b6.

refers to what is primary, regarding any appellation of what is,[17] or to the universal in the sense of 'all-comprehensive'.'

In the second definition there is a shift from 'in an unqualified sense' to 'essential' or 'by nature'. The juxtaposition of ἁπλῶς to φύσει is frequently found. So when discussing (*Anal. Post.* I 2, 71b34-72a5) the requirements for the premisses of a demonstrative proof, Aristotle remarks that they should depend (ultimately) upon primitive truths which are 'prior and more familiar', meaning, not that they are so in relation to us and, thus, nearer to sense perception, but that they are so by nature, *simpliciter* and far away from sense perception.[18] In *Topica* VI 4, there is a similar association of true definition (through *genus* and *differentiae*) with a thing's essential nature (141b24), which is 'prior *simpliciter* and requires exceptional understanding to be grasped' (141b13-14).

The word ἁπλῶς also occurs in *De caelo* I 9 where Aristotle discusses the contradistinction between something's shape (μορφή, which term is used as an equivalent of εἶδος) in itself and the one in combination with matter. This distinction is telling, Aristotle argues, since e.g. the form (as such) of the sphere is one thing and the golden or bronze sphere is another, for when we state the essential nature (τὸ τὶ ἦν εἶναι) of the sphere we do not include its material in the definition, because it does not belong to its essence. If the universe is a particular, there will still be a distinction between the being of 'the particular universe' and 'universe' taken by itself (ἁπλῶς i.e. *qua* εἶδος). So there is a difference between 'this universe' (*i.e.* ours) and 'universe taken *qua* εἶδος; the latter stands for form and shape (εἶδος καὶ μορφή), the former for a form that is combined with matter.[19] In *Phys.* VIII 7, 261b4-5, with respect to

17 καθ' ἑκάστην κατηγορίαν τοῦ ὄντος. The common rendering 'within each Category' (Oxford translation) is senseless. Aristotle means to say that if you name an entity, say stone or health, and so on, ἁπλῶς it is stone, health etc. in an unqualified sense (e.g. 'health *simpliciter* ' at *Top.* VI 4, 142a11). In the sense of 'all-comprehensive' 'stone ἁπλῶς' means the class of all stones. For the key notion κατηγορία (= 'name' or 'appellation/nomination' rather than 'predicate') see De Rijk (1980) and (1988) *passim.*

18 *A.Post.* I 2, 71b33-72a5: 'Things are prior and more familiar in two ways: for it is not the same to be prior by nature and prior in relation to us, nor to be more familiar <*simpliciter*> and more familiar to us. I call prior and more familiar in relation to us what is nearer to sense perception, prior and more familiar *simpliciter* what is further away. What is most universal is furthest away, and the particulars are nearest; and these <two kinds> are mutually opposite'.

19 *Cael.* I 9, 277b31-278a15.

becoming and passing away, a similar opposition between their being as such (ἁπλῶς) and their being instantiated in particulars (καθ' ἕκαστον) is made.

The general idea in all these passages is that the phrase '**[x]** taken ἁπλῶς' is used by Aristotle to stand for an entity irrespective of its being instantiated in matter, and that its counterparts[20] stand for **[x]** as instantiated in matter. Now, any material instantiation—one must keep in mind that for Aristotle, anything sensible *is* instantiated in matter[21]—is temporal. Therefore, the notion of ἁπλῶς naturally comes close to that of timelessness.[22]

In point of fact, one sometimes finds the notions of ἁπλῶς and 'universality' opposed to the temporality of particular instantiations. Thus, when discussing the nature of the universal syllogistic premiss (e.g. 'A belongs to all B'), Aristotle explains (*Anal. Pr.* I 15, 34b7ff.) that we must understand the phrase 'belonging to all of a subject' not with reference to any time (μὴ κατὰ χρόνον ὁρίσαντας), but ἁπλῶς, hence 'timeless', for that is the way to get hold of the material genuine syllogisms are made of. The author expressly insists that in such cases 'universality must be taken simply', that is not limited in terms of time.[23] The phrase (οὐ χρόνῳ διορίζοντας at b18) seems to rule out time and temporal instantiation and to imply timelessness, rather than merely temporal indefiniteness or omnitemporality. To Aristotle of course, unlike Plato, no transcendent domain of being is implied when he uses the notion of timelessness. In his view, this notion is merely instrumental in *our conceiving* the things of the outside world, *viz.* our taking (at times, e.g. when framing apodeictic syllogisms about them) their immanent natures abstracted from these natures' inherence in these things, in order to draw, and to justify, non-contingent conclusions about them.[24]

Aristotle's remark at 16a18 ('either simply or with reference to

---

20 viz. '**[x]** κατὰ μέρος', '**[x]** μεμιγμένον', and so on.

21 *Cael.* I 9, 278a11: 'whatever is sensible subsists altogether in matter.'

22 Ackrill (1963) 115 also considered (and rejected) the suggestion that ἁπλῶς 'alludes to the timeless or to the omnitemporal present tense'; see above, p.120.

23 *A.Pr.* I 15, 34b17-8: τὸ καθόλου ληπτέον ἁπλῶς καὶ οὐ χρόνῳ διορίζοντας.

24 For Aristotle, all epistemonic inquiry starts from particulars of the outside world, but they are always taken, then, as instances of the universal nature(s) immanent in them. Therefore, the 'ἁπλῶς-consideration', by which they are taken *simpliciter* or detached from their being materialised, is of utmost importance for the epistemonic inquiry. See De Rijk (1995) 78-102.

time') should be interpreted along the same lines, i.e. in terms of timelessness vs. temporality. What he means to say is that the 'being' added to verbal expressions or thoughts, which provides them with truth-value, may either be the timeless being belonging to the connotatum of the term involved, or it may refer to the temporal instantiations and instances.[25] Thus, statements of various content may be made.[26]

This interpretation will find some support in Aristotle's discussion of ῥῆμα, which in chapter 3 of his treatise, is said to 'additionally signify time'.[27]

4. *On the semantics of ὄνομα ('name')*

In the opening line of *De interpretatione*, Aristotle had announced (16a1-2) that it was necessary to 'posit' what an ὄνομα, a ῥῆμα, a λόγος etc. is. In ch. 2, 16a19 he starts the discussion concerning the first component of the statement-making expression, which is called ὄνομα. In the wake of Plato, Aristotle's ὄνομα is used to stand for a one-word expression, or 'significative word', always with the strong connotation of 'referring to' or 'representing' some thing (whether connotatively or denotatively).[28] It may be rendered 'name' in English, in the general sense of 'designation'. Its semantic function is to indicate something and to bring it up for discussion.

Name is defined (2, 16a19-21) as [1] 'an articulate sound, [2] significant [3] by convention, [4] without time, [5] none of whose

---

[25] 'Manhood' and 'triangularity' are 'instantiations' inhering in the 'instances' 'man' and 'triangle', respectively.

[26] Cf. the opening lines of the next quotation from Boethius.

[27] The first of the three explanations of our phrase mentioned by Boethius (II, 51.2-10) seems to be very close to the one argued for above: '[...] vel simpliciter vel secundum tempus. Hoc vero idcirco addidit quod in quibusdam ita enuntiationes fiunt ut quod de ipsis dicitur, **secundum substantiam** proponatur, in quibusdam vero hoc ipsum 'esse' quod additur, non substantiam sed **praesentiam quandam** significet. Cum enim dicimus 'Deus est', non eum dicimus nunc esse, sed tantum in substantia esse, ut hoc ad inmutabilitatem potius substantiae quam ad tempus aliquod referatur.' Cf. Trendelenburg (1892) 53: 'ἁπλῶς simpliciter eam affirmationis vel negationis necessitatem indicat, quae quasi maior omni tempore dominetur; cujus modi genus praesenti efferre solemus; κατὰ χρόνον contra enunciatum certo quodam tempore cohibet.'

[28] For Plato's semantics of ὄνομα and ῥῆμα see De Rijk (1986) 217-82; (1987) 27-33; 53. —It should be remarked that in these passages, my unfortunate rendering 'imitation' and 'to imitate' for μίμησις and μιμεῖσθαι must be corrected into 'representation' and 'to represent'; see Kardaun (1983).

parts is significant separately.' The ingredients [1] and [2] are quite in line with what is said in the opening chapter, and [3] alludes to the expositions in Plato's *Cratylus*.[29]

From the semantic point of view the *differentiae* indicated by phrases [4] and [5] are the most interesting, because they are meant to mark off the name against ῥῆμα and λόγος. (Following Aristotle, I will postpone the explanation of phrase [4] 'without time' to the next section). With feature [5] Aristotle, to my mind, only intends to contrast the name,—as at 3, 16b6-7 the ῥῆμα *-qua* one-word expression with λόγος, because, when taken by themselves, their parts ('letters')—unlike those of λόγος—are semantically incomplete and, accordingly, do not fulfil the requirement of being properly significative.[30]

Expressions such as 'not-man' give rise to some difficulties. They are not genuine names, nor are they a λόγος or a negative statement. On the other hand, they *are* significant by themselves, the only difference to ordinary names being that they indicate only a vague, indefinite connotatum[31] and may denote, consequently, 'a wildly various range of objects'.[32]. So they are not entirely denied the label 'name' and are called by Aristotle 'indefinite names'.[33]

Finally, Aristotle rules out the inflexions of names (i.e. oblique cases of nouns, such as 'Philo's' or 'to-Philo') as candidates for counting as names. They do not bring up the entity signified by the name properly, as e.g. 'Philo's' may primarily refer to his wife, or a son or daughter of his, or one of his possessions or properties, anything other, that is, than the man himself. That is why only the name in the nominative form is called κλῆσις, *i.e.* 'calling case', as in *A. Pr.* I 36, 48b39-49a1, where Aristotle claims that the terms of the syllogism are always to be stated in 'the calling-up-forms of the names' (κατὰ τὰς κλήσεις τῶν ὀνόματων), e.g. 'man', 'good', 'contraries', not 'of-man', 'of-good', 'of-contraries'.

---

29 For the semantic impact of this dialogue see De Rijk (1986) 217-53.

30 Weidemann (1994) 166.

31 See *De int.* 10, 19b9: 'for what it signifies is in a way one thing, but indefinite.' Obviously, when actually used, its *denotatum* may be quite precise, e.g. in '*this* not-man is a tree'.

32 Ackrill (1963) 118. See also Boethius II, 62.3-19; 69.29-70.3.

33 Boethius II, 62.19-63.14. For Plato too, the indefinite name has a descriptive force. See De Rijk, (1986) 165ff.; 170ff.

5. *On the semantics of ῥῆμα ('attribute')*

As a technical tool ῥῆμα (literally 'what is said' or 'assertible') is identified as 'that <*sc.* ῥῆμα> which additionally signifies time, no part of which is significant separately, and which is[34] always a sign of things *qua* being said of something else'.

The wording of this formula requires some comment. It must strike the reader that the first part of the definition of λόγος, which will be presented by Aristotle in chapter 4, runs entirely parallel to that given of ὄνομα (in chapter 2) in that each of them commences with their common generic part, *viz.* 'articulate significative sound which ...'. What Aristotle says here about ῥῆμα, however, does not start from that generic part, he rather *posits* (notice the use of θέσθαι at 16a1, and its being alluded to at 19b14)[35] ῥῆμα as 'the one which ... etc.'[36] This wording strongly suggests that Aristotle is not defining ῥῆμα in general, but instead identifies the ῥῆμα as intended in the present treatise as 'that <*sc.* ῥῆμα> which additionally signifies time, no part of which ... etc.'. Quite understandably so, because e.g. Plato's ῥῆμα is not necessarily a one-word expression[37], so that it would not meet the second condition ('no part of which is significant in its own right') for being a ῥῆμα in the sense Aristotle has determined just now.

The features [1] and [3] are interesting from the semantic point of view. What is meant by 'to additionally signify time'? Aristotle explains (16b8-9) this by opposing ὑγιαίνει to (the name) ὑγίεια: 'By 'additionally signifying time' I mean this: *health* is a name, but *is-healthy* a ῥῆμα, because it additionally signifies something as obtaining *now*.' He apparently intends to say that as a name ὑγίεια refers to the entity 'health', but in bringing it up only *qua* form, whereas ὑγιαίνει refers to health as a form *actually inhering* in something else, hence as a form that is materialised or actualised and manifests itself in temporal conditions. According to Aristotle,

---

34 The Greek language does not allow one to connect more than one relative clause with an antecedent, and instead has the paratactical construction *esti de* ('and it is'). See Kühner-Gerth (1904) 2.432f.

35 At 10, 19b14 Aristotle qualifies the notion ῥῆμα by saying 'ῥήματα according to what we laid down'.

36 It is worthwile to note that Boethius finds it useful to begin his comments on this lemma by presenting the 'integra definitio' (II, 66.3-6: 'Verbum est vox significativa secundum placitum, que consignificat tempus ... etc.').

37 See De Rijk (1986) 222-234.

no form exists unless it is materialised in something else as its subject-substrate.[38] This need not prevent us, however, from referring to a form as such, irrespective of its being immanent in a substrate. For that matter, Aristotle's vivid discussion with Plato about his Master's Separate, Transcendent Forms, as well as his own reflections in his *Metaphysics* about true substance, could not possibly take place without bringing up 'forms as such' *in abstracto.* Now, in such discussions, names designate entities regardless of their being immanent in temporal substrates ('without time'), whereas by using ῥήματα this ontological state is focussed on.

The third feature ('is always a sign of things *qua* being said of something else') is closely linked up with the first one, and is in a way its counterpart. Whereas the first raises the question of an entity's ontological state as something that is immanent in a subject-substrate and hence temporally determined, the third refers to the matching grammatico-semantical situation, namely that, in keeping with this ontological state, the entity is also examined inasmuch as it is *assigned to* this subject-substrate.[39] Thus Aristotle implicitly presents his basic view—opposed to that of Plato—that what is signified by a ῥῆμα is a non-subsistent entity. So a ῥῆμα always implies a reference to the subsistent substrate which the significate it designates inheres in.[40] Quite naturally, then, these two features of ῥῆμα are explained by Aristotle as being closely related.[41]

Next, Aristotle deals with two kinds of ῥῆμα-like expressions which, however, are not entitled to bear the label properly, *viz.* negative expressions such as οὐχ - ὑγιαίνει, and inflexions of ῥῆμα, *i.e.* its preterite and future tenses. He proposes to call the former ἀόριστα ῥήματα. Though they have time-reference and their significates include a connotation of temporality and always their

---

38 *Cael.* I 9, 278a11.

39 Though the addition (at 16b10) ἢ ἐν ὑποκειμένῳ (found in Porphyry and some manuscripts, and defended by Montanari (1988, 193-9) is perhaps not authentic, it is perfectly in keeping with what Aristotle has in mind in this chapter.

40 The two conditions are explained by Boethius (II, 66.9-22; 67.7-21; 68.1-31) along the same lines.

41 '[...] because it additionally signifies something as obtaining now, *and* is always a sign of what is said of something else, that is, of a subject-substrate' (16b9-10), reading, with a number of manuscripts (and Porphyry), καθ' ἑτέρου λεγομένων instead of ὑπαρχόντων (Minio-Paluello). See Weidemann (1994) 173.

holding of something else, they are different[42] and can only be classed as ῥήματα in a qualified sense.

There is some discussion about the precise meaning of 'indefinite ῥῆμα'. Ackrill considers it a 'misnomer'.[43] It should be noted at the outset that Aristotle's account of it (at 16b15) is rather obscure: 'Because it [*sc.* the indefinite ῥῆμα] holds indiscriminately of anything, whether being or not being.' Ackrill and Weidemann are of the opinion that the indefinite ῥῆμα is in fact a sentence-fragment, containing an ordinary ῥῆμα together with the negative particle, which serves to make the statement of which it is part a negative one.[44]

I prefer, however, to take ἀόριστον ῥῆμα in a similar way as 'indefinite name'. On this assumption, it must refer to an expression that equals an ordinary ῥῆμα, save for the latter's definite way of referring to the significate involved. The indefinite ῥῆμα thus signifies some kind of being in an indefinite manner, e.g. 'being not-healthy' (16b11) or 'being not-just' (20a31). One should be aware that, just as in the case of indefinite names, there is no empty designation involved, but really an ontic value, despite the minimal information given about its nature. The 'characteristic' designated by the indefinite ῥῆμα is so vague even that 'it can be said of things that are and things that are not, indiscriminately', meaning that e.g. 'not-healthy' and 'not-just' may stand for any existent thing that lacks health as well as for what does not exist at all.

That precisely reflects the double meaning of ἀόριστον elsewhere in Aristotle. In *Physics* II 5, 196b23ff., when discussing, for instance, the different ways in which a thing's cause may be indicated, he distinguishes the (determinate) *per se* designation from the plurality of indeterminate, incidental designations. *E.g.* the cause of a house (architect) may be *per se* designated as 'housebuilder' or by one of the man's incidental attributes as 'the pale entity' or 'the musical'; in the latter case the cause is an indefinite one (ἀόριστον, b 28), not *qua* cause, but as to how it is

42 I agree with the common interpretation of this passage, but, to my mind, it is necessary to remedy the harsh construction by supplying (at b13, after ὑπάρχει) the words ⟨διάφερει δέ>, which may have been omitted due to haplography.

43 Ackrill (1963) 120; also Weidemann (1994) 177.

44 Ackrill (1963) 120-1; Weidemann (1994) 177. See also p. 133 below.

being referred to. In *Physics* V 1, 225a20-25, the author uses both senses of the indefinite term 'not-being', which may stand for unqualified not-being ('what is not'), as well as 'what-is-not' taken in a certain sense, *viz.* 'what is not-white' or 'what is not-good'.

In my view, it is wrong to assume that the phrase 'holding indiscriminately of what is and what is not' refers to the existence or non-existence of the subject of the sentence in which the indefinite ῥῆμα is actually used. Rather, only the applicability of the indefinite ῥῆμα's own significate itself is concerned, irrespective of its actually occurring in a sentence. Of this significate it is said that it either applies, or does not.[45] In this connection it should be kept in mind that in chapters 2 and 3 Aristotle is discussing ὄνομα and ῥῆμα as *potential* ingredients of a statement-making expression and thus he focusses on the things they refer to, each in its own *specific* way. Of course, to determine what, in accordance with their specific nature, each of them contributes to the λόγος, and the statement-making expression when "is' or 'is not' is added' (16a17-8), remains the ultimate aim of the observations made in these chapters.

The other candidates for the label 'ῥῆμα in a qualified sense' are its inflexions. In fact, they fulfil the condition of being said of something else, but do not meet the requirement of holding *now*, that is, at the time of the utterance, but refer to the inherence of the characteristic in the past or the future. Ackrill is right in remarking that the opposition of the inflexions of the ῥῆμα to the ordinary ῥῆμα is not at all parallel to that between names and their inflexions. Unlike name inflexions, which do not refer to what the name stands for, and only indirectly connote it, the inflexions of ῥῆμα really refer to the same entity as the ῥῆμα, albeit with a different time-reference.

The two first lines of the next passage (16b19-20), which deals with the ῥῆμα when uttered just by itself, give rise to less difficulty than is commonly assumed, if only they are interpreted along the forementioned lines. The phrase 'when uttered just by itself' is wrongly taken to mean 'when taken out of a certain statemental context'.[46] Rather it only is about the absence of the two features that

---

[45] Therefore, the reference made by Ackrill (1963, 120) and Weidemann (1994, 177) to *Cat.* 10, 13b27-35, where it is said that if Socrates does not exist 'Socrates is not sick' is true, is beside the point.

[46] Cf. Weidemann (1994) 178.

make up the specific difference between ὄνομα and ῥῆμα, *viz.* the latter's additional time-reference and its being said of something else, including its attributive use, as e.g. in 'white man'. On this assumption, the ῥῆμα *is* merely a name, because, just like a name, it only brings up its significate as an ontic value,[47] detached from its being immanent in something else and without implying the subject-substrate of which it is said. The fact that the ῥῆμα in that position does signify something does not yet *eo ipso* imply that the entity involved is, or is not, the case. This is quite in line with what has been said earlier (16a13-8) about ὀνόματα and ῥήματα, 'when nothing further (*viz.* 'is' or 'is not') is added'.

What remains to be discussed are the final sentences of this chapter, in which the author tries to support his claim about the ῥῆμα when taken on its own, by an 'anticipative refutation'[48] concerning the verb 'to be'. Not even the verb 'to be' (or 'not to be'), which on the face of it seems to really imply 'being-the-case', affords a counter-example to invalidate my claim, Aristotle argues,[49]—not even if you use, without a further addition, the term ὄν ('be-ing'), which *qua substantivated* neuter word does imply the idea of something actually being there.[50] Why not? Because, according to Aristotle (16b23-5), even the verb 'to be', including its nominal participle, 'is nothing' (an empty notion, that is), and merely helps to signify[51] a certain σύνθεσις, which cannot be conceived of without the things combined.

A final remark should be made on the rendering of ῥῆμα. The rendering 'verb' does not reflect adequately the semantic function

---

47 In Aristotle's words: 'it signifies something: the speaker arrests his thinking and the hearer acquiesces (i.e. 'comes to understand')'. Aspasius rightly defends this interpretation on the level of name-giving: when hearing a single word, the hearer's mind is not in suspense and, like the speaker, the hearer has a determined entity in his mind. This operation has nothing to do as such with framing statements; see Boethius II, 74.9-33. Cf. Aristotle, *Phys.* VII 3, 247b11-2: 'We are said to know and to understand owing to our thought coming to acquiesce and arriving at a standstill.' For the historical context of the expression see De Rijk (1986) 268, n. 26.

48 I refer by this term to Aristotle's habit of supporting a claim by invalidating a seemingly strong counter-example. Cf. Ackrill (1963) 114; 123; Weidemann (1994) 156; 163; 181.

49 I have to leave Weidemann's (1994, 180-5) interesting attempt to emend the *locus corruptus* 16b21-3 out of consideration now.

50 The sentence οὐδ' ἐὰν τὸ ὂν εἴπῃς ψιλόν should be read *in parenthesi, pace* Weidemann (1994) 186.

51 For this sense of προσσημαίνειν cf. ch. 10, 20a13. For σύνθεσις see below, p.131-133.

Aristotle has in mind when using ῥῆμα, because it indiscriminately stands for any attributive determinant of an entity referred to by a name, whether it is nominal[52] or verbal. Therefore, the neutral rendering 'attribute' seems to be the most appropriate in English.[53]

6. *On the semantics of λόγος (both 'statable complex' and 'statement')*

Chapter 4 opens with the definition of λόγος, the definiens of which has been arranged in a similar way as that of ὄνομα : 'a significant articulate sound some part of which is significant in separation—as an expression, not as an affirmation'(16b26-8). This addition, which aims at marking off the main difference between λόγος and its components, ὄνομα and ῥῆμα, is explained by Aristotle in the next lines where he points out, quite in line with 16b21-2, that e.g. the name 'man' taken as part of a λόγος signifies something, but leaves the question of its being the case undecided, whereas when 'something' (*viz.* 'is' or 'is not') is added, it makes up an genuine affirmation or negation. Next, the non-statement-making significant expressions, such as prayers, threats and commands[54] are ruled out, because they all lack truth-value.

The Greek word λόγος, which is the verbal noun deriving from a root that, roughly speaking, always connotes an orderly procedure, discernment, or the speaker's intention to 'clear up' some situation, has several meanings.[55] One of its primary meanings is 'account', which includes 'speech' (as a means of 'giving an account' or 'accounting for'), as well as the more sophisticated 'argument'.

It should be kept in mind, however, that λόγος does not stand as such for 'statement', and may also refer to phrases, such as 'beautiful horse' (16a22) or a definiens, such as 'two-footed land animal' (17a13). As is clear from chapter 5, 17a9ff., the sentential functor 'is' or 'is not' should be added to the name and the attribute—which

52 Nominal ῥήματα are found at 16a15; 20a32; 20b2.

53 The rendering 'Aussagewort', which some German interpreters rightly prefer to 'Verb' or 'Zeitwort', hits the mark, provided it is not associated (as in Weidemann, *passim*) with the notion 'sentential predicate'. That this association is wrong is clear from 1,16a15, as well as from its function within the λόγος, which has a broader sense than 'sentence'; see our next section.

54 Cf. *Poet.* 19, 1456b10-1.

55 For a survey of its various senses see De Rijk (1986) 225-31.

together make up a λόγος or 'assertible (or statable) complex'—to turn the λόγος from simply an assertible complex into a statement-making expression. It is really important to distinguish between these two senses of λόγος.[56]

In order to make sense of Aristotle's semantics of λόγος it is very important to understand correctly the anatomy of the Aristotelian statement-making expression. The Aristotelian proposition is commonly taken to be an expression with the (modern) '*S=P*' structure, to the effect that, like the copula in '*S=P*', the functor 'is' ('is not') is held to be dyadic, and to act as that which combines (*copulat* in Latin) the subject-term with the predicate-term. However, there is an alternative view[57] to the effect that the verb 'is' is a monadic functor which, when added to an 'assertible or statable complex' (i.e. a λόγος expressing a state of affairs), makes up a statement by solely asserting that this state of affairs is really the case. In my view of things, any dyadic function (as '*copula*') is out of the question, since the λόγος by itself is already a composite expression combining ὄνομα and ῥῆμα. Much evidence may be put forward in support of this view.

[1] To begin with, Aristotle never speaks of 'is' as *copula*, nor is this verb ever brought up under a special name. Besides, 'is' and 'is not' are always said to *be added to* the combination already formed of an ὄνομα and a ῥῆμα, whereas there is never any suggestion that Aristotle takes these functors *as themselves performing* the combination of an ὄνομα and a ῥῆμα.[58]

[2] Secondly, it is relevant to recognise what Aristotle means when he says (at 16b24) that 'it (the verb 'is', and 'is not' as well (!); see 16b22) helps to signify some σύνθεσις, which cannot be thought of without the things combined.' Now, the word σύνθεσις is basically used either to refer to a compound structure ('composite') of physical things or to the mental act of uniting two or more concepts. This logico-grammatical use is twofold: either σύνθεσις *only refers* to an (alleged) composite, or it *asserts this composite as being the case* or '*obtaining*'.[59] The term διαίρεσις,—which in

---

[56] They are opposed by Aristotle as λόγος and λόγος ἀποφαντικός (17a8ff.; for Plato's λόγος εἰρήμενος at *Tht.* 189a3-4, see De Rijk (1986) 309-16).

[57] Matthen (1983) 125-31; De Rijk (1987) 43f.; 50-2; 60, n. 60.

[58] Notice that in as far as 'is' is concerned, Aristotle always uses (16a15; 16a18; 16b30; 17a12; 19b25; 19b30;19b38; 20a9; 20a14; 20a36; 21a21; 21b6; 21b21; cp. 21b27-30) the passive verb προστίθεσθαι, never the active verb συντίθεναι.

[59] See De Rijk (1987) 45-50, where more evidence from Aristotle's other

De int. occurs only once, *viz.* in the opening chapter (16a12-4)—, must be explained as the denial of the σύνθεσις referred to by the assertible complex, rather than as a separation of its components. Thus, the procedure of speaking truly (ἀληθεύειν) and speaking falsely (ψεύδεσθαι) is basically a matter of asserting or denying rightly—or wrongly, respectively—an assertible complex, to the effect that to assert or to deny amounts to giving one's assent to, or dissent from one and the same assertible complex, respectively. For example,

'obtains (obtained, will obtain) [man *plus* paleness]'

or

'does (did, will) not obtain [man *plus* paleness]',

meaning indiscriminately *'a man being pale is (was, will be) the case' (='a man is [was, will be] pale') or *'a pale man existing is (was, will be) the case' (='there is [was, will be] a pale man').[60]

A happy consequence of the alternative view is that the term ὑποκείμενον can be taken to stand for 'substrate' (referred to by the name), rather than for sentential subject, as the '*S=P*' device would suggest. Thus, it is not necessary to oppose, as Weidemann does,[61] the use of this term at 19a38 to that at 21b28-2, where his rendering 'sentential subject' will not do at all.[62]

Aristotle's semantics is often censured, but a lot of criticism may turn out to be beside the point, if the alternative interpretation is followed. Here are three examples:

—Aristotle is commonly reproached for failing to distinguish between the 'copulative' and 'existential' uses of 'to be'[63]. This distinction, however, turns out to be anachronistic, because the functor meaning 'obtains [$(x)f$]' is monadic and combines both uses indiscriminately.

---

works is adduced.

[60] For the whole statement procedure see *De int.* 1, 16a12-8; *A. Pr.* I 46, 52a24-38; *Metaph.* Δ 7, 1017a31-5; E 4, 1027b18-1028a1; *De an.* III 6, 430a27-b6 (this passage includes time-differentiation), and the discussion in De Rijk (1987) 48-50. At *Phys.* V 1, 225a21, non-being taken κατὰ σύνθεσιν ἢ διαίρεσιν appears to concern 'that-which-is-not' in the sense that it is the assertion of a false assertible complex or the denial of a true one. Cf. *Metaph.* E 2, 1026a35; Θ 10, 1051b1; N 2, 1089a28.

[61] Weidemann (1994) 158.

[62] 'Being' is said (at b29) to act as ὑποκείμενον to the modifiers δύνασθαι and ἐνδέχεσθαι in a similar way as in 'being a pale man', 'pale' and 'man' do; see De Rijk (1987) 35 and 55, n. 25.

[63] Ackrill (1963) 119; 123; also Weidemann (1994) 174; 190.

—Ackrill's[64] claim that Aristotle fails to distinguish between the predicative and the assertive functions of the ῥῆμα (as used in a statement) is also pointless, for a similar reason; see our foregoing analysis of the statement-making expression.
—The problems raised by Ackrill and Weidemann[65] concerning Aristotle's (putative) use of the indefinite ῥῆμα in statements disappear as soon as the '*S=P*' structure is abandoned.

7. *Conclusion*

Aristotle's semantics of the statement-making expression as occurring in *De interpretatione* is quite modest indeed, but serves its purpose well enough for the narrow scope of issues he has to deal with, given his main intention, *viz.* to set against Plato's ontology his own view of how to speak about 'things' that really are the case.[66] The semantics as set out in *De interpretatione* is suitably supplemented by the semantics of name-giving found in the *Categories* and the doctrine of categorisation[67], which enables Aristotle to develop a method of scientific inquiry, without having to take recourse to Platonic transcendent Forms.[68]

Bibliography

(1) *Primary works*

Aristoteles graece ex recensione I. Bekkeri. Edidit Academia Regia Borussica. Aristotelis Opera, vol. I-II (Berlin 1831; reprint Darmstadt 1960)
Ross, W.D. (ed.), *The Works of Aristotle translated into English.* (Oxford, 1928ff.)
Aristotelis *Categoriae* et *Liber de interpretatione* . Recognovit brevique adnotatione critica instruxit L. Minio Paluello (Oxford, 1949 1956^2)
A.M.S. Boethii *Commentarii in librum Aristotelis* Περὶ ἑρμηνείας. Recensuit Carolus Meiser. Pars posterior secundam editionem et indices continens (Lipsiae 1880)

64 Ackrill (1963) 119; 150-1.
65 Ackrill (1963) 120-1; Weidemann (1994) 177. See also above, p. 126.
66 For Plato's view see *Soph.* 260e4-264b9, and De Rijk (1986) 194-354. It is noteworthy that in the technical treatise *A.Pr.* the syllogistic premisses are not framed along the lines of *De int.*, but by using the verb ὑπάρχειν instead of εἶναι.
67 See De Rijk (1988) *passim.*
68 See De Rijk (1995) 78-102.

(2) *Secondary literature*

Ackrill, J.L. (1963) Aristotle's *Categories* and *De Interpretatione.* Translated with Notes (Oxford).

Bonitz, H. (1870) *Index aristotelicus* (Berlin 1870; reprint Graz 1955).

Kardaun, Maria S.J.M. (1993) *Der Mimesisbegriff in der griechischen Antike.* Neubetrachtung eines umstrittenen Begriffes als Ansatz zu einer neuen Interpretation der platonischen Kunstauffassung. Koninklijke Nederlandse Akademie van Wetenschappen. *Verhandelingen Afdeling Letterkunde,* Nieuwe Reeks, deel 153 (Amsterdam/Oxford/New York).

Kühner, R. - Gerth, B. (I, 1898^3; II, 1904^3) *Ausführliche Grammatik der griechischen Sprache.* Zweiter Teil: Satzlehre. 2 Bde (Hannover/Leipzig; reprint Hannover 1983).

Matthen, M. (1983) 'Greek Ontology and the 'Is' of Truth', *Phronesis* 28: 113-35

Montanari, E. (1988) *La sezione linguistica del Peri hermeneias di Aristotele.* Vol. II: *Il commento* (Firenze).

Rijk, L.M. de (1980) 'On Ancient and Medieval Semantics III: The Categories as Classes of Names', *Vivarium* 18: 1-62.

—— (1986) *Plato's Sophist. A Philosophical Commentary.* Koninklijke Nederlandse Akademie van Wetenschappen. *Verhandelingen Afdeling Letterkunde,* Nieuwe Reeks, deel 133 (Amsterdam/Oxford/New York).

—— (1987) 'The Anatomy of the Proposition. *Logos* and *Pragma* in Plato and Aristotle', in L.M. de Rijk and H.A.G. Braakhuis (eds.), *Logos and Pragma.* Essays on the Philosophy of Language in Honour of Professor Gabriel Nuchelmans, (Nijmegen) 27-61.

—— (1988) 'Categorization as a Key Notion in Ancient and Medieval Semantics', *Vivarium* 26: 1-18.

—— (1995) 'Ockham as the Commentator of *His* Aristotle: His Treatment of *Posterior Analytics*' in Fernando Dominguez, Ruedi Imbach, Theodor Pindl and Peter Walter (eds.), *Aristotelica et Lulliana* magistro doctissimo Charles H. Lohr septuagesimum annum feliciter agenti dedicata (The Hague) 77-127.

Trendelburg, F. (1892^9) *Elementa logices aristotelicae* (Berlin).

Weidemann, H. (1994) *Aristoteles, Peri Hermeneias.* Uebersetzt und erläutert. *Aristoteles. Werke in deutscher Uebersetzung* hrsg. von Hellmut Flashar. Band 1, Teil II (Berlin).

Wieland, W. (1970) *Die aristotelische Physik.* Untersuchungen über die Grundlegung der Naturwissenschaft und die sprachlichen Bedingungen der Prinzipienforschung bei Aristoteles. 2. durchgesehene Auflage mit einem Nachwort (Göttingen).

THEOPHRASTUS FR. 184 FHS&G: SOME THOUGHTS ON HIS ARGUMENTS

IAN G. KIDD

This is an old hobby horse, much ridden and rightly so, for arguments concerning the eternity or destructibility of the cosmos became a stock topic over a long period of the history of Greek philosophy, the response and arguments coloured by the philosophical stance of each proponent. In modern scholarship, this fragment, located at Philo, *De aeternitate mundi* 117–149, has evoked widely, not to say wildly conflicting views with regard to context, provenance, influence and reliability from scholars such as Zeller and Von Arnim on,[1] and has been much revived in the last decade, with an important article by David Sedley on 'Theophrastus and Epicurean Physics' about to appear. Since Jaap Mansfeld has himself richly engaged in the struggle, [2] it will seem imprudent or even impudent for an intruder to this particular paddock to offer him some thoughts on the matter. The imprudence will be only too obvious to him, but I hope he may excuse it remembering our common fascination with the problems of fragmentary evidence and a shared appreciation of their extreme difficulty and danger; and the impudence will have to be forgiven in the light of a long and much-valued friendship. And my contribution is very limited, and skates over or ignores many detailed issues.

As with all fragments, it is best to keep distinct reporter, context and reference. Since the only reporter who names Theophrastus for these arguments is Philo, not only should we allow for Philonic intrusion, but also in general distinguish later influence of the

---

[1] E. Zeller, 'Der Streit Theophrasts gegen Zeno über die Ewigkeit der Welt', *Hermes* 11 (1976) 422–9; H. von Arnim, *SVF* 1.106; but on the other hand, H. von Arnim, 'Der angebliche Streit des Zenon und Theophrastos', *Jahrbücher für classische Philologie,* 39 (1893) 449–467.

[2] E.g. 'Providence and Destruction of the Universe', *Studies in Hellenistic Religions,* ed. M.J. Vermaseren (Leiden 1979) 129–188; '*Physikai doxai* and *Problemata physika*' in *Theophrastus, His Psychological, Doxographical and Scientific Writings,* Rutgers University Studies in Classical Humanities 5 (New Brunswick 1992) 63–111; 'A Theophrastean Excursus on God and Nature and its Aftermath in Hellenistic Thought', *Phronesis* 37 (1992) 314–335.

arguments themselves from the original Theophrastean *Sitz im Leben*. To begin with, Philonic authorship has been denied for *Aet.*, but I am persuaded that David Runia's arguments for genuineness are valid;[3] so we do have a general context of authorship, and this offers some control over language and presentation.

The presentation of the arguments should first briefly be put in local context. *Aet.* begins (like Aristotle's *De Caelo* 1.10, but quite differently) with a tripartition of views: that the cosmos is created and destructible, for which Democritus, Epicurus and most Stoics are named (§§7–9); that it is uncreated and indestructible, citing Aristotle as innovator, or perhaps Pythagoreans (§§10–12); that it is created but indestructible, the view of Plato (§§13–16). After interpretations of the Platonic position,[4] Philo launches into a main exposition of the Peripatetic view and argument (§20ff). But it becomes clear that the main attack is against the Stoa (§47ff). At §55 he refers to the theories of the 2nd cent. BC Head of the Peripatos, Critolaus. At §75 he returns to the main attack on the Stoics, citing Boethus of Sidon, Panaetius and Diogenes of Babylon, seeming to add incidentally at §113ff an attack on atomistic modes of destruction. Then it is at that point (§117ff) that Theophrastus is brought on with his classification of the four main arguments used by proponents of the coming-into-being and destructibility of the cosmos, and the counter arguments against these.

What is immediately obvious is the 2nd cent. BC weight of evidence in Philo. Plato is there, of course, but *Timaeus* was common coin. But the case of Aristotle is curious. He is named only once as the possible innovator of the uncreated and indestructible theory (§§10–12). When we come to the main arguments for this (§20ff), Philo appears to know nothing of the important arguments in *De Caelo* 1.10–12, but presents others which have now been classified as fragments of Aristotle's *De Philosophia* (F19abc Rose and Ross; F916 Gigon). This may well be so, but no particular source is named. Earlier (§§10–12), where Aristotle was named, Philo seems to make a point of saying that what he had read was Ocellus, presumably meaning the Περὶ τῆς τοῦ παντὸς φύσεως,[5] a work again of the mid-2nd c. BC apparently, and something of a

[3] David T. Runia, 'Philo's *De Aeternitate Mundi:* The Problem of its Interpretation', *Vigiliae Christianae* 35 (1981) 105–151.

[4] For the strategic importance of this for Philo, see Runia, *art. cit.*

[5] Ed. R. Harder, Neue Philologische Untersuchungen 1 (Berlin 1926).

Peripatetic/Pythagorean mixture (though Philo regarded it as older than Aristotle). So clearly it has to be kept in mind that the Theophrastean evidence may be filtered and embroidered.

The fragment itself is structured in three parts: (1) (lines 1–4, §117)[6] the explicit statement that Theophrastus said that those asserting the coming-to-be and destruction of the cosmos were led astray by four arguments cited as the greatest or most important (μέγιστα), then succinctly listed: (i) unevenness of the land; (ii) withdrawal (ἀναχώρησις) of the sea; (iii) dissolution (διάλυσις) of each of the parts of the whole; (iv) destruction (φθορά) of whole classes (κατὰ γένη) of land animals. (2) (4–89, §§118–131) The second part fleshes out each of the four arguments in turn. This part is led into by indirect speech still dependent on Theophrastus (4, §118), but immediately lapses into straightforward narrative indicatives, interspersed with things like 'as I said' (12, §119), and 'they say' (18, §120; 80, §130). (3) The third section (90–204, §§132–149) presents arguments to counter the previous arguments, again in order. The language at least of this section could quite naturally be taken to be from Philo, but it is Philo's practice to present the arguments of others in his own way.[7] Clearly we have to accept Part (1) as Theophrastus, but in what follows, how much is Theophrastus, and how much Philo? This obvious question has interested scholars since Von Arnim accepted only the first sentence as Theophrastus.[8] Given the complexity of transmission, the answer is unlikely to be simple.

There is little doubt Parts (2) and (3) have at least been contaminated linguistically, and in detail, and by embroidery. Certainly Philo expresses himself in his own language. Much has been made of the Stoic vocabulary in Argument (iii) (45–52, §125) as being also Philonic. But I can give a more clear-cut example. In Argument (i) we read that if land did not come to be but was always there from eternity, it would have been flat, worn smooth

[6] In references to the fragment, I give the line numbers of F184 FHS&G (on this edition see below n. 25) followed by section numbers of Philo, *Aet.*

[7] Runia, *art. cit.* (n.3) 130.

[8] Von Arnim, *art. cit.* (n.1). Compare also, J.B. McDiarmid, 'Theophrastus on the Eternity of the World', *TAPA* 71 (1940) 239–247. W. Wiersma (*Mnemosyne* III 8 (1940) 234–243) argued again that only Part (1) can be trusted, since Parts (2) and (3) can be shown linguistically and in prose rhythm to be strongly Philo, and they do not always match consistently with (1).

by the rain (12–13, §119). But the Greek for 'flat' is not, as one would have expected, ὁμαλός or πεδίον, but λεωφόρος (13, §119): everywhere would have been broad highway, or motorway. This extraordinarily flamboyant phrase[9] brought me up short until I discovered that it was a favourite metaphor in Philo for the smooth main highway leading to virtue and to God.[10] Of course, later language does not disprove earlier argument. But some of the language seems tied up with the argument, like the Stoic (or Philonic) vocabulary in Argument (iii) (see below). And indeed some arguments themselves, such as the latter part of the extended argument in Argument (ii), appear out of tune with the earlier part (see below). There are suspicious details of examples or illustrations which reappear in later popular clusters (e.g. in the counter arguments for Argument (ii), see below); and most notoriously, from animal marvel lore, the extended with graphic and technicolour detail but hardly apposite illustration of nineteen lines to Argument (iii), of snakes in India twining themselves round elephants, and by draining their life blood, killing them, only to perish themselves when the dying elephant fell on top of them (59–77, §§128–129). It is true that Theophrastus himself was into marvel literature (Frs. 218, 236 FHSG); but much of the strange illustrative detail in Philo has its cluster of popular echo in Diodorus Siculus, Strabo, Seneca (*NQ*), Pliny, Lucan, and Aelian.

But, of course, later embroidery of detail or illustration in the expanded arguments of Part (2) does not disqualify the spines of argument from being original. Indeed the transmission of philosophical arguments, like the transmission of anecdotes, invites such embroidery. And it can be proved with certainty that the expansion of arguments in Part (2) does not come from Philo, because the extended argument (iii) is reproduced in Lucretius 5. 235–317, and Philo's extended argument (iv) recurs in Lucretius 5.324–350. Furthermore, these two arguments follow in Philo and

---

[9] In earlier philosophical Greek I can only bring forward the Pythagorean γνώμη: τάς τε λεωφόρους μὴ βαδίζειν (58C6, 1.465.32 D-K; D.L. 8.17). Philo himself quotes it at *Prob.* 2.

[10] For the metaphorical use relating to the highway leading to virtue and to God: *Opif.* 69, 144; *Leg.* III 253; *Post.* 31, 102, 154; *Deus* 61, 143, 165, 182; *Agr.* 101; *Conf.* 19; *Her.* 70; *Congr.* 28; *Fug.* 203; *Abr.* 7; *Jos.* 142; *Mos.* II 138; *Decal.* 50; *Spec.* I 355; *Spec.* II 202; *Spec.* III 185; *Spec.* IV 62, 155, 167; *Virt.* 51; *Legat.* 216. Philo also uses λεωφόρος literally, e.g. *Det.* 2; and twice referring to Moses' parting of the waters: *Mos.* I 177; *Contempl.* 86.

Lucretius in the same immediate sequence. There must therefore be an ultimate common source. The common source cannot be Epicurus, because Philo's source is certainly not Epicurean, but anti-Epicurean, and rather Peripatetic/Pythagorean with noticeable 2nd c. BC influences. Also, apart from embroidery, the framework of argument in Argument (iii) on destruction of elements, for example, is different in Philo and Lucretius. The evidence suggests the possibility of different intermediary sources or influence, but a common ultimate source; and the simplest solution for that is Theophrastus.

As for the counter arguments of Part (3), they were the whole point, not only of Philo introducing Theophrastus' four arguments, but of Theophrastus in the first place introducing the four most important arguments so that *he* could counter them, because the arguments supported a dogma to which he was opposed. So, I am prepared to believe that at least the spines of the arguments do derive from Theophrastus.

If the argument is granted so far, it would be interesting to survey very briefly the peculiar characteristics of the four arguments themselves with their counter arguments, attempting carefully to distinguish original spine from later accretions. This is particularly important because of an initial major misdirection in the study of this evidence by Zeller,[11] who assigned the arguments selected and attacked by Theophrastus to Zeno of Citium; and the whole fragment was then sanctified by Von Arnim as a Stoic fragment (*SVF* 1.106).[12] We must, however, distinguish between the Theophrastean *Sitz im Leben* and the subsequent history of the argument. Both are interesting, but should not be confused. So, to a brief review of the arguments and their counters:

Argument (i) (4–17, §§118–119) is a cracker. If land did not come to be but was there from eternity, it would have been worn smooth with no mountains or hills; for rain from eternity would have worn it level (4–17, §119). Although, of course, mention of the destructive power of rain on earth occurs elsewhere,[13] its use as a cosmic argument is not surprisingly lacking elsewhere. It smacks

---

[11] *Art. cit.* (n.1).

[12] A position still entertained until at least quite recently: e.g. A. Graeser, *Zenon von Kition* (Berlin 1975) 187–206.

[13] E.g. Lucr. 5.255f; but there it makes earth pass into another element (water), and so relates more to Argument (ii).

of rhetorical debate. It is however a geological argument derived from observation, and is countered by meteorological observation and theory: the continual but slow (and hardly perceptible) cyclical evolution of geographical features, whereby mountains are not only worn down but recreated by fire and earthquake (93ff, §132ff).[14]

Argument (ii) (18–40, §§120–123) depends on the observation of the constant diminishing or withdrawal of the sea. This is again established by geographical evidence: rising of islands, shell deposits inland, etc. All this occupies nineteen lines of text. The disturbingly brief concluding argument takes up only four lines: if the sea diminishes, so too the earth will diminish. This seems crazy on observational grounds; if sea diminishes, the land area increases, and vice versa. But we now seem to be talking of sea, earth, air diminishing in the sense of being used up (ἀναλωθήσεται, 38, §123) and ending up in the one οὐσία, fire. Now, ignoring the fearful confusion between geographical/meteorological phenomena, elements and principles, this seems a brief Stoic tail later pinned onto, and wagging, the donkey of the first part. For after all, the first part is already in Aristotle. Indeed, that the sea had a beginning, and the wetness finally all dried up by evaporation, was attributed by Theophrastus himself to the Presocratics Anaximander and Diogenes of Apollonia (according to Alexander, F221 FHS&G), a theory countered by Aristotle in *Meteor.* II.1ff. But the actual tying of the argument of the sea drying up to the creation and destructibility of the cosmos is countered already by Aristotle in *Meteor.* II.3, 356b6ff. And he specifically links the argument of sea perishing by drying up to Democritus (356b10ff = 68A99a Diels). As for the observational *evidence* for the sea drying up and changes of sea and earth areas, Aristotle cites it (*Meteor.* I.14, 351a19ff) as evidence for an orderly cycle where one geological element reciprocally gives way to another. Interestingly, he has no mention of Theophrastus' inland shell deposits, but they do turn up in Olympiodorus, *Comm. on Meteor.* on 351b22 (p.116 Stüve). The Theophrastean counter arguments (129–158, §§138–142) are again based purely on geographical observation of sea encroachment. It is true that the examples chosen by Philo were later popular: for Sicily being previously attached to Italy: D.S. 4.85.3; Strabo 6.1.6;

---

[14] Earthquakes also certainly interested Theophrastus.

Sen. *NQ* 6.30.3; Pliny *NH* 3.86; but these make clear that the tradition is an old one. For Helice and Bura exampled as cities swallowed by sea, compare Polyb. 2.41.7; Strabo 8.7.2; Ovid, *Metam.* 15.293f; Pliny *NH* 2.206; Pausanias 7.24.5f and 12f; 7.25.8; Amm. Marc. 17.7.13. Interestingly for Theophrastus, the disappearance of Helice and Bura was also associated with earthquakes as well as sea. But although popular around Philo's time, the cited instances of Bura and Helice are referred by Seneca (*NQ* 6.23.4; 7.5.3–4) specifically to Aristotle and Callisthenes, Aristotle's nephew. The story of Atlantis (150ff, §141) of course comes from Plato, *Tim.* 24E, 25CD.[15]

Argument (iii) (41–79, §§124–129) seems a more general argument, that of parts/whole correspondance in genesis and destruction. If parts are perishable, the whole will perish. But all parts of the cosmos are perishable, therefore the cosmos is perishable. This is illustrated by running through the four elements, but again by observation as meteorological phenomena: the strongest stones crumble and dissolve; water if stagnant become noisome; air can become tainted, fire extinguished. Historical reference for this argument surfaces strongly in hellenistic philosophy. It is certainly Epicurean, for it recurs in considerable detail in Lucretius 5.235–317; but Stoic too, for Philo presents it in Stoic garb. It is true that some of the Stoic vocabulary is also Philonic, but it can hardly be denied that the framework is also Stoic in physical destruction through the loosening of the πνευματικὸς τόνος as ἕξις (47), and the death of water as if the removal of soul. In any case the argument is independently given as Stoic by D.L. 7.141 (*SVF* 2.589).[16] However, the main Theophrastean counter argument to this (160ff, §143), is that Argument (iii) would hold if and only if *all* parts perished together at the same time. But that is not so in the cosmos when an element individually changes to another. But *that* is normal Aristotelian doctrine frequently expressed.[17]

---

15 D.T. Runia, *Philo of Alexandria and the Timaeus of Plato,* Philosophia Antiqua 44 (Leiden 1986) 84f thinks the reference may come from Philo rather than Theophrastus. But this is debateable, and even if it does come from Philo, does it matter?

16 Which incidentally displays exactly the same reaction to the Theophrastean counter argument that Sedley claims for Lucretius and Epicurus, i.e. change of elements into each other *is* destruction.

17 Ar. *GC* II.4, 331a12ff; *De Caelo* I.10, 280a16ff; III.6, 304b23ff; *Meteor.* II.3, 357b27ff.

Argument (iv) (80–89, §§130–131) is based on the coevality of the human race and the cosmos: if the cosmos were eternal, the human race would be eternal. But man's origin is recent because the arts and crafts must be coeval, and they are clearly recent. Therefore the cosmos was generated.[18]

Again, this argument shows up in Epicurean garb at length in Lucretius 5.324–350. But it is hardly confined to that. The argumentative link between the eternity of the human race to the eternity of the universe is in Ocellus, Περὶ τῆς τοῦ παντὸς φύσεως, 38ff Harder, whom Philo had been reading, and so is likely to have gone further back in Peripatetic discussion. Anyway, the counter arguments to this, dissociating the history of the two by maintaining that the human race is continuous, although liable to partial destruction by fire and water, while the arts are periodically destroyed and have to be recreated, certainly have earlier reference. The cycles of destruction from fire and water are linked to Philolaus (Stob. I.20.1, p.172.6ff W.);[19] while the continuity of human beings but destruction and rediscovery of τέχναι are already in Plato (e.g. *Tim.* 22c–23b; *Laws* 3.677a–d), and Aristotle (*Meteor.* 1.14, 351b8ff; *Metaph.* Λ.8, 1074b10ff; *Pol.* II.8, 1269a4ff).

Even in such a brief and superficial skating over the four arguments selected by Theophrastus, and even with the savagely curtailed evidence available to us today, what strikes one is the range of philosophical provenance involved. The allocation of the arguments to precise origins seems impossible, and the attempt to do so perhaps misguided. I strongly believe that we oversimplify the historical transmission of ideas, forgetting not only written evidence we no longer possess, but also the strong influence of oral communication and discussion. The form and range of the arguments suggest that Theophrastus probably selected *types* of argument that were cullable from the whole range available to him (after all they were the four μέγιστα); i.e. from predecessors (so-called Presocratics, Plato), his own master (Aristotle), and surely contemporary models from debate, which might include incipient Epicurean and Stoic discussion; I do not mean settled dogma, but exploratory oral discussion.[20] It need not even refer to full-blown

---

18 It is interesting to note that the logical form of the agument is: P, Q; –Q, .: –P, i.e. *modus tollens.* So also Argument (i).

19 See now Carl A. Huffman, *Philolaus of Croton* (Cambridge 1993) 261ff.

20 We know that much of Zeno's teaching was oral; I.G. Kidd, *Posidonius,*

theories, nor even to influence in one direction or another, but rather centred on contemporary *reaction* to a common topic. This was certainly one such, namely πότερον ὁ κόσμος ἀίδιος ἢ οὔ, as we perfectly well know from Aristotle, *Top.* 105b24; 104b9, b17. And that context (*Top.*1.14) makes clear that such propositions were the subject of common formal debate, both rhetorical and philosophical. There were clearly a number of such fashionable common topics producing lively reaction in the contemporary Schools, and not only in natural philosophy. For example, in moral philosophy one could hazard: the relativity of goods; whether virtue can be lost or not; the moral status of anger. Moreover, the structure of the Theophrastus fragment in Philo, comprising several arguments with their counter arguments supplied for debate, is typical of Theophrastus, as Jaap Mansfeld has shown.[21]

That is old ground. What is much more interesting is why one should choose *these* four arguments to illustrate the topic of the eternity or destructibility of the cosmos; and they are underlined as the four most important (μέγιστα). For they are indeed a strange collection. Furthermore, the stark fact is that the character of the arguments as given by Theophrastus and their counters, is in the sharpest contrast to those not only of Plato in *Timaeus,* but, and more relevantly, to those of his master Aristotle on the subject. Aristotle's examination of the different views on the topic, and his own arguments in *De Caelo* 1.10–12 are constructed completely through logical and conceptual analysis, and opponents are attacked for logical inconsistency. And this is also true, although the details are different, of the so-called 'Aristotelian arguments', usually taken to be from *De Phil.,* from earlier in Philo, *Aet.* 20ff. But in marked contrast, the arguments that were selected by and appealed to Theophrastus for selection, and so also the arguments (which is perhaps even more important) by which they were countered, depend on observation of geological, geographical and meteorological phenomena with empirical appeal of instance, not on metaphysical argument. I have argued at length elsewhere,[22] that this is precisely the characteristic approach of his *Meteorology.* So this attempt to penetrate to the *Sitz im Leben* of the fragment

---

vol.II *Commentary* on F165.4EK; cf. T91, T99, F166EK.

21 Mansfeld, '*Physikai doxai* and *Problemata physika*', (see above n. 2) 67ff.

22 'Theophrastus' *Meteorology,* Aristotle and Posidonius' in *Theophrastus, His Psychological, Doxographical and Scientific Writings,* 294–306.

suggests that it tells us more about Theophrastus himself than about the arguments or their sources.

As for the *Nachleben* of the arguments, the result is even more striking, for far from being transmogrified into a Stoic fragment, it seems to have been the Epicureans who took most account of it. This is no monopoly, of course, for the evidence indicates derived grounds of argument gong on in all the major Schools, on what after all continued to be a central topic. But the extensive use of Theophrastus' arguments by Lucretius chimes in exactly and significantly with what happened to Theophrastus' *Meteorology*, about which we now know much more from the invaluable find of the Arabic translation extract, edited by Hans Daiber.[23] I have argued elsewhere,[24] that it was Theophrastus' *Meteorology* (which is marked by similar characteristics of argument, very different from Aristotle, as those of our *De Aeternitate* fragment) which was again extensively used by Lucretius, and that this is in sharp contrast, for example, to the Stoic Posidonius, whose *Meteorology* was a recognisable development from the *Meteorology* of Aristotle. This position is now reinforced by the history of the Theophrastus fragment from Philo. One wonders whether Lucretius had direct access to Theophrastus. Whether he did or not, the splendid new edition of Theophrastus' fragments[25] has opened new light on the transmission of ideas in the 1st c. BC.

St. Andrews

---

23 H. Daiber, 'The *Meteorology* of Theophrastus in Syriac and Arabic Translation;' in *Theophrastus: His Psychological, Doxographical and Scientific Writings*, 166–293.

24 Kidd, *art. cit.* (n. 22). So also, J. Mansfeld, 'A Theophrastean Excursus on God and Nature and its Aftermath in Hellenistic Thought', *Phronesis* 37 (1992) 314–335.

25 *Theophrastus of Eresus, Sources for his Life, Writings Thought & Influence*, edd. W.W. Fortenbaugh, P.M. Huby, R.W. Sharples, D. Gutas, 2 vols., Philosophia Antiqua 54 (Leiden 1992).

RICERCHE SULLA TRASMISSIONE DELLE *DIVISIONI ARISTOTELICHE*

TIZIANO DORANDI

Multa Dircaeum levat aura cycnum,
tendit ... quotiens in altos
*nubium tractus ...**

Chi abbia una qualche familiarità con l'opera di Jaap Mansfeld sa bene come anche una sola sua nota possa celare quantomai inaspettati e suggestivi spunti per ulteriori succose ricerche. Questo è il caso del mio contributo il cui germe è già tutto nella frase di una nota dell'articolo: '*Physikai doxai* e *problemata physica*: Da Aristotele ad Aezio (ed oltre)':[1]

> Ciò che vale per questo trattatello [*scil.* lo pseudo-aristotelico Περὶ ἀρετῶν καὶ κακιῶν o Περὶ ἀρετῆς] vale anche per i *Placita* e per le *Divisioni aristoteliche*. Bisogna tentare di rendere conto delle pluralità delle tradizioni in gioco; ha poco senso cercare di ricostruire una singola *Urquelle*.

È prendendo lo spunto da questa frase che vorrei, dunque, indagare la tradizione delle così dette *Divisioni aristoteliche* (d'ora in poi: *DA*) in vista di una nuova edizione—mia o di altri—che sostituisca quella vecchia e ormai superata di Hermann Mutschmann.[2]

La trasmissione delle *DA* è duplice. Da un lato esse sopravvivono in tre codici medievali, dall'altro sono conservate, in maniera affatto indipendente, da Diogene Laerzio. Si tratta di redazioni diverse di un unico *corpus* o, forse, di singoli e distinti *corpora*, che

---

* *Caro Jaap ti chiederai perché anch'io ti abbia "tradito" accogliendo l'invito a partecipare a questo volume miscellaneo: "Il cui diritto all'esistenza" tu-wilamowitzianamente—riterrai "non ancora del tutto accertato". Ma come dimostrare, seppure in maniera affatto inadeguata, un minimo della affettuosa riconoscenza e della stima infinita che mi legano a te? Il tema del mio intervento trova origine in una delle tue illuminanti ricerche e ha come recondita speranza quella di aprire un dialogo con te: che non sia solo ideale! Perché—e mi auguro di non apparire troppo presuntuoso e irriverente nella mia scoperta allusione—almeno una volta l'anno bisogna io appaghi il desiderio, che mi tormenta tutto l'anno, di discutere con te di storia della filosofia antica.*

[1] Mansfeld (1993) 370 n. 80.

[2] Mutschmann (1906).

vanno considerati e studiati, il più delle volte, ciascuno per sé. Ma prima è opportuno descrivere i testimoni.

Comincio con Diogene Laerzio (**DL**). A conclusione della *Vita di Platone* (3.80-109), **DL** trascrive un *corpus* di 32 divisioni che presenta come la testimonianza di Aristotele sulla maniera in cui Platone divideva le cose (3.80: διῄρει δέ, φησὶν 'Αριστοτέλης, καὶ τὰ πράγματα τοῦτον τὸν τρόπον. Cf. 109: ὧδε καὶ τὰ πρῶτα διῄρει κατὰ τὸν 'Αριστοτέλην). In questo caso, la tradizione delle *DA* è inscindibilmente legata a quella dell'intero complesso delle *Vite* laerziane e deve essere, pertanto, studiata in tale contesto.

Le ricerche recenti di Knoepfler[3] hanno gettato nuova luce sul dibattutissimo problema della storia del testo laerziano e i suoi risultati, sebbene siano fondati sull'indagine di una sola biografia e quindi richiedano ulteriori verifiche sistematiche sulle restanti parti dell'opera, considererei, in linea di massima, convincenti. Li ripropongo in forma estremamente sintetica.

Tra i manoscritti *vetustiores* si distingue **B** (*Neap. Burb. gr.* III B 29: s. XII), la cui superiorità deriva non solo dal fatto che è il più antico dei manoscritti integri, ma anche da quello che discende da un *codex* perduto scritto in onciale (dunque anteriore all'anno 800 *ca.*). Nonostante i suoi numerosi errori minori, la tradizione che questo manoscritto offre—non ancora contaminata (se si escludono gli interventi seriori di $\mathbf{B^2}$) dalle correzioni cui andò soggetto l'antenato comune di **P** (*Paris. gr.* 1759 s. XIII *ex.*) e di **F** (*Laur.* 69.13: s. XIII *in.*)—è superiore a quella dei rappresentanti della così detta "vulgata" e a quella degli altri due *vetustiores*, cioè **P** (con il quale è, tuttavia, strettamente imparentato) e **F**, un manoscritto bizzarro e variamente apprezzato. I tre manoscritti *integri* più antichi ebbero un archetipo in comune (**Ω**), distinto da quello dei codici degli *excerpta*, che rimontano tutti a **Φ** (*Vat. gr.* 96: s. XII *in.*), un testimone, comunque, non molto lontano da **Ω**. Le differenze che caratterizzano i due rami della tradizione portano a concludere che l'*autographon excerptoris*, modello di **Φ**, e che risale al s. XI o XII, non era quello di **BPF**, cioè **Ω**, che viene quindi a occupare la posizione di subarchetipo in rapporto al vero e proprio archetipo **X**, capostipite comune di **Φ** e **Ω**. **Φ** discende da **X** attraverso l'intermediario di un manoscritto traslitterato e forse, in più punti, corretto (**χ**) verso il 1100. Simili conclusioni e i risultati delle ricerche più recenti su

[3] Knoepfler (1991).

alcune famiglie della "vulgata" (il cui capostipite Knoepfler designa con la sigla **α**, da non confondere con la prima classe di manoscritti di Martini), hanno consentito allo studioso di delineare i rapporti tra i codici laerziani in uno stemma.[4] Per quanto concerne la localizzazione spazio-temporale dei testimoni, Knoepfler distingue un ramo italo-greco, rappresentato da **BPF** e i loro discendenti, e un ramo orientale rappresentato da **Φ** copiato a Bisanzio. Si può supporre che la tradizione orientale non rimase del tutto sconosciuta in Occidente e che esercitò una influenza indiretta sulla formazione della "vulgata", che si sarebbe ugualmente diffusa in Oriente per l'intermediario di **P**, dopo essere stato corretto, sulla base di **α** (recensione $\mathbf{P^4}$); dall'Oriente, **P** sembra sia stato riportato in Italia da Guarino Veronese. A Firenze, da $\mathbf{P^4}$ fu copiato il *Laur.* 69.35 (**H**), uno degli esemplari utilizzati da Ambrogio Traversari per la sua traduzione latina.

A partire da quanto sopra esposto Knoepfler trae alcuni principi sui quali deve fondarsi la costituzione del testo di **DL** e, di conseguenza, quello delle *DA* nella recensione che da **DL** ci è stata trasmessa.[5] La ricostruzione dell'archetipo (**X**) sarà possibile solo quando **Φ** è conservato; in tutti gli altri casi bisogna contentarsi di ricostituire il subarchetipo (**Ω**), il cui testo può, talvolta, coincidere con quello dell'archetipo. A fondamento del testo è da porre la lezione di **B** correggendone gli errori veniali con l'aiuto di **PF** (quando vi sia concordanza). L'accordo di **B** con **P** o con **F** riporta alla lezione del subarchetipo anche qualora **Φ** appoggi la lezione dell'altro manoscritto. Nei casi in cui i tre codici primari divergano fra loro e manchi la testimonianza di **Φ** né sia possibile dare meccanicamente la preferenza a **B**, si opterà per la lezione che è più vicina a quella di **B**. Con il ricorso alla testimonianza della "vulgata", l'editore potrà altresì rendersi conto di quale manoscritto, fra **F** e **P**, trasmette il testo autentico (immune cioè dalla revisione di **ω'** nel caso di **P** o di **ω** nel caso di **F**). Tale situazione rende, infine, ben evidente che, se talora si riesce a correggere un errore di **Ω** grazie al ricorso a **Φ**, una lezione corrotta di **X** si potrà emendare solo con l'eventuale ricorso alla tradizione indiretta o al *iudicium*. Ma con un testo come quello di Diogene Laerzio l'invito

---

4 Knoepfler (1991) 154.

5 Knoepfler (1991) 163–164. *Condicio sine qua non* per la validità di queste conclusioni è l'accettazione dello stemma tracciato da Knoepfler, una cui verifica è in corso da parte di chi scrive.

alla cautela e a non abusare dell'arte congetturale non è mai superfluo.

Questo è sufficiente a proposito della *recensio* laerziana. Passiamo ai tre manoscritti.

M (*Marcianus gr.* 257 s. XIII *ex.* o s. XIV *in.*).[6] Questo codice, unico testimone conosciuto dell'altra redazione delle *DA* fino a Mutschmann, presenta sotto il titolo Διαίρεσις Ἀριστοτέλους (non Διαιρέσεις Ἀριστοτέλους Rose/Mutschmann) una raccolta di 69 divisioni (ff. 251^r-254^r). Il testo delle divisioni in **M** è sfigurato da numerosi errori, imprecisioni e lacune; anche se in misura minore di quanto finora supposto.

Stretta parentela con **M** mostra **A** (*Parisinus gr.* 39 s. XIII), che tramanda un gruppo di sole 39 divisioni sotto il titolo Διαίρεσις Ἀριστοτέλους (ff. 168^v-172^v).[7] Rispetto a **M**, **A** conserva un numero ridotto di divisioni (omette [22], [27], [35]-[37], [42]-[44], [46], [48]-[57], [59]-[69]);[8] è infestato da diverse lacune; abbrevia il testo di [41], dopo di cui presenta, inoltre, due frammenti allotrî (f. 172^r 7-172^v 4);[9] qualche volta restituisce solo i primi due dei quattro termini di cui è costituita una divisione 'normale' ([1]-[3], [7], [9], [38]-[39]); in altri casi manca la sola ricapitolazione ([4]-[6], [8], [10]-[12]); in altri ancora il terzo termine è mescolato, seppure solo in parte, con il primo ([11], [58]).

Infine **L** (*Leid. Voss. gr.* Q 11 s. XIV, prima metà). Esso trasmette (ff. 92^r-96^r) un *corpus* di 61 divisioni rispetto alle 69 di **M** sotto il titolo anonimo Περὶ διαιρέσεως scritte da due mani distinte, ma databili entrambe alla prima metà del XIV sec.[10] **L** non è né fratello né discendente né imparentato direttamente con **M** come dimostra la diversità di errori e lacune. La differenza più evidente è nel numero minore di divisioni conservate: mancano in **L** le otto divisioni [35], [63] e [64]-[69] la cui assenza—se si eccettua [35], accidentalmente omessa—può essere voluta: [63] costituisce, infatti,

---

6 Cf. Rossitto (1984) 13 s. n. 3.

7 Boudreaux (1909), che per primo ne scoprì l'esistenza. Indico il manoscritto con la sigla **A** invece che con **P** (come finora fatto) per evitare confusione con il *Paris. gr.* 1759 di Diogene Laerzio, ugualmente siglato **P**.

8 La numerazione, fra parentesi quadre, è quella di **M**, che contiene la raccolta più completa.

9 E non tre come scrive Boudreaux (1909) 222 n. 5 seguito da Moraux (1977) 126. La seconda e la terza aggiunta costituiscono, infatti, un unico testo. Cf. *infra*, 150–152.

10 Moraux (1977), che per primo ne ha scoperto l'esistenza.

in un certo modo, un doppione di [51], mentre [64]-[69] formano un gruppo compatto i cui membri sono saldamente legati l'uno all'altro con caratteristiche che non sono le stesse che ispirano le restanti divisioni. Al posto di quel nucleo, **L** riporta una appendice, nella quale Moraux scorge tracce di influenza neoplatonica, e che è costituita da una διαίρεσις ψυχῆς μετὰ ὁρισμοῦ e da un ὅρος νοός.[11] Alcune lezioni di **L** possono servire talora a correggere quelle corrotte di **M** o **A**.

Il testimone più sfruttato delle *DA*, anche perché conosciuto da più tempo, è **M**. Esso è stato posto a fondamento delle edizioni di quell'opera, come unico testimone della tradizione parallela a **DL**, fino a quella recente curata da Gigon,[12] che continua a ignorare sia **A** sia **L**.

È ormai accertato che **M A L** tramandano una seconda 'redazione' delle *DA*. I tre manoscritti devono, comunque, essere indagati singolarmente al fine di metterne bene in risalto le caratteristiche portanti e meglio definirne gli eventuali legami e rapporti.

Comincio con **M A**. Per Boudreaux, **A**, per certi aspetti, inferiore a **M**, è a questo manoscritto imparentato, come prova la presenza di errori congiuntivi e il fatto che le divisioni sono riportate nella stessa sequenza; esso risale, tuttavia, a un modello comune in maniera probabilmente indipendente. Lo dimostrerebbero i casi in cui **A** fornisce la lezione originale, sfigurata in **M**; quelli in cui aiuta a eliminare dal testo di **M** alcune intrusioni o a ripararne omissioni, tra cui anche il testo della ricapitolazione di cinque divisioni ([26], [28], [30]-[32]). Il caso, infine, di [10] dove **A** presenta un testo superiore a quello raffazzonato di **M**. Per Moraux,[13] la parentela fra i due codici è evidente anche se assai lontana. **A** tramanda, infatti, una scelta di divisioni spesso in forma abbreviata soprattutto nella terza parte di quella che è la struttura canonica completa di una divisione: 1. Indicazione dei membri della divisione (διαρεῖται ... εἰς τρία, τέσσαρα); 2. Enumerazione di questi membri; 3. Spiegazioni relative a ogni membro, spesso con una serie di esempi introdotti da οἷον; 4. Ricapitolazione, che riproduce, in linea di massima, l'enumerazione di 2. In **A** la ricapitolazione

---

[11] Sono riprodotte da Moraux (1977) 126. Esse dovranno figurare nella nuova edizione delle *DA*.

[12] Gigon (1987) F 83.

[13] Moraux (1977) 101, 103–104.

compare solo per le divisioni [26], [28], [30]–[32], casi in cui, curiosamente, manca negli altri testimoni. Poiché le ricapitolazioni svolgono, più o meno, la stessa funzione dell'enumerazione, c'è da chiedersi se queste cinque aggiunte risalgano al modello di **A** oppure siano state introdotte da un anonimo redattore.[14]

La dipendenza di **A** e **M** da un capostipite comune appare sicura. Resta, semmai, da vedere fino a che punto sia lecito correggere il testo di **M** a partire dalle lezioni di **A** e viceversa; se cioè le differenze che distinguono i due manoscritti siano da imputare al fatto che **A** ha trasmesso meglio il suo modello oppure se derivino da una recensione (?) diversa con cui **A** o il suo antenato (o antenati?) hanno contaminato il testo comune anche a **M**, o meglio se non siano interventi personali del suo copista (che in questo caso avrebbe svolto anche il ruolo probabile di redattore). Si tenga conto che la datazione dei due manoscritti impedisce di postulare una derivazione di **A** da **M** e che una derivazione di **M** da **A** è altresì impossibile.

Prendo in considerazione le caratteristiche di **A** rilevate da Boudreaux. La presenza di un numero inferiore di divisioni, l'omissione di uno dei membri che costituiscono la divisione tipo, il rimaneggiamento della struttura o la tendenza a abbreviare può bene essere imputata sia al modello di **A** sia al copista (redattore?) stesso. Se alcune omissioni e errori comuni a **A** e a **M** si spiegano come verificatisi in maniera accidentale, diversamente da Boudreaux giudicherei, invece, i luoghi in cui **A** conserva la lezione corretta rispetto a **M**. Non è affatto escluso che le lezioni di **A** siano frutto di congettura (lo confermerebbe il fatto che, nella quasi totalità delle occorrenze gli studiosi successivi avevano proposto le medesime correzioni). Lo stesso discorso può valere, talvolta, per quei casi in cui **A** consente di eliminare intrusioni o riparare omissioni in **M**. Per l'aggiunta delle cinque ricapitolazioni, ha ragione Moraux a lasciare la questione in sospeso. Quanto a [10], non parlerei, con Boudreaux, della versione di **A** come della genuina rispetto a quella rimaneggiata di **M**, ma piuttosto di un caso di tradizione ritoccata (rispetto a **M** e a **L**), non esente essa stessa da eventuali corruttele (Νείλου).[15]

Qualche chiarimento relativamente ai rapporti fra **M** e **A** ritengo possa venire dallo studio delle due inserzioni allotrie dopo [41]. La

---

[14] Moraux (1977) 104 conclude con un *non liquet*.

[15] Per la questione, vd. Rossitto (1984) 157–158.

seconda (παρακαλῶ πρῶτον πάντων... θεῷ τὰ τετολμημένα), come sono riuscito a appurare, è una citazione letterale dall'omelia di Severiano di Gabala, *In incarnationem Domini.*[16] Più difficile l'identificazione della prima—che trascrivo:

> *ἐγώ εἰμι ἐγώ εἰμι καὶ ἕως ἂν καταγηράσατε ἐγώ εἰμι* (*LXX* Is. 46, 4) *δεῖ γὰρ αὐτὸν βασιλεύειν ἄχρις οὗ ἂν θῇ πάντας τοὺς ἐχθροὺς αὐτοῦ ὑπὸ πόδας αὐτοῦ* (*NT* 1 Cor. 15.25). τὸ *ἕως* οὐ χρόνου δηλωτικὸν, ἀλλ' ἰδίωμα τῆς θείας γραφῆς. ση(μείωσαι)· ταῦτα διὰ τὸ *καὶ οὐκ ἐγίνωσκα αὐτὴν ἕως οὗ ἔτεκε τὸν υἱὸν αὐτῆς τὸν πρώτοτοκον* (*NT* Matth. 1. 25)· *πρώτοτοκος ἐκ νεκρῶν* (*NT* Col. 1. 18). εἰπὲ καὶ τὰς ὀκτὼ ἀναστάσεις.[17]

L'εἰπέ mi porterebbe a pensare che siamo di fronte a un appunto anonimo per un sermone. Si tratta, dunque, di due frammenti derivati da un contesto cristiano la cui estraneità alle *DA* è indubitabile, ma la cui sopravvivenza ben si spiega in questa sezione di **A**, il solo manoscritto in cui le *DA* sono precedute e seguite da materiale di contenuto prevalentemente teologico.[18] Resta da chiedersi a chi debba essere imputata l'inserzione di questi brani, a quel punto del manoscritto, a interrompere la sequenza delle *DA*: se al copista (redattore?) di **A** o già al suo modello. Se si accetta la seconda ipotesi e si mantiene ferma una derivazione di **A** e **M** da un comune antenato, sebbene lontano, la mancanza di questi frammenti in **M** si potrebbe spiegare sia ammettendo che **M** abbia volontariamente omesso quelle parti estranee oppure presupponendo un testimone intermedio fra **A** e il suo modello. Ma se, come ho suggerito, il primo frammento è quanto resta di un anonimo appunto per una predica, ben più probabile mi appare l'eventualità che i due passi siano stati aggiunti direttamente dal copista di **A**. Quello che mi sembra derivi, comunque, in maniera evidente dalla identificazione di queste due citazioni e dalla stessa struttura di **A** è la prova concreta di una sicura circolazione delle *DA* all'interno di *milieux* cristiani, d'altra parte, già presupposta.[19]

---

[16] *PG* 59. 697, 69–698, 11 (riferita parzialmente e con varianti anche da Fozio, *Bibl.* cod. 277. 520a 27–42 [8. 142, 27–143, 42 Henry], che la attribuisce a Giovanni Crisostomo). Cf. *Clavis Patrum Graecorum* 2 n° 4240.

[17] Posso richiamare a confronto: Didym., *fr. Ps.* F 1054, 5 ss. Mühlenberg; Thdt., *interpr. in Pauli ep.*, *PG* 82.356, 25–28; Didym., *Trin.* 3, *PG* 39.832, 39–833, 5. Per le ὀκτὼ ἀναστάσεις: Georg. Mon., *Chron.*, 1. 315, 1–316, 2 De Boor.

[18] Sulla struttura composita di **A**, cf. l'*Inventaire sommaire* di Omont, 1.7. Ma la mescolanza eterogenea dei testi in esso contenuti meriterebbe di essere approfondita anche in rapporto con la presenza delle *DA*.

[19] Cf. la bibliografia citata alla n. 44.

Vengo ora ai rapporti, ben più complessi, di **L** con **A** e **M** (o **AM**). La scoperta di **L** ha gettato luce sul problema della tradizione delle *DA* e non soltanto per il contributo che da questo terzo codice può venire per la costituzione del testo, ma anche per meglio spiegarne la diffusione e i canali della trasmissione. **L** è un manoscritto indipendente da **A** e **M**: la differenza più notevole che distingue **L** da **M** consiste nel fatto che il primo contiene un numero inferiore di divisioni. Per Moraux[20] l'assenza, in particolare, delle ultime sei ([64]-[69]) dipenderebbe non dal fatto che il modello di **L** era mutilo, quanto piuttosto dal fatto che **L** risale a un ramo della tradizione, che non conosceva l'esistenza di questa appendice; essa sarebbe stata nota solo al tronco da cui derivò **M**. Come **A**, **L** non è esente da errori, ma consente anche, in molti casi, di correggere luoghi corrotti di **M** e di colmarne lacune.[21] Pur con la dovuta cautela dettata dal fatto che alcune divergenze non possono essere imputate alla negligenza del copista, ma tradiscono l'intervento di un redattore, si deve ammettere l'importanza del contributo di **L** per sanare talvolta il testo difficile e malamente alterato delle *DA*.

Le differenze fra i tre manoscritti risultano dalla collazione pubblicata da Moraux.[22] I criteri che lo studioso enuncia a proposito dell'uso che si può fare dei tre testimoni per la ricomposizione dell'*Urtext* delle *DA* non possono, tuttavia, assumere il valore di principi validi in assoluto:[23]

> Comme L représente une autre branche de la tradition, il a souvent conservé le texte original là où M présente une lacune. Et quand c'est L qui a, par distraction, laissé tomber un morceau de texte entre deux mots identiques, on trouve d'ordinaire le texte complet dans M (éventuellement dans P *[= A]*). La comparison des deux branches de la tradition permet donc, dans bien de cas, de reconstruire le texte de l'archétype, que ni MP *[= A]* ni L n'ont conservé dans sa pureté première.

Sul fondamento di queste premesse, Moraux propone un nuovo testo parziale per [36], [53], [56] o completo per [22], [38], [40], [45], [51], [54] combinando insieme lezioni di **M** e di **L**. Non posso

---

[20] Moraux (1977) 102.

[21] Una delle caratteristiche di **L** è la presenza di titoli per le singole divisioni escluse [26]–[27]. Nel caso di [13], [16], [19] e [41], i titoli sono riportati a margine. **A** ha il titolo solo di [1], **M** di [2]. Per quanto riguarda **DL** ci sono sporadiche tracce di titoli in **B** e in **P** (sistematicamente cancellati dal quarto correttore **P**^{4}).

[22] Moraux (1977) 105–114.

[23] Moraux (1977) 114–115. Le esplicazioni in corsivo sono mie.

discutere nei dettagli tutti i casi i cui Moraux ha operato sulle *DA*. Noto solo che talvolta i suoi tentativi hanno dato origine a una ricostruzione dubbia sia dal punto di vista testuale sia soprattutto dal punto di vista filosofico, come ha chiarito la Rossitto nelle pagine del suo commento.

Più cautamente e con maggiore verisimiglianza, argomenta la Rossitto:[24]

> L compie interventi molto significativi sul testo, dando l'impressione di volerlo rendere più coerente, o addirittura di correggerlo: ad esempio esso ripristina spesso nella spiegazione l'ordine in cui i termini appaiono succedersi negli elenchi iniziale o finale, o risulta "confermare" congetture di studiosi moderni, il che può essere considerato piuttosto una prova di congettura da parte del copista, che non tradizione genuina o non inquinata del manoscritto.

Riserve avrei, semmai, sulle sue ulteriori conclusioni—ma di questo in seguito:

> Il grado di "perfezione" che (L) sembra presentare parla a sfavore di una sua maggiore fedeltà al testo primitivo rispetto a M, il quale, in virtù delle sue non infrequenti, ma nemmeno decisive, incongruenze, e della sua rozzezza, rimane in fin dei conti la versione delle *Divisioni*, tuttora maggiormente affidabile.

Fin qui lo *status quaestionis* sui manoscritti.

L'edizione di Mutschmann, le cui debolezze non dipendono solo dalle cattive conoscenze della tradizione laerziana,[25] è stata messa in crisi dalla scoperta delle raccolte di **A** e di **L**. Né tantomeno soddisfa l'attesa riedizione delle *DA* approntata da Gigon, insieme con i restanti frammenti di Aristotele.[26] Lo studioso riproduce, infatti, le due versioni delle *DA* di **M** e **DL**, la prima a partire dalle edizioni di Rose e di Mutschmann e da una rinnovata autopsia di **M**, la seconda tenendo presente il testo stabilito da Hicks, dagli Editori di Basilea e da Long e suggerendo, in entrambi i casi sporadiche correzioni.[27] Purtroppo, Gigon non ha utilizzato né **A** né **L** né ha apportato sostanziali miglioramenti.

L'edizione delle *DA*, qualunque sia il loro valore intrinseco, resta, pertanto, ancora un *desideratum* nella storia della filologia classica e

---

[24] Rossitto (1984) 25 n. 38.

[25] Cf. Biedl (1955) 28. Severa, ma giusta, la recensione di Praechter (1910).

[26] Cf. Rossitto (1989) 213–215.

[27] Gigon (1987) 318.

della filosofia antica. Ma come affrontare il problema? Su quali principi fondare il nuovo testo critico? Non è possibile rispondere a queste domande se non si imposta prima correttamente (non dico, si risolve) la questione ancora più spinosa e ostica della origine di questa raccolta, del genere letterario e della sua eventuale paternità. Sono questioni interrelate fra loro e già ampiamente dibattutte, ma che solo ora si avviano a trovare una risposta soddisfacente.

Le liste antiche dell'opere di Aristotele attestano l'esistenza di scritti il cui titolo riporta nell'àmbito delle *Divisioni*: Διαιρέσεις σοφιστικαὶ δ (DL 29; H 31*; A —) Διαιρέσεις ιζ (DL 42; H 41; A 58* ?) Διαιρετικῶν α (DL 43; H 42; A —) Διαιρετικὸν α (DL 63; H —; A —). E questi dati parrebbero confermati da **M** e **A** e da **DL**: **M** e **A** nel titolo stesso (Διαίρεσις 'Αριστοτέλους), **DL** nelle parole che premette alla raccolta (3.80: διῄρει δέ, φησὶν 'Αριστοτέλης, καὶ τὰ πράγματα τοῦτον τὸν τρόπον) e nella conclusione (109: ὧδε καὶ τὰ πρῶτα διῄρει κατὰ τὸν 'Αριστοτέλην). Ma la paternità aristotelica delle *Divisioni* e la loro identificazione con una delle opere citate, seppure in una versione in larga misura riscritta e rimaneggiata, è stata spesso accolta con scetticismo.[28]

Per primo, Rose pubblicò nell'*Aristoteles Pseudepigraphus*[29] il testo delle *DA* nella redazione di **M** insieme con i frammenti degli scritti di Aristotele che non erano rientrati nel *corpus* di Bekker, giudicandoli tutti spuri. Nelle due edizioni successive della sua opera, Rose, pur mantenendo ferma la propria convinzione dell'inautenticità dei frammenti, non riprodusse più il testo delle *DA* nella rubrica intitolata Διαιρέσεις e si limitò a un semplice rinvio a **DL** (F 111^2 = 114^3) e a **M** (F 112^2 = 115^3).[30] Le *DA* rivendicò a Aristotele Heitz.[31] Egli distinse, peraltro, due raccolte di *Divisioni*: la prima—una esposizione di divisioni platoniche—rappresentata dal testo di **M** e **DL**; la seconda dalle divisioni citate nei cataloghi delle opere di Aristotele e nella testimonianza di Alessandro di Afrodisia. **M** e **DL** conserverebbero una raccolta di divisioni di origine peripatetica, interpolata da autori cristiani, dove, accanto a molte cose indegne di Platone e Aristotele si intravedono ancora elementi più

[28] Dettagliata e documentata analisi in Rossitto (1984) 13–26.

[29] Rose (1863) 677–695.

[30] Rose^2 F 110–112 e Rose^3 F 113–115. F 112 =113 è un passo di Alex. Aphr., *in Top.*, 242, 1–9 Wallies (*CAG* 2.2), che Gigon (1987) F 622 assegna piuttosto alla Τῶν ἀγαθῶν διαίρεσις.

[31] Heitz (1868) 91–112, 118–119.

antichi, risalenti forse allo stesso Aristotele. Se Suckow[32] considerò le *DA* come opera genuina di Aristotele, in generale, prevalse l'opinione che si trattasse piuttosto di una raccolta di dottrine platoniche e aristoteliche (Susemihl), della rielaborazione di un'opera composta nell'àmbito della Academia antica (Zeller) o un manuale scolastico in essa usato (Christ). Un giudizio più favorevole sullo scritto dette invece Hambruch,[33] che individuò in alcune *DA* (**M** [37], [64]-[69]) l'esposizione di regole logiche comuni a Platone e alla sua scuola, che rimontavano alla Academia antica, ma che erano state utilizzate anche da Aristotele nei *Topici*. Lo studioso mise, inoltre, in evidenza alcune analogie fra le *DA* e le esposizioni delle lezioni orali di Platone, quale quella *Sul bene*, e il Περὶ τἀγαθοῦ di Aristotele, nonché con i frammenti dell'altro suo scritto perduto Περὶ ἐναντίων. Sulla falsariga dei risultati di Hambruch si pose Mutschmann nella *Praefatio* alla sua edizione: per molte *DA* è possibile postulare una derivazione diretta da Platone; altre si presentano come la rielaborazione di dottrine dei dialoghi platonici risalente al suo insegnamento orale e trascritte dai suoi discepoli, tra i quali lo stesso Aristotele, che vi aggiunse qualcosa di suo e ne adattò i contenuti al proprio pensiero. È difficile stabilire a quando risalgono gli interventi di Aristotele: la presenza giustapposta di elementi della fase platonizzante e di altri di una fase più matura farebbero pensare a una rielaborazione diacronica. Alcune *DA* sono frutto di manipolazioni seriori dovute all'intervento di editori peripatetici e talvolta anche cristiani. Nel complesso, ci troveremmo di fronte a un compendio di filosofia a uso delle scuole la cui relativa facilità e il cui livello elementare sarebbero dovuti proprio a questa destinazione. Se le *DA* analizzate da Hambruch erano finalizzate all'insegnamento della dialettica, le altre erano destinate, invece, alle esercitazioni retoriche. Le analogie fra alcune *DA* e i resti del Περὶ τἀγαθοῦ aristotelico furono approfonditi da Wilpert,[34] che intravide nelle *DA* una esposizione academica delle dottrine non scritte di Platone. Lo studioso segnalò anche interessanti coincidenze e differenze con il libro Δ della *Metafisica* e il Περὶ ἐναντίων. Le *DA*, in ultima analisi, sono—a suo avviso—una rielaborazione delle dottrine orali di Platone nata nella Academia per le cure di un discepolo sul genere del Περὶ τἀγαθοῦ

32 Suckow (1855) 96ss.
33 Hambruch (1904).
34 Wilpert (1941) 236–241, (1949) 108, 149, 183.

di Aristotele. Favorevole alla paternità aristotelica delle *DA* sembrerebbe fosse Ross, a meno a quanto si può ricavare dalla sua edizione degli *Aristotelis Fragmenta selecta*, dove le due redazioni dello scritto (**M** e **DL**) vengono menzionate nella sezione sulle opere di logica sotto il titolo Διαιρέσεις.[35] I rapporti con l'insegnamento orale di Platone ha ulteriormente sviluppati Krämer[36] per **M** [67]-[68] e **DL** [32], divisioni nelle quali lo studioso individua una probabile relazione delle dottrine non scritte di Platone elaborata da Aristotele.[37] E accanto a queste, le *DA* mostrano corrispondenze anche con il pensiero di altri Academici antichi, talvolta rivisitato attraverso il ripensamento di Aristotele. Una svalutazione globale delle *DA* ha riproposto Moraux:[38] si tratterebbe di un manuale mediocre, senza originalità, ricolmo di piattezze, banalità e inezie, anche se fondato su un sostrato che alla lontana risale a Platone e a Aristotele. Per Gigon,[39] le *DA* sono un *excerptum*, con fini protrettici, di materiale derivato da distinti dialoghi di Aristotele; il loro carattere prevalentemente etico mostra stretti parallelismi non solo con i trattati aristotelici, ma anche con i dialoghi platonici. Esse sono, dunque, da restituire a Aristotele e da ricondurre nell'âmbito della Academia Antica dove egli soggiornò a lungo, restandone influenzato e a sua volta influenzandola. Infine, la Rossitto[40] ha cercato di dimostrare che le *DA* hanno un grado di "aristotelicità" non inferiore a quello delle altre opere scritte da Aristotele durante il periodo academico e ne ha spiegato la peculiare natura con la loro destinazione scolastica. Innanzitutto le *DA* mostrano numerose coincidenze di contenuto con quanto Aristotele afferma nelle sue opere, soprattutto quelle che possono essere fatte risalire al periodo giovanile sia quelle frammentarie (*Protreptico*) sia quelle conservate (i *Topici*, il libro Δ della *Metafisica* e le *Categorie*); ma non mancano neppure significativi paralleli con le due *Etiche* e la *Retorica*. In secondo luogo, le *DA* presentano analoghe coincidenze sia con le dottrine degli Academici antichi (Speusippo, Senocrate, Ermodoro) sia soprattutto con alcuni *Dialoghi* di Platone e con le sue dottrine orali; e, nondimeno, influssi dalla *Rhetorica ad Alexandrum*

---

35 Ross (1955) 101–102 = F 12 (**DL**) e 3 (**M**).

36 Krämer (1983) 141–142.

37 Gaiser—seguito da Krämer, in studi successivi—allarga il numero a **M** [23], [67]–[68] e **DL** [27], [32].

38 Moraux (1977) 1–127.

39 Gigon (1987) 318.

40 Rossitto (1984) 27–33.

di Anassimene di Lampsaco, da Isocrate, dai *Magna Moralia* e dallo pseudo-aristotelico *De virtutibus et vitiis*. Tutto ciò induce a pensare che nelle *DA* siano confluite: "Classificazioni di carattere dialettico e retorico più diffuse all'interno, ma non meno all'esterno, dell'Accademia platonica del IV secolo", un ambiente con il quale doveva avere buona familiarità colui che ha costituito il *corpus* delle *DA*, che si presenta come una raccolta di gruppi di classificazioni non totalmente eterogenei fra loro, perché legati da divisioni "di passaggio" e soprattutto perché riconducibili a un: "Denominatore comune, rappresentato dal loro carattere retorico e dialettico".[41] Non deve meravigliare che l'organizzatore di tutto questo materiale in un unico scritto sia stato lo stesso Aristotele: egli vi avrebbe aggiunto proprie dottrine e l'avrebbe uniformato dal punto di vista terminologico negli anni del suo soggiorno nell'Academia, in preparazione dei suoi corsi di retorica e di dialettica. Il metodo di lavoro adottato e i fini sono simili a quelli che Aristotele applica nel libro Δ della *Metafisica*. La tesi che le *DA* costituiscano, invece, un anonimo "manuale di filosofia elementare" è stata suffragata da Mansfeld[42] portando a confronto—accanto ai manuali appartenenti alla famiglia dei *Placita*—il caso del Περὶ ἀρετῶν καὶ κακιῶν o Περὶ ἀρετῆς dello ps.-Aristotele sia nella versione abbreviata sia in quella seriore riveduta con integrazioni stoiche, nota con il titolo Περὶ παθῶν e attribuita a Andronico di Rodi.[43] L'ipotesi non è nuova, ma i confronti che Mansfeld adduce sono quanto mai significativi e un'interpretazione delle *DA* come "manuale a uso scolastico" spiega, meglio di ogni altra, aspetti della trasmissione di quel testo e è da questa confortata.

Ma il dibattito sulla paternità aristotelica o meno delle *DA* svolge, in un certo qual modo, un ruolo secondario. Il *corpus* (o i *corpora*?), messo insieme da anonimi redattori, contiene, effettivamente, materiale originale derivato da tradizione scritta o orale risalente a Platone, Aristotele e a altri membri interni o esterni all'Academia. Quello che mi sembra evidente è, tuttavia, il fatto che, nelle redazioni in cui sono oggi leggibili, le *DA* difficilmente possono essere considerate al pari di altri frammenti di opere perdute di Aristotele. Nemmeno se si suppone una pessima trasmissione, riesco a intra-

---

41 Rossitto (1984) 30–31.
42 Mansfeld (1993) 317, 326–327.
43 Mansfeld (1993) 370 n. 80.

vedere come loro unica fonte uno scritto originario di Aristotele in cui egli avrebbe organizzato materiale di diversa provenienza (ma questo vale anche per un qualunque altro autore specifico). Pure ammettendo, infatti, che all'origine ci fosse una o più opere di Aristotele, gli infiniti passaggi e rimaneggiamenti cui i testi sono stati sottoposti le hanno talmente sfigurate, che è ben faticoso intravederne la struttura stessa—non parlo della forma né tantomeno della lingua.

Delle *DA* circolarono già nella tarda antichità redazioni distinte, inquinate e interpolate da "redattori" e da "maestri di scuola",[44] arricchite di esempi o semplificate nella loro struttura e nel loro dettato: la raccolta giunta a **DL** e un accenno in uno scolio allo *Hexaemeron* di Basilio[45]—scoperto da Pasquali, e correttamente utilizzato da Mansfeld[46]—ne provano la diffusione nel mondo tardo-antico.

All'origine di queste diverse redazioni bisogna ammettere una pluralità di modelli non attribuibili a un determinato autore (p. es.: Aristotele). Si può pensare a più scritti (p. es.: i trattati aristotelici ricordati nei cataloghi delle sue opere, Platone, Anassimene e Isocrate) dai quali anonimi maestri o redattori hanno ricavato—più o meno indipendentemente—il loro materiale; ma anche—e mi sembra ipotesi più consona con le realtà di cui disponiamo—a una o più raccolte anonime, patrimonio di scuola che, come il citato Περὶ ἀρετῶν καὶ κακιῶν pseudo-aristotelico, avevano la funzione di manuali: "Per studenti di filosofia, ma anche per studenti di retorica".[47]

A partire da queste premesse, devono essere impostati i criteri ecdotici per la nuova edizione. L'indipendenza di **DL** nei confronti di **M** è stata riconosciuta fino da Rose e ammessa dagli editori e studiosi successivi, che pubblicarono **DL** separatamente (Rose, Heitz, Gigon) o su una colonna parallela al testo di **M** (Mutsch-

44 Rose (1863) 678, Mutschmann (1906) XXXIII e Moraux (1977) 121 n. 13 vi hanno scorto interpolazioni cristiane. Ne ridimensiona la presenza Gigon (1987). Cf. Rossitto (1984) 133 e *supra* 150–152.

45 *Schol. in Bas. Hexaem.* XIX Pasquali (1910/1986) 200, 4–5 (= 545, 4–5): ἐν ταῖς Ἀριστοτέλους εἰς Πλάτωνα ἀναφερομέναις διαιρέσεσιν κεῖται αὕτη τῶν τεχνῶν ἡ διαφορά. Il riferimento è a [8].

46 Mansfeld (1993) 370–371 nn. 81 e 83.

47 Mansfeld (1993) 370 n. 81. Una situazione simile è stata postulata da Souilhé (1930) 155–158 a proposito degli ὅροι pseudo-platonici.

mann).[48] **DL** rappresenta una tradizione a sé, la cui origine può essere ravvisata in una raccolta precedente la composizione delle *Vite* laerziane (prima metà del s. III d.C.) e posteriore a Aristotele. Restano gli altri tre testimoni. Mutschmann, che conosceva solo **M**, vi intravide una seconda recensione, che pubblicò a fianco di quella di **DL**, da lui considerata primaria. La situazione è divenuta più complessa con la scoperta di **A**, prima, e di **L**, dopo. Già Boudreaux riconobbe in **A** una tradizione vicina a quella di **M** e suggerì di utilizzarne il contributo per correggere quelli che riteneva errori o omissioni meccaniche di **M**, ma che sono piuttosto, in molti casi, omissioni volontarie e sintomatiche di influenze di diverse scelte "redazionali" o "scolastiche". Questo significa che, sebbene i due manoscritti siano tra loro imparentati e, in un certo qual modo, costituiscano un'unica famiglia, non sempre le loro lezioni possono essere mescolate a formare un *Urtext*. Similmente per la testimonianza di **L**. Le lezioni di **L** risultano talvolta utili per riparare guasti di **M** (e di **A**) qualora siano corruttele di origine meccanica; anche in questo caso, si deve, comunque, evitare di incorrere nella tentazione di ricostruire, a ogni costo, un *Urtext*. Per le *DA*, ci troviamo, dunque, di fronte almeno a due redazioni diverse e distinte di un testo originale la cui forma e struttura spesso non può essere stabilita con certezza. Non si deve dare la preferenza, in assoluto, all'una o all'altra delle tradizioni, ma il contributo di ciascuna deve essere considerato di per sé. Questo comporta, come prima conseguenza pratica, l'invito al *futurus editor* di pubblicare il testo delle due redazioni delle *DA* su pagine parallele: su quella di sinistra la redazione di **DL**, su quella di destra il testo **M A L** (oppure **M A**, **M L**, **M** o **L** soltanto). Il tutto può essere più o meno così rappresentato:

Pagina sinistra	Pagina destra
DL	**M A L**
-----------	--- --- ---
-----------	--- --- ---
-----------	--- --- ---

48 Le differenze analizza la Rossitto (1984) nelle pagine del suo commentario.

L'editore sarà talvolta costretto a riprodurre su colonne parallele le distinte 'versioni' dei singoli manoscritti perché troppo divergenti; in altri sarà sufficiente stampare il testo di **M** sulla prima colonna e, a fianco, solo le 'varianti' di **A** o **L**; in altri ancora potrà presentare il ricostruito *Urtext* limitandosi a segnalare eventuali minime diffenze in apparato. Il confronto fra i codici consentirà altresì di correggere vicendevolmente corruttele meccaniche, di migliorare incertezze testuali o risolvere dubbi.

Per rendere più chiaro il discorso, cerco di definire graficamente la mia suggestione. Una cosa vorrei risultasse evidente e cioè che questo schema non è né uno *stemma codicum* né ha l'ambizione di rappresentare una ricostruzione, dettagliata e sicura in tutti i particolari, della nascita e delle tappe progressive di formazione delle due redazioni delle *DA* giunte fino a noi. Esso troverà conferme o smentite nel lavoro di cesello che costituisce il momento della *recensio* di qualsiasi testo antico:

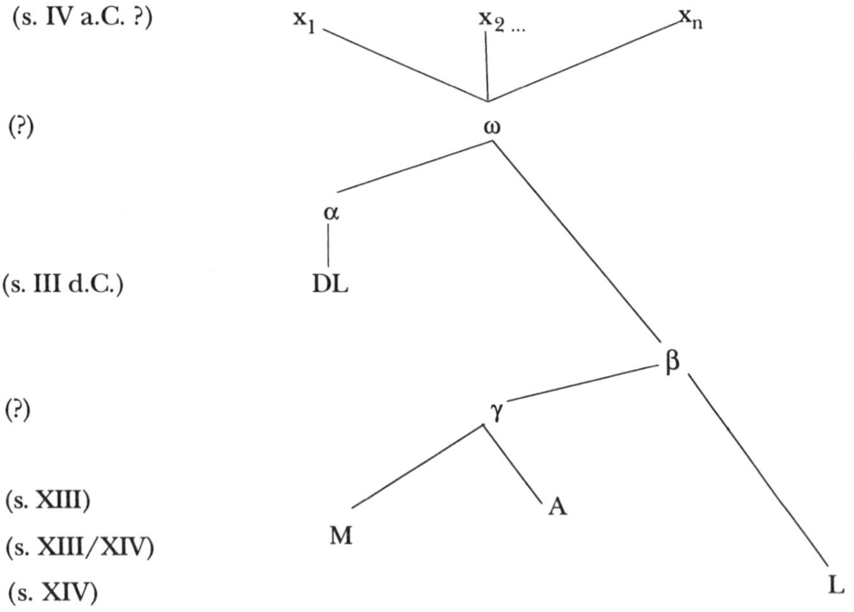

Con $\mathbf{x_1}$, $\mathbf{x_2}$, ..., $\mathbf{x_n}$ indico la serie molteplice di fonti (anonime o non) che costituirono il sostrato materiale dal quale derivò la successiva tradizione "scolastica" (**ω**), da intendere come un ipotetico bacino collettore, la cui ricostruzione risulterà spesso difficile o disperata a causa della fluidità di quell'opera, ma la cui esistenza non può essere negata. Da **ω** attinsero, in tempi diversi e con modalità diverse, i singoli redattori (**α β γ**), in maniera diretta o attraverso modelli intermedi, non sempre né sicuramente identificabili o postulabili.

A mo' di conclusione propongo, infine, quattro esempi di come intenderei dovessero essere pubblicate le *DA*. Si tratta di una divisione ([10]) tramandata da tutti e quattro i testimoni, di due da tre (**DL M L** [36] e **M A L** [30]) e di una da due (**M L** [22]). Non è necessario proporre divisioni conservate da **DL** e **M**; né esistono casi di *DA* note da **M A**.[49]

---

49 Alla fine di ogni esempio segnalo la bibliografia e mi soffermo su una scelta di problemi testuali.

[10] DL M A L

DL
Titulus deest

διαιρεῖται δὲ ἡ εὐγένεια εἰς εἴδη τέτταρα. ἓν μέν, ἐὰν ὦσιν οἱ πρόγονοι καλοὶ κἀγαθοὶ καὶ δίκαιοι, τοὺς ἐκ τούτων γεγεννημένους εὐγενεῖς φασιν εἶναι· ἄλλο δέ, ἐὰν ὦσιν οἱ πρόγονοι δεδυναστευκότες καὶ ἄρχοντες γεγενημένοι, τοὺς ἐκ τούτων εὐγενεῖς φασιν εἶναι. ἄλλο δέ, ἐὰν ὦσιν οἱ πρόγονοι ὀνομαστοί, οἷον ἀπὸ στρατηγίας, ἀπὸ στεφανιτῶν ἀγώνων· καὶ γὰρ τοὺς ἐκ τούτων γεγεννημένους εὐγενεῖς προσαγορεύομεν. ἄλλο εἶδος, ἐὰν αὐτός τις ᾖ γεννάδας τὴν ψυχὴν καὶ μεγαλόψυχος, καὶ τοῦτον εὐγενῆ φασὶν εἶναι· καὶ τῆς γε εὐγενείας αὕτη κρατίστη. τῆς ἄρα εὐγενείας τὸ μὲν ἀπὸ προγόνων ἐπιεικῶν, τὸ δὲ δυναστῶν, τὸ δὲ ἐνδόξων, τὸ δὲ ἀπὸ τῆς αὐτοῦ καλοκἀγαθίας

Bibl Mutschmann (1906) 12-13; Boudreaux (1909) 223-224; Moraux (1977) 106; Rossitto (1984) 151-158

[36] DL M L

DL
Titulus deest

τὸ ἀγαθὸν εἰς τέτταρα γένη διαιρεῖται· ὧν ἓν μὲν λέγομεν εἶναι τὸν τὴν ἀρετὴν ἔχοντα ἰδίᾳ ἀγαθόν· ἄλλο δὲ αὐτὴν τὴν ἀρετὴν καὶ τὴν δικαιοσύνην λέγομεν ἀγαθὸν εἶναι· τρίτον δέ, οἷον σιτία καὶ γυμνάσια τὰ πρόσφορα καὶ φάρμακα· τέταρτον δέ φαμεν εἶναι ἀγαθόν, οἷον αὐλητικὴν καὶ ὑποκριτικὴν καὶ τὰ τοιαῦτα. ἀγαθοῦ ἄρα τέτταρα εἴδη ἐστί· τὸ μὲν τὸ τὴν ἀρετὴν ἔχειν, ἕτερον δὲ αὐτὴ ἡ ἀρετή, τρίτον δὲ σιτία καὶ γυμνάσια τὰ ὠφέλιμα· τέταρτον δὲ αὐλητικὴν καὶ ὑποκριτικὴν καὶ ποιητικὴν ἀγαθὸν λέγομεν εἶναι

Bibl Mutschmann (1906) 30-31; Moraux (1977) 110, 121; Rossitto (1984) 244-247

M	A	L
Titulus deest	*Titulus deest*	διαίρεσις εὐγενείας
διαιρεῖται ἡ εὐγένεια εἰς τρία· ἔστι γὰρ αὐτῆς ἓν μὲν ἀπὸ ἐνδόξων καὶ ὀνομαστῶν γονέων γεγονέναι, οἷον ἀπὸ βασιλέων καὶ ἀρχόντων [γεγονέναι] ἢ ἄλλην τινὰ δόξαν ἐχόντων· τὸ δὲ ἀπὸ σπουδαίων καὶ δικαίων, οἷον ἀπὸ Ξενοφῶντος καὶ Νείλου καὶ τῶν τοιούτων καὶ μεγαλοπρεπὴς καὶ δίκαιος καὶ τὰ ἄλλα τὰ τοιαῦτα. τῆς εὐγενείας ⟨ἄρα⟩ ἓν μὲν ἐστι τὸ ἀπὸ ἐνδόξων καὶ ὀνομαστῶν προγόνων γεγονέναι ἕν δὲ τὸ ἀπὸ σπουδαίων καὶ δικαίων, ἓν δὲ τὸ ἀπ᾽αὐτῆς τῆς τοῦ ἔχοντος ἀρετῆς	διαιρεῖται ἡ εὐγένεια εἰς τρία· ἔστι γὰρ αὐτῆς ἓν μὲν ἀπὸ ἐνδόξων καὶ ὀνομαστῶν γονέων γεγονέναι, ἓν δὲ ἀπὸ σπουδαίων καὶ δικαίων, ἓν δὲ ἀπ᾽αὐτῆς τῆς τοῦ ἔχοντος ἀρετῆς. ἔστι δὲ τὸ μὲν ἀπὸ ἐνδόξων, οἷον ἀπὸ βασιλέων καὶ ἀρχόντων, τὸ δὲ ἀπὸ σπουδαίων καὶ δικαίων, οἷον ἀπὸ Ξενοφῶντος καὶ Νείλου καὶ τῶν τοιούτων, τὸ δὲ ἀπ᾽αὐτῆς τῆς τοῦ ἔχοντος ἀρετῆς, οἷον ἐὰν ᾖ γενναῖος καὶ μεγαλοπρεπὴς καὶ δίκαιος καὶ τὰ ἄλλα τὰ τοιαῦτα	διαιρεῖται ἡ εὐγένεια εἰς εἴδη τρία· ἔστι δὲ αὐτῆς ἓν μὲν ἀπὸ ἐνδόξων καὶ ὀνομαστῶν γονέων γεγονέναι, ἓν δὲ ἀπὸ σπουδαίων καὶ δικαίων, ἓν δὲ ἀπ᾽αὐτῆς τῆς τοῦ ἔχοντος ἀρετῆς. ἔστι δὲ τὸ μὲν ἀπὸ ἐνδόξων καὶ ὀνομαστῶν γεγονέναι, οἷον ἀπὸ βασιλέων καὶ ἀρχόντων τιμήν τινα καὶ δόξαν ἐχόντων· ἀπὸ δὲ σπουδαίων καὶ δικαίων, οἷον ἀπὸ Ξενοφῶντος καὶ Νείλου καὶ τῶν τοιούτων καὶ μεγαλοπρεπὴς καὶ δίκαιος καὶ τὰ τοιαῦτα

L conferma l'espunzione di [γεγονέναι] proposta da Jensen. Aperta rimane la questione se Νείλου (S. Nilo) abbia sostituito un originale Γρύλου, il figlio di Senofonte morto a Mantinea (Rose, Wendland, Rossitto) oppure se sia corruzione per Νειλέου o Νεικίου (Sudhaus) o Νελέως (? Gigon). Cf. Rossitto [1984], 157-158.

M L

Titulus deest in **M** (διαίρεσις ἀγαθοῦ **L**)

διαιρεῖται τὸ ἀγαθὸν εἰς τέσσαρα· ἔστι γὰρ αὐτοῦ ἓν μὲν ἀρετὴ καὶ δικαιοσύνη, ἓν δὲ τὸ ἔχον ἀρετήν, ἓν δὲ τὸ συμφέρον, ἓν δὲ τὸ τερπνὸν καὶ τὸ ἥδεσθαι ποιοῦν· οἷον ἀρετὴ μὲν καὶ δικαιοσύνη ὅτι τούτων ἑκάτερον ἀγαθὸν λέγεται εἶναι[1], ἓν δὲ τὸ ἔχον ἀρετὴν, οἷον ἵππος καὶ ἄνθρωπος καὶ τὰ τοιαῦτα· καὶ γὰρ τούτων ἕκαστον λέγεται ἀγαθὸν εἶναι, ἐὰν ἔχῃ τὴν ἀρετήν. τὸ δὲ συμφέρον, οἷον γυμνασία καὶ φαρμακεία καὶ τἆλλα τὰ πρὸς ὑγείαν καὶ εὐεξίαν· καὶ γὰρ τούτων ἕκαστον λέγεται ἀγαθὸν εἶναι ᾧ[2] ἂν συμφέρῃ. τὸ δὲ τερπνὸν καὶ τὸ ἥδεσθαι ποιοῦν, οἷον ὑποκριτὴς καὶ αὐλητὴς καὶ τῶν βρωμάτων ἔνια καὶ τὰ τοιαῦτα· ὁ γὰρ ὑποκριτὴς καὶ αὐλητής, οὐ τῷ ὠφελεῖν ἀγαθὸν λέγεται[3] ἀλλὰ τῷ τέρπειν [τοῦ ἀγαθοῦ εἶναι]

1 **M**: λέγεται **L** — *2* **M**: ὡς **L** — *3* **M**: ἀγαθὸν εἶναι λέγεται **L**

L conferma l'espunzione di [τοῦ ἀγαθοῦ εἶναι] in **M** (glossa?) proposta da Wendland. La corretta deduzione di Moraux relativa alla lacuna per *saut du même au même* di **M** è fondata su false indicazioni di Mutschmann. La frase incriminata è, infatti, tramadata da **M**; l'omissione risale a Mutschmann o a Wilke (che collazionò **M**). Cf. Rossitto (1984) 244-245. Non necessarie le correzioni di Gigon a **M**: δικαιοσύνη [ὅτι] ἀγαθὸν λέγεται εἶναι τούτων ἑκάτερον e εὐεξίαν ⟨πρόσφορα⟩.

[30] **M A L**

M	**A**	**L**
Titulus deest	*Titulus deest*	διαίρεσις ἀγαθοῦ
διαιρεῖται τὸ ἀληθὲς εἰς τρία. ἔστι γὰρ αὐτοῦ ἓν μὲν τὸ πρᾶγμα ἀληθὲς εἶναι, ἓν δὲ τὸν λόγον, ἓν δὲ καὶ τὸ συναμφότερον.	τὰ συναμφότερα	
ἔστι δὲ τὸ πρᾶγμα ἀληθὲς ὅταν ᾖ οὕτως ἔχον καὶ οὐκ ἄλλως,	τὸ μὲν πρᾶγμα τοῦτο ἀληθὲς μὴ ἄλλως	τὸ μὲν πρᾶγμα ἀληθὲς εἶναι μὴ ἄλλως
οἷον τὸ τὸν θεὸν ἀθάνατον εἶναι· οὕτως γὰρ ἔχει τὸ πρᾶγμα καὶ οὐκ ἄλλως.		οὕτως γὰρ ἔχει .... τοῦτον ὄν *omittit*
τὸ δὲ λέγειν ʽοὗτος ἐστὶν ἀληθὴς λόγοςʼ τοῦ ἀληθοῦς ἐστιν·	τοῦτο ἀληθὲς	
ἔστι γὰρ ὁ λόγος πρᾶγμα ὑπὸ τὸν λόγον τοῦτον ὄν. τὸ δὲ λέγειν ὅτι ʽοἱ ἄνθρωποι ἔμψυχοί εἰσιʼ καὶ ὁ λόγος ἀληθής ἐστι καὶ τὸ πρᾶγμα	καὶ τὸ πρᾶγμα τοῦ ἀληθοῦς ἄρα τὸ μέν ἐστι τὸ πρᾶγμα ἀληθὲς, τὸ δὲ τὸν λόγον εἶναι ἀληθῆ, τὸ δὲ τὰ συναμφότερα καὶ τὸ πρᾶγμα καὶ τὸν λόγον ἀληθῆ εἶναι	

Bibl Mutschmann (1906) 49-50; Boudreaux (1909) 223; Moraux (1977) 109; Rossitto (1984) 223-230

L'aggiunta dell'elenco finale in **A** non prova che questo debba essere reintegrato in **M** e **L**. Cf. Rossitto (1984), 225-226. Non necessarie le correzioni di Gigon in **M**: τὸ δὲ λέγειν, 〈...〉 ʽοὗτος ἐστὶν ἀληθὴς λόγοςʼ [τοῦ ἀληθοῦς ἐστιν].

[22] **M L**

Titulus deest in **M** (διαίρεσις τῆς τῶν ὄντων ὀνομασίας **L**)

διαιρεῖται ἡ τῶν ὄντων ὀνομασία εἰς πέντε. ἔστι γὰρ αὐτῶν τὰ μὲν ὥσπερ ἓν πρὸς πολλά, τὰ δὲ ὡς πολλὰ πρὸς πολλὰ καὶ πρὸς ἕν, τὰ δὲ ὡς ἀνόμοια πρὸς ὅμοια, τὰ δὲ ὡς ὅμοια πρὸς ὅμοια, τὰ δὲ ὡς ἓν πρὸς ἕν. ἔστι δὲ τὸ μὲν ὡς ἓν πρὸς πολλὰ οἷον τάχιστος καὶ μέγιστος καὶ κάλλιστος καὶ τἄλλα τὰ τοιαῦτα. τὰ δὲ ὡς πολλὰ πρὸς πολλὰ καὶ πρὸς ἕν, οἷον πλείω τάδε τῶνδε καὶ μείζω τάδε τῶνδε καὶ καλλίους οἵδε τῶνδε καὶ τἄλλα τὰ τοιαῦτα. τὰ δὲ ὡς ἀνόμοια πρὸς ὅμοια, οἷον πατὴρ πρὸς υἱοὺς καὶ δεσπότης πρὸς δούλους καὶ τἄλλα τὰ τοιαῦτα. τὰ δὲ ὡς ὅμοια πρὸς ὅμοια, οἷον ἀδελφοὶ πρὸς ἀδελφοὺς καὶ φίλοι πρὸς φίλους καὶ τὰ τοιαῦτα. τὰ δὲ ὡς ἓν πρὸς ἕν, οἷον καλλίων ὅδε τοῦδε καὶ θάσσων ὅδε τοῦδε καὶ τὰ τοιαῦτα

Bibl Mutschmann (1906) 46-7; Moraux (1977) 107-108, 115; Rossitto (1984) 186-192

Ho riprodotto il testo stabilito da Moraux. **L** conferma la lacuna per *saut du même au même* in **M** già individuata e parzialmente restaurata da Rose. Il testo di **L** può essere accolto anche se *exempli gratia* a colmare la lacuna; non è esclusa, infatti, una diversa disposizione degli esempi o un numero variato. Più sicura la proposta di integrare la frase finale nella redazione di **L** sfigurato, di nuovo, da una piccola lacuna per *saut du même au même* (ὅδε ... ὅδε).

... Ego apis Matinae
more modoque,
grata carpentis thyma per laborem
plurimum, circa nemus uvidique
Tiburis ripas operosa parvos
*carmina fingo.**

BIBLIOGRAFIA

Biedl, A. (1955) *Das Grosse Excerpt Φ. Zur Textgeschichte des Laertios Diogenes* (Città del Vaticano)

Boudreaux, P. (1909) "Un nouveau manuscrit des *Divisiones Aristoteleae*", *Revue de Philologie* 33: 221-224

Gaiser, K. (1963) *Platons ungeschriebene Lehre* (Stuttgart) *Testimonia Platonica*

Gigon, O. (1987) *Aristotelis Opera. III: Librorum deperditorum fragmenta* (Berolini et Novi Eboraci)

Hambruch, E. (1904) *Logische Regeln der Platonischen Schule in der Aristotelischen Topik* (Berlin)

Heitz, E. (1868) in *Aristotelis Opera omnia graece et latine* (Parisiis)

Knoepfler, D. (1991) *La Vie de Ménédème d'Érétrie de Diogène Laërce. Contribution à l'histoire et à la critique du texte des Vies des Philosophes* (Basel)

Krämer, H.J. (1983) *Ältere Akademie* in Flashar, H., ed., *Die Philosphie der Antike,* 3. *Ältere Akademie, Aristoteles, Peripatos* (Basel–Stuttgart)

Mansfeld, J. (1993) "*Physikai doxai* e *problemata physica* da Aristotele ad Aezio (ed oltre)" in Battegazzore, A.M., ed., *Dimostrazione, argomentazione dialettica e argomentazione retorica nel pensiero antico* (Genova) 311-382

Moraux, P. (1977) "Témoins méconnus des *Divisiones Aristoteleae*", *L'Antiquité Classique* 46: 100-127

Mutschmann, H. (1906) *Divisiones quae vulgo dicuntur Aristoteleae* (Lipsiae)

Pasquali, G. (1910/1986) "Doxographica aus Basiliusscholien", *Nachrichten der Akademie der Wissenschaften in Göttingen*, phil.-hist. Kl.: 194-228 = *Scritti filologici* (Firenze) 1, 539-574

Praechter, K. (1910) Rec. di Mutschmann (1906), *Berliner Philologische Wochenschrift* 30: 387-395

Rose, V. (1863) *Aristoteles Pseudepigraphus* (Lipsiae)

Ross, W.D. (1955) *Aristotelis fragmenta selecta* (Oxford)

Rossitto, C. (1984) *Aristotele e altri. Divisioni.* Introd., trad. e comm. (Padova)

——(1989) Rec. di Gigon (1987), *Elenchos* 10: 213-215

Suckow, F.G.G. (1855) *Die wissenschaftliche und künstlerische Form der Platonischen Schriften in ihrer bisher verborgenen Eigenthümlichkeit dargestellt* (Berlin)

Souilhé, J. (1930) *Platon, Oeuvres complètes. Dialogues apocryphes*: 13.3 (Paris)

Wilpert, P. (1941) "Neue Fragmente aus Περι τἀγαθοῦ", *Hermes* 76: 236–241

——(1949) Zwei aristotelische Frühschriften über die Ideenlehre (Regensburg)

CNRS, Paris

* Una stesura dell'articolo ha letto con la consueta disponibilità e sostanziali suggerimenti, soprattutto per la costituzione dello 'stemma', il Prof. R. Kassel (Köln). Di alcuni punti ho discusso con profitto con i miei colleghi e amici L. Brisson (Paris), R. Chiaradonna e E. Spinelli (Roma).

PART FOUR

HELLENISTIC AND EARLY ROMAN PHILOSOPHY

THE CATALOGUE OF CHRYSIPPUS' LOGICAL WORKS

Jonathan Barnes

At the end of his brief *Life* of Chrysippus, Diogenes Laertius remarks that

> since his books have a very high reputation, I have decided to record here the list of them arranged by subject. They are these. (VII 189)

There follows an articulated catalogue of Chrysippus' works.

Diogenes has a standing interest in the writings of his subjects, an interest which he implicitly avows in his preface (I 16). Almost all the *Lives* refer to what their subjects wrote;[1] and in the vast majority of them Diogenes presents a book-list. The list of Chrysippus' writings stands out on three diverse counts. First, it is articulated into sections and subsections,[2] and the articulation is based on philosophical principles.[3] Secondly, it is incomplete: the end of Book VII is missing from all surviving manuscripts of Diogenes[4]—and with it half the Chrysippean bibliography.[5] Thirdly, it is exciting; for it appears to offer us information about Chrysippus' philosophical activities, and in particular about his logical activities, which we cannot find elsewhere—it parades his terminology; it shows where his interests lay; it indicates the structure which he gave to his philosophical work.[6]

---

1 Exceptions: Myson, Anaximander, Anaximenes, Archelaus, Socrates, Eubulides, Diodorus, Menedemus of Eretria, Lacydes, Lycon, Menedemus the Cynic, Melissus, Leucippus, Anaxarchus. Occasionally—and particularly if the subject wrote nothing (e.g. Arcesilaus, IV 32; Carneades, IV 65)—the reference is brief (e.g. Polemo, IV 20; Bion, IV 47; Clitomachus, IV 67; Eudoxus, VIII 89).

2 Other articulated lists: Plato (IV 57–66), Heraclides Ponticus (V 86–88), Antisthenes (VI 15–18), Diogenes of Sinope (VI 80), and Democritus (IX 46–49).

3 Compare e.g. the list of Democritus' works (drawn up by Thrasyllus): IX 46–49. Contrast e.g. the Platonic tetralogies: III 57–66.

4 On the loss see Mansfeld (1986) 308–312; Dorandi (1992).

5 What survives lists some 350 titles: in all, Chrysippus wrote 'more than 705' works (VII 180; ὑπὲρ πέντε καὶ ἑπτακόσιά ἐστιν: a bizarre remark—change πέντε to πεντηκόντα? or delete πέντε καί ?).

6 Odd then that it has accumulated so little literature Numerous scattered comments, of course; and annotated translations in Italian (Gigante (1983); Baldassarri (1985)), German (Hülser (1987/8)) and French (Hadot (1994)).

The catalogue appears to offer such information. But what is its pedigree? What authority does it possess?

Diogenes does not name his source; but we can guess it. On the one hand, we know that Apollonius of Tyre 'published the table of the philosophers of Zeno's school and of their books' (Strabo, XVI 2. 24 (757 C)),[7] a work which must have included a catalogue of Chrysippus' writings. On the other hand, Apollonius is an author whom Diogenes cites more than once.[8] Diogenes, like many another scholar, sometimes cites sources which he knows only at second hand; but nothing hints that he did not himself read Apollonius; and in any event it is eminently reasonable to believe that his list came from Apollonius, either directly or indirectly.

What do we know about Apollonius? Next to nothing.[9] His date is roughly fixed; for Strabo describes him as living 'a little before us', which presumably puts him in the first part of the first century BC[10]—and Philodemus cites him in the *Index Stoicorum* (col xxxvii), which cannot be dated much later than 50.[11]

Scholars generally assume that he was a Stoic philosopher; and a popular view makes him a follower of Apollodorus of Seleucia.[12] He wrote about the Stoics, and part of the work betrayed at least a quasi-philosophical interest in the subject. No doubt you might

But apart from Dyroff (1896) and Brunschwig (1991) I know of no sustained study.—The present paper will, I hope, eventually form part of a larger work. I am indebted to several friends and colleagues; and in particular to Keimpe Algra, whose comments enabled me to correct a number of errors in the penultimate version of the paper.

7 ἐκ Τύρου δὲ Ἀντίπατρος καὶ μικρὸν πρὸ ἡμῶν Ἀπολλώνιος ὁ τὸν πίνακα ἐκθεὶς τῶν ἀπὸ Ζήνωνος φιλοσόφων καὶ τῶν βιβλίων. There is no reason to think that Strabo's phrase is, or is intended as, a book-title; and the πίναξ was surely presented in Apollonius' work *On Zeno*, which was in more than one book (see Diogenes Laertius, VII 2, 6): so Mejer (1978) 75, n.33; Hahm (1992) 4166 n.207.

8 See VII 1, 2, 6, 24, 28. (For the spurious correspondence between Antigonus and Zeno at VII 6 see Crönert (1906) 28–29; Dorandi (1994) 9 and n. 41.)

9 On Apollonius see e.g. Goulet (1989a); Dorandi (1994) 6, 33. —Hahm (1992) argues that Apollonius was Diogenes' primary source not only for the catalogue but also for the biographies of Zeno and his six followers and for the Stoic doxography: like most essays in Laertian *Quellenforschung*, this will persuade no-one but its author.

10 Strabo uses the same phrase of Antiochus (XVI 2.29 (759C)), whose dates are c. 130–68/7; cf. e.g. VIII 7.5 (387C), XII 3.41 (562C)—events datable to the early 60s.

11 Dorandi (1990) 2334–2335.

12 So Dyroff (1896) 39–41; cf. Crönert (1906) 80, 180; Baldassarri (1985) 12–16 (see also Hülser (1987) LXXXVII).

have a philosophical interest in the Stoics without being a Stoic—or even a philosopher. Nonetheless, it is not a bad guess that Apollonius was a Stoic.

Why a follower of Apollodorus? The argument is this. The catalogue regularly uses the word τόπος to mark areas or divisions of its subject matter; and 'Apollodorus calls these parts (i.e. the three parts of philosophy) τόποι, while Chrysippus and Eudromus call them μέρη and others call them γένη' (Diogenes Laertius, VII 39). So when Apollonius talks of τόποι he is using a terminology peculiar to Apollodorus; and hence he was probably a member of his school.

Evidently, the argument is at best frail. In fact it is worthless; for in the catalogue the word τόπος is not used in its Apollodoran sense. Apollonius speaks, say, of 'the logical τόπος concerning πράγματα' (VII 190), thereby referring to that area or part *of logic* which deals with 'objects signified'. Thus logic itself is not designated a τόπος: rather, logic has τόποι. Apollonius uses the word τόπος in its standard sense. He does not use it in its special Apollodoran sense.

Allow that Apollonius was a Stoic, and that he was Diogenes' source for the Chrysippean catalogue. Did he compile the catalogue himself?

Diogenes provides book-lists for the other Stoics whose lives he records—Zeno (VII 4), Aristo (VII 163), Herillus (VII 166), Dionysius (VII 167), Cleanthes (VII 174-175), and Sphaerus (VII 178). The lists are short, and unlike the Chrysippean list they are not articulated. But it is an economical conjecture that they all derive from Apollonius. Now the catalogue of Aristo's works ends with '*Letters* —4 books'; after which Diogenes makes the following comment: 'But Panaetius and Sosicrates say that only the *Letters* are his, the other items belonging to Aristo the Peripatetic' (VII 163).[13] The comment presupposes that Panaetius and Sosicrates had a list of Aristo's putative writings. On chronological grounds it is unlikely that this list came from Apollonius.[14] It follows that there was a catalogue of Aristo's writings in existence before Apollonius

---

13 Panaetius is mentioned in similar contexts at II 64 (Aeschines of Sphettus), 85 (Aristippus), and III 37 (Plato). For Sosicrates see II 85 (Aristippus) and VI 80 (Diogenes of Sinope).

14 Panaetius died in 110/09 (Dorandi (1991) 41–42); Sosicrates' dates are uncertain—but he probably flourished in the second century (Giannattasio Andria (1989) 73–75).

published his *On Zeno*. And if for Aristo, surely also for Zeno and Cleanthes ... and Chrysippus?

Hence Apollonius did not himself compile the Chrysippean list—or at any rate, he was not the first to compile such a list. Perhaps there were catalogues in the library of the Stoa, which Panaetius and Sosicrates had consulted? Perhaps Apollonius merely prepared these for public consumption, adding a few embellishments of his own?[15] All this is lamentably vague; but I doubt if we should speak with confidence of Apollonius as the compiler of the Chrysippean catalogue.

However that may be, there are more important questions to broach: in particular, how close is the catalogue to Chrysippus himself? Did the compiler arrange the works to reflect the scope and structure of Chrysippus' logical interests, or does the articulation of the catalogue tell us more about the compiler's own interests? Did he copy Chrysippus' titles, or did he (in some or all cases) invent titles of his own?[16] It is generally assumed without argument that the catalogue gives us reliable information about Chrysippus. Here is an argument. It starts from a remote origin.

The catalogue presents all the minor problems which beset any text of Diogenes. There are also two major problems. First, the logical section of the list ends by observing that the total number of books in Chrysippus' logical *oeuvre* was 311 (ὁμοῦ τὰ πάντα τοῦ λογικοῦ τια′: VII 198). But if you count the works which Diogenes lists you will not readily arrive at that figure. Secondly, the ethical part of the catalogue—the surviving fraction of the ethical part—contains several titles which apparently point to a logical rather than an ethical content: *On Divisions* and *On Contraries*, for example; or *On Dialectic* and *On the Objections to the Dialecticians*. Can these really be titles of works whose main effort was devoted to ethics?

Why not amalgamate the two problems? Suppose that a few pages in a manuscript copy of Diogenes worked loose and were

---

[15] Note that Strabo says that he *made them public* (ἐκθείς), not that he collected the materials for them.

[16] We should not assume without ado that Chrysippus entitled his writings. Note e.g. that Plotinus gave no titles to any of his essays—those of his pupils who managed to get hold of copies gave them different titles (Porphyry, *Vit. Plot.* 4: see Brisson *et al* (1982), 283, n.1). Similarly, Galen did not give titles to writings which he sent to his pupils and friends, and he complained that these works were later in circulation under different titles (*Lib. prop.* XIX 10–11 K). Many of Chrysippus' works are addressed to pupils and friends.

later replaced in the wrong order; and that this disorderly copy is the source of our modern text. Then if we cunningly rearrange the pages we may, at one blow, save the arithmetic at VII 198 and restore to their proper place the logical works which now appear in the ethical part of the list.[17]

First, let us look more closely at the arithmetic. The first four logical τόποι contain, by my count, 118 works divided into 263 books. (But in at least three places the manuscripts offer variant readings for the book numbers,[18] so that the transmitted total is between 261 and 265.) The total includes four works in eight books which are marked as spurious; and it is not clear whether they should be included in the arithmetic. In addition to the contents of the first four τόποι, there are the 39 books mentioned at VII 198. Hence in all there are 303 books, plus or minus two (or 295, plus or minus two, if we do not count the spurious items).[19] Thus we are between 18 and 6 short of the desired total of 311.

It is easy to emend the text: for example, read τα΄ ('301') instead of τια΄, and then take the lower of the variant readings. But the possibilities are so many, and corruption of numerals is so common,[20] that it is a waste of time to play the numbers game. Hence it is tempting to observe that the transmitted numeral is not wildly out, to conclude that Chrysippus' logical bibliography contained about 300 books, and to abandon as delusory the hope of establishing a precise figure.

But this leaves aside the second of the two major problems. Roughly speaking, the apparently logical items in the ethical part of the catalogue are the contents of the second, third, fourth and fifth συντάξεις of the first ethical τόπος and the contents of the first and second συντάξεις of the second τόπος. In all, they amount to 26 works in 70 books. Suppose that the text were rearranged so that all these items appeared in the logical section: then the total number of logical books would be about 370. (And should we emend τια΄—to τοα΄?[21])

---

[17] For an example of this sort of thing see Egli (1967) 3.

[18] I rely on the notoriously unreliable OCT: doubtless there are variant readings for many more than three titles.

[19] I have counted as carefully as I can, and three times. But scholars differ, even in their addition. E.g. Dörrie (1970) col. 151, finds 298 books; Baldassarri (1985) 5, counts 305; Hadot (1994) 336, gives 300.

[20] As Galen observes: *Antid.* XIV 31-32 K.

[21] Egli's reordering of the catalogue purports to yield a grand total of 321

It would be absurd to deny that some of these 70 books should in some sense be counted as part of Chrysippus' logical *oeuvre*. *On Dialectic, to Aristocreon*, whatever else it contained, surely included some Chrysippean reflexions on dialectic;[22] the works on definitions, on species and genera, on division must have published some logical reflections;[23] again, there are titles dealing with etymology and poetry and rhetoric, all of which fell under the generous Stoic conception of λογική.[24] But it does not follow that these titles should be transplanted to the logical section; and in point of fact no simple hypothesis of mechanical corruption is satisfactory and no simple textual transposition resolves the problem.[25] Complex hypotheses are delightful to construct—and impossible to justify. If the text of Diogenes is seriously disorganised, then we can no longer (or not yet) hope to put it right.

That being so, we might as well ask whether the second major problem cannot be solved without textual surgery.[26] Well, consider the rubric to the second ethical τόπος: it is the area concerned with 'reason in general and the arts and virtues which are constituted by it' (VII 201); that is to say, the rubric announces that the section will contain logical material. Hence it would be quite unwarranted to transfer the first σύνταξις of this τόπος to the logical part of the catalogue—or the second σύνταξις, which contains titles bearing on the arts or virtues of dialectic and rhetoric. Similarly with the first ethical τόπος; for this τόπος deals with 'the articulation of ethical concepts' (VII 199), and hence with matters on the borders of logic.

In brief, the rubrics to the first two ethical τόποι suggest that they collected items dealing with the logical aspect of ethics. No need then to blench if some of the titles promise a logical content.

A question remains: on what grounds did the compiler of the

---

items; so he emends to τκα′. But I am not sure how he does his arithmetic. Moreover, his selection of 'logical' works from the ethical part is capricious.

[22] But see below, p. 177.

[23] The topics are within the scope of logic: e.g. Diogenes Laertius, VII 60, 61, 61.

[24] E.g. Diogenes Laertius, VII 60, 41.

[25] It is enough to note that the rubrics attached to the apparently logical τόποι are all ethical: if we transfer the titles, we must leave the rubrics behind; and this scotches the straightforward hypothesis that a folio dropped out of an early manuscript and was stuck back in the wrong place.

[26] 'The fact that the arrangement in the bibliography is disturbing need not entail that it has been disturbed' (Mansfeld (1986) 358 n. 147).

catalogue assign, say, *On Dialectic* to ethics? Assume that the work said *something* about logical matters—otherwise its title would be wholly misleading. Assume, too, that it contained at least *some* ethical content—otherwise its position in the ethical section is inexplicable. Why, then, assign it to ethics rather than to logic? (No doubt it is absurd even to guess at such questions. But what the hell, archie, what the hell.)

Chrysippus did not secure the three parts of philosophy each in a watertight compartment, and his thought often seeped from one to another—he could touch on physical and ethical matters in his logical writings, on logical and physical matters in his ethical writings, on logical and ethical matters in his physical writings.[27] It is clear, then, that the compiler will have faced problems once he determined to order his catalogue according to the standard tripartition of philosophy. Now the logical section contains virtually no maverick titles: virtually all the titles clearly suggest a logical content. Perhaps, then, the compiler, convinced of the superiority of ethics to logic and of physics (or theology) to ethics, decided to adopt the following principle: any work which dealt substantially with physical matters would be placed in the physical section of the catalogue, whatever its title; of the remaining works, any which dealt substantially with ethical matters would be placed in the ethical section of the catalogue, whatever its title; and the rest would be ranked under logic. This is at least a rational principle and it explains (better than any other hypothesis I have come across) the puzzling entries in the ethical section.[28]

If some such suggestion is right—and, more generally, if the catalogue in its present form is not seriously disturbed—, then we may plausibly draw two merry consequences. First, the compiler must have taken his task seriously; for he could have had no reason to place a work entitled *On Dialectic* in the ethical part of the catalogue unless the content of the work convinced him that there, despite its title, it belonged. In other words, the catalogue was not

[27] Thus in his account of Stoic logic Diocles mentions, *inter alia*, texts from Chrysippus' *On the Soul* and *Physics* (Diogenes Laertius, VII 50, 54, 55).

[28] See e.g. Long (1978) 117–118, who appeals to the idea that 'the study of dialectic, for Chrysippus at least, is an integral part of moral conduct'. Such an idea might lead you to range *all* logical titles under the heading of ethics; but it does not yet explain how you could place some of them under ethics while leaving most in an independent section on logic.

constructed on the basis of titles alone: the compiler must have had some knowledge of the contents of the works he was cataloguing—he must have unrolled at least a few columns of text.

This claim remains plausible even if the catalogue has been substantially deranged. For some of the titles in the logical section itself are puzzlingly placed.[29] Had the compiler looked no further than the title of, say, *Πιθανὰ Συνημμένα*, he could have had no reason to place the work in the first—and no doubt introductory—τόπος.[30] Its position suggests that he must have troubled to form some idea of its contents.

Secondly, the book-titles must come from Chrysippus and not from any compiler; for a compiler would surely have given each work a title appropriate to the position it was to hold in his list. If you have an untitled work which you intend to place in the first ethical τόπος, you will not call it *On Dialectic*: you will give it a name which fits its place—for example, *Dialectical Matters bearing on Ethics.*

This second claim also remains plausible even if the catalogue is seriously disturbed. Suppose that the compiler found an untitled work which, on the basis of its contents, he decided to place in the first part of the logical section: would he have given it the bald title *Plausible Conditionals*?

With these two claims I have returned to my sheep: the catalogue has an honest pedigree. No doubt the compiler made mistakes: he certainly missed a few works,[31] and he probably misplaced others. No doubt the list has been damaged in transit. Certainly there are titles whose import remains opaque to us. Nonetheless, we may properly boast that we possess a fairly competent and a fairly well preserved and a fairly intelligible list of Chrysippus' logical writings. In particular, we may confidently use the titles as evidence of Chrysippus' own logical lexicon; and we may plausibly discern in the catalogue a general indication of Chrysippus' logical interests—of the topics he did and did not discuss, of

[29] You might, of course, hypothesize serious *local* disruptions (compare the case of Aristotle's catalogues); but I have not managed to contrive an interesting hypothesis in this vein.

[30] On the work—the title of which is usually misunderstood (e.g. Hadot (1994) 338)—see Barnes (1985).—The Mss. give no subtitle to the first τόπος: von Arnim (1903) II 4, rightly suggested something like 'Λογικοῦ τόπου <τοῦ περὶ τὴν διάρθρωσιν τῶν λογικῶν ἐννοιῶν>' (misreported by Hülser (1987) 172).

[31] See Hülser (1987) 190–191.—I assume that he was trying to give a bibliography of Chrysippus' works rather than, say, a list of the Chrysippean holdings in some library.

the breadth and depth of his researches, of the relative weight which he gave to different parts of the subject.

The individual titles must wait on a detailed commentary. Here, a word on Chrysippus' logical interests. And first let it be underscored that there are limits to the inferences we may draw from the list.[32] For ancient book-titles—even when they were not deliberately allusive or fanciful—do not invariably give exact information about the contents of the books to which they are affixed. First, titles were sometimes incipits. Protagoras' *On the Gods* was so-called because it began with the words Περὶ μὲν θεῶν ...: it was not a work about the gods at all.[33] (I have wondered whether *On Dialectic, to Aristocreon* did not begin: 'On dialectic, O Aristocreon, I here say nothing; for my subject is ethical ...'.) Secondly, titles are often vague, so that one and the same name could be attached to books of very different stamp: consider, say, Περὶ Ὅρων or Περὶ Ὁρμῆς.[34] Thirdly, ancient philosophers were less subject-bound than scholars (modern and ancient) care to imagine. Poor Plato was incapable of sticking to a single topic: ancient scholars felt obliged to list his Πολιτικός as a 'logical' work;[35] modern scholars have wearied themselves and their readers with fatuous efforts to discover what the *Phaedrus* is 'about'. In the case of Chrysippus we know that there was logical material in works which we should classify—and which the ancient catalogue classified—as works on physics; and we might recall the chagrin which Dionysius of Halicarnassus felt when he contemplated the contents of the books entitled Περὶ συντάξεως (*Comp. verb.* 31-32).

Nonetheless, the catalogue does allow a few banal inferences. First, Chrysippus wrote a large number of logical works: at least 130 essays or treatises, amounting to over 300 rolls. Aristotle's *Organon* consists of six works in fifteen books. Chrysippus' logical *oeuvre* was twenty times the length of the *Organon*.[36]

Secondly, three aspects of logic received especial attention. Chrysippus liked puzzles: twelve works in 23 books on the Liar;

---

32 Brunschwig (1991) 80, is perhaps too sanguine on this point.

33 See Nachmanson (1941) 50–52; compare Dyroff (1896) 14–15. Note also Galen, *Lib. prop.* XIX 11 K.

34 See Dyroff (1896) 14–21.

35 Diogenes Laertius III 58; see Dyroff (1896) 14–15.

36 But not twenty times the length of Aristotle's logical *œuvre*, much of which is lost.

another nine works in another 26 books on other puzzles; seven works in 17 books on amphiboly. In all, more than a sixth of his logical production. Again, there are some eighteen works in 35 books on arguments—on the various forms of inference and syllogism which the Stoics recognised and investigated. (More than it seems, since technical logic uses little papyrus.) Finally, there are some twenty works in 46 books on the elements of arguments: on the various forms of complex proposition (five works in 12 books on conditionals); on simple propositions; on predicates and names. Chrysippus devoted as much paper to the elements of arguments as to the arguments themselves—and here his work has no parallel in the Peripatetic tradition, where this aspect of what we call 'philosophical logic' was scarcely studied.

Thirdly, it is plain—and unsurprising—that most of Chrysippus' works were technical essays or treatises on particular points within logical theory. Almost all of these works are wholly lost. What we are accustomed to refer to as the 'fragments' of Stoic logic are mainly drawn from summaries and allusions and polemical caricatures. Much of this material surely derives from handbooks, and the handbooks themselves derived in the end from the original works of Chrysippus and his followers. But none of the subtleties of the originals was conserved: the account of Stoic logic in Diogenes Laertius is, for us now, richly informative; but it is also the thinnest of gruels—and although it is one of our main pieces of evidence for Stoic logic, it is not a piece of Stoic logic.

Finally, what of the organisation of the catalogue? In particular, does it perhaps reflect the way in which Chrysippus himself organised his logical studies?[37] Does it perhaps follow the arrangement of topics in one of Chrysippus' own introductory books on logic? We can no longer read these books; but Diogenes Laertius offers us two general accounts of Stoic logic, the summary at VII 42-48 and the longer version at VII 49-82,[38] and we can at least compare the structure of these accounts with the arrangement of the catalogue.

Here is a pretty crude and tentative description of the three items:

---

[37] So Tieleman (1992) 246; and a hint in Mansfeld (1986) 363–4.

[38] On which the fundamental article is Mansfeld (1986); see also Cellu-prica (1989) (but I remain stubbornly convinced that the whole account comes from Diocles of Magnesia ...).

The Catalogue:[39]

I LOGIC

A: Introductory

B: Πράγματα

1. Simple ἀξιώματα
2. Complex ἀξιώματα
3. Non-ἀξιώματα
4. Incomplete λεκτά
5. πτώσεις

C: Λέξεις

1. Questions of usage
2. Elements and syntax
3. Ambiguity

D: Λόγοι

1. Forms of argument
2. Arguments
3. μεταπίπτοντες
4. Hypotheses
5. The Liar
6. The Liar
7. Other paradoxes
8. The Nobody
9. Sophisms
10. συνηθεία

E: Miscellaneous

II ETHICS

F: Introductory

1. Definitions
2. Definitions etc
3. Definitions etc
4. Etymology
5. Poetics

G: Κοινὸς λόγος

1. General

---

39 A–H are the τόποι, numbered sections are συντάξεις. My names for τόποι derive from the text; I have invented names for the συντάξεις.

2. Dialectic
3. The Virtues

H: The Good and the Bad

1. Pleasure

The Long Account (Diogenes Laertius, VII 49-82):

A*: Epistemology

1. φαντασία
2. αἴσθησις
3. ἔννοια
4. The κριτήριον

B*: Περὶ φωνῆς

1. φωνή
2. λέξις
3. στοιχεῖα
4. The parts of speech
5. The virtues of λέξις
6. Poetry
7. Definition
8. Division etc
9. ἀμφιβολία

C*: Περὶ πραγμάτων

1. λεκτά
2. The parts of λεκτά
3. Complete λεκτά
4. ἀξιώματα
5. λόγοι
6. Puzzles

The Summary (Diogenes Laertius, VII 41-48) :

A+: The Parts of Logic

B+: Rhetoric

C+: Dialectic

1. The parts of dialectic
2. φωνή
3. συλλογισμοί
4. Epistemology
5. Dialectical virtues

The summary is too thin to allow detailed comparisons. But it seems that: C+ 1 answers roughly to A; C+ 2 matches C (and also B*); C+ 3 corresponds to D and to C* 5; C+ 4 goes with A*; and C+ 5 fits with G. One thing is plain: if the summary derives from a single source (as it surely does), then the source organised the material in a manner very different both from the catalogue and from the long account.

As for the catalogue and the long account, it is worth observing, first, that they agree in one significant peculiarity: both follow an unorthodox ordering of the parts of philosophy: <logic, ethics, physics>. The order <logic, physics, ethics> is ascribed by Diogenes to Zeno and to Chrysippus (VII 41); and according to Sextus, *PH* II 13, it was the order favoured by most Stoics.[40] (But Sextus also says that the order <logic, ethics, physics> was in general the most common (*M* VII 22); and at *Stoic. rep.* 1035A–F Plutarch takes Chrysippus to task for inconsistently adopting now one and now another order.[41])

But this apart, the long account and the catalogue differ dramatically.[42] At the first level of specificity, nothing in the catalogue corresponds to section A*, on epistemology, in the account. Epistemological topics were surely discussed in some of the items which the catalogue ranges under ethics; and I guess that others were covered in the lost section on physics, perhaps in a subsection on psychology. But it is striking that the catalogue, so far as we know, did not imagine a special place for what many ancient and modern critics have taken to be the glory, jest and riddle of the Stoic world. Section C in the catalogue answers to B* in the account, while B and D together cover C*. In the long account we are told that 'most are agreed in thinking that the study of dialectic starts from the area concerned with utterances' (VII 55). The word 'most' suggests that there were at least a few deviant thinkers; and the compiler of the catalogue may have been among them.

Take next the subdivisions of B* and C*: B* 1 has no clear counterpart in the catalogue—although some of the items in C 1 are pertinent;[43] B* 2 answers to part of C 1; B* 3, and perhaps B* 4,

---

40 It is the order which Sextus himself follows in *PH* and in *M* VII-XI.

41 On all this see Ierodiakonou (1993).

42 See Mansfeld (1986) 357–8, 371–3.

43 It is generally supposed that Diogenes of Babylon was the first Stoic to take the study of φωνή seriously.

to C 2; and B* 5 to another part of C 1. B* 6-8 are matched in the ethical section of the catalogue, namely in F 5, F 2, and F 3; and B* 9 corresponds roughly to C 3. C* 1 perhaps answers to A. C* 2 goes with B 4 and B 5; C* 3 with B 3; and C* 4-5 with B 1-2. C* 5 corresponds to D 1-2, and C* 6 to D 5-9. There are thus several subsections in the catalogue which do not appear to be matched in the account—scarcely odd, given the jejune character of the account. More noteworthy are the differences in arrangement.

Finally, a sample from the lowest level of specificity—compare C* 4 with B 1-2. In the table, the left column gives the order of events within C* 4, the right column the corresponding titles in the catalogue.[44]

(i) Simple)(non-simple ἀξιώματα	B 1: περὶ ἀξιωμάτων [**7**], περὶ τῶν οὐχ ἁπλῶν ἀξιωμάτων [**8**]
(ii) Simple ἀξιώματα	
a. Negations	B 1: περὶ ἀποφατικῶν [**10**]
b. Denials	
c. Privatives	B 1: περὶ τῶν κατὰ στέρησιν λεγομένων [**12**]
d. Categoricals	
e. Determinates	B 1: περὶ τῶν καταγορευτικῶν [**11**]
f. Indefinites	B 1: περὶ τῶν ἀορίστων ἀξιωμάτων [**13**], περὶ τῆς διαφορᾶς τῶν ἀορίστων [**14**]
(iii) Non-simple ἀξιώματα	
a. Conditionals	B 2: περὶ ἀληθοῦς συνημμένου [**18**], πρὸς τὸ περὶ ἀκολούθων [**20**]
b. Quasiconditionals	
c. Conjunctions	B 1: περὶ τοῦ συμπεπλεγμένου [**9**]
d. Disjunctions	B 2: περὶ ἀληθοῦς διαζευγμένου [**17**], (?) περὶ τοῦ διὰ τριῶν [**21**]
e. Causals	
f. Comparatives	
g. Conditionals	

44 Numerals in bold give the position of the item in the catalogue: the first logical τόπος contains six items, so that [**7**] is the first item in the second τόπος.

h. Quasiconditionals
i. Causals
(iv) Modal ἀξιώματα
a. Plausible
b. Possible/impossible B 2: περὶ δυνατῶν [22]
c. Necessary/non-necessary

No doubt the differences between the two columns were not as great in reality as they appear in the table—thus, for example, the fact that no *title* in the catalogue corresponds to 'categoricals' in Diocles' account hardly implies that Chrysippus had nothing to say on the topic. Nonetheless, real differences remain, and some at least of them are to be explained by the fact that the account refers to Stoic logicians who worked after Chrysippus.

From this spattering of factlets, what to infer? Suppose (as seems pretty plausible) that the arrangement of items in the account reflects a Stoic handbook on logic. Suppose (as seems mildly plausible) that the arrangement in the catalogue also reflects a Stoic handbook.[45] In that case, the account certainly reflects a post-Chrysippean handbook; and the catalogue certainly reflects a different handbook—and probably an earlier handbook. Hence—a leap but not an Olympic leap—the catalogue may well reflect a Chrysippean handbook.

In truth, this final argument is made of gossamer. But the question of the structure of the catalogue is in any event of less concern that the questions of its scope and its terminology.

Small beer, alas. And I had wished to offer a large vodka.

Geneva

Bibliography

Arnim, H. von (1903) *Stoicorum Veterum Fragmenta* (Leipzig, 1903–05)
Baldassarri, M. (1985) *La logica stoica: testimonianze e frammenti – II: Crisippo* (Como)
Barnes, J. (1985) 'ΠΙΘΑΝΑ ΣΥΝΗΜΜΕΝΑ', *Elenchos* 6: 455–467
Blumenthal, H., and Robinson, H.M. (edd.) (1991) *Aristotle and the Later Tradition,* Oxford Studies in Ancient Philosophy supplementary volume (Oxford)

[45] Other suppositions, of course, are readily imagined—especially if the compiler was himself an amateur of the subject.

Brisson, L., Goulet-Cazé, M.-O., Goulet, R., and O'Brien, D. (edd.) (1982) *Porphyre: la vie de Plotin,* I (Paris)

Brunschwig, J. (1991) 'On a Book-Title by Chrysippus: "On the Fact that the Ancients Admitted Dialectic along with Demonstrations"', in Blumenthal and Robinson (1991)

Celluprica, V. (1989) 'Diocle di Magnesia fonte della dossografia stoica di Diogene Larzio', *Orpheus*: 10, 58–79

Crönert, W. (1906) *Kolotes und Menedemos* (Munich)

Dörrie, H. (1970) 'Chrysippos', *Paulys Realencyclopädie der classischen Altertumswissenschaft* suppt XII (Stuttgart)

Dorandi, T. (1990), 'Filodemo storico del pensiero antico', in Haase (1990)

Dorandi, T. (1991) *Ricerche sulla cronologia dei filosofi ellenistici,* Beiträge zur Altertumskunde 19 (Stuttgart)

Dorandi, T. (1992) 'Considerazioni sull'*index locupletior* di Diogene Laerzio', *Prometheus* 18: 121–126

Dorandi, T. (1994) *Filodemo: storia dei filosofi—la Stoà da Zenone a Panezio (PHerc. 1018),* Philosophia Antiqua 60 (Leiden)

Dyroff, A. (1896) *Über die Anlage der stoischen Bücherkataloge,* Programm des ... Gymnasiums zu Würzburg (Würzburg)

Egli, U. (1967) *Zur stoischen Dialektik* (Basel)

Giannattasio Andria, R. (1989) *I frammenti delle 'Successioni dei filosofi',* Università degli studi di Salerno, quaderni del dipartimento di scienze dell'antichità 5 (Naples)

Gigante, M. (1983) *Diogene Laerzio: Vite dei filosofi* (Rome/Bari, 2nd edn.)

Goulet, R. (1989a) 'Apollonios de Tyr', in Goulet (1989b) 294

Goulet, R. (1989b) (ed.) *Dictionnaire des philosophes antiques* I (Paris)

Goulet, R. (1994) (ed.) *Dictionnaire des philosophes antiques* II (Paris)

Haase, W. (1990) (ed.) *Aufsteig und Niedergang der römischen Welt* II.36.4 (Berlin)

Haase, W. (1992) (ed.) *Aufsteig und Niedergang der römischen Welt* II.36.6 (Berlin)

Hadot, P. (1994) 'Liste commentée des oeuvres de Chrysippe (D.L. VII 189–202)', in Goulet (1994) 336–356

Hahm, D. (1992) 'Diogenes Laertius VII: On the Stoics', in Haase (1992)

Hülser, K.-H. (1987/8) *Die Fragmente zur Dialektik der Stoiker* (Stuttgart/Bad Cannstatt)

Ierodiakonou, K. (1993) 'The Stoic Division of Philosophy', *Phronesis* 38: 57–74

Long, A.A. (1978) 'Dialectic and the Stoic Sage', in Rist (1978)

Mansfeld, J. (1986) 'Diogenes Laertius on Stoic Philosophy', *Elenchos* 7: 295–382 (reprinted in Mansfeld (1990))

Mansfeld, J. (1990) *Studies in the Historiography of Greek Philosophy* (Assen)

Mejer, J. (1978) *Diogenes Laertius and his Hellenistic Background,* Hermes Einzelschriften 40 (Wiesbaden)

Nachmanson, E. (1941) *Der griechische Buchtitel,* Göteborgs Högskolas Årsskrift 47 (Göteborg)

Rist, J.M. (ed.) (1978) *The Stoics* (Berkeley/Los Angeles/London)

Tieleman, T.L. (1992) *Galen and Chrysippus—Argument and Refutation in the* De Placitis *Books II–III,* Quaestiones Infinitae 3 (Utrecht)

CICERO'S ROPE

R. J. HANKINSON

> Substitute for the time honoured 'chain of causation', so often introduced into discussions upon this subject, the phrase 'a rope of causation', and see what a very different aspect the question will wear. (J. Venn, *The Logic of Chance*, London 1866, 320)

Metaphor plays a central role in the conceptual scaffolding of our metaphysics. This is particularly the case the further removed from the realm of ordinary experience are the phenomena being discussed and analysed (consider the cases of 'wave' and 'particle' in current high-energy physics); but it is also true at a less recherché level. The choice of metaphors is not only conditioned by the particular presuppositions of those who coin them, but also affects the way in which that conceptual structure develops and then ramifies through the wider linguistic community.

In this paper I wish to consider the origins of Venn's hallowed causal metaphor of the chain. Effects of previous causes become in their turn causes of subsequent effects, and so on in a continuous series; every member in the series depends causally upon its predecessor. The notion is ubiquitous; and even where the metaphor is not actually invoked, the idea that causation involves a sequence of distinct entities standing in a certain relation to one another is never far from the surface.[1]

Both the metaphor and its associated conceptualization of causation are usually ascribed to the Stoics, and this has been the case since antiquity. I shall argue that such an ascription is mistaken, and if accepted encourages a wholly unwarranted and misleading reading of the Stoics' actual views on the matter, which are (the polemic of later Peripatetics such as Alexander notwithstanding) very much closer to those of Aristotle than has been generally

[1] Compare Hume's celebrated account: although Hume never employs the chain metaphor, his definition of a cause as 'an object, followed by another, and where all the objects similar to the first are followed by objects similar to the second' (*Enquiry Concerning Human Understanding* VII 2; cf. *Treatise* I iii 15) clearly conceptualizes causes and effects as distinct, discrete entities, something which the chain-metaphor at the very least encourages.

allowed by scholars both ancient and modern. In fact the Stoics' use of metaphor encourages a quite different picture of the metaphysics of causation, one which stresses the continuity of processes, rather than relations between discrete events. Finally I will indicate some points of contact between the Stoic position, as I understand it, and one particular modern anti-Humean account of causation, that of Wesley Salmon.[2]

I

Aristotle's treatment of causation and explanation makes little or no use of metaphor: but I wish to begin by sketching some particular aspects of it for the purposes of subsequent comparison with the Stoic account with which this paper is primarily concerned.

Aristotle's famous doctrine of the four causes is at once familiar and frustratingly elusive. Much modern attention has been focussed on the legitimacy of translating Aristotle's *aitia* as 'cause';[3] I shall not here contribute (except perhaps indirectly) to that rather sterile discussion, beyond noting that, for Aristotle, αἰτίαι properly so-called are intensional items (i.e. it matters how you pick them out), while causal contexts in ordinary language at least (*pace* Anscombe)[4] appear to be extensional (i.e. they tolerate the substitution within them of co-referring terms); on the other hand Aristotle allows that the results of such substitutions within the contexts of *aitiai* will yield what he calls 'incidental causes', αἰτίαι κατὰ συμβεβηκός (*Phys.* II 3, 195a29-b12). Thus, if a builder is the efficient cause of a house's being built, and the builder happens to be Callias, then Callias is the incidental efficient cause of the building; to be an incidental cause is simply to be a cause picked

---

[2] See in particular W. Salmon, 'Causality: production and propagation', in P.D. Asquith and R.N. Giere (eds.) *Proceedings of the 1980 Biennial Meeting of the Philosophy of Science Association*, 1980, 2.49-69 (repr. in E. Sosa and M. Tooley (eds.) *Causation* (Oxford 1993) 154-77: my references are keyed to their pagination); 'Probabilistic causality', *Pacific Philosophical Quarterly* 61 (1980) 50-74 (repr. in E. Sosa and M. Tooley (eds.) *Causation* (Oxford 1993); and 'An "at-at" theory of causal influence', *Philosophy of Science* 44 (1977) 215-24.

[3] Cf. e.g. M. Hocutt, 'Aristotle's four becauses', *Philosophy* 49 (1974) 385-99; G.R.G. Mure 'Cause and because in Aristotle', *Philosophy* 50 (1975) 356-7; R. Sorabji, *Necessity, Cause and Blame* (London 1980) chs. 1-3.

[4] G.E.M. Anscombe, 'Causality and extensionality', *Journal of Philosophy* 46 (1969) 152-9; see on this issue J.L. Mackie, *The Cement of the Universe* (Oxford 1974) ch. 10.

out under a description which does not perspicuously link the cause to the effect.

This strongly suggests that Aristotle's principal concern is to relate causes to their effects in such a way as to make the link between them intelligible: it is *because* Callias is a builder (has internalized the τέχνη of building) that we may anticipate, under the appropriate circumstances, his producing a house (cf. *Metaph.* H 7-9). Similarly, it is because Callias's father contained within himself the human form (and, in virtue of being male, was able to transmit it), that he produced Callias. Causing, at least of the intelligible kind, is the transmission of form; *aitiai* are explanations: but they are causal explanations.

Occasionally things just occur or arise spontaneously, and in these cases there is no communication of form from one thing to another. Rather, the form simply emerges from the appropriate matter in virtue of its inherent tendencies (although some things never arise without the mediation of form—stones never spontaneously arrange themselves into a house: *Metaph.* H 9, 1034a9-21). And while we might say (although perhaps strictly speaking we should not do so) in the case of such accidentally emergent structures that they exhibit form, they have not come to do so as a result of any form-transmitting process.

This is, I think, the key to understanding an obscure passage of *Metaph.* Z, where Aristotle is discussing various types of accidental or coincidental occurrence:

> That there are principles and causes which are generable and destructible without their being for them any process of generation and destruction is obvious; for otherwise everything will be of necessity, since what is in the process of being generated or destroyed must have a cause which is not accidentally its cause. Will this occur or not? Yes, if such and such happens, but not if it does not. And this will occur if something else does. And so if time is constantly subtracted from a limited temporal extent, we will clearly arrive at the present. This man, then will die by violence if he goes out; and he will do this if he is thirsty; and he will be thirsty if something else happens... For instance he will go out if thirsty, and he will be thirsty if he eats something spicy; and this is either so or not; so he will either of necessity die or not die.... Everything, then, that is to be will be of necessity; e.g. it is necessary that someone who is alive must some time die, since something has already occurred <sc. to necessitate it>, namely the existence of contraries in the body. But whether he dies by disease or by violence is not yet determined, but depends on the happening of something else. Evidently then the process goes back to a particular source but this does not itself indicate anything further

> <in the past>. This, then, will be the source of what happens by chance, and will have nothing else as the cause of its coming to be. (1: *Metaph.* Z 3, 1027a29-1027b14)

This text has been much discussed, and there is little agreement as to its import. My translation is tendentious (although not I hope unwarrantedly so). What Aristotle is saying here (if I am right) is not that some occurrences are uncaused or unnecessitated,[5] but rather that some cannot be properly explained, where proper explanation has to do, as we have seen, with the propagation (in one way or another) of form. It is not that the hapless individual's death is uncaused—it is rather that the causal chain (as we might say) that leads from his predilection for hot foods *via* his consequent thirst and his desire to slake it to his unfortunate meeting with the ruffians at the well is not such as to instantiate, in its totality, any generally-repeating process.[6] That is why the causes in such chains come to be without any process of generation: there is nothing, prior to the coincidence, which can be said in any generally illuminating way to be leading up to it. In this sense, nothing leads up to it.

The crucial point is that coincidences are intersections of processes: κινήσεις.[7] Aristotle devotes most of the second half of the *Physics* to an analysis of κινήσεις: but for our purposes the important thing about them is that they have beginnings, middles and (most importantly) ends (*Phys.* V 1, 224a34-b16, 225a12-34). Not all

---

[5] These do not (necessarily) come to the same thing: see Sorabji (*op. cit.*, n. 3), chs. 1-3; I do not, however, agree with Sorabji's interpretation of this passage. See D. Frede, 'Aristotle on the limits of determinism: accidental causes in *Metaphysics* E 3', in A. Gotthelf (ed.) *Aristotle on Nature and Living Things* (Bristol/New Brunswick) 1985, for an account with which I am more in sympathy.

[6] Compare Aristotle's other canonical example of coincidence: happening to run into someone who owes you money and recovering your debt: *Phys.* II 5, 196b24-197a5; see W. Charlton, *Aristotle's Physics I, II* (Oxford 1970) 105-11, for a useful discussion of this and related passages.

[7] It is not clear that all such intersections are coincidences for Aristotle, since some might be held to be predictable from within the working-out of a particular process—indeed I am tempted to see the generation of substantial form as having this structure. Here two processes (that in the male and that in the female) intersect; but while the particular manner, time and place of their intersection is not predictable from within either process, that there will be such intersections presumably is; moreover, in the appropriate way, the creation of a new substantial form is instantaneous, and not itself the subject of generation in time. This is speculative, and needs more working out than I can give it here. However I note, proleptically, that if this is right, then the Aristotelian and the Stoic accounts will be even more closely related.

changes are κινήσεις, however (*Phys.* V 2); in particular, instantaneous changes from one state to another do not qualify (although they may, as in the case of the generation of substances, occur as a result of processes). Processes have an internal cohesion and a natural direction. They may be as simple as the falling of earth to its natural place[8] or as complex as those involved in animal metabolism; but they share a crucial characteristic. Once begun, their progress towards their ends is natural, intrinsic to the order of things, and will (other things being equal) result in the process's successful completion.

When the process fails to fulfil itself, that failure will be neither uncaused nor utterly inexplicable; but it will be attributable to factors external to the development of the form itself. Thus not all acorns become saplings and not all saplings oaks; in some cases the oak form will have been insufficiently firmly imprinted in the original woody matter (for various reasons: *Gen. Anim.* IV 4-6), in others external conditions will have been unpropitious (drought, insufficient sunlight) or directly inimical (lightning, squirrels).

All of this suggests that for Aristotle it is the processes which are basic.[9] Processes are not simply aggregates of discrete events, describable in some suitable four-dimensional spatio-temporal language[10] (indeed, I am inclined to think that the concept of an event, at least as it is deployed in contemporary analytical philosophy, is quite alien to the ancients). And while processes evidently have temporal stages which stand in relations of succession to one another, on this metaphysical view there is no temptation to suppose with Hume that what causation amounts to is the *mere* sequence of discrete events (and hence to make the causal relation utterly mysterious), nor either to imagine that somehow each such event is metaphysically dependent in some way upon its predecessor. Equally, the difficulty that Russell felt to be fatal to the entire concept of causation, namely that causally-significant events

8 The fact that Aristotle refers to such natural motions as involving the perfection of form becomes perfectly intelligible on the interpretation being offered: *Cael.* IV 3, 310a32-b1; cf. I 8, 276a23ff.

9 This may sound bizarre: of course on Aristotle's own account it is the category of substance which is fundamental, and in terms of which everything else must be explained (cf. e.g. *Cat.* 1-5; *Metaph.* H); but the upshot of my suggestion is that Aristotelian substances (or most of them) may be regarded as processes.

10 For a sophisticated modern defence of this philosophical position, see D.Wiggins, *Sameness and Substance* (Oxford 1980), esp. 25-6.

must be instantaneous and that hence between any two distinct events conceived of as cause and effect a third potentially disruptive event may be intruded,[11] ceases (insofar as it ever did) to trouble.

One final point bears noting. We are so inclined to suppose that causes in general precede their effects that we tend to overlook the fact that Aristotle hardly treats of the temporal succession of causes and effects at all. Occasionally Aristotle will offer examples of the *aitia*-relation where what is explanatory precedes what is to be explained, most notably the example of efficient causation at *A.Po.* II 11, 94a36-b8: the Persians made war on the Athenians because the latter had attacked Sardis. But this is a rarity (moreover, the example itself is unhappy, and badly fits Aristotle's programme in the passage).[12]

In *A.Po.* II 12, where he apparently deals with temporal considerations, Aristotle is concerned only with the appropriate tenses to employ in different explanatory accounts—and indeed explicitly says (95a36) that the middle term (which does the explaining by binding together subject and predicate in the *explanandum*) must be coeval with what it explains.

Aristotle, then, for theoretical reasons rarely even suggests that causes may precede their effects. Perhaps the nearest he gets to it is text **1**: but the whole point of that, if I am right, is to deny that, in any strong sense, causes do precede their effects. To be sure, as we would see it at least, earlier events are causally relevant to later ones—but they are so for Aristotle because they are part of intelligible processes. When those processes intersect in unforeseen ways there is created a new (instantaneous) cause, but that cause is itself the cause of something else instantaneous and cotemporal with it, namely the initiation of a new process. Finally consider Wicksteed's translation of ἀρχὴ κινήσεως, Aristotle's description of the efficient cause, as 'initiating the process':[13] initiation sounds like triggering, setting a train of events in sequence—but that is quite alien to Aristotle's sense. Rather the ἀρχὴ is the *source* of the

---

11 B. Russell, 'On the notion of cause', *Proceedings of the Aristotelian Society* 13, 1912/13, 1-26 (repr. in Russell, *Mysticism and Logic*, New York 1918); see the discussion in Mackie (*op. cit.*, n. 4), 143-54.

12 See W,D. Ross, *Aristotle's Prior and Posterior Analytics* (Oxford 1949) and J. Barnes, *Aristotle's Posterior Analytics* (Oxford, 1994^2) *ad loc.*

13 In *Aristotle: The Physics*, Loeb Classical Library (Harvard 1920), in particular at *Phys.* II 3, 194b29ff.

process or change, what drives it; and such sources are coeval with their effects.[14]

II

Metaphor is strikingly absent from Aristotle's treatment of these issues;[15] not so from the Stoics'. For the Stoics, everything that occurred in the world was the result of the working out of fate, εἱμαρμένη:

> Chrysippus described (in the second book of his *On the Cosmos*) the substance (ουσία) of fate as the pneumatic power[16] which governs everything in orderly fashion (τάξει τοῦ παντὸς διοικητικήν).... Elsewhere he describes it in several ways, as the *logos* of the cosmos, the *logos* of the things which are governed by providence in the cosmos, or the *logos* according to which things that have occurred have occurred, things which are occurring are occurring and things which will occur will occur. (**2**: Stobaeus I 79.1-12, = *SVF* 2.913, = 55M L&S)

That image of government, διοίκησις, is found elsewhere in texts reporting the Stoic position:

> Fate is a continuous cause (αἰτία εἰρομένη) of things, or the *logos* in virtue of which the world is administered. (**3**: DL 7.149; cf. **8** below)

But more important for our purposes is the metaphor of the continuous thread, the αἰτία εἰρομένη (cf. the λόγος εἰρόμενος of Arius Didymus Fr. 29, = *SVF* 2.528). Hicks in the Loeb translates: 'Fate is defined as an endless chain of causation, whereby things are, or as the reason or formula by which the world goes on', which seems to me to be multiply misleading. Nothing in the Greek corresponds to Hicks' 'endless';[17] 'whereby things are' is a needless

---

14 This is partly what causes Aristotle's notorious difficulties with projectile motion: if the spear continues to move after it leaves contact with the thrower's hand, something must still be pushing it (*Phys.* VIII 10, 266b29-267a11).

15 Unless you count as metaphoric the ἀρχὴ in his standard expression for the efficient cause, ἀρχὴ κινήσεως.

16 I.e. the power manifested in the *pneuma*, the all-pervasive dynamic constituent of the universe which is responsible for its cohesion: cf. e.g. D.L. 7.138-9 (= *SVF* 2.634, 47O LS); Cicero, *ND* 2 22 (= 47C LS); Galen, *Plen.* VII 524 Kühn (= *SVF* 2.439, 47F L&S); Plutarch, *Comm. Not.* 1085c-d (= *SVF* 2.444, 47G L&S); see also 47 I-M L&S; and see further below.

17 Although the Stoics do think that the sequence of causes is endless (see n. 18, and text **10**, below): Alexander fastens upon this aspect of their theory in order to argue that such an infinite sequence of causes would render the cause (or explanation) unknowable, since knowledge just is knowledge of the primary cause: *Fat.* 25, 196.1ff Bruns, = *SVF* 2.949. Alexander here confuses the

over-translation; but most serious is the intrusion of the metaphor of the chain.

The word εἰρομένη is the passive participle of εἴρειν, to string together, as of necklaces (cf. *Od.* 15.460, 18.296); in grammar and rhetoric, the λέξις εἰρομένη is a continuous or running style, as opposed to the classical periodic construction of balanced, antithetical clauses (cf. Aristotle *Rhetoric* III 9, 1409a24ff.). The metaphorical emphasis here is on the continuity of the process, not the discrete identity of its parts.[18] Cognate with εἴρω is the noun εἱρμός, defined in LSJ as 'train, series, sequence'; and the Stoics regularly described Fate as an εἱρμός of causes, seeking to discern an etymological link between εἱρμός and εἱμαρμένη (cf. Chrysippus, reported by Diogenianus: *SVF* 2.914).

The εἱρμός metaphor is undoubtedly Stoic: it figures in all the major doxographical accounts of the Stoic position, and is probably original to the school (at all events, I can find no earlier traces of it). Aëtius remarks that

> the Stoics say that fate is an εἱρμός of causes, i.e. an ineluctable ordering (τάξις) and connection (ἐπισύνδεσις). (**4**: I 28.4 Diels, = *SVF* 2.917)

Nemesius objects that:

> if fate is a sort of ineluctable εἱρμός of causes, as the Stoics define it (i.e. an unalterable τάξις and ἐπισύνδεσις), ends will come about not for the sake of any advantage, but simply in accordance with their own motion and necessity. (**5:** *Nat. Hom.* 37, 299, = *SVF* 2.918)

And Alexander notes:

> still, they [sc. the Stoics] agree that all things that occur in accordance with fate do so in accordance with order (τάξις) and consequence (ἀκολουθία), and have within themselves some sequentiality. (**6**: *An. Mant.* 25, 185.1-3 Bruns, = *SVF* 2.920; cf. Alex. *Quaest.* I 4)

But, it may be objected, an εἱρμός is a string *of beads* (cf, the passages from the Odyssey cited above): surely the weight of the metaphor might equally well fall upon the individual items which are strung together? And if that is the case, then the metaphor of

---

infinity of temporal sequence with an infinity of metaphysical ordering: only if the Stoics were committed to the latter (which they are not) would knowledge, even on this Peripatetic account, be threatened.

18 Cf. Critolaus, *ap.* Philo. *Aet.* 70 (= *SVF* 2.913): 'since according to the best students of nature fate is without beginning or end, stringing together the causes of everything without cessation or intermission'.

the chain is perfectly appropriate. The Stoics will, after all, be seeking to emphasize the fact that causal sequences are sequences of distinct events, like the beads on a necklace, somehow joined together.

I think that this conclusion can and should be resisted. It is worth reiterating the connection of εἱρμός with εἴρω and εἴρομαι: it is a verbal noun, capturing the process of the stringing together. More significantly, however, consider the other expressions that are used alongside εἱρμὸς αἰτιῶν, presumably by way of exegesis. In the texts cited above (*SVF* 2.917-20), we have τάξις, ἐπισύνδεσις, and ἀκολουθία. Gellius reports that:

> in the fourth book of his *On Providence*, Chrysippus says that 'fate is a certain natural, eternal ordering of the whole, in which things are consequent upon and follow one another, and in which the interweaving is ineluctable'. (**7**: *Noct. Att.* 7.2.3, = *SVF* 2.1000, = 55K L&S).

Plotinus writes that those who believe in:

> the interweaving (ἐπιπλοκή) of causes with one another, the εἱρμός from above, and the invariable consequence of later occurrences upon earlier ones... evidently introduce fate in another manner [sc. from that of the astrologers].[19] (**8**: *Enn.* 3.1.2, = *SVF* 2.946; cf. *ibid.* 3.1.4, = *SVF* 2.934)

In the course of elaborating an objection (unjustified as it will turn out) to the Stoic account, namely that it makes every prior event a cause of every subsequent one, absurdly (since thereby day would be the cause of night, and summer of winter: *Fat.* 25, 194.25ff., 195.13ff. = *SVF* 2.948; **22** below), Alexander speaks of them as:

> positing a certain binding together (ἐπισύνδεσις) and cohesion (συνέχεια) of causes, and holding this to be the reason why nothing comes to be causelessly. (**9**: *Fat.* 25, 195.4-5 Bruns, = *SVF* 2.948).

A page later, he asks:

> how could it not be absurd for them to say that causes are infinite, and that the εἱρμός and ἐπισύνδεσις of them has no first or last

---

[19] Plotinus's account is in many ways puzzling. He apparently contrasts with astrological determinists two groups of people who hold similar views about the interconnectedness and ineluctability of fate; and then (at the end of *Enn.* 3 1 2) he remarks that the second of these two groups should be further subdivided between 'those who make everything dependent upon a single principle' and those who do not (cf. *ibid.* 4-7). It is far from clear where, if anywhere, orthodox Stoicism is supposed to fit into this picture. But by Plotinus's syncretist age, original orthodoxies had become watered down, and distinctions blurred; there is, at any event, little doubt that the language that Plotinus adopts here originates with the Stoics.

> member? (**10**: *ibid.* 196.1 Bruns, = *SVF* 2.949; see **14** below; and nn. 17, 18 above)

'Binding together', 'cohesion' and 'interweaving', along with 'ordering' and 'consequence', clearly do not emphasize the supposedly discrete nature of each cause in the sequence.

Latin texts reporting or reflecting Stoic doctrine support this. Cicero writes:

> I call 'fate' what the Greeks call εἱμαρμένη: and ordering and sequence of causes (*ordinem seriemque causarum*), since cause being connected to cause brings things to be out of itself; it is an everlasting truth which flows from all eternity. (**11**: Cicero, *Div.* 1 125, = *SVF* 2.921, = 55L L&S; cf. Servius *ad Verg. Aen.* 3.376, = *SVF* 2.920)

And Augustine:

> 'Those (i.e. the Stoics) who call by the name of 'fate' not the arrangement of the stars but rather the connection and sequence of causes (*conexionem seriemque causarum*).... attribute the ordering of causes itself and that particular connection to the will and power of God the supreme'. (**12**: *CD* 5.8, = *SVF* 2.932)

Moreover, this emphasis is buttressed by considerations deriving from the Stoics' analysis of the causal relation.[20] Sextus Empiricus reports that

> the Stoics say that every cause is a body which becomes a cause to a body of something incorporeal. For instance the scalpel, a body, becomes the cause to the flesh, a body, of the incorporeal predicate 'being cut'. (**13**: *Adv. Math.* 9.211, = *SVF* 2.341, = 55B L&S; cf. *SVF* 1.89, 2.336)

Causes are bodies, effects are predicates (or rather attributes). Thus it cannot be the case in any straightforward manner that the effect of a previous cause may itself in turn be the cause of a subsequent effect.[21] Causation is not, then, to be understood on the model of a sequence of events, each of which brings about its successor, as in a row of falling dominoes.[22] That may be how opponents such as

---

[20] On the Stoic analysis of causation, see M. Frede, 'The original notion of cause' in J. Barnes *et al.* (eds.) *Doubt and Dogmatism* (Oxford 1980); see also J. Barnes, 'Skepticism and causation', in M.F. Burnyeat (ed.) *The Skeptical Tradition* (California 1983); and R.J. Hankinson, *The Ancient Concept of Explanation*, Oxford, forthcoming, ch. 7; and 'Causation and explanation' and 'Determinism and indeterminism, both in J. Barnes, J. Mansfeld, M. Schofield (eds.) *Cambridge History of Hellenistic Philosophy* (Cambridge, forthcoming).

[21] As noted by F.H. Sandbach, *The Stoics* (Bristol 1989^2) 81-2; I disagree with Sandbach, however, in his characterization of Stoic effects as events.

[22] Although there are ancient analogues to such a notion: cf. Galen, *On the Differences of Symptoms* VII 47-9 Kühn. In such sequences, Galen stipulates that

Alexander seek to paint their doctrine in order to refute it (day causing night, summer winter, and so on: *SVF* 2.948); but it is not how the Stoics themselves saw matters.

At this point we may examine Alexander's treatment of the issue in a little more detail:

> they [sc. the Stoics] say that this cosmos, which is a unity encompassing everything within itself and which is governed by a living, rational and intelligent nature, has an eternal government of things in accordance with a certain prior εἱρμός and τάξις, with the prior things being the causes of those which occur after them. In this manner all of them are bound together with one another, and nor does anything occur in it without something else following from and being linked to it causally. Nor can any one of the subsequent events be detached from those which precede it so as not to be consequent upon and bound to one of them; but rather everything which occurs is succeeded by something else which is necessarily causally dependent upon it, and everything which occurs has something prior to it upon which it is causally dependent. For nothing in the cosmos can either exist or come to be without a cause since nothing within it is detached or separated from everything that has come before. For if any uncaused process were introduced, the cosmos would be torn apart and divided and would no longer remain a unity, forever governed according to one ordering and administration; and such an uncaused process would be introduced if everything which exists and comes to be were not to have preceding causes which they followed of necessity. They say that this would be similar to something's coming to be out of nothing without a cause, and similarly impossible; and being of such a kind, the government of the totality goes on actively[23] and without cessation from infinity to infinity. (**14**: *Fat.* 22, 191.30-192.17 Bruns, = *SVF* 2.945, = 55N L&S)

That is Alexander's report of Stoic doctrine: and it is by no means entirely unfair. For the Stoics, a cosmos is a totality of totally interrelated items, no one of which can be affected without some effect upon all of the others: everything is linked by συμπάθεια, joint affection, which accounts for the unification of the whole (Cleomedes 1 1, = *SVF* 2.534, 546), for which the Stoics adduced as evidence the dependence of the tides and of the behaviour of animals on the moon, and which formed the cornerstone of their theological cosmology (Sextus *Ad. Math.* 9.78-85, = *SVF* 2.1013).

---

each item causes its immediate successor 'primarily and essentially', its more remote consequents 'secondarily and incidentally', 'thirdly and incidentally', and so on.

[23] Reading ἐνεργῶς with Usener and von Arnim, against the MSS. reading ἐναργῶς preferred by Long and Sedley.

The universe as a whole is a rational animal, all of whose parts are responsive to its overall will, which is the source of its διοίκησις and is identified with God (Cicero, *ND* 1.39, = *SVF* 2.1077, = 54B L&S; DL 9.148, = *SVF* 2.1022, = 43A L&S). Indeed, God is identical with intelligence and fate (*ibid.* 135. = *SVF* 1.102, = 46B LS), and is even identified with the cosmos itself (*ibid.* 137, *SVF* 2.526, cf. 527-8). God's rule of the universe is accomplished by his pervading it through and through in the form of *pneuma*, the subtle, dynamic mixture of fire and air responsible for intelligence and sensation (Alexander, *Mixt.* 216.14ff., = *SVF* 2.473, = 48C L&S; 224.14ff., = *SVF* 2.442, = 47I L&S; *ibid.* 226.34ff., = *SVF* 2.475; DL 7 151, = *SVF* 2.479, = 48A L&S; cf. n. 16 above). This *pneuma* is also responsible for the very cohesion of physical objects (*ibid.* 223.25ff., = *SVF* 2.441, = 47L L&S).[24]

We now need to see what implications this physics has for the Stoics' overall view of causation. That the Stoics introduced new categories into causal analysis is undisputed, although quite which categories (and what they were intended to do) is a matter of much less agreement. But it is reasonably clear at all events that the Stoics distinguished between containing (or sustaining) causes (αἴτια συνεκτικά), causes which were coeval with their effects and necessary and sufficient for them, and antecedent causes (αἴτια προκαταρκτικά). Sextus almost certainly has the Stoics in mind when he attributes the following account to an unnamed group of Dogmatists:

> causes are containing (συνεκτικά) if, when they are present the effect is present, when they are removed the effect is removed, and when they are decreased the effect is decreased (thus they say that the application of the noose is the cause of the strangling);... and some of them have said that things present can be causes of things future as well as their antecedents (προκαταρκτικά): for instance protracted exposure to the sun of fever. (**15**: *PH* 3 15-16)

---

24 Something Galen at any rate thinks requires no explanation, solidity simply being the property of being cohesive (*On Containing Causes* 6.3); *pace* Galen, there is nothing absurd in treating solidity as a derived property, dependent upon the presence of continuously active *pneuma* in sufficient concentrations in the appropriate passive material. Nor does Galen succeed in showing that the doctrine is viciously regressive on the grounds that *pneuma* is, for the materialist Stoics, itself a physical stuff (*ibid.* 6.4; cf. *SVF* 2.439-42). These issues are more fully explored in my *opp. citt.*, n. 20 above. For the Stoics' division of the material of the world into active and passive components, associated with fire and air and earth and water respectively, see *SVF* 2.524, 299, 300, 311, = 44A-C L&S.

This distinction is elaborated by Clement:

> when antecedent causes are removed the effect remains, whereas a containing cause is one during whose presence the effect remains and on whose removal the effect is removed. (**16**: *Str.* 8 9 33, = *SVF* 2.351, = 55I L&S)

Αἴτια συνεκτικά are no longer simply the immanent causes of persistence and coherence:[25] they are the sustainers of processes as well.

But evidently if there is to be a succession of causes in any way at all, not all causes can be αἴτια συνεκτικά on this model. That the Stoics did allow that, in some sense, causation embodied consecutive relations, is not in doubt. The question is: what form do those relations take?

Alexander, in **14** and elsewhere, seeks to foist upon them the unpalatable conclusion that every precedent event is the cause of every subsequent one; but there is no reason to suppose that the Stoics accepted this consequence, nor that they were in any way committed to it. Similar (although less sweeping) concerns are voiced by Cicero:

> 'cause' should not be so understood as to make whatever precedes a thing its cause, but what precedes it actively: the cause of my playing ball was not my going down to the campus, nor did Hecuba's bearing Alexander make her the cause of the death of Trojans, nor was Tyndareus the cause of Agamemnon's death because he was Clytemnestra's father. (**17**: *Fat.* 34).

Mere prerequisites should not be confused with causes as such. But he goes on to note that the Stoics:

> say that there is a difference between whether a thing is of such a kind that something cannot be brought about without it, or such that something must necessarily be brought about by it. None of the causes mentioned therefore is really a cause, since none by its own force brings about that of which it is said to be the cause; nor is that which is a condition of a thing's being brought about a cause, but that which is such that when it is present that of which it is the cause necessarily is brought about. (**18**: *ibid.* 36, = *SVF* 2.987)

Finally, we may quote Cicero's report of Chrysippus's own causal distinctions, deeply puzzling though it is:[26]

> 'some causes ', he says, 'are perfect and principal, others are auxiliary and proximate. Hence when we say that everything takes

---

[25] Which Galen says was the original Stoic sense: *Adv. Jul.* XVIIIA 278-9 Kühn, = *SVF* 2.355; cf. *idem Syn. Puls.* IX 458 Kühn, = *SVF* 2.356.

[26] I offer an interpretation of it in my *op. cit.* (n. 20), ch. 7, § 1d.

> place by fate from antecedent causes, we should not be taken to mean by perfect and principal causes, but by auxiliary and proximate causes'. Accordingly he counters the argument which I have just set out as follows: 'if everything comes about by fate it does follow that everything comes about from prior causes: not, however, from principal and perfect but from auxiliary and proximate causes'. (**19**: *ib.* 41, = *SVF* 2.974, = 62C L&S)

The 'auxiliary and proximate causes' presumably at any rate include antecedent causes.[27]

Elsewhere Chrysippus is explicitly said to have identified fate with a sequence of antecedent causes. Plutarch objects that if Chrysippus allows that antecedent (rather than perfect or containing) causes are the source of fate, and that is identical with God, God will not be all-powerful, since antecedent causes are weaker than their perfect cousins (*Stoic. Rep.* 47, 1056b-c, = *SVF* 2.997; cf. ps.-Plut. *Fat.* 11, 574d, = *SVF* 2.912; Cicero *Top.* 59). But Plutarch's objection can be blunted in the following manner. Consider Chrysippus's celebrated example of the distinction he has in mind, reported by both Cicero (*Fat.* 42-3, = *SVF* 2.974, = 62C L&S) and by Gellius (*Noct.Att.* 7 2 6-13, = *SVF* 2.1000, = 62D L&S): once it has been set in motion on a smooth surface, a cylinder will continue rolling for a while. Its beginning to roll is caused by something external to it, an antecedent cause which predates the rolling (and ceases to exercise its influence before the cessation of the rolling: cf. Clement, *Str.* 8.9.33, quoted above). However it continues to roll, according to Cicero, *suapte vi et natura,* as a result of its own force and nature, or, in Gellius's version, *quoniam ita sese modus eius et formae volubilitas habet,* because its form and rollable shape are thus. No cylinder will start rolling simply in virtue of its own rollability—yet, once it is rolling it is its *volubilitas* (in a state of actuality) which accounts for its continuing to roll, a persistent, immanent cause which lasts as long as the rolling: i.e., an αἴτιον συνεκτικόν.

The Greeks had nothing comparable to the modern concept of inertia. Things don't just go on and on until something stops them: if something is happening, something must be making it happen. There is thus no radical distinction in type between what we would think of as temporally-extended events (such as the cylinder's rolling) and genuine processes, such as the maturation of an oak tree. If this is correct, first impressions notwithstanding, the

---

27 The situation is complicated, however, and controversial: compare the different accounts offered in the works cited in n. 20 above.

Stoic account has much in common with that of Aristotle sketched earlier.

That impression is strengthened by further consideration of the role and nature of the antecedent cause. By contrast with containing causes (which are internal to their objects and identified at least partially with their nature or form),[28] antecedent causes are external to the objects affected, and are responsible for the actualization of some particular propensity they have. Thus the irruption of an antecedent cause into the tranquil life of the object, disturbing it and rousing it into action, is not something predictable or explicable from within the object itself on the basis purely of an understanding of its intrinsic properties. That a cylinder has a tendency to roll is not accidental to it—that it starts to do so at 2.30 on Thursday afternoon in response to a kick given it by a passing Stoic is. For all that, *sub specie aeternitatis* and the total structure of the world, that kick is not undetermined or accidental—indeed, it is only to be expected.

That, ultimately, is why Chrysippus wants to identify fate with antecedent causes: from the point of view of understanding why certain processes are initiated at certain times, we need to understand their antecedent causes—or, more precisely, we need to know why and when one particular process embodied in an object impinges upon another object, setting a second process in train. The internal propensities of things to act, considered purely in and of themselves, are inert,[29] and cannot account for the dynamic structure of things. Not that antecedent causes are against nature: indeed, as part of the overall harmonious totality of things which is the universe, they could not be. But the Stoics distinguish between two senses of 'nature':

> sometimes by 'nature' they mean that which holds together (συνέχουσαν) the cosmos, sometimes that which is responsible for the growth of things on earth. Nature is a constitution (ἕξις) which moves of itself, and brings to completion and sustains (συνέχουσα) what results from it in accordance with the seminal principles in a determinate time, and produces things of the same type as those from which they came. (**20**: DL 7.148, = *SVF* 2.1022, = 43A L&S)

---

[28] Frede (*art.cit.*, n. 20 above, 243) is thus clearly right to describe the αἴτιον συνεκτικόν as 'the Stoic analogue to Aristotle's formal cause'.

[29] Strictly speaking, this is false: the internal propensities are ἕξεις of the objects, which are themselves to be identified with the structure of the *pneuma* within them, and that *pneuma* is intrinsically dynamic. But this sort of dynamism is of a different type to that exhibited by macroscopic objects in action, even though those actions too are ultimately traceable to *pneuma*.

This passage resonates with unmistakable Aristotelian echoes: compare his definition of nature as 'an internal principle of motion'[30] (*Phys.* II 1, 192b8-193a10); and note the conception of generation as the transfer of form embodied in the final clauses. On the other hand, it also illustrates the Stoics' un-Aristotelian view of the perfect harmony of the whole, which is, in fact, a single organism. Each natural individual in the world has its own nature (its own structure and set of functions, which are in fact its containing causes), just as do the parts of a living body; but the overall goal of nature as a whole is to work towards their complete, harmonious interaction. Entirely congruently, for the Stoics, moral progress consists in the ever-closer assimilation of the individual's nature and will to the nature and will of the whole, in order to secure the εὔροια βίου, the smooth flow of life which is human happiness (*SVF* 2.184, 554; 3.4, 11), and which is what, in the long run, is accomplished by ineluctable fate:

> Chrysippus the Stoic said that there was no difference between what was necessitated and fate, saying that fate was an eternal, continuous, and ordered movement. (**21**: Theodoretus *GAC* 6.14, = *SVF* 2.916)

III

What is the upshot of all of this? First of all, I have been trying to bring out the Stoics' own emphasis on the essential continuity of the processes involved. Where the working out of one process abuts spatio-temporally against a suitably-disposed body, another process is set in motion: and here the one (or rather the object in which the process is embodied) may be said to be the cause to the other of the new process (entirely congruently with the canonical form of Stoic causal sentences: see above, p. 194). Thus the Stoics are by no means committed to supposing, as Alexander would have them absurdly do, that every temporally precedent stage of every process is the cause of every subsequent stage,[31] although for the Stoics any particular stage of a process will in a sense be causally relevant to others, since they will, other things being equal, be inferable from

---

[30] Or 'change', or 'process': κίνησις.

[31] I say 'absurdly': Alexander evidently considers it absurd, and it seems to me at least to do violence to our ordinary notions of causing; yet some (notably Mackie, *op. cit.*, n. 4 above, ch. 8) at least entertain the thesis. At all events, it is irrelevant to the Stoics.

it. Moreover, they reject the Aristotelian orthodoxy that properly so called no cause may precede its effect: for them, in contrast with the Peripatetics (if my account above is correct), antecedent causes are causes not just of the initiations of processes, but of the processes themselves and of their outcomes.

Nor are the Stoics to be saddled with a picture in which causes and effects are essentially discrete events, on the Humean model, whose relations are consequently obscure. Containing causes, responsible for the continuous persistence and evolution of things and processes, are themselves continuous. Antecedent causes do indeed precede their effects, but are themselves parts of other processes. Alexander claims that the Stoic doctrine forces them to suppose that winter causes summer (*Fat.* 25, 194.30ff., = *SVF* 2.948; **22** below);[32] but they are under no compulsion to suppose any such thing. The orderly progression of the seasons (as well as the alternation of day and night) is simply a continuous, repeating process. In fact, the Stoics will explain it in much the same way as Alexander does, as 'being caused by the motion and rotation of the divine body, and its inclination in virtue of the ecliptic, in accordance with which the motion of the sun is equally responsible for all of the aforementioned phenomena' (*ibid.* 195.11-13): DL.7 151-2, = *SVF* 2.693 (cf. *SVF* 2.694-6).[33]

Alexander's attempt to foist an uncongenial picture of the causal structure of things upon the Stoics is, however, underlined by his own use of a particular metaphor—which takes us back to where we started. Twice he characterizes the Stoic view, in which (so he alleges) earlier events invariably bring about later ones, as involving events being related to one another δικὴν ἁλύσεως, in the manner of a chain. Here unequivocally (by contrast with the case of εἱρμός, investigated above), we have our time honoured metaphor.

---

[32] My colleague Steve White suggests that this example, as well as that of night causing day, might have seemed particularly *ben trovato* for the Peripatetics, with their insistence that opposites could not be the cause of opposites (a widely-held ancient principle: cf. Plato, *Phaedo* 101b); however Alexander also cites cases which do not involve opposites (walking being caused by standing up, the Isthmian games by the Olympian: *Fat.* 25, 194.29ff.).

[33] There is, however, a difference of emphasis: for the Peripatetics, the unity of the cosmos is preserved by the regular heavenly rotation, rather than, as in the Stoic account, by the interpenetration of intelligent *pneuma*: Alexander, *Mixt.* 10, 223.9ff., 11, 226.24ff., = *SVF* 2.441, 1048 (cf. *SVF* 2.470-5); moreover, the Stoics reject the Peripatetic postulation of a divine fifth element, the ether, of which the heavenly bodies are made.

ἅλυσις is not a very common word: but it clearly means a chain in the literal sense of a set of interlocking links.[34] Alexander first refers to

> their first thesis [cf. **14** above], namely that of all the things that are, some become causes of things after them,[35] and things depend upon one another in this way, namely with the second depending upon the first in the manner of a chain (δικὴν ἁλύσεως), which is what they take to be the essence of fate... (**22**: *Fat.* 23, 193.4-8, = *SVF* 2.945)

The second passage occurs immediately after his explanation of the true causes of summer and winter:

> nor is it the case, because day is not the cause of night and nor is winter of summer, and these things are not interwoven (ἐμπέπλεκται) with one another in the manner of a chain (ἁλύσεως δικὴν), that they would come to be without a cause,[36] nor that if they did not come to be in this way the unity of the cosmos and of everything which exists and comes to be within it, would be torn apart. (**23**: *ibid.* 25, 195.13-16, = *SVF* 2.948; cf. **14** above)

What are we to make of this? Even if the chain-metaphor as it is

---

[34] Cf. Hdt. 9 74 (the Athenian hero Sophanes secures himself to the ground in battle with an anchor tied to his corslet by means of a chain); Polybius 3 82 8, 32 3 6, of chains used for securing captives: note the idiom *eis halusin agein*, to throw into chains: *ibid.* 4.76.5, 20.10.7-8, 21.5.3.

[35] Both text and translation here are problematic. Sharples (*Alexander of Aphrodisias on Fate*, London, 1983, 71) accepts Bruns' text (ὡς πάντων τῶν ὄντων αἰτίων τινων γινομένων τῶν μετὰ ταῦτα) and translates 'that all the things that are become causes of some of the things after them' (i.e. everything that exists comes to be a cause for at least something subsequent to it); but this seems to me to be an impossible construal of the Greek. On the other hand, my translation, while a good deal less tendentious as an interpretation of Stoic doctrine, does not seem capable of doing the work Alexander requires of it (his subsequent counterexamples consist of cases where something fails to be the cause of anything subsequent, cases which would not be ruled out by my translation of the thesis here). Sharples is no doubt influenced by considerations of what Alexander needs to say for his argument (and text **8**, to which Alexander refers here, certainly suggests, although it does not explicitly state, that the thesis in question is that everything is a cause for some subsequent event). There is an alternative textual tradition (ὡς τῶν τῶν ὄντων αἰτίων, *etc.*) which would encourage the translation 'of the causes of things, some occur of things subsequent to them', i.e. some causes precede their effects, would be equally unexceptionable as an account of Stoic doctrine, but equally incapable of bearing the weight of Alexander's argument here. Alexander may perhaps have intended first to argue, on general Peripatetic principles, against the thesis that *any* cause can precede its effect, before turning to attack the stronger claim that everything has some subsequent effect.

[36] The text is once again problematic, but the difficulties are not pertinent to our purposes. See Sharples (*op. cit.* n. 32) for useful comments *ad loc.*, as elsewhere.

deployed here does not carry any particular Humean connotations of the discreteness of the individual events in the chain, it clearly suggests (and is intended to suggest) a transitivity in the transmission of causal power from one item to the next, in the manner of falling dominoes (above, p. 194), which is equally inimical to the picture I have been trying to establish on the Stoics' behalf.

It should be repeated that ἅλυσις is not a common word; and it is very rare indeed in philosophical contexts.[37] I know of no text outside *Fat.* which deploys it as a causal metaphor at all, much less of any which ascribes it to the Stoics, and for this reason I am tempted to suppose that it is Alexander's own contribution (or possibly borrowed from earlier polemical exchanges, now lost, involving anti-Stoic philosophers, perhaps Academics). If this is right, the image is not originally Stoic at all, and rather derives from the unsympathetic and unwarranted interpretations of their intellectual opponents of the certainly authentically-Stoic εἱρμός metaphor.

There is to my knowledge only one text that tells against this supposition:

> fate, which the Greeks call εἱμαρμένη, was defined by Chrysippus, the chief Stoic philosopher, in roughly the following terms: 'fate', he said, 'is a certain everlasting and unalterable sequence (*series*) and chain (*catena*) of things turning around and interweaving itself through its eternal orderings of consequence, out of which it is fixed and interconnected'. These are Chrysippus's actual words, if my memory serves me aright... (**24**: Aulus Gellius, *Noct. Att.* 7.2.1-2, = *SVF* 2.1000)

Note that Gellius is quoting from memory here, which he admits is fallible. Moreover, he is quoting in Latin: he has already made a mental translation of Chrysippus's original Greek, in contrast with his practice elsewhere of quoting the Greek directly (as he does a few lines later: **7** above). I suggest that *catena* here is his infelicitous rendering of εἱρμός (compare *SVF* 2.916-21, quoted above); and that this constitutes another route by which the image of the chain, with its unwelcome suggestions of the transitive metaphysical dependence of later links upon earlier, as well as of their discreteness, found its way into the tradition.

---

[37] I have come across only three instances in all of the Aristotelian commentators, and although they have metaphorical significance, none has anything to do with causation. They are Simplicius, *in Phys.* 10 877.10, 878.23 (discussing various different ways in which things can be joined together); and Alexander, *in Meteor.* 3.2 217.7, discussing types of chemical combination.

IV

I hope, then, to have demonstrated that the Stoics did not adopt the chain as a metaphor for continuing causal sequence and dependence: and for good reasons. John Venn sought an alternative metaphor, that of the rope. If I am right, this is, in effect, very much the force of the Stoic εἱρμός, properly interpreted. There is, however, one text which explicitly mentions ropes:

> it is not the case that the things which are going to be simply spring into existence; rather the passage of time is like the unwinding of a rope (*rudentis explicatio*),[38] producing nothing new, but merely unrolling each thing for the first time. (**25**: Cicero, *Div.* 1 127, = *SVF* 2.944, = 55O L&S)

The unfolding of time simply brings to light what is already implicit in the structure of things, a picture reinforced by a passage a page or so earlier:

> since this is the case, nothing occurs which was not going to be, and in the same way nothing is going to be for which nature does not already contain causes productive of it. (**26**: *ibid.* 1.125-6, = *SVF* 2.921 = 55L L&S: follows **11** above)

Wesley Salmon, who quotes Venn as the *envoi* to his article ('Causality', art.cit., n. 2 above), might as felicitously have cited Cicero. In this article he seeks to undo what he takes to be the damage done to our philosophical accounts of causation by an uncritical acceptance of the Humean model. Causation, in his view ('Causality' 155-6), primarily involves two types of process, production and propagation. Production involves the creation of something new, propagation the transmission of something already existing. Moreover, production consists in the interaction of processes, 'the means by which structure and order are *propagated* or transmitted from one space-time region of the universe to other times and places' (169). For Salmon, processes, not events, are ontologically fundamental (170-1).

There is, of course, much in Salmon's position which has nothing whatever to do with the Stoics. Salmon is expressly concerned with developing an account that will apply to *probabilistic* causation,[39] a concept without parallel in the ancient world, not least

[38] Intriguingly, von Arnim's index to *SVF* reads: rudens: = ἅλυσις, repeating Gellius's mistake.

[39] Cf. the articles cited in n. 2 above.

because the elaboration of any such notion with any degree of rigour requires an understanding of statistics, something notoriously beyond the ancients' competence.[40] But if I am right there are structural similarities between the two views that are more than merely adventitious, and which are instructive in a number of ways. Salmon's interactive 'productions' are more than merely superficially reminiscent of the Stoics' antecedent causes;[41] while his 'propagations' bear more than passing comparison with the sorts of process which for the Stoics exhibit containing causation.[42]

The contributors to this volume were asked to write on some subject intersecting with the philosophical interests of Jaap Mansfeld. Given the extraordinary catholicity of those interests, such an injunction was, as the editors themselves pointed out, not a hard one with which to comply. They did, however, suggest that we might focus our attention 'on historical aspects of the study of ancient philosophy', aspects which Jaap has done so much to illuminate. I have sought to fulfil that brief; and I hope that my attempts to draw illuminating comparisons between ancient and modern views will not appear to have adulterated the pure doxographical spirit so clearly distilled by Jaap and his colleagues in Utrecht.

Thus I do not wish to suggest, absurdly, that all causal wisdom is owed ultimately to the Stoics. But a crucial aspect of their fundamental metaphysics of the matter seems to me, as presumably it would also to Salmon and others of his ilk, fundamentally on the right lines, in contrast with what has been for the past couple of centuries the dominant account in the Anglo-Saxon philosophical world (which is in any case the only philosophical world which takes such things seriously). In philosophy, no less than in the wider world, one who is ignorant of history is doomed to repeat it.[43]

University of Texas at Austin

---

[40] See I. Hacking, *The Emergence of Probability* (Cambridge 1975) for an excellent historical survey of the concept.

[41] As they are also, if I am right, of Aristotle's coincidences, and perhaps also of his account of other types of generation: see n. 7 above.

[42] And they too bear comparison with Aristotle's account of the transmission of form.

[43] I should like to thank Jennifer Hankinson for helpful comments of both a strategic and a stylistic nature.

ARISTIPP UND SEINE ANHÄNGER IN ROM

CARL JOACHIM CLASSEN

Die Letzten, die sich zur Lebensweise des Aristipp und den Lehren seiner Anhänger bekannten[1], waren—etwa in der Zeit des ersten Ptolemäerkönigs—Hegesias, Annikeris und Theodoros und eine Generation später deren Schüler, die uns fast ausnahmslos nicht mehr namentlich bekannt sind[2]. Seit der Mitte des dritten Jahrhunderts v. Chr. gibt es in den uns erhaltenen Quellen keine Hinweise mehr auf eine weitere, jüngere Generation von Kyrenaikern, und bezeichnenderweise findet schon kurz vorher der Spott über sie mit Alexis sein Ende[3]. Unter den übrigen Dichtern erinnert nur der gelehrte Elegiker Hermesianax an Aristipp und zwar an dessen Liebe zu Laïs (frg. IV A 94 Giannantoni = frg. 2, 95-98 Diehl), während Timon Aristipp und dessen τρυφερὴ φύσις ebensowenig verschont wie andere Philosophen (frg. IV A 51 Giannantoni = frg. 27 di Marco).

Von den Philosophen selbst werden in den ersten beiden Generationen nach Aristoteles—sieht man von Epikur ab—nur biographische Einzelheiten überliefert etwa von Phainias in der Schrift über die Sokratiker (frg. IV A 1 Giannantoni = frg. 31 Wehrli), vielleicht beiläufig von Chamaileon (frg. IV H 11 Giannantoni[4]) und von Philipp dem Megariker (frg. IV E 5 Giannantoni = frg. 164 A Döring[5]); dasselbe gilt auch für Kallimachos (frg. IV H 27 Giannantoni = frg. 438 Pfeiffer). Nur Bion von Borysthenes, der zeitweilig Schüler des Theodoros war (frg. IV H 28 =

---

[1] Die Zeugnisse und Fragmente sind zusammengestellt und teilweise auch erläutert von E. Mannebach (1961) und G. Giannantoni (1990).

[2] Annikeris hatte noch einen Bruder Nikoteles und einen Schüler Poseidonios (frg. IV G 2 Giannantoni).

[3] Frg. IV A 9 Giannantoni = frg. 37 Kassel Austin; zur Bezeichnung σοφιστής s. Giannantoni (1958) 21; 31-32; Classen (1986) 193; 212. Alexis frg. IV A 71 Giannantoni = frg. 241 Kassel Austin läßt sich nicht mit Sicherheit auf Aristipp beziehen.

[4] Wehrli schreibt Chamaileon die Bemerkung über Theodoros' Tod nicht mehr zu (frg. 35), s. auch Mannebach (1961) frg. 266. Zu den älteren Berichten über Aristipp s. Classen (1986) 267-271 mit Anm. 13-39 (zuerst 1958) und Döring (1988) 62-69.

[5] Eine genaue Datierung ist nicht möglich.

test. 19 und 3 Kindstrand), gibt in seinen Diatribai eine Anekdote über Aristipp wieder (frg. IV A 79 Giannantoni = frg. 40 Kindstrand[6]), während Teles in seinen Diatriben Aristipp ein Dictum zuschreibt, das sonst anderen zugewiesen wird (frg. IV A 103 Giannantoni = p. 29, 13—30, 1 Hense).

Sogar die Autoren, die in den folgenden Generationen über die Schulen der Philosophen und deren Doxai berichten, oder auch die Philosophen selbst zeigen ein erstaunlich geringes Interesse an den Lehren der Kyrenaiker: Es wird auf Lehrer-Schüler-Beziehungen verwiesen, z.B. von dem nicht sicher datierbaren Antisthenes von Rhodos in seinen Φιλοσόφων Διαδοχαί (frg. IV H 13 Giannantoni = frg. 5 Giannattasio Andria), und es werden Schriftenverzeichnisse überliefert (frg. IV A 144 Giannantoni = Sotion frg. 6 Wehrli, Panaitios frg. 123 v. Straaten und Sosikrates frg. 10 Giannattasio Andria), außerdem biographische Einzelheiten etwa von dem Historiker Idomeneus, einem Schüler Epikurs (frg. IV A 15 Giannantoni = frg. 26 Angeli, s. auch frg. 27 Angeli[7]), und vor allem Anekdoten, die oft Tadel an Aristipp und seinen Anschauungen spürbar werden lassen und Polemik, aber auch Rechtfertigungen, von Sotion (frg. IV A 17 und 96 Giannantoni = frg. 4 und 5 Wehrli) oder Hegesander in seinen Hypomnemata (frg. 17, 26 und 36 Giannantoni = frg. 17, 1 und 18 Müller), wie auch sonst die Berichte und Zitate oft durch Hinweise auf Gegensätze oder Ähnlichkeiten oder durch Polemik bestimmt sind[8].

---

[6] Zur Formulierung οἱ περὶ τὸν Βίωνα vgl. Kindstrand (1976) 150-151 (ad loc). Eine Anekdote erzählt auch der Historiker Istros in seiner literarisch nicht leicht einzuordnenden Schrift Περὶ ἰδιότητος ἄθλων (frg. IV E 2 Giannantoni = FGrHist 334 frg. 55 Jacoby); da sie nicht zu einem Anhänger der Lebensweise Aristipps paßt und auch von einem Kyrenäer Eubotes erzählt wird (bei Aelian *VH* 10, 2, der kurz darauf den Kyrenäer Aristoteles erwähnt: *VH* 10, 8 = frg. IV E 3 Giannantoni), ist sie wohl nicht auf den Kyrenaiker Aristoteles zu beziehen, von dem der Megariker Philipp spricht.

[7] Zu Idomeneus s. jetzt M. Erler (1994) 244-246, auch zu Epikur (29-202) und dessen anderen Schülern, z.B. Metrodoros (216-221); auch der mit diesem Diog. Laert. 10, 136 genannte, wohl ins 2. Jahrhundert zu datierende Diogenes von Tarsos scheint die Kyrenaiker erwähnt zu haben (= frg. IV A 200 Giannantoni); daß Diogenes Laertios dessen Schriften selbst noch benutzt hat, ist allerdings wenig wahrscheinlich, wie M. Giusta (1963) 121-122 mit Recht betont.—Von den früheren Historikern hat wohl nur Theopomp Aristipp in seiner Polemik gegen Platon genannt (FGrHist 115 frg. 259 = frg. IV A 146 Giannantoni); sein Vorwurf deutet übrigens auf die Existenz von Schriften Aristipps, vgl. auch Döring (1988) 68.

[8] Zur Polemik vgl. Antigonos von Karystos frg. IV A 161 Giannantoni = p.

Dagegen bleibt sehr allgemein, was etwa Hippobotos[9] oder Panaitios über die Auffassung der Kyrenaiker von der ἡδονή sagen (frg. IV A 172 Giannantoni = Panaitios frg. 49 v. Straaten und Hippobotos frg. 4 Gigante) oder Kleitomachos zu den von den Kyrenaikern nicht akzeptierten Teilen der Philosophie (frg. IV A 172 Giannantoni = frg. 10 Mette), anders übrigens als Sotion (frg. IV A 168 Giannantoni = frg. 7 Wehrli)[10]. So zeigt sich, daß Aristipp und seine Anhänger bei den Griechen nicht völlig in Vergessenheit gerieten, man ihnen aber andererseits nur ein begrenztes Interesse entgegenbrachte. Denn wenn uns auch nur wenige Trümmer der hellenistischen Literatur vorliegen, so dürften diese doch ein einigermaßen richtiges Bild von dem geben, was man von Aristipp und den Kyrenaikern wußte, was man über sie dachte und welche Bedeutung man ihnen beimaß[11].

Ähnlich wie Panaitios ist Kleitomachos hier besonders wichtig, weil er die Brücke zu den Römern schlägt: Er kann nicht nur von den Erlebnissen der Teilnehmer an der Philosophengesandtschaft in Rom berichten, er widmet dem Konsul L. Marcius Censorinus und dem Satiriker Lucilius nach Ciceros Zeugnis philosophische

---

118 v. Wilamowitz und den nicht sicher datierbaren Theodoros (zu ihm Mejer (1972) 76; 78-79) frg. IV A 15 Giannantoni; s. ferner *PapHerc* 418 frg. 4, 10-14 (= frg. IV A 72 Giannantoni; dazu W. Crönert (1906) 19). Parallelen werden z.B. zu dem Stoiker Ariston notiert (frg. IV A 107 und 166 Giannantoni = SVF I frg. 349 und 353 v. Arnim).

9 Zu seiner Einteilung der Philosophenschulen s. frg. I H 6 Giannantoni = frg. 1 Gigante; vgl. auch die Aufzählung der Schulen durch Herakleides, den 'Pythagoreer' (bei Joseppos, *lib. mem.* 143 = frg. I H 6 Giannantoni), dessen Gleichsetzung mit Herakleides Lembos durch H. Usener von Wehrli (1978) 17-18 mit guten Gründen bestritten wird.

10 Der vor Kleitomachos genannte Meleagros Περὶ δοξῶν (frg. IV A 172 Giannantoni) begegnet nur hier und ist nicht sicher zu datieren; dagegen ergibt sich die Datierung von Nikolaos und Sotion (frg. IV A 202 Giannantoni) aus ihrer Polemik gegen Diokles, der seinerseits dadurch datiert wird, daß Meleagros von Gadara ihm seinen Kranz widmet, s. Martini (1905) 798-801; Diokles (cf. frg. IV A 30 Giannantoni) wird von Diogenes Laertios zweimal Magnes genannt 7, 162 und 7, 48, wo zugleich seine Schrift mit dem Titel Ἐπιδρομὴ τῶν φιλοσόφων begegnet, der 10, 11 verkürzt (Ἐπιδρομή) erscheint, während Diogenes sonst von Βίοι τῶν φιλοσόφων spricht (2, 54; 82) oder Diokles ohne Buchtitel erwähnt (mehrfach) und stets ohne Herkunftsangabe (mit Ausnahme der oben angegebenen zwei Stellen); Euseb kennt Diatribai eines Diokles von Knidos (frg. IV H 29 Giannantoni), dessen Identität jedoch nicht geklärt ist, vgl. Kindstrand (1976) 169.

11 Bekanntlich erwähnt auch Ps.-Demetr. *de eloc.* Aristipp zweimal (288 und 296 = frg. IV A 14 und 148 Giannantoni); doch ist die Datierung dieser Schrift weiterhin umstritten, so daß hier auf eine Einordnung verzichtet werden muß.

Schriften[12]. Lucilius ist dann der erste Römer, der—soweit die trümmerhafte Überlieferung uns zu urteilen erlaubt—Aristipp erwähnt (frg. IV A 145 Giannantoni = frg. 800 Krenkel[13]) und zwar ein Buch, das Aristipp dem Tyrannen Dionys geschickt habe, wieder ein Stück Biographie oder wohl eher eine Anekdote. So stellt sich die Frage, welche Kenntnisse die Römer später von Aristipp und seinen Anhängern hatten und wie sie zu ihnen gelangt sein mögen.

In seinen frühen Schriften spielt Cicero nur einmal auf Aristipp an, und zwar auf einen der Aussprüche über den Umgang mit überflüssigem Reichtum (*inv.* 2, 176 = frg. IV A 83 Giannantoni); und eine Anekdote, die z.B. Vitruv (6,1, 1) und Galen (*Protr.* 5) auf Aristipp beziehen, führt er sogar nur mit der unbestimmten Formulierung *ut mihi Platonis illud, seu quis dixit alius, perelegans esse videtur (rep.* 1,29 = frg. IV A 50 Giannantoni) ein. Auch später begegnen Anekdoten fast nie, nur in den Tuskulanen eine kühne Antwort des Theodoros auf eine Drohung des Königs Lysimachos (1,102 = frg. IV H 8 Giannantoni) und in einem Brief an Paetus Aristipps berühmter Ausspruch über sein Verhältnis zu Laïs (*fam.* 9,26, 2 = frg. IV A 95 Giannantoni).

Von der Philosophie Aristipps und der Kyrenaiker spricht Cicero zum ersten Mal in seiner Übersicht über die sokratischen Schulen (*de orat.* 3, 61-62 = frg. I H 4 Giannantoni): Neben Platon und Antisthenes nennt er Aristipp, begnügt sich hier allerdings nicht (wie bei Antisthenes) mit einem Hinweis auf die besondere Vorliebe für bestimmte Inhalte der sokratischen Dialoge und einem weiteren auf die von ihm ausgehende *Cyrenaica philosophia;* er charakterisiert außerdem Aristipps und seiner Schüler Umgang mit den eigenen Anschauungen knapp, ehe er sie den zeitgenössischen Vertretern ähnlicher Lehren gegenüberstellt[14]: Das offene Bekenntnis zur Lust, das jene früher einmal ablegten (*simpliciter defenderunt*), scheint ihm den Vorzug zu verdienen gegenüber

[12] Cicero *ac. pr.* 2, 137 und 102 (= test. 18 Marx).

[13] Krenkel (1970) 445 verweist auf Diog. Laert. 2, 82 und vor allem 2, 84 (= frg. IV A 144 Giannantoni); frg. 716-718 Krenkel spricht Lucilius übrigens auch von *Socratici carti.*

[14] Nachdem Cicero zunächst eindeutig vom älteren Aristipp gesprochen hat, wählt er für die späteren Kyrenaiker bewußt das seltene *posteri,* das er *fin.* 5, 13 für die späteren Vertreter des Peripatos verwendet, von denen er sagt ... *ita degenerant, ut ipsi ex se nati esse videantur.*

denen, *qui nunc voluptate omnia metiuntur,* also den Epikureern, die sich doch weder voll zur *voluptas* noch zur *dignitas* (der Menschen) bekennen.

Erst in den philosophischen Schriften der letzten Jahre spricht Cicero ein wenig häufiger von Aristipp, dessen Lebensweise, dessen Anschauungen und den Lehren der Schüler. Allerdings berührt er nur wenige Aspekte und seine Formulierungen bleiben meistens sehr allgemein. Eine Prüfung der einzelnen Stellen zeigt zunächst, daß bald Aristipp allein, bald Aristipp und die Kyrenaiker, bald diese allein genannt werden, und zwar oft so, daß sie mit anderen Philosophen verglichen oder kontrastiert werden.

Genaueres Hinsehen lehrt, daß Cicero nur einmal die Schrift eines Kyrenaikers anführt, den Ἀποκαρτερῶν des Hegesias (*Tusc.* 1, 84 = frg. IV F 4 Giannantoni), also nie ein Werk des älteren oder des jüngeren Aristipp, und sehr vorsichtige Formulierungen wählt, wenn er die Meinungen oder Lehren Aristipps oder der Kyrenaiker erwähnt. Wo er sich auf den älteren oder jüngeren Aristipp bezieht, gebraucht er gern Wendungen wie *Aristippi est* oder *voluptas illa Aristippi*[15] oder Ellipsen[16], ähnlich bisweilen auch bei den Kyrenaikern[17]. Für den älteren oder jüngeren Aristipp wählt er daneben je einmal *dicit* und *dicere* (*fin.* 2, 19 und *Tusc.* 2, 15 = frg. IV A 183 und 204 Giannantoni), einmal *ducit,* einmal *ponit* in *voluptate ... non dolere:* (*fin.* 2, 41 und 2, 19 = frg. IV A 185 und 183 Giannantoni) und einmal *sententia* (*fin.* 2, 19, s. auch *Tusc.* 2,15 = frg. IV A 183 und 204 Giannantoni), das er daneben auch einmal für Aristipp und die Kyrenaiker verwendet (*sententiae ... : fin.* 2, 39 = frg. IV A 185 Giannantoni)[18], einmal für diese allein (*Tusc.* 3, 52 = frg. IV A 208b Giannantoni); für sie finden sich außerdem *posuerunt, censuerunt* und *censent*[19], *non recusant* und *negant* (*fin.* 2, 114 und

15 *Fin.* 1, 23 (= frg. IV A 180 Giannantoni) und 2, 35 (nicht bei Giannantoni); s. ferner *fin.* 2, 18 und 20 *illud Aristippeum (genus); fin.* 2, 34-35 ... *fines ... Aristippo simplex voluptas, ... unus Aristippi vel Epicuri ... Aristippo voluptas; fin.* 5, 20 ... *principes: voluptatis Aristippus* (= frg. IV A 183, 184 und 187 Giannantoni), auch *ac. pr.* 2, 139 *Aristippus ... solum corpus tuetur* (s. auch *fin.* 2, 18) = frg. IV A 179 (und 183) Giannantoni.

16 *Fin.* 1, 26 und 2, 18 (*quam Aristippus*) = frg. IV A 181 und 183 Giannantoni.

17 *Fin.* 1, 39: *conclusum est ... contra Cyrenaicos; Tusc.* 3,31: *accipio ... a Cyrenaicis haec arma* = Frg. IV A 182 und 208a Giannantoni.

18 Für sie zusammen auch *simpliciter defenderunt* (*de orat.* 3, 62, s.o.); ... *esse voluerunt, quorum princeps Aristippus, ... unde Cyrenaici (ac. pr.* 2, 39) = frg. I H 4; IV A 178 und 185 Giannantoni.

19 *Off.* 3, 116: *Cyrenaici atque Annicerii ... omne bonum in voluptate posuerunt*

ac. pr. 2, 76 = frg. IV A 186 und 209b Giannantoni) sowie *putant* und *putent (ac.* 2, 142; 2, 20 und *Tusc.* 3, 76 = frg. IV A 209a, 209c und 208c Giannantoni). Für Theodoros[20] (immer zusammen mit Diagoras) gebraucht er *putaverunt, deorum naturam sustulerunt* und *deos esse negabant (nat. deor.* 1, 2; 1, 63 und 1, 117 = frg. IV H 19a; 19b und 19c Giannantoni). Dagegen heißt es in den Tuskulanen *a Cyrenaico Hegesia sic copiose disputatur* (1, 83 = frg. IV F 3 Giannantoni), unmittelbar bevor dessen Buch erwähnt wird.

Auffällig ist weiterhin, daß Cicero gelegentlich, wenn auch selten genug, den älteren Aristipp eindeutig bezeichnet, etwa als Schüler des Sokrates (*ac. pr.* 2, 131 = frg. IV A 178 Giannantoni[21]), nie jedoch den von den Griechen als μητροδίδακτος charakterisierten Enkel (cf. e.g. Strabo 17, 3, 22 und Diog. Laert. 2, 83 und 86 = frg. IV B 1 und IV A 160) und daß er nur einmal einen Aristipp (den älteren oder den jüngeren) mit den Kyrenaikern unmittelbar zusammennimmt (*fin.* 2, 39 = frg. IV A 185 Giannantoni), ihn sonst aber deutlich von ihnen absetzt[22] oder allein von Aristipp[23] oder allein von den Kyrenaikern[24] spricht; eine Systematik bei der Verwendung der einzelnen Bezeichnungen ist nicht erkennbar[25].

Schließlich fällt auf, daß sich das, was Cicero über Aristipp und die Kyrenaiker sagt, auf sehr wenige Themen beschränkt, und auf sehr vage und allgemeine Aussagen über diese Themen, und weiter, daß er deren Anschauungen in der Regel neben die anderer Philosophen rückt, sei es daß diese vergleichbare oder entgegengesetzte Positionen vertreten. Diese Beobachtungen erlauben die Vermutung, daß Cicero weder je ein Werk des älteren noch des

---

virtutemque censuerunt; Tusc. 3, 28 und 52 = frg. IV A 189; 208 a und 208 b Giannantoni.

[20] Zweimal erzählt Cicero Anekdoten von Theodorus, *Tusc.* 1, 102 und 5, 117 (= frg. IV H 8 und 7 Giannantoni) und einmal von Antipater (*Tusc.* 5, 112 = frg. IV C 1 Giannantoni).

[21] Vgl. ferner *de orat.* 3, 62 (s.o.), *Tusc.* 2, 115 *Socraticus Aristippus* und auch *off.* 1, 148 *si quid Socrates aut Aristippus contra morem ... fecerint* (= frg. I H 4; IV A 204 und 83b Giannantoni).

[22] *Ac. pr.* 2, 131; *fin.* 1, 23; *off.* 3, 116 = frg. IV A 178; 180; 189 Giannantoni.

[23] Cf. *ac. pr.* 2, 139; *fin.* 1, 26; 2, 18-20; 34-35; 41; 5, 20; *nat. deor.* 3, 77 = frg. IV A 179; 181; 183; 184; 185 (am Ende); 187; 161a Giannantoni.

[24] Cf. *ac. pr.* 2, 20; 76 (*Cyrenaei*); 142; *fin.* 1, 39; 2, 114; *Tusc.* 3, 28-31; 52; 76 (Konjektur) = frg. IV A 209c; 209b; 209a; 182; 186; 208a; 208b; 208c Giannantoni.

[25] Dort wo die *Cyrenaici* allgemein genannt werden, wird fast stets gegen Epikur polemisiert.

jüngeren Aristipp gelesen hat, sich aber auch nicht auf Handbücher mit Darstellungen der einzelnen Philosophenschulen stützt, sondern auf Passagen bei anderen Philosophen, die sich auf Aristipp und dessen Anhänger berufen oder gegen sie polemisieren.

Damit wird zugleich die Frage aufgeworfen, welche Anschauungen und Lehren der Kyrenaiker Cicero überhaupt kennt und warum er sie erwähnt.

Die erkenntnistheoretischen Probleme, die Cicero in den *Academica* erörtert, geben ihm Anlaß, mehrfach von den Kyrenaikern zu sprechen. Zunächst verweist Lucullus in seiner Rechtfertigung der Möglichkeit von Erkenntnis, die er mit Ausführungen über die Zuverlässigkeit der Sinne beginnt, auf den 'inneren Tastsinn', der Schmerz oder Lust empfindet und mit dem, wie er hinzufügt, für die Kyrenaiker das einzige Wahrheitskriterium gegeben ist (*ac. pr.* 2, 20 = frg. IV A 209c Giannantoni). Ganz ähnlich klingt die Beschreibung, die Cicero selbst in seiner Entgegnung von der Lehre der Kyrenaiker gibt, die er hier als *minime contempti philosophi* bezeichnet (*ac. pr.* 2, 76 = frg. IV A 209b Giannantoni[26]); sie könnten, wie er sagt, nur erfassen (erkennen), was sie mit dem inneren Tastsinn spürten, und er fügt hinzu, sie wüßten nicht, welche Farbe oder welchen Klang etwas habe, sie empfänden nur, daß sie irgendwie betroffen seien. Gegen Ende des Dialogs schließlich kommt Cicero noch einmal auf die Position der

---

[26] Die Lesart *Cyrenaei* überrascht (und wurde schon von Lambin 1573 durch Konjektur in *Cyrenaici* geändert, das einige Editoren in den Text aufgenommen haben); denn die Griechen unterscheiden Κυρηναῖος (Einwohner von Kyrene) und Κυρηναϊκός (Anhänger der Philosophie der Kyrenaiker). Döring (1988) 35-37 bestreitet dies unter Berufung auf die Formulierung, mit der Diogenes Laertios 2, 83 (= frg. IV A 144 Giannantoni) die erste Liste der Schriften Aristipps einleitet, und glaubt, daß Diogenes 2, 86b-93 (= frg. IV A 172 Giannantoni) "referiert, ... was er als orthodoxe, auf den Auffassungen Aristipps basierende Lehre in seiner Quelle bzw. seinen Quellen verzeichnet fand" (35). Er erklärt nicht, warum Aristipp in den Quellen so oft von den Kyrenaikern getrennt wird (s. auch o. Anm. 14 und 22) und z.B. überall dort, wo es um erkenntnistheoretische Probleme geht, Cicero, Plutarch oder Sextus Empiricus nie von Aristipp, sondern stets nur von den Kyrenaikern sprechen bzw. Aristokles von οἱ ἐκ τῆς Κυρήνης oder οἱ κατ' Ἀρίστιππον (τὸν Κυρηναῖον) (Döring (23): "die nach allgemeiner Auffassung in der Nachfolge des Aristipp aus Kyrene philosophieren") und daneben von οἱ περὶ τὸν Ἐπίκουρον ἐκ τῆς Ἀριστίππου διαγωγῆς ὁρμώμενοι (frg. IV A 209-219 Giannantoni). Ich bin eher geneigt, an jeweils einmalige Irrtümer bei Cicero und Diogenes zu glauben (*ac. pr.* 2, 76 und Diog. Laert. 2, 84 = frg. 209 und 144 Giannantoni).

Kyrenaiker zurück (*ac. pr.* 2, 142 = frg. IV A 209a Giannantoni). Er beginnt die Schilderung der Uneinigkeit der Philosophen für den Bereich der Dialektik, ehe er eine Reihe weiterer Meinungen referiert, zunächst, indem er Protagoras und die Kyrenaiker einander gegenüberstellt—Protagoras, der die Auffassung vertritt, daß für jeden wahr ist, was ihm als wahr erscheint[27], und die Kyrenaiker, die *praeter permotiones intumas nihil putant esse iudicii.* Zum dritten Mal begnügt sich Cicero mit einer sehr allgemeinen Formulierung, um die erkenntnistheoretische Position der Kyrenaiker zu charakterisieren, und verzichtet erneut darauf, sie im einzelnen vorzustellen, zu erörtern oder zu widerlegen.

Häufiger erinnert Cicero in den Diskussionen ethischer Fragen an Aristipp, den älteren oder den jüngeren, und an die Kyrenaiker. Kurz vor der eben zitierten Stelle in den *Academica* wendet er sich anläßlich der Vielfalt der Meinungen, die die Philosophen über Gut und Böse vortragen, nach vielen anderen, die er teilweise für nicht mehr bedeutsam hält (*ac. pr.* 129: *illa quae relicta ... videntur;* 130: *abiecti*), denen zu, die seit langer Zeit und oft vertreten worden sind: *alii voluptatem finem esse voluerunt, quorum princeps Aristippus, qui Socratem audierat, unde Cyrenaici, post Epicurus, cuius est disciplina nunc notior nec tamen cum Cyrenaicis de ipsa voluptate consentiens.* (*ac. pr.* 2, 131 = frg. IV A 178 Giannantoni). Wichtig ist hier, wie mir scheint, der Hinweis, daß den Zeitgenossen eher die Auffassung Epikurs geläufig ist—die Kyrenaiker sind offenbar weitgehend vergessen. Wenn Cicero trotzdem betont, daß Epikur ihrer Auffassung von der *voluptas* nicht voll zustimmt, so will der Skeptiker hier die Meinungsvielfalt mit einem weiteren Beispiel illustrieren. Denn die Formulierung *voluptas finis est,* ist so allgemein, daß sie für Aristipp ebenso wie für Epikur gelten kann, und so stellt Cicero auch beide wenig später als Alternativen nebeneinander: *labor eo ut adsentiar Epicuro aut Aristippo* (*ac. pr.* 2, 139 = frg. IV A 179 Giannantoni). Anschließend erläutert er dann allerdings Aristipps Position, um ihn mit dem Stoiker Zeno kontrastieren zu können: *Aristippus quasi animum nullum habeamus corpus solum tuetur, Zeno, quasi corporis simus expertes, animum solum complectitur.*

Ähnlich kann Cicero Epikur gleich zu Beginn seiner Darlegungen über die Hilflosigkeit vieler Philosophen aus verschiedenen Schulen in den Tuskulanen unmittelbar an Aristipp heranrücken

---

[27] Zu Protagoras s. Classen (1989).

(2, 15 = frg. IV A 204 Giannantoni[28]), weil er sich auf die sehr allgemeine Aussage *summum malum dolor* beschränkt, der er ähnlich knappe Formulierungen zu anderen Philosophen entgegensetzt.

Auch in seiner einleitenden Kritik an Epikur in *de finibus* bedient sich Cicero, sobald er sich der Ethik zuwendet, nur sehr allgemeiner Formulierungen für die Kyrenaiker: Der Grundsatz, daß *voluptas* und *dolor* alles bestimmen, was wir erstreben oder meiden, wird vor Epikur auch schon von Aristipp vertreten und von den Kyrenaikern besser und freimütiger verteidigt (1, 23 = frg. IV A 180 Giannantoni), eine Bemerkung, die er durch einen sehr scharf kritisierenden Zusatz ergänzt. Ähnlich heißt kurz darauf ... *voluptatem ... summum bonum ... ante Aristippus, et ille melius (sc. quam Epicurus)* (1, 26 = frg. IV A 181 Giannantoni). Damit greift Cicero auf, was er schon bei der ersten Vorstellung Aristipps und seiner Anhänger in *de oratore* über sie und Epikur sagte: daß sie zusammengehören und daß die Kyrenaiker ihre Position freimütiger, rigoroser (d.h. wohl ohne Rücksicht auf die Konsequenzen, mögen sie auch noch so abstoßend sein) vertreten, anders als Epikur und dessen Anhänger, von denen es dort heißt *dum verecundius id agunt, nec dignitati satis faciunt, quam non aspernantur, nec voluptatem tuentur, quam amplexari volunt (de orat.* 3, 62[29]), während Cicero hier von dem *voluptas*-Begriff der Kyrenaiker sagt *eius modi esse iudico, ut nihil homine videatur indignius (fin.* 1, 23).

Dagegen läßt Cicero Torquatus ein wenig später nicht nur den Unterschied zu den Kyrenaikern durch den Hinweis betonen, der mit Hilfe der unbewegten Hand der Chrysippstatue gewonnene Schluß richte sich gegen sie, nicht gegen Epikur, er legt dem Epikureer noch eine Überlegung in den Mund, die die *voluptas*-vorstellung der Kyrenaiker deutlicher werden lassen soll (*fin.* 1, 39 = frg. IV A 182 Giannantoni): "Wenn allein das Lust sei, was die Sinne gleichsam kitzele—um es einmal so zu formulieren—und mit Süßigkeit auf sie zuströme und in sie hineingleite, dann ... könne kein Teil des Körpers zufrieden sein mit der Freiheit vom Schmerz ohne eine angenehme Lustbewegung." Offensichtlich ist Cicero mit der Definition der *voluptas* (ἡδονή) als λεία κίνησις vertraut (cf. Diog. Laert. II 86 = frg. IV A 172 Giannantoni), und dies wird durch mehrere Passagen im zweiten Buch *de finibus*

---

28 Zu *enervata muliebrisque sententia* s. Görler (1974) 79, s. auch 50.

29 Vgl. auch *fin.* 2, 14 (= frg. IV A 186 Giannantoni): *verecundius/constantius.*

bestätigt, z.B. *eam voluptatem ... quam Aristippus, id est, qua sensus dulciter ac iucunde movetur* oder ... *in ea voluptate, quae maxima dulcedine sensum moveret* oder ... *optabile esset maxima in voluptate ... versari, cum omnes sensus dulcedine omni quasi perfusi moverentur* (*fin.* 2, 18; 39 und 114 = frg. IV A 183; 185 und 186 Giannantoni) oder durch eine Formulierung in den *Academica: revocat virtus .., pecudum illos motus esse dicit* (2, 139 = frg. A IV 179 Giannantoni).

Die angeführten Stellen lassen zugleich zwei andere Aspekte erkennbar werden, die immer wieder begegnen, wo Cicero von der *voluptas* Aristipps oder der Kyrenaiker spricht: Einerseits äußert er oft scharfe Kritik[30] an Aristipps Deutung der zugleich als *finis* oder *summum bonum* bezeichneten *voluptas,* da sie menschenunwürdig sei. Dafür verweise ich neben *de orat.* 3, 62 und *ac. pr.* 2, 139 auf *fin.* 1,23 (*ut nihil homine videatur indignius*), *fin.* 2, 18 (*voluptatem ... quam etiam pecudes, si loqui possent, appellarent voluptatem*), *fin.* 2, 40 (*ut tardam aliquam et languidam pecudem ad pastum et ad procreandi voluptatem hoc divinum animal ortum esse voluerunt, quo nihil mihi videtur absurdius*) und *fin.* 2, 114 *qui est autem dignus nomine hominis, qui unum diem totum velit esse in genere isto voluptatis?* (= frg. I H 4 und IV A 179; 180; 183; 185 und 186 Giannantoni)[31].

Zum anderen rückt Cicero neben die *voluptas*-vorstellung Aristipps und der Kyrenaiker gern eine oder mehrere andere vom *finis* oder vom *summum bonum,* etwa das Freisein vom Schmerz (*non dolere, vacuitas doloris, sine dolore esse*[32]) oder *virtus* oder *honestas*[33], oder mehrere wie *doloris vacuitas* und *frui principiis naturalibus* (*fin.* 2, 35, vgl. *fin.* 5, 17 = frg. IV A 187 Giannantoni). Offensichtlich erscheint Aristipps *voluptas* Cicero besonders geeignet, um eine bestimmte Position in der ethischen Diskussion gegenüber anderen zu markieren, und so begegnet er mehrfach neben Hieronymos und Karneades (*fin.* 2, 35 sowohl mit Epikur—wie auch *ac. pr.* 2, 131 neben Hieronymos und Kalliphon—wie ohne Epikur), aber auch Epikur ohne Aristipp (*fin.* 4, 49; 5, 87; *Tusc.* 5, 84). Daraus wird deutlich, daß es Cicero bei solchen Reihungen nur ganz allgemein

---

30 Diese Kritik spiegelt sich nicht nur in Anekdoten und Aussprüchen—auf die Cicero fast völlig verzichtet—sondern auch in der Charakterisierung der Aristippanhänger als ἄσωτοι, an die er *nat. deor.* 3, 77 erinnert (= frg. IV A 161 Giannantoni).

31 Vgl. dazu auch Görler (1974) 70-71.

32 Cf. *fin.* 2, 18-20; 34; 39 und 41, auch schon 1, 37-39 (frg. IV A 183, 184, 185 und 182 Giannantoni).

33 Cf. *fin.* 2, 34 und 2, 19 (= frg. IV A 184 und 183 Giannantoni).

um die jeweiligen Grundsätze geht, nicht um die Einzelheiten der verschiedenen Systeme[34].

Auch die Frage, ob eine These von dem älteren oder dem jüngeren Aristipp oder von allen Kyrenaikern vertreten wurde, stellt Cicero nicht. Ihm genügt es, eine ethische Position anführen zu können, deren Verfechter die *voluptas—simplex, sola, summa*—als *summum bonum,* als *finis* ansahen, *expers honestatis, quae maxima dulcedine sensum movet,* und entsprechend *dolor* als *summum malum*[35], und eine weitere, nach der—im Gegensatz zu anderen—nicht jedes Unheil Betrübnis aufkommen läßt, sondern nur unvermutetes und nicht erwartetes[36], ferner eine erkenntnistheoretische, nach der der innere Tastsinn als einziges Wahrheitskriterium anzusehen ist, und eine 'theologische', nach der die Existenz der Götter geleugnet wird und für die es ihm nicht so wichtig ist, sie mit den übrigen Anschauungen der Kyrenaiker zu verknüpfen, als zwei Repräsentanten zu nennen, neben Diagoras auch Theodoros[37].

Fassen wir zusammen. Wie andere Römer, frühere, gleichzeitige und spätere, kennt Cicero einige Anekdoten über Aristipp und dessen Anhänger, die deren Lebensklugheit und Unabhängigkeit illustrieren[38]. Außerdem ist er mit einigen philosophischen Grundsätzen Aristipps und der Kyrenaiker vertraut, vor allem mit ethischen, auf die er sich in der Regel bezieht, um gegen sie und Epikur oder mit ihrer Hilfe gegen Epikur zu polemisieren oder um Meinungen und Anschauungen anderer Philosophen durch Vergleich oder Kontrast deutlicher herauszuarbeiten. Den Versuch, alle Lehren der Kyrenaiker zusammen zu erfassen und als

---

[34] Das gilt auch für die kurze Bemerkung *off.* 3, 116 (= frg. IV A 189 Giannantoni).

[35] *Simplex: fin.* 2, 34; *sola: fin.* 2, 41; *summa: fin.* 2, 41; *summum bonum: fin.* 2, 19; *finis: ac. pr.* 2, 131; *expers honestatis: fin.* 2, 35; *quae maxima dulcedine sensum movet: fin.* 2, 39 (cf. auch *fin.* 1, 39 und *fin.* 2, 18); *dolor: Tusc:* 2, 15 (= frg. IV A 184; 185; 183; 178; 182 und 204 Giannantoni).

[36] Cf. *Tusc.* 3, 28-31; 52; 75-76 (= frg. IV A 208 Giannantoni).

[37] Cf. *nat. deor.* 1, 2; 1, 63; 117 (= frg. IV H 19 Giannantoni).

[38] Von den früheren ist nur Lucilius zu nennen (frg. 800 Krenkel = frg. IV A 145 Giannantoni), von den gleichzeitigen nur Vitruv (6, 1, 1 = frg. IV A 50 Giannantoni), von den späteren Horaz (frg. IV A 45; 80; 100 Giannantoni), Valerius Maximus, Seneca, Apuleius, Gellius, Porphyrio, Ausonius und Ps.-Caesius Bassus (= frg. IV A 47; 65; 104; 49; 45; 80; 100; 81 Giannantoni); zu Aristipps Lebensart s. Tertullian *apol.* 46, 16 (= frg. IV A 54 Giannantoni); Anekdoten aus Ciceros Werken geben Laktanz und (zu Theodoros) Valerius Maximus und Seneca wieder, aus Gellius (zu Aristipp) Augustin: frg. IV A 83 und 95, H 8 und A 49 Giannantoni.

philosophisches System zu verstehen (oder gar zu widerlegen), unternimmt Cicero nicht. Dafür hatte er mehrere Gründe. Zum einen ist nicht sicher, wie weit die Kyrenaiker ein umfassendes philosophisches Lehrgebäude entwickelt hatten[39], zum anderen kannte Cicero offenbar keine Gesamtdarstellung, sondern nur Einzelheiten, und zwar aus der Polemik anderer Schulen, außerdem vielleicht auch aus Handbüchern, in denen vergleichbare und entgegengesetzte Lehrmeinungen zusammengestellt waren; vor allem aber gab es, wie er selbst gelegentlich bemerkt, in seiner Zeit keine Kyrenaiker mehr (*off.* 3, 116 = frg. IV A 189 Giannantoni); vielmehr waren Epikur und dessen Anhänger an ihre Stelle getreten und verbreiteten ihre vielfach sehr ähnlichen Anschauungen mit großem Erfolg (*Tusc.* 4, 6)[40]. Gegen sie glaubte Cicero sich mit seinen philosophischen Schriften wenden und sie teilweise auch mit Hilfe der Kyrenaiker bekämpfen zu müssen.

Auch später zeigen die Römer wenig Interesse an der Philosophie der Kyrenaiker, mögen einzelne auch dieses oder jenes Detail aus Ciceros Darstellungen reproduzieren[41]. Nur bei Seneca findet sich etwas Neues, eine Untergliederung der Ethik, die er wohl einem der an solchen Dingen interessierten Handbücher entnimmt, ohne auf sie einzugehen (*epist.* 89, 12, s. Anm. 39). Wenn Horaz dichtet

---

[39] Vgl. Kleitomachos frg. 10 Mette; Sotion frg. 7 Wehrli und Sen. *epist.* 89, 12 (= frg. IV A 172 und 168 Giannantoni). Außerdem ist, wie Döring (1988) 69 mit Recht betont, anzunehmen, daß die Lehre der 'eigentlichen' Kyrenaiker (vor Annikeris, Hegesias und Theodoros) erst allmählich ihre endgültige Form in der Generation des jüngeren Aristipp fand. Entsprechend wird sie in den einzelnen Phasen ihrer Entwicklung in verschiedener Weise von ihren Gegnern angegriffen worden sein (zu Aristoteles s. Döring (1988) 69 Anm. 146), was die spätere Überlieferung, soweit sie sich auf polemische Äußerungen stützte, geprägt haben dürfte.

[40] Wenn Epikur und seine Anhänger auch oft in die Nähe von Aristipp und den Kyrenaikern gerückt werden, so ist nicht zu vergessen, daß Epikur und seine Schüler immer wieder gegen sie polemisieren, was hier nicht im einzelnen belegt zu werden braucht.

[41] Vgl. Val. Max. 8, 9 *ext.* 3 aus Cic. *Tusc.* 1, 83 (= frg. IV F 5 und 3 Ginannantoni), ferner Quint. *inst.* 12, 23-24; Min. Fel. 8, 1-2; Lact. *inst.* 3, 7, 7; 3, 8, 6-10; 7, 7, 11; *epit.* 28, 3; 34, 7; 63, 1; *ira* 9, 7; 10, 47; Arnob. *nat.* 4, 29; Aug. *c. acad.* 3, 11, 26; *c. Iulian.* 4, 14, 72; *civ.* 8, 3; 18, 41; Eucher. *epist. ad Val.* p. 724 Migne (= frg. IV A 190; IV H 21; IV A 191; 193; 194; 195; 192; IV H 20; H 22; IV A 210; 188; I H 13b; 13c; IV A 196 Giannantoni); s. dazu auch die von mir angeregte, nicht veröffentlichte Magisterarbeit von B. Ch. Weber, *Die Rezeption der Lehren des Aristipp und der Kyrenaiker durch die Römer*, Göttingen 1993.

nunc agilis fio et mersor civilibus undis
virtutis verae custos rigidusque satelles,
nunc in Aristippi furtim praecepta relabor
et mihi res, non me rebus subiungere conor (*epist.* 1, 1, 16-19),

so verrät er nicht Kenntnis der Philosophie der Kyrenaiker (*praecepta*), sondern illustriert seine eigene Unabhängigkeit, die sich am Aristipp der Anekdoten orientiert und es ihm erlaubt, ebenso mit dessen Worten über Laïs zu spielen (18-19) wie auch einmal eine 'stoische' Position einzunehmen (16-17)[42].

Die lebensbejahenden Gedanken und Lehren Aristipps und der Kyrenaiker, von Epikur verdrängt und zur Bedeutungslosigkeit verurteilt, noch ehe die griechische Philosophie nach Rom kam, haben dort nie selbständig Fuß fassen können. Sie haben den Römern allein dazu gedient, die Lehren anderer Schulen klarer zu beschreiben oder die Philosophie zu bekämpfen, der sie selbst hatten weichen müssen.

Göttingen

[42] Die Debatte zwischen Traina (1991), Gigante (1993) und wiederum Traina (1994) soll hier nicht fortgeführt werden. Die Gefahr einer 'sopravvalutazione' Aristipps ist nicht zu verkennen.

BIBLIOGRAPHIE

Fragmentsammlungen außer denen von v. Arnim, Hense, Jacoby, Kassel-Austin, Müller, Pfeiffer und v. Straaten:

Angeli, A. (1981) 'I frammenti di Idomeneo di Lampsaco', *Cronache Ercolanesi* 11: 41-101.
Di Marco, M. (1989) *Timone di Fliunte. Silli* (Roma).
Döring, K. (1972) *Die Megariker* (Amsterdam).
Giannantoni, G. (1958) *I Cirenaici* (Firenze).
—— (1990) *Socratis et Socraticorum Reliquiae* I-IV (Napoli).
Giannattasio Andria, R. (1989) *I frammenti delle 'Successioni dei filosofi'* (Napoli).
Gigante, M. (1983) 'Frammenti di Ippoboto', in *Omaggio a Piero Treves,* a cura di A. Mastrocinque (Padova) 151-193.
Kindstrand, J.F. (1976) *Bion of Borysthenes* (Uppsala).
Krenkel, W. (1970) *Lucilius. Satiren* I-II (Leiden).
Marx, F. (1904-1905) *C. Lucilii Carminum Reliquiae* I-II (Leipzig).
Mannebach, E. (1961) *Aristippi et Cyrenaicorum Fragmenta* (Leiden).
Mette, H. J. (1985) 'Kleitomachos von Karthago', *Lustrum* 27: 142-148.
Wehrli, F. (1969) *Die Schule des Aristoteles* IX: *Phainias von Eresos. Chamaileon. Praxiphanes* (Basel).
—— (1978) *Die Schule des Aristoteles,* Supplement II: *Sotion* (Basel).

Die Abkürzung frg. ist von mir weitgehend auch dort verwandt worden, wo genau genommen nur Nachrichten, also *testimonia,* vorliegen.

Aufsätze und Monographien:

Classen, C. J. (1986) *Ansätze. Beiträge zum Verständnis der frühgriechischen Philosophie* (Würzburg).
—— (1989) 'L'ἀλήθεια di Protagora', *Rivista di Filosofia* 70: 163-188.
Crönert, W. (1906) *Kolotes und Menedemos* (Leipzig).
Döring, K. (1988) *Der Sokratesschüler Aristipp und die Kyrenaiker* (Stuttgart).
Erler, M. (1994) 'Epikur', in *Die Philosophie der Antike Band 4. Die Hellenistische Philosophie,* hgg. v. H. Flashar (Basel) 29-490.
Gigante, M. (1993) 'Quel che Aristippo non aveva detto', *La Parola del Passato* 48: 267-280.
Giusta, M. (1963) 'Passi dossografici di morale epicurea nel X libro di Diogene Laerzio', *Atti della Accademia delle Scienze di Torino. Classe di Scienze Morali, Storiche e Filologiche* 97: 120-174.
Görler, W. (1974) *Untersuchungen zu Ciceros Philosophie* (Heidelberg).
Martini, E. (1905) 'Diokles', *Paulys Realencyclopädie der classischen Altertumswissenschft,* hgg. v. G. Wissowa 5 (Stuttgart) 798-801.
Mejer, J. (1978) *Diogenes Laertius and His Hellenistic Background* (Wiesbaden).
Traina, A. (1991) 'Orazio e Aristippo. Le *epistole* e l'arte di convivere', *Rivista di Filologia e di Istruzione classica* 119: 285-305.
—— (1994) 'In Aristippi praecepta relabor', *Eikasmos* 5: 243-246.

LUCRETIUS ON THE ORIGIN AND DEVELOPMENT OF POLITICAL LIFE (*DE RERUM NATURA* 5.1105–1160)

P. H. Schrijvers

Lucretius' sketch of the origin and development of political life, which forms part of his general history of the beginnings of human life and civilisation, gives rise to the following two questions on which this brief article, dedicated to a good friend and highly esteemed colleague, will focus: (1) Is his account a purely theoretical reconstruction or is it based on historical evidence in spite of its anonymous character? (2) Is Lucretius, as an orthodox follower of Epicurus, exclusively following the doctrine of his Master, or does the Roman poet belong to the category of *polyhistores* who make use of all relevant sources and doctrines to create their own, new, synthesis?

A quick and global view on the paragraph 5.1105-1160 of *De Rerum Natura* leads to two rather evident impressions: Lucretius presents a series of 'political' constitutions which are more or less characterized by the position of power of certain individuals or social groups, and this list is drawn up as a process of historical evolution in which each form of government grows out of another. I shall start to identify the different individuals and groups whose changing positions were the cause of the political evolution. I use the word 'political' in the ancient, etymological sense of 'belonging to' or 'concerning the *polis*', the city, because the foundation of cities (*urbes*) and also of citadels (*arces*) is stated expressly by Lucretius at the beginning of his political story (5.1108 *condere coeperunt urbis arcemque locare*).[1]

At the start he mentions the superiority of certain individuals who excelled in intelligence and inventiveness. These anonymous inventors who introduced all sorts of novelties, are called 'kings' (1109 *reges*).[2] In the beginning their rule seems to have

---

[1] In the same way, Lucretius mentions the cities at the beginning of his next paragraph on religion (5.1162); it is the origin of civil religion he is dealing with.

[2] For the topical character of this list of qualities and activities of the so-

been fair because they parcelled out fields to each man and divided flocks among them, according to their inborn qualities: beauty, strength, intelligence (5.1110-1111). In accordance with the ancient, traditional definition of δικαιοσύνη their measures may be considered an act of distributive justice.[3] In spite of the fair character of their rule these so-called kings did not feel secure; they founded citadels as strongholds and refuges *for themselves* (5.1109 *praesidium reges ipsi sibi perfugiumque*). Moreover, at a later moment, this kingship became arrogant (1137 *sceptra superba*) and in the end the kings were dreaded overmuch by the population (1140 *nimis ante metutum*). Ancient political thought and historical writing have their stereotyped descriptions: being frightened and frightening others at the same time is what characterizes the *tyrant*.[4] In the view of Lucretius these kingships, good at the start, changed gradually into tyrannies (second form of government implied by his text).

In his description of the good kings Lucretius mentions a category of men distinguished by their inborn qualities, by their *aretai*. Here the poet seems to define the class of *aristocrats*. After the invention of property and the discovery of gold the privileged position of real aristocracy was taken over by 'the richer men' (5.1115 *divitioris*), the plutocrats, and—according to traditional definitions in the political thought of the Ancients—wealth is the characteristic feature and basis of *oligarchy*.[5]

These oligarchs (the wealthier people are in my opinion subject in line 1120: *at claros homines voluerunt se atque potentis*) wished to be famous and powerful and started to contest the supremacy of the

---

called kings compare Polybius 6.7 (and the comm. by Walbank): ... ποιοῦνται μετὰ ταῦτα τὴν αἵρεσιν τῶν ἀρχόντων καὶ *βασιλέων* ... κατὰ τὰς τῆς *γνώμης* καὶ *τοῦ λογισμοῦ διαφοράς*...τὸ μὲν οὖν παλαιὸν ἐνεγήρασκον ταῖς βασιλείαις οἱ κριθέντες ... *τόπους* τε διαφέροντας *ὀχυρούμενοι* καὶ *τειχίζοντες* καὶ *χώραν κατακτώμενοι*, cf. 5.1107-1110 and Th. Cole, 'The Sources and Composition of Polybius VI', *Historia* 13 (1964) 450-451.

[3] Cf. Polybius on the good king (6.6.11) διανεμητικὸς...τοῦ κατ'ἀξίαν ἑκάστοις and Aristotle *VV* 1250a12 δικαιοσύνη δὲ ἐστιν ἀρετὴ ψυχῆς διανεμητικὴ τοῦ κατ'ἀξίαν, *SVF* 3.262 ἐπιστήμη ἀπονεμητικὴ τῆς ἀξίας ἑκάστῳ

[4] Cf. Polybius 5.11.6 on the tyrant: *τυράννου* μὲν γὰρ ἔργον ἐστὶ τὸ κακῶς ποιοῦντα τῷ φόβῳ δεσπόζειν ἀκουσίων, *μισούμενον καὶ μισοῦντα* τοὺς ὑποταττομένους, and Cicero, *De rep.* 2.45 (*rex ille*) *cum metueret ipse poenam sceleris sui summam, metui se volebat.*

[5] Cp. Aristotle, *Pol.* 2.8.5, 1273a; 6.8, 1294a10, Polybius 6.8.5, Plato, *Rep.* 8.551a, and in general H.-O. Weber, *Die Bedeutung und Bewertung der Pleonexie von Homer bis Isokrates* (diss. Bonn 1967).

kings. Envy and ambition caused internal struggles between these richer men who longed to rule the world with royal power, and the kings who wanted to keep and to defend their position at the top (line 1130 *quam regere imperio res velle et regna tenere*[6] does not refer in a rather pleonastic way to one single category of ambitious men but to the two different categories of opponents). These internal struggles caused the fall of the kings (old and new ones all together) and the break-down of kingship as a regular institution (1136-1137 *ergo regibus occisis subversa iacebat/pristina maiestas soliorum et sceptra superba*). The situation (and the power) passed to the utmost dregs (*faex*) of disorder (*turbas*) and general violence (or rule passed to the lowest dregs of the mob).[7] At last, mankind worn out by leading a life of violence submitted itself to the constitutional state with its legislation and magistrates introduced by some anonymous legislators (5.1143-1147). The expression *magistratum creare* ('the appointment of magistrates by the people') shows that in Lucretius' view the political evolution finally led to a *democratic republic.*

Let us summarize: one finds in Lucretius' political history six categories of people who successively had supreme power or tried to obtain it, and therefore six forms of government succeeding each other: kingship—tyranny / aristocracy—oligarchy / ochlocracy—democracy. The conception of political evolution through six forms of government (three principal forms—kingship, aristocracy, democracy—degenerating resp. into tyranny, oligarchy, ochlocracy) was rather well-known in Antiquity and has been called the μεταβολὴ πολιτειῶν ('change of constitutions'). The idea was developed and systematized e.g. by the Greek historian Polybius in his famous book 6 and borrowed by Cicero in his *De Re Publica.* Modern studies of the sources of Polybius establish that the Greek historian made a new synthesis from certain ideas one finds already—in the course of the 5th century—in the works of

---

6 Bailey's translation of *regna tenere* ('to sway kingdoms') is misleading and pleonastic; *velle regna tenere* describes in my opinion the aspirations of the original kings 'to keep their kingdoms'.

7 5.1140-1141 *res itaque ad summam faecem turbasque redibat,/ imperium sibi cum ac summatum quisque petebat.* There is a problem of interpretation here, concerning the more abstract or concrete sense of the words *res* ('situation' or 'reign'), *turbas* ('disorder' or 'mob') and *redibat* ('passed to' or 'returned'—to the anarchic situation of primitive times) in these lines (cf. the commentaries of Bailey and Costa *ad loc.*). However this may be, in my opinion the Latin words *faex* and *turba* allude to the technical term 'ochlocracy'.

Herodotus, Thucydides, Xenophon and the Sophists, and in the 4th century in the political works of Plato, Aristotle and the Peripatetic scholar Dicaearchus of Messene (one also finds traces of this theory in works and fragments belonging to the Stoic tradition).[8] Actually, my paraphrase of Lucretius' text is not based on the commentaries of Lucretius by Bailey and Costa[9]—who give us too exclusively the rather slightly attested, Epicurean background of Lucretius' account—but on the commentary of Polybius VI by Walbank. It appears that the concept of μεταβολὴ πολιτειῶν I just mentioned, was rather popular in the time of Lucretius. We may suppose that the intellectual aristocracy of late-republican Rome—who formed the reading public of the *De Rerum Natura*[10]—were acquainted with this political theory. Therefore, this reading public was able to recognize Lucretius' political story as a new version of a well-known doctrine, presented this time by an Epicurean author. The originality of Lucretius lies in this new arrangement and application of traditional ideas, e.g. in the reversed order of ochlocracy and democracy, the latter growing out of the former one and not in the opposite direction: democracy turning into ochlocracy, as Polybius and Cicero affirm. According to the judgment of Cicero, Lucretius is *multis luminibus ingenii, multae tamen artis,* that means in our context: *multae artis politicae.*

Before analysing Lucretius' view on the origin of democracy I must make a short digression on the topic of physical beauty which the poet mentioned as one of the natural qualities of the first privileged aristocrats (cf. 5.1111, 1114, 1116). The second part of book 5 of the *De Rerum Natura* dealing with the origin and rise of mankind and human civilisation belongs to a definite class of ancient texts we might call 'archeologies', in the ancient sense of the word ἀρχαιολογία: explanatory stories about τὰ ἀρχαῖα / τὰ παλαιά, 'reconstructions of prehistoric developments'. So we have the Archeology by Thucydides (the first 20 chapters of book 1), the archeologies written by the Greek historians Dicaearchus of Messene and Diodorus Siculus (at the beginning of their histories),

---

8 Cf. Th. Cole, *art. cit.*, H. Ryffel, *Metabole Politeioon, Der Wandel der Staatsverfassungen* (Bern 1949), G. J. D. Aalders, *Die Theorie der gemischten Verfassung im Altertum* (Amsterdam 1968).

9 C. Bailey, *Titi Lucreti Cari De Rerum Natura Libri Sex* (Oxford 1947, repr. 1963), vol. 3.1498ff., C.D.N. Costa, *Lucretius De Rerum Natura V* (Oxford 1984).

10 Cf. M.R. Gale, *Myth and Poetry in Lucretius* (Cambridge 1994) 89-90.

the 6th book of Polybius, and we find similar reconstructions of the shadowy past in philosophical works (Plato's myth of Protagoras, the 3th book of his *Laws*), Aristotle's archeology at the beginning of his *Politics*: for both historians and philosophers in different ways the temporal ἀρχή reflects the archetypal essence.

In their descriptions of more or less primitive times which represented a level of civilisation less advanced than their own, all these Greek authors could not ignore the oldest written documents from their own past: the Homeric epics, and also the Hesiodic poems (the *Erga kai Hemerai* containing a very popular version of human evolution or rather of human deterioration: the story about the sequence of golden, silver, bronze and iron age). Homer was for the Ancients in all senses the first historian and also the first ethnographer.

For his reconstruction of prehistory Thucydides used more than once the Homeric epics; one finds references to the story of the Cyclopes—the first antisocials in human history—in serious, politico-philosophical discussions by Plato and Aristotle;[11] in his analysis of kingship, in book 3 of his *Politics* (3.5.14,1285 b 3), Aristotle had no choice but to analyse the heroic kingship of the Homeric *basileis*; Dicaearchus explicitly discussed the historical value of mythical stories transmitted by the poets;[12] probably, the idea of a primitive monarchy, based on brute force, as starting point in Polybius' archeology, has its roots in the same story about the Cyclopes.[13]

Against the background of the influence exercised by Homer on many a Greek archeology and also on ancient ethnographical descriptions (cf. Strabo) it is not surprising that physical beauty, mentioned by Lucretius as a distinctive quality, was also pointed out as such in hellenistic commentaries on Homer and in ancient ethnographical treatises.[14]

---

11 Cf. Plato, *Leges* 3.680b, Aristotle, *Pol.* 1252b19, and in general P. H. Schrijvers, 'Intertextualité et Polémique dans le *De Rerum Natura* (V 925-1010), Lucrèce vs. Dicéarque de Messène', *Philologus* 138 (1994) 295 and note 18.

12 Cf. P. H. Schrijvers, *art. cit., passim.*

13 Cf. Polybius, 6.5.7 and Aalders, *op.cit.* 100.

14 Cf. Ps. Plut. *De vita et poesi Homeri* 136: μάλιστα ... τὴν τῆς ἀρετῆς δόξαν συνίστησιν, ἐν οἷς τὸν ᾿Αχιλλέα ποιεῖ οὐ μόνον ἀνδρεῖον ἀλλὰ καὶ *κάλλιστον* τὸ εἶδος, Onesicritus (*FGrH* 134 F 21) βασιλέα τε γὰρ τὸν κάλλιστον αἱρεῖσθαι φησιν Ὀνησίκριτος (ἐν δὲ τῇ Καθαίᾳ καινότατον ἱστορεῖται τὸ *περὶ τοῦ κάλλους* ὅτι τιμᾶται διαφερόντως...), Pomponius Mela 3.86 *mos est cui potissimum pareant specie ac viribus legere.* Beauty as a human value has been discussed also by Aristotle in his

In my opinion one finds other traces of Homeric influence on the Archeology of Lucretius. The situation described in the lines 5.1107-1110 (the foundation of cities and the parcelling out of fields) is repeated by the poet in the summary which concludes his prehistory (5.1440-1447):

> Iam validis saepti degebant turribus aevom,
> et divisa colebatur discretaque tellus,
> iam <maris> velivolis florebat navibus pontus,
> auxilia ac socios iam pacto foedere habebant,
> carminibus cum res gestas coepere poetae
> tradere; nec multo prius sunt elementa reperta.
> Propterea quid sit prius actum respicere aetas
> nostra nequit, nisi qua ratio vestigia monstrat.

Actually, the existence of the Homeric epics presupposes the existence of the phenomena mentioned in the lines 1440ff. (cities, division of lands, navigation etc.). The final summary implies also a further development of the first two stages of social life (line 1025 mentions the first pact of cooperation and mutual defense, line 1155 the first pact of submission resulting in general peace: *communia foedera pacis*)[15] : at the end a pact (treaty) of submission (to one chief, and when we fill in the anonymous picture, it will be to king Agamemnon) and of cooperation between cities has been concluded (1143 *iam pacto foedere*). The lines 5.324-327 show that Lucretius considered the Theban War and the Fall of Troy as historical events which occurred at the beginning of the world, the earth and the human kind:

> Praeterea si nulla fuit genitalis origo
> terrarum et caeli semperque aeterna fuere,
> cur supera bellum Thebanum et *funera Troiae*
> non alias alii quoque res *cecinere poetae?*

The final summary alludes to the content of the Iliad and in a very sophisticated way the allusion is reinforced by the stylistic formulation of line 1442: the use of the epic epithet *velivolus* and the collocation *mari's pontus* (I am following here Housman's emendation which has been defended forcefully by Timpanaro)[16] which

---

Politics (cf. 1282b14) and *Ethics*. The ancient discussion seems to be linked also to the well-known locution καλοκἀγαθός.

[15] Cf. for the terminology J. Kaerst, 'Die Entstehung der Vertragstheorie im Altertum', *Zeitschrift für Politik* 2 (1909) 505ff.

[16] S. Timpanaro, 'Lucrezio V 1442 (e I 314, e V 1203)', *Rivista di Cultura Classica e Medioevale* 19 (1977) 730ff. (cf. Housman, *Classical Papers* II 436-438 =

translates the Homeric expression ἁλὸς πόντος.[17] Here the Homeric style echoes the event. As a matter of fact one finds other allusions to the Homeric epics in Lucretius' description of the first primitive period of mankind (5.948-949 *templa Nympharum*—*Od.* 13.103 ἄντρον ...ἱρόν νυμφάων), the antisocial, 'Cyclopic' way of life (5.958ff.–*Od.* 9.108)[18] and also, in my opinion, in the paragraph we are talking about (lines 1125-1128, esp. the locution *in Tartara taetra*)[19]:

> et tamen e summo, quasi fulmen, deicit ictos
> invidia interdum contemptim in Tartara taetra;[20]
> invidia quoniam, ceu fulmine, summa vaporant
> plerumque et quae sunt aliis magis edita cumque;

In accordance with his regular practice Lucretius' allusion to poetic myth (cf. the explicit reference to the Myth of the Giants in 5.117ff. and the harangue against Jupiter's thunderbolt, 6.421-422) is followed immediately by a reference to the same phenomenon presented now as a natural and even common event (5.1127-1128).

I should like to conclude my digression on Lucretius and Homer by pointing out that in his treatise entitled *On the Good King according to Homer*—which has been dated 59-55 B.C., so before the death of Lucretius[21]—the Epicurean philosopher-poet Philodemus likewise mentions physical beauty as a distinctive trait of the Homeric heroes and also their mutual envy as a source of internal troubles.[22] I conclude for the moment that this first part of Lucretius' story about political evolution has in some lines a definitely Homeric colouring.

Journal of Philology 25 (1897) 243-245).

[17] The prosody of line 1442 seems rather primitive but may reflect, in a sophisticated way, the primitive stage of poetry described.

[18] Cf. P. H. Schrijvers, *art. cit.* (n.11) 288-304.

[19] These lines have not been analysed sufficiently by M.R. Gale, *op.cit.* 188-189.

[20] Cf. Homer, *Iliad* 8.13 ἤ μιν ἑλὼν ῥίψω *ἐς Τάρταρον ἠερόεντα* (cf. *Hom.H. Merc.* 256, 374), Lucretius, 3.966 *nec quisquam in b a r a t h r u m nec T a r t a r a deditur atra*, and *Iliad* 8.14 *τῆλε μάλ', ἧχι βάθιστον ὑπὸ χθονός ἐστι β έ ρ ε θ ρ ο ν.*

[21] I am following at this point the dating proposed by O. Murray and followed by T. Dorandi, *Filodemo, Il buon re secondo Omero* (ed., transl., comm, Napoli 1982).

[22] coll. 38 [τὸν δ' 'Α]χιλλέα καὶ κάλλιστον, coll. 29 καὶ τὸ ζηλότυπον [δ'] ἀπεῖναι δεῖ...(cf. Dorandi *ad loc.*). In line 5.1120 the Latin word *potentes* may be a translation of the Greek term δυνάσται (cf. also G.J.D. Aalders, 'The Political Faith of Democritus', *Mnemosyne* IV 3 (1950) 304 on the Greek terms δυνάσται / δυναστεία).

We turn now to the lines 5.1141-1160. As Lucretius tells us, the human beings, worn out with leading a life of violence, lay faint from their feuds and therefore gave in all the more easily, even of their own will, to strict ordinances and laws (5.1145ff). The institution of official, criminal justice, surveyed by a chosen magistrate, limited the excesses of bloody vendettas and personal revenge (cf. 1146 *ex inimicitiis*, 1149 *ulcisci*). I should like to point out that, as Albrecht Dihle has shown in his monograph entitled *Die Goldene Regel* (dealing with popular morality),[23] Greeks and Romans were well aware of the primitive and/or exotic character of the *lex talionis*; they generally considered the institution of regular, criminal justice as a real progress in the history of human civilisation. In the ethical and rhetorical thought of the Ancients the impulsive feeling of anger is linked, as in Lucretius' text (1148-1149 *ex ira...ulcisci*), to the act or urge of avenging an outrage, often in a rather excessive way.[24] Plato formulates in his *Protagoras* (324 b) a twofold opposition between revenge (τιμωρία) and punishment (κόλασις): revenge is considered an irrational and even bestial action, punishment is or ought to be a rational and thoughtful act; revenge is concentrated on the injustice suffered in the past, punishment has a preventive effect for the future.[25] In my opinion, one finds this twofold opposition again in the lines of Lucretius (cf. 1151 *metus poenarum*) although he adds that the aspect of revenge is not completely absent in official, criminal justice (cf. 1153 'violence and hurt for the most part fall on the head of him from whom they had their rise').

We may establish that the number of strictly Epicurean ideas in Lucretius' story of political evolution is rather limited. With reference to the lines 1117-22 our commentaries duly quote some parallels with the opinions of Epicurus. But we must take into account that the depraving effects of avidity, of money and envy (πλεονεξία, φθονός) are very common themes in ancient literature

---

23 A. Dihle, *Die Goldene Regel* (Göttingen 1962) 14, note 1 and ch. 5 'Prinzipielle Ueberwindung des Vergeltungsdenkens'; cf. also the studies by R. Hirzel, *Die Talion* (*Philologus*, Suppl.Bd. 11, 1907-1910, 407-482) and *Themis, Dike und Verwandtes, Ein Beitrag zur Geschichte der Rechtsidee bei den Griechen* (Leipzig 1907).

24 Cf. Aristotle, *Rhet.* 2.2.1378a31 Ἔστω δὴ ὀργὴ ὄρεξις μετὰ λύπης *τιμωρίας*.

25 οὐδεὶς γὰρ κολάζει τοὺς ἀδικοῦντας πρὸς τούτῳ τὸν νοῦν ἔχων καὶ τούτου ἕνεκα, ὅτι ἠδίκησεν, ὅστις μὴ ὥσπερ θηρίον ἀλογίστως *τιμωρεῖται*. ὁ δὲ μετὰ λόγου ἐπιχειρῶν *κολάζειν* ... τοῦ μέλλοντος χάριν, cf. Seneca, *De ira* 1.16.21 *nemo prudens punit quia peccatum est, sed ne peccetur.*

and moral philosophy. At the end of Lucretius' story one finds again the Epicurean notion of 'treaty' (συνθήκη, 1155 *foedera*), qualifying in general the institution of law, civil justice and magistrates. From line 1154 onward Lucretius repeats Epicurus' opinion according to which it is not easy for one who by his act breaks the common pact of peace, to lead a calm and quiet life.[26] Probably, under the influence of the reproaches made by the Stoics—they accused the Epicureans of committing or approving crimes as long as they were sure to escape criminal justice[27]—Lucretius reinforces Epicurus' opinion (as far as we know from the fragmentary tradition) by referring to a common experience which he had mentioned already in his explanation of dreams: men often betray themselves by talking in their dreams (4.1018-1019).

The lines 1156ff. mention the notice of gods and men which a criminal might escape (*etsi fallit enim divum genus humanumque...*). This reference to the gods, coming from an Epicurean poet, need not surprise us;[28] Lucretius' argument has a narrative form in which a change of viewpoint (in modern terminology: of the so-called focalisation) is quite normal. Of course it is the criminal who hopes the gods will ignore him. By means of this reference Lucretius succeeds in connecting the paragraph on political change to the next one dealing with the origin of belief in gods. In this new argument topics from his political story return: e.g. the fear of the gods inspired in proud kings by their bad conscience (1122-1125), and,—as Lucretius explains at the opening of the paragraph on religion—men saw in their dreams the glorious shapes of beings, who—like the first human aristocrats—possessed noble beauty and ample strength. I should like to point out that this implied similarity between gods and aristocrats ('godlike men') has been mentioned explicitly by Philodemus in his treatise *On the Good King according to Homer* (cf. the paraphrase of the columns 37-39 given by the most recent editor T. Dorandi). I may add that, syntactically and semantically, line 1156 *etsi fallit...* is not an everyday expression in Latin—as Costa claims in his comment—, but has a definite Greek flavour: the use of *fallit* with a personal

---

[26] Cf. Bailey p. 1504, Costa p. 129.

[27] Cf. the discussion by P.A. Van der Waerdt, 'The Justice of the Epicurean Wise Man', *Classical Quarterly* 37 (1987) 409ff.

[28] As it did Bailey (see his comment on this line). Lucretius' line may allude to Hesiod, *Op.* 265-268 (well known in Antiquity), cf. 268 οὐδέ ἑ λήθει on the all-knowing and all-seeing God.

subject and with the gods as object, in the sense of 'being ignored, escape', is quite unusual in Latin literature and has been built on the regular use of the Greek verb λανθάνειν (τοὺς θεούς / τὸν θεόν).

By means of this analysis of the paragraph concerning the origins and the evolution of political life I hope to have shown how much Lucretius has drawn from an ensemble of common ideas which were rather widespread in later hellenistic times among Greek and Roman intellectuals who belonged officially to different philosophical schools. Like Philodemus, Lucretius tried to integrate Epicureanism in the *paideia*, in the general civilisation of his times. Leaving aside the relationship between Lucretius and Philodemus, I am not able to point out the direct sources of Lucretius' argument. Therefore, I used expressions like 'the ensemble of common ideas' or 'ancient thought in general'.[29] Methodologically, it is very important to make a sharp distinction between sources/ideas attested before or *only* after Epicurus' lifetime,[30] although the very fragmentary state of the transmission of Epicurus' works makes the problem of Lucretius' factual dependency on Epicurus rather intractable. In any case, these direct of indirect sources were Greek.

Although Lucretius' reconstruction of political change is wholly anonymous, without any precise chronology or localisation,—and so without any explicit trace of ethnocentrism. But this impression is misleading. His theoretical analysis has been inspired by real, factual history which certainly is *not* Roman. The change from kingship to democratic republic by the way of a chaotic, ochlocratic interval is without any parallel in Roman history. Moreover, Lucretius would have been blatantly anachronistic if, in his reconstruction of the origins of political life, he had referred to Roman history, the development of which is clearly later in time than Greek history. Of course, some lines that contain a more generalised moral message about jealousy and wealth may have been applied to the Roman, late-republican situation (the poet said himself that at a more general level history repeats itself, 5. 1135 *nec*

[29] Cf. the terms 'allgemeines Bildungsgut/ Kulturgut' in W. Spoerri's monograph *Späthellenistische Berichte über Welt, Kultur und Götter* (Schweiz. Beitr. zur Altertumswiss. 9, Basel 1959).

[30] Cf. my discussion in 'Philosophie et Paraphrase, Lucrèce et les Sceptiques', in *La Langue Latine, langue de la philosophie* (Coll. Ecole Française de Rome 161, Rome 1992) 125-140.

magis id nunc est neque erit mox quam fuit ante),[31] but chronologically this history did not start in Rome. Content and style of the first part of Lucretius' story have more than once a Greek flavour as if the period of the Homeric kings and their mutual envy hides itself under the surface of the text. Subsequently, aristocrats, oligarchs, great legislators who bring the internal troubles and vendettas to a close, in general tend to evoke events in Greek history: the legislations introduced by a Solon of Athens or a Dracon, the bloody revenge, subject of many a Greek tragedy about the House of Atreus. The cities mentioned in the beginning seem to be Greek *poleis*, not Roman *urbes* which in fact did not yet exist in these earlier times.

In spite of many a reference I made to the Greek historian Polybius I do not think that he was a primary source for Lucretius; this Greek historian combined the doctrine of political change with the concept of a cyclic return (*anakyklosis*) which is not emphasized in Lucretius' story (it is only mentioned in 5.1135). I think the underlying presence of Greek history and the theory of μεταβολὴ πολιτειῶν point to another Greek scholar, a Peripatetic who influenced also Lucretius' description of the savage and antisocial life of primitive man (as I tried to prove in my recent article in *Philologus*),[32] a scholar who, in Roman, republican times, was known as the author of a rather famous Archeology: the first chapters of his *Life of Greece*; this Greek scholar did make use of poetical testimonies, had a reputation as a historical critic of the Homeric epics and was rather well-known for his treatise entitled *Tripolitikos* dealing with the three principal forms of government: in short, once again I am persuaded that Lucretius' story might be influenced—directly or indirectly—by Dicearchus of Messene.[33]

Leiden

---

[31] In a more general and allusive way, 'Lucretius' model for such a constitutional development in some ways resembles that of Rome' (Costa, p. 128), and '*superbus* was the regular Latin epithet for the tyrant; cf. Tarquinius Superbus' (Bailey *ad* 5.1137); for more allusions to the contemporaneous, Roman situation see D.P. Fowler, 'Lucretius and Politics', in M. Griffin - J. Barnes (ed.), *Philosophia Togata, Essays on Philosophy and Roman Society* (Oxford 1989) 120-150.

[32] Cited above in note 11.

[33] Cf. the collection of testimonies by F.Wehrli (*Die Schule des Aristoteles*, Heft 1, *Dikaiarchos*), the subdivisions of which obscure somewhat the *unity* of Dicaearchus' philosophical and scientific activities.

PHILOSOPHICAL INNOVATION IN LUCRETIUS?

H. B. Gottschalk

There are various ways in which a philosophical or scientific system—I am using this word loosely, to denote any body of beliefs felt by its adherents to be connected and interdependent—can be modified. Individual doctrines or theorems can be altered or abandoned in order to meet criticism or to assimilate new data or problems which may have arisen after the system was first formulated; such changes are obvious and relatively easy to explain. Or there may have been less palpable changes of attitude which leave the official, written doctrines unaltered but make their adherents approach them in new ways; these are manifested as changes in the way in which the old doctrines are stated, changes of emphasis and balance and, where they concern ethical beliefs, may lead to changes of behaviour. Most of the changes undergone by Greek philosophy in the Roman world are of the second kind, and most of this paper will be concerned with them. Epicureans, in particular, were reluctant to criticise or tamper with the doctrinal legacy contained in Epicurus' writings, and Lucretius wanted nothing more than to be a faithful mouthpiece of his master's gospel (*DRN* 3.3). But first I want to discuss one purely doctrinal modification, partly in order to illustrate the distinction I have just drawn, but also because it may shed some light on the way in which Epicurus' teaching was taken up by his followers and on the kind of sources Lucretius may have used.

In the course of his description of the soul (3.230 ff.), Lucretius tells us that it is composed of four substances: *aura* or *ventus* (282), terms which represent the Greek πνεῦμα and should be translated as 'breath' (so M.F. Smith) rather than 'wind'; *vapor* or *calor* ('heat', τὸ θερμόν); *aer*; and the mysterious fourth, unnamed substance which is finer than any of the other three and the source of those movements giving rise to sensation and thought. These four substances combine to form a single, unified soul, but each retains its own power within the whole, and at 3.282 ff. the first three are said to produce different emotional states (πάθη): heat, anger; breath or wind, fear; and air, placidity. The same fundamental doctrine is found in the doxographical tradition represented for us by Aëtius (ps-Plutarch, Stobaeus and Theodoretus) and in Plutarch's *Ad. Colotem.*[1] We can safely say that it was accepted as standard by Epicureans from at least the first century BC.

However, when we turn to Epicurus' own writings, we find something different. In his *Letter to Herodotus* (§63), he says that the soul is composed not of four but of *three* substances: it is a 'fine body ... most like wind or breath (πνεῦμα) with a certain admixture of heat , in some respects like the one, in some like the other; and there is a third component far exceeding even these in fineness ...' This last is clearly the same as Lucretius' fourth substance, but instead of three there are only two 'earthly' substances, *pneuma* and the 'hot stuff'. Together these add up to something very like the Stoic concept of *pneuma* or, for that matter, the Holy Spirit of the Pentecost miracle which manifested itself first as the sound of rushing wind and then as tongues of fire. These two qualities were regularly associated with the 'life-giving spirit' in the late classical and Hellenistic periods.

Comparing this with Lucretius' account, we can see that he has gained his extra component by treating 'air' as something different from *pneuma,* although he defines *pneuma* (here meaning 'wind') as 'air set in motion' in the section of his work dealing with meteorology (6.685). The question now is, what caused him to make this change. While the view that *pneuma* is the carrier of sensation and other vital functions was widely accepted in the Hellenistic era, the precise nature of this substance remained an open question. Aristotle's remarks on this topic were unclear and those of Epicurus studiously vague, as we have seen. Later researchers, medical men even more than philosophers, tried to solve this problem. It seemed fairly obvious that the material basis of the vital *pneuma* must be the air we take in when we breathe, but that the two were not identical; the air had to undergo some kind or processing or 'concoction' to turn it into *pneuma.* One anonymous third-century writer, a Peripatetic with a strong interest in medicine, tried to describe the difference by saying that the outer air is 'tame' (πραύς) and becomes *pneuma* after being taken into the organism.[2] Others

---

1 Aëtius 4.3.11, *DG* 388; Plut. *Adv.Col.* 1118e = Usener, *Epicurea* 314–5.

2 Ps.-Arist.*Spir.* 483a33 τὸ γὰρ ὅλον [sc. πνεῦμα] οὐκ ἀήρ, ἀλλὰ συμβαλλόμενόν τι πρὸς ταύτην τὴν δύναμιν ὁ ἀήρ. b6 ἔξω μὲν γὰρ πραύς, ἐμπεριληφθεὶς δὲ πνεῦμα.

believed that there might be several kinds of *pneuma*, of different degrees of purity and vitality, in the same organism. It is against this background that we must see Lucretius' innovation. Probably it originated as an attempt to update Epicurus' teaching by an adherent with medical interests, perhaps a professional physician; since the change does not affect any fundamental philosophical issue, it was not seen as a threat to the system, and it may even have been sanctioned by Epicurus himself. As for Lucretius, there is no need to suppose that he turned to a different source for this part of his poem from the one he followed elsewhere;[3] he could have used a copy of some work of Epicurus with annotations like those found in the extant version of Epicurus' Letters. There is only one feature of Lucretius' account still needing to be explained: he connects heat with *aer*, not with *pneuma*. This is not found in the doxographical parallels and runs counter to the views of all other Hellenistic writers on the subject I know, including Epicurus. I suspect that here Lucretius simply made a mistake.

The other kind of change I mentioned is much harder to pin down, but every reader can feel it immediately; change not of doctrine, but of the way the doctrine is understood and of the responses it arouses. They are not the result of philosophical debate, but of differences of temperament and circumstance, and often throw more light on the character of individual thinkers than on the philosophies they profess or the arguments used to underpin it. Changes of this kind affect Lucretius' reading of every part of Epicurus' philosophy. In an interesting article published last year, K. Summers has shown that Lucretius' attitude to the religion of his day was much more hostile than that of Epicurus.[4] But it is a fact that their teaching about the gods and their mode of existence is identical. The difference lies in their responses to that dogma and must be due to a difference of temperament or perhaps to differences between the religious practices of the societies in which they lived. Yet it remains true that Lucretius' attitude was different from his master's, and on one occasion at least this bias led Lucretius to make a philosophical blunder which Epicurus avoided. Both begin their account of the natural world by laying down that nothing comes out of nothing (*Ep.Herod.* 38, *DRN* 1.150). This is a

---

[3] As Heinze and Bailey (*Commentary* p. 1025) do.

[4] K. Summers, 'Lucretius and the Epicurean tradition of piety', *Classical Philology* 90 (1995) 32–57.

fundamental principle which, until the advent of quantum mechanics, was regarded as the basis of all science and philosophy. Epicurus states it without embellishment and tries to establish its truth by induction—if it were not true, anything could spring from anything. He then goes on to establish that the only things which exist in their own right are matter and void, and all other existing things are derivatives or accidents of them. Lucretius clearly means to reproduce Epicurus' argument, but vitiates it by adding one word to his premiss: *nullam rem e nilo gigni* divinitus *umquam.* In this form, his premiss loses its universality and can no longer be inferred from the inductive evidence he adduces; for God is not 'nothing', and the fact that particular things are always seen to come from other particular things, does not prove that there is not a deity (instead of another particular thing) at the beginning of the chain. Moreover, since his avowed purpose is to disprove divine creation (1.159), the presence of this word in his premiss makes the argument circular. Lucretius' eagerness to give his demonstration an extra anti-religious twist has betrayed him into formulating his initial postulate in a way that renders it invalid.

Lucretius' view of Roman religion could be regarded as an intensification of Epicurus' attitude. In other ways, the psychological differences between them are more marked, and some of them touch the very roots of their philosophy. For example, Lucretius describes the contemplation of nature as thrilling and a source of god-like pleasure:[5]

> *His ibi me rebus quaedam divina voluptas*
> *percipit atque horror, quod sic natura tua vi*
> *tam manifesta patens ex omni parte retecta est.*

And he pictured Epicurus as a heroic figure, a victorious fighter for the truth who burst out of the confines of the world to slay the dragon *Religio* by the force and vigour of his mind:[6]

> *Ergo vivida vis animi pervicit, et extra*
> *processit longe flammantia moenia mundi ...*
> *quare religio pedibus subjecta vicissim*
> *obteritur, nos exaequat victoria caelo.*

---

[5] 3.28. The expression has a Greek precedent, as well as the Latin ones adduced by Bailey and the other commentators: Pindar *Nem.* 1.56 ἔστα δὲ θάμβει δυσφόρῳ τερπνῷ τε μιχθείς, of Amphytrio on seeing the serpents killed by the infant Herakles.

[6] 1.72 ff. Note the use of *vis* in both places.

But this is far from the impression we get from Epicurus' own writings. He holds that the study of nature would be superfluous if we could banish our fears without it (*KD* 11); in the *Letter to Herodotus* he insists that its only purpose is to obtain a calm life (ἐγγαληνίζειν, §37) and warns his readers to confine themselves to the study of general principles and not to delve too deeply into details, as this might cause them amazement (θάμβος) if they met problems they cold not solve (§79). For Epicurus, it seems, *horror* was not compatible with pleasure. Thus we are faced with two opposed attitudes to the purpose of natural philosophy: on one side, a zestful pursuit of a vision which will reveal the truth about the universe and free men from the terrors of superstition, on the other, a purely defensive search for 'scientific' support for a rather timid ideology. One reason, perhaps, why Lucretius' poem is great literature and Epicurus' works are not. Some of Lucretius' most memorable lines are those which state the terrifying aspects of his vision in the most dramatic terms:

> *Principio mare ac terras caelumque tuere:*
> *quorum naturam triplicem, tria corpora, Memmi,*
> *una dies dabit exitio multosque per annos*
> *sustentata ruet moles et machina mundi.* (5.91 ff.)

Contrast this with the anodyne, matter-of-fact statement in the *Letter to Herodotus:*

> And in addition to what we have already said, we must believe that worlds, and indeed every limited compound body which continuously exhibits a similar appearance to the things we see, were created from the infinite, and that all such things, greater and less alike, were separated off from individual agglomerations of matter; and that all are again dissolved, some more quickly, some more slowly, some suffering from one set of causes, others from another. (§73, tr. Bailey)

This is the kind of thing we might expect from a government spokesman after some embarrassing disaster.

We can also observe a difference between the attitudes of Lucretius and Epicurus to public life. Epicurus taught that the tranquillity his philosophy aimed at could only be achieved by retiring from the world and living quietly in a community of friends (*KD* 14). This doctrine was hotly debated in the Hellenistic era; most Stoics took the opposite view and there were many professed Epicureans, Greeks as well as Romans, who did not follow Epicurus' precept.

Lucretius did, and in several places he warns his readers against seeking salvation in political or military power: this will not, he emphasises, free men from their fears of death or the gods, but rather induce new fears and cut off the possibility of attaining the peace of mind they need for happiness.[7] Nevertheless, he seems to have had some reservations. In his prayer to Venus (1.42 ff.) he asks for peace because neither he nor Memmius could be happy doing philosophy at a time when their country seemed to need their active service; this in an age when even the Stoic Athenodorus recommended that those who found the times too hard should retire from political involvement.[8] The attitude implied by Lucretius' prayer is typically Roman; it has a parallel in a remark of Cicero's, that the poet Archias came to Italy at a time when the arts were cultivated in Rome 'because the Commonwealth was at peace'.[9] While Lucretius regularly preaches against greed and luxury, he nowhere urges those of his contemporaries who felt they had a duty to participate in public life, to abstain from doing so.[10] His philosophy could not altogether prevail against the instinct of a Roman aristocrat. No doubt he would have justified his own abstention from politics by the argument, used by Athenodorus and later Cicero (*Div.* 2.1), that his writing was the greatest benefit he could confer on his fellow-Romans.

Apart from this, Lucretius' teaching on ethics, natural philosophy and, in so far as he deals with it, epistemology, is completely orthodox; he had neither the desire nor the ability to make any original contributions here. There are un-Epicurean features, notably a tendency to personify nature manifested in such expressions as *natura creatix* or *natura daedala rerum* or even *tanta stat praedita culpa*

---

[7] 2.37 ff., 5.1125 ff. I am grateful to Monica Gale for drawing my attention to the second passage, which I omitted in the first version of this paper, but would interpret it in a different way from hers; see n.10 below.

[8] Athenodorus *ap.* Sen. *Tranq. An.* 3. See further M. Pohlenz, *Die Stoa,* (Göttingen 1948) 1.242, 2.124 f.; *idem, Kleine Schriften* (Göttingen 1956) 1.287 ff.

[9] Cic. *Pro Archia* 3.5: *Erat Italia tum plena Graecarum artium ac disciplinarum, studiaque haec ... et hic Romae propter tranquillitatem rei publicae non neglegebantur.*

[10] Monica Gale has suggested that 5.1129 ff. contains such a recommendation, but here, as in bk. 2, Lucretius only warns against ambition because of the *invidia* it arouses and recommends the life of a private citizen as a means of attaining tranquillity: *ut satius multo iam sit parere quietum quam regere imperio* ... (note the emphatic position of *quietum* at the end of the line and the clause). This is compatible with the position adopted at 1.41 ff., that some may feel an obligation to sacrifice their immediate peace of mind in order to benefit their community by public service.

[natura]. But these do not lead him to depart from a strictly mechanistic account of causation; they do not signify a modification of Epicurus' doctrine but are part of the poetical form Lucretius has given to his exposition. However, this brings us to the greatest departure from his master's teaching. In the 'ancient quarrel between poetry and philosophy' Epicurus was as uncompromising as Plato. He warns his followers against the snares of poetry, with its tales of a world controlled by jealous deities and of a dire existence after death, and tells them to avoid all 'culture'.[11] But Lucretius, author of the fullest exposition of Epicurean philosophy that has come down to us, made a poem of it, a poem, moreover, which is no dry piece of versified argument like the poem of Parmenides, but used all the devices of high poetry and openly acknowledged its debt to Empedocles, a myth-maker if ever there was one. The paradox is pointed up by a passage where Lucretius warns Memmius not to be put off by *vatum terriloquis dictis* (1.102 f.). It has become customary to translate *vatum* here by 'bards' or even 'priests', [12] but this is mistaken. There are several passages where Epicurus advises his followers not to be put off by fears arising from μῦθοι;[13] the writers of 'myths' were poets, and when Lucretius goes on to give examples of the 'terrifying sayings' against which he wants to warn Memmius, he refers to accounts of the underworld given by Ennius (1.115 ff.). The term *vates* is ambiguous, and Lucretius may have chosen it in order to give an anti-religious twist to Epicurus' warning; it would then be a parallel to the insertion of *divinitus* in line 150, with less disastrous consequences.[14] But the immediate reference is to the stories of poetry, and the paradox of a poet warning his readers against poetry is something we should embrace, not fudge. Lucretius did not regard himself as a

---

[11] *Ap.* Diog. Laert. 10.6 = fr. 163 Usener. Παιδεία includes all kinds of non-philosophical literary activity.

[12] 'Bards': Bailey; 'seers': Munro; 'priests': Diels, M.F. Smith. But Knebel (1831²) and Binder (1868) have *Dichter*.

[13] *Ep. Her.* 81, *KD* 12. Note that the Greeks mostly speak of μῦθοι in the plural and never use the singular as a collective noun to denote a privileged group of fictions endowed with some kind of mystical collective significance. To speak of Lucretius', or any other ancient writer's, use of or attitude to 'myth' (or *der Mythos*) in this sense, is at best anachronistic and could be seriously misleading.

[14] Another reason for his choice may have been that *vates* could have a contemptuous meaning in Lucretius' time (see Munro and Bailey *ad loc.*). But this would not fit well with his immediately citing Ennius, in most honorific terms.

poet of quite the same kind as the rest: when staking his claim to poetic fame, his first boast was that he 'taught about great issues and freed minds from the bonds of religion', his second that he 'wrote clear poetry about an obscure subject'. The poetic quality of his work, *musaeo contingens cuncta lepore,* comes last and is justified by the famous image of the honey on the cup of bitter medicine.[15]

This raises the question of the relationship between the form and content of his work. There was a time when it was thought that he began by wanting to write a poem, looked for a subject and chose Epicurus' philosophy; some nineteenth-century writers, including Macaulay and Mommsen, even suggested that his choice was a mistake and complain that he wasted so much poetic talent on an inherently dull subject, while Munro devotes a whole page of rhetoric to demonstrating that Epicureanism is a better subject for poetry than any of the alternative systems available to Lucretius.[16] Of course this is arrant nonsense. If one thing is clear from his poem, it is that Lucretius decided to write about Epicureanism because he saw it as the key to the salvation of mankind. His choice of poetry as his vehicle, in an age when prose had long been the normal medium for serious philosophical writing, must mean that, in his own situation, it seemed to offer some palpable advantage over prose. Our task is to determine what this advantage may have been.

Lucretius' purpose was to write in a way that would attract the audience he was aiming at, the narrow, highly sophisticated circle of the Roman upper class in which he and Memmius, the dedicatee of his poem, moved. Now prose treatises on philosophy or other instructional subjects seem to have had a low literary status, rather like textbooks or what the trade calls 'academic books' to-day, and according to Cicero, the only Latin prose works on philosophy produced up to that time, by the Epicureans Catius and Amafinius, were too shoddily written to appeal to sophisticated readers, although he admits that they had a wide popular following.[17] Those philosophers who aspired to be men of letters wrote dialogues or open addresses to named individuals, which could be

---

15 1.93 ff, = 4.6 ff. Clarity (σαφήνεια) was the one quality on which Epicurus insisted in his *Rhetoric* (*ap.* Diog. Laert. 1013).

16 Th. Mommsen, *Römische Geschichte* (Berlin 1882^7) 3.595 f. H.A.J. Munro, in the introduction to vol. II of his edition (London 1900^4) 5 ff.

17 Cic. *Ad fam.* 15.16, 19; *Tusc.* 4.3.6, *Acad.* 1.3.6. But Quintilian (*Inst.* 10.1.124) describes Catius as *levis quidem sed non iniucundus auctor.*

taken as 'partial dialogues'. Didactic poetry, on the other hand, was a flourishing genre with a long and honourable history; in Rome, it had been practised by eminent poets and versifiers from Ennius to Cicero. Lucretius could have written a dialogue or series of dialogues, like Cicero a few years later, but they were not trying to do the same thing. Each of Cicero's works is centred on a problem or set of connected problems, and Cicero's purpose was to confront the views about it of all the important schools; this was something for which the dialogue form was eminently suitable, but it involved a good deal of selection and re-arrangement of his material, and some distortion was inevitable. Lucretius wanted to give an account of one system of philosophy, as complete and accurate as he could make it. The Epicurean writings he followed were very much in the textbook tradition, consisting of systematic, point-by-point exposition with very few literary graces. As material for an urbane dialogue they were unpromising, but since the basic structure of a didactic poem is straight narrative, they could fit into that almost paragraph by paragraph, as a comparison between the *DRN* and Epicurus' letters shows. Their monotony could be relieved by alternating didactic with descriptive passages, the use of illustrative similes and variations in stylistic levels, devices which would have seemed merely precious in a prose work.

In one respect at least, Epicurus' work lent itself particularly well to this treatment. Similes played a prominent part in epic and didactic poetry from Homer onwards, but Empedocles had put them to new use.[18] Instead of treating them as mere decorations, he used them as analogies to illustrate and explain phenomena which could not be directly observed. Aristotle and his followers had doubts about the probative value of this method, but Epicurus sanctioned it.[19] Lucretius exploited this opening to the full. He expanded Epicurus' analogies into splendid word-pictures to provide relief for the more technical passages, but they are integrated into his argument, not otiose distractions. Thus he transforms Epicurus' exposition while remaining true to his intentions.

Naturally the form of Lucretius' epic had some effect on its content. Aristotle's complaint that 'nature' seemed to mean little more for Democritus than 'what always happens', can be transferred to

---

[18] Cf. O. Regenbogen, 'Eine Forschungsmethode antiker Naturwisenschaft', in *Kleine Schriften,* ed. F. Dirlmeier (München 1961) 156 ff.

[19] *Ap.* Diog. Laert. 10.32, etc.

Epicurus without much injustice, but Lucretius personifies her as 'creator' and 'maker of things', as we have seen. Empedocles would seem to have influenced his outlook as well as his poetic technique. But even Epicurus, in an expansive moment, was able to 'thank blessed nature for making the necessities of life easy to obtain'.[20] In spite of this, nature never became an independent force, but remained an epiphenomenon of the mechanical interaction of atoms.

To conclude, the *DRN* contains one substantive but minor modification of Epicurus' original teaching, almost certainly not the work of Lucretius himself; occasional mistakes which we can attribute, with a high degree of probability, to the poet; and an extra anti-religious twist which did not entail any doctrinal change. Lucretius' poetical vision transcends the mechanical character of his system and almost brings it alive, while his hero-worship of Epicurus introduces a personal element into his poem not found in Epicurus' treatises. But this is something that goes beyond his philosophy.[21]

University of Leeds

---

[20] Fr. 469 Usener.

[21] A version of this paper was read at a meeting of the Leeds International Latin Seminar, on the theme 'Roman poetry and the philosophy of its time', February, 1996, and I am grateful to the participants, especially Monica Gale, for their comments. Needless to say, I am solely responsible for the views and any errors it contains.

PART FIVE

IMPERIAL PHILOSOPHY

L'*OIKEIÔSIS* SOCIALE CHEZ EPICTÈTE

Brad Inwood

Il y a peu de philologues qui ont fait autant que Jaap Mansfeld pour traverser les frontières nationales et linguistiques du monde savant. En hommage à cet esprit d'internationalisme, j'ose offrir la petite discussion qui suit, convenable (je l'espère) à cette occasion et par son thème et par le fait que celle-ci répresente la première fois que j'ai pu offrir une communication dans une langue étrangère.[1]

Le monde socratique peut être perçu comme étant un monde dur et égoiste. En vertu de la prescription du 'soin de l'âme', le soi est au centre de l'univers moral de chacun, ce qui rend problématique nos relations avec les autres. Ceci est clair dans un passage du *Gorgias* qui déconcerte souvent ceux qui l'aborde pour la première fois. À 458a, Socrate dit qu' il vaut mieux être réfuté soi-même que réfuter quelqu' un d'autre dans la mesure où 'il est plus avantageux pour un homme d'être délivré du plus grand des maux que d'en délivrer autrui'. Quel signe plus clair que l'éthique socratique accorde la plus grande importance au soin de soi-même? Et pourtant c'est Socrate lui-même qui a défendu l'idée—jusqu' à la mort, en fait—qu' il vaut mieux souffir une injustice qu' en infliger une. Quel signe plus clair pourrait-on trouver à l'effet que Socrate prend comme point de départ un respect fondamental pour autrui?

Voilà un problème bien connu, qui se présente à maintes reprises dans la tradition socratique. En effet, il est possible que ce problème aide à expliquer la mode actuelle parmi les philosophes pour les études de la φιλία chez Platon et Aristote. De toute façon, il y a dans le stoïcisme une tension entre les vertus orientées vers soi-même qui sont fondamentales dans toute éthique eudémoniste, et les vertus orientées vers autrui qui jouent un rôle significatif dans les théories antiques de la moralité. Cette tension devient plus aiguë avec la doctrine stoïcienne de l'*oikeiôsis*. Un écart peut toujours se former entre la conception de l'homme en tant qu' animal qui part

---

[1] Je dois remercier Carlos Lévy pour l'encouragement qu' il m' a donné et Jean Baillargeon, qui a traduit le texte anglais. Partout j'emploie les traductions 'Budé' des textes anciens, tout en modifiant legèrement celles de Souilhé pour Epictète.

d'une tendance à la préservation de soi, et la conception de l'homme en tant qu' animal social. Dans plusieurs contextes on peut fermer l'écart, et pour certains auteurs ce problème est périphérique ou même n'existe pas. Mais à mon avis, ceci n'est pas le cas pour Epictète. Il insiste catégoriquement sur la nature irréductiblement sociale de l'homme. Ceci est vrai, même si on voit régulièrement chez lui une certaine dureté et un manque de considération envers les autres êtres humains, leur bien-être et leurs intérêts. La tendance de se soucier premièrement de soi-même que Socrate manifeste dans le *Gorgias* se retrouve de manière prononcée à travers les entretiens compilés par Arrian, et pourtant Epictète ne cesse jamais de proclamer la fraternité des hommes. Il est évident que la nature des liens sociaux est à la fois intéressante et profondément problématique pour Epictète. La solution aux problèmes soulevés par la nature des liens sociaux est seulement implicite dans les *Entretiens*, et cependant je crois qu' on peut l'articuler de sorte à montrer à la fois que sa 'théorie sociale' s'accorde avec le stoïcisme plus ancien, et que Epictète apporte sa propre contribution à ces problèmes. Epictète accepte avec enthousiasme la théorie stoïcienne traditionnelle des valeurs, et approuve sans réserve la cosmologie théologique stoïcienne. Ce sont là les deux éléments de base de sa théorie sociale.

Je vais commencer par donner un aperçu de l'évidence qui montre que les relations sociales présentaient beaucoup d'intérêt pour Epictète. Il écrit à maintes reprises que τὸ πιστόν et τὸ αἰδῆμον sont indispensables pour notre bien-être, et ces deux traits de caractère sont essentiellement sociaux: c'est seulement à l'intérieur d'une matrice de relations et de conventions sociales que l'on peut comprendre ces traits de caractères. On trouve une illustration de la dimension sociale de τὸ πιστόν et τὸ αἰδῆμον dans *Entretien* 1.5.3-5. Une condition pathologique que Epictète appelle 'pétrification' ou 'nécrose' est considérée en rapport avec les deux aspects de la personne, le corps et l'âme; et à l'intérieur de l'âme, une autre division est considérée, soit la division entre l'intellect (τὸ νοητικόν) et le sens de la honte (τὸ ἐντρεπτικόν). Epictète emploie la stratégie socratique/ platonicienne (qui consiste à exploiter le contraste entre le corps et l'âme) de sorte à produire un bon résultat rhétorique. Epictète met ensuite en contraste notre fonction purement intellectuelle (en vertu de laquelle nous pouvons comprendre ou suivre un argument) avec notre sens social: nous pensons que la faiblesse intellectuelle est un signe de misère (κακῶς ἔχειν), mais nous considérons aussi la 'nécrose' sociale, ou l'insensibilité, comme un indice de force de caractère. Il n'y a pas de doute que le contexte de ce passage est polémique, mais il est quand même certain que les relations sociales sont présentées comme étant tout aussi importantes pour le bien-être humain que la santé physique ou intellectuelle. Ces termes (τὸ πιστόν et τὸ αἰδῆμον) reviennent souvent.[2] En particulier, ils figurent de façon saisissante dans 2.4.1, où Epictète maintient que l'homme est fidèle par nature, que la πίστις est un trait caractéristique des êtres humains. De la même façon, dans 2.10.22-3 il maintient catégoriquement que nos sens de la honte et du respect, notre sens de la fidélité, notre tendance affective,[3] notre disposition à aider les autres et notre esprit de retenue sont tous des traits naturels, et que la faiblesse de ces traits constituent une pénalité et un mal. Nos relations sociales ont une importance qui gouverne même nos habitudes d'hygiène personnelle (4.11.14-18)—c'est en vertu de nos liens sociaux fondamentaux que la vie cynique n'est pas la meilleure vie pour tous les êtres humains, mais seulement pour une minorité d'entre eux. Nos instincts sociaux sont, comme d'autres stoïciens l'ont affirmé, une partie de notre nature sans laquelle nous ne pouvons réaliser notre nature et atteindre le bonheur.

Epictète présente régulièrement des arguments contre ce qu' il considère comme les implications anti-sociales de la pensée épicurienne. Dans 2.20, 3.7, 1.23 et ailleurs Épicure devient la cible de la langue hargneuse de Epictète, simplement parce que sa théorie est incapable d'appuyer ou d'expliquer l'importance évidente des relations sociales qui sont au coeur du bien-être humain. Un troisième indicateur de la très grande importance naturelle des relations sociales est l'emploi que fait Epictète des σχέσεις. Ces relations—avec les dieux, avec ses parents, avec ses frères et soeurs, ses enfants, et ses concitoyens—constituent la matière du deuxième

---

[2] Mais il faut noter 1.4.18-20 où Epictète dit qu' un resultat du retrait des choses externelles est la préservation de τὸ πιστόν et τὸ αἰδῆμον. Si Epictète n'utilise pas 'choses externelles' dans un sens très étroit ici, ce passage met en relief la tension entre les relations sociales positives et le retrait en soi-même.

[3] τὸ στερκτικόν, probablement la même chose que la φιλοστοργία de 1.11, où Epictète donne un argument assez long à l'appui de l'idée que la φιλοστοργία parentale est un de nos dons naturels. Il est à noter aussi qu' à 3.7.27 la tendance humaine de rougir est offerte comme preuve que le sens de τὸ αἰδῆμον est naturel pour les êtres humains.

champ d'études (3.2.4). De tels σχέσεις sont sous la supervision de Zeus (3.11.6); elles sont indispensables pour la bonne conduite (4.6.26, cf. 4.12.16-17); on lit dans le *Enchiridion* que nos καθήκοντα sont 'mesurés' (παραμετρεῖται) par nos relations (*Ench.* 30). Dans 3.7.25. ss., Epictète énumère les principales responsabilités d'un homme: l'activité civile, le mariage, élever des enfants, la piété, prendre soin de ses parents, et ainsi de suite. L'*Entretien* 1.2 est encore plus clair sur ce sujet: à maintes resprises dans ce texte Epictète met l'accent sur l'idée que notre place dans un contexte social aide à déterminer le rôle et les devoirs que chacun de nous doit remplir. Nous ne pourrions même pas concevoir ce que c'est que de faire des décisions morales sérieuses si nous ne connaissions pas notre place dans la société.

De toute évidence donc, Epictète attribue une très grande valeur aux liens que les êtres humains entretiennent en société. Ces liens sont naturels, surveillés par Zeus, indispensables au bien-être humain, et constituent la clé pour la compréhension de nos καθήκοντα. Tout comme son maître Musonius, Epictète semble se soucier sincèrement de la sécurité et de l'intégrité de l'organisation sociale—quoiqu' il ne va peut-être pas aussi loin que le consulaire Cicéron. Cependant l'attitude d'Epictète n'est pas aussi simple que cela, et son attitude envers les liens sociaux elle non plus n'est pas aussi simple. Prenons quelques moments pour considérer les tendances de sa pensée qui vont à l'encontre de la valorisation de la dimension sociale des êtres humains.

Examinons d'abord *Entretien* 1.1. En soulignant le fait que nous maîtrisons seulement notre vie mentale, que nous contrôlons nos impressions, il se tourne dans les sections 14 ss. vers les erreurs que nous faisons tous dans le cours de notre vie. Notre vie mentale est à proprement parler la seule chose dont nous sommes capables de prendre soin, et à laquelle nous pouvons nous consacrer. Néanmoins nous essayons avec insistance de nous occuper de plusieurs choses, et par conséquent nous nous donnons trop de soucis. Nous prenons un souci pour notre corps, nos possessions matérielles, notre frère, notre ami, notre enfant et notre esclave. Nos intérêts sont si nombreux qu' ils nous accablent. Ici, comme dans 4.1 (surtout 65 ss.), Epictète souligne que pour être libre de tracas et pour atteindre la tranquillité, il faut se détacher de tout sauf notre vie mentale. La famille, les amis, les relations sociales, et même nos propres corps sont dans la même catégorie que nos possessions matérielles: nous

nous en occupons au péril de notre bonheur. Comme il le dit dans 4.1.100, les forces cosmiques ont le contrôle de mes possessions, mes meubles, mes enfants, et mon épouse. C'est une erreur que de se soucier excessivement de ces choses-là, non seulement parce que ça menace notre bonheur personnel, mais aussi parce qu' un tel souci ne correspond pas à la volonté de Zeus. Le fondement des πάθη est l'intérêt que l'on prend pour les choses externes, y compris un autre être humain; et une vie tourmentée par les passions ne peut pas être une vie heureuse. Epictète exprime cette idée dans 3.24.58-9 en disant qu' il n'y a aucun avantage à être affectueux envers notre famille si cela nous cause de la misère. Nous devons même aimer nos enfants avec un certain recul, de sorte à être indifférent à leurs souffrance et à leur mort (3.24.84-89).

Il y a un problème semblable du point de vue de l'enfant. Je pense ici au chaptre 30 de l' *Enchiridion.* Epictète insiste beaucoup dans ce chapitre sur l'idée que nous avons une affiliation naturelle (οἰκείωσις) avec un père, et non pas avec un bon père. Notre relation avec lui—comme c'est le cas avec un frère—est naturelle et basée fermement sur la *oikeiôsis* qui nous définit en tant que membres de l'espèce humaine. Les relations sociales que nous avons avec notre père, notre frère, notre voisin, notre concitoyen, ou notre officier supérieur sont des relations réelles—et dans ce passage il y a une suggestion à l'effet que nous partons de nos relations les plus intimes pour développer nos autres relations—mais elles sont limitées par les frontières de notre caractère moral. Nous ne traitons pas notre semblable d'une manière qui pourrait compromettre notre propre bonheur. Pour Epictète, nous ne devons rien faire, même pour le bénéfice de nos relations les plus intimes, qui puisse compromettre le bénéfice moral. La βλάβη socratique est le seul mal véritable.

Epictète est donc un véritable eudémoniste socratique. Socrate pensait que c'était un plus grand bien d'être libéré du mal que de libérer autrui; de la même veine, Epictète recommande en toute franchise que chacun de nous devrait 'jurer de se tenir soi-même en plus haute estime que n'importe qui' (1.14.17). Epictète soutient, tout comme Aristote et Platon, que cet intérêt personnel ne correspond pas à ce que nous appelons l'égoïsme. Mais on ne peut pas nier la preférence pour le soi; voir 3.3.5:

> Voilà pourquoi on préfère le bien à tous les liens du sang. Mon père n'est rien pour moi, mais seulement le bien. 'Peux-tu être aussi dur?' La nature m'a fait ainsi. Telle est la monnaie que dieu m'a

> donnée. Aussi, le bien vient-il à s'opposer au beau et juste, tout s'en va, père, frère, patrie, et tout le reste. Mais quoi? vais-je, moi, négliger mon propre bien pour que tu en jouisses, et vais-je te céder la place? En échange de quoi? 'Je suis ton père.' Mais non un bien....

Et ça serait une erreur de penser qu' il s'agit d'un bien transcendant et impersonel qui contraint nos obligations sociales; en effet, on lit dans 3.4.10: 'nul ne m'est plus cher que moi-même'.

Une des illustrations les plus vivides de la détermination de Epictète à minimiser l'importance des relations sociales pour le bonheur humain se trouve dans un passage où il recommande un modèle d'entraînemement mental conçu pour nous aider à atteindre le bon degré de détachement: dans 4.1.111-2 il nous conseille de 'pratiquer ceci du matin jusqu' au soir:...

> Commence par les plus petites choses, par les plus fragiles, un pot, une coupe, puis, poursuis de la sorte jusqu' à une tunique, à un cabot, à un vieux cheval, à un bout de champ; de là, passe à toi-même, à ton corps, aux membres [ou parties] de ton corps, à tes enfants, à ta femme, à tes frères. Regarde bien de toutes parts pour tout rejeter loin de toi; purifie tes jugements pour que rien de ce qui ne t'appartient pas ne s'attache à toi, ne fasse corps avec toi, ne te cause de la souffrance, si on vient à te l'arracher.[4]

Ceci constitue une inversion frappante des notions que nous connaissons du passage familier de Hièrocle,[5] qui préconise la stratégie opposée, selon laquelle nous devrions renforcer nos liens avec les autres en allant de l'extérieur vers l'intérieur, en apportant chaque niveau de relations sociales plus proche du centre, c'est-à-dire notre âme et notre centre moral. L' ἄσκησις de Epictète préconise le contraire: nous ne devons pas accorder plus d'importance à ceux qui nous sont les plus chers que nous n'accordons à un morceau de vaisselle ou un vieux manteau. Nous ne trouverons une meilleure illustration de la profonde indifférence de ce Stoïcien austère face à l'ensemble de nos liens sociaux.

En tant qu'êtres humains, nous sommes inévitablement déchirés. D'une part, notre tendance fondamentale est de poursuivre notre propre bien, ce qui est nous est réelement avantageux. Nos relations avec les choses exterieures nous rendent vulnérables, et donc on ne peut pas permettre qu' elles deviennent trop importantes. Si nous faisons l'erreur d'accorder trop de valeur aux choses externes, y compris ces êtres humains qui nous sont les plus intimes et dont

---

[4] On peut comparer l'expression plus brève de cette idée dans *Enchiridion* 3.

[5] Dans Stobée 4.671-673 (=texte 57G dans A.A. Long et D.N. Sedley, *The Hellenistic Philosophers*, Cambridge 1987).

les vies sont les plus rapprochées de la nôtre, alors nous courtisons la misère.[6] D'autre part, nos relations humaines constituent une partie vitale de ce que nous sommes en tant qu' êtres humains. C'est difficile, sinon impossible, de découvrir ce que nous sommes et ce que nous devons faire si nous n'avons pas une conception adéquate de nos liens naturels et indissolubles avec les autres. Les autres êtres humains ne sont pas seulement les objets de nos affections; ils sont aussi des éléments constitutifs et indispensables de notre vie morale. Il est difficile d'imaginer une vie caractérisée par la sorte d'indifférence aux autres préconisée par Epictète.

Je ne veux pas suggérer que Epictète n'offre aucune résolution à la tension dans ses travaux que je viens d'esquisser si brièvement. Il n'en est pas ainsi, et je veux me pencher sur une tentative de réconcilier ces tendances opposées de la pensée d'Epictète.[7] Mais il est important, je crois, de partir de l'idée qu' il y a bel et bien une tension ici, notamment parce que nous devrons éviter d'être séduits trop facilement par l'attrait de l'optimisme stoïcien. Il serait facile de s'endormir dans une fausse sécurité, et de présumer qu' il est tout simplement raisonnable d'avoir beaucoup d'intérêt et même d'inquiétude pour les autres. Epictète montre que tel n'est pas le cas. Il soutient qu' un trop grand souci pour les autres est une source de misère, et que notre intérêt rationnel pour notre propre bonheur peut parfois prescrire une cruelle indifférence aux autres êtres humains. ('Quel mal y a-ti'l à dire tout bas, en embrassant ton enfant 'demain tu mourras'' 3.24.88). Dans sa théorie quelque chose d'aussi simple que l'affection d'un père envers son fils peut présenter un problème théorique profond, une théorie qui montre que nous devons souvent choisir entre nos engagements envers les autres et notre tendance vers le bonheur.

Les moyens disponibles à Epictète pour réconcilier ces deux tendances ne lui appartiennent pas tout seul. En effet, plus nous regardons les choses de près, plus nous verrons une continuité avec le stoïcisme ancien. Considérons d'abord la contribution apportée par la théorie stoïcienne de la valeur. Cette théorie est basée sur la distinction cardinale entre deux sortes de valeur qui sont considérées

---

6 Cf. B. Inwood, 'Why do fools fall in love?' *Bulletin of the Institute of Classical Studies* (London) 1996, et M. Nussbaum *The Therapy of Desire* (Princeton 1994) ch. 10.

7 Cf. A. Bonhöffer, *Die Ethik des Stoikers Epiktet* (Stuttgart 1894) 4-5, 158-9. J'ose offrir dans cette discussion-ci une solution complémentaire aux remarques de Bonhöffer, qui son très à propos mais trop brèves.

comme étant radicalement incommensurables. D'abord, il y a ce que nous serions peut-être tentés d'appeler la valeur 'morale' (quoiqu' il est important de noter que les stoïciens n'utilisaient pas cette étiquette pour désigner la catégorie, ni même une étiquette que l'on peut traduire en ces termes). Les seuls membres de cette catégorie sont les choses bonnes et mauvaises, soit la vertu, le vice, et ce qui 'participe' à la vertu ou au vice. Puis, il y a le domaine des choses indifférentes, des choses qui ont une sorte de valeur, mais pas une sorte de valeur qui soit de quelque façon ou à quelque degré pertinente pour le bien-être ou la misère de l'agent. Quelques instances typiques de ces valeurs sont la vie et la mort, la santé et la maladie, le plaisir et la douleur, une belle apparence et la laideur, la force physique et la faiblesse, la richesse et la pauvreté, une bonne et une mauvaise réputation, une grande ou une petite naissance, les talents naturels, les habiletés, même le progrès moral et son contraire (D.L. 7.106.), etc. C'est certainement le genre de valeurs auxquelles la majorité de l'auditoire non-spécialisé d'Epictète accordent de l'importance. Un stoïcien tel Epictète peut considérer les objets de ces soucis humains ordinaires comme rien de plus que des préférences: les néologismes inventés pour ce genre de valeur sont 'préférées' et 'dé-préférées' (προηγμένα, ἀποπροηγμένα). Aucune de ces choses n'importent au bonheur humain, peu importe à quel point notre attachement à ces valeurs est naturel.

Il y a aussi, et c'est bien connu, une autre catégorie de choses, les choses qui sont 'absolument indifférentes', les choses qui n'éveillent jamais nos désirs. Par exemple, que le nombre de cheveux sur notre tête soit pair ou impair, ou la position précise d'un de nos doigts lorsqu' il est étendu (D.L. 7.104-105). Mais la puissance inquiétante et paradoxale de l'axiologie stoïcienne devient évidente lorsque l'on réfléchit sur le fait que ces bagatelles sont dans la même catégorie générale que la vie et la mort: étant indifférentes elles sont, quant à leur valeur, plus proches de la santé et de la richesse que la santé et la richesse ne le sont du bien. On trouve ici une dichotomie radicale au niveau des valeurs entre la catégorie des vertus et des vices et le reste des choses auxquelles une personne normale accorde raisonnablement de l'importance. Ceci est signe que l'éthique stoïcienne est et doit être prise comme étant une théorie radicale et subversive. L'étrangeté des idées de Epictète n'a rien de nouveau. Quand il affirme qu' il n'y a aucun mal à se dire à soi-même (et dire à son enfant) que l'enfant pourrait mourir demain, c'est choquant, mais pas surprenant.[8] Il n'y a aucun mal ici parce que le seul mal véritable est le vice et que la mort de qui que ce soit est une affaire indifférente. Nous pouvons 'dé-préférer' cet événement, mais si nous le considérons comme une chose mauvaise nous compromettons notre tranquillité. Quand nous sommes invités à commencer avec les bagatelles de la vie (4.1.111), un pot, une coupe, une tunique, et à les considérer comme n'ayant aucune importance, et de mettre ensuite dans cette catégorie un animal familier, notre cheval, ou un bout de champ, Epictète nous encourage alors à se rappeler que même les choses préférées comme celles-là sont indifférentes, qu' elles sont dans la même catégorie que le nombre de cheveux sur notre tête. Et quand il passe aux choses indifférentes préférées qui sont plus proches de nous, c'est-à-dire nos propres corps et les vies des membres les plus chers de notre famille, encore une fois il nous rappelle simplement que les seules valeurs qui peuvent avoir un effet sur notre bonheur sont les valeurs 'morales', soit la vertu et le vice. C'est pour cette raison que nos passions peuvent être animées par des erreurs concernant les valeurs—c'est parce que nous pouvons croire que d'autres êtres humains sont indispensables à notre bonheur que nous éprouvons le chagrin ou la peur, le désir ou le plaisir.

Epictète illustre cette idée avec beaucoup d'insistance dans l' *Entretien* 2.17, avec le cas de Medée. Dans les sections 18 ss. Epictète fait référence à sa croyance erronée que Jason est indispensable à son bonheur. À partir de cette croyance mal fondée son raisonnement était néanmoins correct: Medée avait 'une représentation exacte de ce qu' est pour quelqu' un l'échec de ses désirs' (2.17.19). Donc elle tua ses propres enfants. Epictète vient tout près de faire l'éloge de Medée pour la grandeur de son âme: comme un philosophe, elle a agi conformément à ses croyances—mais une de ces croyances était mal fondée. La morale de cette histoire nous donne un frisson—la vie d'un de nos enfants ne fait pas le poids si on la compare avec la poursuite de ce que l'on considère comme étant notre 'bien', ce que nous pensons être indispensable à notre propre bonheur.

Mais on peut se poser la question suivante: la vertu et le vice ne doivent-ils pas être concrétisés dans les êtres humains? N'est-ce pas cela que les stoïciens veulent dire lorsqu' ils parlent de 'ce qui

---

[8] Voir 3.24.88.

participe à la vertu'? La vertu et la sagesse d'un autre être humain ne sont-elles pas dignes que l'on y porte un intérêt authentique? Bien sûr qu' elles le sont. Mais selon les stoïciens, les membres de notre famille et nos concitoyens ne sont pas vertueux, et nous ne le sommes pas non plus. Seule une personne sage et vertueuse possède la valeur la plus haute, et alors seulement aux yeux d'un autre sage.[9] Or quelle est l'importance pour nous des chances qu' ont les autres d'atteindre la vertu? N'y a-t-il pas une valeur 'morale' spéciale dans le potentiel pour la vertu, et dans le progrès vers la vertu? Encore une fois, la réponse est dure. Le progrès moral se trouve dans la catégorie des choses indifférentes. Le fait que votre vie ou votre épouse est menacée n'est pas plus sérieux parce que vous ou elle est plus près de la vertu que quelqu' autre victime. Seule une personne sage aurait une plus grande importance, et alors ça serait seulement la vertu de la personne qui aurait de l'importance, pas sa vie.

Cependant cette façon de voir le problème ne le résoud pas, mais ne fait que le pousser plus loin en arrière dans l'histoire de l'école stoïcienne, ce qui nous rappelle que le problème des relations sociales n'est pas apparu plus tard dans l'histoire de l'école, au moment où elle s'est tournée vers des affaires plus pratiques. Je fais allusion, bien sûr, à la fausse idée que la théorie sociale est apparue comme un sujet digne d'intérêt au moment de la fondation du soi-disant *Portique Moyen* de Panaetius, un stoïcisme qui s'intéressait à la moralité pratique et qui par là se distinguait de l'ancienne école. À mon avis il n'y a jamais eu une telle 'fondation', et aucune discontinuité dans la pensée éthique stoïcienne.[10] On peut donc s'attendre à trouver dans la pensée stoïcienne ancienne des signes précurseurs des problèmes et tensions que l'on trouve chez Epictète. Et je pense que nous en trouvons effectivement.

La théorie stoïcienne de *oikeiôsis* pose qu' il y a deux aspects, ou même deux formes, de cet instinct primordial.[11] D'abord, il y a une

---

[9] Voir 2.22.1-3 et la discussion ci-dessous.

[10] Cf. M. Schofield, *The Stoic Idea of the City* (Cambridge 1991); Schofield démontre une pareille continuité—et développement—dans l'histoire de la philosophie politique stoïcienne.

[11] Voir A.A. Long et D.N. Sedley, *The Hellenistic Philosophers* (Cambridge 1987) 1.350-4 et J. Annas, *The Morality of Happiness* (Oxford 1993) 265. Travaux fondamentaux sur *oikeiôsis*: M. Pohlenz, 'Grundfragen der stoischen Philosophie', *Abhandlungen der Göttingen Gesellschaft*, phil.-hist. Klasse 3.26 (1940) 1-122; S.G. Pembroke, 'Oikeiosis', *Problems in Stoicism* ed. A.A. Long (Londres 1971) 114-149; H. Görgemanns, '*Oikeiosis* in Arius Didymus' (et le commentaire de

affiliation à soi-même et à la préservation de soi (la soi-disant *oikeiôsis* personnelle) qui est la base de notre poursuite du bien et de l'avantageux, ces valeurs dont la possession assure le bonheur, qui est le but ou *telos* dominant de la vie humaine. Et il y a aussi une seconde affiliation naturelle, et celle-ci nous lie avec les autres êtres humains—cette relation naturelle que tous les stoïciens considéraient comme l'explication ultime de la nature intrinsèquement sociale de l'homme. Qu' il puisse y avoir un conflit entre ces deux affiliations dans des circonstances particulières est clairement possible—et les stoïciens étaient conscients de cette possibilité. Il semble que Chrysippe pensait que ce conflit ne pouvait pas être ultime et insoluble, et que la réconciliation des deux affiliations fondamentales se trouve dans la relation entre nous-mêmes et notre progéniture. Comme je l'ai soutenu il y a quelques années,[12] il parta probablement de nos relations en tant que parents à nos enfants. Ils sont (selon Plutarque, *St. Rep.* 12) des 'parties' de nous-mêmes; si nous sommes conçus par nature pour s'occuper de nous-mêmes et de nos parties constitutives, alors nos enfants—étant des parties de nous-mêmes—nous sont égalements chers.

Cette relation biologique est évidemment naturelle, etsi c'est bien le cas, alors la nature providentielle dont nous sommes les produits devrait garantir qu' il n'y aura pas de conflit entre notre amour de soi et l'amour de nos enfants. Cette affiliation à nos enfants devient alors le fondement de notre souci général et impartial pour l'ensemble des hommes. À l'époque de Hièrocle (col. 9 de l' *Ethikê stoicheiôsis*) il y avait même un terme courant pour cette relation: notre 'affiliation de famille' (συγγενικὴ οἰκείωσις) est la base de notre affection pour les autres—c'est στερκτική, la base pour φιλοστοργία.

B. Inwood), *On Stoic and Peripatetic Ethics* ed. W.W. Fortenbaugh (New Brunswick NJ et Londres 1983) 165-201; G. Striker, 'The Role of *oikeiosis* in Stoic ethics', *Oxford Studies in Ancient Philosophy* 1 (1983) 145-167; B. Inwood, 'Hierocles: theory and argument in the second century A.D.', *Oxford Studies in Ancient Philosophy* 2 (1984) 151-184; J. Brunschwig, 'The cradle argument in Epicureanism and Stoicism', *The norms of nature,* edd. G. Striker et M. Schofield (Cambridge et Paris 1986) 113-144. Récemment J. Annas (*The Morality of Happiness* 262-276 et 'Aristotle's political theory in the Hellenistic period', *Justice and Generosity,* edd. A. Laks et M. Schofield [Cambridge 1995] 74-94), propose une liaison étroite entre l' *oikeiôsis* et le concept post-Kantien de 'impartiality'. Je ne suis pas convaincu; voir mon compte-rendu, dans *Ancient Philosophy* 15 (1995) 647-665.

12 'The Two Forms of *oikeiôsis* in Arius and the Stoa', W.W. Fortenbaugh, (ed.), *On Stoic and Peripatetic Ethics: the work of Arius Didymus* (New Brunswick NJ et Londres 1983) 190-201.

La réconciliation envisagée entre les affiliations personnelle et sociale dans le stoïcisme, donc, met l'accent sur la relation entre l'enfant et le parent, et en particulier sur l'idée que l'enfant est (à l'origine au moins) une partie du parent. Une telle relation ne garantit pas automatiquement et sans prémisses additionnelles l'élimination du conflit que la théorie requiert. Après tout, il y a une possibilité réelle qu' une de mes parties sera en conflit profond avec moi-même pris comme un tout: un organe cancéreux menace le tout et doit être excisé. Pourquoi donc cette réconciliation est-elle censée réussir dans le stoïcisme ancien? Rien ne nous le dit directement—il y a en effet très peu d'évidence directe sur ceci—mais le texte central de Diogène Laèrce (D.L. 7.85 ss.) nous donne un indice valable. Ce texte présente un argument sur la nature de l'*oikeiôsis* personnelle qui est basé sur une assomption fondamentale concernant une Nature créatrice dont les opérations sont contraintes par les canons de plausibilité rationnelle: ça ne serait pas plausible (εἰκός) que la nature produise une créature et la laisse se débrouiller toute seule, en lui donnant ou bien aucune tendance à la préservation de soi, ou bien des tendances auto-destructives. De manière semblable, Ciceron nous dit qu' il serait irrationnel que la nature décide de prévoir la reproduction de l'espèce, pour ensuite abandonner les enfants sans pourvoir à leurs besoins (*Fin.* 3.62):

> Or il serait forcément contradictoire que la nature voulût la reproduction des êtres et ne fît rien pour que les êtres reproduits fussent l'objet d'une affection. Même chez les animaux se peut très bien remarquer cette action de la nature: à voir la peine qu' ils se donnent pour mettre au monde et pour élever leurs petits, il semble que l'on entende la voix de la nature elle-même. (tr. Jules Martha)

Évidemment l'affection parentale est le moyen par lequel la Nature a assuré la survie de l'espèce. Au vingtième siècle nous sommes plus enclins à considérer la rationalité de ces arrangements comme un aspect *a posteriori* de la biologie évolutionniste, mais dans le monde ancien le modèle de l'artisan dominait. Ainsi les stoïciens pouvait plausiblement offrir la rationalité de la Nature (ou Zeus) comme une explication authentique de certaines caractéristiques favorisant l'adaptation et la survie de l'espèce, telles que la tendance à la préservation de soi et le soin de nos enfants.

Epictète, comme les anciens stoïciens, traite la convergence de la *oikeiôsis* personnelle et des liens sociaux comme une partie du plan rationnel de Zeus. Dans l' *Entretien* 1.9.11 il souligne l'égoïsme fondamental de la nature humaine. L'animal humain, selon Epictète, fait tout pour son propre bien. Mais il avance aussi l'idée qu' il est nécessaire que cet intérêt personnel soit satisfait de sorte à rendre service aux autres. Et le fait que ceci est une dimension inévitable de la vie humaine est assuré par le fait que Zeus est contraint de la même manière—sa nature, étant rationnelle, n'est pas en principe différente de la nôtre.

> Ce n'est pas de l'égoisme, car telle est la nature de l'animal: il fait tout pour lui-même. Mais le soleil aussi fait tout pour lui, et du reste Zeus lui aussi. Quand Zeus, par example, veut être 'le dieu qui répand la pluie' et 'le dieu qui produit les fruits' et 'le père des homme et des dieux', tu vois qu' il ne peut réaliser ces actes et mériter ces appellations sans être utile au bien commun. D'une façon générale, il a disposé de telle sorte la nature de l'animal raisonnable qu' elle ne puisse obtenir aucun bien particulier sans contribuer à l'utilité commune. Ainsi n'est-il plus antisocial de tout faire pour soi-même. Qu' attends-tu, en effet? Qu' on renonce à soi-même et à son propre intérêt? Et comment l'affiliation à soi (ἡ πρὸς αὑτὰ οἰκείωσις) serait-elle encore un seul et même principe pour tous les êtres humains? (1.19.11-15) [13]

Il faudrait noter que le rôle *paternel* de Zeus est lié à l'exigence qu' il réalise un équilibre entre les motivations égoïstes et désintéressées; il en va de même pour son rôle de bienfaiteur (Zeus qui amène la pluie). Mais ceci n'est pas surprenant, puisque le fils de Zeus, Hercule, était un autre bienfaiteur de la race humaine, et dans 1.6.30-36 il est clair que l'épanouissement de soi de Hercule passe par le service aux autres. Pour Epictète, ceci est le propre d'un animal rationnel.

Il est encore plus important de souligner la dernière question rhétorique. Ceci est la seule façon qu' il puisse y avoir un principe unique et cohérent pour tous, et ce principe doit être ἡ πρὸς αὑτὰ οἰκείωσις, une affiliation à soi-même. La tendance à la préservation *de soi* est à la base de nos relations sociales, mais les deux sont liées inextricablement. Avant de finir je vais explorer ce rapport, en vue de montrer pourquoi la réconciliation du souci orienté vers soi-même et du souci orienté vers les autres doit être fondé sur la primauté du souci pour soi-même. Il deviendra évident, je l'espère, que la théorie d'Epictète rend explicite quelque chose qui se trouve caché dans les textes fragmentés du stoïcisme ancien.

J'ai souligné que Epictète considère la réconciliation de l'*oikeiôsis* personnelle et de l'*oikeiôsis* sociale comme une exigence ration-

---

[13] J'ai modifiée legèrement la traduction de Souilhé ici.

nelle, sans laquelle le monde ne pourrait être considéré comme un tout intelligible. Et j'ai insisté sur l'idée que le modèle de l'artisan qui déploie une prévoyance intelligente est indispensable au sens stoïcien de l'organisation et de l'administration cosmique (διακόσμησις). Une comparaison intéressante vient à l'esprit si on réfléchit sur le mythe du *Protagoras* de Platon. Le manque de prévoyance d'Epiméthée a presque laissé l'humanité dans la situation que les stoïciens considéraient comme implausible, dans la mesure où elle est irrationnelle. Quand les moyens disponibles pour la préservation de soi furent épuisés, les besoins de l'humanité n'avaient pas été satisfaits. L'organisation sociale fut la première tentative pour combler cette lacune, mais il s'avèra qu' il manquait aux hommes les ressources nécessaires pour la vie sociale—ce qui mena presque à la disparition de l'espèce. Seule l'intervention de Zeus, qui donna aux hommes la justice et le respect devant les autres (ἀιδώς) pouvait les sauver. Ce mythe, raconté par Protagore, montre jusqu' à quel point les instincts sociaux (y compris l'esprit de honte devant les autres—comme τὸ αἰδῆμον chez Epictète) sont essentiels pour la survie de l'humanité. Traduit dans le langage du naturalisme stoïcien, ce mythe illustre la nécessité rationnelle des liens sociaux. Dans un mythe on peut imaginer que Epiméthée est incompétant, qu' il permet que l'humanité risque sa disparition; on peut imaginer que le Zeus de Protagore choisit *volontairement* s'il va sauver les hommes ou non; mais on ne peut parler ainsi du Zeus stoïcien—sa nature (comme la nature des dieux de Platon) est *réellement* contrainte par la rationalité. Puisque l'on ne peut concevoir que la Nature permette l'existence d'une espèce incapable de survivance, son caractère rationnel peut servir d'explication réelle.

Tout ceci confirme davantage, je pense, que la situation difficile où se trouve Epictète est la même que celle où se trouvait toute la tradition Socratique. Il doit considérer que les liens sociaux constituent une composante essentielle de notre nature, ancrée aussi profondément dans nos natures que notre tendance à la préservation de soi et l'amour de soi. Et cependant, tout comme ses prédecesseurs, il doit également considérer que la tendance individuelle pour l'*eudaimonia* est l'intérêt dominant, plus important que les liens interpersonnels les plus forts, ceux que nous avons avec nos enfants. (Je sais que j'ai beaucoup mis l'accent sur ces relations, presque à l'exclusion des autres liens sociaux. C'est parce que les stoïciens considéraient que les relations familiales étaient fondamentales pour l'ensemble des relations sociales; on peut facilement faire une critique *a fortiori* de la cohérence de toute la pensée sociale stoïcienne si leurs idées sur les relations entre parents et enfants sont mal fondées. On voit l'importance de ces relations pour Epictète par le fait qu' il les invoque souvent, et aussi par la façon qu' il passe de ces relations à des thèmes moraux plus généraux; je pense, par exemple, à l' *Entretien* 1.11 *De l'affection familiale*—φιλοστοργία).

Il reste à se demander si Epictète a fait du progrès par rapport au *statu quo* dans le stoïcisme, et s'il a apporté une contribution personnelle à la théorie qui sous-tend la thèse stoïcienne sur les liens sociaux. Je crois que oui, et que sa contribution à la pensée stoïcienne vient du modèle qu' il développa à partir des relations entre parents et enfants.

Réfléchissons un moment sur le modèle des relations entre parent et enfant proposé par les stoïciens anciens. Nous nous soucions de nous-mêmes d'abord et avant tout, et nous nous soucions de nos enfants parce qu' ils sont des *parties* de nous. Nos parties nous sont certainement indispensables, mais elles ne sont pas nous—en tant que parties elles sont non-pas-autres que nous, comme diraient les stoïciens (voir Sextus *M* 9.336).[14] Certaines parties sont indispensables pour nous-mêmes en tant que totalités (nos poumons, par exemple), tandis que des autres parties ne le sont pas (nos pieds, par exemple). Certes, il se peut que l'on doive enlever une partie afin que le tout survive. Epictète fait référence dans 2.6.10 au fait que Chrysippe reconnaissait explicitement le rôle subordonné des parties comme le pied, et il approuve sa doctrine. Notre pied, étant une partie, a moins d'importance qu' une personne, qui est le tout pertinent; le pied se salierait volontiers—ou accepterait d'être estropié, suivant la suggestion (non publiée) de A.A. Long[15] de πηροῦσθαι pour πηλοῦσθαι—si les intérêts du tout l'exigeaient. Il en va de même pour les êtres humains qui font parties de la totalité cosmique (voir aussi 2.10); si c'est nécessaire, un agent rationnel sacrifiera au tout n'importe lequel de ses indifférents préférés. Et la

---

[14] Voir J. Barnes, 'Bits and Pieces' dans *Matter and Metaphysics* (edd. J. Barnes et M. Mignucci, Naples 1988) 223-294, et 'Partial Wholes' (dans *Ethics, Politics and Human Nature,* edd. E.F. Paul, F.D. Miller Jr., et J. Paul, Oxford et Cambridge MA 1991, 1-23). Barnes commence 'Bits and Pieces' avec une reconnaisance de l'importance de la relation entre la partie et le tout dans l'éthique stoïcienne—du début jusqu' à la fin de l'histoire de l'école.

[15] Une suggestion de Long avancée à son seminaire sur l'éthique stoïcienne à Berkeley au printemps de 1982, mais qu' il n' a pas inclu dans *The Hellenistic Philosophers* (Cambridge 1987).

vie de n'importe qui, même celle d'un membre intime de notre famille, ne vaut pas plus que ça.

Nos enfants sont des parties, au moins dans le sens que c'est en tant que parties de nous-mêmes qu' ils revendiquent le plus fortement notre affection. Si l'on peut dans certains cas se passer d'une de nos parties, on peut se passer encore plus d'un enfant. Et si l'on peut se passer d'un enfant, on peut se passer encore plus d'un autre être humain! Et pourtant, l'enfant est une partie de nous-mêmes; il n'est pas 'autre' que nous. Je pense que cette perspective sur nos vies nous permet de bien comprendre la tension entre l'*oikeiôsis* personnelle et l'*oikeiôsis* sociale. L'idée que nos enfants sont des parties explique pourquoi nous nous soucions tellement d'eux, pourquoi notre intérêt pour nos enfants est dans la plupart des cas et dans la plupart des circonstances égal à notre interêt personnel. Mais cette idée explique aussi pourquoi, en dernière analyse, le moi vient en premier. Mes enfants, après tout, ne sont pas des 'autres moi'. (Il est intéressant de noter que seuls les hommes sages peuvent être vraiment des amis et donc des 'autres moi' l'un pour l'autre, de sorte qu' un homme sage a une raison de considérer qu' une autre personne a une importance égale à la sienne, et alors seulement si cette personne-là est sage elle aussi—d'où la rareté du dilemme confronté par les deux sages sur la planche, mentionné par Cicéron, *De Officiis*, 3.89-90)

La conception des enfants pris comme des parties réalise exactement ce que l'on veut. Elle explique à la fois pourquoi ils sont si importants et pourquoi ils peuvent être relégués au second rang en cas de conflit. Et si nos relations avec les autres êtres humains (notre *oikeiôsis* sociale) sont dérivées et formées à partir de nos relations avec nos enfants, alors ces relations aussi s'inscrivent bien dans ce modèle. On peut présumer que Epictète a emprunté ce modèle à ces prédecesseurs. Sa propre contribution à la conception de ce problème se trouve, je pense, dans son développement de l'idée des relations entre parent et enfant. Plus que la plupart des stoïciens dont nous connaissons les textes, Epictète considère que Zeus est une personne, un père pour l'espèce humaine. L'idée homérique du Zeus 'père des dieux et des hommes' fait partie de l'arrière-plan; comme plusieurs stoïciens Epictète retient et justifie les aspects de la tradition poétique qui conviennent à sa théorie. Epictète, comme Cléanthe avant lui (dans l'*Hymne à Zeus*) et Marc Aurèle plus tard (qui a lui-même été influencé par Epictète), soulignait le caractère personnel de nos relations avec Zeus. Zeus est souvent un 'tu'—un *Du* Buberien, un autre individu dont le rapport avec nous est celui d'un parent.

Nous, les êtres humains, sommes des parties de la totalité cosmique, des parties ainsi que des alliés de Zeus, comme le dit Sénèque (*Ep.* 92.30). Ce statut que nous avons comme parties du Cosmos s'accorde bien avec le statut que nous avons comme enfants de Zeus. Plus on met l'accent sur le fait que nous sommes les enfants de Zeus, plus il est naturel de penser que notre relation avec nos semblables est une relation fraternelle, une relation avec nos frères (et soeurs). Dans ce modèle, les autres êtres humains deviennent nos frères (et soeurs). La notion que tous les hommes sont frères a son origine dans la pensée stoïcienne, puisque nous pouvons être frères seulement si nous avons un parent en commun; les images cosmologiques stoïciennes présentent la source la plus riche de cette imagerie de la relation entre parent et enfant.

Epictète trouve qu' il est naturel de mettre l'acccent sur la conception cosmologique où Zeus est un parent quand il se penche sur l'attitude humaine erronée face à la perte d'un être bien-aimé, c'est-à-dire le chagrin. Dans l' *Entretien* important 3.24 le souci de dieu pour les humains est paternel (3.24.3) lorsqu' il rend notre bonheur indépendant des choses qui sont hors de notre contrôle:

> À cette fin, il leur a donné des moyens dont certains appartiennent en propre à chacun et les autres lui sont étrangers. Tout ce qui peut être entravé, enlevé, violenté, ne nous appartient pas en propre; tout ce qui est libre d'entraves nous appartient en propre. Quant à la vraie nature du bien et du mal, dieu, ansi qu' il convenait à celui qui veille sur nous et nous protège à la manière d'un père, nous l'a donnée en propre.

Il faut penser à la cosmologie stoïcienne (3.24.10-11); Epictète dit, écoutons les philosophes:

> ils [disent] que cet univers n'est qu' une seule cité, que la substance dont il est formé est unique et qu' il doit y avoir une révolution périodique où les choses se cèdent mutuellement la place, où les unes se dissolvent tandis que d'autres viennent au monde, où les unes demeurent au même lieu tandis que d'autres se mettent en mouvement. Et tout est rempli d'amis: d'abord de dieux, puis également d'hommes que la nature a rapprochés les uns des autres: les uns doivent vivre ensemble, tandis que d'autres doivent se quitter, se complaisant parmi ceux qui vivent avec eux et sans s'attrister de voir s'éloigner les autres.

Comme le montrent les carrières d' Ulysse et de Hercule, les gens se déplacent, ils meurent. Pourquoi n'est-ce pas une infortune? En partie parce que c'est un état de choses naturel et inévitable. Mais ce que Epictète dit au sujet de Hercule est plus important. Il était constamment guidé par le savoir:

> en effet, que nul homme n'est orphelin, mais que tous ont un père, qui, sans jamais cesser, prend soin d'eux. Car ce n'étaient pas de simples mots qu' il avait recueillis, quand il entendait dire que Zeus est le père des hommes, lui qui, en vérité, le regardait comme son père et l'appelait ainsi et, le regard fixé sur lui, accomplissait toutes ses actions. C'est pourquoi il a pu vivre heureux partout. Mais il est impossible d'associer le bonheur et le regret des choses absentes. Car l'être heureux doit recevoir tout ce qu' il désire; il doit ressembler à un homme repu: il ne doit éprouver ni la soif ni la faim. 'Ulysse, pourtant, regrettait son épouse et, assis sur un rocher, il pleurait.' Et toi, tu ajoutes foi à tout ce que dit Homère et à ses fables? S'il est bien vrai qu' Ulysse pleurait, qu' était-il de plus qu' un infortuné? Or, quel homme de bien peut être infortuné? En vérité, l'univers est bien mal gouverné si Zeus ne veille pas à ce que ses propres concitoyens soient heureux comme lui. Non, il n'est pas permis et il est impie de penser cela, mais si Ulysse pleurait et se lamentait, il n'était pas un homme bon. Qui, en effet, peut être bon, s'il ignore qui il est? Et qui le sait, s'il a oublié que tout ce qui vient à l'existence est périssable et que, pour les hommes, vivre ensemble n'est pas toujours possible? Quelle sera la conclusion? C'est que désirer l'impossible est le fait d'un esclave, d'un sot; c'est agir comme un étranger, qui combat contre dieu avec les seules armes qui soient à sa disposition, ses propres jugements (3.24.15-21)

Mais céder au chagrin, c'est se battre contre dieu:

> Par conséquent [du fait que le chagrin d'autrui n'est pas à moi, mais seulement le mien] je le ferai cesser à tout prix, car cela dépend de moi; pour celui des autres, j'essaierai, suivant mes forces, mais je n'essaierai pas à tout prix; sinon, je combattrai contres les dieux, je me mettrai en opposition avec Zeus, je serai en contradiction avec lui pour le gouvernement de l'univers. Et la peine de cette lutte contre dieu et de cette désobéissance, ce ne sont pas les enfants de mes enfants qui la paieront, mais moi-même, de jour et de nuit, quand mes rêves me feront tressauter, quand je vivrai dans le trouble, tremblant à la moindre nouvelle, avec la paix de mon âme (mon ἀπάθεια) suspendue aux lettres des autres (3.24.23-24).

Ce n'est pas un accident si dans cet *Entretien* Epictète considère ensuite la relation de Socrate avec ses enfants (3.24.60 ss.)—il les aimait, malgré son indifférence notoire face à leur destin dans ce monde (voir la fin de l'*Apologie*). Il se souvient qu' il doit aimer ses fils 'comme le fait un homme libre, gardant à l'esprit qu' il doit être un ami des dieux d'abord et avant tout'. L'amitié divine, ou la φιλία par rapport à ce qui est purement rationnel, a la priorité sur nos amours et affiliations humaines. Il y a d'autres entretiens où ces thèmes se retrouvent de la même façon—par exemple 1.9, où l'on contraste la conscience de la parenté divine avec les relations sociales humaines. Notre citoyenneté humaine dans une petite ville est basée sur nos liens de parenté avec nos semblables, et notre citoyenneté dans la *cosmopolis* est basée de la même façon sur notre parenté avec dieu. Le divin est le paradigme pour la vie terrestre; nos relations cosmiques sont à la fois le modèle et la cause de nos relations humaines—et ce qui est plus important, le divin nous aide à comprendre que l'expérience humaine est un système rationnel et cohérent.

En soulignant que Zeus remplit le rôle du père commun de tous les hommes, Epictète augmente et renforce les fondements de la théorie stoïcienne des relations humaines. Nos liens avec les autres hommes ne sont pas, comme les autres stoïciens le pensaient, seulement une extension de l'affection parentale aux autres êtres humains par le biais d'une analogie faible et diluée (comme le suggère les cercles en expansion de Hiérocle); cette façon de promouvoir la fraternité des hommes fut attaquée par le commentateur anonyme du *Théétète*, et cette critique nous fait penser aux commentaires d'Aristote sur les relations familiales artificielles dans la *République* de Platon. Plutôt, cette relation est ancrée dans une application nouvelle de la métaphore des relations familiales, dans laquelle la figure principale est Zeus dans le rôle du père. Ce modèle aide aussi à expliquer nos relations sociales aux autres hommes, et rend compte *et* de leur caractère naturel *et* de leur place secondaire. Le lien le plus fort dans n'importe quelle famille ancienne (d'un point de vue idéologique) est le lien entre père et fils; les relations entre frères (et soeurs) doivent leur existence même à la primauté de la relation paternelle. La primauté de notre relation avec Zeus le père est un symbole, pour ainsi dire, de la primauté de la cohérence rationnelle dans nos vies. Et tout comme la primauté de la relation parent-enfant met les liens entre frères (et soeurs) en perspective, la primauté de la cohérence rationnelle dans nos vies détermine que toutes les autres relations—σχέσεις—sont secondaires. Ces thèmes sont très importants dans le discours que je vais explorer en guise de conclusion, l' *Entretien* 2.22 intitutlé *De l'amitié*.

Epictète prend comme point de départ un argument raisonnable (εἰκότως) modelé sur celui que Chrysippe a employé pour fonder la rationalité de notre inclination à la préservation de soi dans D.L. 7.85 ss. Nous aimons (φιλεῖν) ce que nous prenons au sérieux; ceci est raisonnable, puisqu' il serait absurde de prendre au sérieux ce qui est mauvais pour nous ou ce qui ne présente aucun intérêt pour nous. Ainsi nous prenons au sérieux seulement ce que nous considérons bon, et si nous prenons quelque chose au sérieux, il s'ensuit que nous l'aimons. Par conséquent, seule une personne qui connaît le bien peut réellement savoir comment être un ami. Seul un homme sage peut donc être un ami ou éprouver de l'amitié.

Cette position strictement rationnelle est ensuite contestée par l'interlocuteur imaginaire d'Epictète, qui dit 'Écoutez, je ne suis pas un homme sage, et pourtant j'aime mon enfant'. Epictète doit, dans ce qui suit, montrer que l'amour d'un fou n'est pas vraiment de l'amour. Mais il commence par isoler la cause de la folie de son interlocuteur. C'est qu' il se trompe au sujet de la valeur des choses: il s'agit d'une erreur axiologique. Le résultat de cette erreur est la passion et la misère, l'instabilité et l'inconsistance, un panorama toujours changeant de réactions aux événements de la vie. Quand l'interlocuteur reconnaît son erreur, Epictète lui demande de reconnaître les mauvaises conséquences de cette inconsistance sur l'amitié. Quand notre attention se déplace de l'amour de notre ami à l'amour de l'argent, notre attitude change. La comparaison avec les chiens est pertinente:

> Eh quoi! As-tu jamais vu des petits chiens se caresser et jouer entre eux, ce qui te faisait dire: 'Il n'y a rien de plus amical'? Mais pour voir ce qu' est l'amitié, jette entre eux un morceau de viande et tu le sauras. Jette aussi entre toi et ton fils un bout dc champ, et tu sauras combien ton fils est impatient de t'enterrer et combien tu souhaites, toi, la mort de ton fils. Et tu diras au contraire: 'Quel enfant j'ai élevé! Il y a longtemps qu' il m'enterre.' (2.22.9-10)

Viennent ensuite d'autres exemples d'amour instable, qui proviennent des tragédies greques, l'*Alcestis* et les *Phoenissae* en particulier. Quand n'importe quelle chose qui revêt de l'importance pour nous affaiblit le lien entre deux amis, alors ce qu' ils valorisent vraiment devient évident, et l'amitié meurt. Les seules amitiés réelles sont celles partagées par des gens qui savent la valeur réelle des choses, puisque même les relations entre frères et soeurs et entre parent et enfant sont vulnérables. Le paradoxe stoïcien selon lequel seuls les sages peuvent être des amis (voir D.L. 7. 124) reçoit ici un sens concret.[16]

---

[16] On pourrait comparer la façon dont Sénèque rend ces paradoxes réels dans le *De Beneficiis* (voir mon 'Politics and Paradox' dans *Justice and Generosity,* edd. M. Schofield et A. Laks, Cambridge 1995) ou la stratégie très différente de Cicéron dans le *Paradoxa Stoicorum* (voir W. Englert, 'Bringing Philosophy to the Light: Cicero's *Paradoxa Stoicorum*' in *The Poetics of Therapy* ed. M. Nussbaum (Edmonton 1990 = *Apeiron* 23 no.4).

Selon Epictète, ceci est tout à fait naturel:

> En règle générale—ne vous faites pas d'illusion—tout être vivant n'a rien qui lui soit plus cher que son propre intérêt. Dès lors, quoi que ce soit qui lui paraisse y faire obstacle, s'agirait-il d'un frère, ou d'un père, ou d'un enfant, ou d'un être aimé, ou d'un amant, il le hait, il le rejette, il le maudit. Car il n'est rien que, par nature, il aime autant que son propre intérêt. C'est là son frère, ses parents, sa patrie, son dieu. (2.22.15-6)

L'histoire révèle que même les dieux ne sont pas exempts de la colère d'un être humain qui pense que ses intérêts ont été lésés. Ainsi une fausse conception de mes intérêts réels détruit même les liens humains les plus forts (18-21). Les grandes guerres du passé sont basées sur de telles erreurs (20-23), et donc l'on ne peut pas penser que même les plus sincères et enthousiastes déclarations d'amitié sont sécures. En effet, l'on ne peut compter sur les relations humaines si les agents en question sont des fous sans vertu (25). Une évaluation de la force de n'importe quel lien social ne peut être faite à partir de critères traditionnels (26-29); elle doit passer par un examen des valeurs morales profondes des hommes en question. Savent-ils quels sont leurs intérêts réels? Si oui, alors il se peut fort bien qu' ils soient des amis authentiques, et qu' ils aient la fidélité et le respect (πίστις, αἰδώς) qui constituent le fondement des relations humaines (30). Il n'y a pas d'autre base solide pour les liens sociaux authentiques, pas même les liens qui semblent avoir duré le plus longtemps et être les plus forts.

Epictète termine en décrivant la fausse opinion sur la valeur des choses externes:

> Telle fut la force sauvage, telle fut la force destructrice de l'amitié, celle qui ne permit plus à une femme d'être une épouse, à une mère d'être vraiment mère. Et que celui d'entre vous qui a sincèrement à coeur ou de témoigner lui-même son amitié à quelqu' un, ou de se gagner l'amitié d'un autre, extirpe ces jugements, qu' il les haïsse, qu' il les banisse de son âme à lui. De la sorte, il n'aura point tout d'abord à s'adresser à lui-même de reproches, à lutter contre lui-même, à se repentir, à se tourmenter; de plus, il n'entrera pas en lutte avec son prochain, absolument pas avec celui qui lui ressemble, et vis-à-vis de celui qui lui est dissemblable, il sera tolérant, condescendant, doux, indulgent, comme envers un ignorant, comme envers un homme qui se fourvoie en matière capitale; il ne sera dur pour personne, car il comprendra parfaitement le mot de Platon: 'C'est toujours malgré elle qu' une âme est privée de la vérité.' Dans le cas contraire, vous agirez en tout comme agissent les amis: vous boirez ensemble, vous vivrez sous le même toit, vous naviguerez de conserve et vous pourrez avoir les mêmes parents. Oui, et les serpents aussi. Mais amis? vous ne le serez pas plus qu' ils ne le sont tant que vous conservez ces jugements sauvages, ces jugements pervers. (2.22.33-37).

Et c'est ici que nous devons terminer, avec le diagnostic final d'Epictète sur la nature des liens sociaux. Dans sa théorie, les liens sociaux doivent être secondaires, ils ne peuvent être au même niveau de valeur que l'*oikeiôsis* fondamentale que chacun a envers soi-même. Et ceci est dû au fait qu' une appréciation adéquate de notre propre bénéfice est essentielle à la stabilité morale de n'importe quel animal rationnel. Étant ce que nous sommes, tels que Zeus nous a crées, il nous est impossible de poursuivre un autre but fondamental; notre relation naturelle avec notre propre bien-être doit être le point de départ de tous nos engagements. C'est pourquoi il dit que seule l'*oikeiôsis* personnelle peut être le principe *unique* de la vie morale; si nous mettons les relations sociales au même niveau, nous ne pouvons plus maintenir notre équilibre.

Il s'avère donc inévitable dans la théorie stoïcienne que l'amitié réelle, la φιλία stable, doive s'obtenir au prix du détachement affectif. À fin de montrer de la loyauté et du respect réels envers nos semblables—même pour les membres de notre famille—nous devons également cesser de s'en faire s'ils nous quittent, s'ils rivalisent avec nous, s'ils nous trahissent, ou s'ils meurent. En effet, la confusion axiologique est la source de la haine autant que de l'amour, et c'est aussi l'adversaire de la stabilité rationelle.

Ainsi nous vivons dans un monde cruel, où les relations humaines ne peuvent jamais être idéales—nous pouvons avoir la consistance et l'affection réciproque, mais pas en même temps que la passion profonde. Ou bien il est possible d'avoir des liens passionnels et dévoués, mais seulement au prix d'une troublante instabilité. On peut se demander comment un Zeus bienveillant pourrait créer un monde comme celui-là. Le Zeus tout-puissant ne peut-il pas faire mieux que ça pour ses enfants?

Je termine avec deux pensées. (1) Il se peut que Zeus n'ait pas voulu faire mieux. Dans les affaires affectives, comme pour tout le reste, nos goûts sont différents et il est possible que *notre* monde est réellement celui que Zeus voulait créer. Mais (2) Zeus se trouve probablement sous les mêmes contraintes que cet autre artisan divin, le Démiurge de Platon. Comme lui, et comme tous les artisans, le Zeus stoïcien doit travailler avec les matériaux qu' il a sous la main, et il n'est pas vraiment tout-puissant. Et nous, les êtres humains, nous devons nous débrouiller avec le meilleur des mondes possibles.

National Humanities Center, North Carolina
et Université de Toronto

THE HUNT FOR GALEN'S SHADOW

Alexander of Aphrodisias, *De anima* 94.7-100.17 Bruns Reconsidered

TEUN TIELEMAN*

1. After long years of comparative neglect, Galen of Pergamon (129-c. 210 CE) is being re-discovered as a philosopher in his own right. This re-appraisal is to be applauded, not least because he was taken seriously as a philosopher in his own day and beyond.[1] In fact, our earliest extant testimonies—a mere handful—concern his influence in regard to philosophical, not medical matters. Most notable are those from (or relating to) the important Peripatetic philosopher Alexander of Aphrodisias, who was Galen's junior by about a generation.[2] These testimonies have encouraged a comparison between their surviving writings from a doctrinal point of view. Thus Donini has argued convincingly that Alexander at *De anima* 24.18-26[3] engages in an (implicit) polemical dialogue with Galen (notably his *Quod animi mores*) on the view of the soul as a harmony of the body.[4]

The question of Galen's presence also arises in regard to the closing section of the *De anima* (94.7-100.17), which is concerned with the question where in our body the centre of command, or, as it was called, the 'regent part' (ἡγεμονικόν) of the soul, is located.[5] Alexander presents a battery of arguments in favour of the Aristotelian view that the regent part resides in the heart rather than the

* I regard it as an honour and a privilege to be able to dedicate this article to my esteemed teacher on his sixtieth birthday.

1 See Nutton (1984); cf. also Temkin (1973) 51ff., Frede (1981) 66.

2 Alexander dedicated his *De fato* to the emperors Septimius Severus and Caracalla (164.3 ff. Br.), who exercised joint rule between 198 and 209 CE. These are the only firm dates we have with regard to his life and career; cf. Todd (1976) 1. It is a fair assumption that he was born in the 150's or 160's. Galen was born in 129 and presumably died some time after 210: see Nutton (1984) 323; *id.*, (1987) 46 ff.

3 References give page- and line-number of the standard edition by I. Bruns in the *CAG*-series (Suppl. II, pars I, Berlin 1887).

4 Donini (1974) 148ff.; *id.*, (1982) 226-8, 232; cf. Mansfeld (1990) 3108n.217.

5 On this long-standing controversy in ancient philosophy and medicine see Mansfeld (1990), Tieleman (1996) xxxiiiff.

brain. A few decades earlier,[6] Galen had devoted no less than four books (viz. I-III and VI) of his *On the doctrines of Hippocrates and Plato* (hereafter *PHP*)[7] to the same issue. Drawing on his dialectical skills and extensive anatomical knowledge, he delivered a thundering vindication of the Platonic tripartition and trilocation. That is to say, he established the brain as the seat of Plato's rational part (commonly identified with the regent part[8]), refuting in the process the main Stoic and Peripatetic arguments in favour of the cardiocentric theory.

Naturally enough, it has been suggested that Alexander wrote the last section of *De an.* in conscious opposition to Galen.[9] Some scholars have even commented unfavourably on the strength of what is considered Alexander's response to Galen's challenge.[10] In view of what is otherwise known of Alexander's reactions to Galen's work[11] and of the impact of *PHP*,[12] it is quite plausible that Alexander had the argument of *PHP* forced upon his attention.

---

[6] *PHP* books I-VI were written during Galen's first stay in Rome, i.e. between 162 and 166 CE, see De Lacy (1978) 46-48. Alexander's *De anima* is usually dated to the final period of his career; see Moraux (1978) 304-5; Donini (1982) 231; cf. *supra*, n. 2.

[7] References give book-, chapter- and paragraph-numbers in Ph. De Lacy's edition (*CMG* V 4,1,2, 3 vols. Berlin 1978-82)

[8] Cf. Alex. *De an.* 98.24f., Gal., *PHP* II 5.81.

[9] Todd (1977); Moraux (1978) 293; Donini (1982) 232; Mansfeld (1990) 3109 n. 223.

[10] Moraux (1978) 293; Donini (1982) 231.

[11] Alexander, *In Top.* 549.24 Wallies mentions Galen alongside Plato and Aristotle as an authority whose views count as ἔνδοξα suitable for dialectical discussion. He composed two tracts against Galen's (lost) *On the First Mover* and *On Possibility* respectively. The former has been preserved in an Arabic abstract; see Rescher-Marmurra (1965). One of the Arabic mss. contains a notice saying that Galen wrote to Herminus a letter in which he criticized Aristotle's theory of motion; see Pines (1961) 23, Rescher and Marmurra (1965) 57f. Herminus was Alexander's teacher, see Simpl. *De caelo* 430.32ff. Heiberg. He may be identical to the Peripatetic philosopher and pupil of Aspasius, whom the young Galen heard lecture in Pergamum, *Aff. Dig.* 8.4, p.28.15f. De Boer. See further Moraux (1984) 361ff. On Alexander's affiliations with (proximate) contemporaries cf. also Sharples (1990). The identification of Alexander with Alexander of Damascus (*De praecogn.* 5.9-15 Nutton; *De Anat. Admin.* 2.216.6-8 K.)—first made in Arabic sources—is today generally rejected; see Todd (1976) 4ff. esp. 6 n.29, Sharples (1987) 1179 with nn. 18-21.

[12] See esp. *PHP* VII 1.1-4: books I-VI circulated among Peripatetics, Stoics and physicians and, if we may believe Galen, had already convinced some of these opponents. On the Peripatetic section of his audience see also II 3.23. In fact, books I-VI were written at the request of a Peripatetic, viz. Flavius Boethus, see *Lib. Prop.* 1, *SM* II p.96.19ff. Müller; cf. also *De praecogn.* 2.24, 5.9, 5.19 with Nutton *ad loc.*

This claim is not invalidated by the fact that Alexander does not refer explicitly to Galen in the *De an.* Both Alexander and Galen follow the common practice of avoiding names of contemporary opponents when dealing with their arguments.[13] For example Alexander directed his tract on the theory of motion against Galen without mentioning him by name.[14]

But it is one thing to assume that Galen looms in the background of Alexander's argument; it is quite another to substantiate and illustrate this assumption on the basis of textual evidence. In fact, a negative conclusion has been reached by Accattino in the most recent and fullest available discussion on the matter.[15] This discussion takes the form of an extensive critique of three parallels adduced by Todd.[16] These parallels, Accattino argues, fail to establish the thesis that Alexander uses arguments or ideas of Galen.[17] However, the removal of Todd's trio of parallels does not settle the issue satisfactorily. What we need is a systematic treatment involving more material from Galen. Oddly enough, neither Todd nor Accattino pays much attention to what might be called Galen's formal contribution to the controversy over the seat of the regent part—the *PHP*.

In the following pages, I will reconsider the relation between the closing section of the *De an.* and what is to be found in Galen's writings, most notably the *PHP.* I shall argue that Alexander does respond to specific arguments he had read in Galen. Meanwhile Accattino's critique may stand as a reminder of the strict criteria needed for assessing 'parallels' in terms of historical relations. Mere resemblances are not good enough. Many current arguments and ideas used in the controversy over the regent part were traditional and hence not confined to Galen and Alexander.

---

13 Tieleman (1996) 67ff., Sharples (1987) 1178f. The exegetical style of later ancient philosophy entailed a heavy concentration on the *ipsissima verba* of the past masters, notably Plato, Aristotle and Chrysippus. *PHP* books I-VI, with their extensive quotations, are a case in point. Likewise Alexander presents his *De an.* as an explication of Aristotle's doctrine (2.4-9). In much philosophical polemicizing of the period, contemporary opponents are thus involved without being explicitly or separately refuted.

14 See Rescher and Marmurra (1965), esp. 59.

15 Accattino (1987).

16 Todd (1977), esp. 117f., 121-3. See *infra*, nn. 33, 55.

17 In fact Todd (1977) 123 does not even claim that Alexander had read Galen but merely propounds an indirect kind of relation, i.e. one mediated by other authors.

Medical insights may have reached Alexander by a different route. The case for direct influence should therefore rest on specific features of Alexander's argument which are most easily explicable by reference to Galen. As will be shown, this question involves not only individual arguments and passages but also Alexander's overall strategy .

My argument is structured as follows. I shall begin by presenting some observations on the overall design and strategy of Alexander's demonstration (§ 2). Next I shall compare his arguments concerned with the nutritive and other faculties of the soul with the relevant passages in Galen (§ 3). This is followed by a few observations on Alexander's rebuttal of two encephalocentric arguments at the end of his demonstration (§ 4). Finally I shall draw some conclusions with special reference to Alexander's dialectical procedures (§ 5)

2. Alexander turns to the question of the seat of the dominating part (ἡγεμονικόν) of the soul (94.7-11) at the end of his work—a placement which attests to its importance:

> Where is the regent part of the soul, i.e. in which part of the body ? And does the soul reside in a substrate (ὑποκειμένῳ) that is numerically one, having differentiations only as to powers (δυνάμεις) and conceptually, or are the powers of the soul also separated from one another by location?

This scheme of options is common ground between Alexander, Galen and such Platonists as Porphyry and Iamblichus. As such, it provides a suitable point of departure.[18]

Alexander goes on to posit the general principle that in all things in which one thing is 'more perfect' (τελειότερον) and another 'less perfect' (ἀτελέστερον), the less perfect becomes perfect through a certain *addition*; hence where is the imperfect thing, there must also be the 'more perfect' one (94.11-13; cf. 28.14ff.). Alexander applies this to the psychic functions, starting with the least perfect among them, viz. the nutritive (θρεπτική) power. In an ascending series, each of the following functions is inferred from the presence of the preceding one. Thus the perceptive faculty, Alexander argues, cannot be located separately from the nutritive one (96.19-23).[19] And in the same section he argues that since the

---

[18] Gal. *PHP* VI 2.5, Porphyry Fr. 253 Smith; Iambl. *De an. ap.* Stob. *Ecl.* pp. 368.12-369.4 W. Cf. also Alex. *De an.* 94.1-3.

[19] Cf. Arist. *Iuv.* 3, 469a8ff.

heart is the source of taste and touch, the other senses must reside there too (96.25-8).[20] The series culminates in the theoretical intellect (ὁ θεωρητικὸς νοῦς), being the perfection of the soul (99.6).

This scheme constitutes so to speak the skeleton of the demonstration as a whole. It is fleshed out by additional arguments establishing the location of each of the main functions independently of the others. This concatenation of functions corresponds to the order in which the individual powers are treated in the main body of the work (27.1-92.11, recapitulated at 92.12-94.6): Alexander successively deals with the nutritive (94.17-96.10), the perceptive (96.10-97.15), the appetitive-cum-motive (97.15-99.1) and cognitive (99.1-10) powers. Each of these main powers is further subdivided, and the resulting sub-species are linked by inferences as well. We must note in particular his ploy of proceeding by *small* transitions, including those from one main function to another. Thus at 98.29-99.2 we have the following sequence: where is the appetitive (ὀρεκτικόν), there is also the volitional (βουλητικόν); and where is the volitional, there is the deliberative and rational (βουλευτικόν τε καὶ λογιστικόν) faculty.

The ordering of the main functions is loosely modelled on Aristotle's *De an.* Books II and III. As to the steps made from one function to another it is also worth comparing individual passages such as Arist. *De an.* B 2, 413b21-4[21] and the hierarchy of five functions, *ibid.* 3, 414a31-33. But the prominence given by Alexander to this inferential sequence is no doubt due to the influence of the (originally Sceptical) little-by-little argument or *sôritês*.[22]

Here Alexander was anticipated by Chrysippus' demonstration of the cardiocentric view in his *De an.*, from which Galen has preserved extensive quotations in *PHP* books II and III. In his account of what he regards as common opinion, Chrysippus started from the perception of certain passions, notably inflamed anger (ὀργή), arising in the heart. But then:

---

20 Cf. Arist. *Iuv.* 3, 469a13-17.

21 'In insects which have been cut in two each of the segments possesses both sensation and local movement; and if sensation, necessarily also imagination and appetition; for where there is sensation, there is also pleasure and pain; and where these, necessarily also desire' (Oxford transl.).

22 On the *sôritês* in general see Barnes (1982); Burnyeat (1982). For Chrysippus' use of it see *SVF* 2.665; cf. 1003, 1005, Cic. *ND* 2.164-166. Cf. Burnyeat (1982) 337f.

> given the fact that inflamed anger arises there, it is also reasonable that the other desires are there, and indeed the rest of the passions and the deliberations and whatever resembles these (*PHP* III 2.5 = *SVF* 2.890; cf. Alex. *De an.* 97.1-3).[23]

Galen tells us (III 2.4) that Chrysippus used this mode of reasoning throughout his demonstration, thus indicating, ones presumes, that the Stoic developed this common pattern of thought further in the light of considerations of a more philosophical and scientific kind.[24] The argument exemplifies Chrysippus' use of the *sôrites* for constructive purposes, just as he appropriated the Sceptical technique of *diaphônia*.[25] The use made of *sôrites* by Chrysippus and Alexander in this particular context is an effective means of countering the Platonic tripartition.[26]

3. Let us now take a closer look at those of Alexander's arguments which invite comparison with the relevant parts of *PHP*. Given the relation posited between things of greater or lesser perfection (see above) it is of prime importance for Alexander to establish the presence in the heart of the lowest or nutritive faculty: 'where the nutritive power is, there are also the more perfect ones' (94.17). Obviously, the nutritive faculty, being at the bottom of the scale, cannot be inferred from the presence of another one. Thus he devotes considerably more space to the principle of nourishment than to any of the other faculties (94.11-96.10).

Alexander begins by pointing to the need for a large supply of hot and wet material as indispensable for life and hence for the nutritive soul, affirming that the heart meets this requirement (94.17-20; cf. 96.5-8).[27] This passage (as well as 39.21-40.3, to which he refers) is closely similar to an argument paraphrased and criticized by Galen at *PHP* II 8.30ff.[28] For chronological reasons Galen cannot be attacking Alexander.[29] We are dealing with a traditional Peripatetic (and Stoic) argument reiterated by Alexander, who gives no sign of taking note of Galen's objections.

---

23 Also quoted at *ibid.* III 5.2 (*SVF* 2.89), II 7.11 (*SVF* 2.887).

24 *PHP* III 5.43-44 (= *SVF* 2.899); cf. III 3.7 with Tieleman (1996) 249 ff.

25 For the *diaphônia* see esp. Chrys. *ap.* Gal, *PHP* III 1.10-15 (*SVF* 2.885) with Mansfeld (1990) 3167ff. See also, *infra*, n. 61.

26 On Plato as Chrysippus' main butt see Tieleman (1996) 140f.

27 *PA* Γ 4,665b, *Iuv.* 4, 469b7ff.

28 See Tieleman (1996) 67ff.

29 *Supra*, nn. 2, 6.

Alexander next (94.21-6) draws an analogy between plants and animals with respect to growth and nourishment. In plants these physiological processes are directed from a single principle located between roots and stem. In animals too the nutritive and generative principles are identical. In them, Alexander briskly concludes, it is the heart which is the starting point of growth and nourishment. In other words, the nutritive power resides in the heart. Again, there is a parallel in Galen. At *PHP* VI 3.10-26 he draws what is unmistakably the same analogy. Although the passage of Alexander is much more concise than Galen's rather elaborate version, their arguments run clearly parallel. Of course, Galen argues that the liver, not the heart, is the analogue of the spot between the stem and roots of plants. The procedure of arguing from analogy, or similarity, can be traced back to the Aristotelian *Topics*.[30] But this elaborate application to the anatomy of plants and animals seems to be original with Galen.[31] Alexander simply reverses the argument into one in favour of the heart.

The plant analogy remains in force, though less prominently, in Alexander's subsequent observations, which concern the *structure* of the blood-vessels (94.26-95.6).[32] The blood is the ultimate form of nutriment, and the source of the vessels is the heart. But Alexander qualifies the conclusion that the heart is, or contains, the principle of nourishment by assigning to the liver a preparatory role in the digestive process. It is this view of the functions of the two organs which Galen refutes at some length at *PHP* VI 4. Alexander however does not seem to take this refutation into account.[33]

We should also note that Alexander goes on to point to the fact that the blood-vessels that grow from the heart are thicker near the source and ramify into ever thinner outshoots the farther they are removed from this source (95.4-6).[34] Galen continues his plant analogy (VI 3.13ff., cf. 6.43-44) in exactly the same way: the roots

---

30 *Top.* A 13, 105a20ff.

31 But Galen may owe something to the analogy between animals and plants drawn by Aristotle at *Iuv.* 2, 468a13ff., where the nutritive part is associated with the middle part of the body; cf. also *ibid.* 3, 468b17ff.

32 Cf. the phrase αἱ φλέβες ... ἐκ ... τῆς καρδίας ... ὡς ἐκ ταύτης τὴν ἀρχὴν ἔχουσαι τῆς βλαστήσεως. Alexander, like Aristotle, does not differentiate between arteries and veins, speaking of φλέβες ('vessels') only.

33 On this parallel cf. Todd (1977) 118, Accattino (1987) 455ff.

34 Cf. also Arist. *PA* Γ 5, 668b36ff.

of plants are structurally similar to the veins sprouting from the liver. So once again we may conclude that Alexander uses an argument of the same form to arrive at an opposite conclusion.

But this is not the end of our list. Alexander's next argument (95.6-8) resembles the one following in Galen (VI 6.20ff.), viz. the nutritive principle must be in the organ which is the first to be articulated in the embryo. Alexander claims that it is the heart for which this is observed (φαίνεσθαι) to hold true, whereas Galen argues that the observation of an embryo of a goat *in utero* confirms that the liver is the source of the veins. Alexander also points to the fact that the heart is the last organ to stop functioning. The idea that the heart is the first to move and the last to stop (so that its activity coincides with life itself) belonged to the traditional repertory of cardiocentric arguments. It is cited and criticized by Galen at II 8.23-24. Here, however, it serves to establish the location in the heart of the soul *tout court.* I assume that Alexander restricted the scope of this argument to the nutritive power because, as we have noticed, he is in need of arguments for the presence in the heart of this power in particular.

Alexander, *De an.* 94.17ff and Galen, *PHP* VI 3-7 run to a large extent parallel both as to the individual arguments used and as to the order in which they are presented. The relation between the two texts is characterized by the reversal of Galen's arguments. That is to say, Alexander argues that the indications adduced by Galen apply to the heart, not the liver (cf. 95.1-2). The term 'reversal' is all the more appropriate since Galen too constantly opposes the heart and the liver as competing alternatives.[35]

But there is more to be said. In Galen the distinctive properties of the liver and heart serve as signs (σημεῖα, τεκμήρια) of the essential nature of these organs.[36] This particular way of combining philosophical methodology—i.e. a basically Platonist method of division-cum-definition—with anatomical lore is peculiar to Galen, notably the argument of *PHP.*[37]

Alexander's battery of arguments concerned with the principle

---

[35] This is of course because he directs his argument against the Erasistrateans and Peripatetics, see e.g. VI 6.3ff. On the influence of Aristotelian physiology on Erasistratus cf. *Nat. fac.* III 4, p.165.7ff. Helmreich.

[36] See Tieleman (1996) 55ff., 60ff.

[37] See esp. the logical and methodological sections in Middle Platonist handbooks, notably Alcin. *Did.* c.5 and Clement, *Strom.* VII, esp. 7.17-21 on the role of properties as signs.

of nourishment is not yet exhausted. He continues with a few arguments (95.12-96.15) which are used by other authors to establish the location of the regent part. As far as Galenic parallels are concerned, we now have to switch from *PHP* VI to II. At II 4 Galen takes issue with a set of Stoic and Peripatetic arguments 'from position' (II 4.6ff., cf. Arist. *PA* Γ 4). According to Alexander, the heart must contain the principle of life since it occupies the midmost position in the body, which is *safest* and least vulnerable to ailments (95.12-16; cf. Arist. *PA* Γ 4, 665b25ff.).[38] Galen does not discuss this particular train of thought, though he speaks broadly of various possible arguments from position (II 4.12ff.). Alexander points to the chest (θώραξ) as the proper body of animal on which the organs have, as it were, grown; the common psychic faculty must be in the common bodily part.[39] Galen, for his part, refers to an (otherwise unknown) argument which appeals to the middle position of the heart *in* the chest (II 4.14).[40] Galen refers to the originally Aristotelian[41] argument that the heart lies in the middle of the body for the sake of an even distribution of the powers (δυνάμεων) sent out from the heart (II 4.12). Alexander uses this argument at 95.19-24, but restricts its scope to the distribution of nutriment and the nutritive principle for the reasons indicated above.[42]

At 96.10ff. Alexander proceeds to the second faculty of the series, viz. the perceptive (αἰσθητική) faculty. He argues that the nutritive and the perceptive powers must necessarily be located in one and the same place, or else animals would have two souls instead of one (and by the same token lose their individuality).[43] For Galen

---

38 This point is also made with regard to the perceptive faculty, 98.20ff.

39 This could reflect Arist. *Iuv.* 2, 468a13ff., where Aristotle says that the nutritive principle resides in the middle part of the body: some animals (wasps, bees) can be seen to survive for some time without heads or food receptacle (viz. the upper and lower parts of their structure). Cf. Alex. *De an.* 100.8ff. on which see *infra* p. 13f.

40 This may however reflect Aristotle's observation that in animals the place of the heart is in the middle of the breast (whereas in man it inclines slightly to the left), *PA* Γ 4, 666b7-9.

41 Arist. *PA* Γ 4, 666b18-20, 666a14-15; *MA* 9, 702b12-703a3; cf. Simpl. *In Arist. De caelo* p. 514.11-3 Heiberg.

42 But cf. Arist. *Iuv.* 4, 469a24ff. where the same argument is also used with regard to the nutritive-cum-perceptive function only.

43 Cf. 99.5 ff. where Alexander says that this implication is not inescapable in the case of the theoretical intellect: we may accept that it exists separately from the other functions without having to assume two souls—which is impossible. The fact that he takes into account a counter-argument is typical of his method, see *infra*, p. 278.

the doctrine that the psychic powers determine the shape of the bodily organs is related to—and justified by—a *scala naturae* expressed in terms of the three Platonic parts of the soul: plants possess only the desiderative part,[44] non-rational animals have the desiderative and the spirited part, human have the rational on top of the other two.[45] Here the non-rational parts of the soul coincide with the kind of soul possessed by non-rational animals. This *scala naturae* thus brings out the status of the non-rational (i.e. the desiderative-cum-spirited) as a distinct part of the soul.[46] This emphasis is typical of Galen, who, in *PHP* and elsewhere, describes the parts or forms (εἴδη) of the soul as distinct in kind (γένει) and being (οὐσία). On occasion he even speaks—in a way which is unwarranted by the Platonic text—of a plurality of souls.[47] So here too Galen would seem to be the most likely target of Alexander's critique.[48]

---

[44] Cf. Pl. *Tim.* 77b with Gal., *In Tim.* 11.24-27 Schröder. In the context Galen connects this point to his view that the desiderative part is different in essence (οὐσία) from the rational part; *pace* those who posit one essence with three powers (δυνάμεις) Plato speaks of forms or parts. This may be directed against Platonists like Severus who were swayed by Peripatetic criticism to abandon soul-partition in order to save the unity (and immortality) of the soul; cf. Deuse (1983) 104ff.

[45] *PHP* V 6.37-9, where Galen ascribes this Platonizing chain of being to Posidonius (F144 E-K). Posidonius, for his part, conceived of the soul in terms of powers (δυνάμεις) not parts, let alone separate souls; like Aristotle and most Stoics he assigned the powers (i.e. the regent part) to the heart. See *PHP* V 4.3; 7.9-10; 7.50; VI 2.5 (Posid. Frs. 142, 144, 145, 146 E-K).

[46] See *supra*, n. 18 with text thereto. Similarly, Alex. *De an.* 27.8ff. (who of course speaks of δυνάμεις), Nemes. *Nat. hom.* 16, 73.3-6 Morani.

[47] *PHP* V 4.3, 7.9-10; 7.50; VI 2.5, *In Hipp. Epid.* p. 272.22-273.1 Wenkebach-Pfaff. For a plurality of souls distinct in essence see esp. *De meth. med.* X, 635.6ff. K., *In Plat. Tim.* Fr. II 1.87 Schroeder. Cf. also *De moribus*, p. xvi Walzer, where Galen presents it as one of the options available in the debate concerned with the structure of the soul. On his conception of the soul against the backdrop of contemporary Platonism cf. the concise discussion of Deuse (1983) 100ff.

[48] It might be supposed that Alexander's target was the Pythagoreanizing Platonist Numenius of Apamea, who is known to have distinguished between a rational and a non-rational soul: Numen. *ap.* Porph. *ap.* Stob. *Ecl.* I 49.25a (350.25-351.1 Wachsmuth) = Numen. fr. 44 Des Places, Porph. fr. 253 Smith (272.18 ff.). Here Numenius is mentioned as one among a plurality of authorities, who remain anonymous but may include Galen; cf. Nemesius referred to *supra*, n. 46. Numenius' *floruit* is generally dated to around 150 CE or the later 2nd century CE; Frede (1987) 1038 f. So as far as chronology is concerned he might have been Alexander's butt. But on closer thought this seems far less likely. The cosmic perspective motivating Numenius' doctrine is something quite different from the anatomical and physiological aspects highlighted by both Galen and Alexander. On Numenius's conception of the soul

But can we be reasonably confident about this anti-Galenic purport? Is Alexander not barring a purely theoretical implication? We would prejudge the issue if we were to argue that Alexander knew this implication as being distinctive of Galen. Clearly the anti-Galenic motivation of this passage has to gain plausibility at least to some extent from the indications to the same effect provided by other passages. But if we add this passage to our list, it can be seen to fit into the general pattern exhibited by Alexander's way of dealing with Galenic views and arguments. As such, it presents another instance of a straightforward reversal of Galen's position. The point is well-chosen. Galen's emphasis on the spatial separation of the parts of the soul gave rise to serious problems as to their coherence and interactions on the physiological level—a problem he never adequately faced.[49]

Finally I wish to call attention to 98.7-9:

> One could learn that the regent part of the soul is in the heart also from the structure (κατασκευῆς) of the organ itself, which it has received from Nature, which does nothing without reason.

Again, the colouring of this passage immediately recalls Galen. What we have here is Galen's 'strong' teleology encapsulated in his oft-repeated adage 'Nature does nothing without reason'.[50] Considered in this light, distinctive properties of organs have to pertain to their essence or function. This teleological perspective is associated by Galen with the form, or structure, of organs in particular.[51] In *PHP* it is a distinctive property of the heart that it is connected with all the arteries, just as the brain is the centre of the nervous system (*PHP* I 7). The liver is designated as the structural centre of the veins with the same purport (*PHP* VI 5).

Of course, in a by now familiar way, Alexander draws a

---

see Deuse (1983) 62ff., esp. 79ff., Frede (1987) 1070 ff. At this stage, moreover, he was not yet a factor on the philosophical stage; see the evidence surveyed by Frede (1987) 1034 ff. Alexander, at any rate, nowhere refers to him explicitly.

[49] Cf. Mansfeld (1991) 138ff.

[50] I do not of course wish to imply that this dictum is confined to Galen, cf. e.g. Arist. *De an.* 9, 432b21, 12 434a31, *PA* B 13, 658a5, Γ 1, 661b24; Alex. *Fat.* 178.12, *De an.* 27.9, 13, 28.5. The theme of Nature's design in shaping the organs of the body is also prominent in Alexander's preface, 2.10-25.

[51] Cf. also *De usu partium* X 5.6, vol. 2, p. 75 Helmreich, *Nat. fac.* III 8, p. 227.19ff., Helmreich. Similarly, Alex. *De an.* 2.19-20, in a context strongly reminiscent of Galen's *De usu partium*, a work which, if we may believe Galen, was popular among Aristotelians, see *Lib. Prop.* 2, p.100.18-23 Müller.

conclusion opposite to that of Galen, arguing that the properties of the heart indicate that it is the seat of the regent part. Most notable is his reference to 'nerves' (νεῦρα) on the heart, following Aristotle, *PA* Γ 4, 666b14-16 (98.15; cf. 76.14ff.). It was Galen who had devoted much effort in subverting this supposed observation, arguing that what Aristotle saw were nerve-like tissues rather than nerves and that the presence of nerves (if granted) is not peculiar to the heart anyway (*PHP* I 8.3-15; 10.6-10; II 8.26-28).

4. Having established the heart as the seat of the regent part, Alexander turns to the arguments advanced in favour of the brain (99.30-100.17). On the whole these, he says, are 'empty'. Nonetheless, he singles out for treatment two of them which 'lay claim to a certain degree of plausibility' (100.1-2). The first appeals to clinical experience: mental disease is cured by tending to the head, just as mental afflictions result from disease or damage of the same organ. Alexander for his part points to the principle that all parts are connected through sympathy, which he backs up with an appeal to the rational design of the body: '... since every organ is beautifully adapted (scil. to the other parts)' (100.3-4). In other words, the idea of sympathy demolishes those arguments which infer the presence of psychic functions from certain physical effects or affections.[52] Thus it can also be used against the stock cardiocentric argument—used by Alexander himself (97.1-3)—which appeals to the physical effects attendant on certain passions, notably the pulsation of the heart in anger or fear.[53] Galen too invokes the principle of sympathy when confronted with this argument (*PHP* II 7). On the other hand he himself appeals to the effect of afflictions of the head.[54] In addition, we should once again note the distinctively Galenic colouring of much of Alexander's subject-matter.[55] So it seems that Alexander again turns the tables

---

[52] The history of this rejoinder can be traced back to a treatise as early as the Hippocratic *On the sacred disease* (later 5th cent. BCE), ch. 17; cf. 14.

[53] Chrysippus, arguing in his *On the soul* in favour of the cardiocentric position, is sensitive to the counter-argument from sympathy too: see *PHP* III 5.41ff. with Tieleman (1996) 252ff.

[54] See further the part played by *sympatheia* at *Loc. aff.* III 5, with Mansfeld (1990) 3110.

[55] Cf. also *Loc. aff.* III 5, 8.158.1ff. K., *Meth. med.* XIII 21, 10.928.2-932.17 K. with Mansfeld (1990) 3141ff., 3110 n. 225. Todd (1977) 122f. suggests that Alexander's argument is based on his misunderstanding of *Caus. Symp.* 7, 1.137 K., but this seems less likely; cf. Accattino (1987) 467f. Likewise Todd (1977)

on Galen. His point about sympathy produces a stalemate between a pair of evenly matched (counter-)arguments.

A similar strategy is followed with regard to experimental observations of animals which stay alive for some time after their hearts have been removed, thus warranting, it seems, the inference that the heart cannot be the seat of the soul. Observations of this type, Alexander points out, can be adduced in support of either side of the debate (100.9: κοιναὶ πρὸς ἀμφότερα[56]). Cases of animals (e.g. the tortoise and the chameleon) that can dispense with a heart for some time are balanced by others (not specified) which survive, or at least do not die instantly from, decapitation.[57] Alexander adds that both the heart and brain when removed often continue to exercise their proper functions too (100.9-13). In other words, insofar as these observations are concerned, the stalemate between the opposing views persists.

Galen had adduced an observation of the same kind. Sacrificial bulls whose heart lies already on the altar move and bellow in panic until they die through loss of blood (*PHP* II 4.45-9). He adds that the excised heart continues pulsating, thus indicating its proper function—independent of the brain—in accordance with the Platonic tripartition (*PHP* II 4.48).[58] Likewise he establishes the mutual independence of the heart and the brain through experiments whereby the vessels (veins, arteries, nerves) connecting the two organs are intercepted (*PHP* II 6, III 6). This point is echoed by Alexander, who stresses that either organ, when separated from the rest of the body, often continues to exercise its proper functions. In the case of the brain, he may be thinking of the continuation of the perceptive powers in certain kinds of animals. However this may be, Alexander urges against those who point to the continued

121f. assumes that the same passage has inspired *De an.* 98.20-24 (on so-called 'cardiac disease'). But Alexander's point about not allowing oneself to be misled by terminology has a closer parallel at *PHP* II 8.3-17 (on καρδαλγία).

[56] Cf. *PHP* IV 1.5, where Galen accuses Chrysippus of 'taking both sides' (ἐπαμφοτερίζων) in the debate over the number of parts of the soul. On the affinities between the methodologies of Galen and Alexander, cf. also *infra*, n. 61.

[57] Similarly Cic. *ND* II 24 (*SVF* 1.513), Tert. *De an.*15.6; cf. Mansfeld (1990) 3111f.

[58] Galen associates the pulse - as a non-rational motion independent of the brain and essentially different from voluntary motion, with anger, fear and sexual arousal as characteristic of the Platonic spirited part, cf. e.g. *PHP* III 1.30ff., VIII 1.23; cf. II 7.17ff.

activity of the brain that the same holds good of the heart. If intended as a rebuttal of Galen, this is beside the point, for the latter—in accordance with the Platonic trilocation—assigns to either organ its own distinctive motion. So the issue is not that of function vs. loss of function. But if Alexander fails to meet Galen's argument, that does not mean that he did not respond to it. It is noteworthy that Alexander says that each organ, when removed from the body, retains its 'proper activities (οἰκείας ἐνεργείας, 100.12f.)'. This very point is stressed by Galen in the context of the same kind of observations, where it supports his anatomically based Platonic tripartition (*PHP* II 4.49; II 6.10).[59]

Alexander's claim that arguments of this type tell in favour of neither alternative recalls his view of the purpose of a dialectical investigation in search of the truth in an Aristotelian manner. The ability to discern the strong points—and argue oneself—in favour of one of two opposed positions is integral to his concept of dialectic.[60] This made him hospitable to the Sceptical technique of *diaphônia*. But the Aristotelian dialectician cannot of course rest content with a stalemate of conflicting views and arguments, i.e. he tries to balance the arguments pro and con in order to determine which of two tenets is to be accepted, or at least preferred. Jaap Mansfeld has established and analysed Alexander's use of this technique on the basis of his *De fato*.[61] For our purposes it is interesting to note that it is part of this procedure that Alexander is interested not only in arguments or facts supporting either of the views at issue, but also in points to be scored against *both of them*. Those of the two positions which appears more vulnerable to these objections, and hence more complicated or muddled, is the one to be discarded in favour of the other. Indeed, the thesis to be accepted becomes clearer insofar as the alternative can be shown to be muddled.[62] Hence the exposure of the invalidity of both the encephalocentric and cardiocentric arguments from sympathy at

---

59 Cf. also *PHP* I 6.10, III 6.5, V 3.5, VI 6.44.

60 *In Top.* 27.7–29.16 Wallies; *In Met.* 173.5-174.7 Hayduck.

61 The procedure of starting from an existing disagreement with a view to eventually accepting one of the available options can be traced back to Chrysippus; see *supra*, n. 25. Mansfeld (1987) 185 f. points to *PHP* V 4.1, where Galen argues that one should suspend judgement whenever opposed views are of more or less equal credibility, but that if one of them turns out to be far more credible than the other, we have to assent to it as being *true*.

62 See esp. *Fat.* 164.21-165.8 Br. with Mansfeld (1987) 184 f.

100.2-13. But, as we have noticed, the preceding argument too bristles with rebuttals of what can be found in Galen's work.

5. What are we to conclude from the preceding survey of resemblances and differences ? Many of the arguments used by Alexander had started their career in Aristotle's *PA* Γ 3-4 and *Iuv.* 2-4 and found their way into the traditional debate concerned with the seat of the soul, where they served, often in a somewhat modernized form, on the Peripatetic side. Alexander uses some of these without adapting them to meet Galen's objections. It would however be rash to assume that he did not know, or chose to ignore, Galen's critique and simply drew on a repertoire of traditional Peripatetic arguments. Not only would such a *dialogue des sourds* be implausible in the light of his knowledge of Galen's work.[63] Alexander has been shown to use specifically Galenic notions and arguments and to do so in a way which can best be explained on the assumption that he had indeed read the Galenic passages I have been referring to.[64]

Large parts of Alexander's argument read like an inverted mirror image of Galen's demonstration in *PHP* books II and VI. The reason is that Alexander applies the technique of turning Galen's arguments and concepts against him, just as he elsewhere appropriated Stoic concepts and arguments to anti-Stoic ends.[65] This is the familiar technique of reversal (περιτροπή) in its wider sense of taking a statement of one's opponent and turning it against him.[66]

The opposition of two alternative views (or arguments) is also at issue in the so-called *Placita* tradition as reconstructed by Diels in his *Doxographi Graeci*.[67] Jaap Mansfeld has demonstrated Galen's knowledge of this tradition on the basis of *De locis affectis* III 5.[68]

---

63 See *supra*, n. 11.

64 See *supra*, p. 3.

65 Cf. Todd (1976) 27f., Moraux (1984) 335-6, 359, Sharples (1987) 1178 with further references.

66 The wider sense gained currency under the influence of the rhetorical tradition; cf. e.g. Arist. *Rh.* B 23, 1398a3-4. The technical term περιτροπή stems from dialectic, where it designates self-refutation in the narrower sense of refuting a thesis from its own contents. One of the most famous instances in ancient philosophical literature occurs in Pl. *Th.* 171a-b, where Protagoras' Man is the Measure-thesis is turned against itself. See further Burnyeat (1976), esp. 65.

67 Berlin 1879; several reprints. A new study devoted to the so-called doxographic tradition is being prepared by Jaap Mansfeld and David T. Runia.

68 Mansfeld (1990) 3141ff.

Here Galen presents a list of issues—including that of the location of the regent part—which runs closely parallel to the relevant sections in the *Placita* tradition as to both content and wording. Interestingly enough, Galen says that the many different statements about the regent part are the subject of dialectical disputation, thus affording a rare glimpse of the *Sitz im Leben* of doxographic schemas.[69] In addition, we must note the question-type familiar from the *Placita* tradition, which opposes two alternatives ('whether P or not-P' or 'whether X or Y'). This recalls the so-called θέσις ('theoretical problem', 'general question') as a concept of ancient dialectic and rhetoric.[70] Indeed, Clement of Alexandria (150-c. 215 CE), *Strom.* 8.14.4 mentions the question of the location of the regent part ('The regent part: is it in the heart or in the head?') as a typical instance of a θέσις. A θέσις is marked by its stress on the opposition between two views at issue. Both of them are presented, though one is eventually to be preferred. Clearly, this suits Alexander's concept of dialectic.[71]

It may not be too far-fetched to compare the Δικτυακά ('Hunting-Net Arguments') by Dionysius of Aegae, in which fifty medical theses were both defended and refuted in a way reminiscent of the much earlier Δισσοὶ λόγοι ('*Double Arguments*,' *DK* 90).[72] Unfortunately, only the *theses* have been preserved (Photius, *Bibl.* Codd. 211 and 185).[73] But these certainly attest to the gambit of opposing and reversing *medical* tenets. No. 49 is: ὅτι οὐ περὶ καρδίαν τὸ διανοητικόν, ἀλλὰ περὶ κεφάλην καὶ ὅτι ἀνάπαλιν. Other theses (viz. nos. 36-50) are also similar or identical to those discussed by Galen in *PHP* and Alexander in the final section of the *De an.* Thus nos. 41 and 42, concerned with the question whether or not the heart or the liver is the source of the veins, correspond to *PHP* VI 3-6 and *De*

---

69 *Loc. aff.* 8.157.17-18 K.

70 On the relation of doxography to the θέσις see Mansfeld (1990) 3193ff. See further Throm (1932); Runia (1981) 116f.

71 For Alexander's view on the θέσις see *In Top.* 78.21-83.2; cf. also 27.12ff., 82.19ff. Wallies. At 76.1ff. (in the section dealing with the wider concept of πρόβλημα) we have three physical issues familiar from the *Placita* tradition, which he of course knew: 'whether the world is eternal or not'; 'whether the world is spherical or not', 'whether the soul is immortal or not'; see Aëtius, *Plac.* II 4, II 2, IV 6.

72 Photius' preface indicates pairs of argument and counter-argument, see p.336.1-6 Deichgräber. 'Antilogies' of this type were subsumed under the θέσις, see Alex. *In Top.* 27.17f. Wallies with Throm (1932) 170f.

73 Also printed, with a brief introduction, by Deichgräber (1930) 335-340.

an. 94.25ff.[74] No. 48 dealt with the question whether or not the heart is the source of the nerves (cf. *PHP* I 8, 10; *De an.* 98.15).[75] The formulation in terms of polarities recalls the theses in the doxographic texts. The phrase καὶ ὅτι ἀνάπαλιν ('and in reverse', 'and contrariwise') may indicate the reversal of argumentation exemplified by the (lost) pairs of arguments.

According to Photius, Dionysius' booklet was 'quite useful for dialectical exercise and the knowledge of some doctrines belonging to medical theory' (*Cod.* 185). It has been assumed that the pairs of arguments were designed to induce suspension of judgement.[76] But we have to be cautious in drawing precise conclusions about historical affiliations. The exact dates and identity of the author of the Δικτυακά must remain uncertain (though the issues listed seem to presuppose Galen's work).[77] But it is tempting to assume that the lost arguments reflected the same kind of method as is followed by Alexander in the closing section of his *De an.*

To conclude. We have found a number of parallels which relate Alexander's argument to Galen's in the various ways I have been arguing. In the light of this evidence we may, in Alexander's own fashion, tip the scales in favour of the thesis that *De an.* 94.7–100.17 is primarily designed as a response to Galen. Particularly striking are Alexander's use of the *sôritês* and his technique of inverting Galen's arguments. Thus Alexander succeeds in exposing a few weak (and blind) spots of Galen's position, especially those relating to the spatial separation between the 'parts' of the soul. The cardiocentric view still had a future lying ahead.*

Utrecht University

---

74 See *supra*, p. 271f.

75 See *supra*, p. 276.

76 For this reason the author has been identified with a Dionysius who was a Methodist physician of the 1st cent. CE. Alternatively, he has been described as an Empiricist and Sceptical doctor. But his identity must remain uncertain. Eustathius, *In Il.* 1192 (= vol. 4, p. 355.10-13 Van der Valk) aligns the author of the Δικτυακά with the dialecticians and the Sceptics; cf. Deichgräber (1930) 336.

77 E.g. No. 15 at *Cod.* 185 'that heat does not vary in quality' clearly states the view of Lycus of Macedonia as discussed by Galen, *Adv. Lyc.* c. 3, pp. 8.15-14.4 Wenkebach. Lycus belonged to the generation of Galen's teachers; cf. *De anat. admin.* 2.449f., 470 K.

* I should like to thank Keimpe Algra, Han Baltussen and David Runia for their comments on an earlier version. Research for this article was made possible by a fellowship of the Royal Dutch Academy of Arts and Sciences.

Bibliography

Accattino, P. (1987) 'Ematopoiesi, malatti cardiaca e disturbi mentali in Galeno e in Alessandro di Afrodisia', *Hermes* 115: 454-473.

Barnes, J. (1982) 'Medicine, experience and logic', in J. Barnes et al. (eds.) *Science and Speculation. Studies in Hellenistic Theory and Practice* (Cambridge 1982) 24-68.

Burnyeat, M.F. (1976) 'Protagoras and Self-Refutation in Later Greek Philosophy', *Philosophical Review* 85: 1, 44-69.

——, (1982), 'Gods and Heaps', in M. Schofield and M.C. Nussbaum (eds.), *Language and Logos.* Studies in ancient Greek philosophy presented to G.E.L. Owen (Cambridge).

Deichgräber, K. (1930) *Die Griechische Empirikerschule. Sammlung der Fragmente und Darstellung der Lehre* (Berlin).

Deuse, W. (1983) *Untersuchungen zur mittelplatonischen und neuplatonischen Seelenlehre*, Mainz.

De Lacy, Ph. (ed.) (1978–84) *Galen: On the Doctrines of Hippocrates and Plato, Corpus Medicorum Graecorum* V, 4, 1, 2 (Berlin).

Donini, P., (1974) *Tre studi sull'Aristotelismo nel II sec. d. C.*, Torino.

——, (1982), *Le scuole, l'anima, l'impero: la filosofia antica da Antioco a Plotino*, Torino.

Frede, M. (1981) 'On Galen's Epistemology', in V. Nutton (ed.), *Galen: Problems and Prospects* (Cambridge) 65-86; repr. in *id.*, *Essays in Ancient Philosophy* (Oxford 1987) 279-98.

——, (1987) 'Numenius', *ANRW* II 36.2, 1034-75.

Mansfeld, J., (1988) 'Diaphonia: the Argument of Alexander *De fato* Chs. 1-2', *Phronesis* 33: 181-207.

——, (1990) 'Doxography and Dialectic: The *Sitz im Leben* of the *Placita*', *ANRW* II 36.4, 3056-3229.

——, (1991) 'The Idea of the Will in Chrysippus, Posidonius, and Galen,' in J.J. Cleary (ed.), *Boston Area Colloquia on Ancient Philosophy* series, Vol. V, 107-45.

Moraux, P. (1978) 'Le "De anima" dans la tradition grecque. Quelques aspects de l'interprétation du traité de Théophraste à Thémistius', in G.E.R. Lloyd and G.E.L. Owen (eds.) *Aristotle on Mind and the Senses* (Cambridge) 281-324.

——, (1984) *Der Aristotelismus bei den Griechen.* 2. Band. Der Aristotelismus im I. und II. Jh. n. Chr. (Berlin/New York).

Nutton, V. (1984) 'Galen in the eyes of his contemporaries', *Bulletin of the History of Medicine* 58 (Baltimore) 315-24; repr. as Study nr. III in *id.*, *From Democedes to Harvey: Studies in the History of Medicine.* Variorum Reprints (London 1988).

——, (1987) 'Galen's Philosophical Testament: "On my own opinions" ', in J. Wiesner (ed.), *Aristoteles. Werk und Wirkung* (Berlin–New York) 2.27-51.

Pines, S. (1961) 'Omne quod movetur necesse est ab aliquo moveri: A Refutation of Galen by Alexander of Aphrodisias on the Theory of Motion', *Isis* 52: 21-54.

Rescher, N. and Marmura, M.E. (1965) *The Refutation by Alexander of Aphrodisias of Galen's Treatise on the Theory of Motion.* Translated from the Medieval Arabic Version, with an Introduction, Notes, and an Edition of the Arabic Text. Islamic Research Institute, Islamabad, Pakistan.

Runia, D.T. (1981) 'Philo's De aeternitate mundi: The problem of its Interpretation', *Vig. Chr.* 35: 105-151; repr. in *Exegesis and Philosophy: Studies on Philo of Alexandria* (London 1981).

Sharples, R.W. (1987) 'Alexander of Aphrodisias: Scholasticism and Innovation', in W. Haase (ed.), *Aufstieg und Niedergang der Römischen Welt* II 36.2 (Berlin–New York) 1177-1243.

——, (1990) 'The school of Alexander ?', in R.R.K. Sorabji, *Aristotle Transformed; the Ancient Commentators and their Influence* (London), 83-111.

Temkin, O. (1973) *Galenism. Rise and Decline of a Medical Philosophy* (Ithaca/London).

Throm, H. (1932) *Die Thesis. Ein Beitrag zu ihrer Geschichte und Entstehung* (Paderborn).

Tieleman, T. (1996) *Galen and Chrysippus on the Soul. Argument and Refutation in the* De placitis *Books II-III.* Philosophia Antiqua 64 (Leiden).

Todd, R.B. (1976) *Alexander on Stoic Physics* (Leiden).

——, (1977) 'Galenic Medical Ideas in the Greek Aristotelian Commentators', *Symbolae Osloenses* 52: 117-34.

DOTI NATURALI, ABITUDINI E CARATTERE NEL *DE FATO* DI ALESSANDRO

PIERLUIGI DONINI

Di Alessandro di Afrodisia lo studioso a cui è dedicato questo volume ebbe occasione di occuparsi più di una volta; tuttavia lo scritto *De fato* è fra le opere del commentatore fino a oggi l'unica cui Jaap Mansfeld abbia dedicato un intero saggio. Non ripeterò qui quale importanza abbia quel lavoro in vista dell'interpretazione complessiva dello scritto; prenderò invece in considerazione un piccolo suggerimento, a mio giudizio estremamente fecondo, che Mansfeld diede in quelle pagine. Egli prometteva allora di ritornare successivamente sulla questione: il che non essendo finora avvenuto, spero di fare cosa non sgradita al destinatario del presente volume se mi servo dello spunto da lui fornito non certo con la pretesa di indovinare le sue intenzioni, ma nella speranza di far progredire la discussione e di attenuare intanto una notevole difficoltà di interpretazione che a suo tempo io stesso avevo sollevato.[1]

Occorre in primo luogo ricordare i termini del problema, che concerne la possibilità di riconoscere ad Alessandro e al suo trattato una sostanziale coerenza di pensiero fra le due parti in cui lo scritto si articola (cioè i capitoli 1-6[2] contenenti la dottrina del fato che Alessandro considera aristotelica e la parte rimanente con la sua lunga polemica contro il determinismo). L'obiezione che molti anni addietro[3] avevo mosso ad Alessandro era che trattando nel cap.6 il carattere degli uomini come risultante dalla 'naturale costituzione'[4] dell'anima (e quindi come portatore del destino, almeno

[1] Il saggio di Mansfeld cui mi riferisco è '*Diaphonia* : the Argument of Alexander *De Fato* Chs.1-2', *Phronesis* 33 (1988) 181-207. Come la tesi illustrata in quel lavoro contribuisca a chiarire la natura e le finalità del *De fato* ho argomentato nel saggio citato qui sotto (n. 23) 5043 n. 54.

[2] O meglio, a rigore, 3-6 dato che Mansfeld, *art. cit.*, ha persuasivamente mostrato che entrambi i capitoli 1-2 servono come proemio.

[3] Nel libro *Tre studi sull'aristotelismo nel II secolo d.C.* (Torino 1974) 164-165 e 171-173.

[4] *De fato* 6, p. 170,17.20. Se Alessandro può parlare di una costituzione naturale (*physikè kataskeue*) dell'anima, mi pare sicuro che egli si riferisce implicitamente alla sua dottrina dell'anima come risultante dalla mescolanza degli elementi (per cui cfr. *De anima* p. 2,25–11,13).

nelle intenzioni di Alessandro ormai dimostratosi identico alla natura)[5] egli contraddiceva insieme Aristotele e se stesso: il suo maestro, in quanto il commentatore attribuiva unilateralmente alle doti naturali il peso determinante nella formazione del carattere ignorando il fatto che nelle *Etiche*[6] Aristotele aveva spiegato che il carattere è il risultato delle abitudini contratte fin dalla prima fanciullezza nel corso dell'educazione e in generale dei processi di socializzazione; e poi anche se stesso, in quanto nelle pagine successive del trattato (e specialmente nei capitoli 27–29) Alessandro avrebbe molto più correttamente riprodotto la teoria aristotelica ridimensionando, o meglio addiritura tacendo l'apporto delle doti naturali in vista della formazione del carattere morale e facendo derivare l'*ethos* dalle abitudini contratte dopo la nascita. Non è poi necessario riferire qui anche tutti gli interventi successivi nella discussione, dato che sia la difesa di Alessandro tentata da qualche studioso,[7] sia i rilievi che a mia volta mossi a questi tentativi ritenendo di confermare le mie precedenti obiezioni[8] mi sembrano oggi non conclusivi e forse diventano completamente superflui qualora si raccolga e si sviluppi il suggerimento espresso nell'articolo di Mansfeld. Il quale fu appunto l'unico a notare[9] che gli esempi di cui Alessandro si serve nel cap.6 (pp. 170,21–171,4) al fine di provare l'identità del fato con il carattere naturale sono tutti quanti 'esempi di κακίαι nel senso di Aristotele *EN* II–V'.

---

[5] Questo è appunto il risultato della discussione del *De fato* nei capitoli 3, p. 166,15–6, p. 170, 9. Non dico nulla in questa sede dell'altra maggiore difficoltà del cap.6, il rapporto fra la natura di cui Alessandro parla nelle pagine ora citate e 'l'*oikeia physis* di ciascuno' (individuo o tipo?) di cui parla nel seguito della pagina 170.

[6] *EN* II, 1-4; cfr. *EE* II 1 (1220a 13 sgg.) - 2.

[7] Mi riferisco soprattutto a P. Thillet e all'introduzione alla sua edizione del *De fato*, Alexandre d'Aphrodise, *Traité du destin* (Paris 1984) CXV-CXXI—ma a dire il vero io non avevo affatto detto, come apparirebbe dal sunto di Thillet a p. CXVI, che la natura 'détermine totalement chaque individu' secondo la teoria esposta nel cap. 6. Avevo spiegato a p. 164 del libro citato sopra (n. 3) che la causalità naturale secondo Alessandro è operante solo per la maggior parte dei casi e che il caso di Socrate, di cui Alessandro parla alla fine del capitolo, p. 171,11-16, è appunto una delle eccezioni ammesse dalla regola del 'per lo più'. Ho così l'impressione che la critica che mi muove A. Zierl, in Alexander von Aphrodisias, *Ueber das Schicksal* (Berlin 1995) 160, dipenda piuttosto dalla lettura delle pagine di Thillet che da quella del mio libro.

[8] Nel saggio 'Il De fato di Alessandro. Questioni di coerenza', in *Aufstieg und Niedergang der römischen Welt*, herausg. von W. Haase und H. Temporini, II. 36.2 (Berlin-New York 1987) 1246-1247.

[9] *Art.cit.* (n. 1) 182 n. 4 *sub fin.*

Questa preziosa osservazione ha soltanto bisogno di essere difesa e precisata per quanto riguarda il tipo del καρτερικός che compare in 170,25 sgg.;[10] esso infatti, cioè il tipo dell'uomo resistente o dotato di fermezza, non è di per sé presentato come un carattere vizioso nei libri dell'*EN* dedicati all'analisi delle virtù etiche e anzi compare nella tabella delle virtù in *EE* II 3, 1221a 9 come una medietà buona fra gli estremi della mollezza e della κακοπάθεια (che è l'attitudine a sobbarcarsi ogni fatica, pena o strapazzo). Se invece, come appare da 170,26, Alessandro ha trasferito sulla καρτερία precisamente quell'attitudine al κακοπαθεῖν che per l'*EE* caratterizzava un estremo vizioso, sembra chiaro che egli ha inteso farne appunto una qualità non positiva; e lo spunto per una simile valutazione può essergli venuto da *EN* VII (= *EE* VI) 7, 1150a 36 dove egli trovava che per Aristotele la continenza (ἐγκράτεια), che è già di per sé non identica alla virtù (secondo *EN* VII 1, 1145a 36) e di questa è certamente meno apprezzabile, era comunque a sua volta ancora preferibile alla καρτερία. Era facile concludere che in questo modo per Aristotele la καρτερία veniva a trovarsi a due gradi di distanza dalla virtù etica. Il carattere eccessivo che Alessandro, o quanto meno la sua scuola, attribuiva al καρτερικός è del resto con ancora maggior chiarezza fatto rilevare dall'opuscolo sul fato conservato al termine della *Mantissa.*[11] Di conseguenza, siamo effettivamente autorizzati a interpretare tutti gli esempi di Alessandro a p.170,21–171,4 come riferiti a caratteri inferiori alla virtù etica e genericamente identificabili con il vizio.[12]

Si aggiunga ora a tutto ciò la considerazione che nel cap.6 del *De fato* l'unico esempio di un carattere che fuoriesce dal condizionamento naturale e 'grazie all'esercizio fondato sulla filo sofia' risulta alla fine 'migliore della sua natura' (171,11-16) è quello di Socrate: dunque il caso raro e positivo di un individuo

---

[10] Il suo nome è integrato da Bruns a 170,25 sulla base del riscontro fornito dall'opuscolo sul fato in *Mantissa* 185,29. L'integrazione si può considerare sicura (curiosamente invece Thillet, p.10,25 della sua edizione, preferisce un plurale).

[11] P.185,29 ὑπερβολή. Sulla questione d'autenticità dell'opuscolo non è qui necessario pronunciarsi .

[12] Si noti per di più che nella proposizione di 171,4-7, che è evidentemente destinata a commentare tutta l'esemplificazione precedente includendo dunque anche il caso della *karteria,* Alessandro parla di 'mali presenti' riferendosi a quelle situazioni in cui ognuno dei tipi illustrati sarebbe meritatamente caduto. Questo conferma il loro carattere comune, negativo perché o identico o assimilabile al vizio.

eccezionale[13] il quale smentisce la regola del 'per lo più' che vincola invece la maggior parte dell'umanità al destino già segnato nella costituzione naturale dell'anima. La situazione presupposta da Alessandro nel cap. 6 è pertanto chiara: l'idea fondamentale è che il destino è identico alla natura interpretata nel senso, perfettamente ammissibile per un aristotelico,[14] di una causalità che opera solo per la maggior parte dei casi e non di necessità, ammettendo dunque eccezioni. In quanto è un agente naturale, 'per lo più' il carattere iscritto nella costituzione naturale dell'anima determina la qualità morale e il destino degli uomini; ma questo condizionamento ha soltanto esiti moralmente deteriori: i caratteri condizionati dalla costituzione naturale (cioè quelli della maggior parte degli uomini) sono caratteri moralmente inferiori alla virtù. Le eccezioni previste dalla statistica aristotelica sono invece quelle di chi è capace di *migliorare* la propria natura grazie all'educazione ricevuta—o anche, eventualmente, grazie a un'autoeducazione filosofica, come sembra probabile che si debba pensare relativamente a Socrate. Si registra allora immediatamente una prima, benché ancora solo parziale concordanza fra il cap. 6 e il 27, dato che anche secondo quest'ultimo testo l'esistenza di uomini virtuosi è cosa estremamente rara:

> infatti non vediamo che in possesso delle virtù sono tutti, oppure la maggior parte degli uomini (il che sarebbe il segno delle cose che accadono conformemente a natura); ma bisogna contentarsi di trovarne anche uno solo, il quale mediante l'esercizio[15] e

---

[13] Il che P. Thillet *op.cit.* (n. 7) CXVII n. 4 sembra voler mettere in dubbio. Confesso di non comprendere bene le sue argomentazioni e osservo a mia volta che, se la costituzione naturale determina 'per lo più' la sorte degli uomini (come Alessandro più volte ripete nelle pp. 170-171), ci devono per forza di logica essere anche dei casi che sfuggono alla regola del 'per lo più' e allora mi sembra del tutto legittimo considerare questi casi come 'eccezioni' (cioè eccezioni alla regola, alla norma, alla maggioranza statisticamente rilevata). Che Socrate sia precisamente una di queste eccezioni non mi pare che possa essere materia di dubbio: egli è appunto riuscito a essere 'migliore della sua natura' (171,16). Del resto, se non si considerasse eccezionale il suo caso, si perderebbe anche un importante motivo di concordanza con il cap. 27 (si veda il seguito della discussione sopra nel testo).

[14] Cfr. p.es. Aristot. *Rhet.* I 10, 1369a 35-b 2; *Phys.* II 8, 198b 35 ; *An.pr.* I 3, 25b 14 (altri passi in Bonitz, *Index aristotelicus* 836a 43-48). Quanto ad Alessandro, che la natura ammetta eccezioni è ripetutamente segnalato in *De fato* 6: cfr. specialmente 169,28-170,9; 170,14-16 e forse anche 16-18, se *para* nella linea 17 deve essere interpretato come vuole R.W. Sharples, *Alexander of Aphrodisias on Fate* (London 1983) 47 e 129.

[15] ἄσκησις, come nel caso di Socrate in 6, p. 171,16. Alla p. 198,23 leggo e traduco ἀναγκαῖον seguendo il ms. Marciano, Bruns e Orelli. Sharples

l'insegnamento mostra la naturale superiorità dell'uomo sugli altri animali, dato che da sé aggiunge quel che è necessario e che mancava alla nostra natura (198,19-23).

L'accordo con il cap. 6 è qui davvero notevole: prevalenza statistica dei caratteri deteriori; rarità estrema delle persone virtuose; la virtù raggiunta mediante l'esercizio e l'educazione; l'incapacità della *physis* a conferire da sola la virtù—su tutti questi punti i due testi implicano o sostengono le stesse posizioni, per di più sempre all'interno della generale nozione aristotelica della natura come agente che opera 'sempre o per lo più' . C'è tuttavia un aspetto della questione per il quale la coincidenza delle tesi espresse da Alessandro nei due passi non è totale. Nel cap. 6 la possibilità di migliorarsi rispetto a quanto comporterebbe la natura appare sì fuori della normalità statistica (è infatti quanto rimane al di fuori del 'per lo più', che opera nel senso di vincolare la maggior parte dell'umanità al suo carattere naturale); ma non è così drasticamente limitata come nel cap. 27 a un solo individuo: Socrate è certamente un caso eccezionale, ma nel cap. 6 non è detto che sia anche l'unico. Come spiegare questa difformità di posizioni?

Ora la tesi dell'estrema rarità degli uomini virtuosi può essere fatta derivare anche da Aristotele, è vero;[16] ma la formulazione di Alessandro in *De fato* 27, p. 198,20 sembra davvero eccessiva per un aristotelico e di fatto viene a coincidere con la tesi stoica. Il risultato è paradossale: il medesimo autore che si sforza lungo tutto il trattato di distinguere la filosofia aristotelica da ogni possibile versione del determinismo enuncia in quel passo una proposizione che altrove rimprovera aspramente agli avversari stoici di aver sostenuto;[17] e la enuncia senza che nemmeno ve ne sia la stretta necessità: non gli bastava forse dire che gli uomini per bene non essendo tali per natura—perché allora sarebbero buoni tutti quanti gli uomini, o almeno la loro maggioranza—il loro numero si restringe a un piccolo gruppo? Perché mai dire, invece, 'a uno solo'? Può ben darsi, dunque, che sugli avversari di quella filosofia la pressione

(seguito poi da Zierl) accetta invece l'avverbio ἀναγκαίως di tradizione indiretta. Si introdurrebbe così una nozione di necessità assoluta che mi sembra quanto di più sgradito ed estraneo all'aristotelismo ci possa essere per Alessandro. 'Αναγκαῖον si intende invece facilmente nel senso di *Metaph.* Δ 5, 1015a 22-26: è 'quel che è necessario perché il bene si realizzi'.

16 Come osserva Sharples, *op.cit.* (n. 14) 162.

17 Cfr. *De fato* 28, p. 199,16 sg.

delle tesi stoiche fosse ancora fra il secondo e il terzo secolo tale, da imporre come ovvie persino tesi che a una riflessione critica attenta avrebbero dovuto essere rifiutate; ma è anche vero che nel complesso del *De fato* la concezione di Alessandro non è comunque pienamente identificabile con quella stoica. Può essere assimilata alla posizione stoica la tesi che ci siano, o che siano esistiti, soltanto uno o due uomini per bene; ma certamente Alessandro non accetta mai il corollario stoico che ne consegue a proposito della rimanente umanità—che si tratterebbe cioè di una massa di stolti, folli e malvagi tutti ugualmente immersi nell'errore e nel vizio. Ben lontano da queste convinzioni, Alessandro le censura anzi esplicitamente in una pagina del *De fato*.[18] La sua convinzione[19] sembra dunque piuttosto essere che l'umanità comune si trovi in una condizione che è certamente ancora lontana dalla virtù, ma si colloca tuttavia in una posizione in qualche modo mediana fra la virtù e il vizio completo. Quel che allora occorre ammettere è che, almeno in vista dell'argomento del cap.6, Alessandro ha deciso di non tenere conto di alcuna differenza fra i caratteri che risultano comunque inferiori alla virtù: tutti risultano assimilati dal fatto di essere legati al carattere naturalmente costituitosi nell'anima.

Prima di proseguire nell'analisi del nostro problema vorrei segnalare un aspetto interessante dell'esemplificazione di Alessandro a p. 171, perché esso può avere qualche importanza in relazione alla (ancora irrisolta) questione del rapporto fra il trattato maggiore e l'opuscolo sul fato incluso nella *Mantissa*. Nel suo articolo Mansfeld segnalò[20] come 'a flagrant contradiction of major importance' il fatto che nella pagina del trattato l'esempio di Socrate serve a illustrare la rilevante eccezione che si può introdurre al dominio del fato sulle vite umane, mentre nell'opuscolo (p. 185,14 sg.) lo stesso Socrate (in compagnia di Callia) è presentato come esempio della regola generale che il fato governa gli individui. E apparentemente questa contraddizione dovrebbe allora corroborare il sospetto[21] che l'opuscolo non sia opera di Alessandro, ma di un suo scolaro. Dopo aver accettato per qualche tempo l'osservazione di Mansfeld sono ora giunto alla conclusione che essa è infondata e

---

[18] Cap. 28, p. 199,18-22.

[19] Come si potrebbe anche indurre da altre pagine della sua opera. Si veda in proposito il mio saggio citato sopra (n. 8) 1254-1256.

[20] 182 nota 4, *sub fin.*

[21] Espresso da Mansfeld nella stessa pagina già citata qui sopra, n. 20.

che l' uso del nome di Socrate nei due esempi non può servire a discriminare in nulla le due diverse opere in cui lo leggiamo. Questo perché, come mostra precisamente il fatto che esso compaia abbinato con il nome di Callia, nell'opuscolo il nome di Socrate deve essere letto, secondo l'uso aristotelico ben noto,[22] senza alcun preciso riferimento al personaggio storico: è soltanto un modo di riferirsi a persone reali, ma la cui individuazione precisa è irrilevante: è l'equivalente, insomma, dei nostri Tizio, Caio o Sempronio. Diversa sarebbe stata l'importanza del caso se l'opuscolo avesse citato Socrate in riferimento o alla stessa situazione in cui compare nel trattato (il giudizio espresso su lui da Zopiro), o comunque a un episodio preciso della vita del personaggio storico di quel nome.

Siamo forse ora in grado di capire il ragionamento di Alessandro benché esso rimanga largamente implicito e possiamo finalmente rendere conto in modo coerente tanto delle affermazioni del cap. 6, quanto di quelle dei capitoli 27-29. E' verissimo, infatti, che in questa serie di capitoli, apparentemente contraddicendo il 6, si riconduce la formazione del carattere all'educazione, all'esercizio, alle abitudini e non più alla natura; ma si doveva aggiungere (cosa che finora nessuno ha fatto) che in quei capitoli Alessandro intende parlare soprattutto e, anzi, quasi esclusivamente della formazione dei caratteri virtuosi, cioè del modo in cui si diventa φρόνιμοι : solo pochissimi e brevissimi sono gli accenni alla formazione dei caratteri viziosi (e di questi ci occuperemo in un secondo tempo). Se dunque il cap. 6—quando sia stato debitamente interpretato l'esempio di Socrate—concorda con 27-29 quanto all'ammissione che una personalità virtuosa, formata come tale dalle abitudini contratte con l'esercizio e l'educazione, è realmente un'occorrenza molto rara e rappresenta un'eccezione alla regola che dice che la maggioranza degli uomini è inferiore alla misura della virtù, tutto il discorso di Alessandro può assumere una sua coerenza anche se lascia implicite troppe cose e sorvola inoltre su difficoltà tutt'altro che marginali. Il significato complessivo potrebbe essere questo.

Il fato è davvero identico alla natura, come vuole il cap. 6, e cioè è identico negli uomini al destino già iscritto nella costituzione naturale della loro anima. Ma questo dominio del fato non si estende alla totalità degli uomini: come prevede la dottrina di Aristotele, la natura può funzionare come agente decisivo soltanto per una

---

22 Cfr. Bonitz, *Index aristotelicus,* 359b 56 e 741b 45.

maggioranza di casi. Dunque, soltanto per la maggior parte dei suoi rappresentanti individuali l'umanità non andrà al di là del carattere iscritto nella costituzione naturale (e fatale) dell'anima: le cui potenzialità devono però essere state pensate da Alessandro come di per sé unicamente negative. Questa è infatti l'inevitabile illazione che dobbiamo trarre dal cap. 6. Ma come pretendere allora senza contraddirsi che sia anche vero (come sostiene il cap. 27, p. 198,29) che 'i caratteri degli uomini diventano di questa o quella qualità in forza delle differenti abitudini'? Bisogna semplicemente ammettere che Alessandro abbia sottinteso una premessa di questo tipo: se non si contraggono buone abitudini, è inevitabile contrarre invece quelle contrarie e cattive. Se dunque c'è mancanza totale di buona educazione, o se l'educazione impartita risulti male impostata e carente, la maggioranza dell'umanità non assumerà affatto quelle buone abitudini che potrebbero correggere le potenzialità negative della costituzione naturale: contrarrà invece abitudini cattive; ma a loro volta queste non faranno altro che confermare e irrigidire quanto era già iscritto nel patrimonio naturale della costituzione psichica degli individui. In tal modo non risulterà falso né dire (come accade nel cap. 6) che il carattere è negli uomini fissato dalla costituzione psichica assegnata dalla natura: questo è infatti vero per la maggioranza dell'umanità, per la quale il risultato finale dei processi di assuefazione è purtroppo perfettamente conforme ai presupposti naturali; né dire (come invece accade nel cap. 27) che i caratteri umani divengono tali o talaltri in conseguenza delle differenti abitudini contratte: quest'affermazione è infatti vera incondizionatamente per quanto riguarda le (poche) persone virtuose e i *phronimoi*, che divengono tali soltanto grazie alle buone abitudini assunte dall'esercizio e dall'educazione; e rimane vera in modo qualificato riguardo alla moltitudine dei non-virtuosi, nei quali le cattive abitudini contratte per difetto di educazione portano alle conseguenze estreme il patrimonio naturale del carattere.

Giunti a questo punto del nostro ragionamento è facile tuttavia indovinare un'obiezione. Ammesso che si elimini in tal modo la contraddizione che si era creduto di scoprire fra le due parti del trattato di Alessandro e che tanto nel cap. 6 quanto in quelli successivi (27-29) il commentatore si attenga costantemente all'idea che il carattere è già naturalmente determinato nella maggioranza degli uomini che rimane inferiore al livello della virtù, mentre è prodotto dalle buone abitudini in coloro che riescono a diventare persone per bene—ammesso dunque tutto questo, che ha a fare però una simile concezione con Aristotele? Al quale sembra ovviamente impossibile attribuire una siffatta bipartizione e distinzione dei modi in cui gli uomini svilupperebbero il loro carattere; impossibile, in particolare, attribuire una simile accentuazione della rilevanza delle doti naturali e per di più soltanto in vista dello sviluppo di un carattere moralmente deteriore. Certamente l'obiezione sarebbe ragionevole, né io intendo dire ora che la teoria di Alessandro corrisponde perfettamente a quella di Aristotele. Ma credo di dover aggiungere ancora, nonostante tutto, un ulteriore argomento a discarico di Alessandro: che cioè egli poteva in buona fede esser convinto di aver offerto un'interpretazione e una sistemazione adeguata e coerente del punto di vista di Aristotele.

A proposito del contributo che le doti naturali potrebbero dare alla formazione del compiuto carattere degli uomini il pensiero di Aristotele è infatti abbastanza oscillante[23] e non chiaramente definito; per modo che Alessandro aveva ragione di trovarsi in difficoltà davanti alle diverse proposizioni aristoteliche relative al problema e, secondo la sua radicata tendenza, doveva allora cercare di proporne un'interpretazione unificata e tale da giustificare il maggior numero possibile dei testi aristotelici che trattavano della questione. L'aspetto che forse a noi sembrerà il più arrischiato di tutti nell'interpretazione di Alessandro—vale a dire il giudizio così radicalmente negativo dato a proposito delle potenzialità naturalmente presenti nell'anima—poteva dunque essere da lui giustificato quanto meno fondandosi sul testo di *EN* VI (= *EE* V) 13, 1144b 4-9 secondo cui ciascun tratto del carattere è già naturalmente presente negli uomini, ma tuttavia 'disgiunto dal senno appare manifestamente dannoso', tanto da poter essere paragonato da Aristotele alle qualità degli animali, oltre che dei bambini. Posto che il conseguimento del 'senno'[24] richiesto per trasformare gli

---

[23] Mi sia consentito a questo proposito rinviare al mio libro *Ethos. Aristotele e il determinismo* (Alessandria 1989) cap. 5. Per la tendenza di Alessandro a offrire interpretazioni capaci di armonizzare e far concordare fra loro tutte le tesi e le proposizioni aristoteliche devo rinviare al mio saggio 'Testi e commenti, manuali e insegnamento: la forma sistematica e i metodi della filosofia in età postellenistica', in *Aufstieg und Niedergang der römischen Welt*, herausg. von W. Haase und H. Temporini, II.36.7 (Berlin-New York 1994) 5041. Il *De anima* offre abbondanza di esempi in proposito: il commento di P. Accattino–P.L. Donini a questo trattato (che è attualmente in corso di stampa) ne segnala un gran numero.

[24] *Nous* in VI 13,1144b 9.

'abiti naturali' in vere e proprie virtù dovrebbe essere unicamente il risultato dei processi educativi correttamente impostati—questa è appunto la lezione generale che si dovrebbe ricavare dall'*EN*—Alessandro aveva qualche buona ragione per indurre che l'assenza di quei processi non poteva far altro che condurre all'acquisizione di cattive abitudini; e aveva anche ragione, oltre a ciò, di pensare che queste cattive abitudini non sarebbero state altro che l'inevitabile (naturale e anche, secondo lui, fatale) sviluppo di quanto era già naturalmente iscritto nella costituzione originaria dell'anima: se appunto egli aveva posto come fondamento della sua costruzione la dichiarazione di *EN* VI 13 a proposito del naturale fondamento di ogni tratto del carattere individuale, ma anche della negatività di qualsiasi aspetto di tale carattere che rimanesse dissociato dalla corretta razionalità. E infine, tenuto conto delle lamentele di Aristotele a proposito della scarsa cura che le città greche dedicavano alla formazione dei cittadini[25] (una situazione che difficilmente poteva apparirgli migliorata ai tempi suoi), aveva ragione anche di concluderne che per la maggior parte degli individui sarebbe stato fatale il rimaner vincolati al carattere già determinato dalla natura; mentre le eccezioni previste dalla regola di quel fatale 'per lo più' gli permettevano di soddisfare d'altra parte l'esigenza aristotelica tante volte chiaramente espressa, che cioè la virtù morale ripetesse la sua origine dalle abitudini e dall'educazione. La concezione che Alessandro si era fatta del carattere e dei modi della formazione di esso potrebbe dunque davvero essere rimasta la stessa per tutto il trattato ed essere ricondotta all'esigenza di trovare una sistemazione coerente[26] per i differenti giudizi dati da Aristotele a proposito delle doti naturali. Nelle pagine in cui doveva enunciare una dottrina 'aristotelica' del fato gli risultava utile limitare la propria considerazione alla maggioranza dell'umanità che non andava oltre il suo carattere naturale; nelle pagine in cui doveva parlare

---

[25] *EN* X 9, 1180a 24-30.

[26] Un esempio significativo: in *EN* II 1, 1103a 18 sgg. Aristotele nega che le virtù etiche siano 'per natura' (φύσει) e non fa alcun cenno all'esistenza di particolari doti innate del carattere, né negative, né positive; osserva però che le virtù nascono in noi 'che siamo naturalmente preparati a riceverle' (πεφυκόσι δέξασθαι) e siamo poi portati a compimento dall'abitudine. Alessandro riecheggia da vicino questo passo a 198,3-6 parlando di un'attitudine e di una potenza ricettiva delle virtù che la natura ci avrebbe concesso, ma (ovviamente) non ne tiene alcun conto nel cap. 6, dove invece poteva valersi degli accenni agli 'abiti naturali' reperibili nel VI libro dell'*EN*.

specificamente del carattere virtuoso poteva invece prendere in considerazione l'eccezione costituita dalla minoranza delle persone per bene e rendere così giustizia alla teoria aristotelica che derivava il carattere dalle abitudini.

Non credo che si avrebbe ragione di obiettare alla spiegazione che ho qui proposto l'eccessiva quantità dei passaggi che essa integra o supplisce nel ragionamento di Alessandro (cioè, che Alessandro non dice mai esplicitamente che l'assenza delle buone abitudini comporterebbe automaticamente che se ne contraggano di cattive; o che non segnala mai esplicitamente di aver inteso rendere ragione di questo o di quel passo aristotelico concernente le doti naturali). Si deve tenere conto di due fatti—e di entrambi insieme. In primo luogo, il *De fato* non è un commentario ad alcun testo aristotelico, ma uno scritto in cui Alessandro riassume ed espone le proprie vedute relativamente a un'importante questione largamente dibattuta nella filosofia dal IV secolo in poi; che alcuni passaggi del ragionamento e gran parte dei riferimenti[27] al testo aristotelico restino impliciti è perciò semplicemente quanto ci si deve attendere da un'opera che non può raggiungere il livello di tecnicità che è invece tipico dei commentari.[28] In secondo luogo, se è vero che il *De fato* non è un commentario ad alcuna opera di Aristotele, non meno vero è tuttavia che la sua composizione presuppone certamente il lavoro di esegesi tipicamente svolto da Alessandro nei suoi commentari: qualsiasi pagina dell'opera è il risultato evidente[29] di una puntuale riflessione su qualche testo del corpus aristotelico. E se anche non fosse sicuro che Alessandro compose un commentario all'*EN* (come invece giustamente insiste a ricordarci Mansfeld),[30] una lettura nemmeno troppo approfondita

---

[27] Salvo casi episodici come quelli di 166,23 o di 167,20.

[28] Si confronti con quello del *De fato* il caso del trattato *De anima* che può essere messo in relazione al precedente commentario allo scritto di Aristotele dallo stesso titolo (in proposito, si veda l'introduzione di Accattino—Donini al *De anima* nell'edizione ricordata sopra – n. 23). Anche senza arrivare a parlare di carattere 'semipopolare' del *De fato* (per il quale cfr. Thillet, *op. cit.*, – in n. 7 – CXXV) e pur ammettendo con Sharples, *op.cit.*, (n. 14) 18 che il libro contiene anche parti di elevata tecnicità, rimane il fatto che in esso Alessandro non si impegna direttamente mai nell'esegesi di testi aristotelici che siano richiamati esplicitamente e analizzati parola per parola, come invece accade nei commentari.

[29] Il commento di Sharples basta a suggerirlo. Sul metodo di lavoro di Alessandro mi sia consentito di rinviare ancora una volta al commento di Accattino-Donini al *De anima* di prossima pubblicazione.

[30] *Art.cit.* (n. 1) 182 n. 4, cfr. anche R.W. Sharples, 'Alexander of Aphro-

del suo trattato sul destino dovrebbe bastare a suggerirci che egli doveva aver lungamente e seriamente meditato sulle pagine di almeno quella fra le tre etiche del Corpus (certamente, inoltre, su un'*EN* che includeva già i libri comuni).[31]

Ma è infine doveroso che aggiungiamo a questa difesa della coerenza di Alessandro anche l'ammissione che l'interpretazione ora proposta non è in grado di eliminare tutte le difficoltà. Sull'origine del vizio i capitoli 27-29 del *De fato* hanno, come si è detto, qualche raro accenno che non è sempre possibile far concordare con la tesi generale che ho creduto di attribuire ad Alessandro. Una spiegazione è possibile trovare per l'implicito accenno di p. 198,29;[32] ma l'esordio del capitolo 27 rimane sotto molti aspetti problematico:

> coloro che sono in possesso delle virtù furono a se stessi causa dell'acquisizione della virtù in quanto, invece[33] di trascurarlo, scelsero quel che è meglio; e press'a poco così (παραπλησίως) coloro che si trovano nei vizi (197, 6-8).

L'idea di un'originaria opzione (ἑλόμενοι!) a favore della virtù è forse difficilmente riconducibile ad Aristotele e alla sua etica;[34] tuttavia essa appare alquanto più attendibile in Alessandro, special-

---

disias: Scholasticism and Innovation', in *Aufstieg und Niedergang der römischen Welt* II.36.2, herausg.von W. Haase und H. Temporini (Berlin-New York 1987) 1186. Che Alessandro avesse una conoscenza anche di *EE* e *MM* non era dimostrabile secondo F. Dirlmeier, in Aristoteles, *Magna Moralia* (Berlin 1958) 103-104, ma si veda ora il commento di Accattino-Donini a proposito di *De an.* p. 89,1-7.

31 La conoscenza, quanto meno, del II e del III libro dell'*EN* risulta chiara dal cap. 27 (si veda anche qui sopra, n. 26) e quella delle definizioni e dell'analisi delle virtù dianoetiche nel libro VI risulta indubitabile p.es. da passi come *De an.* 66,16-20. 80, 24–81,9.

32 Sopra, p. 291.

33 Tutte le edizioni posteriori a Bruns accettano qui la congettura ἀντί.

34 Quanto di più vicino si può trovare a quest'idea è probabilmente la (problematica e limitativa) dichiarazione di *EN* III 5, 1114b 22-24 che 'noi uomini siamo in qualche modo corresponsabili' dei nostri abiti morali—un passo molto discusso, su cui si vedano da ultimo D. Frede, 'Necessity, Chance, and 'What happens for the most part' in Aristotle's Poetics', in *Essays on Aristotle's Poetics,* ed. A. Oksenberg Rorty (Princeton 1992) 203, inoltre il mio libro citato sopra (n. 23), 102-103. Molto più plausibile sarebbe invece stato per Alessandro sostenere la tesi più modesta della semplice 'volontarietà' degli abiti etici: cfr. R. Sorabji, *Necessity, Cause and Blame. Perspectives on Aristotle's Theory* (London 1980) 266-69; inoltre il mio saggio 'Volontarietà di vizio e virtù (Aristot. *Eth. Nic.* III 1-7)', in *Etica, politica, retorica. Studi su Aristotele e la sua presenza nell'età moderna,* a cura di E. Berti e L.M. Napolitano Valditara (L'Aquila 1989) 3-21.

mente se si tiene conto del modo in cui è illustrato l'esempio di Socrate nel cap. 6, p. 171,11-16: in quel caso si può probabilmente davvero parlare di un'autonoma scelta[35] dell'individuo di migliorarsi e di darsi un'educazione filosofica, tanto più se si trattava per Socrate prima di tutto di rifiutare le limitazioni che le sue naturali tendenze gli avrebbero imposte. E non mancano in Alessandro alcuni altri accenni che fanno pensare che per lui una scelta fondamentale di vita, una conversione alla virtù o alla filosofia come frutto di decisione personale fosse diventata una nozione ovvia e una prospettiva reale:[36] egli avrebbe così felicemente risolto un punto che Aristotele (in un ben diverso quadro storico) aveva lasciato quanto meno poco chiaro. Ma ciò che nel passo di 197,6-8 risulta perfettamente oscuro o, a essere sinceri, completamente inattendibile è il trattamento riservato all'origine del vizio: che cosa può infatti significare la proposizione che 'press'a poco così' (cioè press'a poco come nel caso dell'origine delle virtù: non si può intendere altrimenti) andrebbero le cose anche per le persone che si trovano a essere viziose? Per mantenere un'analogia con il caso della virtù si deve pensare che in qualche momento della loro esistenza vi sia stata da parte di esse (che numericamente devono per di più rappresentare la grande maggioranza dell'umanità!) una consapevole scelta di attenersi al carattere naturale e una rinuncia formale ad assumere buone abitudini. Ma sarebbe grottesco immaginarlo e infatti Alessandro non lo dice: dice semplicemente che le cose andrebbero 'press'a poco allo stesso modo',[37] lasciando

---

[35] Cfr. spec. 171,13 προαίρεσις κατὰ τὸν βίον.

[36] Così sono indotto a pensare anche da 170,24 con l'accenno a 'qualcosa di più bello' che si realizzerebbe nel vizioso. La costituzione del testo in questo passo è estremamente difficile (si veda l'apparato di Sharples), ma forse qualcosa di meglio di quanto finora si è tentato è ancora possibile suggerirlo. Veramente impossibile mi pare la soluzione di Thillet, nel cui testo bisognerebbe comunque correggere l'accento del verbo a p.10,24 scrivendo ἐκπέσῃ. Sennonché non sembra che ἐκπίπτω possa mai avere un significato transitivo e causativo—suggeritomi dal fatto che Thillet traduce 'l'ait fait sortir de son vice'—e bisognerebbe dunque dare al verbo il solito suo significato intransitivo: qualcosa di più bello che realizzandosi nel vizioso 'cade fuori', fuoriesce dalla malvagità, un' espressione tortuosa e innaturale, dato che il senso che ci attendiamo è invece precisamente quello assunto dalla traduzione di Thillet. Questo senso si può ottenere, certo, con la congettura di Diels (accolta infatti da Sharples) ἐκσείσῃ, che è però alquanto lontana dalla lezione tradita εκπισητησ. Come mi suggerisce oralmente Gianfranco Gianotti, si potrebbe allora pensare a ἐκπιέσῃ: 'comprima fuori, costringa a uscire' (cfr. Polibio 18.32.3).

[37] Παραπλησίως mi pare meglio tradotto da Thillet (à peu près) che da

dunque intuire che esiste una qualche differenza fra il caso dell'origine della virtù e quello del vizio, ma guardandosi bene dal precisarla. In realtà, nei capitoli 27-29, in cui si ricollegava più chiaramente alla tesi aristotelica dell'origine degli abiti morali (tutti, sia quelli virtuosi, sia quelli viziosi) dai processi di assuefazione, Alessandro era in certo senso costretto a sottolineare l'esistenza di una fondamentale identità fra le modalità di formazione della virtù e quelle del vizio; ma doveva anche nello stesso tempo non smentire in maniera troppo evidente quanto aveva già esplicitato nel cap. 6 a proposito dell'origine dei caratteri viziosi in contrapposizione a quello del saggio Socrate: di qui, da questo disagio, viene probabilmente la formulazione generica e reticente della linea 197,8.

Notevole sembra un altro passaggio del ragionamento di Alessandro nel cap. 27, in cui c'è un'allusione inequivocabile, ma anche alquanto problematica, alla teoria del cap. 6. Nel corso di un argomento inteso a mostrare che le virtù non nascono in nessun senso per natura, Alessandro osserva (a 197,30—198,3) che

> niente di impossibile bisogna richiedere alla natura (essa è infatti la misura del possibile e dell'impossibile; infatti la virtù è perfezione e compimento sommo della *natura propria* di ciascuno ed è impossibile che qualcosa che è imperfetto sia nella perfezione, ma quel che è stato generato è imperfetto non appena generato).

Il concetto di οἰκεῖα φύσις, natura propria, è precisamente quello che appare centrale nella teoria del fato esposta nel cap. 6; sennonché, là la natura propria è unicamente collegata al carattere deteriore e al destino delle persone non virtuose, tanto da indurci a pensare che quel che si ha alla nascita come costituzione naturale dell'anima sia destinato a tradursi in un carattere vizioso ogni volta che non intervenga l'educazione (o l'autoeducazione) mediante le buone abitudini. Nei casi eccezionali in cui questo intervento ci sia, l'opera dell'educazione consisterebbe allora essenzialmente nel cancellare o radicalmente emendare il carattere naturale (così appunto ci dice anche l'esempio di Socrate) e nessun positivo contributo questo carattere dovrebbe poter dare alla costituzione della personalità virtuosa. Infatti, coerentemente con queste assunzioni, implicite o esplicite che siano, lo stesso cap. 27 insiste a presentare il contributo che la natura darebbe alla virtù soltanto nei termini di

---

Sharples (similarly). Non è infatti ὁμοίως, né ὡσαύτως.

una 'capacità *ricettiva*'[38] della virtù stessa: la mera attitudine a far sviluppare in sé la virtù grazie alle buone abitudini e all'insegnamento. Ma, perché si possa parlare della stessa virtù come del compimento e della perfezione (*teleiotes*) della *natura propria* di ciascuno, occorre invece che quella natura propria sia stata pensata da Alessandro almeno in questo passo del cap. 27 in modo non esclusivamente negativo, ma quanto meno neutro: intendendo cioè le doti della costituzione naturale come qualcosa di ambiguo e realmente suscettibile di essere completato anche nel senso migliore.[39] Di qui si intuisce quanto risultasse difficile per Alessandro la normalizzazione e la sistemazione delle tesi aristoteliche; e altri scritti inclusi nelle raccolte delle sue opere minori confermano che egli stesso, o qualche suo scolaro, deve essersi affaticato più volte e senza troppo successo sull'arduo problema delle doti naturali e della loro valutazione in sede di etica.[40]

Non è il caso di infierire ancora su Alessandro insistendo sul fatto che nemmeno una volta che si siano spiegate così, come appunto egli cercò di fare nel *De fato,* le modalità di formazione dei caratteri virtuosi e viziosi la sua difesa dell'autonomia e del potere di autodeterminazione da parte dell'uomo diviene realmente più forte; infatti, anche concessagli da parte nostra la possibilità dell'opzione originaria in favore del bene e della virtù, rimane comunque il guaio che il carattere del φρόνιμος ormai costituitosi come tale risulterà non meno vincolante di quello (considerato espressione del 'fato', cioè della natura) della moltitudine dei non-saggi. Non

---

38 δύναμίς τε καὶ ἐπιτηδειότης δεκτική 198,5 – chiaro ricordo, come si è detto (sopra, n. 26), di EN II 1.

39 Nel senso, dunque, in cui parla delle doti naturali la *Politica* VII 13, 1332b 1-3. Sono però evidenti le ragioni per cui Alessandro non poteva adottare in modo esplicito questa soluzione: a parte il fatto che la *Politica* parla della presenza innata solo di 'alcune' doti e non di tutte, se Alessandro avesse ammesso che tali doti erano fondamentalmente ambigue e potevano essere risolte in meglio o in peggio soltanto dai processi di assuefazione, avrebbe anche dovuto rinunciare a identificare il fato con una natura a cui non poteva più attribuire la forza di determinare il corso successivo degli eventi quanto meno nella maggior parte dei casi. L'intera sua teoria dell'identità tra fato e natura avrebbe così dovuto limitarsi alla sola considerazione del livello della generazione nelle specie biologiche senza poter discendere alle qualità degli individui umani (o, tutt'al più, dei tipi). Per qualche ragione (cfr.anche qui sotto, nota 41) egli credette di non potersi limitare a questo livello, dove certamente la sua teoria sarebbe potuta risultare più aristotelica e più coerente.

40 Cfr. il mio libro del 1974 cit. sopra (n. 3) 165-170.

c'è nulla da aggiungere, su questo punto, a quanto era già stato notato nelle precedenti ricerche sul problema del determinismo in Aristotele e più specificamente nel *De fato*.[41]

Università di Milano

---

[41] Cfr. la mia messa a punto del problema nel saggio citato sopra (n. 8) soprattutto 1249-1258; e da ultimo le chiare osservazioni di D. Frede, *art. cit.* (n. 34) 203 a proposito del carattere deterministico che si può riconoscere all'etica di Aristotele—Vorrei ancora aggiungere una precisazione. Nei miei precedenti interventi, soprattutto nel libro citato sopra (n. 2), avevo ricondotto all'influenza di Galeno la teoria esposta nel *De fato* che assume un'identità fra il carattere naturale e il destino. Non vedo contraddizione fra quell'ipotesi e il suggerimento che dò oggi e che mira a ricondurre all'interpretazione sistematica dei passi aristotelici sulle doti naturali l'origine della concezione alessandrista. E' infatti perfettamente concepibile che Alessandro, influenzato da Galeno (di cui comunque conosceva qualcosa), o da una precedente tradizione peripatetica (per cui cfr. *Mant.* 186,28-31), si fosse convinto dell'importanza del carattere naturale legato alla costituzione dell'anima e che credesse in buona fede di poter ricostruire la medesima concezione anche muovendo dalle opere di Aristotele, di cui si sentiva comunque tenuto a offrire una spiegazione che appianasse ogni incoerenza e oscurità. Del resto Galeno stesso, nello scritto *quod animi mores etc.* (p. 51,12 sgg. Müller), si appella ad Aristotele e cerca di includere la teoria aristotelica fra i garanti della sua tesi deterministica. Un caso perfettamente analogo a quello del *De fato* è fornito dalla teoria alessandrista dell'origine dell'anima dalla mescolanza degli elementi corporei: Alessandro la trovava già presente nella tradizione peripatetica e in Galeno, ma, d'altra parte, credeva anche di poterla ricavare da un preciso testo di Aristotele. Riferimenti ai testi e alla letteratura in Sharples, *art. cit.* (n. 30) 1203.

ALCINOUS' EPISTEMOLOGY

DAVID SEDLEY

When it came to epistemology, doctrinal Platonists in antiquity faced a daunting task. They had somehow to integrate into a single theory at least three very disparate-looking treatments of the relation between knowledge and opinion:

(1) the *Meno*'s apparently successful account of knowledge as a species of correct opinion (*doxa*);

(2) the *Theaetetus'* self-acknowledged failure to find out what species of correct opinion knowledge could possibly be;

(3) the seemingly unbridgeable separation of knowledge from opinion in both *Republic* V and the *Timaeus.*

In some recent work,[1] I have tried to explore how this task of integration was tackled by three rival groups of Platonists—the sceptical Academics of the Hellenistic age, who aimed to show that Plato rejected the possibility of knowledge; the anonymous commentator on the *Theaetetus,* who makes the *Meno* the authoritative Platonic text on knowledge; and the group which he most strongly opposes, best represented for us today by chapter 4 of Alcinous' *Didaskalikos,* an epitome of Plato's thought composed in the first or second century AD.[2] In the present article, in order to

---

[1] G. Bastianini, D. Sedley, edition of Anonymous Commentary on Plato's *Theaetetus,* in *Corpus dei papiri filosofici greci e latini,* vol. III (Florence 1995), 227-562; D. Sedley, 'Three Platonist interpretations of the *Theaetetus*', in *Form and Argument in Later Plato,* ed. C. Gill, M.M. McCabe (forthcoming, Oxford 1996).

[2] Citations of the *Didaskalikos* are from the Budé edition by J. Whittaker and P. Louis, *Alcinoos, Enseignement des doctrines de Platon* (Paris 1990), to whose notes and apparatus I am heavily indebted. Equal thanks are due to the splendid English translation and commentary by John Dillon, *Alcinous, The Handbook of Platonism* (Oxford 1993). Both of these should be consulted for full details of the Platonic allusions in Alcinous' text, and for many other aspects not covered in the present article. Other helpful recent work on this chapter includes R.W. Sharples, 'The criterion of truth in Philo Judaeus, Alcinous and Alexander of Aphrodisias', in *The Criterion of Truth,* ed. P.M. Huby and G. Neal (Liverpool 1989) 231-56; and L.P. Schrenk, 'Faculties of judgment in the *Didaskalikos*', *Mnemosyne* 44 (1991) 347-63. On the date of *Did.* I suspend judgement for now. It may seem unwise not to acquiesce in the schooled intuitions

develop a fuller account of how this last party handled the task, I shall be analysing the Platonic exegesis propounded in *Didaskalikos* chapter 4.

Their outline position seems to have been as follows. Platonic *epistêmê*, as explained in the *Republic* and *Timaeus*, has Ideas as its objects, while the sensible world is the object of mere *doxa*. These two faculties of *epistêmê* and *doxa* were jointly taken to map onto what in the Hellenistic age had come to be known as the topic 'on the criterion'—that is, the principles and means of cognition in general. The *Theaetetus* was held to deal with only one half of this topic, albeit the half which had become the central focus of Hellenistic debates on the criterion: that is, the part which deals with sensory cognition.[3]

The *Theaetetus* fails to find a definition of knowledge, but the failure is interpreted as a calculated one. The search fails precisely because what it in fact addresses itself to is the epistemology of the sensible world, whereas knowledge has the Ideas as its proper objects. Consequently, while it fails as an account of knowledge, the *Theaetetus* succeeds as an investigation of the sensible world's epistemological structure and of the cognitive faculties which bear on it. It is to be plundered, not as a radical (and aporetic) re-investigation of *epistêmê*, but as Plato's most fully elaborated account of sensory cognition.

As for real *epistêmê* of the Ideas, it is held by this group of Platonists that that topic is not tackled in the *Theaetetus* but in the immediately succeeding dialogue, the *Sophist*. Their critic, the anonymous commentator on the *Theaetetus*, sums up their view at the beginning and end of the following passage (2.11-39):

> Some of the Platonists have thought that the dialogue was on the topic of the criterion, in view of the considerable space it also

---

of Dillon (*op. cit.*) xii-xiii and P.-L. Donini, 'Testi e commenti, manuali e insegnamento: la forma sistematica e i metodi della filosofia in età postellenistica', *ANRW* II 36.7 (1994) 5027-5100, pp. 5057-8, who plead for a date in the second century AD on the basis of comparisons with known Platonists from Plutarch to Numenius. Nevertheless, it seems to me that we still know far too little about first-century AD Platonism to exclude even so early a dating. One thing, at least, has ceased to be controversial, and that is the restoration of the author's name to the transmitted 'Alcinous', in place of Freudenthal's century-old conjecture 'Albinus'.

3 I leave aside here the question how they managed to accommodate, or discount, the *Meno*'s definition of knowledge as a species of correct *doxa*. On this, see my *art. cit.* (n. 1).

> devotes to the investigation of this. That is wrong. Rather, the declared aim is to speak about simple uncompounded knowledge, and it is for this purpose that he necessarily investigates the criterion. By 'criterion' in the present context I mean the criterion *through* which we judge, as an instrument; for it is necessary to have that whereby we will judge things; then, whenever this is accurate, the permanent acceptance of the things which we have judged properly becomes knowledge.
> These people, on the other hand, say that, having made it his declared aim to investigate knowledge, in the *Theaetetus* he shows what its objects are not, while in the *Sophist* he shows what its objects are.

On this view, then, the *Theaetetus* is about the 'criterion'. It tells us much about sensory cognition, but all that it reveals about real knowledge is something negative, what its objects are not, namely sensibles.

Such a view seems to fit closely the epistemological reading of Plato advocated in *Didaskalikos* chapter 4, which is itself, significantly, introduced as being 'on the criterion'.[4] The chapter's opening distinction between the criteria 'through which' and 'by which' judgement is exercised is inspired primarily by *Theaetetus* 184-185, where the senses are relegated to the former, purely instrumental, role, while the judging mind is dignified with the genuine cognitive agency which the latter role confers on it.[5]

The chapter's account of *epistêmê* reflects, not the *Theaetetus*, but the *Republic, Timaeus* and *Phaedrus*. Knowledge is of Ideas, not sensibles. What is especially distinctive of Alcinous' approach is the elaborate parallelism which he constructs between the intelligible and sensible worlds and, correspondingly, between intellectual and sensory cognition. The inspiration for this parallelism undoubtedly lies in the *Republic* and *Timaeus*.

The nature of the parallelism can be seen in the chart which follows.

---

4 Alcinous, *Did.* 154.8-9.

5 However, as Dillon notes (*op. cit.* [n.2] 61), the most direct source of the actual expression at 154.15-16, τὸ δὲ δι' οὗ ὄργανον κριτικὸν..., is *Republic* IX, 582d, δι' οὗ γε δεῖ ὀργάνου κρίνεσθαι (already called a κριτήριον back at 582a).

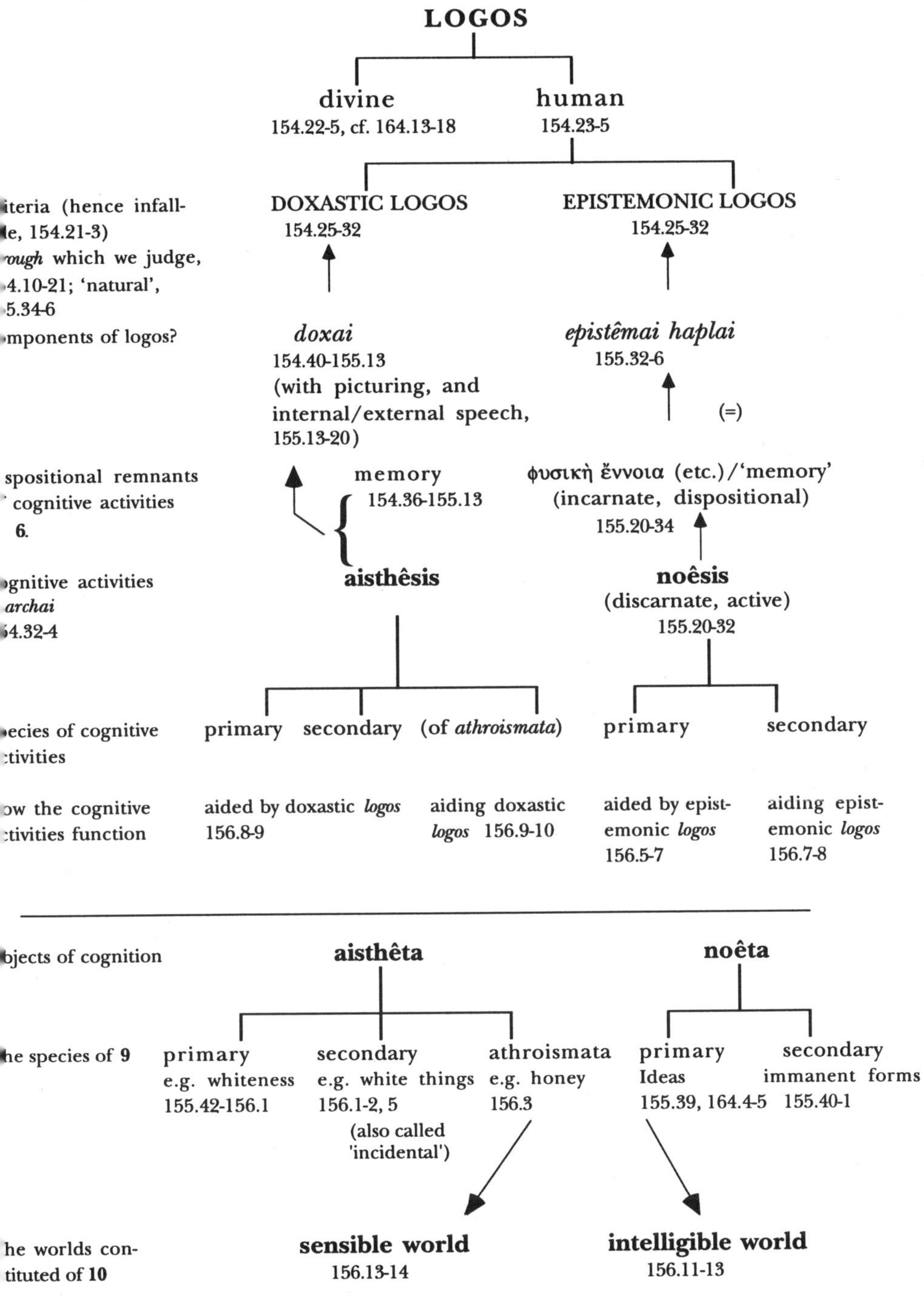
LOGOS
divine
154.22-5, cf. 164.13-18
human
154.23-5
iteria (hence infall-
le, 154.21-3)
rough which we judge,
4.10-21; 'natural',
5.34-6
DOXASTIC LOGOS
154.25-32
EPISTEMONIC LOGOS
154.25-32
mponents of logos?
doxai
154.40-155.13
(with picturing, and internal/external speech, 155.13-20)
epistêmai haplai
155.32-6
(=)
spositional remnants
cognitive activities
6.
memory
154.36-155.13
φυσικὴ ἔννοια (etc.)/'memory'
(incarnate, dispositional)
155.20-34
gnitive activities
archai
4.32-4
aisthêsis
noêsis
(discarnate, active)
155.20-32
ecies of cognitive
tivities
primary
secondary
(of athroismata)
primary
secondary
ow the cognitive
tivities function
aided by doxastic logos
156.8-9
aiding doxastic logos 156.9-10
aided by epistemonic logos
156.5-7
aiding epistemonic logos
156.7-8
bjects of cognition
aisthêta
noêta
he species of 9
primary
e.g. whiteness
155.42-156.1
secondary
e.g. white things
156.1-2, 5
(also called 'incidental')
athroismata
e.g. honey
156.3
primary
Ideas
155.39, 164.4-5
secondary
immanent forms
155.40-1
he worlds con-
tituted of 10
sensible world
156.13-14
intelligible world
156.11-13

In lines 1-8 the operations of perception are shown on the left, those of intellection on the right. The vertically descending lines are used to divide genera into species, while the ascending arrows show the causal chains by which reason (*logos*) is derived from the primary cognitive activities. Lines 9-11 convey the structure of the respective worlds on which perception and intellection operate. Here the vertically descending lines again divide genera into species. The arrows joining line 10 to line 11 convey the composition of the two worlds.

Following *Timaeus* 29b, there are two kinds of human *logos* (line 3), corresponding respectively to the sensible world and the intelligible world (line 11):

> This latter [i.e. human, as opposed to divine, λόγος] is also of two kinds. One kind concerns intelligibles, the other perceptibles. The one which concerns intelligibles is 'knowledge' [ἐπιστήμη] and 'epistemonic reason' [ἐπιστημονικὸς λόγος], while the one which concerns perceptibles is 'doxastic [δοξαστικός] reason' and 'opinion' [δόξα]. Hence epistemonic reason has firmness and duration, because it concerns principles which are firm and enduring, while the persuasive and doxastic has a good deal of 'likelihood' [εἰκός], because it does not deal with enduring things. (154.25-32)

Doxastic *logos* is derived from *aisthêsis*, epistemonic *logos* from *noêsis* (lines 6-3 of the chart). Our next task is to reconstruct these parallel processes, by which the two kinds of *logos* are formed. It will be convenient to reverse Alcinous' order and begin with the formation of 'epistemonic' *logos*:

> Intellection [νόησις] is the activity of the intellect when it contemplates the primary intelligibles. This seems to be of two kinds. One kind is before the soul came to be in this body, when it was contemplating the intelligibles, while the other is after its introduction into this body. Of these, the intellection that took place before the soul came to be in a body was called just that, 'intellection', but once the soul had come to be in a body, what had then been called intellection was now called a 'natural conception', being a sort of intellection stored away in the soul. So when we say that intellection is the starting point of epistemonic reason, we do not mean what we now call intellection, but the one when the soul was separate from the body, which, as we said, was then called intellection but is now called a natural conception. The natural conception is also called by Plato 'simple knowledge' and 'the soul's wingedness', and sometimes 'memory'. It is out of these simple bits of knowledge that natural and epistemonic reason is constituted, being present in us by nature. (155.20-36)

Start on the right-hand side of the chart in line 6 with the cognitive activity of νόησις. This is the discarnate soul's direct apprehension of the Ideas, as described in the *Phaedrus*. When the soul is incarnated, this same apprehension becomes (line 5) a set of buried memories or innate conceptions. Severally, they are (line 4) simple pieces of knowledge (ἐπιστῆμαι ἁπλαῖ), but jointly (line 3) they constitute epistemonic reason. This last identification draws on the common Hellenistic notion of human reason as constituted by a comprehensive set of *ennoiai* or conceptions. Thus our epistemonic or scientific reason is, roughly speaking, an innate capacity to handle *a priori* concepts, thanks to our souls' pre-natal acquaintance with the Ideas.

An apparent anomaly must be tackled. In the lines just quoted, Alcinous seems at pains to emphasize that 'intellection' (*noêsis*) is a term reserved for pre-natal direct acquaintance with the Ideas. Yet he starts this very same passage by allowing, on the contrary, that there are two species of *noêsis*, of which one is prenatal contemplation of Ideas while the other in the incarnate soul's latent memory of those same Ideas. Moreover, later in the chapter he is ready to use *noêsis* in yet another sense, namely the incarnate soul's active contemplation of Ideas (156.5-8)—a usage, of course, with excellent Platonic credentials. It is only within the confines of the present context, the transition from pre-natal contemplation to post-natal epistemonic *logos*, that the restricted usage is imposed. Why so? The answer will, I think, become clear from the parallel process by which doxastic *logos* is formed. *Logos* serves as a criterion of truth because it is a stock of fundamental concepts—empirical concepts in the case of doxastic reason, *a priori* concepts in the case of epistemonic reason—which furnish a standard against which reasoning may be judged. In both cases this relies on the presumption that the criterion in question is not itself the outcome of any process of reasoning. Only thus are the dangers of circularity or infinite regress averted—just the same requirement that had underlain Hellenistic notions of the criterion from Epicurus (*Letter to Herodotus* 37-8) onwards.[6] It is for this reason that

[6] On the Hellenistic notion of a criterion, see esp. Gisela Striker, Κριτήριον τῆς ἀληθείας, Nachrichten der Akademie der Wissenschaften in Göttingen, Phil.-hist. Kl., (Göttingen 1974) 2, 47-110; and 'The problem of the criterion', in *Epistemology*, ed. S. Everson, Companions to Ancient Thought (Cambridge 1990) 143-60.

the process from pre-natal direct acquaintance with Ideas (line 6) to the incarnate soul's framework of *a priori* concepts (line 3) must be mediated by nothing more than the virtually automatic downloading of the pre-natal knowledge into an innate disposition to understand. *Noêsis* in the sense of the incarnate soul's intellectual activity must be allowed to play no part here (even though, when we move from line 6 to line 7 it will be precisely this kind of *noêsis* that comes under scrutiny).

The whole picture is shaped by the need for the transition from the original cognitive act, *noêsis,* to the epistemonic criterion of truth to run in the closest possible parallel to the transition, on the left side of the chart, from the original cognitive act, *aisthêsis,* to the doxastic criterion of truth. It is to this that we must now turn. We start back in line 6 with the cognitive act of *aisthêsis* (which, unlike *noêsis,* is essentially incarnate):

> Perception is an affection of the soul through the body, whose primary function is to report from the faculty affected. When there is engendered in the soul a perceptual imprint, i.e. a perception, through the sense organs, and then this does not fade through length of time, but endures and is preserved, its preservation is called 'memory'. (154.34-40)

Aisthêsis, after its occurrence, leaves a memory trace (line 5; the parallelism to innate knowledge of Ideas, on the right-hand side, is emphasized by noting that even the same term, 'memory' can be used for both),[7] and a set of such memory traces leads eventually to doxastic *logos* (line 3). Where epistemonic *logos* was about intelligibles, doxastic *logos* is said to be about perceptibles. It seems clear that, whereas your epistemonic *logos* is your ability to handle a stock of *a priori* concepts, your doxastic *logos* is your capacity to operate with a set of empirical concepts, derived from repeated sense-experiences. Alcinous' examples include 'horse' and 'fire'. There is no reason in principle why there should not be both a doxastic and an epistemonic conception of the very same thing—both an empirical grasp of what fire is, based on previous experiences though touch and sight, and (as in *Timaeus* 51b) an intellectual grasp of fire's essence, its Idea. The question is not directly addressed, but since Alcinous elsewhere has no trouble in admitting Ideas even of sensible qualities like sweet and hot (180.4-5)

---

7 For 'memory' used of innate ideas, cf. *Phdr.* 249c5, 250a5.

there seems every reason to suppose that he would allow both kinds of conception to co-exist in parallel.[8]

What is the path from *aisthêsis* to doxastic *logos*? The text is inexplicit, and in constructing my diagram I was long hesitant as to whether memory (line 5) leads to doxastic *logos* (line 3) directly, or in partnership with *doxa* (line 4). The reason for hesitation is as follows. *Doxa* is described as the conscious and fallible process by which we compare a sense-impression to pre-existing memory traces and identify an item, either correctly or incorrectly, saying to ourselves e.g. 'That is a horse':

> Opinion is the combination of memory and perception. For when we first encounter some perceptible, and from it we get a perception, and from that a memory, and later we encounter the same perceptible again, we connect the pre-existing memory with the subsequent perception, and say within ourselves 'Socrates!', 'Horse!', 'Fire!', etc. And this is called opinion—our connecting the pre-existing perception[9] with the newly produced perception. And when these, on comparison, are in agreement, an opinion turns out true, but when they differ, false. For if someone who has a memory of Socrates encounters Plato and is led by some resemblance to think he is encountering Socrates again, and then, taking the perception that comes from Plato as coming from Socrates, connects it with the memory he has of Socrates, the opinion turns out false. The thing in which the memory and the perception occur Plato likens to a wax block. (154.40-155.13)

Most of this is, of course, squarely based on the Wax Block model in Part II of the *Theaetetus*. But since it is emphasised (in accordance with the spirit of the *Theaetetus* passage) that *doxa* can be wrong as well as right, it is not easy to see how it can in turn become an adequate basis for doxastic *logos*. For doxastic *logos* is a 'criterion' of truth. It is one species of human *logos*, and human *logos* as a genus is explicitly said by Alcinous to be 'infallible so far as the recognition of things is concerned' (154.23). This perhaps surprising description is in fact required by the very notion of a criterion, which must in its nature be something by which the true is unfailingly distinguished from the false. But how can mere doxastic *logos* achieve such reliability? Alcinous, echoing the

---

[8] For such a reading of Plato, cf. Plutarch fr. 215d Sandbach, and Dominic Scott, *Recollection and Experience* (Cambridge 1995) 18-23 and ch. 2.

[9] I here translate the tranmitted text, τὴν προυποκειμένην [*sc.* αἴσθησιν] (155.4-5). Whittaker and Dillon both adopt Heinsius' supplement <μνήμην>, maybe rightly, but since the μνήμη is itself a stored perception the transmitted reading, if less satisfactory, is not impossible.

Timaeus, admits that doxastic *logos* has an inherent instability because of the unstable nature of its objects (154.31-2). But he still insists, if I understand him correctly, that it does not make mistakes in recognizing things (κατὰ τὴν τῶν πραγμάτων γνῶσιν ἀδιάψευστος).[10] I assume that he means the following. Your empirical conception of, say, horses, being built on a series of sense-perceptions, conveys to you facts about horses which are inherently subject to change—their colours, shapes, movements etc., as distinct from their totally unchanging essence. Thus in many ways it is unreliable, and can offer nothing better than the kind of 'likelihood' promised by the *Timaeus*. But despite this instability, if you have adequate sensory experience of horses (whether or not you use it successfully) you have the capacity unfailingly to *recognize* a horse when you see one. You will lack scientific ('epistemonic') knowledge of what a horse is, but your doxastic grasp of horses will be entirely adequate for *recognitional* purposes. This criterial reliability, it might be thought, would be more credible if doxastic *logos* were the mechanical product of repeated sense-experiences, than if we have to suppose that the passage from sense-experience of horses to a doxastic grasp of 'horse' is mediated by conscious *doxai* about horses, some of them mistaken. That would maintain the parallel with the right-hand side of the diagram, where, as I have emphasized, no active intellectual judgement is permitted to mediate the passage from discarnate knowledge to innate *a priori* concepts.

On the other hand, it may be that the path to doxastic *logos* is after all mediated by *doxai*, but only by a very simple subset of them, the minimal recognitional *doxai* where we do not simply see horses and fires but also, as in Alcinous' own examples, identify them as horses and fires.[11] Later on we will encounter evidence that *doxa* must indeed intervene in this way.

---

[10] I propose this in preference to Dillon's translation 'the other [viz. human reason] is only free from error *when it is engaged in the cognition of reality*' (*op. cit.* [n. 2] 5, with my emphasis added; on p. 63 he uses the plural 'realities'), presumably meaning that only the epistemonic species of human reason is infallible. I suspect that the Greek terminology chosen is too loose to imply such a restriction; there is no sign in Alcinous' usage of this enriched Neoplatonic sense of πράγματα. For γνῶσις in the sense 'recognition', cf. *Did.* 173.43.

[11] For Antiochus' similar use of simple recognitional judgements as a foundation for the criterion of truth, cf. Cicero, *Academica* II 21, aptly cited here by Dillon.

Regardless of these and other details, it seems clear that Alcinous is presenting us with an elaborated cognitive analysis of the two modes of thought, that of *doxa* and that of *epistêmê*, which the *Republic* graphically introduces to us with its parallelisms between the lower and upper parts of the divided Line and between the worlds inside and outside the Cave. The next question is where the epistemology of the *Theaetetus* fits into this picture.

We have already seen how Part II of the *Theaetetus*—in particular the Wax Block analogy—is treated by Alcinous as Plato's canonical account of *doxa* in the sense specified in the *Republic*, fallible empirical cognition. We can now add that *Theaetetus* Part I is used as Plato's guide to the epistemological structure of the sensible world. A distinction is first made (l.c. diagram lines 6-7, right-hand side) between primary and secondary *noêsis*, distinguished (lines 9-10) by their objects, these being transcendent Ideas in the case of primary *noêsis* and immanent forms in the case of secondary *noêsis*:

> Therefore, there being both epistemonic and doxastic reason, and both intellection and perception, there are also the objects of these, namely intelligibles and perceptibles. And since of intelligibles some are primary, namely the Ideas, and others secondary, namely enmattered forms which are inseparable from the matter, intellection will also be of two kinds, namely that of primary and that of secondary intelligibles. (155.36-42)

An analogous set of distinctions is then made for *aisthêsis* (lines 6-7 and 9-10):

> And again, since of perceptibles some are primary, namely qualities like the colour whiteness, others accidental, like the object coloured white, and, posterior to these, the aggregate (ἄθροισμα), e.g. fire, honey, so too of perception one kind, called 'primary', will be of primary perceptibles, and the other, called 'secondary', of secondary perceptibles. (155.42-156.5)

For once Whittaker's excellent apparatus on the Platonic and Aristotelian antecedents is incomplete. He cites Aristotle *De anima* II 6, which is certainly the correct antecedent for the terminology of 'accidental' perceptibles, but overlooks the passage's far more profound dependence on *Theaetetus* 156d-157c.[12] There Socrates can

[12] Whittaker (*op. cit.* [n. 2] 86 n. 65) does note the occurrence of *athroisma* at *Tht.* 157b9, but does not appear to regard the present passage as alluding to it. Dillon (*op. cit.* [n. 2] 70-1) is more attuned to the Theaetetan echoes, including 157b9. However, he emphasizes 182a—rightly, but at the expense of the more important 156d-157c.

be read as making exactly the threefold division of perceptibles which Alcinous describes. In Socrates' chosen example of perception, that of seeing a white object, the object is said to become 'filled around with whiteness' when seen, but to become itself not 'whiteness' but 'white'. That carefully-worded distinction already supplies Alcinous' own distinction between the primary perceptible, 'whiteness', and the secondary perceptible, 'the white thing' (τὸ λευκόν).[13]

After distinguishing primary and secondary perceptibles, Alcinous adds a third item, the *athroisma* or aggregate, exemplified by honey, which combines flavour, texture, colour etc. in a single complex item. This too directly echoes the passage at *Theaetetus* 156d-157c, which ends with the designation of complex objects like man and stone as *athroismata* of simple perceptible properties. (Some have read this sentence in the *Theaetetus* as the phenomenalist thesis that such objects are nothing more than bundles of sensible properties. But Alcinous' physics, based on the theory of elements in the *Timaeus*, precludes the possibility that he is *reducing* physical objects to mere bundles of sense-properties in this way; his claim is purely about the epistemological status of sensible substances.)

This tripartite division of perceptibles is a remarkably ambitious edifice to build on *Theaetetus* 156-157. What is its purpose? The answer begins to emerge only in line 11. We need at this stage to consider the exceptionally off-putting passage which introduces the materials of lines 7-8 and 11:

> Now the primary intelligibles are judged by intellection (νόησις), not without epistemonic reason, by means of a kind of comprehension (περίληψις) and not discourse (διέξοδος); the secondary intelligibles are judged by epistemonic reason, not without intellection. The primary perceptibles and the secondary perceptibles are judged by perception, not without doxastic reason; the aggregate is judged by doxastic reason, not without perception. And the intelligible world being a primary intelligible, while the perceptible world is an aggregate [ἄθροισμα], the intelligible world is judged by intellection 'with the help of reason'—i.e. not without reason—, while the perceptible world is judged by doxastic reason not without perception. (156.5-14)

---

13 Even Alcinous' variant term for the primary perceptible, ποιότης or 'quality', is so named for the first time later on in the *Theaetetus*, at 182a. That this, in the context of *Did.* ch. 4, is a specifically Theaetetan usage is confirmed in ch. 11, where Alcinous uses ποιότης more broadly for any quality at all.

The intelligible world, on the right-hand side, is composed of Ideas, grasped by primary *noêsis*.[14] However, on the left-hand side, the sensible world is composed not of primary or secondary *aisthêta*, but of *athroismata*. That is, I take it, the sensible world is not properly grasped as a complex set of colours, flavours etc. (primary perceptibles); nor is it properly grasped as a complex set of white things, sweet things etc. (secondary perceptibles). If it were composed merely of either primary or secondary perceptibles, the proper cognitive route to it would be the direct exercise of perception, albeit (as line 8 reminds us on the left-hand side) with the aid of doxastic *logos*. That is, if the sensible world were composed merely either of colours, flavours etc., or of white things, sweet things, etc., we would be left simply to register these with our sense organs, although doxastic *logos* would be called in to enable us to identify such sensibles for what they are—white, sweet etc. That would make the study of the sensible world a most primitive and unrewarding project.

However, the sensible world is not properly analysed as consisting of these simple sensibles. As line 11 indicates, the sensible world is composed of objects—mountains, animals, stars etc.—each of which is, epistemologically speaking, a complex *athroisma* of colours, odours etc. Such objects cannot be grasped by simple sense-perception, which (as *Theaetetus* 184-186 demonstrates) is incapable of synthesizing its own data by placing them in any sort of relation to each other. Such synthetic judgements are, rather, argued by Socrates there to be the work of *doxa* (187a). In other words, the *Theaetetus* itself has an epistemology which establishes that the sensible world is properly studied, not by mere *aisthêsis*, but by *doxa* which uses *aisthêsis* as its instrument. And this fits beautifully with the celebrated epistemological declaration in Alcinous' favourite dialogue, the *Timaeus* (28a), that whereas that-which-always-is is graspable νοήσει μετὰ λόγου, 'by intellection with the help of reason', that-which-becomes is δόξῃ μετ' αἰσθήσεως ἀλόγου δοξαστόν, 'opinable by opinion with the help of irrational perception'. That is why Alcinous is so careful to state, at 156.9-10, that the *athroisma* is judged by 'doxastic *logos* not without perception'. It is true that *Timaeus* 28a makes the sensible world graspable, not by doxastic *logos*, but *doxa* itself. But since the *Timaeus* is explicit

[14] That this primary intellection is non-discursive is Alcinous' interpretation of περιληπτόν at *Tim.* 28a1-2, represented by his περιλήψει at 156.6.

soon after (29b) that the intelligible and sensible worlds each have their own appropriate kind of *logos*, Alcinous is confident that *doxa* at 28a is simply a shorthand for 'doxastic *logos*'. He has already carefully prepared the ground for this equivalence by telling us earlier (154.28-9, p. 304 above) that doxastic *logos* is sometimes simply called *doxa*.

(This realization that *doxa*, and not bare sense-perception, is required if we are to have cognitive access to *athroismata*, can now be fed back into our earlier inquiry as to whether the passage from *aisthêsis* (line 6) to doxastic *logos* (line 3) need be mediated by *doxa*. Since doxastic *logos* deals with complex perceptual items like fire and man, there should now be no doubt that mere sense-perception can never be a sufficient foundation for it, and that *doxa* must be indispensable to the process of its formation.)

Alcinous' exegetical strategy is hideously complicated. But if we persevere in tracing it, we can begin to see how thoroughly he and his fellow-proponents of the interpretation have integrated the epistemology of *Theaetetus* Parts I and II into a global reconstruction of Plato's two-world system. On his view, the *Theaetetus* may profess to be an inquiry into knowledge, but in reality it is Plato's fullest account of perceptual cognition and its objects, demonstrating the parallel structures of the intelligible and sensible worlds. In this way it analyses the type of reason to which we may appeal in a cosmological investigation like that conducted in Alcinous' own favourite dialogue, the *Timaeus*. Matters of no small importance are at stake:

> The aim of physics is to learn what is the nature of the universe; what sort of animal man is and what place he has in the world; whether god exercises providence over things in their entirety; whether this god has others subordinate to him; and what the relation of human beings is to the gods. (161.3-7)

To reconstruct what cognitive capacity, in Plato's view, entitles us to reason about such questions is no mean achievement.[15]

Cambridge

---

[15] I have benefited from discussion of this material in the *Didaskalikos* seminar held at Cambridge in May 1995, and in the Séminaire Léon Robin at the Sorbonne in December 1995. My thanks to participants in both seminars—including, at the former, the honorand of this volume Jaap Mansfeld, whose expertise and good will contributed so much to the entire occasion.

'A SIMPLE PHILOSOPHY' ALEXANDER OF LYCOPOLIS ON CHRISTIANITY

PIETER W. VAN DER HORST

'Christianity is a simple philosophy.' This is the opening line of Alexander's Πρὸς τὰς Μανιχαίου δόξας.[1] When Jaap Mansfeld and I translated and annotated this neglected treatise in 1973, we paid some attention to Alexander's way of describing Christianity and Jesus, but some aspects still deserve a closer look.[2] This early anti-Manichaean work by a Platonist philosopher was probably written towards the end of the third century CE, in the period when Manichaean missionaries[3] were trying to gain a foothold in Egypt,[4] an attempt that was crowned with success, as the Coptic Manichaica from the Fayyum and the recent find of numerous Manichaean papyri in Kellis in the Dakhleh oasis bear witness. It is the radical dualism of this new religion that was Alexander's main target, but

---

[1] P. W. van der Horst & J. Mansfeld, *An Alexandrian Platonist Against Dualism: Alexander of Lycopolis' Treatise 'Critique of the Doctrines of Manichaeus' translated with an introduction and notes* (Leiden 1974; originally published as an article in the short-lived journal *Thêta-Pi* 3 (1974) 1-97) 48. The Greek of the opening line is: Ἡ Χριστιανῶν φιλοσοφία ἁπλῆ καλεῖται. Our translation—which I slightly altered in the text above—is based on the assumption that καλεῖσθαι is here the equivalent of εἶναι, as is often the case; see LSJ *s.v.* καλέω II 2, and C. J. Ruijgh, 'L'emploi onomastique de ΚΕΚΛΗΣΘΑΙ', in *Miscellanea tragica in honorem J. C. Kamerbeek* (Amsterdam 1976) 333-397.

[2] Even though A. Villey in his recent commentary has paid more attention to the matter than we did; see his *Alexandre de Lycopolis: Contre la doctrine de Mani* (Paris 1985).

[3] The first of which was Pappos (2, p. 4 Br.), a close friend of Mani himself; see S. N. C. Lieu, *Manichaeism in the Later Roman Empire and Medieval China* (Tübingen 1992, 2nd ed.) 103, and Villey, *Alexandre* 109-11.

[4] The earliest attempts took place during Mani's lifetime (216-277), especially in the Lycopolitan area; see G. Stroumsa, 'The Manichaean Challenge to Egyptian Christianity', in B. A. Pearson & J. E. Goehring (eds.), *The Roots of Egyptian Christianity* (Philadelphia 1986) 307-19. A sure indication of the movement's presence in Egypt by the final decades of the third century is the circular letter of Theonas (?), bishop of Alexandria, from ca. 280, in which he warns Christians against 'the madness of the Manichaeans' (τῆς μανίας τῶν Μανιχέων); the text has been preserved in *P.Ryl.Gr.* 469 (the quote is in line 30) and is printed in A. Adam, *Texte zum Manichäismus* (Berlin 1959, 2nd ed.) 52-4 (ed. pr. by C. H. Roberts, *Catalogue of the Greek and Latin Papyri in the John Rylands Library*, vol. 3, Manchester 1938, 38-46).

since he regarded Manichaeism as a Christian sect,[5] he pays some attention to Christianity as a whole as well. And he does so in a way that shows some resemblances to, but also marked differences from, the other well-known Greek thinkers who attacked Christianity before, during, and after his time, i.e. Celsus, Porphyry, and Julian.

The fact that Alexander calls Christianity a philosophy is less remarkable than it might seem at first sight. Not only Christians themselves called their religion a *philosophia*, some of their opponents did so as well.[6] As several scholars have demonstrated,[7] in the Hellenistic and Roman period the term *philosophia* underwent a semantic development that, as Armstrong put it, 'accounts for the strong ethical emphasis and, to the modern mind, disconcertingly close connexion between philosophy and religion which we find in nearly all the thinkers of the period, in the Greek pagans just as much as in the adherents of revealed religions.'[8] It should be added, however, that the emphasis on moral and religious concerns in these 'philosophies' often implied a decrease in attention to logic (and physics as well, albeit to a lesser degree). And it is precisely a lack of logical rigour, with its implications for physics, that Alexander sees as one of the weaknesses of Christianity (and Manichaeism). He complains that Christianity is 'chiefly devoted to ethical instruction' (1, p. 3 Brinkmann)[9] but that, as far as clear and coherent theories and ideas about God are concerned, it gets

---

[5] Rightly so, as we now know from the Cologne Mani Codex, where it is explicitly stated that Mani was educated in an Elchesaite milieu; see, e.g., Lieu, *Manichaeism in the Later Roman Empire* 1-85.

[6] For references see A. J. Malherbe, 'Not in a Corner': Early Christian Apologetic in Acts 26:26, *The Second Century* 5 (1985/86) 197 n. 20.

[7] A. M. Malingrey, *Philosophia. Étude d'un groupe des mots dans la littérature grecque des Présocratiques au IVe siècle après J.-C.* (Paris 1961); R. L. Wilken, *The Christians as the Romans Saw Them* (New Haven-London 1984) 72-83; A. Villey, *Alexandre* 93-95.

[8] A. H. Armstrong, Introduction, *The Cambridge History of Later Greek and Early Medieval Philosophy* (Cambridge 1967) 5. Since the dossier on *philosophia* consists mainly of pagan and Christian evidence (although Malingrey, *Philosophia* 87-8, did pay some attention to Philo), I add some Jewish material at random by pointing out how Josephus speaks about the religious movements in the Judaism of his time (Essenes, Pharisees, Sadducees, Zealots) as *philosophiai*, and how he speaks about the Jewish religion in general as 'our philosophy': *Ant.* XVIII 9; 11; 23; *Bell.* II 119; 166; *C. Ap.* II 47.

[9] We still (have to) use Brinkmann's old Teubner edition (Leipzig 1895) but a new critical text is badly needed. Villey's new chapter division makes more sense than Brinkmann's from a logical point of view but does not facilitate reference.

no further than enigmatic talk and allusions. Theology requires logic, but logic is not at all part of the Christian heritage. The truism that 'the productive cause is the most honourable, the most important, and the cause of all beings' (1, p. 3 Br.) is apparently all that Christian philosophy has been able to produce. Even worse is the fact that also in ethics, the domain that the Christians devote most of their attention to, they sidestep the difficult issues. They do not know the important distinctions between various forms of vice and virtue, of disposition and affection, that Greek philosophy (esp. the Stoic school) had developed,[10] and consequently are unable to provide 'the principles according to which each individual virtue should be acquired' (1, p. 3 Br.). So even their best—ethical instruction—is of a lamentably deficient nature. Nonetheless, Alexander has to admit, it is effective: many ordinary people who follow these ethical instructions make great progress in virtue, their characters receive an imprint of piety, and they are gradually led towards a desire for the good. So on the very first page of his treatise Alexander not only debunks Christianity as a philosophy, he also concedes—and unreservedly at that—that the effects of this simple ethical instruction are impressive. And he says so because this is his own experience: ἐκ τῆς πείρας ἔστι μαθεῖν (1, p. 3 Br.). This gives us an important clue to Alexander's attitude towards Christianity. It seems to indicate that he knew many (uneducated) Christians in his own environment whose doctrines he scorned, but whose way of life he could not but admire. In the following pages we will see that this ambiguous attitude may be seen at several turns in his work.[11]

Now we should bear in mind that late third century Egypt was a country that witnessed the rise of Christian monasticism. One of the first Egyptian Desert Fathers (though, as we shall see, not the very first), the long-lived Antony (ca. 250-355), withdrew in the early seventies of the third century from the inhabited world to the desert and the mountains of the Egyptian hinterland. Before the end of the century many believers followed his example. Their life was ascetic, often to the extreme, their goal was meditation in

[10] See M. Giusta, *I dossografi di etica*, 2 vols. (Turin 1962-67). A similar critique is voiced by Celsus *ap.* Origen, *CC* I 4.

[11] It should be kept in mind here that Alexander's positive view of Christian ethical instruction stands in contrast to his very negative view of the Manichaean position that education and punishment should be abolished; see van der Horst-Mansfeld, *An Alexandrian Platonist* 44-5.

order to become as free as possible from bodily desires and so to draw closer to God. The *Historia monachorum in Aegypto,* in spite of its often hagiographic character, gives us a lively picture of the impressive zeal and remarkably self-effacing attitude of many of these early hermits (and of the cenobites not much later).[12] Other examples could be cited, for instance the even earlier anchorite Paul of Thebes (reportedly ca. 228-341),[13] whom Antony met in the desert. Antony is mentioned here first because some of his writings are extant, namely various letters and sermons.[14] What is striking in these documents is that, although they do contain some simple theological ideas, the main emphasis is on ethical instruction. So this contemporary of Alexander illustrates exactly what our philosopher writes about: poor doctrine—often called *philosophia*![15]—combined with an impressive lifestyle. And this is also the impression one receives from other documents of the early monastic movement. There is in these humble Coptic anchorites an enormous zeal, a total dedication to the search of God, an extremely strict ethics (often bordering on the bizarre), combined with a lack of intellectual training.[16] Meetings with people like Antony and his admirers could not fail to have inspired Alexander's ambiguous attitude. We do not know exactly when Christian monasticism spread to Lycopolis (modern Assiut), but it is very probable that our author (could have) got acquainted with this phenomenon in this city as well. One of the most famous Desert Fathers was John of Lycopolis who lived there probably only slightly later than Alexander but who was certainly not the town's first Christian or first monk.[17]

---

[12] See A.-J. Festugière, *Historia monachorum in Aegypto* (Brussels 1961); N. Russell, *The Lives of the Desert Fathers* (London-Oxford 1980); P. W. van der Horst, *Woestijn, begeerte en geloof. Het leven van de eerste monniken in Egypte. De* Historia monachorum in Aegypto *vertaald en toegelicht* (Kampen 1995).

[13] See I. S. Kozik, *The First Desert Hero: St. Jerome's* Vita Pauli (Mount Vernon 1968); M. Naldini in *Dictionnaire encyclopédique du christianisme ancien* (ed. A. di Berardino, Paris 1983) vol. 2, 1951-2.

[14] See T. Orlandi in *Dictionnaire encyclopédique du christianisme ancien,* vol. 1, 169, and S. Rubenson, *The Letters of St. Antony* (Lund 1990; non vidi).

[15] For references see P. Courcelle, 'Verissima philosophia', in *Epektasis (FS Jean Daniélou)* (Paris 1972) 655-6, nn. 15-19.

[16] Several of the documents make clear that many of the Desert Fathers were illiterates. See R. S. Bagnall, *Egypt in Late Antiquity,* Princeton 1993, 246-260.

[17] That Alexander's remarks could not be directed against his philosophically trained (near-)contemporaries such as Origen and Pierius ('the new Origen'), is rightly stressed by Villey, *Alexandre* 96.

A short comparison with Galen may be instructive here. In a 10th century Arabic chronicle by Agapius[18] Galen is reported to have written the following: 'The people called Christians have built their doctrine upon enigmatic indications and miracles. But as far as their actions are concerned, they are not inferior to the genuine philosophers. For they love continence, keep fasts and prayers, and avoid unjust actions. Among them there are men who do not pollute themselves with women.'[19] If this testimony is genuine,[20]—which it probably is since it is independently confirmed by several other sources—we have here a striking agreement between Galen and Alexander.[21] Both of them do not hold the Christian doctrine in high regard, but they do show appreciation for the way of life of (some) Christians. And Galen also specifically says that his high regard for their way of life (not inferior to that of philosophers!) was primarily inspired by their asceticism and strict ethical norms, which is exactly what we surmised to be the case with Alexander.[22]

It would seem that Alexander not only had knowledge of the impact of Christian ethics on the lives of simple people, but that he was also acquainted with Christian theories about history, especially the history of the Christian church in the first 250 years. He says that 'this simple philosophy has been split up into numerous factions by its later adherents' and that 'the number of issues has increased just as in sophistry' (1, p. 3 Br.).[23] This was not his own invention, for in the century before he wrote this, several Christian writers had developed this theory of the gradual 'heresification and schismatization' of the church after its initial 'orthodox' start

---

[18] A passage overlooked by R. Walzer, *Galen on Jews and Christians* (Oxford 1949) 56-74, although he does mention several other Oriental authors who attribute similar statements to Galen (see esp. the quotes at 57 and 65; cf. p. 15).

[19] I quote the translation by S. Pines, *An Arabic Version of the Testimonium Flavianum and its Implications* (Jerusalem 1971) 74.

[20] For the debate see Pines, *Arabic Version* 73-82.

[21] Walzer, *Galen* 72-3, already noted the parallel.

[22] In contrast, most of the other second century critics of Christianity speak in a very negative sense about Christian morality. See for references R. J. Hoffmann, *Celsus. On the True Doctrine. A Discourse Against the Christians* (Oxford 1987) 12-24.

[23] The final words καθάπερ ἐν τοῖς ἐριστικοῖς point to a parallel in the history of philosophy and are reminiscent of the passages from the second century Middle Platonist Numenius to the effect that the entire history of the Academy after Plato had been one of strife and lack of agreement on any essential topic (fragments 1 - 4 Leemans = frgs. 24-27 des Places = Eusebius, *PE* XIV 5-8).

with an unadulterated gospel. A good example is found in Alexander's earlier compatriot and fellow Platonist, Clement of Alexandria, who says in his *Strom.* VII xvii 106-7 that the Lord founded the Catholic Church in the times of Tiberius and that it is evident from the high antiquity and perfect truth of this church that the later heresies, from the times of Hadrian and Antoninus onwards, were new inventions and therefore falsifications of the original truth.[24] This myth of Christian origins became immensely influential. In fact it remained the standard Christian view for some 1500 years until it was subverted at the end of the 17th century when Gottfried Arnold published his important *Unparteiische Kirchen- und Ketzerhistorie* (1699-1700).

Now one could of course argue that Alexander's observation of the splitting up of the Christian philosophy into numerous factions can simply be explained by the fact that in his days Egyptian Christianity was indeed split up into numerous sects, as the Nag Hammadi Codices, the Kellis papyri, the Coptic Manichaica, the other early Coptic literature, and the writings of the Graeco-Egyptian Churchfathers bear witness. All of these testify to such a great variety and wide divergence of opinion in Christian Egypt that any observer could have come to the same conclusion as Alexander.[25] This view does not hold, however, for the simple reason that a wide variety of viewpoints, and even the fact that the various Christian parties themselves argued that they and only they were continuing the original unity of doctrine, would not automatically lead to a conclusion by an outsider to the effect that an original 'simple philosophy' was adulterated only by later (ἐπιγενόμενοι is Alexander's term) depraved adherents. So it would seem that Alexander's view derives from Christian authors or theorists, the more so since he joins them in accusing the 'dissenters' of 'theoretical imprecision' (1, p. 4 Br.) which formed the basis of the decline of

---

24 See also the fragment of Hegesippus (*floruit* 3rd quarter of the 2nd cent.) in Eusebius, *Hist. Eccl.* IV 22, 4-5, where this author says that the earliest Church leaders 'used to call the Church a virgin for this reason that she had not yet been seduced by listening to nonsense,' but soon afterwards this process of corruption and heresy started. Cf. also the similar statements in the slightly later Irenaeus, *Adv. Haereses* III 4. See S. J. D. Cohen, 'A Virgin Defiled. Some Rabbinic and Christian Views on the Origin of Heresies', *Union Seminary Quarterly Review* 35 (1980) 1-11, and esp. A. Le Boulluec, *La notion d'hérésie dans la littérature grecque IIe-IIIe siècles*, vol. 2 (Paris 1985).

25 See W. Bauer, *Orthodoxy and Heresy in Earliest Christianity* (London 1972) 44-60 (though no longer up to date).

their ethical instruction and of the inclination to strife of the common people in the Church, thereby contradicting what he had earlier said about the low level but high results of the moral teachings of Christianity.[26]

In his refutation of Manichaeism, the second part of the book which forms the bulk of the treatise (§§ 5-26 Br. = §§ 14-42 Villey), Alexander begins by saying that he is at a loss how to proceed.[27] Like the other Christians, Alexander implies, Manichaeans too employ no proper methods in their theories and do not care for proof, an argument that recalls Galen's repeated objection to Christian faith. The fact that they do not use generally accepted rational arguments makes it wellnigh impossible for him to refute them. It is interesting to see that one of the arguments of his opponents seems to have been that they do not need to give proofs because the basis of their reasoning is 'their old and new Scriptures which they believe to be divinely inspired' (5, p. 8 Br.). It is most interesting to observe that the term Alexander uses here is θεόπνευστος. This is a word of very rare occurrence. As far as we know, it first occurs in the New Testament passage *2 Timothy* 3:16 and, apart from the innumerable instances in the Churchfathers who borrowed the term from *2 Timothy*,[28] the very few other occurrences are either from Jewish writings or also based upon this New Testament passage. It is, therefore, probable that Alexander either knew that passage itself or had read the term in a Christian or Manichaean writing that had borrowed it from the New Testament. He does not hide his scorn for this kind of appeal to divine authority and revelation,[29] arguing that under these circumstances 'all normal rules are abandoned' because 'the role attributed by Greek philosophers to the postulates, namely the underived propositions upon which proofs are based, is represented among these

---

[26] To be sure, it cannot be excluded that Alexander borrowed the idea from Celsus; see *CC* III 10, V 63.

[27] He adds the sour remark that this deceitful philosophy has unfortunately been successful in making some of his fellow-students to converts, a situation comparable to that in Plotinus' school where some of his friends had adopted gnostic ideas, much to his annoyance (*Enn.* II 9,10). See on this remark the observations by Lieu, *Manichaeism* 152-3.

[28] See G. Lampe's *Greek Patristic Lexicon* s.v.

[29] Like Julian. For Julian's repugnance to the notion of revelation see A. Meredith, 'Porphyry and Julian Against the Christians', *ANRW* II 23, 2 (Berlin 1980) 1140-1 (1119-49).

people by the voice of the prophets' (5, p. 9 Br.). This remark is a further indication that in his anti-Manichaean struggle he uses arguments that were originally directed against Christianity in general.[30] Our conclusion is confirmed by the fact that Alexander here refers to the Old Testament as well, whereas he knew that this document was completely rejected by the Manichaeans and certainly not regarded as 'divinely inspired' by them; on the contrary, they regarded 'the prophets' as inspired by the devil.[31]

The same can be seen again in a later passage (10, p. 16 Br.), where Alexander says that the Manichaeans are even worse than the mythographers who are responsible for the stories of Uranus' castration and Kronos' swallowing his own sons, since their theory of a continual war of matter against God is too crude to admit of allegorical interpretation and is actually taken literally by them. Here, too, we have a traditional anti-Christian argument, already found in Celsus, who not only adduces the same examples (Uranus, Kronos, etc.) but also says that the Christian writings are incapable of being interpreted allegorically and are therefore manifestly very stupid fables (*ap.* Origen, *CC* IV 48-50). And when a little further on Alexander states that the Manichaean theory of God's anger and his desire for vengeance against matter is untenable from a philosophical point of view—since πάθη of this kind 'are absurd even in connection with the good man, let alone in connection with the Good itself' (10, p. 17 Br.)—he again echoes

---

30 See, *inter multos alios*, W. Nestle, 'Die Haupteinwände des antiken Denkens gegen das Christentum', *Archiv für Religionswissenschaft* 37 (1941/42) 72 (51-100). In general it can be said that, in spite of the many differences between Celsus, Porphyry, Julian, and Alexander, what they have in common is a strong resentment against fideism. See also the remarks by A. H. Armstrong, 'Man in the Cosmos. A study of some differences between pagan Neoplatonism and Christianity', in *Romanitas et christianitas. Studia J. H. Waszink oblata* (Amsterdam-London 1973) 5-14, and by R. T. Wallis, *Neoplatonism* (London 1972) 101-105. On Alexander see also G. Stroumsa, 'Titus of Bostra and Alexander of Lycopolis: A Christian and a Platonic Refutation of Manichaean Dualism', in R. T. Wallis & J. Bregman (edd.), *Neoplatonism and Gnosticism* (New York 1992) 337-349 (340: 'The philosopher is ill at ease developing dialectical arguments against a protagonist who does not accept the rules of the game').

31 See Villey, *Alexandre* 194-5. My interpretation of the passage makes unnecessary Villey's forced explanation that 'the old scriptures' refers to the apocrypha and pseudepigrapha in use among the Manichaeans, however true it may be that these writings enjoyed a great popularity among them; see J. C. Reeves, *Jewish Lore in Manichaean Cosmogony. Studies in the* Book of Giants *Traditions* (Cincinnati 1992).

one of Celsus's anti-Christian arguments to the effect that ascribing human emotions like anger to God is ridiculous (*ap.* Origen, *CC* IV 71-73), an argument that Origen has a hard time refuting.[32]

I further wish to draw attention to an interesting aspect of Alexander's polemic on the *aeternitas mundi* in ch. 12 (p. 19 Br.), a view firmly rejected by the Manichaeans. He quotes Zeno[33] to the effect that the universe will be destroyed by fire, and opposes this by a quote from 'a subtle thinker' (Theophrastus?, Eudemus?) who is said to have argued against Zeno: 'What I for one have seen yesterday and a year ago and an even longer time ago, and what I similarly see today, I do not see to have suffered at all through the fire of the sun. But in the course of time some little damage should have been done if we are to believe that the whole universe will ever be destroyed by fire.' A similar answer, Alexander says, is valid against the Manichaeans as well, namely: 'But evil has not in the slightest respect grown less. It hasn't: it was there formerly in the time of the first man to be born, where brother killed brother, and even now it is still there; wars are the same and desires are even more complicated. Now it would be reasonable that these things, if they did not altogether cease, should at least grow less, if we are to trust that in the long run they will ever cease. As, however, they are the same as formerly, what confidence in future events can be possible on this basis?' (12, p. 19 Br.). Now, apart from the fact that, as Mansfeld had already noticed,[34] Alexander's predecessor Celsus had already adduced against the Christians the same argument that 'in the existing world there is no decrease or increase of evils either in the past or in the present or in the future' (*CC* IV 62), two things have to be noticed here. The first is a striking agreement between the argument here and the one we find in one of the last New Testament documents to be written, namely *2 Peter,* ch. 3. In this pseudonymous letter (probably from the early

[32] For a concise history of the problem see P. W. van der Horst, 'Philo Alexandrinus over de toorn Gods', in A. de Jong & A. de Jong (edd.), *Kleine encyclopedie van de toorn* (Utrecht 1993) 77-82.

[33] Honesty demands that we state explicitly that our claim in 1973 to have discovered here a new and authentic fragment of Zeno overlooked by Hans von Arnim (van der Horst-Mansfeld, *Alexandrian Platonist* 74 n. 294) was invalid. More than 50 years earlier the great Arthur Stanley Pease had already detected it (*Classical Philology* 1921, 200). We note that Villey too has overlooked Pease's contribution.

[34] *Alexandrian Platonist* 75 n. 299.

second century) we find the following situation:[35] The author tries to refute opponents, Christian opponents that is, who find it impossible any longer to believe in the second coming (the *parousia*) of the Lord,[36] and who say: 'Where is the promise of his coming? For ever since the fathers[37] died, all things continue as they were from the beginning of creation!' (v. 4). He then goes on to demonstrate that, despite the apparent unchangeability of all things, the world will in the end certainly be destroyed by fire and the elements will be dissolved by it (a Stoic motif). In his reply there are also a number of references to the early chapters of the book of Genesis (esp. to chs. 1 and 6 in vv. 5-7), probably induced by his opponents' reference to the Patriarchs. This would seem to be not without significance. The opponents of the NT author use the immutable nature of the cosmos as an argument against the idea of a final conflagration (and the second coming of the Lord), and this is very similar to Alexander's argument.[38] In his counterattack, the author of *2 Peter* refers to the two biblical stories in Gen. 1 and 6, not unlike Alexander's reference to the two biblical stories in Gen. 1 and 4. For—and that is the second aspect to be noticed—his words about 'the time of the first man to be born, when brother killed brother' are undeniably a reference to the creation myth in Gen. 1-2 and to the story of Cain's murder of Abel in Gen. 4. Why should Alexander use biblical references in his refutation of those who think the world will be destroyed by fire? Could it be that, because he regards the Manichaeans as Christians, he tries to beat them with arguments that were being used within Christian circles in the debate over the eternity or the destructibility of the world?[39] That such a debate was going on in some Christian circles is apparent not only from the passage in *2 Peter* 3, but also, for instance, from passages such as *1 Clement* 23:3 and *2 Clement* 11:2,

---

35 See the discussion in P. W. van der Horst: 'The Elements Will Be Dissolved With Fire.' The Idea of Cosmic Conflagration in Hellenism, Ancient Judaism and Early Christianity, in my *Hellenism—Judaism—Christianity: Essays on Their Interaction* (Kampen 1994) 227-251, esp. 243-248. Further R. J. Bauckham, *Jude, 2 Peter* (Waco 1983) 300-301.

36 A problem caused by the so-called 'Parousieverzögerung'.

37 I.e., probably, the Jewish Patriarchs (Abraham, Isaac, and Jacob).

38 On Alexander's anti-Stoic stance see Mansfeld in *An Alexandrian Platonist* 47.

39 But note that prior to Alexander Celsus too had referred to 'the plot of brothers against one another' (*ap.* Origen, *CC* IV 43 and V 59) as did Julian after him (*C. Galil.* 347 A-C = fr. 84 Masaracchia).

where the authors combat 'the double-minded, who doubt in their heart, and say: These things we heard of old in the days of our fathers also, but behold we have grown old and none of these things has happened to us!' These people doubt God's promises, among which that of a new world, because they have never seen any of them come true. Other Christians, who did not doubt God's promises, still found it difficult to believe in a destruction of the universe by fire, since as an act of punishment, inspired by anger, it seemed to be to them not θεοπρεπής.[40] So they took recourse to allegorical interpretation of the biblical texts concerned (e.g., Origen).[41] The debate between these diverging Christian groups or individuals was no doubt waged with constant recourse to the Scriptures. It cannot be ruled out that this is the background of Alexander's at first sight rather surprising[42] presentation of an argument that makes reference to Scriptural passages.[43]

There is another passage in which Alexander shows his knowledge of the Bible, sc. ch. 24 (p. 36 Br.), where he draws attention to the fact that there are some parallels to the idea of Christ's self-sacrifice: 'To say in accordance with the doctrine of the Church that he gave himself up for the remission of our sins has a certain plausibility in the eyes of the many[44] because of historical parallels: in Greek history where we often read about people giving themselves up in order to save their cities;[45] also Jewish history, which prepares the son of Abraham for being sacrificed to God,[46] contains an example of such a tale.' That Alexander knew the story of Genesis 22 seems beyond doubt at first sight,[47] but we have to raise the question whether perhaps he knew the story (only or

---

40 O. Dreyer, *Untersuchungen zum Begriff des Gottgeziemenden in der Antike* (Hildesheim-New York 1970).

41 See my essay 'The Elements ...' 250.

42 Surprising also because in ch. 24 (p. 35 Br.) Alexander appears to know that the Manichaeans rejected the Old Testament.

43 This may have been one of the facts that contributed to the long-standing but erroneous view, inaugurated by Photius (*Contra Manichaeos* I 11), that Alexander was *the bishop* of Lycopolis, which is the reason why his treatise was also printed in Migne's *Patrologia Graeca* (vol. 18), published in 1856, even though I. de Beausobre had decisively refuted this view as early as 1734 (*Histoire critique de Manichée et du manichéisme*, vol. I 236-7).

44 *Not* of Alexander himself, that is.

45 A parallel drawn already by Celsus in *CC* I 31.

46 A clear reference to the so-called *aqedat Yitschak* ('the binding of Isaac') in Genesis 22.

47 Julian also knew the story, *C. Galil.* 343C-D = fr. 83 Masaracchia.

also) as expanded in Jewish (or Christian) interpretation, for he mentions Isaac ('the son of Abraham') as an example of 'people giving themselves up,' whereas the biblical story portrays Isaac as just a completely passive object of God's command and his father's activity. In post-biblical Jewish sources of the Roman period, however, we find the motif that Isaac cheerfully volunteered to be the sacrifice God wanted to have, and that he did this for the welfare of his people, the Jews. To quote just one of the many examples, *Targum Pseudo-Jonathan*, an Aramaic (strongly paraphrastic) translation of the Bible from late antiquity (but containing many older traditions),[48] renders Gen. 22:10 ('Then Abraham put forth his hand and took the knife to slay his son.') as follows: 'Isaac spoke up and said to his father: 'Tie me well lest I struggle because of the anguish of my soul, with the result that a blemish will be found in your offering, and I will be thrust into the pit of destruction.' The eyes of Abraham were looking at the eyes of Isaac, and the eyes of Isaac were looking at the angels on high. Isaac saw them but Abraham did not see them. The angels on high exclaimed: 'Come, see two unique ones who are in the world: one is slaughtering and one is being slaughtered; the one who slaughters does not hesitate, and the one who is being slaughtered stretches forth his neck'.'[49] In the first century pseudo-Philonic *Liber Antiquitatum Biblicarum* XVIII 5 the soteriological aspect is stressed. Here it is even said that God chose the people of Israel on account of Isaac's blood (*pro sanguine eius*)! Even though Alexander seems to be aware of the fact that the biblical story does not describe the actual sacrifice of Isaac ('Jewish history ... *prepares* the son of Abraham for being sacrificed to God'), the sheer fact that he mentions this tradition on a par with the Greek stories of heroes sacrificing themselves in order to save their cities strongly suggests that he was also aware of the soteriological interpretation that this story was given in post-biblical Jewish exegesis.[50] If this is correct, it could mean that Alexander not only

---

[48] See U. Glessmer, *Einleitung in die Targume zum Pentateuch* (Tübingen 1995) 181-196.

[49] See for this translation and notes M. Maher, *Targum Pseudo-Jonathan: Genesis* (The Aramaic Bible, vol. Ib, Edinburgh 1992) 79-80. The Aramaic original is in *Biblia Polyglotta Matritensia, ser. IV: Targum Palaestinense in Pentateuchum, Lib. 1: Genesis*, ed. A. Diez Macho (Madrid 1988) 143.

[50] Sh. Spiegel, *The Last Trial. On the Legends and Lore of the Command to Abraham to Offer Isaac as a Sacrifice: The Akedah* (Woodstock 1993 = New York 1967), offers many examples of this exegesis. The best bibliography on the *aqedah* to date is by B. Cozijnsen and P. Wansink at the end of their contribution to

knew the Bible, together with various Christian writings and traditions, but was perhaps also acquainted with Jewish haggadic material, either oral or written, or with Christian variants of these interpretations.

This impression is strengthened by ch. 25 (p. 37 Br.) where Jewish tales are favourably compared with Manichaean ones. In this case he remarks that 'when the history of the Jews speaks of the angels who consorted with the daughters of men in order to have sexual intercourse, this way of telling the story hints at the nurturing faculties of the soul which comes down hither from above.' This reference to the famous but enigmatic passage in Gen. 6:1-4 is revealing in a number of respects. Firstly, the biblical text does not speak about 'angels' but about 'sons of God' who had sexual intercourse with earthly women. The Septuagint also reads here οἱ υἱοὶ τοῦ θεοῦ, although there is a widely attested but certainly secondary variant ἄγγελοι, a reading supported by Josephus, *Ant.* I 73,[51] but evidently an interpretation meant to get rid of the somewhat embarrassing 'sons of God.'[52] This interpretation of 'sons of God' as angels was later adopted also by the Christians, so it is hard to decide whether Alexander learned this interpretation from Jewish or from Christian sources (a LXX ms he knew?). Secondly, he interprets the angels as αἱ θρεπτικαὶ δυνάμεις τῆς ψυχῆς who come down from above. Though Philo's interpretation of the biblical verse (*Gig.* 6-18, on Gen. 6:2) is rather different from Alexander's, what they have in common is that the angels are here taken in an allegorical sense as the souls, or functions of the souls, of men. It may well be that Alexander is here drawing on a Jewish Alexandrian tradition of interpretation of Gen. 6:1-4, although it should be added that this biblical passage has evoked such an

---

M. van den Berg *et al.* (edd.), *Uit de sjoel geklapt. Christelijke belangstelling voor joodse traditie* (Hilversum 1986) 143-5.

[51] Philo has the mixed reading 'angels of God' (*Gig.* 6), although at *Quaest. Gen.* I 92 he remarks that 'Moses sometimes calls the angels 'sons of God' because they are made incorporeal.' See D. Winston & J. Dillon, *Two Treatises of Philo of Alexandria* (Chico 1983) 236: 'It seems as if someone in the Alexandrian tradition was offended, as well he might be, by the idea of God having sons, and glosses 'sons' by the less offensive term ἄγγελοι.' But the phenomenon was certainly not restricted to Alexandria, as the Targumim show (see the references in the next note).

[52] See J. W. Wevers, *Notes on the Greek Text of Genesis* (Atlanta 1993) 75-6; Ph. S. Alexander, 'The Targumim and Early Exegesis of 'Sons of God' in Genesis 6', *Journal of Jewish Studies* 23 (1972) 60-71.

enormous amount of speculation and literature among both Jews and Christians in antiquity that, again, it is hard to decide what exactly his source was. Nonetheless, we may conclude that he was acquainted not just with the Bible but also with Jewish and/or Christian interpretations of it.[53]

It is conspicuous that the biblical passages we have seen Alexander referring to are almost all from the early chapters of Genesis. This aspect deserves some additional comments. Recently Giancarlo Rinaldi has collected all the references to the Bible in pagan Graeco-Roman authors of the imperial period.[54] This useful catalogue contains 715 entries of which no less than 96 pertain to Genesis. That is to say that some 13.5% of the biblical references in pagan literature of these centuries is to Genesis, which is quite disproportionate in view of the fact that the book of Genesis takes up no more than some 4.4% of the Bible (i.e., OT and NT). That is to say that Genesis is referred to more than three times as often as might be expected on average. The first book of the Bible seems to have been much better known among pagan authors than any other book of the Old Testament.[55] When we take a closer look at the 96 entries for Genesis, we see that no less than 63 of them are references to what I called the early chapters, i.e. the so-called 'Urgeschichte' in Gen. 1-11.[56] These are exactly the chapters that most of Alexander's references are to: Gen. 1, 4 and 6 (the only exception being Gen. 22). So Alexander neatly fits into the general pattern we see elsewhere. The unknown author of the *Poimandres*,

---

[53] J. Geffcken, *Der Ausgang des griechisch-römischen Heidentums* (Darmstadt 1963 = Heidelberg 1929) 77, even goes as far as saying that Alexander was 'gleich sovielen Genossen seiner Sekte voll Interesse für die Juden.' For Julian's treatment of Gen. 6:2 see *C. Galil.* 290B-D = fr. 67 Masaracchia. Does Alexander refer to the famous myth about the giants in Gen. 6:1-4 because he knew that the Manichaean *Book of the Giants* had been inspired, albeit indirectly, by that passage? See Reeves, *Jewish Lore* 20-1. Perhaps Reeves somewhat too confidently states that it is clear that 'Alexander was acquainted with both Jewish and Christian literature' (21).

[54] G. Rinaldi, *Biblia Gentium. Primo contributo per un indice delle citazioni, dei riferimenti e delle allusioni alla bibbia negli autori pagani, greci e latini, di età imperiale* (Roma 1989).

[55] For comparison's sake: in Rinaldi's list Exodus has 23 entries, Isaiah 16, Daniel 40 (but all of them from Porphyry!); from the NT Matthew has most entries: 106 (cf. John 65).

[56] The number of references to Gen. 1-11 would even have been much higher if Rinaldi had included the many allusions to these chapters in the Hermetic tractate *Poimandres*, which he did not for unclear reasons stated at p. 52 n. 27.

who was a somewhat earlier compatriot of Alexander, also draws mainly upon the chapters of the 'Urgeschichte,'[57] as is also done by some Gnostic writers (see esp. the *Apocryphon of John*).

Let us finally turn to an interesting and curious passage where Alexander, after having argued that moral progress is possible, says the following: 'This was, I believe, correctly understood by Jesus, and this is why, in order that farmers, carpenters, masons, and other skilled workers should not be excluded from the good, he instituted a common circle of all these people together, and why, by means of simple and easy conversations, he led them towards an understanding of God and helped them to achieve a desire for the good' (16, p. 24 Br.). In the first place, it is clear that Alexander sees in Jesus here (and elsewhere) 'nullement un rédempteur transcendant, mais plutôt un professeur de morale populaire.'[58] Rather, Jesus is here depicted as a kind of latter-day Socrates who also used to have conversations with δημιουργοί.[59] Secondly, the contents of the list of 'farmers, carpenters, masons, and other skilled workers,' who formed the circle of Jesus' disciples, is hard to explain, but it may point in the direction of which kind of people belonged to the Christian communities in Alexander's own environment. The fact that the final words of this passage literally echo the words of ch. 1, where he said that he had seen with his own eyes that Christian ethical instruction, in spite of its low theoretical level, nevertheless led people by degrees towards 'a desire for the good,' seems to indicate that it is again his own experiences with Christians that makes him enumerate here the sorts of people Jesus was able to attract to his teachings.[60] Here we can see a marked difference with his predecessor Celsus, who had said that 'Jesus collected around him ten or eleven infamous

---

[57] See the extensive discussion of this matter by C. H. Dodd, *The Bible and the Greeks* (London 1964 = 1935) 99-248.

[58] Villey, *Alexandre* 279. Cf. also Alexander's remark in ch. 24 (p. 36 Br.): 'To have Christ submit to passion to make something manifest is utter foolishness, when words are sufficient for the teaching and the knowledge of what is.'

[59] Compare Porphyry's remark that Jesus was one of the wise men of the Hebrews (from *De philosophia ex oraculis haurienda*, quoted by Augustine, *Civ. Dei* XIX 23). Geffcken, *Ausgang* 77, reckons Alexander among those who 'Porphyrios' Gerechtigkeit gegen Christus selbst noch weiter entwickelt haben.' On Porphyry's praise of Jesus see also Wilken, *Christians* 148-56, 159-60.

[60] It is notable that in the third-century *Acts of Thomas* 2 the apostle Thomas is also presented as a carpenter. In the Gospels Jesus is himself the son of a carpenter.

men, the most wicked tax-collectors and sailors, and with these he fled hither and thither, collecting a means of livelihood in a disgraceful and importunate way' (*CC* I 61); and, similarly, in *CC* II 46: 'When he was alive he won over ten sailors and tax-collectors of the most abominable character.'[61] And especially in *CC* III 59-69 Celsus mocks Jesus' and the Christians' love for 'sinners' and tries to demonstrate that this leads to the church's being nothing but a band of criminals.[62] Not so Alexander. Of course, his enumeration of the professions of Jesus' followers implies that they were lower class people, who for that very reason needed 'simple and easy conversations' but, contrary to Celsus, he does believe that Jesus was succesful in bringing these simple people to a higher level and a genuine 'desire for the good.'[63]

Even though the subject under consideration deserves more of an in depth treatment than was possible in this short paper, we may briefly summarize our provisional findings. Alexander had some knowledge of the Bible but it was not extensive (especially when compared with that of his predecessor Celsus and his contemporary and fellow-Platonist Porphyry, not to speak of the later Julian). It cannot even be excluded that all the biblical references in his work are based on hearsay, not on his own reading. The (only?) biblical books he appears to have had some knowledge of were Genesis and the Gospels (as usual among pagan authors with some knowledge of the Bible), and perhaps also of *2 Timothy*. But this

---

61 The Gospels mention four fishermen ('sailors') and one tax-collector as Jesus' disciples. In *CC* I 62 Origen rejoins that a sailor is not the same as a fisherman and, moreover, that, contrary to the suggestion by Celsus, of the majority of the disciples we do not at all know what were the trades by which they earned their living. Yet the designation 'fishermen' for the apostles (and sometimes for Christians in general) is found more often; see J. H. Waszink, *Tertulliani De anima* (Amsterdam 1947) 119. On Celsus' (and others') uncertainty about the number of disciples see W. Bauer, 'Das Apostelbild in der altchristlichen Überlieferung', in E. Hennecke & W. Schneemelcher (edd.), *Neutestamentliche Apokryphen*, vol. 2 (Tübingen 1971, 3. Aufl.) 11-12.

62 *CC* III 55 makes clear that it is probably also Celsus' own experiences with Christians in his environment that colours his depiction of Jesus' followers. Cf. also Lucian, *De morte Peregrini* 13. See on this topic further W. Bauer, *Das Leben Jesu im Zeitalter der neutestamentlichen Apokryphen* (Tübingen 1909, repr. Darmstadt 1967) 426-7.

63 Unlike Alexander, Celsus heaps scorn upon the person of Jesus; for a list of references see S. Benko, 'Pagan Criticism of Christianity During the First Two Centuries A.D.', *ANRW* II 23, 2 (Berlin 1980) 1102.

knowledge apparently did not inspire him to vehement attacks on the Bible, in sharp contrast to Celsus, Porphyry, and Julian. He had some knowledge of Christian, but possibly also of Jewish, exegetical traditions. Even though he found Christian doctrine inferior from a philosophical point of view, he was positive about the effects of Christian ethical preaching and he praised Jesus' efforts to bring common people to 'a desire for the good.'[64] This might make us wonder why he was so circumspect and mild in dealing with Christianity and its founder. Could it have been at least in part motivated by the fact that some of his own students belonged to the Christian church?[65]

Utrecht

---

64 'Une telle bienveillance n'était pas courante', says P. de Labriolle, *La réaction païenne. Étude sur la polémique antichrétienne du Ier au VIe siècle* (Paris 1950, 10th ed.) 317.

65 It should be noted that in the three centuries after Alexander Christian students in the Alexandrian Platonist school were increasingly a common phenomenon. On the interactions taking place and the compromises reached between the Alexandrian form of Neoplatonism and Christianity see L. G. Westerink, *Anonymous Prolegomena to Platonic Philosophy* (Amsterdam 1962) X-XXV, and R. Sorabji, 'The Ancient Commentators on Aristotle', in R. Sorabji (ed.), *Aristotle Transformed: The Ancient Commentators and Their Influence* (London 1990) 1-30, esp. 10-15. Note the interesting but bold and hypothetical statement by I. Hadot in the same volume: 'Alexander, the head of the Platonic school of Lycopolis, refutes the Manichaeans because the Manichaeans attended his courses' (287).

I owe thanks to the following colleagues for their useful comments on the first draft of this paper: Keimpe Algra, Jan den Boeft, Roelof van den Broek, Peter Lautner, David T. Runia (who also kindly checked my English), and Leonard V. Rutgers.

PART SIX

DIALECTIC AND DOXOGRAPHY

A 'DIALECTICAL' ARGUMENT IN *DE ANIMA* A 4

On Aristotle's use of *topoi* in systematic contexts*

HAN BALTUSSEN

1. *Introduction*

Aristotle's introductory discussions of earlier views on specific philosophical issues have been studied from different angles. One fairly recent line of investigation makes use of his handbook on dialectic, the *Topika.*[1] This has proven profitable in many ways, but has also created a (minor) problem of terminology. Whenever the introductions are labelled 'dialectical', the meaning of this term is usually considered as sufficiently clear. However, it hardly ever receives an explicit definition.[2] It seems to take on at least two basic meanings: 1. Aristotle engages in a critical debate (διαλέγεσθαι) and aims at scrutinizing the views;[3] 2. Aristotle makes use of certain techniques (*diairesis, aporia, diaphônia*) indicated as useful in the *Topics*, which provide the structure for the selection and presentation of earlier *doxai*. These are very general ways of clarifying his approach and are for the most part based on a few passages in the *Topics* (mainly the programmatic books A and Θ).[4]

My objective in this paper is a modest one: (1) I will explore the possibility of defining the label 'dialectical' more accurately than has been customary hitherto,[5] and (2) I will argue that the actual *topoi* of the central books of the *Topics* deserve more attention as an aid for analysing the *doxai*-discussions.[6] Among several illustrative

---

* It is my pleasure to offer this paper to Jaap Mansfeld, *vero magistro.*

1 Fundamental paper by Weil (1951). See Baltussen (1993) ch. 2 for further literature.

2 His approach in these passages has also been labelled 'doxographical' or even 'historical'. For some remarks on these (problematic) terms see section 2.

3 For this function of dialectic see *Top.* 101b4 ἐξεταστική and *Rhet.* 1354a5 ἐξετάζειν καὶ ὑπέχειν λόγον.

4 On *diairesis* see Mansfeld (1990) 3062n; on *aporia* cf. *Top.* 145b1f., on *diaphônia* (not an Aristotelian term!) see esp. Mansfeld (1990) 3060, 3063, 3092 ff.

5 Mansion (1961) 41 calls his method in *Phys.* A 'préparation dialectique' without further clarification; not so Mansfeld (1990) 3063 who speaks of overviews 'for dialectical purposes' or of 'a dialectical discussion (which may even be purely didactic) ...' (*ibid.* 3064) (cf. n. 4).

6 I prefer the expression '*doxai*-discussion' instead of 'doxography' because

examples which might be adduced for this purpose,[7] Aristotle's discussion of the views on the soul is very useful one with some especially interesting aspects. The general features which make *De anima* A 2-4 a good example of a dialectical *doxai*-discussion (in the sense described above) are well-known and hardly need extensive discussion here.[8] However, some aspects of a more technical nature may illustrate that the influence of the dialectical method goes beyond the obvious fact of classification and selection of *doxai*. I will call attention to one specific point which to my knowledge has received little attention so far.[9] In tracing these details in Aristotle's criticisms I shall argue that our understanding of specific forms of argument may profit from comparison with the *Topics*. Thus I also hope to show how we may further qualify the term 'dialectical', while bearing in mind Aristotle's own conception of dialectic.[10]

2. *A note on terminology*

Since it may not be apparent why Aristotle's approach towards previous views may be labelled 'dialectical' (rather than 'historical' or 'doxographical'), some introductory remarks on terminology are called for. In our view the alternative terms bring in connotations (and analyses) which are either anachronistic or inappropriate, and may actually be misleading in our understanding of Aristotle's (and Theophrastus') actual procedure.

In modern studies the term 'doxography' appears to mean 'a description or summary of what philosophers have said', where

---

it highlights the role of *doxa* and at the same time draws a distinction between *doxai*-discussions and *doxai*-collections (cf. below n. 8).

[7] Modern studies using the technical elements are e.g. Schickert (1977) 48 ff. (on the *Eudemus/De an.* A), Morsink (1982), Beriger (1989) 81 ff. (on *Metaph.* M 1-3).

[8] The use of *endoxa* —the mark of applied dialectic— as views endorsed by 'reputable men' (*Top.* 100b21-23) is more than apparent: apart from adducing qualified opinions (see esp. 407b4-5, 13, 27) Aristotle adds a positive formulation of a better perspective which itself is backed up by endoxic views (408a34-b20). Compare 408a10 where he characterizes the discussion as the *testing* of views (εὐεξέταστος).

[9] Despite many remarks on dialectical aspects Hicks (1907) does not mention it.

[10] Irwin's distinction (1988) 19 ff., 116 between 'strong dialectic' and 'pure dialectic' seems less appropriate, because it does not take its cue from Aristotle. It has met with strong criticism, see e.g. D.W. Hamlyn, *Philosophy* 65 (1990) 465-476, R. Wardy, *Phronesis* 26 (1991) 86-106.

particular stress is on the *reporting* of the *doxai*.[11] It is not hard to see that this would be a rather narrow description for Aristotle's approach (who adds criticisms and also uses generally accepted opinions). Also, the origin of the term is significant. It is thought that Hermann Diels introduced the terms *doxographia/doxographi* to characterize the form in which post-Peripatetic collections of *doxai* were cast, while deriving their contents from the material available in Peripatetic writings.[12] What Diels had in mind is illustrated by the way in which he edited the Aëtius text in his *Doxographi Graeci* (*DG*). Diels's intention has been stated as follows:

> Diels himself ... seems originally not to have used *doxographia* nor *doxographus* as an adjective but only *doxographi* to denote the authors of books about the physical and metaphysical opinions of ancient philosophers, as contrasted to authors of biographies (cf. *DG* 145-46), [...] The main characteristic of all these *doxographi* is that they report the philosophical doctrines according to subject in such a way that the view of each philosopher ... is given as a separate entry under a general 'chapter heading'.[13]

I note that initially the term referred to a (post-Theophrastean) 'genre' of *doxai*-collections which became common in the Hellenistic period for several purposes. When and where the term became used to denote 'any report of philosophical *doxai*', even in Aristotle and Theophrastus, is not our concern. It will be enough to point out here that the expression acquired a wider application which is not completely free of misleading connotations and should be used with qualification in the case of the Peripatetics.[14]

The question of whether Aristotle's approach can be called 'historical' was already debated a few decades ago.[15] No doubt it is correct to state that Aristotle had great interest in all kinds of transmitted knowledge. But this hardly justifies that we regard Aristotle and his followers as historians in the modern sense of the word. The concept of a 'history *of philosophy*' is fairly recent (18th century) and any comparison with Aristotle's method from that perspective is bound to be anachronistic. Both subject (theories, not events)

---

[11] Cf. Passmore (1967) 226, Mejer (1978) 81, Rorty (1984).

[12] If Mejer (1978) whom I follow here is correct. See the next note.

[13] Mejer (1978) 81f. For *doxographi* see e.g. Diels (1879) title page, 114, 145, 178, 225. Diels may also have used the term in respons to the question of the *Preisfrage* of the Academy in Berlin (*DG* introd., v) 'inquiratur ... qui auctores ... sint' and by analogy with the Latin 'placitorum scriptores' (*ibid.* p. iii).

[14] My own suggestion (1993, 21) is to speak of *critical endoxography*.

[15] See Stevenson (1974) with further literature.

and methodology (justification of sources and the aim of being objective) show that he did not self-consciously aim at such an approach.

It could be argued that Aristotle's investigations into the political constitutions bring him closer to the historian than anything else.[16] Here as in biology his 'investigations' (ἱστορίαι) are of a descriptive character, providing a first collection of the facts.[17] His conviction that not knowledge of the particular, but of the universal, was essential must have guided him: by supplying himself with the necessary material he would then be in a position to perform the inductive reasoning towards the universal.[18] Clearly, then, ἱστορία is a term of wide application.[19] It can hardly support the view that Aristotle was a historian *sensu stricto*.[20] Considerations such as these must (and did) lead to the view that Aristotle did not write (and did not intend to write) history of philosophy.[21] The main reason is that Aristotle is very selective in what he thinks is useful for his own purposes.[22]

Since it is clear that the terms just discussed are problematic, I propose to concentrate on the term 'dialectical' as the one which offers the least problems. For this we may take a look at the *Topics*, where we find a connection between arguments and *doxai* (e.g. *Top.* A 14)[23] and a statement which presents Aristotle's different

---

16 It is said of the works on politics and laws. See the references in n. 22.

17 Of course they are more concerned with facts than his *doxai*-discussions. On *historia* see the thorough study by Zoepffel (1975) from which I take over some conclusions.

18 In this respect there is a parallel with the basic principles of dialectic, see e.g. *Top.* 105a12-20; 108b10-12. For a more elaborate exposition on the role of the universal in linking history and Aristotle's general theory of knowledge see Zoepffel (1975) 17 ff.

19 Zoepffel (1975) 33.

20 Even the famous passage in *Poetics* A 9, which brings the term *historikos* close to what we would interpret as 'historical', cannot alter this conclusion. Zoepffel (1975: 14f.) argues persuasively that in this passage, where Aristotle calls poetry 'more philosophical than history, because it says more on the universal, whereas history deals with the particular', the emphasis of the comparative form is on poetry; hence it does not follow that (1) it also goes with the particular thereby 'saving' a bit of the universal for history nor that (2) poetry is philosophical in an absolute sense.

21 As Barnes has put it (1987, 25): 'These accounts have a historical purpose and they are written with a philosophical intention; but they are not, properly speaking, 'histories of philosophy''.

22 Meier (1930), von Fritz (1958), Weil (1965), Huxley (1973) 282 all use the term 'historical'. More careful views are found in Reinhardt (1954) 82 ff., Braun (1973) 16, 20f.

23 Note that even the Greek commentators made a connection between certain 'doxographic' discussions in Aristotle and the mandate of *Top.* A 2

options for the use of dialectic, viz. (1) training, (2) everyday discussions, (3a) philosophy (where it may have several functions), one of which is (3b) the search for *archai* in all fields of investigation (*Top.* A 2.101a25-b4).

Admittedly these are very general descriptions, but the inference seems warranted that modes (2), (3a) and (3b), which represent several stages of increasing technical complexity, build on—and therefore reflect—the features of (1). And while (2) may have left its traces mainly in rhetoric, (3a) and (3b) are very likely to be found in Aristotle's philosophical research. They are different modes of the same *technê* and may be regarded as offshoots of the same stem.[24] I would prefer to use the term 'dialectical' with reference to these, i.e. Aristotle's own, options. In my view it is against this general background that we should try to establish to what extent certain features of his treatment in the *doxai*-discussions warrant use of the term 'dialectical'. I will now proceed to deal briefly with some examples of how such technical features are applied in a systematic context.

3. *A case in point:* De an. *A 2-4*

The following aspects in *De an.* A 2-4 are indications for the use of dialectical tactics.

(I) The combination and confrontation of views exemplifies the use of well-known and accepted views in philosophical investigation; it creates an implicit scale of agreement[25] and disagreement[26] on certain questions, which helps to make a decision on the issue. The cases of agreement (related views) and disagreement (*diaphônia*) resemble collections of views and contrary arguments from the sophistic period.[27] In this way the problematic issues and the arguments with good (*endoxic*) support can be found.[28]

(II) The aspect of definition and linguistic analysis is worked

---

(Simplicius, *In Phys.* 47.22 Diels; *id. In De caelo* 523.25-27 Heiberg; Alexander, *In Metaph.* 174.3 Hayduck; Asclepius, *In Metaph.* 140.7 Hayduck).

24 In the same sense as Aristotle himself calls rhetoric a 'kind of offshoot' of dialectic (*Rhet.* 1356a25, οἷον παραφυές τι).

25 On ξύσματα, 404a3 Atomists and a18 Pythagoreans; on στοιχεῖα, 404b11 Empedocles and b17 Plato; on κίνησις 406b17 Democritus and b26f. Plato.

26 Democritus vs. Anaxagoras ~ corporeal vs. incorporeal.

27 Cf. Mansfeld (1986) 17, 46. See also *De an.* 407b4-5 καθάπερ εἴωθε τε λέγεσθαι καὶ πολλοῖς συνδοκεῖ; 407b27 δόξα ... πιθανὴ πολλοῖς;

28 No doubt these are *endoxa* of the *sophoi* (*Top.* 100b21-24; cf. 104a33-36).

out in different ways. For instance, in dealing with the question whether 'movement' is a characteristic of the soul (406a4 ff.) Aristotle examines the meaning of the phrase 'being moved' (406a4 διχῶς δὲ κινουμένου παντός). Of the two possible meanings—being moved 'either in virtue of something else', i.e. indirectly, 'or in its own right', i.e. directly—the first is clarified by common usage: '*we say* that something is moved indirectly when it is in something' (καθ' ἕτερον δὲ λέγομεν κτλ.) and an example from navigation ('as sailors in a ship').[29] It concerns essential and accidental movement (see below (b)). When this distinction has been stated (διχῶς δὴ λεγομένου), Aristotle turns to applying this distinction to the question at issue.

The step from διχῶς δὲ κινουμένου παντός to διχῶς δὴ λεγομένου marks the transition from descriptive preparation to (formal) analysis. Here some crucial distinctions, originating in Aristotle's physical and dialectical theory, direct the argument and conclusions reached.[30] They may be summarised as follows:

(a) there are four basic types (species) of movement to be distinguished (406a11-12; analysis according to species—κατ' εἴδη, see especially *Top.* B 2.109b14 and cf. *Top.* A 15.106a9 ff.; Δ 1.121b1 ff.);
(b) Aristotle opposes essential to accidental movement (cf. n. 29), and
(c) natural versus forced movement (division according to opposites, see *Top.* A 15.106a10f.; *Top.* B 8.113b15 ff.; E 6.135b7 ff.);
(d) observed fact leads to a reasonable assumption (ἐπεὶ φαίνεται ..., εὔλογον ... 406a30-31) but only to prove the unacceptable consequences of the position (the soul leaving and entering the body, b1-5);[31]
(e) accidental movement is then further explored (b5 ff.).

(III) Another example of dialectical tactics is the rather elaborate critique of Empedocles at 408a19 ff., where Aristotle is in the process of treating the question whether soul is a *harmonia* (a 'hot topic' in contemporary discussions). He reproduces (in indirect speech)

---

[29] On the use of καθ' ἕτερον instead of κατὰ συμβεβηκός see Hicks (1907) 241: 'καθ' ἕτερον ... enables A. to include the case of the passenger, who is, strictly speaking, neither a part nor an accident of the ship [...] his motion ... is as much conditioned by that of the ship as if he were the ship's mast or its tonnage'.

[30] Hicks points to some parallels with the *Physica*: 2.1, 192b13-15, 22; 8.4, 254b14.

[31] Similar terminological distinctions are at the basis of the discussion of soul as 'harmonia' at 407b27 ff., 'a further theory which has come down to us, commending itself to many minds as readily as any that is put forward' (esp. b31 and 408a5). See also section (III).

the line of reasoning behind this view—the body consists of opposites, a *harmonia* is a blending (κρᾶσις) or combining (σύνθεσις) of opposites, the soul is a *harmonia*. In his view (407b32 ff.) *harmonia* must either mean a ratio (λόγος) between or a combination (σύνθεσις) of components, but the soul is (α) neither of these (b33) and (β) this theory cannot explain the cause of motion.

The emphasis on terminology is important, as Aristotle thinks it is preferable to apply the term *harmonia* to health or in general to bodily excellence (408a1). In the ensuing paragraph (408a5 ff.) he goes even further and distinguishes two senses of *harmonia*. Much is now made of the meaning of 'combination' (σύνθεσις), positing that 'there are many combinations of the parts, and they combine in many ways' (a11f.). Aristotle asks for clarification as to how the intellect combines with a part of the body, what the relation is with the appetites, and denies that the mixture in flesh is identical to that in bone.[32]

The argument(s) concerning part and whole and concerning 'combination' (σύνθεσις) in *Top.* Z (which deals specifically with definition) contain the 'blue-print' so to speak for the tactics in our passage in the *De an.*: regarding composition one should state its *method* (150b22-26) and *what kind* is meant (151a22-25). We may compare:

De an. 408a11-12[33]	*Top.* 150b22; 151a20-5 (OCT)
πολλαί τε γὰρ αἱ συνθέσεις τῶν μερῶν καὶ πολλαχῶς· τίνος οὖν ἢ πῶς ὑπολαβεῖν τὸν νοῦν χρὴ σύνθεσιν ἢ καὶ τὸ αἰσθητικὸν ἢ ὀρεκτικόν; ὁμοίως δὲ ἄτοπον καὶ τὸ τὸν λόγον τῆς μίξεως εἶναι τὴν ψυχήν· οὐ γὰρ τὸν αὐτὸν ἔχει λόγον ἡ μίξις τῶν στοιχείων καθ' ἣν σὰρξ καὶ καθ' ἣν ὀστοῦν.[34]	ἔτι [sc. ἐπισκοπεῖν] εἰ μὴ εἴρηκε τὸν τρόπον τῆς συνθέσεως. [...] πάλιν εἰ τὴν τούτων σύνθεσιν εἴρηκε τὸ ὅλον, οἷον τῆς ψυχῆς καὶ τοῦ σώματος σύνθεσιν ζῷον, πρῶτον μὲν σκοπεῖν εἰ μὴ εἴρηκε ποία σύνθεσις, καθάπερ εἰ σάρκα ὁριζόμενος ἢ ὀστοῦν τὴν πυρὸς καὶ γῆς καὶ ἀέρος εἶπε σύνθεσιν. οὐ γὰρ ἀπόχρη τὸ σύνθεσιν εἰπεῖν, ἀλλὰ καὶ ποία τις προσδιοριστέον[35]

---

32 The standard distinction Aristotle makes (*PA* B 1) between *homoiomerê* and *anhomoiomerê*, that is between materials of which the smallest part is of the same nature as a larger quantity and those which break up into different elements.

33 A good parallel is 408b11: ... ἀλλοίωσιν, ποία καὶ πῶς, ἕτερός ἐστι λόγος.

34 'There are *many* combinations of the parts, and they combine *in many ways*. Of what is thought or the sensitive or the appetitive faculty the composition? And what is the composition which constitutes each of them? It is equally absurd to identify the soul with the ratio of the mixture; for the

In both passages the difference between the composition of bone and flesh on the one hand, and that of the elements on the other is emphasized.

The passage—aimed against Empedocles as we see in 408a19—constitutes, as it were, a miniature case of διαπορῆσαι πρὸς ἀμφότερα. Three questions in the form of a dialectical πρόβλημα (disjunctive question: πότερον ... ἢ) are stated (408a20-24):

> (i) Is the soul a ratio or is it something else, which, being distinct, comes to be in the parts ?
> (ii) Is Love the cause of any and every mixture or of a mixture in the right proportion?
> (iii) If the latter, is Love the proportion itself or something other and distinct from it?
> Such then are the difficulties involved in this view. (tr. Hicks, modified)

We should note how the difficulties are spelled out, though not all the options are fully explored. Hicks (*ad* a24, p. 271) rightly points out that 'the whole criticism tends to pass into a discussion of antinomies similar to those which fill *Metaph.* B, where arguments *pro* and *contra* are impartially stated and no decision is given *ex cathedra*'. Aristotle emphasizes the need for characterization in terms of identity and difference. He elaborates on one point, confronting it with observed facts (408a24-28):

> (a) if the soul is distinct from the proportion [cf. (iii) above], why is it destroyed together with the essence of the flesh and that of the other parts of the living being?
> (b) Further, if each of the parts does not have a soul of its own –unless the soul is the ratio of the mixture– what is it that perishes when the soul leaves the body?

The whole passage constitutes a kind of *diairesis* in which disjunctive options are followed through (thus (iii) follows (ii), (a) is connected to (iii) and (b) to (i)). The question dealing with the scheme parts-and-whole takes up one of the initial questions of *De an.* A 1 and illustrates how the earlier views sometimes fail to comply to Aristotelian standards. The most interesting point in

mixture of the elements which makes flesh has a different ratio from that which makes bone.' (tr. Hicks, modified; italics mine).

[35] 'see if he has failed to state the manner of combination ... First, see whether he has omitted to state the kind of composition, as (e.g.) in the definition of flesh or bone as the combination of fire, earth, and air. For it is not enough to say it is a composition, but you should also go on to define the kind of combination'.

Aristotle's discussion is that he shows that both the acceptance and the denial of the theory cause serious difficulties.[36] Thus the dialectical exploration of this view has shown it should be dismissed—which is in line with the original method stated at the outset (403a20-25).[37]

(IV) One other aspect of Aristotle's criticisms deserves to be mentioned here. Aristotle's most frequent complaint we read concerns inadequacy of formulation (lack of clarity). Thus he may point out that more distinctions should be made (A 4, 408b32-409a20 διαφέρειν δεῖ etc.); or he may complain about the formulation of earlier views. This point is nearly always expressed in the phrase οὐ καλῶς/ὀρθῶς λέγειν.[38] The same formulation occurs in programmatic passages such as *Top.* A 2 and *De an.* A 2. The turn of phrase ἱκανῶς—καλῶς—ὀρθῶς λέγειν, 'stating things well etc.' is very frequent in endoxic contexts.[39] A more programmatic illustration of this attitude is the remark in (again) *Top.* Z, viz. in the concluding part of ch. 14 [my italics]:

> In dealing with any definition, it is a most important elementary principle to make a shrewd guess in one's mind at the definition of the object before one or else *to take* over some *happily expressed definition.* For it necessarily follows that, with a model [Cf. *Top.* Z 1-2; Θ 3], as it were, before one, one can see anything that is lacking which the definition ought to contain and any needless addition, and thus be the better provided in the points to attack.[40]

We may take this dialectical rule as a fundamental instruction, since the rules on definition clearly belong to the core of dialectic.[41] The way in which Aristotle formulates his criticisms in the course of investigating earlier views (which in his view are part of

---

[36] Hicks (1907) 271; Ross (1961) 197.

[37] διαποροῦντας ... τὰς τῶν προτέρων δόξας ... <u>εἰ δέ τι μὴ καλῶς</u> [sc. εἰρημένα], τοῦτ' <u>εὐλαβηθῶμεν</u>. Cf. on this passage Mansfeld (1990) 3202.

[38] Cf. Beriger (1989) 84; Hicks *ad loc.*

[39] I.e. contexts in which *endoxa* are prominent. For (οὐ) ἱκανῶς in a systematic context see e.g. *De caelo* 270b12, 291a32, 308a24; *Phys.* 191b36; *HA* 513a14; *EN* 1136a10; *Pol.* 1335a41. For (οὐ) καλως / (οὐ) ὀρθῶς in a logical context see e.g. *Cat.* 8a29-31; *Top.* 101b10-13; *Soph. El.* 175a20, b13, 183b15.

[40] *Top.* 151b17-23: πρὸς ἅπαντας δὲ τοὺς ὁρισμοὺς οὐκ ἐλάχιστον στοιχεῖον τὸ πρὸς ἑαυτὸν εὐστόχως ὁρίσασθαι τὸ προκείμενον ἢ <u>καλῶς εἰρημένον ὅρον ἀναλαβεῖν</u>· ἀνάγκη γὰρ ὥσπερ πρὸς παράδειγμα θεώμενον τό τ' ἐλλεῖπον ὧν προσῆκεν ἔχειν τὸν ὁρισμὸν καὶ τὸ προσκείμενον περιέργως καθορᾶν ὥστε μᾶλλον ἐπιχειρημάτων εὐπορεῖν

[41] I think this 'rule' goes beyond the level of dialectical exercises. The reason is that in *Top.* A. Aristotle states that his main tools for dialectical analysis are the four predicables (genus, differentia, accidens, definition), which '*in a way all are concerned with definition*' (τρόπον τινὰ ὁρικά, 102b34f.).

'apparent facts', *ta phainomena*) and solving the difficulties shows how the discussion moves quickly from the abstract (or logical) level to the concrete level and back again, that is to say, between theoretical considerations and existing views. Such an approach he no doubt regarded as legitimate, given the nature of dialectic as 'a technique independent of any specific field of investigation' (*Rhet.* 1358a10-35).

The importance of the function of dialectic is further clarified in the same passage (*Rhet.* 1358a21-26), when Aristotle connects it to dialectical moves geared to find starting-points (*archai*) within a philosophical inquiry (= mode 3b mentioned above):

> these [general commonplaces] have no special subject-matter, and will therefore not increase our knowledge of any particular class of things (*genos*). On the other hand, the better the selection one makes of propositions suitable for special commonplaces the nearer one comes, unconsciously, to setting up a science that is distinct from dialectic and rhetoric. One may succeed in stating the required principles, but one's science will be no longer dialectic or rhetoric, but the science to which the principles thus discovered belong. (Rev. Oxf. Tr.)

Here Aristotle indicates how the formal moves of rhetoric and dialectic give a science or field of investigation direction and substance: these can contribute to the attainment of starting-points, thus setting up a science in a well-founded manner.

4. *Conclusion*

Our starting-point was the query concerning the use of certain (modern) labels for Aristotle's discussions of earlier views. Among the three most frequently used—'historical', doxographical', 'dialectical'—the term 'dialectical' was chosen as the one causing the least problems. Because the term still needed further qualification, we opted for an approach in which Aristotle's own position was studied as found in his work on dialectic, the *Topics.*

We saw that Aristotle indicates four areas in which dialectic may be used (*Top.* 101a25-b4)[42] and suggested that the basic level of training (γυμνασία) is traceable in all three other areas mentioned.[43] With this in mind it was urged that we exercise caution in using the term 'dialectical'.

---

[42] For a new interpretation of this passage see Smith (1993).

[43] Viz. (2) everyday encounters (cf. *Rhet.* 1354a4f), (3a) philosophy and (3b) search for *archai* in all the sciences.

As one possible route towards clarifying the label we have briefly analysed some passages in *De an.* A with a view to the statements in the *Top.* which give dialectic a role in such contexts. This revealed, among other things, an interesting parallel between the 'rules' from a *technê* (*Top.*) and a treatise of systematic nature (*De an.*). Not only does it provide counter-evidence to the view that dialectic was superseded by the *Analytics*,[44] it also gives the label 'dialectical' a fuller meaning by taking more aspects of the dialectical method into account.

I end with a few concluding remarks. The *Topics* may still be regarded as a valuable tool for analysis when it comes to interpreting the nature of Aristotle's arguments. The example given above may seem somewhat tenuous on its own, but it does not stand alone.[45] This is not to say that Aristotle was slavishly following his own codifications of the handbook, but merely expresses the conviction that the *topoi* give us a clue to many of his lines of reasoning, in particular when it comes to critical evaluations of his predecessors. My argument has been that we should use the term 'dialectical' with some care, especially in making clear which of its different aspects is meant. In other words, the more general features of presentation (the use of *endoxa*, the opposing of views) should not be given a too dominant role in defining what dialectic is at the cost of more technical ones (formal arguments for criticism, technical terms). The first category is important in making a philosophical point by way of enhancing contrast, the second helps to establish to what extent certain arguments really represent the critic's own views or are merely 'logical'. Both aspects of the method can be found in Aristotle and both deserve attention in their own right.*

Utrecht

---

44 On this point see also Baltussen (1993) 16-18.

45 Cf. above n. 7 (not all on *doxai*-discussions).

* I am grateful to K.A. Algra, D.T. Runia and T.L. Tieleman for some very useful remarks on an earlier version of this paper.

Bibliography

Baltussen, H. (1993) *Theophrastus on Theories of Perception. The Argument and Purpose in the De sensibus* (diss. Utrecht).

Barnes, J. (1987) *Early Greek Philosophy* (Penguin Classics).

Beriger, A. (1989) *Die aristotelische Dialektik. Ihre Darstellung in der 'Topik' und den 'Sophistischen Wiederlegungen' und ihre Anwendung in 'Metaphysik' M 1-3.* (Heidelberg).

Braun, L. (1973) *L'histoire de l'histoire de la philosophie* (Paris).

Fritz, K. von (1958) 'Die Bedeutung des Aristoteles für die Geschichtsschreibung', *Entretiens Fondation Hardt,* Tome iv (Vandroeuvres-Genève) 83-128.

Hicks, R.D. (1907) *Aristotle. De anima* (with tr. intr. notes) (Oxford, repr. Amsterdam, 1965).

Huxley, G. (1973) 'Aristotle as an Antiquary', *GRBS* 14: 271-286.

Irwin, T.H. (1988) *Aristotle's First Principles* (Oxford).

Mansfeld, J. (1986) 'Aristotle, Plato, and the Pre-Platonic Doxography and Chronography' in Cambiano (ed.), *Storiografia e Dossografia nella Filosofia Antica* (Torino) 1-59.

——, (1990) 'Doxography and Dialectic. The *Sitz im Leben* of the 'Placita'', *ANRW* II 36.4 (1990) 3056-3229.

Mansion, S. (1961) 'Le rôle de l'exposée et de la critique des philosophies antérieures chez Aristote', in S. Mansion (ed.), *Aristote et les problèmes de la méthode* (Louvain/ Paris)

Meier, M. (1930) 'Aristoteles als Historiker', in: *Philosophia Perennis I,* Festschrift Josef Geyser (Regensburg) 39-54.

Mejer, J. (1978) *Diogenes Laertius and his Hellenistic Background* (Wiesbaden).

Momigliano, A. (1978) 'Greek Historiography', *History and Theory* 17: 1-28.

Morsink, J. (1982) 'The Mandate of Topics I.2', *Apeiron* 16: 102-128.

Passmore, J. (1967) 'Historiography of philosophy', in *Encyclopedia of Philosophy,* ed. P. Edwards (New York-London).

Reinhardt, K. (1954) 'Philosophy and History among the Greeks', *Greece & Rome* 1: 82-90.

Rorty, R. (1984) 'The Historiography of Philosophy: four genres', in R. Rorty, J.B. Schneewind & Q. Skinner (eds), *Philosophy in History. Essays on the Historiography of Philosophy* (Cambridge-London-New York) 49-75.

Ross, W. D. (1961) *Aristotle. De anima* (Oxford).

Schickert, K. (1977) *Die Form der Wiederlegung beim frühen Aristoteles* (München).

Sichirollo (1966) *Dialegesthai-Dialektik, von Homer bis Aristoteles* (Hildesheim).

Smith, R. (1993) 'Aristotle on the uses of dialectic', *Synthese* 96: 335-358.

Stevenson, J.G. (1974) 'Aristotle as Historian of Philosophy', *Journal of Hellenic Studies* 94: 138-143.

Weil, E. (1951) 'La place de la logique dans la pense aristotélienne', *Revue de Métaphysique et de Morale* 56: 283-315 [= 'The Place of Logic in Aristotle's Thought', in: J. Barnes e.a. (edd), *Articles on Aristotle, 1. Science* (London 1975) 88-112]

Weil, R. (1965) 'Philosophie et histoire. La vision de l'histoire chez Aristote', *Entretiens Fondation Hardt,* Tome xi (Vandroeuvres-Genève) 161-189.

Zoepffel, R. (1975) *Historia und Geschichte bei Aristoteles,* Abh. Heidelberger Akad. der Wiss., Phil.-hist. Kl., Abh.2.

THEOPHRASTUS' *DE SENSIBUS* ON PLATO

A. A. Long[1]

Theophrastus' *De sensibus* is a unique source of information concerning earlier Greek philosophers' opinions on sense perception and perceptible properties.[2] If his work had not survived, we would lack details pertinent to understanding Parmenides' obscure lines on human thought (fr. 16 DK), and we would know very little

---

[1] I offer this paper as a sixtieth birthday present to my friend Jaap Mansfeld. As the world's greatest expert on the doxography of Greek philosophy, he will be the first to spot its shortcomings and the first to build on anything of value it contains.

Much of my material was presented to the Theophrastus conference, which took place on Lesbos in August 1989. I am grateful for the comments from participants that I received on this occasion, and also to Tom Rosenmeyer, who helped me to improve this final version. After I had submitted it, the editors recalled my attention to H. Baltussen's chapter, 'Theophrastus' *De sensibus* and Plato's *Timaeus*', which forms part of his doctoral dissertation, *Theophrastus on Theories of Perception. Argument and Purpose in the De sensibus,* written under the direction of Jaap Mansfeld and Hans Gottschalk, and published as vol. VI of *Quaestiones infinitae. Publications of the Department of Philosophy, Utrecht University* (Utrecht 1993). Although there is some overlap in the material we discuss and in our respective findings, our approaches are so different that I find it best to let my original text stand for the most part. My purpose is largely limited to comparing Theophrastus' reports on Plato, as clearly as possible, with the relevant passages of the *Timaeus*. Baltussen's study offers much more in the way of attempts to explain and partly justify Theophrastus' procedures.

[2] Assessments of Theophrastus' accuracy in the *De sensibus* vary considerably. Citing Stratton (n. 3 below), Charles Kahn wrote: 'The performance of Theophrastus here [i.e. his treatment of Plato], in the sole case where we can fully control his use of source material, is fine enough to justify a modern editor's praise of the "high accuracy" of his "dispassionate and marvellously impartial report", *Anaximander and the Origins of Greek Cosmology* (New York 1960) 21. Yet, Statton himself also admitted that Theophrastus, in his criticism of Plato, 'seems oftener to miss the point' (p. 53). For a very different assessment, cf. J. McDiarmid, who, in his article 'Theophrastus on the Presocratic Causes', *HSCPh* 61 (1953) 133, wrote: 'The fragments considered disclose no evidence that Theophrastus employed his knowledge of the Presocratics in such a way as to exercise independent judgment about them ... He has frequently misrepresented his source and has exaggerated the faults present in it. It must be concluded that, with regard to the Presocratic causes at least, he is a thoroughly biased witness and is even less trustworthy than Aristotle'. To place this comment in perspective, note J. Mansfeld's comment in his *Studies in the Historiography of Greek Philosophy* (Assen–Maastricht 1990) 24: 'There is no doxography in the proper sense of the word in Aristotle or Plato, or even in Theophrastus, because the *doxai* at issue are presented from a systematical point of view in order to further the discussion of problems of a systematical nature'.

about the relevant doctrines of Alcmaeon, Anaxagoras and Democritus. Theophrastus' lengthy treatment of Empedocles includes many points that could not be inferred from the surviving fragments or from other secondary sources. In one instance only, Plato, we are able to compare Theophrastus' reports with his own source. Although he does not name the *Timaeus*, all his information about Plato in the *De sensibus*, as G.M. Stratton observed, seems 'to be drawn exclusively from' that dialogue.[3] Indeed, according to the same scholar, when he deals in the last part of the work (*Sens.* 83-91) with Plato's treatment of perceptibles (αἰσθητά), Theophrastus preserves Plato's order of exposition 'without a single change'. 'This', he continues, 'with the various verbal similarities, makes one almost see Theophrastus at work with the *Timaeus* spread before him'.[4] My purpose in this paper is very simple—to exhibit what happens when we study Theophrastus' treatment of Plato in the *De sensibus* on the basis of Stratton's observation.[5]

At the beginning of the work Theophrastus divides the majority of opinions concerning αἴσθησις into two groups: those that explain it 'by likeness', and those that explain it 'by the opposite'. As proponents of the first explanation he cites Parmenides, Empedocles and Plato. In aligning Plato with Empedocles, Theophrastus follows Aristotle (*De an.* I 2, 404b16) whose justification for the claim is tendentious if not impenetrable.[6] After elaborating on the two types of explanation, Theophrastus makes the following observation:

> As for each particular sense, practically all of them are neglectful, but Empedocles does try to refer them too to likeness (*Sens.* 3).

Theophrastus returns to Plato, after a page on Parmenides, with these words:

---

[3] G.M. Stratton, *Theophrastus and the Greek physiological psychology before Aristotle* (London–New York 1917) 159. Stratton's text, which I draw on here, is substantially that of Diels in his *Doxographi Graeci*. A new Budé text is bring prepared by André Laks and Glenn Most.

[4] *Ibid.* 203.

[5] Baltussen (n. 1 above), p. 129, says: 'We should certainly not imagine Theophrastus at work' in the way Stratton intimated. I demur. For even if, as is probable, Theophrastus is writing on the basis of excerpts of the *Timaeus*, Baltussen himself assumes (p. 127) that 'Theophrastus has consulted the (complete) *Tim.* text', and acknowledges the verbatim character of some of his reports.

[6] Aristotle *ad loc.* refers to 'Plato in the *Timaeus*'. R.D. Hicks, in his great commentary on the *De anima*, comments: 'The reference is to the ψυχογονία in *Timaeus* 34C sqq.', and 'that like is known by like is the assumption underlying the language of *Tim.* 47A-C'. I confess to doubt about both proposals.

> Plato touched on the particular senses to a greater extent, but he did not in fact speak about all of them, but only about hearing and sight (*Sens.* 5).

Theophrastus then gives reports about Plato's account of these two senses, and concludes with this remark:

> Concerning smell, taste and touch he said nothing at all, nor about whether there are other senses beyond these, but he gives a more careful treatment of the perceptibles (*Sens.* 6).

This is an extraordinary statement because Plato's discussion of tactile, gustatory and odoriferous properties (*Tim.* 61e-62c, 65b-67a), which Theophrastus knows very well (see below), includes an account of touch, taste and smell. Why, then, has he suppressed this? (I say 'suppressed' rather than 'ignored' because much later, when Theophrastus charges Democritus and Plato with contradicting themselves in their accounts of the perceptibles (*Sens.* 60-61), he virtually retracts the statement, claiming that 'Plato refers practically all the perceptibles to their [perceptible] effects (πάθη) and to sense perception'!) The answer seems to be that he suppresses Plato's account of touch, taste and smell at this point in his argument because what Plato says about these perceptual processes does not fit the explanation in terms of 'likeness'. According to Plato, these perceptions result from contact with elementary particles that lack the properties we ourselves perceive. In the case of sight and probably hearing too, Theophrastus leads his readers to think that Plato's words justify his being regarded as a 'likeness' theorist. Thus he says that Plato 'makes sight of fire, which is why he also makes colour a kind of flame coming from bodies...' (*Sens.* 5). The 'likeness' explanation is also implicit, I think, in his characterization of Plato's account of hearing, when, going beyond Plato's text, he says: 'He defines hearing through sound'. The idea seems to be that, like Empedocles (*ibid.* 9), Plato took hearing itself to be a sound within the percipient. In regard to seeing colours, Theophrastus explicitly and very misleadingly aligns Plato with Empedocles (*Sens.* 91).[7] He follows Aristotle in treating Empedocles as the paradigm for discussing Plato.

---

[7] Cf. Stratton *op. cit.* (n. 3) 220: 'Theophrastus here does great violence to Plato's doctrine'. See also D.N. Sedley, 'Empedocles' theory of vision', in W.W. Fortenbaugh & D. Gutas, *Theophrastus. His Psychological, Doxographical and Scientific Writings* (New Brunswick–London 1992) 26-31.

Theophrastus' repeated claim in *De sensibus* 5-6 that Plato omitted any treatment of touch, taste and smell influenced one branch of the doxographical tradition. Pseudo-Plutarch and Stobaeus confine their remarks on Plato's perceptual theories to sight and hearing, omitting any reference to him in their doxographies of smell and taste.[8] By contrast, Alcinous' summary of Plato in his *Didaskalikos* includes a close and lucid paraphrase of most of the relevant parts of the *Timaeus*, with no reference to 'likeness' as Plato's generic mode of explanation nor any hint of the omissions alleged by Theophrastus.[9] From Alcinous one has the impression that Plato wrote about the five senses in this order—sight, hearing, smell, taste and touch.

Before pursuing Theophrastus' treatment of Plato in detail, it needs to be emphasized that Plato's organization of the relevant material in the *Timaeus* is far from straightforward. In summary, it goes thus:

44d-45b	construction of the head
45b-46c	construction of the eye and explanation of sight
46e-47c	benefits of sight
47c-d	benefits of sound and hearing ...
53c-61c	the four regular solids, the four corresponding elements and their species and compounds
61c-64a	tactile properties *and their effect on the percipient's body*, in the order: hot cold, hard soft, heavy light, rough smooth.
64a-65b	relation of perceptions to pleasure and pain
65b-66c	gustatory properties and the effects of elementary particles on the tongue
66d-67a	smells and the 'power' of the nostrils
67a-c	'the third αἰσθητικόν (i.e. hearing) and sounds
67c-68d	colours

[8] Cf. H. Diels, *Doxographi Graeci* (Berlin 1879) 4.13.11, Aëtius = Ps. Plut. 4.13 901C, Stob. *Ecl.* 1.52.7. Both texts use the expression Πλατωνικὴ συναύγεια in summarising Plato's theory of sight.

[9] Cf. *Alcinous, The Handbook of Platonism*, ed. J. Dillon (Oxford 1993), chs. 18-19. Alcinous' reports of the *Timaeus* are much clearer and more accurate than those of Theophrastus, especially in the case of sight, though he too omits Plato's description of transmission back to the eye and the soul. Yet, as Dillon notes (144-5), Alcinous seems to have been influenced directly or indirectly by the *De sensibus*. This appears in his treatment of flavours, and also in the Aristotelianism of his allusion to 'natural place' in his account of Plato's theory of weight.

As this summary shows, Plato gives his account of sight many pages before he deals with the other senses and their objects including colour. He returns to sense perception only after he has elucidated the four kinds of elementary particles and their combinations, and explains his reasons thus:

> The various shapes have now been adequately explained with their figures, combinations and mutual transformations. Now we must try to clarify the causes that account for their effects (παθήματα). Our statements must presuppose the existence of sense perception even though we have not yet expounded the generation of the flesh and its properties or of the mortal part of the soul. It is impossible to give an adequate account of these things without the perceptible effects (παθήματα αἰσθητικά) and vice versa, and impossible to treat them both together. So we must first hypothesize the one or the other, and then return later to what we have hypothesized. In order to speak of the properties corresponding to the kinds (of shapes), let us first assume the facts to do with body and soul (*Tim.* 61c-d).

Plato's procedure is complicated, but scarcely confusing. Because sense perception involves interaction between the elementary particles and the soul-body complex, it requires reference to both of these. Having not yet completed his account of the latter, Plato assumes certain facts about it, in order to focus initially on the perceptible effects. Thus, it appears, what Plato will *chiefly* explain, following this methodological passage, is the perceptibles (αἰσθητά in Theophrastus' terminology) and not the accompanying psychophysical processes.

Theophrastus may be registering this when he says: 'He gives a more careful account of the perceptibles' (*Sens.* 6). Reading on (or remembering), he finds Plato discussing the tactile properties but without any explicit word on touch (*Tim.* 61e-63e). Then, after treating of pleasure and pain, Plato remarks:

> This is a more or less complete statement about the (perceptible) effects common to the body as a whole and of the names given to the things that produce them. Now we must try, if we can, to speak about what happens in our specific parts, both the (perceptible) effects and their causes (*Tim.* 65b).

Plato's first sentence refers back to his treatment of tactile properties and touch which, for obvious reasons, he assigns to no 'specific' bodily part. He then discusses flavours and taste, odours and smell, sound and hearing, which he calls 'the third perceptible part in us' (67a, i.e. *specific* part), and 'our fourth and remaining perceptual faculty' (67c)—the faculty for perceiving colours.

Theophrastus had no difficulty in extracting Plato's account of hearing from this passage, and he incorporated some of Plato's remarks on colours in what he says about sight. Given Plato's sign-posting, especially his distinction between touch and 'the specific parts' and his description of hearing as 'the third perceptible part in us', Theophrastus' claim that Plato said nothing about touch, taste and smell is startlingly false. It is also absurd as polemic, because, as I pointed out, Theophrastus contradicts the claim by his subsequent comments and reports.

Plato on sight

The crucial features of Plato's account in *Tim.* 45b-d are as follows:

(1) Day-light consists of non-burning fire.

(2) There is a kindred fire within us.

(3) The out-flow of our own fire-light through the eyes in day time fuses, *like by like* (ὅμοιον πρὸς ὅμοιον), with the external light, and forms a homogeneous visual ray extending from the eye to the object.

(4) The interaction of this visual ray with an object results in movements that are transmitted back into the whole body right up to the soul, and thereby produce sight.

When Plato later deals with colours (*Tim.* 67c-68d), he makes these further points:

(5) Colour is a flame issuing from bodies and consisting of particles.

(6) The visual ray itself consists of particles.

(7) The flame particles, which are so proportioned to our sight as to yield perception (ὄψει σύμμετρα μόρια ... πρὸς αἴσθησιν), depending on their size and interaction with the visual ray generate the spectrum of perceived colours.

(8) The interaction of the two sets of particles is transmitted back to the eye.

What does Theophrastus do with all this? His account runs:[10]

> Sight he makes of fire. (That is why he also makes colour a kind of flame coming from bodies, having its parts commensurate with sight—on the ground that effluence occurs and they must fit into

[10] I adopt Sedley's translation and punctuation of Theophrastus, *art. cit.* (n. 7) 30.

> each other.) It passes out of the eye for a distance and coalesces with the effluence, and that is how we see (*Sens.* 5).

Theophrastus draws this extremely condensed report from both contexts of the *Timaeus.* He begins by alluding to Plato's first point in (3), but he omits the fact that the eye's fire is light and also that what it coalesces with is day-light.[11] Plato adduces the principle of 'like by like' to explain this coalescence. Theophrastus, however, implies that Plato uses the principle for a different purpose—to explain the relation of sight to colour. He takes Plato's reference to the commensurability of colour and visual ray particles to involve an explanation of sight by 'likeness', conflating symmetry of particles to likeness of substance.

If this is regarded as a relatively minor distortion of Plato's theory, such charity cannot extend to the rest of Theophrastus' account. Without Plato's text we would have the impression that he regarded sight as simply the effect of external interaction between the visual ray and a colour effluence, without reference to transmission back to the eye and the soul. That impression is hardly corrected when Theophrastus adds:

> One could classify Plato's opinion as intermediate between those who claim that sight falls upon its object and those who say it is a case of transmission from visual objects to sight (*Sens.* 5).

For Plato the coalescence of colour and visual ray particles begins outside the eye, but seeing occurs as a result of the way that coalescence changes the visual ray and so affects the eye and eventually the soul. By omitting all reference to Plato's points (4) and (8), Theophrastus credits him with a misleadingly crude theory of seeing as the contact between two fires outside the eye.

Plato on sound and hearing

Plato's account of hearing and sound (*Tim.* 67b) is very brief. Following his practice of treating sense perception separately from perceptibles, Theophrastus divides his treatment of Plato's unitary passage between the two parts of *De sensibus.* In regard to the first part he cites Plato almost *verbatim*:

---

[11] Stratton *op. cit.* (n. 3) 161 comments: 'If Theophrastus had borne in mind *Republic* 507C-E, we should not have had his astonishing neglect of *light,* which is so important in Plato's theory of vision'. But Plato's emphasis on light is totally obvious from the *Timaeus* alone.

Plato	*Theophrastus (Sens. 6)*
ὅλως μὲν οὖν φωνὴν θῶμεν τὴν δι' ὤτων ὑπ' ἀέρος ἐγκεφάλου τε καὶ αἵματος μέχρι ψυχῆς πλήγην διαδιδομένην, τὴν δὲ ὑπ' αὐτῆς κίνησιν, ἀπὸ τῆς κεφαλῆς μὲν ἀρχομένην, τελευτῶσαν δὲ περὶ τὴν τοῦ ἥπατος ἕδραν, ἀκοήν.	ἀκοὴν δὲ διὰ τῆς φωνῆς ὁρίζεται· φωνὴν γὰρ εἶναι πληγὴν ὑπ' ἀέρος ἐγκεφάλου καὶ αἵματος δι' ὤτων μέχρι ψυχῆς, τὴν δ' ὑπὸ ταύτης κίνησιν ἀπὸ κεφαλῆς μέχρι ἥπατος ἀκοήν.

By starting his account with the statement, 'Plato defines hearing through sound', Theophrastus gives the erroneous impression that Plato takes hearing (the effect of the motion caused by sound on the percipient's organs and soul) to be *itself a sound*. Thus the unwary reader will take Plato's account of hearing to be an instance of Theophrastus' general characterization of those who explain sense perception 'by effluence and the transmission of like to like' (*Sens.* 1). Apart from this, his report is impeccable and almost verbatim. Here, in contrast with what he says about Plato's treatment of sight, Theophrastus makes it clear that the sensory stimulus has to reach the soul in order to be registered as such. Why his treatment of the *Timaeus* should be so tendentious in the one case and so accurate in the other is a question that is easier to ask than to answer. For the present, I put it on one side, and continue the comparison.

Plato's treatment of sound and hearing continues (*Tim.* 67b) with a brief statement about how sounds vary in pitch, smoothness and volume respectively according to the speed, regularity and size of the motions that produce them. Much later (*Tim.* 80a-b) he gives a fuller explanation of harmony and dissonance. Theophrastus draws briefly on both contexts at *Sens.* 85, where he is dealing with perceptibles. First, substituting δὲ for γὰρ, he repeats word for word the sentence φωνὴν...μέχρι ψυχῆς from *Sens.* 6. Next, he reports Plato's explanation of differences of pitch, but omits Plato's further reference to smooth, harsh, loud and soft sounds. Thus he says nothing about regularity and size as further differentiae of sound-producing movements. He concludes by saying:

> Sounds are in concord when the beginning of the slow sound *is like* the end of the swift one.

This is a cryptic paraphrase of part of Plato's very difficult account, which runs:

> As *to the swift and slow sounds* that appear high and low, *they are* dissonant when the motion they produce in us is dissimilar, and *concordant when that motion is similar.* For the slower sounds catch up with the motions of the earlier and swifter ones, which are already fading and have reached a similar state to the motion that the slower sounds, as they approach later, generate in them; when these slower sounds encounter the others, they do not cause discord by introducing a different movement but *the beginning of a slower movement which accords with the faster one that is ending, and by contributing similarity* they cause a unitary experience in which high and low are blended.

If Theophrastus had to restrict his paraphrase of this to thirteen words, he could scarcely have done better. Even so, his words are so condensed that they do little more than record his favourite preoccupation in *De sensibus*—'likeness' as an explanatory factor in sense perception. In particular, we are left without any understanding of how the two movements come to be 'like' one another, which is Plato's main point.

Plato on tactile properties (Tim. *61e-64a*)

Hot and cold: Theophrastus, *Sens.* 83:

> Plato says that is hot which causes division by the sharpness of its angles.

This is careless and defective. Plato makes 'sharp' the generic property of heat, taking this to be observable from heat's divisive and cutting effects on the body. But he advances the sharpness of the angles of fire *as only one* of four imperceptible properties that account for heat's 'cutting' sensation; the others that he cites are the thinness of its edges, the smallness of its particles and their speed of motion (*Tim* 61e).[12] He does not, as Theophrastus later claims (87) define heat simply 'by shape' (σχήματι).

As regards cold, Theophrastus gives a fairly accurate paraphrase of Plato's account of its production from large liquid particles compressing small ones (*Tim.* 62a-b). We then get a revealing instance of accurate quotation combined with error:

---

[12] Stratton *op. cit.* (n.3) 204 mistakenly refers to 'the three factors to which Plato attributes the cutting power of heat', omitting the 'thinness' of the particles' edges.

Plato	*Theophrastus* (*Sens.* 83)
τῇ δὴ μάχῃ καὶ τῷ σεισμῷ τούτῳ τρόμος καὶ ῥῖγος ἐτέθη, ψυχρόν τε τὸ πάθος ἅπαν τοῦτο καὶ τὸ δρῶν ἔσχεν ὄνομα.	τῇ γὰρ μάχῃ τρόμον καὶ τῷ πάθει ῥῖγος εἶναι ὄνομα.

Theophrastus sticks very closely to Plato's language, but he misrepresents Plato in saying that the feeling of cold is called ῥῖγος. Plato reserves this name together with τρόμος for 'shivering' —'the struggle between the particles'; his name for the agent and feeling of cold is ψυχρόν. More important, Theophrastus fails to remark that the outcome of the struggle between the particles is 'immobility and congealing' (σύνωσις). Thus Plato treats the effects of cold as directly opposite to the cutting caused by heat. If Theophrastus had attended to this point, he would have had little grounds for his objecting (*Sens.* 87) about a lack of congruence between Plato's treatment of hot as distinct from cold.

Hard and soft: Theophrastus (*Sens.* 83) reports Plato, *Tim* 62b6-8 almost *verbatim.* Next, he cites Plato's explanation of 'the small base' characteristic of things that yield, but completely omits what follows—Plato's explanation of non-yielding things (*Tim.* 62b8-c3).

Heavy and light: Next, Theophrastus (*Sens. ibid.*) correctly states Plato's view (*Tim.* 62c) that there is no absolute 'up' or 'down'. He continues:

> Light is what is easily drawn into the place contrary to its nature, and heavy what is so moved with difficulty.

This second statement (which completes Theophrastus' account) is very misleading for two reasons. First, it gives the false impression that Plato takes heavy and light, *in contrast with up and down,* to be objective properties. Secondly, it suggests that, according to Plato, light and heavy have no natural connexion with up and down. Here is the most relevant part of Plato's account:

> What is light or heavy or below or above in one region will be found to become or to be the opposite of what has all these characteristics in the opposite region... Concerning all of these, this one point has to be grasped—that the progression of each thing in the direction of what is kindred to it makes the moving thing heavy and that the region to which it moves is below, and vice versa (*Tim.* 63d-e).

In his subsequent criticism of Plato's doctrine (*Sens.* 88-9), Theophrastus acknowledges Plato's refusal to define heavy and light ἁπλῶς, but he adds, very misleadingly, that 'he defines them 'with respect to what is made of earth'. In fact, Plato no more defines terrestrial weight than weight in any other region. He takes the earth as *a* region by means of which he can explain the principle of relative weight (*Tim.* 63c-d). Theophrastus' critique of Plato, which 'is only repeating Aristotle', as A.E. Taylor says in his commentary on the *Timaeus ad loc.*, gives his readers no opportunity to grasp the radical divergence between Plato's theory of relative weight and the Aristotelian theory of objective weight or lightness as a function of the elements' movement to their natural places.

Rough and smooth: Of these tactile properties Theophrastus says (*Sens.* 83):

> He passes over them, on the ground that they are sufficiently clear, and says nothing.

The first part of this sentence is broadly true, the second totally false. Plato writes (*Tim.* 63e):

> Everyone, I think, who has seen the cause of the sensation of smooth and rough could explain it to someone else; for the latter is a combination of hardness and unevenness, and the former is brought about by a combination of evenness and density.

*Plato on pleasure and pain (*Tim. *64c-d)*

Plato

τὸ δὴ τῆς ἡδονῆς καὶ λύπης ὧδε δεῖ διανοεῖσθαι· τὸ μὲν παρὰ φύσιν καὶ βίαιον γιγνόμενον ἀθρόον παρ' ἡμῖν πάθος ἀλγεινόν, τὸ δ' εἰς φύσιν ἀπιὸν πάλιν ἀθρόον ἡδύ, τὸ δὲ ἠρέμα καὶ κατὰ σμικρὸν ἀναίσθητον, τὸ δὲ μετ' εὐπετείας γιγνόμενον ἅπαν αἰσθητὸν μὲν ὅτι μάλιστα, λύπης δὲ καὶ ἡδονῆς οὐ μετέχον, οἷον τὰ περὶ τὴν ὄψιν αὐτὴν παθήματα. . .ταύτῃ γὰρ τομαὶ μὲν καὶ καύσεις καὶ ὅσα ἄλλα πάσχει λύπας οὐκ ἐμποιοῦσιν, οὐδὲ ἡδονὰς πάλιν ἐπὶ ταὐτὸν ἀπιούσης εἶδος. . .βίᾳ γὰρ τὸ πάμπαν οὐκ ἔνι τῇ διακρίσει τε αὐτῆς καὶ συγκρίσει.

Theophrastus (*Sens.* 84)

ἡδὺ δὲ καὶ λυπηρόν, τὸ μὲν εἰς φύσιν ἀθρόον πάθος, τὸ δὲ παρὰ φύσιν καὶ βίᾳ λυπηρόν, τὰ δὲ μέσα καὶ ἀναίσθητα ἀνὰ λόγον. διὸ καὶ κατὰ τὸ ὁρᾶν οὐκ εἶναι λύπην οὐδ' ἡδονὴν τῇ διακρίσει καὶ συγκρίσει.

Theophrastus' report is a clear and accurate paraphrase of Plato down to the words βίᾳ λυπηρόν. At the corresponding point, Plato says:

> A gentle and slight process is imperceptible (sc. with respect to pleasure and pain).

Theophrastus renders this point too, and then writes:

> Therefore, in seeing there is no pleasure or pain from the cutting and combining.

This sentence too is accurate, but scarcely intelligible without allusion to Plato's full treatment of the point. For what he undertakes to say is that processes such as those involved in sight *are supremely perceptible,* but the disturbance to the visual ray that they involve (cutting etc.) is too slight to cause pleasure or pain.

Plato on flavours (Tim. *65b-66c*)

Theophrastus' report (*Sens.* 84) begins thus:

> As for flavours, Plato mentions four species of water in his treatment of water; the juices include wine, verjuice, oil and honey, and the sensations include the earthy flavour.

Theophrastus' basis for his comment on the juices is the context of the *Timaeus* where Plato discusses types of water (58d-60b). At the end of this passage Plato lists the four types of juice as instances of 'composite water'. Then, at the beginnng of his treatment of taste and flavours, he says (65c):

> First we must explain to the best of our ability what we omitted in our earlier account of juices—the sensations peculiar to the tongue.

The unwary reader of Theophrastus will form the impression that Plato's account of the four juices contributes to his explanation and classification of flavours, and Theophrastus actually says this later (*Sens.* 89) in his criticism, but it does not. Plato makes no use of the types of juices in his treatment of flavours, and when discussing the juices in the earlier passage the only gustatory sensation he mentions is the sweetness produced by honey (60b).

As for what Theophrastus calls 'the earthy flavour' (τὸν γεώδη χυμόν), this too has no authority in Plato's text. Plato does not cite earth as a flavour but as a substance whose particles, depending on their consistency, generate 'astringent (στρυφνά) or 'harsh' (αὐστηρά) tastes' as a result of their interaction with the blood vessels extending from the tongue to the heart '(*Tim.* 65c-d). The corresponding texts continue thus:

Plato	*Theophrastus* (*Sens.* 84)
...γήινα μέρη κατατηκόμενα συνάγει τὰ φλέβια καὶ ἀποξηραίνει, τραχύτερα μὲν ὄντα στρυφνά, ἧττον δὲ τραχύνοντα αὐστηρὰ φαίνεται· τὰ δὲ τούτων τε ῥυπτικὰ καὶ πᾶν τὸ περὶ τὴν γλῶτταν ἀποπλύνοντα, πέρα μὲν τοῦ μετρίου τοῦτο δρῶντα καὶ προσεπιλαμβανόμενα ὥστε ἀποτήκειν αὐτῆς τῆς φύσεως οἷον ἡ τῶν λίτρων δύναμις, πικρὰ πάνθ' οὕτως ὠνόμασται, τὰ δὲ ὑποδεέστερα τῆς λιτρώδους ἕξεως ἐπὶ τὸ μέτριόν τε τῇ ῥύψει χρώμενα ἁλυκὰ ἄνευ πικρότητος τραχείας...	καὶ διὰ ταῦτα συνάγοντα τοὺς χυλοὺς καὶ συγκρίνοντα, τὰ μὲν τραχύτερα στρυφνὰ εἶναι, τὰ δὲ ἧττον αὐστηρά. τὸ δὲ ῥυπτικὸν τῶν πόρων καὶ ἀποκαθαρτικὸν ἁλμυρόν· τὸ δὲ σφόδρα ῥυπτικόν, ὥστε καὶ ἐκτήκειν, πικρόν.

As this comparison shows, Theophrastus gives an accurate paraphrase of Plato's treatment of astringent, harsh, bitter, and salty, but he reverses Plato's order of presenting the latter pair of flavours and omits soda, Plato's illustrative example for explaining the difference between them.

Next he reduces Plato's six-line explanation of 'pungent' (δριμέα) to a single line (*ibid.*):

> Things that are warm and move upward and have a cutting effect are pungent (τὰ δὲ θερμαινόμενα καὶ ἄνω φερόμενα καὶ διακρίνοντα δριμέα).

This telegraphic style is quite inadequate to convey Plato's account:

> Things that share in the mouth's warmth and are softened by it, become inflamed and heat in their turn the thing that heated them, and rising because of their lightness to the senses of the head, cut everything on which they impinge (*Tim.* 65e).

This is a brilliant description of the sensations concomitant on eating spicy food. Theophrastus, having falsely declared that Plato has nothing to say on taste, makes Plato's report virtually unintelligible.

Next, Theophrastus writes (*ibid.*):

> Things that have a seething effect are sharp (τὰ δὲ κυκῶντα ὄξεα).

In his lengthy account (*Tim.* 66a-b) Plato uses the word 'seething' to describe the general effect that (probably) acidic substances have on the blood vessels of the tongue, an effect he actually calls 'bubbles, boiling and fermentation'. He does not characterise the gustatory sensation itself as 'sharp', but says 'the cause of these sensations is called sharp'.[13]

---

[13] Cf. Aristotle's list of flavours at *De sensu* 442a19, which corresponds

Finally, sweet. Theophrastus (*ibid.*):

> Things that in company with the moisture in the tongue cause it to expand or contract into its nature are sweet.

Again his compression of the original is extreme and partly opaque. Plato's account goes:

> When the composition of the things entering (the mouth) in liquid form, being naturally akin to the state of the tongue, smoothes and strokes its roughened parts, and contracts or expands any unnatural contraction or expansion, and makes everything accord with nature as far as possible, and any such remedy for the enforced sensations is pleasant and agreeable, it is called sweet. (*Tim.* 66c).

Half of Theophrastus' report is taken up with the obscure expression σὺν τῇ ὑγρότητι τῇ ἐν τῇ γλώττῃ, yet this fails to bring out Plato's point that the causes of sweet tastes are themselves liquids.

*Plato on smells (*Tim. *66d-67a)*

Plato begins his account of smells by denying that these can be classified according to species (a point he repeats later), and that any of the four primary bodies is perceptible to smell. Smells, he says, occur when air is changing into water, or vice versa. The rest of his account (with the exception of a final sentence about the difference between pleasant and unpleasant smells) is taken up in detail by Theophrastus:

Plato	*Theophrastus* (*Sens.* 85)
εἰσίν τε ὀσμαὶ σύμπασαι καπνὸς ἢ ὁμίχλη, τούτων δὲ τὸ μὲν ἐξ ἀέρος εἰς ὕδωρ ἰὸν ὁμίχλη, τὸ δὲ ἐξ ὕδατος εἰς ἀέρα καπνός· ὅθεν λεπτότεραι μὲν ὕδατος, παχύτεραι δὲ ὀσμαὶ σύμπασαι γεγόνασιν ἀέρος. δηλοῦνται δὲ ὁπόταν τινὸς ἀντιφραχθέντος περὶ τὴν ἀναπνοὴν ἄγῃ τις βίᾳ τὸ πνεῦμα εἰς αὑτόν· τότε γὰρ ὀσμὴ μὲν οὐδεμία συνδιηθεῖται, τὸ δὲ πνεῦμα τῶν ὀσμῶν ἐρημωθὲν αὐτὸ μόνον ἕπεται. δύ' οὖν ταῦτα ἀνώνυμα τὰ τούτων ποικίλματα γέγονεν, οὐκ ἐκ πολλῶν οὐδὲ ἁπλῶν εἰδῶν ὄντα, ἀλλὰ διχῇ τό θ' ἡδὺ καὶ τὸ λυπηρὸν αὐτόθι μόνω διαφανῆ λέγεσθον...	τὰς δὲ ὀσμὰς εἴδη μὲν οὐκ ἔχειν, ἀλλὰ τῷ λυπηρῷ καὶ ἡδεῖ διαφέρειν. εἶναι δὲ τὴν ὀσμὴν ὕδατος μὲν λεπτότερον, ἀέρος δὲ παχύτερον. σημεῖον δὲ ὅτι ὅταν ἐπιφράξαντος ἀνασπῶσιν, ἄνευ ὀσμῆς τὸ πνεῦμα εἰσέρχεται· διὸ καθάπερ καπνὸν καὶ ὁμίχλην εἶναι τῶν σωμάτων ἀόρατον. εἶναι δὲ καπνὸν μὲν μεταβολὴν ἐξ ὕδατος εἰς ἀέρα, ὁμίχλην δὲ τὴν ἐξ ἀέρος εἰς ὕδωρ.

---

exactly to Plato's terms: γλυκύ, ἁλμυρόν, πικρόν, αὐστηρόν, δριμύ, στρυφνόν, ὀξύ.

In his treatment of this passage, Theophrastus offers an impeccable account of Plato's text, accurate, clear and so full that he even includes the proof that the smell of an object vanishes when someone inhales through an obstruction. He also adds a detail Plato omits—the invisibility of the vapour that causes smell. Why is he so careful and patient here and so hasty and careless elsewhere? The question cannot be answered, but before assessing his overall treatment, let us conclude the details with his account of Plato on colours.

*Plato on colours (*Tim. *67c-69a)*

Theophrastus begins his treatment of Plato's fourth 'perceptible' that affects the body's particular parts by repeating (*Sens.* 86) almost verbatim his accurate citation (*ibid.* 5) of Plato's account of colour, which he derived from this passage (*Tim.* 67c6). Omitting Plato's remarks on the different sizes of colour particles and on transparency (*ibid.* 67d3-6), he continues:

> What penetrates sight is white, and what compresses it is black,

drawing almost word for word on *Tim.* 67e5-6. He also alludes with reasonable clarity to the analogy Plato draws between the different particles responsible for the perceptions of black/white, hot/cold and astringent/pungent respectively (*Tim.* 67d7-e2).

Next, he gives his own truncated description of what Plato calls 'brilliant' (λαμπρόν, *Tim.* 68b5), 'fiery white' (τὸ πυρῶδες λευκόν), after which the transmitted text contines: 'and the rest of the colours from these'. Because Plato's account of the rest requires the prior specification of red as the fourth primary colour, we should assume, with Stratton,[14] a short lacuna in which Theophrastus mentioned this. He presumably omitted Plato's explanations of orange, purple, and the other derived colours.

So far, so fairly good. Theophrastus concludes his brief report on colours thus (*Sens.* 86):

> But in what proportions [sc.the rest of the colours are blended], he says one should not state even if one knew them, since we do not have a likely or a necessary account of them. Nor is it at all surprising if on experiment the outcome is different, but god has the power to do this.

---

[14] *Op. cit.* (n. 3) 212.

This is a curiously synthetic report of two independent observations by Plato.[15] At *Tim.* 68b6-8, Plato writes:

> Bright mixed with red and white becomes orange. It would make no sense to state the proportions, even if one knew them, given that no one could be even moderately capable of stating either their necessity or the likely account.

Plato then (*ibid.* 68b8-d2) gives an account of many other colours that are generated by mixtures, and concludes:

> These examples make it more or less clear to what mixtures the other colours must be assimilated in order to preserve the likely account. But if anyone investigating should apply a test to the facts, he would prove his ignorance of the difference between divine and human nature; for god has the knowledge and the power to blend the one into many and to resolve the many into one, but no human being exists now or ever will exist who can do either of these things (*Tim.* 68d2-7).

Theophrastus in his second sentence (cited above) alludes to Plato's warning against experimentation and to the superiority of divine power, but his brevity leaves his readers guessing as to what 'this' is that god can do by way of frustrating the temerarious experimenter.

Conclusions

I now summarise the results of this survey. Theophrastus' reports on Plato's sensory doctrines in the *Timaeus* range from being almost *verbatim* and entirely clear at one extreme to misrepresentation and opacity at the other.

Accurate and clear: hearing, smell, the tactile properties hard and soft, pleasure and pain, the gustatory properties astringent, harsh, bitter, salty, the colours black and white

Venial omissions: explanations of four of the types of sound and of rough and smooth

Damaging omissions: sight

Extreme condensation: sight, concord in sound, no pleasure or pain in seeing, the gustatory properties pungent, sweet and sharp, his concluding remarks about Plato on colours

---

[15] Cf. Baltussen (n. 1), pp. 118-19, who comments cogently on other aspects of Theophrastus' method of excerpting here.

Serious misrepresentation:
1. (general) the attribution to Plato of 'likeness' as *the* explanatory principle, the denial that Plato explains the operations of touch, taste and smell;
2. (particular) the explanations of sight, hot and cold, heavy and light, the first part of flavours

In regard to the general misrepresentations, something has already been said. Theophrastus followed Aristotle in classifying theories of perception in terms of explanation by 'likeness' or its opposite. This damages his treatment of Plato's explanation of sight, but it has little effect on the accuracy of his other reports. The complexity of Plato's arrangement of topics in the *Timaeus* may help to explain Theophrastus' extraordinary claim that Plato has nothing to say about touch, taste and smell, but since his later reports show otherwise the claim seems to be largely gratuitous, motivated by unjustified preconceptions that he subsequently drops. It is hard to see why, even allowing for his polemical leanings, he failed to state explicitly that Plato's account of these and all other perceptual processes except sight is premissed on Plato's theory of the four primary bodies and their particles.

As regards his detailed misrepresentations, the two worst are his treatment of Plato's accounts of sight, and heavy and light. With regard to sight, Theophrastus, by his own words, assimilated Plato to Empedocles (*Sens.* 91). On heavy and light, his Aristotelianism probably helped him to misread Plato's radical account of relative weight. His introduction to Plato's account of flavours is decidedly skewed, but the text at this point is sufficiently difficult to warrant suspicion of corruption and lacunae. The misrepresentations in his account of hot and cold may be due to inadequate note-taking, lapse of memory, desire for brevity, and a combination of these.

Why he should be so full and accurate in some instances and so compressed and inaccurate in others is a question to which I have no satisfactory answer to offer. We need, of course, to take account of his dialectical methodology, his Aristotelianism, the restricted focus of his interest in the doctrines he reports.[16] A case can be

16 For good remarks on all this, cf. H. Baltussen, 'Peripatetic dialectic in the *De sensibus*', in Fortenbaugh & Gutas *op. cit.* (n. 6) 1-19. Baltussen's approach to understanding the basis and methodology of Theophrastus' critical comments is much more sophisticated than that of Stratton and other earlier scholars. Yet he is too kind to his author when he describes Theophrastus'

made, as Han Baltussen shows (n. 1 above, p. 129), for explaining Theophrastus' omissions as due to a deliberate choice of 'only clear-cut statements pertaining to physiology'. Baltussen quite rightly insists too that we not saddle Theophrastus with our own standards for accurate treatment of an author's text. Yet, whatever we say in explanation of Theophrastus' methodology in the *De sensibus*, the validity of his reports as an account of Plato's doctrines remains an issue. If these were consistently inaccurate or tendentious, that would be telling, but they are not. Theophrastus is simply very uneven in his level of accuracy and clarity. I see no reason to presume that his starting-point was an epitome of the *Timaeus* as distinct from a text virtually identical to our own. He may at times be relying on memory or on (by our standards) inadequate excerpts, whether made by himself or by a pupil. But apart from the cases of sight and weight, I do not think that extraneous factors, his Aristotelianism or his explanatory purposes go far to account for the unevenness of his accuracy, clarity and comprehensiveness.

We do not need Theophrastus for studying Plato. We do need him for access to Plato's predecessors. If my findings about his treatment of Plato are extrapolated, they suggest that in every instance we need to be on our guard in the following ways.

First, his general claims about what a philosopher said or did not say may be inaccurate either by omission, inappropriate addition, or by failing to fit the data precisely.

Second, his criticisms of a philosopher should be cited as evidence only in cases where independent corroboration is available.

Third, it should never be assumed without further evidence that any report Theophrastus gives is comprehensive, completely accurate in formulation or adequate in clarity. Much that he says will be correct, but no sound criterion exists within his text for determining exactly where he can be trusted.

Berkeley

---

reports as 'brief, yet very informative' (9) and characterizes his criticism of Democritus and Plato as 'precise and thorough' (11). This apologetic tendency is my only objection to his excellent study of Theophrastus' treatment of the *Timaeus* in his dissertation (n. 1 above.)

ADDITIONAL FRAGMENTS OF ARIUS DIDYMUS ON PHYSICS

DAVID T. RUNIA

For more than a century a minor but not insignificant figure in the study of ancient philosophy has been the doxographer Arius Didymus. Ever since Meineke and Diels presented their hypothesis,[1] it has been customary to attribute the following documents, all located in Eusebius and Stobaeus, to this obscure personage.[2]

1.	Eusebius	*PE* 11.23.2–6	fragment on Plato's ideas taken ἐκ τῶν Διδύμῳ Περὶ τῶν ἀρεσκόντων Πλάτωνι συν-τεταγμένων (a very similar text is found in Alcinous, *Didaskalikos* 12.1);
2.		*PE* 15.15	Stoic fragments on cosmo-theology ἀπὸ τῆς Ἐπιτομῆς Ἀρείου Διδύμου;
3.		*PE* 15.18–20	Stoic fragments on cosmology and psychology ἀπὸ τῶν Ἐπιτομῶν Ἀρείου Διδύμου;
4.	Stobaeus	*Ecl.* 1	large number of fragments on physics pertaining to Aristotle and the Stoics, but without any reference to their source; also at 1.12.2a the same fragment on Plato's ideas that is found in Eusebius;
5.		*Ecl.* 2.1.17	epistemological fragment beginning with Xenophanes, entitled Διδύμου ἐκ τοῦ Περὶ αἱρέσεων;
6.		*Ecl.* 2.7.1–4	untitled introductory discussion on ethics, containing διαιρέσεις by Philo of Larissa and Eudorus and with copious references to philosophers, esp. Plato and Aristotle (= ethical doxography A)[3]
7.		*Ecl.* 2.7.5–12	synopsis of Stoic ethics entitled Ζήνωνος καὶ τῶν λοιπῶν Στωικῶν δόγματα περὶ τοῦ ἠθικοῦ

---

[1] A. Meineke, 'Zu Stobaeus', *Berliner Zeitschrift für das Gymnasialwesen* [= *Mützells Zeitschrift*] 13 (1859) 563–565; H. Diels, *Doxographi Graeci* (Berlin 1879, 1976^{4}) 69–88 (henceforth *DG*).

[2] References to Mras' edition (Berlin 1956) for Eusebius' *Praeparatio Evangelica*, Wachsmuth-Hense for Stobaeus (1884–1912). I omit two references to a Didymus in Clement of Alexandria which are of lesser importance and difficult to integrate in our picture of Arius Didymus. There is also a reference to Didymus' account of Aristotelian doctrine in Priscianus Lydus *Sol. ad Chosr.* 42.39–40 Bywater, but no fragmentary material is furnished.

[3] The useful labels A, B and C for the three ethical doxographies were introduced by D. E. Hahm, 'The Ethical Doxography of Arius Didymus', *ANRW* 2.36.4 (Berlin-New York 1990) 2935–3055; it is fast becoming standard.

		μέρους τῆς φιλοσοφίας (= Ethical dox. B)
8.	*Ecl.* 2.7.13–26	synopsis of Peripatetic ethics entitled Ἀριστοτέλους καὶ τῶν λοιπῶν Περιπατητικῶν περὶ τῶν ἠθικῶν (= Ethical dox. C)
9.	*Flor.* 4.39.28	excerpt on εὐδαιμονία entitled ἐκ τῆς Διδύμου Ἐπιτομῆς identical to *Ecl.* 2.7.17 (and so furnishing the basis of Meineke's source theory).

A further aspect of the Meineke-Diels hypothesis that has long won acceptance was the identification of this Arius Didymus with the Stoic philosopher and confidant of Augustus, Arius of Alexandria (c. 70 to c. 5 BCE).[4] During the last 15 years there has been a gradual realization that the hypothesis has its shaky aspects, but no direct challenge was mounted.[5] This has now come in the form of a fresh and incisively written monograph by Tryggve Göransson, who argues that the identification with the Stoic Arius is unsound, because the direct references to the doxographer listed above *always* use the identificatory name Didymus, but this name is *never* used for Arius the court philosopher.[6] We thus lose our chronological anchor for the doxographer and can only locate him at some time between the mid first cent. BCE and Eusebius.

The Swedish scholar's point is well taken, even if it may not be quite as strong as he thinks it is.[7] Our concern in this article, however, is only with a limited section of the uncontested and contested remains of Arius Didymus' *œuvre,* namely the physical fragments listed under 3. above. In his *Doxographi Graeci* Diels identified a number of such fragments and edited them in an edition

---

4 On this intriguing figure see G. W. Bowersock, *Augustus and the Greek World* (Oxford 1965) 33–35.

5 See the evaluatory articles by C. H. Kahn, 'Arius as a Doxographer', in W. W. Fortenbaugh (ed.), *On Stoic and Peripatetic Ethics: the Work of Arius Didymus* (New Brunswick 1983) 3–13; Hahm, *art. cit.* (n. 3). Both concentrate primarily on the ethical doxographies.

6 T. Göransson, *Albinus, Alcinous, Arius Didymus,* Studia Graeca et Latina Gothoburgensia 61 (Göteborg 1995), esp. 182–226.

7 Effectively what he has done is forcefully remind us of the *hypothetical* character of the identification of the doxographer with the Stoic court philosopher. It cannot be taken *as a fact* that the two are the same person. The problem of the names was already recognized by Diels and Zeller. But this century scholars simply assumed the identification. For a spirited defence of the hypothesis see B. Inwood's review of Göransson's book, *Bryn Mawr Classical Review* 95.12.8 (electronic document). A further important result of his research is that he casts serious doubt on the assumption shared by all scholars since Diels that Ethical doxography A is by the same author as B and C (who, at least in the case of C, *must* be Arius Didymus).

that has been the point of reference ever since.[8] Paul Moraux, to take a prominent example, presents a lengthy analysis of the Aristotelian physical fragments purely on the basis of Diels' identifications, the methodology of which is not even discussed.[9] Göransson states somewhat apodictically that the criteria used by Diels to sift out the Didymean material 'are perhaps not as indisputable as they have been regarded every since',[10] but makes no attempt to embark on this investigation himself.

My intention is to reexamine the question of the separation of the Didymean material on physics in Stobaeus' *Eclogai* afresh. I will argue that Diels' criteria need to be refined and more consistently applied. This will lead to the identification of a number of additional fragments, but also to the removal of a few snippets from Diels' collection. The investigation may be regarded as a preliminary study for a new edition of these physical fragments, which remains a real *desideratum*. It is a joy to be able to dedicate this contribution to my mentor, colleague and friend Jaap Mansfeld on his sixtieth birthday. We have discussed these and related issues on numerous occasions during our joint research on ancient doxography, and have not always been able to reach complete unanimity. So I am sure that he will scrutinize these pages with an even sharper eye than usual.

The disputed fragments we are concerned with are all located in Book I of Stobaeus' *Eclogae*. This book, which unfortunately only survives in a truncated version,[11] contains a vast amount of doxographical material in the area of physics, but gives no indication whatsoever as to where it was drawn from. As we all know, Diels, basing his theory on earlier research but also adding new elements of his own, argued that most of this material was derived from a compendium entitled Περὶ ἀρεσκόντων (*De placitis*) also

---

8 *DG* 449–472. As far as I know, apart from Wachsmuth, on whom more below, no attention has been given to the question of the identification of physical fragments of Arius Didymus in Stobaeus, except incidentally, for example in my own articles cited below in n. 35 & 39.

9 P. Moraux, *Der Aristotelismus bei den Griechen von Andronikos von Rhodos bis Alexander von Aphrodisias, Band I: Die Renaissance des Aristotelismus im I. Jh. v. Chr.* (Berlin-New York 1973) 276–305.

10 *Op. cit.* 220. No doubt he is especially thinking of Diels' criterion of a certain Stoicizing flavour (*DG* 75); see further below n. 19.

11 The prologue is missing; chapters 1–31 are fairly complete, but chapters 32–60 have been considerably abridged by an epitomator, who wrote out only the Platonic and Aristotelian material.

exploited by Theodoret of Cyrrhus, who appears to refer to its author as the otherwise totally obscure Aëtius.[12] An important task that Diels set himself in his *Doxographi Graeci* was to separate this Aëtian material from a second important source of material drawn from the doxographical work of Arius Didymus. The results of Diels' analysis were incorporated by Wachsmuth in the very structure of his edition,[13] which therefore cannot be regarded as an independent piece of work. But we must give the latter scholar credit for subjecting the details of the theory to a thorough examination, which led to a number of minor improvements.

In the light of the sceptical remarks about the Meineke–Diels hypothesis outlined above, it is worth emphasizing that there can be no doubt whatsoever that Stobaeus did make use of a work of Arius Didymus.[14] One of his excerpts shows a strong verbal resemblance to an Didymean fragment preserved by Eusebius (= fr. 36 in Diels' collection). The texts are best placed side by side:[15]

Eusebius *PE* 15.18.3 Mras	Stobaeus *Ecl.* 1.20.1e Wachsmuth
ἀρέσκει γὰρ τοῖς Στωϊκοῖς φιλοσόφοις τὴν ὅλην οὐσίαν εἰς πῦρ μεταβάλλειν, οἷον εἰς σπέρμα, καὶ πάλιν ἐκ τούτου αὐτὴν ἀποτελεῖσθαι τὴν διακόσμησιν, οἵα τὸ πρότερον ἦν. καὶ τοῦτο τὸ δόγμα τῶν ἀπὸ τῆς αἱρέσεως οἱ πρῶτοι καὶ πρεσβύτατοι προσήκαντο, Ζήνων τε καὶ Κλεάνθης καὶ Χρύσιππος. τὸν μὲν γὰρ τούτου μαθητὴν καὶ διάδοχον τῆς σχολῆς Ζήνωνά φασιν ἐπισχεῖν περὶ τῆς ἐκπυρώσεως τῶν ὅλων.	Ζήνωνι καὶ Κλεάνθει καὶ Χρυσίππῳ ἀρέσκει τὴν οὐσίαν μεταβάλλειν οἷον εἰς σπέρμα ⟨εἰς⟩ τὸ πῦρ, καὶ πάλιν ἐκ τούτου τοιαύτην ἀποτελεῖσθαι τὴν διακόσμησιν, οἵα πρότερον ἦν.
	Παναίτιος πιθανωτέραν εἶναι νομίζει καὶ μᾶλλον ἀρέσκουσαν αὐτῷ τὴν ἀϊδιότητα τοῦ κόσμου ἢ τὴν τῶν ὅλων εἰς πῦρ μεταβολήν.

---

12 For Aëtius, Diels' theory and the contributions of his predecessors I refer the reader to volume 1 of the study being prepared by J. Mansfeld and myself entitled *Aëtiana: the Method and Intellectual Context of a Doxographer*. We show that Diels' theory, though deficient in some details, can withstand the attack launched against it by A. Lebedev.

13 Berlin 1884, and since then never superseded.

14 Cf. Göransson *op. cit.* 219–220; note, however, the slight inconsistency between the statements that Stobaeus may have quoted 'from a parallel doxographical tradition' and that 'he demonstrably excerpted Didymus at least once'.

15 I have included Heeren's conjecture in the Stobaean text. *Pace* Diels, it seems to me justifiable in the light of the repeated εἰς πῦρ in the last line.

Eusebius cites *verbatim*, as is his wont, and cites his source (at 15.20.8), whereas Stobaeus leaves his source unnamed and takes the kind of liberties that one might expect from an anthologist. The names of the three Stoics are brought to the fore in order to make the contrast with the other *doxai* clearer. Only the change from αὐτὴν to τοιαύτην might be thought worrying. It could easily be interpreted as a *Verschlimmbesserung*, i.e. Stobaeus cannot imagine the Stoics maintaining a cycle of *identical* worlds. But we must be wary of hyperinterpretation (and how can we be sure that τοιαύτην is not a textual corruption?).

We know, therefore, that Stobaeus (henceforth S) made use of the compendia of both Aëtius (henceforth A) and Arius Didymus (henceforth AD) in his compilation. Most, though not all, of his doxographical information on physics can be reduced to these two sources.[16] Decisive criteria here are comparison with other sources (notably Ps.Plutarch's abridgement of A, henceforth P[17]) and considerations of style and content. The macro-structure of the book is loosely based on A, but the anthologist has seen fit to introduce all manner of structural changes in his material, involving the opposed techniques of coalescence and separation, so that the process of disentangling his original sources has become an immensely complex and often wearisome task. It is thus of vital importance to determine various criteria that allow the two chief sources to be separated. In our view the most significant of these are eight in number. Obviously our list takes as its point of departure the list of ten criteria which Diels outlined in his rigorous and admirably succint analysis.[18] It would seem better, however, to draw up a new and revised list, in which his results are incorporated rather than repeat his list *more scholastico* and comment on each of his criteria individually. Unlike Diels we shall exclude any considerations that are based wholly on content.[19] It needs to be emphasized that these criteria are generalizations, and that for

---

16 These matters can in the present context not be discussed in detail. The reader is referred to the study announced in n. 12.

17 In what follows references are to the Teubner edition of J. Mau, *Plutarchi Moralia* vol. V fasc. 2 pars 1 (Leipzig 1971).

18 *DG* 73–75.

19 I.e. Diels' last three criteria. Diels argues that AD uses Stoic terminology in describing Aristotelian doctrine, but he may well be influenced by his conviction that AD is the Stoic Arius. The criterion of a direct use of Aristotle's *Meteorologica* can only be verified as part of a thorough examination of the meteorology of A's book III.

each one there are exceptions possible. Ideally every lemma found in our sources should be individually analysed, a tedious and time-consuming task. In his *DG* Diels did little more than present the results of his analyses, so often the reasons for his decisions need to be divined.

Here, then, is the list of eight criteria for separating A and AD.
1. The lemmata of AD are often longer than those of A, not only because they enter into more detail, but also because they often combine more than one topic. For example some of the longest lemmata in A are found on the subject Περὶ τάξεως τοῦ κόσμου (cf. P 2.7), e.g. Parmenides at S 1.22.1a, Philolaus at 1d. But they are not even half the length of Chrysippus' long exposé at S 1.21.5 (= AD fr. 31 Diels) on the nature and structure of the cosmos. Because AD treats a number of topics together in a continuous exposé, his fragments often have a more fluent and discursive style than the compact and sometimes crabbed style of A. There are, however, two further complicating factors. Some of the fragments attributed by Diels to AD are so short that the above remarks can hardly be applied. Moreover we have to take into account that S in his coalescing of various chapters in A also groups together subjects that A kept apart. This means that the combinations of AD have to be distinguished from the coalescences of S. As we shall see, this proves to be a highly tricky business.
2. The standard formula of A's *placita* is to have the doxa immediately follow the name-label, whereby the verb of assertion is generally understood (occasionally φησί, ἔφη or ἀπεφήνατο is included). The topic, which is always given in the chapter-title, is sometimes repeated in the first lemma and thereafter it too is generally understood. Sometimes, however, it is even omitted in the opening lemma. Such procedures come much less naturally to AD because he, as far as we can tell, did not have chapter titles[20] and also makes less use of name-labels. Among the fragments of AD in S four different types of lemmata can be observed: (a) those which follow the usual style of the *Placita*, i.e. have the name-label in the nominative at the beginning; (b) those which have the name-label only in the genitive, without a direct grammatical relation to the contents of the lemmata; (c) those which have the name of the

[20] The title Περὶ τέλους at 2.45.11 may not be original, but added either by S or a scribe. See also above n. 7 on doubts as to whether Ethical doxography A in S can be ascribed to AD.

philosopher in the nominative but not at the beginning; (d) those which have the name-label in another case, e.g. accusative in *oratio obliqua* or dative as in the text at 1.20.1e quoted above. In the case of type (a) discrimination is difficult, but remodelling by S can in some cases be demonstrated, particularly by means of his use of characteristic introductory phraseology (e.g. verbs of saying or opining) Type (c) and (d) unambiguously reveal AD because such practices are never found in A.[21] Type (b) was regarded by Diels as furnishing a water-tight criterion, but the evidence in the mss. is less unambiguous than he thought.[22]

3. When S arranges the excerpts he has collected, he often has to add introductory phrases of his own in order to make necessary connections. For example in ¶15 Περὶ σχημάτων he wants to quote *Tim.* 33b on the sphericity of the cosmos. So he adds the words (145.9–11): Πλάτων ἔφησε σφαιροειδῆ τὸν κόσμον ὑπάρχειν. λέγει γὰρ οὕτως ἐν τῷ Τιμαίῳ. We may be fairly certain that there was no such doxa in A.[23] In a number of cases (including this example, as will become clear below), S uses introductory verbs not found in P, a fact which makes his intervention very probable.

4. In the case of AD, because S is taking excerpts from a continuous exposé, they frequently contain δέ as connecting particle. In the ethical *doxai* there are very few lemmata without some kind of connective.[24] In A, on the other hand, the particle is usually only used directly after the name-label if he wants to make a deliberate contrast (see exx. at P 1.22, 1.24, 2.3, in all three cases the 2nd lemma). A third possibility, suggested by the text from ¶15 just cited, is that S feels no need for a connecting particle when he himself inserts introductory connecting phrases.

5. Because the two authors report the views of others, they both make extensive use of indirect speech. But they reveal opposite

---

[21] If so, there are grounds for suspicion. The text at P 5.20 *ad init.* is almost certainly corrupt. The lemma at S 1.50.3 which starts κατὰ τοὺς Περιπατητικούς is attributed to A by Diels *DG* 394, but may well derive from AD.

[22] On this problem see O. Hense, Art. 'Stobaios', *RE* 9 (1916) 2565, who makes clear that this criterion is vulnerable to the interventions of scribes and editors, and so needs to be handled with care.

[23] Cf. P 2.2 886B and S 1.15.6b. If the doxa was in A, then both sources must have changed the label from Plato and the Stoics to the Stoics only. This is less likely than that S added the doxa from his own reading, as he often does in the case of Plato.

[24] One ex. at 2.57.18. There are a number of exx. in the first doxography, e.g. at 39.20, 49.8, 50.11, 52.10, 52.13, 56.8. But see above nn. 7 & 20.

tendencies. AD uses indirect speech almost incessantly. His compendium must surely have been a pain to read. Of the forty fragments in Diels' collection only a handful contain material cast in direct speech.[25] A in contrast often prefers not to linger too long in indirect speech. Exx. of lemmata in A where he reverts to direct speech are: P 1.3 at 876F2 and 877F3, P 1.5 at 879B9, P 2.12 at 888C5 (= S 1.23.3), P 2.20 (= S 1.25.3d), etc. The entire (exceptionally) long passage in P 3.5 at 894B–E is cast in *oratio recta* until for the briefer *doxai* of the Presocratics at the end he returns to *oratio obliqua*. This criterion, we note, was not made explicit by Diels.

6. Detailed comparison of the adaptation of A by P and S respectively is often revealing. P tends to abridge by simply deleting whole lemmata or (less often) by abbreviating longer lemmata. This means he most often retains the original order in A. Comparison of S with P can reveal that S has replaced A with material drawn from AD. For example in S's chapter Περὶ ἰδεῶν, parallel to P 1.10, he changes the order from Plato Aristotle Stoics to Aristotle Plato Stoics.[26] This, together with the fact that the contents of the lemmata are quite different, makes clear that he has inserted the fuller reports of AD (including the passage also found in Eusebius).

7. S tends to begin his chapters with material from A, and group the excerpts from AD towards the end. This characteristic is hardly surprising in light of the fact that he (and the *Placita* in general) rather often begins with Presocratic philosophers, who of course hardly occur in AD's physical fragments.[27] There are also cases, however, where Diels has postulated fragments from AD right in the middle of a series of *doxai* from A (e.g. 1.14.1c, 25.1i). For the brief Chrysippean lemma at 1.8.40b this must be the case, since, as Diels acutely saw, the sentence is repeated at 1.8.42 (at 106.6). In other cases, however, one should be suspicious, as we shall see.

8. Since, to the best of our knowledge, the physical fragments of AD are confined to material on Aristotle and the Stoics (apart from the solitary fragment on Plato just referred to above[28]), it is these

---

[25] E.g. fr. 2, 3, 39.

[26] The reason for the change is rather obscure. A not very flattering suggestion is that he saw the phrase τὰ λεγόμενα εἴδη καὶ τὰς ἰδέας in the Pythagorean lemma (deleted by P), and so decided on a sequence Aristotle (εἴδη), Plato (ἰδέαι).

[27] Heraclitus is twice incidentally mentioned in relation to the Stoic doctrine of the soul at Eus. 15.20.2–3 (= fr. 39 Diels).

[28] Stobaeus mostly prefers to quote Plato in the original.

name-labels which must arouse suspicion. It is striking that the presentation of the views of various members of the Stoic school in S is very rich, whereas in A as represented in P the divergence in Stoic *doxai* is much more limited. It is possible that this was the result of P's efforts at abridgement, i.e. he replaced the names of individual Stoics with the generic name-label. On the basis of the independent evidence in Eusebius we may be certain that AD repeatedly drew attention to the contributions of individual Stoics.[29]

It is on the basis of these eight criteria, combined with thorough analyses of the relevant chapters of Stobaeus' anthology, that we must try to identify the physical fragments of Arius Didymus. Since there is no need to reinvent the wheel, Diels' results should be taken as our starting-point. His collection, published in *DG*, consists of 64 lemmata of greatly varying length, presented as 41 fragments.[30] As noted above, almost all these identifications were taken over and correspondingly labelled in Wachsmuth's text. Diels cautiously stated that his collection was not definitive and might contain errors,[31] adding that the reader will be warned of difficulties in apparatus to his reconstruction. In a footnote he appended the remark that he believed that 'scraps from Didymus were mixed in' and cites six Aëtian passages.[32] This remark is not very precise, and might be mistakenly taken to mean that material from Arius Didymus was excerpted by Aëtius.[33] What he wants to say is that in the case of some texts (all of which we shall examine below), Stobaeus has coalesced together material from both sources in a single lemma. Starting off from Diels, therefore, we shall successively examine the two possibilities open us: first, that he has failed to include material in his collection that should be there, and second, that he has included material that should not be present.[34]

---

[29] See the quote cited above at n. 15. Note that I am not basing my argument on any assumption that AD himself was a Stoic.

[30] *DG* 447–472; the fragment appended at 854 may be considered fr. 41.

[31] *DG* 75: neque tantum vereor ne quid falso in syllogen receperim quantum ne omnia.

[32] *Ibid.* n. 2: frustula ex Didymo admixta credo I 7 31 18 6 23 2 III 1 7 2 3 7 4.

[33] I owe this observation to Jaap Mansfeld.

[34] It will be understood that for reasons of space an exhaustive interpretation of these texts cannot be presented. The analysis concentrates on aspects relevant to the question of identification. For example in the case of the first text I ignore the fact that in P the lemma is attributed to *Socrates and* Plato. The reader is encouraged to have the relevant texts at hand.

I. *Additions to Diels' collection*

The following texts in Stobaeus, which include the six of Diels' footnote, deserve to be considered for inclusion among the physical fragments of AD.

1. ¶1.29b, 37.9–16 W.: Plato. The second half of S's lemma is not found at P 1.7, 881E. Diels, noting the Stoicizing flavour of the phrase λόγοι ἀσωμάτοι, surmised that this section might come from AD. This supposition is almost certainly wrong. The lemma must be interpreted in relation to four surrounding lemmata with differing fortunes in the sources:

Xenocrates	only in S
Plato	short in P, long in S
Aristotle	long in P, short in S
Stoics	identical in P and S
Epicurus	identical in P and S

These five lemmata have a formal feature in common, viz. that in answering the question τίς ἐστιν ὁ θεός they list a a hierarchy of gods at various levels, beginning with the highest god (the same feature also occurs in the well-known doxographies in Cicero *ND* 1.25–41 and Philodemus *De pietate* printed in two columns by Diels in *DG* 531-550). This common feature suggests that the lemmata all come from the same document, which must be A rather than AD. P commonly abbreviates longish lemmata in A. It is unusual for S to abbreviate the Aristotelian lemma; he does this because he will later in the same chapter cite a long quote from the *De mundo*, the authenticity of which he does not doubt.

The final part of the Xenocratean lemma has two features which might suggest derivation from AD. (1) The formula ἀρέσκει δὲ καὶ αὐτῷ is common in AD (twice used in the fragment cited in double columns at n. 15). It is only found once in A, at 5.29.1, where it is used to introduce an additional comment, just as happens here. (2) The final remark that Xenocrates handed a Platonic doctrine down to the Stoics might be thought more in the style of AD than A (cf. again the fragment cited at n. 15). Occasionally, however, A does give information about the provenance and appropriation of doctrines, e.g. at 1.3 877D-F on Epicurus and Democritus. Moreover we have no idea whether AD's treatment of Plato also took developments in the Academy into account.

2. ¶13.1b, 138.9–12: Aristotle. Diels *DG* 64 with great confidence declared that P was wrong in associating Pythagoras and Aristotle on the question of causes (P 1.11.3) and that S, who has separate lemmata for both thinkers, conveys the true picture of the original A. But it is he who is almost certainly wrong. The opening words Ἀριστοτέλης ἔφησεν provides a first clue. The verb in this formula is indicative of Stobaean intervention. It is never found in A, but does occur in 5 fragments of AD as collected by Diels: cf. fr. 20, 21, 26, 34, 35. In all cases but the third it stands at the beginning of the excerpt, i.e. where the anthologist has to cover the traces of his excerpting. In the longer ethical passages from AD in book 2 of S it is not found at all. The use of the formula may thus with some confidence be taken to be S's work (note also the ex. cited above at n. 23), and so supports the hypothesis that S has inserted a fragment from

AD. The formulation as found in S is rather clumsy; both Heeren and Meineke wanted to emend it. If there were originally two lemmata in A, then there is an awkward dilemma: either Aristotle preceded Pythagoras, in which case one would have expected a contrast between Plato τριχῶς and Aristotle τετραχῶς; or Aristotle succeeded Pythagoras, resulting in interference with the διαφωνία between Pythagoras and the Stoics on the materiality of causes. We note too that in S the Aristotelian lemma is followed by three others from AD, of Zeno, Chrysippus, Posidonius; similar sequences are found in ¶8.40–42, 11.4–5, 12.1–2, 17.2–4, 25.4–15. In short both P's and S's arrangements make much more sense if this fragment is assigned to AD.

3. ¶14.1e, 142.1–7: Chrysippus. Diels placed this in A's equivalent of P 1.16 on account of the subject matter and because it follows fairly soon after the Aristotelian lemma from the same chapter (certainly from A since in P). But that lemma is placed there because of coalescence (joined with 3rd lemma in P's 1.12), and it is followed by a lemma from AD. The formula ὁ δεῖνα ἔφασκε is not found in P. It does occur twice in S, here and at 1.15.6a (see next text). Both the verb and the absence of a connecting particle suggest Stobaean intervention (see our remarks above on the 4th criterion). More importantly the lemma seems otiose in P's (and A's) 1.16, which appears to have a simple systematic structure A B A–B, with the third, Aristotelian, lemma inserted as a compromise between the other two positions. Note too how the subject treated in the Chrysippean fragment is much broader than the theme of A's chapter. These considerations all point to AD as the source.

4. ¶15.6a, 146.13–21. This group of five brief lemmata is problematic. Diels included all 5 in his reconstruction of A 1.14. Certainly the short Zenonian lemma at the end seems misplaced. Diels thought it belonged to 1.12 but printed it in 1.14 because of its location in S. The formula Ζήνων ἔφασκε once again points to AD or rather S's adaptation of AD. A difficulty here is that we might have expected the fragment to have been taken from fr. 23 Diels, which discusses Zeno's views on the motion and weightlessness of fire, but it is not found there. The association with the previous Cleanthean lemma which also deals with fire is clumsy but transparent. But this lemma too is problematic. Its position in the Aëtian chapter is not impossible, but one would sooner expect it after the second lemma οἱ ἀπὸ Πυθαγόρου. It is in fact possible that this lemma too comes from AD, but there simply no way to decide. Note finally that the Zenonian lemma is repeated in the mss. at 1.15.6e in the middle of a quite different lemma (at 147.22). This would seem to confirm that it is a *Fremdkörper*, but an ascription to AD is, all things considered, too risky.

5. ¶18.1c, 156.15–25: Aristotle. A real puzzle. The entire lemma in S appears to consist of three parts: (i) a quote on the Pythagoreans contained ἐν τετάρτῳ Φυσικῆς ἀκροάσεως (= lines 8–11); (ii) another quote, this time not *verbatim*, but also concerning the Pythagoreans, located ἐν τῷ περὶ τῆς Πυθαγόρου φιλοσοφίας πρώτῳ (= 11–15); (iii) further *doxai* on space and void introduced καὶ ἐν ἄλλοις λέγει... (= 15–25). Diels rightly suspected some of this material may have come from AD, but printed the entire passage in A nevertheless. But we can fairly sure that the lemma as a whole does not belong together. Both (i) and (ii) deal with the extra-

cosmic void, whereas (iii) discusses place and void in quite general terms, without any cosmological reference. Moreover between (ii) and (iii) the account clearly passes from the views of Aristotle on the Pythagoreans to those of Aristotle himself (although this is not explicitly stated). It is thus logical to conclude that there is break between (ii) and (iii). The style of the third part of the lemma points to AD (note the use of indirect speech). A further hint is supplied by the fact that S has deleted a lemma on Aristotle's views on space in P 1.19. Do the first two parts of the lemma come from A or AD? It is certainly unusual for A to have a lemma containing two complete references, but there are about 15 texts in which he does refer to writings with greater or lesser accuracy.[35] The possibility that S added the learned references is also not so likely because elsewhere he does not cite the Aristotelian corpus or lost works (preferring to use the *De mundo*). The references also do not fit easily into AD's work, which—as far as we know—did not deal with Pythagorean philosophy directly. These considerations point to the conclusion that the first two parts of the lemma come from A and the third part from AD. On the other hand it should be recognized that the differences between P and S in the first part cannot be readily explained on this hypothesis.[36]

6. ¶19.1, 162.19–163.14: Aristotle. Once again Diels thought there might be Arian material in this lemma, but nevertheless printed it as part of his reconstruction of A 1.23. Wachsmuth shows the same vacillation, printing it as A but adding in the apparatus *haec fort. rectius Ario tribuas*. There can be no doubt, however, that, had Diels followed his own criteria, he would have concluded that the entire lemma was from AD. Not only is it very long, but it replaces a very short lemma in P and occurs at the end of the sequence. It is most perplexing that Diels should have printed this piece as part of A. Perhaps he was swayed by the fact that it starts with the name in the nominative, as is usual in A, and is not preceded by the name in the genitive. But the ms. P does add Ἀριστοτέλ (*sic*) in the margin. These genitives, as argued above, are not a reliable criterion.

7. ¶27.7, 226.21–26: Aristotle. Diels in his reconstruction of A 3.1 (*DG* 365) states that he thinks the second part of the lemma in S is Arian since it disagrees with P and is clearly excerpted from *Meteor.* 1.8 346a19ff. He did not, however, include this section in his collection. This passage is the only place in the whole chapter where P and S disagree. We note the use of *oratio obliqua*, even though the second word of the additional section is γὰρ. It is to be concluded that S has added an excerpt from his reading of AD to A.

8. ¶28.1a, 227.17–21: Aristotle. Again the text for A 3.2 in P and S is identical except for the additional Aristotelian material. Diels suspected that it came from AD. Wachsmuth *ad loc.* disagreed, arguing that, since the

---

35 I have listed these in my article 'Xenophanes or Theophrastus? an Aëtian *Doxographicum* on the Sun', in W. W. Fortenbaugh and D. Gutas (edd.), *Theophrastus: his Psychological, Doxographical and Scientific Writings* (New Brunswick 1992) 112–140, on p. 122–123.

36 K. A. Algra, 'Posidonius' Conception of the Extra-cosmic Void: the Evidence and the Arguments', *Mnemosyne* 46 (1993) 484–485 tentatively suggests that it may have been contaminated with material from the Posidonian lemma in the parallel chapter at P 2.9.

material conflicts with views expressed in the *Meteorologica*, it is better to assume a lacuna and attribute the *doxa* to Posidonius. From the formal viewpoint, however, the clues clearly point to AD, not only because of the remaining parallelism between P and S, but also on account of the similarity to S 1.29.1, where the extract on Aristotle from AD (= fr. 12 Diels) has a string of subjects introduced with the exactly the same formula τινας δὲ ὅταν plus subjunctive (admittedly it also occurs occasionally in A, e.g. in the Democritean lemma in the same chapter). It is possible that there is a lacuna in the text or that S made a mistake and added a Stoic fragment from AD to an Aristotelian lemma. It is also possible that AD had an alternative source for Peripatetic meteorological theory.

9. ¶32, 248.7–11: Aristotle. Once again the fact that two explanations of the origin of winds are given in the same lemma indicates that S has coalesced two views, the first from A, the second from AD; cf. Diels *DG* 375, accepted by Wachsmuth *ad loc.* But again the fragment is not found in his collection.

The results so far have been quite remunerative: at least seven fragments should be subtracted from A and added to AD. Six relate to Aristotle, the seventh to Chrysippus. Diels does his reader a disservice by including them in the reconstruction of A, especially because he creates the impression—most blatantly in the case of the Aristotelian lemma in his reconstruction of A 1.23—that A contained more long and detailed lemmata than in actual fact was the case. It also meant that these texts were missing in his fragment collection of AD.

At this point we should note that four of the above texts (nos. 5, 7–9) shed valuable light on the technique of coalescence that S used to weld his doxographical material together. It appears that he not only merges lemmata from different chapters of A, but also is prepared to join together in the same lemma material from both A and AD.[37] This means, I believe, that we should be on our guard in the case of other longish lemmata which Diels attributes wholly to A. I wish to consider three further texts which form part of Diels' reconstruction of A 1.25–29. These chapters are highly complex, and many of Diels' solutions, taken over by Wachsmuth in his edition of S, are rather questionable.

10. ¶5.15, 79.12–20: Chrysippus. The lemma on εἱμαρμένη in its entirety would appear to be to be on the long side for A. From the beginning to γενησέται P (at 1.29 885B) and S run fairly parallel (though P has shortened the reference to Chrysippus' works). The text from μεταλαμβάνει to ἐπιβολάς is probably also Aëtian, since it continues the theme of

---

[37] Diels recognized this in a number of texts on Aristotle, though the presentation in Wachsmuth tends to conceal it: cf. 14.1c, 22.1c, 24.1m, 27.7.

Chrysippean diversity of terminology. But the following words μοίρας δέ introduce a break in thought. Moreover the style, with reversion to *oratio obliqua* and the sequence of single nouns followed by explanatory phrases, reflects the more descriptive, cataloguing style of AD.

11. ¶6.17a, 87.23–88.6: Aristotle. Comparison of the sources and examination of Diels' double columns (*DG* 324–5) reveal a very complicated situation here: P's Aristotelian doxa (at 1.30 885C) can be divided into two parts (let us say K & L). S wishes to begin with the distinction between τύχη and αὐτόματον (cf. the title of his chapter), and so places that part of A's lemma (= L) first. He thus reverses the order of these two parts, separates them (by means of a Platonic lemma slightly longer than what is found in P) and adds sections (let us say M & N) to both. So S's lemma can be represented as L M–Plato–K N. The lemma in P makes good sense, as well as S's continuation καὶ τὴν μὲν τύχην ... βουλευθέντος (= M). But the passage with which S ends, καὶ ὑποθέσεις ... τεταγμένοις (N), is more discursive, It introduces various new elements (e.g. ἀρχαί, τάξις, ἀταξία). It also contains an entire sentence on εἱμαρμένη which seems quite out of place in this chapter. This mixing of themes is characteristic of AD rather than A. We conclude therefore that this final section (= 87.23–88.6 W.) is more likely to derive from AD than A.

12. ¶6.17c, 89.2–5: Theophrastus. If we wish to attribute the Aristotelian passage just dealt with to AD, we must also consider whether the Theophrastean lemma on the next page—in between S interposes an excerpt from Plato's *Laws*—is also derived from him, for it appears to continue the theme of causes discussed in the previous Aristotelian passage, i.e. Theophrastus is reported to add to the causes related to εἱμαρμένη that of προαίρεσις missing in Aristotle. A strong argument in favour of attribution to AD is the verb used, προσδιαρθροῖ. It recurs in a doxographical context in AD at *Ecl.* 2.76.1 (i.e. Ethical doxography B), while elsewhere it occurs only twice in the entire TLG! A lemma referring to Theophrastus would be unique in the physical fragments of AD that we have. But we note that he does occur in the Aristotelian-Peripatetic Ethical doxography C (at 2.140.7 W. = FGS&H fr. 449A). A revised attribution to AD would be consistent with the fact that in the rest of A Theophrastus only occurs as a *reporter* of Presocratic views (S 1.25.1b, on which see Runia *art. cit.* (n. 34), and 1.26.3). The recent editors of Theophrastus' fragments have followed the Dielsian attribution to Aëtius (= FGS&H fr. 503).[38] I submit that the clues point to AD.

The balance of probability, therefore, points to the conclusion that these three lemmata also derive from AD's compendium.

---

[38] Where I would translate the words φέρεται δέ πως 'it contributes in a way' rather than 'he inclines in a way', as done by the editors; see W. W. Fortenbaugh, P. M. Huby, R. W. Sharples, and D. Gutas, *Theophrastus of Eresus: Sources for his Life, Writings, Thought, and Influence*, 2 vols., Philosophia Antiqua 54 (Leiden 1992) 2.329.

II. *Subtractions from Diels' collection*

We turn now to the second category of texts we have to consider, namely those that Diels may have wrongly included in his collection.

1. ¶1.26, 31.12–14: Chrysippus. Diels included this short lemma of 3 lines on the names of Zeus (= fr. 30) because of a general similarity with an extract from AD on the Stoics found in Eus. *PE* 15.15.1–9. There we read that the cosmos is called Zeus because it is the cause of life. A similar connection of the accusative form Δία with the phrase δι' αὐτὸν πάντα is attributed to Chrysippus at Johannes Lydus *Mens.* 4.71 Wünsch (= *SVF* 2.1063, cf. DL 7.147). Here the context appears to be theological rather than cosmological. An argument against Diels' attribution is the fact that S does not use any further material from AD in this chapter. The fragment is in direct rather than indirect speech, but this is also the case for the similar statement in Eusebius. All in all it was wise of Wachsmuth to relegate Diels' attribution to the apparatus. The attribution of such a short fragment to AD is no more than an educated guess.

The remaining texts whose attribution is questionable are all found in fr. 33-34, where Diels has collected together various Stoic extracts on the sun and moon which he thinks S drew from AD rather than from A. Here his assumption that it is possible to separate the material from the sources—which we have taken over in this article—starts to crumble. Some of these fragments are so short that they are stylistically virtually indistinguishable from the telegram-like Aëtian lemmata coalesced together by S. A more complete treatment of the question would require that we make full reconstructions of A's sequence of chapters on the sun and moon. This I have done elsewhere.[39] In the present context I will largely confine my remarks to stylistic and terminological considerations.

2. ¶25.5, 213.13–27: Zeno. I think there can be no doubt that this text is from AD. In the first place it combines information about on the substance of sun *and* moon *and* other stars which A keeps well separate (and S does not coalesce together). Secondly it adds information about kinds of fire that would be difficult to place in A. Thirdly it combines information about the movement and eclipses of sun and moon, whereas in A these are dealt with in separate groups of chapters (which S coalesces in his chapters 1.25 and 1.26 respectively).
3. ¶25.5, 214.1–3: Chrysippus. This lemma is much more difficult precisely because it is so short. It is possible that it represents two lemmata

---

39 In *art. cit.* (n. 35); see also 'Xenophanes on the Moon: a *Doxographicum* in Aëtius', *Phronesis* 34 (1989) 245-269. I hope to return to this problem in a full reconstruction of Book II of Aëtius.

from A joined together. Three arguments favour Diels' attribution. (1) The lemma is placed towards the end of the chapter, and follows two long and (in my view) indubitably Arian texts. (2) The rare term ἀναθυμίαμα is used for exhalation; this is also the case in the other Chrysippean text to be discussed below, whereas in A the term is ἀναθυμίασις (used at least a dozen times, cf. P 2.5 887A, 2.20 890A, 3.1 893A, etc.). (3) The same combination of substance and shape is found in the Chrysippean lemma in the next chapter, where it is complemented with an explanation and definition of the term 'month' which is very difficult to place in A. None of these arguments are decisive, but Diels should be given the benefit of the doubt.

4. ¶26.1i, 219.12–13: Zeno. As argued above (I, text n. 2), the formula Ζήνων ἔφησεν strongly suggests Stobaean remodelling. Moreover the excerpt is almost identical with the Zenonian text from AD in the previous chapter (only the word ἄστρον is added). Diels' attribution is thus justified.

5. ¶26.1i, 219.14–15: Cleanthes. Here the situation is desparate. From the formal point of view the two brief lemmata are identical with what we find in P, except that they are joined together. On grounds of content I have argued elsewhere that the former derives from A.[40] Diels' attribution is probably wrong, though it cannot be proven to be so.

6. ¶26.1l, 219.24–220.2: Chrysippus. As argued under text 3 above, the clustering of lemmata here points to AD. Diels' intuition should be followed.

Conclusions

On the basis of our investigation the following results have been reached.

(1) The criteria that Diels and Wachsmuth used to separate out the physical fragments of Arius Didymus in Stobaeus *Eclogae* book I can be slightly improved. If intelligently and carefully applied, they are equal to their task.

(2) Particular attention should be given to the fact that the anthologist Stobaeus sometimes joins together material from his two sources in one and the same lemma.

(3) In the case of very short fragments formal and stylistic criteria are ineffective. It in fact becomes almost impossible to determine with any degree of certainty whether the texts should be assigned to the one doxographical source rather than the other.

(4) On the basis of the examination carried out above the following ten fragments should be added to Diels' collection.

---

[40] *Ibid.* 258.

a.	5.15, 79.12-20	Chrysippus on the Μοῖραι
b.	6.17a, 87.23–88.6	Aristotle on εἱμαρμένη
c.	6.17c, 89.2-5	Theophrastus on εἱμαρμένη
d.	13.1b, 138.9-12	Aristotle on the four causes
e.	14.1e, 142.1-7	Chrysippus on the divisibility of bodies
f.	18.1c, 156.15-25	Aristotle on place
g.	19.1, 162.19–163.14	Aristotle on motion
h.	27.7, 226.21-26	Aristotle on the milky way
i.	28.1a, 227.17-21	Aristotle on comets
j.	32, 248.7-11	Aristotle on winds

Of great interest is the fact that in one of these texts Theophrastus was mentioned. This confirms that the physical doxography dealt with the thought not only of Aristotle, but also of his Peripatetic successors.[41]

(5) Conversely the following two fragments should be subtracted from Diels' edition.

a.	1.26, 31.12-14	Chrysippus on the name of Zeus
b.	26.1i, 219.14-15	Cleanthes on the moon.

(6) For the assistance of scholars who wish to make use of this important doxographical source, I append below a full list of the physical fragments of Arius Didymus, taking into account the results of this article. The sequence is determined by the following criteria: (i) the philosophers or philosophical school dealt with (Plato-Peripatos-Stoa); (ii) the source (Eusebius, abbreviated as E; Stobaeus, abbreviated as S); (iii) the location in the source (in the editions of Mras and Wachsmuth respectively). In the list I try to separate individual Stoic philosophers as much as I can, splitting up the fragments in Diels' collection in the process.[42] This leads to complications in the case of fr. 36, parts of which are found in both sources.

(7) Finally, I remind the reader of the remark, made at the outset of the article, that a new edition of these fragments is highly desirable.

Leiden

---

[41] Cf. the heading given to the lemma at Stob. *Ecl.* 1.17.2, Ἀριστοτέλους καὶ τῶν ἀπ' αὐτοῦ, and the name-label Ἀριστοτελικοί at 8.40d (but these may have been the work of Stobaeus). The title of Ethical doxography C at 2.116.19–20 is Ἀριστοτέλους καὶ τῶν λοιπῶν Περιπατητικῶν περὶ τῶν ἠθικῶν.

[42] There is no need to try to retain Diels' sequence of fragments, since his ordering is by no means always logical (e.g. why place fr. 16 between 15 and 17?).

APPENDIX

THE PHYSICAL FRAGMENTS OF ARIUS DIDYMUS

No.	*Diels*	*philosopher*	*source*	*subject*
Academy				
1	1	Plato	E 11.23.3-6, 51.18–52.11 & S 12.2a, 135.20–136.13	ideas
Peripatos				
2	–	Aristotle	S 6.17a, 87.23–88.6	*heimarmene*
3	–	Theophrastus	S 6.17c, 89.2-5	*heimarmene*
4	6	Aristotle	S 8.40c, 103.10-16	time
5	7	Aristotelians	S 8.40d, 103.18–104.5	time
6	2	Aristotle	S 11.4, 132.10-25	*archai*: matter
7	3	Aristotle	S 12.1b, 134.18–135.18	*archai*: form
8	–	Aristotle	S 13.1b, 138.9-12	the four causes
9	5	Aristotle	S 14.1c, 141.7-22	simple bodies
10	4	Aristotle & successors	S 17.2, 152.14-17	mixture of bodies
11	–	Aristotle	S 18.1c, 156.15-25	place
12	–	Aristotle	S 19.1, 162.19–163.14	motion
13	9	Aristotle	S 22.1c, 196.5-15	stars consist of ether
14	8	Aristotle	S 24.1m, 204.8-12	motion of the stars
15	10	Aristotle	S 25.4, 212.13–213.13	sun
16	–	Aristotle	S 27.7, 226.21-26	the milky way
17	–	Aristotle	S 28.1a, 227.17-21	comets
18	12	Aristotle	S 29.1, 234.5–235.8	storms etc.
19	14a	Aristotle	S 30.2, 240.13–242.17	haloes and rainbows
20	11	Aristotle	S 31.6, 243.23–245.21	rain and mist
21	–	Aristotle	S 32, 248.7-11	winds
22	13	Aristotle	S 36.2, 249.12–251.27	earthquakes
23	14b	Aristotle	S 39, 253.25–255.7	bodies of water
24	15	Aristotle	S 51.5, 482.11-19	sense-perception
25	17a	Aristotle	S 52.19, 484.15-21	sight and hearing
26	17b	Aristotle	S 54.3, 492.21-22	smell
27	17c	Aristotle	S 55.1, 494.6-7	taste
28	17d	Aristotle	S 56.1, 496.15-23	touch
29	16	Aristotle	S 58, 497.15-25	*phantasia* and criteria
Stoa				
30	29a	unnamed	E 15.15.1-6, 379.12–380.12	cosmo-theology
31	29b	Cleanthes	E 15.15.7, 380.12-14	*hegemonikon* of cosmos
32	29c	Chrysippus	E 15.15.8, 380.15-17	*hegemonikon* of cosmos
33	36a	unnamed	E 15.18.1, 382.22-24	*ekpyrosis*
34	36b	Chrysippus	E 15.18.2, 383.2-7	*ekpyrosis* and change
35	36d	Zeno of Tarsus	E 15.18.3, 383.11-12	*ekpyrosis* doubted

36	36c	Zeno –Cleanthes –Chrysippus	E 15.18.3, 383.7-12 & S 20.1e, 171.2-7	cosmic *ekpyrosis*
37	37	unnamed	E 15.19, 383.15–384.5	cosmic regeneration
38	39a	Zeno	E 15.20.1, 384.7-13	seed and birth
39	39b	Zeno –Cleanthes	E 15.20.2-3, 384.15-24	nature of soul
40	39c	unnamed	E 15.20.4-5, 385.2-7	cosmic soul
41	39d	unnamed	E 15.20.6-7, 385.9-15	soul and body
42	–	Chrysippus	S 5.15, 79.12-20	Moirai
43	26a	Zeno	S 8.40e, 104.7-11	time
44	26b	Apollodorus	S 8.42, 105.8-16	time
45	26c	Posidonius	S 8.42, 105.17–106.4	time
46	26d	Chrysippus	S 8.42, 106.5–107.7	time
47	21	Chrysippus	S 10.16c, 129.2–130.20	elements
48	20a	Zeno	S 11.5a, 132.27–133.5	*ousia* as matter
49	20b	Chrysippus	S 11.5a, 133.6-11	first matter
50	20c	Posidonius	S 11.5c, 133.18-23	*ousia* and matter
51	40	Zeno–Stoics[43]	S 12.3, 136.21–137.6	concepts
52	18a	Zeno	S 13.1c, 138.14-22	cause
53	18b	Chrysippus	S 13.1c, 138.23–139.4	cause
54	18c	Posidonius	S 13.1c, 139.5-8	cause
55	–	Chrysippus	S 14.1e, 142.1-7	divisibility of bodies
56	19	unnamed	S 14.1l, 143.24–144.10	three-dimensional body
57	38a	Zeno	S 17.3, 152.19–153.6	cosmic cycle
58	38b	Cleanthes	S 17.3, 153.7-22	cosmic cycle
59	28	Chrysippus	S 17.4, 153.24–155.14	kinds of mixture
60	25	Chrysippus	S 18.4d, 161.8-26	place
61	22	Chrysippus	S 19.3, 165.15–166.2	motion
62	23	Zeno	S 19.4, 166.4-22	cosmic motion
63	24	Apollodorus	S 19.5, 166.24–167.14	motion
64	36e	Panaetius	S 20.1e, 171.5-7	*ekpyrosis* rejected
65	27a	Posidonius	S 20.7, 177.21–179.5	generation–destruction
66	27b	Mnesarchus	S 20.7, 179.6–17	generation–destruction
67	31	Chrysippus	S 21.5, 184.8–185.24	description of cosmos
68	33a	Zeno	S 25.5, 213.15-27	sun-moon-stars
69	33b	Chrysippus	S 25.5, 214.1-2	sun
70	34a	Zeno	S 26.1i, 219.12-13	moon
71	34c	Chrysippus	S 26.1l, 219.24–220.2	moon
72	35	Chrysippus	S 31.7, 245.23-30	mist etc.

[43] Diels' emendation Ζήνωνος ⟨καὶ τῶν ἀπ'αὐτοῦ⟩ is taken over by Wachsmuth. It is far from certain, but later in the lemma S uses the label οἱ Στωικοὶ φιλόσοφοι.

PART SEVEN

HISTORY OF SCHOLARSHIP

THE TWO PLATOS OF VICTORIAN BRITAIN

John Glucker

A sixty-page survey of the fortunes of Plato in England (and Scotland) since 1804 can be, in the nature of things, only a small map of a vast territory. This is what I attempted to produce, a few years ago, in a long article.[1] Much of it was an attempt to correct misconceptions and put things in perspective. I emphasized the three stages in the rediscovery of Plato in nineteenth-century England: Thomas Taylor's first English translation of the whole of Plato (1804) and its influence on some major literary figures; John Stuart Mill's translations/paraphrases of some dialogues (1834–5) and George Grote's *Plato* (1865), representing a searching, open-ended image; and Benjamin Jowett's translation with introductions of the whole of Plato (1871) as a token of Plato's final 'arrival' on the British academic scene. It was Jowett's image of Plato, 'the father of idealism', rather than the 'negative' and searching Plato of Grote and Mill, which won the day and influenced the whole course of Platonic studies in Britain and beyond.

'It is interesting to speculate,' I wrote, 'on what would have happened if J.S. Mill had translated the whole of Plato.'[2] Hastening on with my bird's-eye view, I did not pose the question as fully as I should have done. It is not only that Mill's translations/paraphrases became more popular than anything he had published before 1834.[3] Grote's *Plato*, published in 1865 and reprinted in 1867, was reviewed in most British journals, and two of the reviews—those in *The Westminster Review* and in *The Edinburgh Review* of 1866—were extremely favourable.[4] Yet Grote's book was only reprinted once again, in 1874, and it exercised little, if any, influence. True, Jowett was an establishment figure, and his part in *Essays and Reviews* made him something of a household name. Yet

---

[1] J. Glucker, "Plato in England, the Nineteenth Century and After", in *Utopie und Tradition, Platons Lehre vom Staat in der Moderne*, ed. H. Funke (Würzburg 1987) 149–210.

[2] Glucker, *op. cit.*, 174.

[3] Glucker, *op.cit.*, 169.

[4] See nn. 59; 60 below and context.

Grote's stature as a scholar was far higher than that of Jowett: as we shall soon see, Jowett himself, in his public utterances, treated him with respect bordering on reverence. Why, then, was Grote's view of Plato consigned to oblivion, and what made Jowett's view become so dominant and seminal?

Limitations of space would render it impossible—even if it were desirable—to give here even a brief sketch of the development of attitudes to Plato since the eighteenth century, and of British philosophy in the nineteenth. References to some standard works will have to do. I shall concentrate on two issues: the nature of the images of Plato presented by Grote (and Mill) and Jowett; and the intellectual climate at the time their works were produced.

Grote's image of Plato is best seen in Chapter VI of his *Plato*, "Platonic Compositions Generally".[5] It is still extremely fresh and readable, after all these years; but here we can only indicate some of its salient points and cite some central passages.

Grote must have been familar with the review of Thomas Taylor's Plato in *The Edinburgh Review* of 1809, where the reviewer regards Plato as a sceptic, citing Cicero, *Acad.* I, 46.[6] He was also aware of other ancient views of Plato as a sceptic: on p. 212, he cites in evidence D.L. 3. 52 and the anonymous *Prolegomena.* His own view is that 'Plato is sceptical in some dialogues, dogmatical in others. And the catalogue of Thrasyllus shows that the sceptical dialogues (Dialogues of Search or Investigation) are more numerous than the dogmatical (Dialogues of Exposition)—as they are also, speaking generally, more animated and interesting.'[7] One would, then, expect Grote to devote equal space, in this chapter, to the discussion of each of these types of dialogue. He does nothing of the sort. Having accepted, in principle, this division of Thrasyllus, he now examines its detailed application to the dialogues.[8] As

---

5 G. Grote, *Plato and the other Companions of Sokrates* (London 1867) vol. 1, 212–280. I shall refer throughout to this second edition, which was available to me. With very slight changes, it is essentially a reproduction of the first.

6 See n. 34 below and context.

7 I shall only mention Grote's total rejection of the possibility of reconstructing any ἄγραφα δόγματα (215–21; 273–4) and his acceptance of all dialogues not athetized in antiquity, and all epistles, as genuine (221–6). The latter, one of the weaker points of his book eagerly seized on by his critics, was probably arrived at mainly because of the value of the epistles to the historian of Greece.

8 On pp. 158–164, he had rejected the 'dramatic' division of Thrasyllus,

against Thrasyllus' list of 22 dogmatic and 14 sceptical dialogues, Grote argues for his own 'more balanced' list of 19 sceptical and 14 dogmatic ones (236). He concludes from this proportion that Plato is 'more negative than affirmative—more ingenious in pointing out difficulties, than successful in solving them'. (236–7)

The discussion of 'philosophy as now understood' which follows (237–8) is crucial for our understanding of the philosophical climate in 1865. Most people, says Grote, ask 'What positive system, or positive truths previously unknown, has he established? ... The philosopher is assumed to speak as one having authority; to have already made up his mind; and to be prepared to explain what his mind is ... Above all, an affirmative result is indispensable.' But '... if philosophers are to be estimated by such a scale, he [Plato] will not stand high up on the list. Even in his expository dialogues, he cares little about clear proclamation of results, and still less about the shortest, straightest, and most certain road for affirming them.'

Almost all the rest of the chapter is devoted to the 'Dialogues of Search', discussing the educational nature of the Socratic ἔλεγχος; the genuine search for the truth by a genuinely ignorant Socrates; the 'negative procedure,' inherited by Plato and the Megarians from Socrates, and its nature as an all-out war against all false pretensions to knowledge; the place of Socrates among the few people in each generation who think for themselves and defy King Nomos (one of Grote's favourite expressions)—including most Presocratics; drama and the dicasteries as places where 'two or more different views of looking at a question' were admitted; and the price paid by Socrates, regarded by the Athenians as a sophist, for expressing his doubts and views (238–267). It is only then, on the last few pages of this long chapter, that Grote has a few words to say on the 'affirmative' aspect of some dialogues. In my longer survey, I had room only for a string of passages from these pages.[9] Here one must quote at far greater length.

---

into tetralogies, as fanciful, but accepted his 'philosophical' division, into sceptical and dogmatic dialogues, as significant. His reconstruction is based on D.L. 3.49–51 and on Alcinous p. 148 Hermann. Jaap Mansfeld, *Prolegomena, Questions to be settled before the Study of an Author, or a Text* (Leiden 1994) 74–97, has argued convincingly that the 'philosophical division' is of Middle Platonic provenance, and is later than Thrasyllus.

9 Glucker, *op. cit.* (n. 1), 171–2.

The negative procedure is so conspicuous, and even so preponderant, in the Platonic dialogues, that no historian of philosophy can omit to notice it. But many of them (like Xenophon in describing Sokrates) assign to it only a subordinate place and a qualified application: while some (and Schleiermacher especially) represent all the doubts and difficulties in the negative dialogues as exercises to call forth the intellectual effort of the reader, preparatory to full and satisfactory solutions which Plato has given in the dogmatic dialogues at the end. The first half of this hypothesis I accept: the last half I believe to be unfounded. The doubts and difficulties were certainly exercises to the mind of Plato himself, and were intended as exercises to his readers; but he has nowhere provided a key to the solution of them. Where he propounds positive dogmas, he does not bring them face to face with objections, nor verify their authority by showing that they afford satisfactory solutions to the negative procedure. The two currents of his speculation, the affirmative and the negative, are distinct and independent of each other. Where the affirmative is especially present (as in Timaeus), the negative altogether disappears. Timaeus is made to proclaim the most sweeping theories, not one of which the real Sokrates would have suffered to pass without abundant cross-examination; but the Platonic Sokrates hears them with respectful silence and commends afterwards. The declaration so often made by Sokrates that he is a searcher, not a teacher—that he feels doubts keenly himself, and can impress them upon others, but cannot discover any good solutions of them—this declaration, which is usually considered as irony, is literally true. The Platonic theory of Objective Ideas separate and absolute, which the commentators often announce as if it cleared up all the difficulties—not only clears up none, but introduces fresh ones belonging to itself. When Plato comes forward to affirm, his dogmas are altogether *a priori:* they enunciate preconceptions or hypotheses, which derive their hold upon his belief, not from any aptitude for solving the objections which he has raised, but from deep and solemn sentiment of some kind or other—religious, ethical, aesthetical, poetical, &c.—the worship of numerical symmetry or exactness, &c. The dogmas are enunciations of some grand sentiment of the divine, good, just, beautiful, symmetrical, &c., which Plato follows out into corollaries. But this is a process in itself; and while he is performing it, the doubts previously raised are not called up to be solved, but are forgotten or kept out of sight. It is therefore a mistake to suppose that Plato ties knots in one dialogue only with a view to untie them in another; and that the doubts which he propounded are already solved in his own mind, only that he defers the announcement of the solution until the embarrassed hearer [*sic*] has struggled to find it for himself. (270–273)

With persons who complain of prolixity in the dialogue—of threads which are taken up only to be broken off, devious turns and "passages which lead to nothing"—of much talk "about it and about it," without any peremptory decisions from an authorized judge—with such complainants Plato has no sympathy. He feels a strong

> interest in the process of enquiry, in the debate per se: and he presumes a like interest in his readers. He has no wish to shorten the process, nor to reach the end and dismiss the question as settled. On the contrary, he claims it as the privilege of philosopical research, that persons engaged in such discussions are noway tied to time; that they are not like judicial pleaders, who, with a klepsydra or waterclock to measure the length of each speech, are under slavish dependence on the feelings of the Dikasts, and are therefore obliged to keep strictly to the point.[10] Whoever desires accurate training of mind must submit to go through a long and tiresome circuit. Plato regards the process of enquiry as being in itself, both a stimulus and a discipline, in which the minds both of questioner and respondent are implicated and improved, each being indispensable to the other: he also represents it as a process carried on under the immediate inspiration of the moment, without reflection or foreknowledge of the result.[11] (274–276)

These passages constitute Grote's summing-up of the chapter, and contain his only reference, in this chapter, to the affirmative aspect of the 'expository' dialogues. A chapter which began with admitting that, in many dialogues, Plato is dogmatic, has ended as one of the clearest and strongest statements in modern literature about Plato as σκεπτικός or ζητητικός in the ancient sense of these words. The dogmas expressed by him are unexamined: in the best case, they are, to him, εὔλογα.

I shall quote one other passage, from Grote's discussion of Plato's *Apology*.

> I have already said... that I cannot take this view [of Socrates' refutations as merely an indirect method for inculcating positive doctrines], either of Sokrates or of Plato. Without doubt, each of them had affirmative doctrines and convictions, though not both the same. But the affirmative vein, with both of them, runs in a channel completely distinct from the negative. The affirmative theory has its roots *aliunde*, and is neither generated, nor adapted, with a view to reconcile the contradictions, or elucidate the obscurities, which the negative Elenchus has exposed. That exposure does indeed render the embarrassed respondent painfully conscious of the want of some rational, consistent and adequate theoretical explanation: it farther stimulates him to make efforts of his own for the supply of that want. But such efforts must be really his own: the Elenchus gives no further help; it furnishes problems, but no solutions, nor even any assurance that the problems as presented admit of affirmative solutions. Whoever expects that such consummate masters of the negative process as Sokrates and Plato, when

---

10 *Theaetetus* 172d4 ff. (Grote's reference).

11 *Republic* 3. 394d (Grote's reference).

> they come to deliver affirmative dogmas of their own, will be kept under restraint by their own previous Elenchus, and will take care that their dogmas shall not be vulnerable by the same weapons as they had employed against others—will be disappointed. They do not employ the negative tests against themselves. When Sokrates preaches in the Xenophontic Memorabilia, or the Athenian Stranger in the Platonic Leges, they jump over, or suppose to be already solved, the difficulties under the pressure of which other disputants had been previously discredited: they assume all the indefinable common-places to be clearly understood, and all the inconsistent elements to be brought into harmony. Thus it is that the negative cross-examination, and the affirmative dogmatism, are (both in Sokrates and in Plato) two unconnected operations of thought: the one does not lead to, or involve, or verify, the other. (292)

The unprejudiced reader who has ever tried the Socratic ἔλεγχος on the arguments of Book X of *The Laws*; or has been puzzled by the string of 'Platonisms' poured forth by Socrates at *Theaetetus* 176a–d, without argument or proof—in a dialogue where almost every statement made by Theaetetus is mercilessly examined by Socrates; or has ever wondered what might have happened to the numerous dogmatic assertions by Socrates of *Republic* II–X, so readily accepted by Glaucon and Adimantus, had they been put to the test of Socrates of Book I—such a reader, whatever his own approach to the dialogues may be, would feel no small measure of sympathy for Grote's 'schizophrenic' picture of the dialogues. In his Preface (p. IX), he writes: '... I have interpreted the numerous negative dialogues in Plato as being really negative and as nothing beyond. I have not presumed, still less tried to divine, an ulterior affirmative beyond what the text reveals—neither *arcana coelestia* like Proklus and Ficinus, nor any other *arcana* of terrestrial character.' I shall leave it to the interested reader to see how consistent Grote remains, throughout the three volumes of his book, to these principles. If his approach strikes some 'modern readers' as somewhat excessive and severe, this may be partly, at least, because 'the modern reader' has been largely conditioned by a very different conception of the Platonic dialogues: indeed, a conception Grote himself warned against in his strong words on 'philosophy as now understood.'

Benjamin Jowett's translation of the whole of Plato was first published in 1871, only six years after the first edition, and four years after the second edition, of Grote's *Plato*. In the Preface to this first edition, two out of its three pages are devoted to Grote. I shall quote most of them, omitting Jowett's disagreement about the Platonic canon, which is beside our main argument:[12]

> I have derived much assistance from the great work of Mr. Grote, which contains excellent analyses of the dialogues, and is rich in original thoughts and observations. I agree with him in rejecting as futile the attempts of Schleiermacher and others to arrange the dialogues of Plato into a harmonious whole ...
>
> If Mr. Grote should do me the honour to read any portion of this work he will probably remark that I have endeavoured to approach Plato from a point of view which is opposed to his own. The aim of the Introductions in these volumes has been to represent Plato as the father of Idealism, who is not to be measured by the standards of utilitarianism or of any other modern philosophical system. He is the poet or maker of ideas, satisfying the wants of his own age, providing the instruments of thought for future generations. He is no dreamer, but a great philosophical genius struggling with the unequal conditions of light and knowledge under which he is living. He may be illustrated by the writings of moderns, but he must be interpreted by his own, and by his place in the history of philosophy. We are not concerned to determine what is the residuum of truth which remains for ourselves. His truth may not be our truth, and nevertheless may have an extraordinary value and interest for us...
>
> It will be seen also that I do not agree with Mr. Grote's view about the sophists; nor with the low estimate which he has formed of Plato's *Laws*; nor with his opinion respecting Plato's doctrine of the rotation of the earth. But I am not going to lay hands on my father Parmenides (*Soph.* 241d), who will, I hope, forgive me for differing from him on these points. I cannot close this preface without expressing my deep respect for his noble and gentle character, and the great services which he has rendered to Greek literature.[13]

So much in public. After all, Grote did have an international reputation; he had been made an honorary Doctor of Oxford University in 1853, and had been Vice-Chancellor of the University of London since 1862. (Jowett was to become Vice-Chancellor of the University of Oxford only in 1882). In private, Jowett could be far more explicit. In a letter to Sir Alexander Grant, written on August 21, 1865, he says:

> I have been reading Grote with very great interest, but with a good deal of disagreement ... I think without fancy that there is more to

[12] *The Dialogues of Plato,* translated into English with Analyses and Introductions by B. Jowett, Fourth Edition (Oxford 1953) vol.1, xxvii–xxix. This part of the Preface is reprinted unchanged from the First Edition.

[13] I think it was Heine who said of Victor Cousin: 'M. Cousin is doing his best to understand German philosophy and interpret it to his countrymen; and I must admit that M. Cousin is a very nice man.'

> Plato than he supposes. I object to a kind of modern rule by which he judges him, and I don't believe Socrates to be a mere professor of negation, as he supposes.[14]

Nine years later, on April 5, 1874, he writes to Lewis Campbell:

> I have been reading Grote and Schleiermacher on the *Republic* ... Grote is really inexcusable in his matter-of-fact and at the same time inconsistent manner of reading Plato, never seeing anything according to its meaning and intention, and defending Plato as paradoxically as he attacks him. He is always thinking, and always thinking wrong.[15]

'Inconsistent manner of reading Plato'—but had not Jowett himself maintained, against Schleiermacher, that 'there is a common spirit in the writings of Plato, but not a unity of design in the whole, *not perhaps a perfect unity in any single dialogue* [emphasis mine. JG]. The hypothesis of a general plan which is worked out in the successive dialogues is an afterthought of the critics who have attributed a system to writings belonging to an age when system had not as yet taken possession of philosophy.'?[16]

What is of greater importance is that Jowett had accused Grote, by insinuation, of reading Plato through utilitarian spectacles, while he, Jowett, did not 'measure him by the standard of any modern philosophical system'. Yet Plato is, for Jowett, 'the father of Idealism...providing the instruments of thought for future generations.' *Which* 'instruments of thought', and for *which* generations? And is 'Idealism', capital I, less of a 'modern philosophical system' than 'utilitarianism', minuscule u?

Jowett refers us to his Introductions to the various dialogues. The interested reader will find in them ample material to exemplify Jowett's approach and compare it with that of Grote.[17] I shall

---

14 E. Abbott and L. Campbell, *The Life and Letters of Benjamin Jowett...* (London 1897) 1.413.

15 *Op. cit.* (n. 14) 2.92.

16 B. Jowett, *op. cit.* (n. 12) xxviii. Did Jowett remember that even the philosophical concept of σύστημα was a Stoic invention?

17 Just two examples for the contrast. In his discussion of *Meno*, Grote (n. 5) 2.14–23, accepts the aporetic end as a genuine aporia, and he emphasizes (23) that nothing is said in that dialogue on the Ideas. Jowett (n. 12), 1.258–263, has a long excursus on the Ideas, which he calls 'the ever-varying expression of Plato's idealism' (263), and which he finds, at least hinted to, in *Meno* as well (260). On *Euthyphro*, Grote 1.322–330, accepts the aporetic end as a genuine expression of Plato's position at the time. Jowett, *ibid.* 307–8, has a ready answer: 'Socrates ... is seeking to realize the harmony of religion and morality, which the great poets Aeschylus, Sophocles and Pindar had unconsciously anticipated, and which is the universal want of all men ... But when we

concentrate on the Introduction to one particular dialogue, which can be regarded as most expressive of Jowett's view of Plato, and may also throw some light on his cryptic expressions in the Preface: his second Introduction to *Sophist.*

In the first edition of Jowett's translation,[18] we have only one Introduction to each dialogue, followed by the Analysis and the translation. In the second edition, a second Introduction, following the analysis, had been added.[19] The second introduction to *Sophist* was further enlarged in the third edition by adding a few paragraphs and sentences, but in all essentials, it remains the same.[20] I shall refer to this second Introduction as it stands in the third edition.

This second Introduction falls into two parts. The first (313–323) is a comparison of 'the identity of being and not—being' in *Sophist* with Hegel's dialectic. The second is a summary—in the mellifluous style so characteristic of Jowett's writings—of Hegel's own dialectic. Already on the first page of the first Introduction—appearing in all three editions—[21] we are given a foretaste of what is to come: '...The kindred spirit of Hegel seemed to find in the Sophist the crown and summit of the Platonic philosophy—here is the place at which Plato most nearly approaches to the Hegelian identity of being and not being.' Things become clearer in the Second Introduction:

> In Plato we find, as we might expect, the germs of many thoughts which have been further developed by the genius of Spinoza and Hegel. But there is a difficulty in separating the germ from the flower, or in drawing the line which divides ancient from modern philosophy. Many coincidences which occur in them are unconscious, seeming to show a natural tendency in the human mind towards certain ideas and forms of thought. And there are many

---

expect him [Euthyphro] to go on and show that the true service of the gods is the service of the spirit [!! JG] and co-operation with them in all things true and good, he stops short; this was the lesson which the soothsayer could not have been made to understand, and which everyone must learn for himself.

18 *The Dialogues of Plato,* translated ... by B. Jowett (Oxford 1871) 3.445–473.

19 *The Dialogues of Plato* etc. (Oxford 1875) 4.401–424. In vol. 1 of this edition, Preface, xi, we are told: 'The Prefaces to the Dialogues have been enlarged, and essays on subjects of modern philosophy having an affinity to the Platonic Dialogues have been introduced.'

20 *The Dialogues of Plato* etc. (Oxford 1892) 4.313–338 (25 pages, as against 23 in the second edition.) In the fourth edition (n. 12) 351–359, that part of the second Introduction which compares Plato with Hegel was still reprinted, but the longer section, devoted to Hegel's own system, was omitted.

21 *Op. cit.,* third edition (n. 20) 283.

speculations of Plato which would have passed away unheeded, and their meaning like that of some hieroglyphic, would have remained undeciphered, unless two thousand years and more afterwards an interpreter had arisen of a kindred spirit and of the same intellectual family. For example, in the Sophist Plato begins with the abstract and goes on to the concrete, not in the lower sense of returning to outward objects, but to the Hegelian concrete or unity of abstractions. In the intervening period hardly any importance would have been attached to the question which is so full of meaning for Plato and Hegel.'[22]

In what follows, Jowett points out some differences between the two, and spells out the similar elements. One of the 'general aspects of the Hegelian philosophy' is presented thus: 'It is the ideal philosophy which, in popular phraseology, maintains not matter but mind to be the truth of things, and this not by a mere crude substitution of one word for another, but by showing either of them to be a complement of the other.'[23]

In such passages, we seem to have the key to those cryptic expressions in the Preface, about Plato 'the father of Idealism—providing the instruments of thought for future generations.' Here he is, indeed, 'illustrated by the writings of the moderns'—or of one of them; but is he, in these passages, really 'interpreted by his own, and by his place in the history of philosophy'? Jowett does his best to point out differences—but in true Hegelian fashion, Plato is taken to be something of a 'prefiguration' of Spinoza and Hegel. To anticipate possible objections, I should point out another part of the second Introduction, in which Jowett cites passages from *Symposium, Republic I,* and *Theaetetus,* to show that the issue of the unity of opposites is not unique to *Sophist,* and concludes: 'And the *Idea* of good is the source of knowledge and also of Being, in which all the stages of sense and knowledge are gathered up and from being hypotheses become realities.'[24] 'The rational is the real and the real the rational'? Clearly, something very similar.

To understand why Jowett's Hegelian Plato won the day in the 1870's, one should take a close—albeit somewhat selective—look at some of the developments in British philosophy in the nineteenth century.

When Thomas Taylor published his Neo-Platonic translation of

[22] Jowett, *op. cit.* (n. 19) 316.
[23] *Op. cit.*, 317.
[24] *Op. cit.*, 322–3.

Plato in 1804, his 'Proclean' conception of Plato was already out of date in academic circles. Taylor's immense influence on some of the greatest English poets of the period[25] was due mainly to the neglect, and general ignorance, of Plato in England during most of the eighteenth century.[26] On the Continent, the Neo-Platonic conception of Plato, which had been the dominant one since Marsilio Ficino, had already been challenged many times over. The influential works of 'the father of modern ecclesiastical history', Johann Lorenz von Mosheim, and of 'the father of the modern historiography of philosophy', Johann Jacob Brucker, had drawn a clear line between Plato and his 'eclectic' interpreters in late antiquity; and in this, they were following in the footsteps of some distinguished predecessors.[27] Mosheim's Plato was the amalgam of Socratic and Pythagorean views, familiar to us from Cicero's *De Re Publica* 1.16 and parallel passages. Brucker's 'Platonic system' was based chiefly on 'Middle Platonic' surveys.[28] What they had in common was a total rejection of the Neo-Platonic image of Plato. Both were read by British scholars.[29] We do not know where the largely self-taught Taylor had obtained his view of Plato.[30] But

---

25 Glucker (n. 1) 155–164.

26 *Op. cit.*, 151–5.

27 On the whole of this issue, the best general survey is still E.N. Tigerstedt, *The Decline and Fall of the Neoplatonic Interpretation of Plato* (Helsinki 1974). It is too brief, and there are gaps. The same author's *Interpreting Plato* (Stockholm 1977) is also too brief, and devotes only two pages to Grote and none to the Mills or Jowett. The proper and extensive history of the modern study of Plato is yet to be written. On Mosheim and Brucker, see *The Decline and Fall* ... 55–61; 62–3, and notes.

28 Tigerstedt, *Decline and Fall* ... (n. 27) failed to notice that in his *Historia Critica Philosophiae* ..., 2 vols. (Leipzig 1742) 1.669, Brucker says that in his survey of Plato's system, he will follow Cicero's *Academicus Primus* (that is, Varro's account, 19–33), Apuleius, and Alcinous, 'qui, ut omnium optime ad ordinem nexumque philosophiae Platonicae attendit, ita dux erit nobis in itinere ...'

29 A shortened version of Brucker appeared in English in 1791, in a translation by William Enfield. The account of Plato appears in vol.1, 199–125, and it contains all the main ingredients of the Latin version. James Mill, in his review of Thomas Taylor of 1804 (see n. 33 and context), is still apparently unaware of Brucker; but in the 1809 review in *The Edinburgh Review*, he already quotes Brucker. See further nn. 45–46 and context.

30 According to the two biographical accounts reprinted in Kathleen Raine and George Mills Harper (eds.), *Thomas Taylor the Platonist* (Princeton 1969) 105–132, Taylor came to Plato through reading Aristotle and his commentators, and what made him opt for the Neo-Platonic view was his reading of Proclus' *Platonic Theology* (112–3 and 125, probably derived from it). The first of these accounts is almost certainly Taylor's own story (see *ibid.* 105,

among the few scholars interested in Plato, this view was already out of date.

Nor was the climate of philosophical opinion in Britain in 1804 favourable to 'the perennial philosophy' or to metaphysics in general. Readers of that neglected genius, Thomas Love Peacock, will remember his many digs at German philosophy, and especially at 'the profound Kant'. On 27 September 1804, Francis Horner, lawyer, scholar, one of the founders of *The Edinburgh Review,* and a future influential politician, wrote to a Scottish friend who proposed to translate Kant into English, and attempted to dissuade him from carrying out his project, since metaphysics had never been a favourite of the British philosophical reader, and its present status—at least in the literary circles in London—was worse than ever before.[31] 1804 was obviously a good year for taking a 'tough-minded', empirical, or even sceptical look at the dialogues of Plato. Even in 1834–5, Mill's translations/paraphrases of some dialogues still had a wide appeal.[32] Had Mill and Grote published their work during those years, they may have created a very different image of the Platonic writings than that which was created by Jowett and others in the 1860's and the 1870's, and became the most influential one for decades. But in 1804 Mill, however precocious he was, had still two years to wait for his own birth, and Grote was still a boy of ten. The only person, during those years, who was capable of expressing a more empirical view of Plato was the father of John Mill and the teacher of both, James Mill.

I have found no external evidence that the reviewer of Taylor's Plato in vol. 14, 1809, of *The Edinburgh Review* [henceforth *ER*] was James Mill.[33] But an earlier review, in *The Literary Journal* [henceforth *LJ*] 3 (1804) 449–61; 577–89, is signed, in both instalments, "M.", which stands for the founder and editor, [James] M[ill]. The style of both reviews is the clear and trenchant style of Mill's

n. *). But is this the whole story?

31 L. Horner, *Memoirs and Correspondence of Francis Horner, M.P.* (Boston and London 1853) 1.282–3.

32 See n. 3 and context.

33 The only full biography of James Mill is still that of Alexander Bain, *James Mill: A Biography* (London 1882). Although Bain deals in a number of places with articles in *ER* which can be ascribed to Mill, this one is never mentioned. Nor is it mentioned in two more recent studies of early *ER* reviewers—I omit the details for lack of space. Kathleen Raine (n. 30) 535, ascribes this review to Mill, but gives no reference to any source. Her words were taken as evidence or near evidence by some more recent scholars.

criticism of literary and philosophical opponents. The structure of both reviews is the same. Both begin with a general stock-taking of the state of the study of Plato in England at the time; both proceed to examine Taylor's Neo-Platonic approach, and to reject it in favour of an open, sceptical approach; and both end with criticisms of Taylor's English and specimens of his mistranslations from the Greek (although each review takes its examples from different dialogues.) Both reviewers (*LJ* 453; *ER* 199) cite with approval Cicero's description of Plato as a sceptic at *Acad.* 1.46.[34] Both reviews (*LJ* 452–3; *ER* 199) describe the positive views expressed in some of Plato's dialogues as 'hypotheses', or 'specimens of investigation',[35] and emphasize the searching and examining nature of Plato's, and Socrates', way of doing philosophy. It is more than a mere probability that both reviews are by the same author.

I have cited elsewhere[36] some passages showing that this view of the 'sceptical' and 'dogmatical' sides of the Platonic dialogues was shared by Grote and John Mill, and suggested James Mill as their 'archetype'. Let us see how James Mill himself regarded these two sides of Plato. I shall cite a passage from each review.

---

[34] In *LJ* 453, the citation begins "cujus (Platonis) in libris". In *ER* 199, it is already "In Platonis Libris". Did the *ER* reviewer copy this citation from the *LJ* reviewer and simplify the 'style of quotation'? In the *LJ* review, the reviewer also quotes 'Varro's' strangely sceptical description of Socrates at *Acad*, 1. 15–16. It appears that, in 1804, Mill had just read this work of Cicero —or had found this particular passage quoted somewhere—and he regarded this statement as having an 'authority sufficient to confirm an opinion respecting the writings of Plato', and as evidence for 'the opinion entertained down to his [Cicero's] time, and entertained by himself, of the philosophy of Plato' (*LJ* 453). By 1809, Mill was too busy with other literary and political schemes (having meanwhile made the acquaintance of Bentham in 1808), and it was easier to quote from his earlier review. John Mill was taught by his father 'several of the orations of Cicero': *Autobiography*, in J.M. Robson *et al.* (eds.), *The Collected Works of John Stuart Mill* (Toronto 1981) 1.14/15. John Mill was also familiar with some of Cicero's letters to Atticus (*ibid.* 48/49), but there is no indication of any acquaintance with Cicero's philosophical works.

I have read through most of the four MS volumes of James Mill's Commonplace Book, presented by his son to the London Library. They date from his years of increasing political involvement and activity in London. Most items are of a political nature, and none is strictly philosophical. The ancient works most frequently quoted are Aristotle's *Rhetoric* and *Politics*, Plato's *Republic*, and Xenophon's *Cyropaedia*. Cicero's *De Natura Deorum* is cited once, on a religious/political issue.

[35] One remembers that Grote, in passages quoted above and elsewhere, also uses these expressions.

[36] Glucker (n. 1) 171–4.

Plato is always understood to deliver his own opinions in the person of Socrates. But in almost all the dialogues of Plato, Socrates, as Cicero remarks, in the quotation above [*Acad.* 1.15–16, quoted earlier on the same page], advances no opinion himself, but refutes the opinions of some other person. It is true he often proposes hypotheses on the subjects under consideration, and contrasts them with those of the person he is examining, in order to puzzle him, and contribute to his refutation. But it scarcely ever appears to be any part of the intention of Plato, that these hypotheses should be considered as the opinions of Socrates, or as his own. It would have been perfectly inconsistent with the character of Socrates to represent him as advancing these or any other hypotheses as his own opinions. It always appears to us in the perusal of these dialogues, that the hypotheses which have been denominated the Platonic visions, and stated as the foundation of what has been called the Platonic philosophy, were introduced for the sake of refutation merely, and that Plato in general adhered to the rule of his master; played with the theories of others; and advanced nothing seriously himself but what concerned virtue. If any authority be sufficient to confirm an opinion respecting the writings of Plato, it is that of Cicero, who expressly affirms that in this respect the practice of that philosopher was conformable to that of his great predecesor, "Cujus (Platonis) in libris," says he, " nihil affirmatur, & in utramque partem multa disseruntur; de omnibus quaeritur, nihil certe[37] dicitur." (*LJ* 452–3).

One of the most remarkable features of the writings of Plato is, that he affirms nothing... In most of the Dialogues of Plato, the object is to refute the tenets and expose the ignorance of some of those sophists who travelled about Greece, under pretence of teaching eloquence and philosophy, and who, in general, filled the minds of the youth with a spirit of mere logomachy, and with the worst impressions of right and wrong, with regard both to public and private life.[38] The ingenuity, the acuteness, the address, the eloquence with which this delicate and important task is performed, render the perusal of these Dialogues among the most improving exercises which can engage a juvenile mind. Hardly any thing, in the way of example at least, can be conceived to sharpen the faculties; to render acute in discerning, and ingenious in exposing, fallacies; to engender a love of mental exercise; and to

[37] All MSS read *nihil certi.* So do all the editions known to me. I have checked all eighteenth-century editions available in London libraries, as well as the 1804 Oxford edition. *Nihil certe dicitur* would mean 'nothing, indeed, is said', or 'nothing is really said'. Both are absurd in themselves, and not what the sentence requires. No sane scholar would offer such a reading as an emendation. It seems clear that the author of the *LJ* review made a mistake in copying this sentence, and the author of the *ER* review copied from the same mistaken copy—or from the *LJ* review. Hardly a coincidence.

[38] This is a view of the sophists which Mill's pupil, Grote, was later to reject, both in his *History of Greece* and in his *Plato.*

> elevate with the ambition of mental excellence [as do these dialogues].[39] In some of the dialogues, as in those with Alcibiades, the object is to expose some of the false impressions which are apt to prevail in the mind of men, and to lead to the most dangerous consequences.[40] In these the skill with which the misapprehension is analyzed; the variety of ridiculous lights into which it is thrown; and the power of argument as well as of satire which is employed to expose it, operate as the stronger sanative. In those of different description, as in the books concerning Polity and Laws, the business is to give specimens of investigation, to let in rays of light, to analyze particular points,and by throwing out queries or hypotheses, to encourage speculation, rather than lay down and establish any system of opinions. Accordingly, Cicero tells us, 'In Platonis libris nihil affirmatur; et in utramque partem multa disseruntur; de omnibus quaeritur, nihil certe dicitur.' (*ER* 119).

We know very little of James Mill's formative years before his arrival in London in 1802. We do know that, during his period in Edinburgh, 1794–5, he was an avid reader of Plato, and borrowed his works again and again from the library.[41] But we have no information concerning his source for the sceptical view of Plato (and no evidence that he was an avid reader—or a reader at all—of Cicero's philosophical works: see n. 30). His chief teacher of philosophy in Edinburgh was Dugald Stuart,[42] and in his published works, Stuart treats Plato clearly as a philosopher with positive opinions and doctrines.[43] When he wrote his *LJ* review,

---

[39] In 1809, John Mill was only three, and was only beginning to read Plato in Greek under his father's tuition: *Autobiography* (n. 34) 8/9. When he was twelve, he studied Plato more properly. His father's opinions on the value of Plato 'to young students', and the impression made on him at the time, are narrated in *Autobiography* 24/5(the 'early draft' is here much shorter than the full draft), in terms similar to those of our *ER* passage. But it has a sentence which was mitigated in the final version: '... and I have ever felt myself, beyond any modern that I know except my father and perhaps beyond even him, a pupil of Plato, and cast in the mode of his dialectics.'

One should, however, also note Mill's words on the limited usefulness of 'negative philosophers' in his essay on Bentham, *Collected Works* (n. 34), vol. 10 (1969) 79–80. Comparing that passage with both James and John Mill's emphasis on the use of Plato for *young* students, one can hardly reconcile this position with the words of praise just quoted from the early draft of the *Autobiography*.

[40] Bentham's famous *Book of Fallacies* springs to mind. It was published only in 1824, but Mill must have known some of its contents from his many conversations with Bentham, and he may well have seen part of the manuscript.

[41] Bain, *op. cit.* (n. 33) 18–19.

[42] Bain, *op. cit.* (n. 33) 13–14.

[43] See, e.g, Sir William Hamilton (ed.), *The Collected Writings of Dugald Stuart* (Edinburgh 1854) 1.48–9, 260–1, 368; 2.368; 4.71, 75, 180, 238.

Mill was familiar with the translation of six dialogues by Floyer Sydenham, of whose scholarship he speaks with great respect.[44] But Sydenham, although he follows the Thrasyllan division of the dialogues into 'sceptical and dogmatical', provides the reader with a view of Plato's dialogues as forming a systematic whole.[45] The author of the ER article is also familiar with Brucker, whom he quotes extensively in disparagement of the Neo-Platonists (*ER* 194–7). But was he familiar with Brucker before 1809? He is not mentioned in the *LJ* review.[46] In any case, Brucker's Plato was no sceptic, but rather a Middle Platonist.[47] One is tempted to think that Mill had read Omer Talon's *Academica* of 1550, in which the author discusses *duas disputationis vias et rationis* of the Academy, the negative one, *in utramque partem,* and the positive *probabilis disputatio,* citing as evidence Cicero, who is his major source in the whole of this work—but also the dialogues of Plato.[48] Be that as it may, one notes that he held this view of Plato four years before he knew Bentham. Thus, the sceptical view of Plato which he was to pass on to John Mill and to Grote was all his own. This is not to deny that, once he came under the spell of Bentham, he began to ascribe to Plato some 'Benthamite' features.[49]

---

44 *LJ* 577.

45 *Dialogues of Plato,* three volumes (London 1767, 1769, 1773.) No translator's name on the title-pages, but each dialogue has a dedication to some public figure, signed by Sydenham. Vol. 1, 5–19, has 'A general View of the Works of Plato,' where the translator's opinions are made clear. Sydenham's translation is a rare book today; but the 'General View' was reprinted by the learned Thomas James Mathhias in his—more accessible—edition of the works of Thomas Gray, vol. 2 (London 1814) 289–296, as an introduction to Gray's own notes on the dialogues.

46 In 1805, James Mill published in London a translation of Charles Villers, *An Essay on the Spirit and Influence of the Reformation of Luther.* On p. 315, Brucker is mentioned—but in a note by the *author.*

47 See n. 28 and context.

48 Audomari Talaei, *Academica* (Paris 1550) 11–15. Talon also cites Quintilian 2.15.26, for the division of Socrates' *sermones* into ἐλεγκτικοί and δογματικοί. On Talon, see Tigerstedt, *Decline and Fall* (n. 28) 36, and C. B. Schmidt, *Cicero Scepticus, a Study of the Influence of the Academica in the Renaissance* (The Hague 1972) 78–91. It is at least likely that the Calvinist Talon, friend and apostle of the Calvinist Ramus, would continue to be popular in Calvinist Scotland even after the decline of Ramism. This should be looked into by someone more familiar with Scottish philosophy and theology than myself. See also next note.

49 See nn. 38–39 and context. In his *A Fragment on Mackintosh* (London 1835) 25, James Mill regards Plato as the originator of Bentham's method of classification. A similar view is expressed by John Mill in his essay on Bentham (n. 38), 88; and in his review of Grote, *Collected Works* (n. 34) 11.405,

Two reviews were hardly sufficient to exercise a wide influence on people's view of Plato—especially since, in the first decade of the century, Plato was still largely ignored in Britain. Although he still considered applying to the chair of Greek in Glasgow as late as 1818,[50] James Mill became, after 1808, almost entirely absorbed by political and economic theory and practice. The task of expounding a sceptical Plato to an unsuspecting British public was left to his two disciples. They, too,were busy men. John Mill published his first Platonic articles in 1834–5, and even they were part of an incomplete project.[51] Grote did not publish his book on Plato until 1865, 'as a sequel and supplement to my History of Greece'.[52] In the meantime, some momentous developments were taking place in British philosophy.

Whether the final 'arrival' of Hegelianism in England should be dated from the publication of James Hutchison Stirling's *The Secret of Hegel* in 1865,[53] or with Benjamin Jowett's reading and disseminating of Hegel's philosophy in Oxford after his long visit to Germany in 1844,[54] is an issue yet to be determined on an examination of the available evidence. In the first half of the century, Utilitarianism was the most prominent philosophical doctrine around. By the 1860's, it was clearly being pushed aside by British Hegelianism, which held the field well into the present century.[55] But 'idealistic' tendencies began to appear in British philosophy—mostly under German influences—much before the 1860's. Sir James Mackintosh became familiar with Kant, Fichte

---

he regards the method of division and classification in dialogues like *Sophist* and *Statesman* as 'an anticipation of Ramus and Bentham'. This, incidentally, may imply some familiarity with Ramus: why not with Talon as well—and perhaps, in both cases initiated by James Mill? Thus, by 1835, James Mill can treat Plato as having positive doctrines—if only in matters of government, where Socrates' exposition in *Republic* appears to agree with his own view (*Mackintosh* 285–290, citing passages from *Rep. III*, and speaking of Plato 'laying it down as a universal truth'.)

50 Bain (n. 33) 165–8.

51 Glucker (n. 1) 167–170.

52 Grote, *Plato* (n. 5) 1.iii.

53 See Amelia Hutchison Stirling, *James Hutchison Stirling, His Life and Work* (London 1912) 114–5, 119–135.

54 Abbott and Campbell (n. 14) 89–92; Geoffrey Faber, *Jowett, A Portrait with Background* (London 1957) 177–183.

55 For a balanced account of these developments and their aftermath, see Frederick Copleston, *A History of Philosophy,* vol. 8 (London 1967). For an analytic philosopher's brief review of British Hegelianism, see G.J. Warnock, *English Philosophy since 1900* (London 1958) 1–11.

and Schelling in the early years of the century, and Sir William Hamilton's essays in the 1830's show close familiarity with Continental philosophy in general. Coleridge's, and Carlyle's, works of the 1820's and 1830's had already made a wide circle of readers aware of the revolutionary nature of much of the new German philosophy. About the same time when Jowett began to acquaint Oxford with Hegel, a group of philosophers in Trinity College, Dublin, began to turn philosophy in their university in the new, 'idealistic', direction. In 1837, William Archer Butler was made the first incumbent of the new chair of Moral Philosophy. His lectures on ancient philosophy, published many years after his death,[56] must date from the 1830's or the early 1840's: they could not have been delivered later than 1847, when he was 'engaged in the preparation of some work on faith'.[57] In them, he shows familiarity with Kant, Fichte and Schelling, who are mentioned by name, and uses some ideas and expressions which may come from Hegel. Butler attempts to reach a compromise between 'the Science of Real Experience' and 'the Philosophy of Induction.' But when he comes to Plato, he sees the Idea of the Good as the main object of Plato's philosophy. 'The predominant quality of Platonic philosophy' is for him 'the perfect union of Absolute Goodness with Absolute Reality.'[58]

One of Butler's successors in Trinity, Thomas Maguire, Professor of Moral Philosophy from 1880 to his death in 1889, was described by his biographer as 'a thorough idealist in philosophy.'[59] In his *Essay on the Platonic Idea* of 1866, and *Lectures on Philosophy* of 1885, he fights the battles of idealism against many an 'empiricist' of the time, and regards Plato and Hegel as the two great champions of idealism. To go back in time, and to return to England: in 1841, Professor William Sewell of Oxford published a book called *An Introduction to the Dialogues of Plato.* Although Sewell has some interesting things to say about the dialogues as works of art, he is sure that Plato expected the intelligent reader to arrive at the 'grand formularies of his doctrine:' a philosophical system, with the Idea at its centre and the education and improvement of

---

56 William Archer Butler, *Lectures on the History of Ancient Philosophy*, ed. W. H. Thompson, 2 vols. (Cambridge 1856).

57 *DNB*, 'Butler, William Archer' (by John Dowden).

58 *Lectures* ..., 1.63.

59 *DNB* 'Maguire, Thomas' (by E.S. Robertson.)

man as its goal. In 1845, George Henry Lewes published the first edition of what was to become a very popular book, *A Biographical History of Philosophy*. Lewes was a professed positivist, but he treats Plato clearly as an idealist, with the Idea of the Good at the centre of his thought, and with his own psychology, dialectic, theology, cosmology and ethics.

Against this background, we should be surprised, not at the failure of Grote's work to exercise any significant influence on the study of Plato in Britain for the next few generations, but at the fact that some of the reviews of it were positive and laudatory. But everyone must have known or guessed that the review in *ER*[60] was written by a close associate, and it was soon revealed that the author was John Mill. As for the favourable review in *The Westminster Review*[61]—what *could* one expect of the 'Benthamites'' periodical, edited for many years by James Mill? The short and cursory review in *The Gentleman's Magazine* and the long and learned review in *The Quarterly Review*,[62] while full of respect for Grote's learning, were entirely opposed to his views of Plato. The *QR* reviewer is clearly an idealist, and he takes Plato's idealism for granted. He ascribes to Plato's 'most exact writings ... the necessity of reconciling the abstract with the concrete, the Ideal with the Actual,' and 'an approach ... to a new and larger idea of knowledge, not merely as the Universal, in which subjective peculiarities are done away [Schelling?], but as the union of all permanent relations in the contemplation of the mind [Hegel?].' Jowett himself could not put it better: indeed, I would not be surprised if it were revealed that Jowett himself was the reviewer. Needless to say, the reviewer dismisses Grote's whole conception of Plato's dialogues as inadequate, and adds: '... it remains for those whose point of view is nearer to Plato's own to vindicate him.' This, of course, is insidious: 'Plato's own point of view' can only be a construct, based on someone's reading of the dialogues. But such expressions show that by 1866, Grote's idealist critics were fighting from a dominant position. Needless to say, Grote is accused again

---

60 *The Edinburgh Review* 123 (1866) 297–364; reprinted in Mill's *Dissertations and Discussions* vol.3 (1867) 275–379, and now in Mill's *Collected Works* (n. 34) vol. 11 (1978) 377–440.

61 *The Westminster Review* 28 (1866) 459–482.

62 *The Gentleman's Magazine* N.S. II (1866) 382–390; *The Quarterly Review* 119 (1866) 109–153.

and again—sometimes explicitly, often by insinuation—of intruding his Radical or Utilitarian views into the dialogues (a thing which he does from time to time,[63] but not as often as one could guess from his reviewers.) And, as if it was not bad enough, in the 1860's, to be a Radical—Grote even served as a Radical Member of Parliament between 1832 and 1841—he was also labelled 'Positivist' by the *Gentleman's Magazine* reviewer. Grote was not a Positivist, but his personal friendship with Comte was well-known, and in the same year as his *Plato*—1865—his good friend and fellow—Utilitarian John Mill published his *Auguste Comte and Positivism.* The reviewer knew his master's crib when he wrote: 'The secularist [i.e. Grote] cannot sympathize with the great thinker who clings with the tenacity of a drowning man ... less to the arguments for the soul's immortality which unassisted reason supplies, than to the belief itself, which so commended itself to his mind and heart.'[64] This sounds almost like Augustine's 'Christian' Plato—with his Christianity brought in by insinuation.

John Mill's laudatory review of Grote's *Plato* was not the only place where he echoed the sceptical image of Plato which he inherited from his father. It is now common knowledge that many of the ideas of *On Liberty* of 1839 were conceived as part of his rebellion against Bentham's proposals for a 'totalitarian democracy', in which the majority has full control of the expression of thought.[65] One may, perhaps, offer the suggestion that much of Chapter II of that work was the result of Mill's reflections on Socrates, Plato, and even the sceptical Academy. I refer not only to the famous passage beginning with the words 'Mankind can hardly be too often reminded that there was once a man called Socrates.'[66] I refer also to the passages beginning 'The beliefs which we have most warrant for...';[67] and 'He who knows only his

---

[63] E.g., in his *Plato* (n. 5) 2.77–89, he takes Socrates' proposal of a 'beatific calculus' in *Protagoras* as a central view of Plato himself. This is one of the issues which his critics jump on, as a proof of Grote's *parti pris* in general.

[64] *Ibid.* 390. Grote also assumed that Plato held such beliefs, often 'from deep and solemn sentiments,' and even from religious sentiments. See, e.g., his *Plato* (n. 5) 1.271. What he was not prepared to do is to accept such beliefs as if they were the essence of Plato's philosophy.

[65] For two recent works, see Isaiah Berlin, *Four Essays on Liberty* (Oxford 1969) 172–206, esp. 175–185; Gertrude Himmelfarb, *On Liberty and Liberalism, the Case of John Stuart Mill* (New York 1974), esp. 3–22.

[66] J.S. Mill, *On Liberty* in *Collected Works* (n. 34) vol. 18 (1977) 235.

[67] Mill, *op. cit.* (n. 66) 232.

own side of the case ...'[68] Such passages are full of sceptical Academic terms like 'assent' and 'suspension of judgement,' and advocate the Academic practice *in utramque partem disputandi.*

But by the 1860's, as we have seen, the game was over. Plato was studied once again in Oxford —and very soon, in the other universities, and the idealists were now in control, both of the academic study of philosophy and of much of public opinion. The idealist image of Plato became canonical, and has been taken for granted since, in various shapes and forms, by most students of Plato and ancient philosophy. Even some analytic philosophers, finding in some of the Platonic dialogues 'prefigurations' of their own discussions, felt it necessary to point out that this is not the way Plato himself regarded what he was doing.[69] It was only recently, in a book on Plato published in 1982, that an analytic philosopher rediscovered the two sides of Plato with which the reader of this article should by now be thoroughly familiar. He calls them, for convenience's sake, Pato and Lato.[70] Was Professor Hare aware of the fact that Grote and Mill had already distinguished between these two sides of Plato more than a century ago?

In the past, I expressed the view that, if I *had* to make a choice, I would rather accept the sceptical Academy's image of the sceptical Plato than any of the, far more influential, dogmatic images of him, from those of Xenocrates and Aristotle to the present day. Meanwhile, a new approach to the Platonic dialogue has made its appearance: reading the dialogue as an organic unity in which drama, narrative, characters and philosophical arguments work together for the purpose of achieving a philosophical discourse in a concrete, human (albeit larger than life) situation.[71] I regard this relatively new approach to Plato as an important and seminal new method, which does justice to the Platonic texts on all their aspects. What made it easy for me to understand this approach and adopt it

---

68 *Op. cit.*, 245.

69 See, e.g., G.E.L. Owen, 'Plato on not-being', in his *Logic, Science and Dialectic,* ed. M. Nussbaum (Ithaca, N.Y. 1986), 104–137, The article was first published in 1970.

70 R.M. Hare, *Plato* (Oxford 1982), esp. 26–7 and 69 ff.

71 Of a number of works, I shall mention two recent ones: Michael C. Stokes, *Plato's Socratic Conversations* ... (London 1986); Ivor Ludlam, *Hippias Major: an Interpretation* (Stuttgart 1991). I do not refer to the rather eccentric use made of the dialogue form by the late Leo Strauss.

was, among other things, my long preoccupation with the sceptical Academy's approach to Plato. I wonder if such a new and fruitful way of reading Plato might not have been discovered earlier, had the British philosophical community adopted Grote's and Mill's image of the sceptical Plato rather than the dogmatic image promoted by Jowett and other idealists.

Tel-Aviv University

DREI BRIEFE WILHELM DILTHEYS AN ULRICH VON WILAMOWITZ-MOELLENDORFF (1908-1910)[1]

WILLIAM M. CALDER III

I

Einleitung

Hochbetagt schrieb Wilhelm Dilthey (1833-1911) die nachfolgenden drei Briefe an Ulrich von Wilamowitz-Moellendorff (1848-1931).[2] Sie weisen eine Reihe von Gemeinsamkeiten auf. Zum einen handeln sie allesamt von Wissenschaftlern des kaiserlichen Berlin, nämlich von Eduard Zeller, Georg Misch, Reinhard Kekule von Stradonitz und Friedrich Hiller von Gaertringen, sowie von einem Projekt der Königlich Preußischen Akademie der Wissenschaften. Zum anderen ist ihnen gemein, daß die genannten Gelehrten überwiegend einerseits der Berliner Universität verbunden waren und andererseits der Königlich Preußischen Akademie der Wissenschaften angehörten.

Zu den zu jener Zeit nach Ausweis der Mitgliederverzeichnisse rund dreißig ordentlichen Mitgliedern der philosophisch-historischen Klasse der Berliner Akademie zählten sowohl der Verfasser

---

[1] Ich danke Prof. Dr. Ulrich K. Goldsmith (Universität Colorado) für seine glänzende Abschrift der schwierigen Texte. Dr. Sven Rugullis (Berlin/Urbana), Oldfather Research Associate (1992/93) hat die deutsche Version der Einleitung geschrieben und viel Material über Dilthey für mich gefunden. Ich bin ihm dafür sehr dankbar. Der honorandus, Prof. Dr. Jaap Mansfeld, hat in einem Brief an mich vom 29. Juli 1980 zum erstenmal versucht, die Briefe zu datieren, und auf wichtiges exegetisches Material hingewiesen. Es ist mir eine echte Freude, die *editio princeps* der Briefe Jaap Mansfeld zu widmen, der so viel für die moderne Wissenschaftsgeschichte, besonders für die Wilamowitzforschung getan hat.

[2] Die Behauptung, zwischen Dilthey und Wilamowitz habe kein Kontakt bestanden, ist falsch. So aber Klaus Oehler, 'Dilthey und die Klassische Philologie', in: Hellmut Flashar – Karlfried Gründer – Axel Horstmann (Hg.), *Philologie und Hermeneutik im 19. Jahrhundert. Zur Geschichte und Methodologie der Geisteswissenschaften* (Göttingen 1979) 190. Für die Druckerlaubnis der Briefe (= Wilamowitz-Nachlaß No. 273) danke ich Dr. H. Rohlfing (Handschriftenabteilung der Niedersächsischen Staats- und Universitätsbibliothek Göttingen).

als auch der Adressat der drei Briefe. Dilthey[3] war 1882 an die Friedrich-Wilhelm-Universität berufen und 1887 als ordentliches Mitglied in die Akademie aufgenommen worden. Wilamowitz, dessen Schwiegervater Theodor Mommsen der Akademie ein halbes Jahrhundert lang angehört hatte, kam 1897 nach Berlin und wurde nach einem gescheiterten Aufnahmeversuch 1899[4] ordentliches Akademiemitglied.[5] Zeller hingegen war bereits 1872 aus Heidelberg einem Ruf nach Berlin gefolgt und noch im gleichen Jahr als ordentliches Mitglied in die Akademie kooptiert worden. Nach seiner Übersiedlung nach Stuttgart im Jahre 1894 blieb er ihr als auswärtiges Mitglied verbunden. Kekule, unter dessen Bonner Studenten sich im Sommersemester 1881 der einstige preußische Thronanwärter und damalige Kaiser Wilhelm II. befand,[6] wurde von diesem 1889, d.h. ein Jahr nach der Thronbesteigung, zum Direktor der Sammlung antiker Skulpturen und Gipsabgüsse bei den Berliner königlichen Museen sowie zum Honorarprofessor und später zum Ordinarius an der Berliner Universität ernannt. Im selben Jahr folgte seine Aufnahme in die Akademie als ordentliches Mitglied[7], deren 'unmittelbarer Protector' Wilhelm II. war.[8] Im dritten Brief wird ferner Friedrich Leo (1851-1914) genannt, der Wilamowitz' Göttinger Kollege gewesen war und seit 1906 als korrespondierendes Mitglied der preußischen Akademie angehörte. In jenem Schreiben wird außerdem Wilamowitz' Schwiegersohn Friedrich Hiller von Gaertringen er-

---

[3] Thomas Kornbichler, 'Wilhelm Dilthey', in: Michael Erbe (Hg.), *Berlinische Lebensbilder. Geisteswissenchaftler* (Berlin 1989) 195-208, 201ff.

[4] Vgl. Theodor Lorenz (Hg.), *Friedrich Paulsen An Autobiography* (New York 1938) 300-301.

[5] Christa Kirsten (Hg.), *Die Altertumswissenschaften an der Berliner Akademie. Wahlvorschläge zur Aufnahme von Mitgliedern von F. A. Wolf bis zu G. Rodenwaldt (1799-1932)* (Berlin 1985) 117.

[6] Hans Schrader, 'Reinhard Kekule von Stradonitz', *Bursians Biographisches Jahrbuch* 35 (1913) 1-40, 20.

[7] SB Akad.Wiss.Berlin (1912) 616; Schader, a.a.O., 22. Der Wahlvorschlag wurde von Alexander Conze (1831-1917) eingebracht und ist lediglich von Johannes Vahlen (1830-1911) mitunterzeichnet. Er beginnt mit folgenden Worten: 'Nachdem es misglückt [*sic*] ist die gegenwärtige vakante Fachstelle für Kunstwissenschaft mit einem Vertreter der Wissenschaft moderner Kunst zu besetzen, wird man zur Besetzung der Stelle einen Vertreter der Wissenschaft antiker Kunst suchen wollen. Demgemäß schlagen die Unterzeichneten Herrn Reinhard Kekulé von Stradonitz, den Nachfolger unseres heimgegangenen Curtius in dessen Ämtern an Universität und Museum, zu dessen Nachfolger auch in der Akademie vor.' (Kirsten, a.a.O., 113).

[8] Adolf von Harnack, *Geschichte der Königlich Preußischen Akademie der Wissenschaften zu Berlin* 1 (Berlin 1900) 1044.

wähnt. Nachdem Wilamowitz 1902 die Leitung der griechischen Inschriftensammlung, welche die Akademie betreute, von Adolf Kirchhoff (1826-1908) übernommen hatte, wirkte Hiller seit 1904 in einer eigens dort für ihn geschaffenen Stelle als wissenschaftlicher Mitarbeiter an den *Inscriptiones Graecae*.[9] Die Abhandlungen und Sitzungsberichte der Preußischen Akademie schließlich erschienen in Kommission bei Georg Reimer, dem Schwiegervater von Mommsen und dem Großvater von Wilamowitz' Gemahlin. Eine Ausnahme in diesem Kreis bildete lediglich Georg Misch. Als einziger der Genannten war er zeit seines Lebens nicht mit der Berliner Akademie verbunden. Dafür hatte er 1905 den Hauptpreis in der 1900 von ihr gestellten *Preisaufgabe über eine Geschichte der Autobiographie* gewonnen. Eingereicht wurden bis zum 31. Dezember 1904 zwei Arbeiten, die beide einen der zwei ausgesetzten Preise erhielten: Mischs Werk gewann den mit 5000 Mark dotierten Hauptpreis, Kurt Jahn für sein unvollständiges Traktat den zweiten Preis in Höhe von 2500 Mark.[10]

Außer diesen personellen Verbindungen besteht eine weitere Gemeinsamkeit der drei Briefe darin, daß sie alle ohne Jahreszahl datiert sind. Der erste wurde durch eine Kritik von Wilamowitz an dem Nachruf auf Eduard Zeller veranlaßt, den Dilthey am 5. April 1908 für die Wiener *Neue Freie Presse* verfaßt hatte. Das zweite Schreiben behandelt Diltheys Sorgen über die Verbindung seiner Tochter Clara mit Georg Misch. Und im letzten Dokument wird weder die Krankheit noch der Tod Reinhard Kekules erwähnt, der nach längerem Leiden am 22. März 1911 verstarb.[11] Damit bildet das Jahr 1910 den *terminus ante*. Der *terminus post* für dieses Schreiben ergibt sich aus Diltheys Angabe 'Grunewald—Siemensstr. 37'. Bis zur Ausgabe für 1909 benennt der Kürschner 'Berlin W, Burggrafenstr. 4' als Diltheys Wohnsitz.[12] Das Verzeichnis der Akademiemitglieder führt Dilthey bereits am 1. Januar 1910 unter der neuen Anschrift.[13] Damit sind die drei Briefe in die Zeit von 1908 bis 1910 zu datieren.

---

[9] SB Akad.Wiss.Berlin physikal.-mathem. Kl. (1936) 158; Leo Stern (Hg.), *Die Akademie der Wissenschaften in der Zeit des Imperialismus*, Teil 1, (Berlin 1975) 161.

[10] SB Akad.Wiss.Berlin (1905) 686-689.

[11] Schrader, a.a.O., 33.

[12] *Kürschners Deutscher Literatur-Kalender auf das Jahr 1909*, 31. Jahrgang (Leipzig 1909) 302.

[13] SB Akad.Wiss.Berlin (1910) IX.

Als letzte Gemeinsamkeit sei erwähnt, daß Dilthey und Wilamowitz nicht nur durch die Berliner Universität und Akademie, sondern gleichfalls durch die zentrale Person des ersten Briefs miteinander verbunden waren, nämlich durch Eduard Zeller (1814-1908). Diltheys Verhältnis zu Zeller ist bekannt.[14] Als junger Privatdozent lernte Wilamowitz ihn durch Theodor Mommsen kennen und—wie bereits zuvor sein Studienfreund Hermann Diels (1848-1922)[15]—schätzen.[16] Davon zeugt auch sein Brief, den er am 7. Dezember 1881 an Zeller richtete:[17]

> gewöhnt daß meinen arbeiten nichts als hohn und rancune gegenüber laut wird, ist mir nächst dem eigenen gewissen die einzige beruhigung daß die männer, auf deren urteil ich den höchsten wert lege, das urteil der tageswelt nicht teilen. es verstand sich bei dieser arbeit[18] von selbst, daß ich an Sie, hochverehrtester herr geheimrat, an Bernays und Usener als leser eigentlich immer dachte.

Angeregt wurde das erste der nachstehenden Schreiben des Geheimen Regierungsrats Dilthey, der 1905 seine Lehrtätigkeit aufgegeben hatte, durch die Reaktion des Wirklichen Geheimen Rates Wilamowitz auf den Nachruf, den Dilthey auf den kurz zuvor verschiedenen Wirklichen Geheimen Rat Eduard Zeller veröffentlicht hatte.[19] Das Thema war ihm wohlvertraut. Nach mehreren Rezensionen und Aufsätzen über das Schaffen Zellers

---

[14] Siehe nur Eduard Zeller, *Erinnerungen eines Neunzigjährigen* (Stuttgart 1908). Vgl. Maximilian Braun, William M. Calder III, Dietrich Ehlers, *Philology and Philosophy: The Letters of Hermann Diels to Theodor and Heinrich Gomperz (1871-1922)* (Hildesheim 1995) 67, 169.

[15] Zu Diels und Zeller siehe Otto Kern, *Hermann Diels und Carl Robert. Ein biographischer Versuch* (Leipzig 1927) 60f., 65, 103-107. Ferner Dietrich Ehlers (Hg.), *Hermann Diels - Hermann Usener - Eduard Zeller. Briefwechsel* (Berlin 1992) mit Nachweisen in Bd. 2, 497 (*sub nomine* Dilthey, Wilhelm).

[16] Ulrich von Wilamowitz-Moellendorff, *Erinnerungen 1848-1914* (Leipzig ²1929) 175, 180.

[17] Ulrich von Wilamowitz-Moellendorff, 'Selected Correspondence 1869-1931', hg. von William M. Calder III, *Antiqua* 23 (Neapel 1983) 301.

[18] Ulrich von Wilamowitz-Moellendorff, 'Antigonos von Karystos', *Philologische Untersuchungen* 4 (Berlin 1881) (Nachdruck Berlin–Zürich 1965).

[19] Wilhelm Dilthey, 'Eduard Zeller', *Neue Freie Presse*, 5. April 1908, 31-35. Dieser Beitrag wurde ursprünglich nicht in Diltheys *Gesammelte Schriften* aufgenommen, weil er nach Meinung des Herausgebers des vierten Bandes, Herman Nohl, gegenüber Diltheys früherem, in die Edition aufgenommenem Beitrag 'Aus Eduard Zellers Jugendjahren' inhaltlich nichts Neues enthalte (578; vgl. Vorwort, VIII). Nohl irrt. 1970 schließlich wurde der Nachruf in dem von Ulrich Herrmann edierten fünfzehnten Band der *Gesammelten Schriften* wiederabgedruckt (267-278).

hatte er bereits 1897, Zellers fünfzigstem Professorenjubiläum zu Ehren, eine Festrede gehalten, in der er dessen Jugendjahre und anfängliche intellektuelle Entwicklung beschrieb.[20] Als Zeller am 19. März 1908 im Alter von 94 Jahren verstarb, hielt sich Dilthey zur Kur in Tirol auf. Dort konnte er, wie er klagte, den Nachruf nur mit Hilfe eines Konversationslexikons anfertigen. Ein Exemplar jenes Artikels sandte er sodann an Wilamowitz, woraufhin dieser wissenschaftsgeschichtliche Ungenauigkeiten monierte. Wilamowitz meinte, dem Artikel entnehmen zu müssen, daß Dilthey Ferdinand Christian Baur (1792-1860), 'dem großen Begründer der modernen, kritischen Erforschung des Urchristentums'[21], und seiner Tübinger Schule, die in Baurs Schwiegersohn Eduard Zeller und in David Friedrich Strauss ihre bekanntesten Vertreter fand, eine 'exakte philologische Methode' zuschrieb.[22] Gegen die Unterstellung eines derart 'gröblichen Versehens' oder 'Schnitzers', wie Dilthey es formulierte, verwahrte sich der 74-jährige. Er suchte zu ergründen, wie seinem Kollegen jener Irrtum unterlaufen sein konnte, und fand sich schließlich damit ab, daß der Altphilologe Wilamowitz ungenau gelesen haben mußte.

Der zweite Brief handelt über die Verlobung der 1877 geborenen Dilthey-Tochter Clara mit Georg Misch (1878-1965), einem Schüler ihres Vaters, der zu jener Zeit sein Leben als Privatdozent für Philosophie an der Berliner Universität fristete, jedoch 1911 in Marburg ein Extraordinariat erhalten und 1916

---

20 Diese Rede wurde unter dem Titel 'Aus Eduard Zellers Jugendjahren' in der *Deutschen Rundschau* (1897, 294-309) veröffentlicht und ist in Diltheys *Gesammelten Schriften*, Bd. 4 (Leipzig/Berlin 1921) 433-450 leicht greifbar.

21 Wilhelm Dilthey, 'Emilie Zeller', *Nationalzeitung*, 17. Mai 1904; wiederabgedruckt in: ders., *Gesammelte Schriften*, Bd. 15 (Göttingen 1970) 265f., 265.

22 Über Baur und seine Schule vergleiche Eduard Zeller, 'Ferdinand Christian Baur', *ADB* 2, 172-179; ders., 'Die Tübinger historische Schule', in: ders., *Vorträge und Abhandlungen* 1 (Leipzig ²1875) 294-389; ders., 'Ferdinand Christian Baur', in: ders, *Vorträge und Abhandlungen*, Bd. 1, 390-479; Ferdinand Christian Baur, *Kirchengeschichte des neunzehnten Jahrhunderts*, hg. von Eduard Zeller (Tübingen 1862) mit Diltheys Rezension in: ders., *Gesammelte Schriften*, 16 (Göttingen 1972) 449-456; Eduard Zeller, *Geschichte der deutschen Philosophie seit Leibniz* (München ²1875) 721, 723, 729 mit der Rezension von Dilthey in: ders., *Gesammelte Schriften* 17 (Göttingen 1974) 322f. Ferner seien Zellers Strauss-Editionen erwähnt sowie sein Aufsatz 'Strauß und Renan', in: ders., *Vorträge und Abhandlungen*, 1. 480-555; s. besonders Eduard Zeller, *Ausgewählte Briefe von David Friedrich Strauß* (Bonn 1895). Zur Tübinger Schule vgl. Horton Harris, *The Tübingen School* (Oxford 1975).

Extraordinarius sowie 1919 in der Nachfolge von Heinrich Maier (1867-1933) Ordinarius in Göttingen werden sollte. Wilamowitz war dieser Brauch aus eigener Erfahrung nur allzugut bekannt. Hatte er nicht selbst 1878 als junger Gelehrter Theodor Mommsens Tochter Marie geheiratet und erlebt, wie später seine eigene Tochter Dorothea den Epigraphiker Friedrich Hiller von Gaertringen ehelichte, der im dritten Brief erwähnt ist? Dilthey konnte mithin bei Wilamowitz nicht nur Verständnis, sondern Mitgefühl erwarten. Auch war der junge Misch für den Altphilologen schon längst kein Unbekannter mehr. Man erinnere sich etwa an Wilamowitz' Besprechung von Mischs erstem Band der *Geschichte der Autobiographie*[23], die aus der erwähnten Preisaufgabe hervorging, oder an die lobende Erwähnung, die dem damaligen Berliner Privatdozenten in Wilamowitz' Schreiben vom 1. August 1908[24] an die nicht lange zuvor in den Ruhestand getretene 'Graue Eminenz' des preußischen Hochschulwesens, Friedrich Althoff (1839-1908), zuteil wurde, dessen Intervention Wilamowitz seinerzeit seinen Lehrstuhl erst in Göttingen, später in Berlin nicht unmaßgeblich zu verdanken hatte.[25] Gleichfalls sind für die Folgezeit mehrere Briefe von Wilamowitz an Misch erhalten.[26]

Als eine Akademiesitzung ausfiel, wandte sich Dilthey mit seinem Anliegen schriftlich an Wilamowitz und verfaßte den letzten Brief der vorliegenden Trias. Ihm kann entnommen werden, wie ein Werk der Akademie entstand. Nach einer Begutachtung

---

[23] Georg Misch, *Geschichte der Autobiographie*, Bd. 1: *Das Altertum* (Leipzig 1907); Wilamowitz, 'Die Autobiographie im Altertum', *Internationale Wochenschrift für Wissenschaft, Kunst und Technik* 1 (1907) 1105-1114; wiederabgedruckt in: ders., *Kleine Schriften* 6 (Berlin/Amsterdam 1971) 120-127.

[24] William M. Calder III / Alexander Kosenina, *Berufungspolitik innerhalb der Altertumswissenschaft im wilhelminischen Preußen. Die Briefe Ulrich von Wilamowitz-Moellendorff an Friedrich Althoff (1883-1908)* (Frankfurt/Main 1989) 161.

[25] Vgl. Karl Reinhardt, 'Ulrich von Wilamowitz-Moellendorff', in: *Die großen Deutschen* 5 (Berlin 1957) 415-421, 417, wo es euphemistisch heißt: 'Der Universitätsgewaltige Althoff verhalf ihm [Wilamowitz] zu seiner Villa in Westend.' William M. Calder III, 'Die Rolle Friedrich Althoffs bei den Berufungen von Ulrich von Wilamowitz-Moellendorff', in: Bernhard vom Brocke (Hg.), *Wissenschaftsgeschichte und Wissenschaftspolitik im Industriezeitalter. Das 'System Althoff' in historischer Perspektive* (Hildesheim 1991) 251-266.

[26] William M. Calder III und Sven Rugullis, 'Ulrich von Wilamowitz-Moellendorff on Wilhelm Dilthey. His Letters to Georg Misch (1914-1928),' *Illinois Classical Studies* 16 (1992) 337-345 = William M. Calder III, *Further Letters of Ulrich von Wilamowitz-Moellendorff* (Hildesheim 1994) 137-145. Vgl. dazu Jaap Mansfeld, 'Two Letters to G. Misch,' *Wilamowitz nach 50 Jahren*, hgg. von William M. Calder III, Hellmut Flashar, Theodor Lindken (Darmstadt 1985) 203-206.

durch Friedrich Leo und durch den 'Hausarchäologen' Kekule wurde das Vorhaben, 'archäologische Arbeiten und Gelegenheitsschriften' zu veröffentlichen, dem Akademieangestellten Hiller von Gaertringen (1864-1947) über seinen Schwiegervater Wilamowitz angetragen. Hiller akzeptierte und veröffentlichte die *Arkadischen Forschungen* zusammen mit Heinrich Lattermann (1882-1914). Das Werk erschien 1911 in Kommission bei Reimer.[27]

II

Briefe

1 [± 19 April 1908]

Hochverehrter Herr College,
Besten Dank für Ihre freundlichen Worte über das zu Zellers Gedächtnis Gesagte.[28] Ich glaubte dem Freunde das schuldig zu sein[29], und so habe ich es in sehr schlechtem Gesundheitszustande und ohne alle Bücher, nur mit Hilfe von ein paar Zahlen aus dem Conversationslexicon niedergeschri[e]ben; selbst meine frühere Rede die Zellers Jugendjahre behandelte war mir nicht zur Hand.[30] So muß ich nachträglich um Nachsicht für das Zugesandte bitten.

---

27 Friedrich Hiller von Gaertringen/Heinrich Lattermann (Hg.), *Arkadische Forschungen* (Berlin 1911).

28 Wilhelm Dilthey, 'Eduard Zeller', *Neue Freie Presse*, 5. April 1908, 31-35. Vgl. die Gedächtnisrede, die Hermann Diels auf Zeller am 2. Juli 1908 in der Akademie vortrug (Abh. Akad.Wiss.Berlin 1908). Über den Verbleib der Briefe Wilamowitz an Dilthey ist mir nichts bekannt.

29 Über sein Verhältnis zu Zeller äußerte sich Dilthey in Briefen an Paul Yorck von Wartenburg. Ende 1883 klagte er: 'Mit Zeller lebe ich gut zusammen, doch eigentlicher geistiger Austausch will sich nicht entwickeln.' Ein halbes Jahr später schrieb er: 'Den Gesprächen mit Zeller fehlt ein belebendes Etwas, ein Hauch, der die Gebeine des Vergangenen auf der Trümmerstätte der Geschichte wieder lebendig macht. Noch gestern saßen wir hier lange auf dem Balkon zusammen. Am meisten lebendig wurde doch wieder unsre Unterhaltung als wir auf die Tübinger Schule kamen: da er einst von dem Genie Baurs persönlich berührt worden ist.' (*Briefwechsel zwischen Wilhelm Dilthey und dem Grafen Paul Yorck v. Wartenburg 1877-1897* [Halle 1923] 37, 46).

30 Aus Anlaß des fünfzigjährigen Professorenjubiläums Zellers hielt Wilhelm Dilthey eine Lobrede, die unter dem Titel 'Aus Eduard Zellers Jugendjahren' in der *Deutschen Rundschau* 1897, 294-309 publiziert wurde. Sie ist wiederabgedruckt in: ders., *Gesammelte Schriften* 4 (Leipzig/Berlin 1921) 433-450.

Aber berichtigen möchte ich doch Ihre Auffassung meiner Worte nach welcher ich 'der Tübinger Schule exacte philologische Methode nachgerühmt' hätte, und darum erlaube ich mir diese Zeilen zu senden, um den Vorwurf eines so gröblichen Versehens über einen Gegenstand dem ich in meiner Jugend und auch später zeitweise viel Zeit gewidmet habe[31] nicht auf mir sitzen zu lassen. Ihre Auffassung konnte leicht—wenn ich meinerseits eine Vermuthung wagen darf—, daraus entstehen, daß Sie etwa p 1. unten u. p 2. oben in den Satz 'Verbindung einer exakten philologischen Methode' nicht[32] die Worte 'Tübinger Schule' im vorhergehenden Satze als Subjekt in Gedanken hinüberbringen.[33] In Wirklichkeit sondere ich gerade seine 'eigenthümliche Stellung' in der Schule darin von Baur u. den anderen Freunden ab. Baur ging ausschließlich von historischen Apercü's aus, unterstützt durch religionsgeschichtliche Vergleichungen. Ich habe das früher in einem größeren Aufsatz ausführlicher dargelegt.[34] Was Zeller selbst betrifft, so glaube ich, als ich die entsprechenden Aufsätze in seinen Jahrbüchern[35] und die Apostelgeschichte[36] durcharbeitete, doch das was ich in meinem früheren aus der Rede entstandenen Aufsatz in der Rundschau[37] näher dargelegt und jetzt in dem Nachrufe wieder angedeutet habe, richtig gesehen zu haben. Wenn man seine Richtung auf 'exakte philologische Methode' eben in den Schranken der Zeit nimmt. Der Grundzug seines Verfahrens bleibt ja immer, auch in der griechischen Philosophiegeschichte die Systematisierung nach

---

[31] Diltheys altphilologische Studien bezeugt Herman Nohl, 'Wilhelm Dilthey', in: *Die großen Deutschen* 4 (Berlin 1957) 193-204, 196. Vgl. Arnold Bork, *Diltheys Auffassung des griechischen Geistes* (Berlin 1944).

[32] So Jaap Mansfeld. Die Lesung ist nicht sicher.

[33] Dilthey hatte geschrieben: 'In dieser Untersuchung Zellers [sc. Zellers *Apostelgeschichte*] zeigte sich aufs glänzendste die Eigentümlichkeit der historischen Methode, durch welche er in der Tübinger Schule seine eigentümliche Stellung behauptet. Sie lag in der Verbindung einer exakten philologischen Methode mit dem großen Zug der Anschauung einer historischen Entwicklung, wie er in dem Geiste Baurs war.'

[34] Wilhelm Dilthey (*Wilhelm Hoffner*), 'Ferdinand Christian Baur', *Westermanns Illustrierte Deutsche Monatsschrift* (1865) 581-599; wiederabgedruckt in: ders., *Gesammelte Schriften* 4 (Leipzig/Berlin 1921) 403-432.

[35] Eduard Zeller war der Herausgeber des *Archivs für systematische Philosophie und Soziologie* sowie der *Theologischen Jahrbücher.*

[36] Eduard Zeller, *Die Apostelgeschichte nach ihrem Inhalt und Ursprung untersucht* (Stuttgart 1854).

[37] Wilhelm Dilthey, 'Aus Eduard Zellers Jugendjahren', *Deutsche Rundschau* (1897) 294-309.

einem festen Schema, und ich habe, so wie man das in diesem Momente durfte, darauf hingewiesen, wie 'geniale Leistungen', die aus einer hochentwickelten Philologie kamen, von ihm theils verwerthet wurden, theils hat er in der ihm eigenen Continuität seiner Arbeit sich mit ihnen abzufinden gewußt, ohne daß er doch selbst Philologe in diesem großen Sinne gewesen wäre.[38] Das wird man bei aller Verehrung für seine große Leistung zugestehen müssen.

Und nun verzeihen Sie diese Weitläufigkeit über etwas das wenn Sie meine Zeilen erhalten schon hinter Ihnen liegt. Aber gerade bei Ihnen möchte ich doch nicht gern im Verdacht eines solchen Schnitzers stehen.

Ich hätte das mündlich gesagt—aber mein Gesundheitszustand ist leider so erbärmlich daß ich an eine Rückkehr nach Berlin noch lange nicht denken kann.

In herzlicher Verehrung
der Ihrige
[gez.] Wilhelm Dilthey

Meran Schloß Labers
Ostern

2 [21 Mai 1908]

Hochverehrter Herr College,
Nehmen Sie meinen besten Dank für die aufrichtigen Worte die Sie Ihrem Glückwunsch zur Verlobung meiner Tochter[39] hinzugefügt haben. Sie begreifen sicher, daß es mir Bedürfniss ist, einige Worte darauf zu erwidern. Sie wissen wie stark und lebhaft

---

[38] In Wilamowitz' *Geschichte der Philologie*, die 1921 erstmals erschien, ist Baur nicht erwähnt. Über Zeller äußert er sich sehr positv. Die Stelle lautet im Nachdruck der dritten Auflage (Leipzig 1959) 67: 'Alles tritt in Schatten vor Eduard Zellers großer Geschichte der Philosophie. Durch ihn dringt ein, was die Tübinger Theologenschule vor den Philologen voraushatte: eine geistige Bewegung durch die Personen der Träger hindurch zu verfolgen, also den geschichtlichen Zusammenhang neben dem Herausarbeiten der einzelnen dogmatischen Systeme.'

[39] Diesem Schreiben ging Wilamowitz' Antwortschreiben auf Diltheys Verlobungsanzeige seiner Tochter Clara mit Georg Misch voraus. Clara Misch veröffentlichte 1930 *Der junge Dilthey. Ein Lebensbild in Briefen und Tagebüchern 1852-1870*, das in zweiter Auflage (Stuttgart/Göttingen 1960) erschien.

ich zu jeder Zeit für meinen künftigen Schwiegersohn[40] eingetreten bin. Und meine Überzeugung von seinen hervorragenden geistigen Gaben und einer seltenen Energie und verzichtenden Ausschließlichkeit in der wissenschaftlichen Arbeit war immer verbunden mit der von seinem Charakter. Daher habe ich, als seine Anfrage[41] kam, nach eingehendem Gespräch mit meiner Tochter meine Einwilligung gegeben, aber mir die Bedingung vorbehalten, daß er ein Extraordinariat oder eine demselben äquivalente Stellung erst erwerbe. Und ich habe meine Überzeugung, daß diese Bedingung nach der Lage der Dinge erforderlich sei, wie sie auf langem aufreibendem Nachdenken beruht, selbstverständlich auch nicht aufgeben können. Meine sehr geliebte und innigst mit mir verbundene Tochter hielt aus Gründen, die ich zwar anerkenne, die mich jedoch durchaus nicht überzeugen können, ein möglicher Weise langes Warten nicht für richtig. Entstand nun hieraus zwischen uns Beiden eine Differenz, so ist doch unsere Liebe zu einander unversehrt aus ihr hervorgegangen, meine Achtung für Misch ist unverändert, und mein Herz und meine Fürsorge sind ganz bei der Verlobung, Ausstattung, Verbindung meiner Tochter, wenn auch mein sehr bedenklicher Gesundheitszustand mich von Berlin fernhält.[42] Ich bin schon seit Jahren sehr leidend, und in diesem Winter hat mein Gesundheitszustand eine gefährliche Form angenommen: zu arbeiten werde ich natürlich immer wieder versuchen, wie sehr es mich auch schädigen mag: ich könnte sonst nicht leben: das muß ich besser wissen als die Ärzte. || Ich habe keinen Grund von diesem ganzen Verlauf irgend etwas zu verhehlen, nachdem gegen meinen Willen durch Unberufene ein thörichtes Gerede entstanden ist.

Nehmen Sie nochmals für
Ihren Brief besten Dank.

---

[40] Georg Misch. Dieser war nach dem Tod Diltheys einer der Herausgeber seiner *Gesammelten Schriften*, beschäftigte sich aber auch monographisch mit seinem Schwiegervater (*Lebensphilosophie und Phänomenologie. Eine Auseinandersetzung der Dilthey'schen Richtung mit Heidegger und Husserl* (Leipzig 1930); *Vom Lebens- und Gedankenkreis Wilhelm Diltheys* (Frankfurt/Main 1947). Vgl. Josef König, 'Georg Misch als Philosoph,' *Nachrichten der Akad. Wiss. Gött. Philol.-hist. Klasse* 7 (1967) 151-243.

[41] Ursprünglich: *sein Antrag.*

[42] Clara Dilthey setzt schließlich ihren Willen durch. Die Eheschließung erfolgte noch 1908 (*Wer ist wer?* 1 [Berlin 1962] 1027).

In aufrichtiger und treuer Verehrung
der Ihrige
[gez.] Wilhelm Dilthey

Meran,
Labers
Südtirol
d. 21.sten Mai

3 Grunewald—Siemensstr. 37

Hochverehrter Herr Kollege.
Beifolgenden Brief Leos hatte ich Ihnen in der Sitzung vorlegen wollen, da ich nun aber vernehme, daß sie verschoben ist, erlaube ich mir, denselben zu übersenden. Die archäologischen Arbeiten und Gelegenheitsschriften sind wie ich voraussetze an Herrn von Kekule[43] gesandt. Hat auch dieser sein Urteil abgegeben, dann hätten Sie vielleicht die Freundlichkeit, die beiden Äußerungen Ihrem Herrn Schwiegersohn[44] vorzulegen, damit derselbe sich äußere, ob er geneigt sei, die Herausgabe zu übernehmen. Man würde dann auch einigermaßen den Umfang abschätzen können und auf Grund davon mit dem Verleger in Verhandlung eintreten.

In Verehrung ergeben
der Ihrige
[gez.] Wilhelm Dilthey

Berlin/Urbana

---

43 Reinhard Kekule von Stradonitz (1839-1911). Zur Korrespondenz zwischen Wilamowitz und Kekule siehe William M. Calder III, 'Ulrich von Wilamowitz-Moellendorff to Kekule von Stradonitz on Friedrich Gottlieb Welcker', *Studi italiani di filologia classica* III 2 (1984) 116-133 = *Further Letters*, 81-95.

44 Friedrich Freiherr Hiller von Gaertringen (1864-1947): vgl. Hiller von Gaertringen, 'Erinnerungen und Betrachtungen eines alten Epigraphikers,' *NJAB* (1942) 108-112 und G. Klaffenbach, *Gnomon* 21 (1949) 274-277.

STEPPING INTO THE STREAM
A Bibliography of the Publications of Jaap Mansfeld (1964–1995)

Note from the editors. This bibliography contains all major publications (books, articles of monograph length, articles, review articles, reviews) published by Jaap Mansfeld in the period 1964-1995. It does not include some minor publications or contributions (such as newspaper reviews) written in Dutch.

1964

[1] *Die Offenbarung des Parmenides und die menschliche Welt*, Philosophical texts and Studies 9 (Assen: Royal Van Gorcum & Comp.), pp. 285 (simultanously published as Ph.D. Dissertation, University of Utrecht, under the direction of C. J. de Vogel).

1965

[2] review of F. Adorno, *La Filosofia antica* I, *Mnemosyne* 18: 291-3.

[3] review of K. Axelos, *Héraclite ou la philosophie, Mnemosyne* 18: 417-9.

1966

[4] 'Parmenides Fr. B 2, 1', *Rheinisches Museum* 109: 95-6.

[5] 'Hermeneutische techniek: Heidegger's methodiek bij de interpretatie van enige vroeggriekse denkers', *Algemeen Nederlands Tijdschrift voor Wijsbegeerte* 58: 19-34.

[6] 'A Reply to Prof. Vollenhoven', *Philosophia Reformata* 31: 124-5.

[7] review of E. Milobenski, *Der Neid in der griechischen Philosophie, Mnemosyne* 19: 431-2.

1967

[8] 'Heraclitus on the Psychology and Physiology of Sleep, and on Rivers', *Mnemosyne* 20: 1-29.

[9] review of H. Cherniss, *Die ältere Akademie, Gymnasium* 74: 362-4.

[10] review of W. N. A. Klever, *Anamnesis en Anagoge, Archiv für Geschichte der Philosophie* 49: 324-6.

[11] review of L. Tarán, *Parmenides, Mnemosyne* 21: 315-9.

1968

[12] review of J. Bollack, *Empédocle* I, *Mnemosyne* 21: 426-8.

[13] review of M. Giusta, *I dossografi di etica* I, *Mnemosyne* 21: 436-8.

[14] review of G. F. Parker, *A Short Account of Greek Philosophy*, *Bibliotheca Orientalis* 25: 224-5.

[15] review of Th. Cole, *Democritus and the Sources of Greek Anthropology*, *Janus* 55: 220-4.

[16] 'Positivistische Hermeneutiek bij Popper', in *Handelingen dertigste nederlandse filologencongres* (Groningen: Wolters-Noordhoff), 65-7 [Abstract].

1969

[17] review article G. E. R. Lloyd, *Polarity and Analogy: Two Types of Argumentation in Early Greek Thought*, *Lampas* 2: 46-57.

[18] review of F. M. Cleve, *The Giants of Pre-Sophistic Greek Philosophy* I-II, *Mnemosyne* 22: 436-8.

[19] review of F. Dieterle, *Platons Laches und Charmides*, *Gymnasium* 76: 93-5.

[20] review of D. J. Furley, *Two Studies in the Greek Atomists*, *Gymnasium* 76: 100-3.

1970

[21] 'σφαιρῆς ἐναλίγκιον ὄγκῳ', in *Akten des XIV. Internationalen Kongresses für Philosophie, Wien 2-9 Sept. 1968*, Bd. V (Wien: Herder), 414-9.

[22] review of É. de Strycker, *Beknopte geschiedenis van de antieke filosofie*, *Mnemosyne* 23: 198-9.

[23] 'Nawoord', in *Grondslagen van het wetenschappelijk denken*, Voordrachten Studium Generale Rotterdam (Rotterdam: Universitaire Pers Rotterdam), 141-51.

[24] 'Naschrift' in Dutch translation with commentary of M. Heidegger, *Wat is dat – Filosofie?* (Tiel-Utrecht: Lannoo), 60-1.

1971

[25] *The Pseudo-Hippocratic Tract ΠΕΡΙ ʽΕΒΔΟΜΑΔΩΝ Ch. 1-11 and Greek Philosophy*, Philosophical Texts and Studies 20 (Assen: Royal Van Gorcum & Comp.), pp. 271.

1972

[26] 'Ambiguity in Empedocles B 17, 3-5: A Suggestion', *Phronesis* 17: 17-39.

[27] 'Three Notes on Albinus (1. Problems of Transcendence. 2. Forms and Qualities. 3. The Descent of Soul)', *Theta-Pi* 1: 61-80; repr. in [125].

[28] 'Man the Measure and Sense-Perception', *Theta-Pi* 1: 128-39.

[29] review of J. Moreau, *Le sens du Platonisme, Gymnasium* 79: 254-5.

[30] 'Literatuurbericht: Wijsbegeerte in de Oudheid, I', *Algemeen Nederlands Tijdschrift voor Wijsbegeerte* 64: 140-58.

[31] 'Literatuurbericht: Wijsbegeerte in de Oudheid, II', *Algemeen Nederlands Tijdschrift voor Wijsbegeerte* 64: 216-33.

1973

[32] *Theorie en Empirie. Filosofie en geneeskunst in de voorsokratische periode.* Assen: Van Gorcum, pp. 38 [inaugural lecture Utrecht University].

[33] 'Notes on Some Passages in Plato's *Theaetetus* (1. The Objects of Knowledge. 2. The Mathematical Passage)', in *Zetesis. Liber amicorum É. de Strycker* (Antwerpen-Utrecht: De Nederlandse Boekhandel), 108-14.

[34] 'Moeite met Plato', *Lampas* 6: 255-66.

[35] review of Th. G. Sinnige, *Matter and Infinity in the Presocratic Schools and Plato, Mnemosyne* 26: 64-70.

[36] review of M. Giusta, *I Dossografi di Etica* II, *Mnemosyne* 26: 75-6.

[37] review of K. Oehler, *Antike Philosophie und byzantinisches Mittelalter*, Gymnasium 80: 324-5.

[38] 'Grieks-wijsgerig commentaar', philosophical comments in Dutch translation with commentary of M. Heidegger, *Brief over het humanisme* (Tiel-Utrecht: Lannoo), 125-9.

1975

[39] (with P. W. van der Horst) *An Alexandrian Platonist Against Dualism: Alexander of Lycopolis' Treatise 'Against the Doctrines of Manichaeus'*, translated with an introduction, notes, and index (Leiden: E. J. Brill), pp. 99; introduction repr. in [125]; simultaneously published at *Theta-Pi* 3: 1-97.

[40] 'Alcmaeon: Physikos or Physician?', in J. Mansfeld and L. M. de Rijk (eds.), *Kephalaion. Festschrift C. J. de Vogel*, Philosophical

Texts and Studies 23 (Assen: Royal Van Gorcum & Comp.), 26-38.

[41] 'Voorsocratici', *Lampas* 8: 318-26.

1976

[42] Review of H. Lloyd-Jones, *Semonides on Women*, *Maatstaf* 24: 71-3.

1977

[43] 106 articles on ancient philosophy, ranging from the very brief to the quite extensive, in K. Kuypers (ed.), *Encyclopedie van de filosofie* (Amsterdam-Brussel: Argus Elsevier); revised and bibliographically updated versions of contributions to the major Dutch general encyclopedia, the *Grote Winkler Prins*, 7th edition (Amsterdam-Brussel: Elsevier), 1966-1975; these have been reprinted in the *Grote Winkler Prins*, 8th entirely revised edition (Amsterdam-Brussel: Elsevier), 1979-84.

[44] 'Aristoteles over waar en onwaar', *Wijsgerig Perspectief* 18: 18-9.

1978

[45] 'Zeno of Citium', *Mnemosyne* 31: 134-78.

[46] review of J. Bollack, *Empédocle* II-III, *Mnemosyne* 31: 207-9.

1979

[47] *Heraclitus: Fragmenten*, bezorgd, vertaald en toegelicht (Amsterdam: Polak en Van Gennep), pp. 79; 2nd rev. ed. 1987.

[48] 'The Chronology of Anaxagoras' Athenian Period and the Date of his Trial. Pt. I, The Length and Dating of the Athenian Period', *Mnemosyne* 32: 39-69; repr. in [134].

[49] 'Providence and the Destruction of the Universe in Early Stoic Thought', in M. J. Vermaseren (ed.), *Studies in Hellenistic Religions*, EPRO 78 (Leiden: E.J. Brill), 129- 88; repr. in [125].

[50] review of H. A. K. Hunt, *The Doctrines of Zeno the Stoic*, *Mnemosyne* 32: 411-4.

1980

[51] 'The Chronology of Anaxagoras' Athenian Period and the Date of his Trial. Pt. II, The Plot against Pericles and his Associates', *Mnemosyne* 33: 17-95.

[52] 'Theoretical and Empirical Attitudes in Early Greek Scientific Medicine', in M. Grmek (ed.), *Hippocratica* (Paris: Editions du CNRS), 371-90.

[53] 'Anaxagoras' Other World', *Phronesis* 25: 1-4.

[54] 'A Pseudo-Fragment of Zeno Stoicus', *Hermes* 108: 255-8; repr. in [134].

[55] 'Plato and the Method of Hippocrates', *Greek Roman & Byzantine Studies* 21: 341-62.

1981

[56] 'Bad World and Demiurge: A 'Gnostic' Motif from Parmenides and Empedocles to Lucretius and Philo', in R. v. d. Broek – M. J. Vermaseren (eds.), *Studies in Gnosticism and Hellenistic Religions. Festschrift G. Quispel*, EPRO 91 (Leiden: E.J.Brill), 261-314; repr. in [125].

[57] 'Hesiod and Parmenides in Nag Hammadi', *Vigiliae Christianae* 35: 174-82; repr. in [125].

[58] 'Protagoras on Epistemological Obstacles and Persons', in G. B. Kerferd (ed.), *The Sophists and their Legacy*, Hermes Einzelschriften 44 (Wiesbaden: Steiner), 38-53.

[59] review of W. Kullman, *Interpretationen zur aristotelischen Theorie der Naturwissenschaft*, *Bibliotheca Orientalis* 38: 219-25.

[60] 'De metafysika van Aristoteles', in C. A. van Peursen – E. J. Petersma (eds.), *Metafysica* (Meppel: Boom), 16-48.

[61] 'De maat en de mensen' (oration on the occasion of the *dies natalis* of Utrecht University), Utrecht, The University, pp. 21.

[62] 'Pythagoras en het oude Pythagoreïsme', *Hermeneus* 53: 80-93.

1982

[63] 'The Cleanthes Fragment in Cicero, *De Natura Deorum* II 24', in J. den Boeft – A. H. M. Kessels (eds.), *Actus*. Festschrift H. L. W. Nelson (Utrecht), 203-10; repr. in [125].

[64] 'Digging up a Paradox: A Philological Note on Zeno's Stadium', *Rheinisches Museum* 125: 1-24; repr. in [134].

[65] review of W. Scheffel, *Aspekte der platonischen Kosmologie*, *Mnemosyne* 35: 168-72.

[66] review of M. Schofield, *An Essay on Anaxagoras*, *Mnemosyne* 35: 360-7.

[67] review of R. B. Todd, *Alexander of Aphrodisias on Stoic Physics*, *Mnemosyne* 35: 388-92.

[68] art. 'Midden-Platonisten', in *Grote Winkler Prins,* 8th entirely revised edition, vol. 15 (Amsterdam-Brussel: Elsevier), 355.

[69] contributions on 'Parmenides', 'Heraclitus', 'Aristoteles', in J. Bor – S. Teppema, (eds.), *25 Eeuwen Filosofie* (Meppel: Boom), 29-40, 57-60 [2nd and 3rd editions in 1985 and 1987].

1983

[70] *Die Vorsokratiker, I: Milesier, Pythagoreer, Xenophanes, Heraklit, Parmenides* (Stuttgart: Philipp Reclam Jun.), pp. 336 [2nd edition 1986].

[71] 'Intuitionism and Formalism: Zeno's Definition of Geometry in a Fragment of L. Calvenus Taurus', *Phronesis* 28: 59-74.

[72] 'Apollodorus on Democritus', *Hermes* 111: 253-8; repr. in [134].

[73] 'Resurrection Added: The *interpretatio christiana* of a Stoic Doctrine', *Vigiliae Christianae* 37: 218-33; repr. in [125].

[74] 'Techne: A New Fragment of Chrysippus', *Greek Roman & Byzantine Studies* 21: 1-10; repr. in [125].

[75] '*Cratylus* 402 a-c: Plato or Hippias?', in L. Rossetti (ed.), *Atti Symposium Heracliteum 1981, I* (Roma: Ed. del Ateneo), 43-55; repr. in [134].

[76] 'Two Heraclitea in Philo Judaeus', *ibid.*, 63-4.

[77] 'The Historical Hippocrates and the Origins of Scientific Medicine; Comments on Joly', in M. Ruse (ed.), *Nature Animated. Papers of the 3rd International Conference on the History and Philosophy of Science, Montreal 1980,* vol. II (Dordrecht: Reidel), 49-76.

[78] review of D. E. Hahm, *The Origins of Stoic Cosmology, Mnemosyne* 36: 193-7.

[79] review of A. A. Mosshammer, *The Chronicle of Eusebius and Greek Chronographic Tradition, Mnemosyne* 36: 202-7; repr. in [134].

[80] review of P. Mastandrea, *Un Neoplatonico Latino. Cornelio Labeone, Mnemosyne* 36: 437-41; repr. in [125].

[81] 'Een brief van Wilamowitz over Nietzsche', *Maatstaf* 31: 115-24; earlier version of [104].

1984

[82] 'Zeno and Aristotle on Mixture', *Mnemosyne* 36: 306-12; repr. in [134].

[83] 'Heraclitus fr. B 63 D.-K.', *Elenchos* 4: 197-205; repr. in [125].

[84] 'Mito Scienza Filosofia: Una Questione di Origini', *Quaderni di Storia* 10: 43-67.

[85] review of H. Grensemann, *Hippokratische Gynäkologie*, *Gnomon* 56: 385-8.

[86] review of M. R. Wright, *Empedocles: The Extant Fragments*, *Canadian Philosophical Reviews* 4: 136-8.

1985

[87] 'Wilamowitz' Ciceronian Philosophy', in W. M. Calder III – H. Flashar — Th. Lindken (eds.), *Wilamowitz nach fünfzig Jahren* (Darmstadt: Wissenschaftliche Buchgesellschaft), 178-221.

[88] 'Some Stoics on the Soul', *Mnemosyne* 37: 443-5; repr. in [125].

[89] 'Versions of the Nobody', *Mnemosyne* 37: 445-7.

[90] .'On Two Fragments of Heraclitus in Clement of Alexandria', *Mnemosyne* 37: 447-51; repr. in [125].

[91] 'Aristotle and Others on Thales, or the Beginnings of Natural Philosophy. With Some Remarks on Xenophanes', *Mnemosyne* 38: 109-29; repr. in [134].

[92] 'Heraclitus, Empedocles, and Others in a Middle Platonist Cento in Philo of Alexandria', *Vigiliae Christianae* 39: 131-56; repr. in [125].

[93] 'Philosophy and Philosophies: A Reply to Leszl and Vegetti', *Quaderni di Storia* 11: 177-83.

[94] 'Myth, Science, Philosophy: A Question of Origins', in W. M. Calder III – U. K. Goldsmith – P. B. Kenevan (eds.), *Hypatia. Festschrift H. E. Barnes* (Boulder Co.: Colorado Associated University Press), 45-65; English version of [84]; repr. in [134].

[95] review of D. O'Brien, *Pour interpréter Empédocle*, *Mnemosyne* 38: 183-8; repr. in [125].

[96] review of H. B. Gottschalk, *Heraclides of Pontus*, *Mnemosyne* 38: 202-8.

[97] review of A. M. Ioppolo, *Aristone di Chio e lo Stoicismo antico*, *Mnemosyne* 38: 209-15.

[98] review of S. Städele, *Die Briefe des Pythagoras und der Pythagoreer*, *Mnemosyne* 38: 215-7.

[99] review of G. Rocca-Serra, *Censorinus. Le jour natal*, *Mnemosyne* 38: 234-6.

[100] review of L. J. Alderink, *Creation and Salvation in Ancient Orphism*, *Mnemosyne* 38: 436-8; repr. in [125].

[101] *Absolutisme en relativisme*, Haarlemse voordrachten XLV

(Haarlem: Hollandsche Maatschappij der Wetenschappen), pp. 32.

1986

[102] *Die Vorsokratiker, II: Zenon, Empedokles, Anaxagoras, Leukipp, Demokrit* (Stuttgart: Philipp Reclam Jun.), pp. 351; vol. I & II reprinted with some bibliographical additions in 1987; reprinted parts (on Anaximander, Heraclitus, Anaxagoras) of this edition have in turn appeared in K.-H. Hartmann (ed.), *Lob der Vergänglichkeit. Gedichte, Geschehen und Gedanken* (Stuttgart: Reclam), 1993, 28-34.

[103] 'Aristotle, Plato, and the Preplatonic Doxography and Chronography', in G. Cambiano (ed.), *Storiografia e dossografia nella filosofia antica* (Torino: Tirrenia Stampatori), 1-59; repr. in [134].

[104] 'Diogenes Laertius on Stoic Philosophy', *Elenchos* 7: 295-382; repr. in [134].

[105] 'The Wilamowitz-Nietzsche Struggle: Another New Document and Some Further Comments', *Nietzsche-Studien* 15: 41-58.

[106] review of F. Decleva Caizzi, *Pirrone. Testimonianze, Mnemosyne* 39: 478-80.

[107] review of D. Pesce, *La Tavola di Cebete* / J. T. Fitzgerald – L. M. White, *The Table of Cebes, Mnemosyne* 39: 484-6; repr. in [125].

[108] review of A. Baumgarten, *The Phoenician History of Philo of Byblus. A Commentary, Mnemosyne* 39: 486-8.

[109] review of D. Winston – J. Dillon, *Two Treatises of Philo of Alexandria, Mnemosyne* 39: 491-3.

[110] 'Heraclitus fr. 111 D.-K.', *Algemeen Nederlands Tijdschrift voor Wijsbegeerte* 78: 234-5.

[111] 'De Centrale Interfaculteit', in H. W. von der Dunk – W. P. Heere – A. W. Reinink (eds.), *Tussen ivoren toren & grootbedrijf. De Utrechtse Universiteit, 1936 – 1986* (Maarssen: G. Schwarz), 492-6.

[112] 'In memoriam C. J. de Vogel', *Algemeen Nederlands Tijdschrift voor Wijsbegeerte* 78: 293-4.

1987

[113] 'Historical and Philosophical Aspects of Gorgias' 'On What Is Not', in L. Montoneri – F. Romano (eds.), *Gorgia e la sofistica*, Siculorum Gymnasium N.S. 38: 243-71; repr. in [134].

[114] 'Theophrastus and the Xenophanes Doxography', *Mnemosyne* 40: 286-312; repr. in [134].

[115] 'Number Nine (Diog. Laert. IX 87)', *Revue de Philosophie Ancienne* 5 (publ. in 1988): 235-48; repr. in [134].

[116] 'Plato over de Vrouw', *Algemeen Nederlands Tijdschrift voor Wijsbegeerte* 79: 119-20.

1988

[117] *Het leerdicht en de paradoxen.* De fragmenten van Parmenides en Zeno, vertaald met inleiding en commentaar (Kampen: Kok-Agora), pp. 166.

[118] 'Philosophy in the Service of Scripture: Philo's Exegetical Strategies', in J. Dillon – A. A. Long (eds.), *The Question of Eclecticism: Studies in Later Greek Philosophy* (Berkeley: University of California Press), 70-102; repr. in [125].

[119] 'Compatible Alternatives: Middle Platonist Theology and the Xenophanes Reception', in R. van den Broek – T. Baarda – J. Mansfeld (eds.), *Knowledge of God in the Greco-Roman World,* EPRO 112 (Leiden: E.J. Brill), 92-117.

[120] 'Diaphonia: The Argument of Alexander *De Fato* Chs. 1-2', *Phronesis* 33: 182-208.

[121] '*De Melisso Xenophane Gorgia*: Pyrrhonizing Aristotelianism', *Rheinisches Museum* 131: 239-76; repr. in [134].

[122] review of M.-O. Goulet-Cazé, *L'ascèse cynique, Classical Review* N.S. 38: 162-3.

[123] review of S.-T. Teodorsson, *Anaxagoras' Theory of Matter,* Göteborg 1982, *Mnemosyne* 41: 395-7.

[124] review of R. W. Sharples, *Alexander of Aphrodisias On Fate, Mnemosyne* 41: 416-9.

1989

[125] *Studies in Later Greek Philosophy and Gnosticism.* A selection of papers and reviews, with preface, index, addenda, and corrections, Collected Studies Series 292 (London: Variorum Revised Editions and Reprints), pp. x + 324.

[126] 'An Echo of Middle Platonist Theology in Alexander's *De fato', Vigiliae Christianae* 43: 86-91.

[127] 'The Stoic Cardinal Virtues at Diog. Laert. VII 92', *Mnemosyne* 42: 88-9.

[128] 'Fiddling the Books: Heraclitus on Pythagoras (DK 22B129)', in K. Boudouris (ed.), *Ionian Philosophy* (Athens), 229-34; repr. in [134].

[129] 'Gibt es Spuren von Theophrasts Phys. op. bei Cicero?', in W. W. Fortenbaugh – P. Steinmetz (eds.), *Cicero's Knowledge of the Peripatos,* Rutgers Studies in Classical Humanities Vol. IV (New Brunswick N. J.–London), 133-58; repr. in [134].

[130] 'Greek Philosophy in the *Geschichte des Altertums*', *Elenchos* 10: 23-60.

[131] 'Stoic Definitions of the Good (Diog. Laert. VII 94)', *Mnemosyne* 42: 487-91.

[132] 'Chrysippus and the *Placita*', *Phronesis* 34: 311-42.

[133] review of J.-H. Kühn – U. Fleischer, *Index Hippocraticus.* Fasc. I: A-Δ. Fasc. II: E-K, *Mnemosyne* 42: 182-6.

1990

[134] *Studies in the Historiography of Greek Philosophy.* A selection of papers and one review, with preface, corrections, addenda, and indices locorum potiorum and nominum (Assen: Van Gorcum & Comp.), pp. x + 482.

[135] 'Doxography and Dialectic: The *Sitz im Leben* of the 'Placita'', including index locorum, in W. H. Haase (ed.), *Aufstieg und Niedergang der Römischen Welt* II Vol. 36.4 (Berlin–New York: De Gruyter), 3056-3229.

[136] 'Greek Philosophy in the *Geschichte des Altertums*', in W. M. Calder III – A. Demandt (eds.), *Eduard Meyer: Leben und Leistung eines Universalhistorikers,* Supplements to Mnemosyne 112 (Leiden: E.J. Brill), 255-84; reprint of [130].

[137] '*Physikai doxai* i *Problemata physika* od Aristotela do Aitija (i kasnije)', *Filosofska Istrazivanja* 37 (Zagreb), 1051-78. Croatian transl. of abridged version of [141] (with summaries in German English French).

[138] '*Physikai doxai* and *Problemata Physika* from Aristotle to Aëtius (and Beyond)', *Synthesis Philosophica* 5 (Zagreb): 469-97 (abridged version of [141] with summaries in German English French).

1991

[139] 'Two Attributions', *Classical Quarterly* 41: 541-4.

1992

[140] *Heresiography in Contert: Hippolytus'* Elenchos *as a Source for Greek Philosophy*, Philosophia antiqua Vol. LVI (Leiden: E.J. Brill), pp. xvii + 391.

[141] '*Physikai doxai* and *Problemata Physika* from Aristotle to Aëtius (and Beyond)', in W. W. Fortenbaugh – D. Gutas (eds.), *Theophrastus: His Psychological, Doxographical and Scientific Writings*, Rutgers Studies in the Classical Humanities, Vol. V (New Brunswick N. J.-London), 63-111.

[142] 'Heraclitus Fr. B 85 D.-K', *Mnemosyne* 45: 9-18.

[143] '*Physikai doxai* et *Problemata Physika* d'Aristote à Aétius (et au-delà)', in A. Laks (ed.), *Doxographie antique, Revue de métaphysique et de morale* 97: 327-64; abridged French version of [141].

[144] 'ΠΕΡΙ ΚΟΣΜΟΥ. A Note on the History of a Title', *Vigiliae Christianae* 46: 391-411.

[145] 'Enige opmerkingen over de 'mens' als *idea* en *eidos* in het griekse denken', in G. Quispel (ed.), *De Hermetische Gnosis in de loop der eeuwen* (Baarn: Tirion), 176-84.

1993

[146] 'The Idea of the Will in Chrysippus, Posidonius, and Galen', in J. J. Cleary (ed.), *Proceedings of the Boston Area Colloquium in Ancient Philosophy* Vol. VII, 107-145 + 153-7.

[147] 'A Theophrastean Excursus on God and Nature and its Aftermath in Hellenistic Philosophy', *Phronesis* 37: 314-35 .

[148] 'Aspects of Epicurean Theology', *Mnemosyne* 46: 172-210.

[149] '*Physikai Doxai* e *Problemata Physica* da Aristotele ad Aezio (ed oltre)', in A. M. Battegazzore (ed.), *Dimostrazione, argomentazione dialettica e argomentazione retorica nel pensiero antico*, Genova, pp.311-382; Italian transl. of revised and amplified version of [141].

[150] review of *Timone di Fliunte: Silli, Mnemosyne* 46: 397-400.

[151] review of L. Zanoncelli, *La manualistica musicale greca, Mnemosyne* 46: 408-9.

[152] review of J. Dillon, *The Golden Chain, Vigiliae Christianae* 47: 305-9.

[153] review of H. Dörrie (- M. Baltes), *Der Platonismus in der Antike.* Bd. I-II, *Mnemosyne* 46: 567-72.

[154] review of M. Tardieu, *Les paysages reliques, Mmemosyne* 46: 572-5.

1994

[155] *Prolegomena. Questions to be Settled before the Interpretation of an Author, or a Text,* Philosophia Antiqua Vol. LVIII (Leiden: E.J. Brill), pp. vii + 252.

[156] 'A Lost Manuscript of Empedocles' *Katharmoi', Mnemosyne* 47: 79-82.

[157] 'Epicurus Peripateticus', in A. Alberti (ed.), *Realtà e ragione. Studi di filosofia antica* (Firenze), 29-47.

[158] 'The Rhetoric in the Proem of Parmenides', in L. Bertelli – P.-L. Donini (eds.), *Filosofia, Politica, Retorica. Intersezioni possibili* (Milano: Francoangeli 1994) 1-11.

[159] review of M. Frede – G. Patzig, *Aristoteles, Metaphysik Z, Mnemosyne* 47: 120-1.

[160] review of Dexippus, *On Aristotle, Categories.* Translated by John Dillon, *Mnemosyne* 47: 287.

[161] review of Alexander of Aphrodisias, *Quaestiones 1.1-2.15.* Translated by R. W. Sharples, *Mnemosyne* 47: 427-8.

1995

[162] 'Critical Note: Empedocles and his Interpreters', *Phronesis* 40: 109-15.

[163] 'Aenesidemus and the Academics', in L. Ayres (ed.), *The Passionate Intellect. Festschrift I. G. Kidd,* Rutgers Studies in the Classical Humanities, Vol. VII (New Brunswick/London: Transaction Publishers), 235-47.

[164] 'Papias over traditie', *Nederlands Theologisch Tijdschrift* 49 (1995): 140-53.

[165] 'Insight by Hindsight. Intentional unclarity in Presocratic Proems', *Bulletin Institute Classical Studies* 42: 225-32.

Major works In Progress

—A new edition, with philological commentary, of the fragments of the Early Stoics, to replace the edition by J. von Arnim, *Stoicorum veterum fragmenta,* Vols. I-III, Leipzig, Teubner 1903-05. Work on this project commenced in 1979.

—*Aëtiana: The Method and Intellectual Context of a Doxographer* (together with D. T. Runia). Work on this project commenced in 1988.

Editorial Work

(1970) *Grondslagen van het wetenschappelijk denken* (Rotterdam: Universitaire Pers Rotterdam), pp. 151.

(1974) *Lampas* 8, fasc. 5 (pp. 318-93) on the Presocratics (contributions in English, German, and Dutch).

(1975) [with L. M. de Rijk] *Kephalaion. Studies in Greek Philosophy and its Continuation. Festschrift C. J. de Vogel.* Philosophical Texts and Studies 23 (Assen: Royal Van Gorcum & Comp.), pp. 234.

(1988) [with R. van den Broek & T. Baarda] *Knowledge of God in the Greco-Roman World,* EPRO 112 (Leiden: E. J. Brill), pp. 290.

(in progress) [with J. Barnes & M. Schofield], *The Cambridge History of Hellenistic Philosophy* (to appear in 1997).

Dissertations supervised

(1983) A. C. J. Habets, *Geschiedenis van de indeling van de filosofie in de oudheid* (Utrecht: The University Press), pp. 223.

(1988) K. A. Algra, *Concepts of Space in Classical and Hellenistic Greek Philosophy,* (Utrecht: Department of Philosophy), pp. viii + 199.

(1990) M. Desbordes, *Introduction à Diogène Laërce. Préliminaires critiques à une lecture de l'oeuvre* (Utrecht: Department of Philosophy), Vol. 1. pp. xxii + 357; Vol. 2, pp. 335.

(1992) T. L. Tieleman, *Galen and Chrysippus: Argument and Refutation in the* De Placitis, *Bks. II-III,* Quaestiones infinitae Vol. 3 (Utrecht: Department of Philosophy), pp. xxx + 287.

(1993) J. N. M. Baltussen, *Theophrastus on Perception. Argument and Purpose in the* De Sensibus, Quaestiones infinitae Vol. 6 (Utrecht: Department of Philosophy), pp. xxii + 306.

Affiliations

Member of the Hollandsche Maatschappij der Wetenschappen

Corresponding Fellow of the Real Academia de Barcelona

Fellow of the Academia Europaea

Fellow of the Koninklijke Nederlandse Academie van Wetenschappen

Member of the Erasmus network Ancient Philosophy

Member of the supervising committee *Symposium Hellenisticum.*

INDEX OF ANCIENT AUTHORS

INDEX OF MODERN AUTHORS